Prisoners of War in Contemporary Conflict

THE LIEBER STUDIES

Professor & Head, Department of Law, Co-Director of the Lieber Institute for Law and Warfare
Colonel Winston Williams

Professor & Co-Director of the Lieber Institute for Law and Warfare
Professor Sean Watts

G. Norman Lieber Distinguished Scholar
Professor Michael Schmitt

Board of Advisors
Honorable John Bellinger
Lieutenant General (ret.) Dana Chipman
Professor Mary DeRosa
Sir Christopher Greenwood
Dr. Wolff Heintschel von Heinegg
Sir Adam Roberts
Professor Gary Solis

Senior Fellows
Professor Laurie Blank
Major General (ret.) Blaise Cathcart QC
Professor Robert Chesney
Professor Geoff Corn
Professor Ashley Deeks
Brigadier General (ret.) Richard Gross
Colonel (ret.) Richard Jackson
Professor Chris Jenks
Professor Eric Talbot Jensen
Colonel (ret.) Michael Lacey
Professor Rain Liivoja
Professor Naz Modirzadeh
Professor Daphné Richemond-Barak
Professor Beth Van Schaack
Professor Matthew Waxman

This is not an official publication of the United States Military Academy, Department of the Army, or Department of Defense. The views expressed in this volume represent the authors' personal views and do not necessarily reflect those of the Department of Defense, the United States Army, the United States Military Academy, or any other department or agency of the United States Government. The analysis presented stems from their academic research of publicly available sources, not from protected operational information.

The Lieber Studies is the flagship publication of the Lieber Institute for Law and Warfare. It is designed to provide scholars, practitioners, and students with in-depth and critical analysis of the most challenging legal issues related to warfare in the 21st Century. Established by the Department of Law of the United States Military Academy at West Point, the mission of the Lieber Institute is to foster a deeper understanding of the complex and evolving relationship between law and land warfare in order to educate and empower current and future combat leaders. It does so through global academic engagement and advanced interdisciplinary research. As such, it lies at the crossroads of scholarship and practice by bringing together scholars, military officers, government legal advisers, and members of civil society from around the world to collaboratively examine the role and application of the law of armed conflict in current and future armed conflicts, as well as that of other regimes of international law in situations threatening international peace and security.

Lieber Institute for Law and Warfare
The Lieber Studies

VOLUME 8

Prisoners of War in Contemporary Conflict

General Editors
PROFESSOR MICHAEL N. SCHMITT
PROFESSOR SEAN WATTS

Managing Editor
PROFESSOR ROBERT LAWLESS

Volume Editors
PROFESSOR MICHAEL N. SCHMITT
MAJOR CHRISTOPHER J. KOSCHNITZKY

OXFORD
UNIVERSITY PRESS

Oxford University Press is a department of the University of Oxford. It furthers the University's objective of excellence in research, scholarship, and education by publishing worldwide. Oxford is a registered trade mark of Oxford University Press in the UK and certain other countries.

Published in the United States of America by Oxford University Press
198 Madison Avenue, New York, NY 10016, United States of America.

© Oxford University Press 2023

All rights reserved. No part of this publication may be reproduced, stored in a retrieval system, or transmitted, in any form or by any means, without the prior permission in writing of Oxford University Press, or as expressly permitted by law, by license, or under terms agreed with the appropriate reproduction rights organization. Inquiries concerning reproduction outside the scope of the above should be sent to the Rights Department, Oxford University Press, at the address above.

You must not circulate this work in any other form
and you must impose this same condition on any acquirer.

CIP data is on file at the Library of Congress

ISBN 978-0-19-766328-8

DOI: 10.1093/oso/9780197663288.001.0001

Printed by Integrated Books International, United States of America

Note to Readers
This publication is designed to provide accurate and authoritative information in regard to the subject matter covered. It is based upon sources believed to be accurate and reliable and is intended to be current as of the time it was written. It is sold with the understanding that the publisher is not engaged in rendering legal, accounting, or other professional services. If legal advice or other expert assistance is required, the services of a competent professional person should be sought. Also, to confirm that the information has not been affected or changed by recent developments, traditional legal research techniques should be used, including checking primary sources where appropriate.

(Based on the Declaration of Principles jointly adopted by a Committee of the American Bar Association and a Committee of Publishers and Associations.)

> You may order this or any other Oxford University Press publication by visiting the Oxford University Press website at www.oup.com.

CONTENTS

Foreword   ix
  Stuart W. Risch
Preface   xiii
Table of Cases   xvii
Table of Treaties   xxi
Contributors   xxix

PART ONE: Prisoner of War Status

1. Prisoners of War (POWs) in Proxy Warfare: The Application of Geneva Convention III to Organized Armed Groups Detaining POWs of Territorial States or Detained as POWs by Territorial States   3
   Marco Sassòli and Eugénie Duss

2. The Application of the Third Geneva Convention in Fluid Conflicts   27
   Laurie R. Blank

3. The Regular Armed Forces, Uniforms, and Prisoner of War Status   51
   Michael N. Schmitt and Christopher J. Koschnitzky

4. "Accompanying the Force" in Modern Armed Conflict   81
   Eric Talbot Jensen

5. *Levée en Masse* in Twenty-First-Century Armed Conflict   97
   Winston S. Williams and Robert Lawless

6. Prisoner of War Status in the Context of Naval Warfare: On the Status of Masters and Crews of Neutral Merchant Vessels   119
   Wolff Heintschel von Heinegg

7. Prisoners of War in Space?   141
   Rob McLaughlin

PART TWO: Prisoner of War Protections and Transfers and Release

8. Protecting Prisoners of War in Contemporary Conflicts   159
   Derek Jinks

9. Military Assimilation and the 1949 Third Geneva Convention on Prisoners of War   181
   Sean Watts

10. The Use of Force Against Prisoners of War: Operationalizing Article 42   211
    Chris Hanna and Bruce "Ossie" Oswald

11. Parole of Prisoners of War Under Article 21 of the Third Geneva Convention: The Past, Present, and Future   235
    Emily Crawford

12. Detention of Suspected Terrorists in Connection with Armed Conflict: A Focus on Release and Repatriation   253
    Pavle Kilibarda and Gloria Gaggioli

PART THREE: History and Perspectives

13. The Lieber Code and Prisoners of War: A Legacy of Practical Humanitarianism   307
    David Wallace and Shane Reeves

14. The Role of Judge Advocates in Prisoner of War and Detention Operations in the U.S. Army: A Short History   323
    Fred L. Borch III

15. The Updated ICRC Commentary on the Third Geneva Convention: A New Tool to Protect Prisoners of War in the Twenty-First Century   343
    Jemma Arman, Jean-Marie Henckaerts, Heleen Hiemstra, and Kvitoslava Krotiuk

16. ICRC Perspectives on the Interpretation of the Third Geneva Convention More Than Seventy Years after Its Adoption   375
    Jean-Marie Henckaerts, Kubo Mačák, Mikhail Orkin, and Ellen Policinski

17. A Perspective on the Updated Third Geneva Convention Commentary from a United States Practitioner   408
    Michael W. Meier

Index   437

FOREWORD

As of this writing, war between nations has again returned to Europe. Although conflicts in the Balkans, Chechnya, and Georgia in the late twentieth and early twenty-first centuries reminded the world that the horrors inflicted upon European nations during two world wars were not just a distant memory, they did not bring about the vigorous international reaction that the current Russian invasion of Ukraine has fostered. In this regard, the role of, and focus on, the laws of armed conflict (LOAC) are generating significant discussion and emphasis. Issues of neutrality, targeting, and protection of civilians are being discussed by scholars, soldiers, diplomats, and news media alike. There is also a renewed focus on an area of LOAC that has not regularly been discussed since before September 11, 2001: the treatment of persons captured or detained on the battlefield of an international armed conflict.

Like most conflicts between States, the current Russian invasion of Ukraine has resulted in the capture of members of the enemy's armed forces by both sides. The information available from both Ukraine and Russia indicate very different efforts, humane or otherwise, as to the treatment of prisoners of war (POWs). Granted, the conflict is only sixty-nine days old at the time of this writing, and the fighting, along with the survival of Ukraine as a nation, remains very unsettled. However, the rules regarding treatment of POWs are not, and cannot be, as unsettled. These rules apply regardless of whether the conflict is just starting, in progress, or has culminated. The treatment of POWs is governed by a thick web of LOAC rules designed to ensure humane treatment of those in captivity from the moment of capture until their release—rules that evolved over time and are grounded in the experience of two world wars and multiple, smaller international armed conflicts. Yet, even as detailed as these rules are, facets of them arguably remain ambiguous, especially as we transition from a twenty-year non-international armed conflict experience of detention activities.

Today in Ukraine, renewed interest in the identity and combatant status of people engaged in fighting is indicative of the overall challenges presented when sorting out privileges and immunities on the modern battlefield. Complex, and currently unanswered, questions facing both belligerents and neutral parties observing the conflict, implicate a wide range of issues regarding a person's status if captured. For example, for how long can a civilian population rise up to repel an invader if there is no end in sight to the invasion, and how should they then be treated if captured? What about foreign military volunteers flocking to Ukraine to join the armed forces and fight as a state-sanctioned militia? Or state-sanctioned paramilitary members from the Russian Wagner group? What about the status of civilian cyber actors who are not physically located in the conflict area but who answered Ukraine's call to attack and disrupt Russian military activities? Finally, what about military forces who enter a neutral's territory seeking aid, logistics, and/or training and those who provide it? These are only a few of the "status" questions that must be considered and addressed, underscoring the complex environment in which we determine when, and how, to apply the law governing POWs.

This challenge is not, of course, new. Questions about POWs have surfaced in every conflict since the dawn of time. For the United States, the Revolutionary and Civil Wars, World Wars I and II, the conflicts in Korea and Vietnam, and the first Gulf War have each presented numerous challenges and questions regarding treatment of POWs. While we may not have always answered them correctly, we have carefully studied what should occur in an effort to properly treat those captured on the battlefield. What we have consistently learned is that the rules governing POWs are complex. In 1979, Howard Levie edited the "Documents on Prisoners of War" for the U.S. Naval War College's International Law Studies. At the time, Mr. Levie, who as an Army Judge Advocate authored the armistice for the Korean conflict and was eminently experienced in the laws of war, noted in his preface that if one follows the documents "through the centuries of recorded history which they represent, there can be little doubt that [one] will observe that there has been, on the whole, a fairly steady improvement in the legal status of these unfortunates." While more documents added to the compilation of laws regarding treatment of POWs may not always be better, the underlying requirement remains true: it is essential for combatants to know the laws and to ultimately treat properly those over whom they take custody and responsibility during armed conflict. Advancing clearly understood scholarly insight into the treatment of persons captured on the battlefield remains one of our most important mandates as national security law practitioners, especially because the detention of combatants, members of organized armed groups, and civilians will raise both familiar and novel issues in the current and future wars.

This volume of the *Lieber Studies* book series, *Prisoners of War in Contemporary Conflict*, and the compilation of articles within, continues the thoughtful and positive evolution of information regarding battlefield detention undertaken by Howard Levie and others over the past centuries. It should be considered essential reading for advancing and clarifying authorities, roles, and responsibilities. It also highlights and reminds us of unique aspects of the evolving character of warfare for the twenty-first century, such as addressing the question of prisoners of war in space. Most importantly, it reminds us that, regardless of how war evolves, those who are captured will always require and deserve protection by the detaining powers supported by others, including the International Committee of the Red Cross.

I offer my most sincere thanks for the combined efforts undertaken by West Point's Lieber Institute for Law and Warfare and the U.S. Naval War College's Stockton Center for International Law to complete this vital project. Their contributions are significant and deserve the highest accolades. In particular, I want to commend the co-editors, West Point's G. Norman Lieber Distinguished Scholar, Professor Michael Schmitt, and Major Christopher Koschnitzky of the U.S. Naval War College's Stockton Center, for leading this effort. I also want to recognize the Strauss Center for International Security and Law at the University of Texas, and its Director and Senior Fellow of the Lieber Institute, Dean Bobby Chesney, for their substantial support of this work. Finally, I must thank each of the renowned contributors whose work made this volume possible. Their commitment to helping us all better understand the law governing POWs is inspiring. It is a commitment that will be realized, most significantly, on the field of battle.

Stuart W. Risch
Lieutenant General, United States Army
The Judge Advocate General

PREFACE

The conflict in Ukraine that began in 2014 has focused global attention on the treatment of prisoners of war (POWs) and other detainees during international armed conflicts. In parallel, the international law governing detention during such conflicts has become a topic of discussion and debate among scholars, practitioners, and the public. The ubiquitous nature of social media has pushed the matter to center stage, as images of, and reports about, captured combatants and others are tweeted, shared, and commented on, while the blog-o-sphere and media provide near real-time analysis. Questions about how the law of detention applies have taken on legal and strategic significance in this war.

West Point's Lieber Institute launched the project that led to this book the international law regarding prisoners of war well before the ongoing conflict descended into nationwide warfare in February 2022. Sadly, the project has become very timely.

The motivating factor for its launch was the International Committee of the Red Cross's (ICRC) release of its 2020 Commentary on the 1949 Geneva Convention Relative to the Treatment of Prisoners of War, which updated the existing 1960 "Pictet Commentary." Initially, the Lieber Institute intended to run an expert-driven workshop focusing on the law governing prisoners of war in order to engage the broader law of armed conflict community on the issues raised in the ICRC's work. Although COVID-19 made it impossible to hold the workshop, the Lieber Institute decided to continue the project in written form.

Of course, the issues of who is entitled to POW status and how they are to be treated are not new. In 1863, Francis Lieber addressed the matter in his so-called Lieber Code, issued as General Order 100 by President Lincoln for Union forces. Article 49 of the Code provides, "A prisoner of war is a public enemy armed or attached to the hostile army for active aid, who has fallen into the hands of the captor, either fighting or wounded, on the field or in the hospital, by individual surrender or by capitulation." The text seems straightforward, but its application was not. For instance, during the Civil War, General Sherman directed that those captured away from the main army had to possess "written orders from some army commander to do some military thing" to qualify for POW status, a condition that went beyond those set forth in the Lieber Code. It would not be the last time that practice on the battlefield and *lex scripta* diverged.

Since then, the law on POWs status has developed appreciably. The 1899 and 1907 Hague Regulations, 1929 and 1949 Geneva Prisoners of War Conventions, and 1977 Protocol Additional I to the 1949 Geneva Conventions directly addressed POWs. Along the way, however, debates over POW status and treatment persisted. Many remain contentious today and new ones have arisen, as evidenced by the ICRC's production of its new commentary.

It must be cautioned that, unlike the ICRC's Commentary, this book is not meant to be a comprehensive treatment of the international law relating to POWs. Rather, it is a collection of *capita selecta* identified by the contributors as meriting examination. These are issues that the individual experts zeroed in on as unsettled, confusing, unaddressed, or problematic.

The book is in three Parts. Part I examines qualification for POW status from two angles. Four chapters deal with types and domains of warfare—proxy, fluid, maritime, and space. The remaining three take on issues regarding the status of detainees cited in Article 4 of the Third Geneva Convention, specifically combatants, civilians accompanying the force, and members of a *levée en masse*.

Discussion then moves in Part II to the treatment to which POWs are entitled. The topics range from a broad survey of key issues regarding POW treatment in contemporary conflicts to narrow topics that have created confusion or proven challenging in practice. The latter group includes so-called military assimilation into the armed forces of the detaining Power, the use of force against POWs, prison of war parole, and the detention of suspected terrorists.

The book concludes with Part III's consideration of the historical relevance of, and perspectives on, the international law governing POWs. Fittingly for a book produced by West Point's Lieber Institute, the part begins with an assessment of the Lieber Code's legacy. A discussion of the historical role that Judge Advocates have played in POW and other detention operations follows.

Part III then turns to perspectives on the event that motivated the project, completion of the ICRC's Commentary on the Third Geneva Convention. It includes two pieces by members of that organization. The first is a reprinted article from the International Review of the Red Cross that was published on the occasion of the Commentary's release. It is followed by a chapter explaining the ICRC's perspective on interpretation of the Third Geneva Convention. The final chapter of the book offers an American assessment of the Commentary by a senior civilian U.S. Army Judge Advocate General's Corp practitioner writing in his personal capacity.

We thank the contributors to this work who "soldiered on" in the face of COVID-driven cancellation of the workshop at which they were to present their work to colleagues, and for their patience and consideration during the book's preparation. Any success of this project is due primarily to their dedication to better understanding of the law surrounding POWs.

The Lieber Institute is also to be commended for its support of the research and commitment to examining these important topics. In particular, we would like to thank Professor Robert Lawless, the Managing Editor of the Lieber Studies series, for his behind-the-scenes efforts that made possible the completion of the project. Special thanks are also due to our copyeditor, Michelle Nichols, who, in the face of personal challenges, stayed committed to completion of the project and ensured a professional product. Finally, this project would not have been possible without the generous co-sponsorship of the Strauss Center for International Security and Law at the University of Texas. In particular, we thank the Strauss Center's Director, Dean Bobby Chesney of the University of Texas School of Law, for making the Center's involvement possible and for his continued service as a Senior Fellow of the Lieber Institute.

History proves that we will likely not predict when the next international armed conflict may erupt. But what we do know is that issues of detention and POW status will matter. As the drafters of the Third Geneva Convention emphasized over seventy years ago, the aim of the law is "to mitigate as far as possible, the inevitable rigours [of a war] and to alleviate the condition of prisoners of war." It is with that lens that scholars and practitioners should continue to consider the rules governing POWs, and with which you should approach this book. After all, for members of the armed forces who go to war, the issues raised in the book are not purely academic; for them, a proper understanding of the law might be the difference between humane treatment and brutality, even between life and death.

Michael N. Schmitt
G. Norman Lieber Distinguished Scholar, West Point
Professor of Law, University of Reading

Christopher J. Koschnitzky
Major, United States Army, Judge Advocate
Military Professor, Stockton Center for
International Law
United States Naval War College

TABLE OF CASES

INTERNATIONAL CASES

Eritrea-Ethiopia Claims Commission

Prisoners of War—Eritrea's Claim, 398n.129
Prisoners of War—Eritrea's Claim 4, 184n.10
Prisoners of War—Eritrea's Claim 17, 13n.39
Prisoners of War—Ethiopia's Claim, 398n.129
Prisoners of War—Ethiopia's Claim 4, 13n.39, 184n.10
Prisoners of War—Ethiopia's Claim 17, 260n.40

Inter-American Commission on Human Rights

Abella v Argentina, 171n.53
Case 10.970 (Peru), 405n.164
Coard v United States, 264n.63
Goiburú v Paraguay, 287n.159

International Arbitration Awards

Great Britain v Costa Rica (Tinoco Claims Arbitration), 269n.90

International Court of Justice

Application of the Convention on the Prevention and Punishment of the Crime of Genocide (Bosnia & Herzegovina v Serbia & Montenegro), 5–6n.5, 6nn.9–10, 7n.15, 345n.8, 379n.18
Case Concerning Rights of Nationals of the United States of America in Morocco (France v United States of America), 384n.50
Kasikili/Sedudu Island (Botswana v Namibia), 345n.8, 379n.18, 391–92
LaGrand (Germany v United States), Provisional Measures, 10n.25
Legal Consequences for States of the Continued Presence of South Africa in Namibia (South West Africa), 391–92, 391n.95
Lockerbie (Libya v United Kingdom), 395–96n.119
Military and Paramilitary Activities in and against Nicaragua (Nicaragua v United States), 4n.1, 6n.9, 171n.50

Oil Platforms (Islamic Republic of Iran v United States of America), 385n.51
Question of the Delimitation of the Continental Shelf between Nicaragua and
  Colombia beyond 200 Nautical Miles from the Nicaraguan Coast (Nicaragua v
  Colombia), 379n.18
Territorial Dispute (Libyan Arab Jamahiriya v Chad), 379n.18

International Criminal Court

Katanga; Prosecutor v, 20n.83
Lubanga Dyilo; Prosecutor v, 5n.3, 17n.66, 21n.90, 28–29n.5, 41n.52

International Criminal Tribunal for former Yugoslavia

Blaškić; Prosecutor v, 10n.25
Delalić; Prosecutor v, 171n.49, 264n.65, 405n.164
Gotovina and Marc; Prosecutor v, 37n.35
Kunarac; Prosecutor v, 405n.164
Milutinović; Prosecutor v, 48n.71
Orić; Prosecutor v, 105n.42
Tadić; Prosecutor v, 3–4, 4n.1, 5, 6–7, 6n.6, 7n.11, 12, 15–16, 16n.60, 17n.66, 18–19,
  20–21, 20n.82, 21n.90, 24, 25, 27n.2, 30n.9, 41n.52, 171n.51, 262n.48, 262n.50,
  271–72, 271n.97, 273n.102, 275–77, 276nn.106–7, 376n.5, 431n.132

International Criminal Tribunal for Rwanda

Akayesu; Prosecutor v, 171n.52, 405n.164

Israeli Military Court

Omar Mahmud Kassem; Military Prosecutor v, 18n.71
Swarka Case, 74, 74n.105

Special Court for Sierra Leone

Sesay; Prosecutor v, 401n.144

Trials of War Criminals before the Nuremberg Military Tribunals

Dönitz; United States v, 127n.36
List; United States v, 48n.70, 127n.36
von Leeb; United States v, 195n.72

United Nations Committee against Torture

T.A. v Sweden, 405n.164

United Nations War Crimes Commission

Tanaka Hisakasu, Trial of General, 195n.72

EU Cases

European Court of Human Rights

Al-Jedda v United Kingdom, 296–97, 297n.199, 297n.200
Aydin v Turkey, 405n.164
Hassan v United Kingdom, 256n.12, 263n.54, 264n.63, 278–79, 279n.120, 285–86, 285n.150, 299n.206
Ilaşcu v Moldova and Russia, 12n.37
Nada v Switzerland, 297–98n.202
Soering v United Kingdom, 261n.46

National Cases

Australia

Turner; R v, 232n.77

Israel

Jaber Al-Bassiouni Ahmed v Prime Minister and Minister of Defence, 388n.76, 389, 389n.82

United Kingdom

Bin Mohamed Ali v Public Prosecutor, 76n.114
Gul; R v, 250n.104
Mohamed Ali v Public Prosecutor, 74–75, 75n.106
Mohammed v Ministry of Defence, 250n.104, 277n.111, 278–79
Oie Hee Koi; Public Prosecutor v, 19n.79

United States

Al-Adahi v Obama, 280, 280n.125, 282n.134
Al-Alwi v Trump, 23n.97
Al-Warafi v Obama, 280, 280n.126
Basardh v Obama, 282, 282nn.133–34
Buck; United States v, 74, 74n.104
Graham v Connor, 231n.72
Hamdan v Rumsfeld, 171n.54, 339–40, 340n.58
Hamdi v Rumsfeld, 23n.97, 90n.41, 280–81, 280n.128, 324n.2
Hudson v McMillian, 231nn.73–74
Lindh; United States v, 76n.114
Noriega; United States v., 179n.100, 205n.136
Quirin, Ex parte, 75, 75n.107, 76n.114, 430–31, 430n.123, 430n.126, 431n.128
Reid v Covert, 88, 88n.31
Sims v Artuz, 231nn.73–74
Territo, In re, 36n.30, 430–31, 430n.123, 430n.127, 431n.129
Whitley v Albers, 231, 231nn.72–73

TABLE OF TREATIES

GENEVA CONVENTIONS

Geneva Convention of 1929 (Convention Relative to the Treatment of Prisoners of War, July 27, 1929)
  generally, 38, 42–43, 65n.69, 84n.14, 87n.26, 185n.13, 193–95, 193n.62, 195n.72, 195–96n.74, 198–99, 243–44, 243n.68, 316n.48, 319, 327, 328, 347–48, 354, 386n.62, 397, 424, 424n.85
  Preamble, 385–86
  Art 2, 319n.68
  Art 10, 194n.64
  Art 11, 194n.65, 198n.86
  Art 23, 194n.66
  Art 25(1), 197n.81
  Art 27, 194nn.68–69
  Art 27(4), 200, 200n.103
  Art 30, 194n.68
  Art 31, 38n.38
  Art 34, 194n.67
  Art 45, 194n.70
  Art 46, 194n.70
  Art 77, 243
  Art 81, 84
Geneva Conventions of 1949
  generally, 5, 38, 87, 143, 162–63, 165, 167n.31, 168n.38, 175, 177, 184–85n.11, 196, 328–29, 333–34, 361n.85, 376, 379, 383–84, 385, 386–87, 391–93, 394–95, 396–97, 399, 400–4, 406–7, 416, 426
  Common Art 1, 293, 293–94n.184, 423–24, 426
  Common Art 2, 33, 336, 341–42, 427
  Common Art 2(1), 426–27
  Common Art 3, 27–28, 32–33, 39, 40, 150n.38, 161, 165, 169, 170–74, 268–69, 274, 277–79, 285, 286–87, 290, 293–94n.184, 329, 336, 336n.46, 337, 341–42, 387, 401, 404–5
Convention (I) for the Amelioration of the Condition of the Wounded and Sick in the Armed Forces in the Field, Aug. 12, 1949 (First Geneva Convention)
  generally, 146–47, 146n.27, 159n.1, 181–82, 182n.3, 386–87, 423n.83, 426n.98
  Preamble, 386n.64
  Art 3, 268n.86, 278n.113
  Art 8, 390, 405–6
  Art 13, 53–54n.13, 349
  Art 14, 349–50n.28
  Art 18(3), 271n.95
  Art 35, 380–82
  Art 38(2), 405–6
  Art 39, 380–82
  Art 49, 175n.81
  Art 55, 384n.43, 403n.156
Convention (II) for the Amelioration of the Condition of the Wounded, Sick, and Shipwrecked Members of Armed Forces at Sea, Aug. 12, 1949 (Second Geneva Convention)
  generally, 120, 146–47, 146n.26, 159n.1, 386–87, 423n.83, 426n.98
  Preamble, 386n.64
  Art 3, 268n.86, 278n.113
  Art 4, 147n.28
  Art 8, 390, 405–6
  Art 12, 147n.29
  Art 13, 53–54n.13, 132, 135, 349

Art 13(5), 120n.7
Art 16, 147–48, 147n.29, 147n.30, 349–50n.28
Art 18, 154n.56
Art 28, 324n.1
Art 50, 175n.81
Convention (III) Relative to the Treatment of Prisoners of War, Aug. 12, 1949 (Third Geneva Convention)
generally, 4, 8, 9–10, 13–16, 17–18, 19, 22, 23, 24, 25, 27n.3, 28, 29, 30, 32–33, 34–35, 39–40, 41, 42, 44–45, 46, 47, 49–50, 52, 52n.5, 62, 65n.69, 69, 71, 80, 85n.16, 98n.4, 106n.50, 120, 146–47, 155, 159n.1, 165–69, 172–73, 176–77, 181–84, 181n.1, 185n.13, 196–97, 201, 202, 203–5, 206–8, 209–10, 230, 235n.1, 243–44, 255–56, 255n.8, 257–58, 270–71, 274, 280–82, 284, 291, 294, 299, 316, 316n.48, 319, 321, 328–29, 328n.21, 334–35, 336, 344–46, 348, 349, 352, 353, 356–57, 358–62, 365, 367, 368–69, 372, 373–74, 378, 379, 383–84, 383n.41, 385–86, 398, 409–10, 413, 417–18, 420–21, 423, 423n.83, 426n.98, 430
Art 2, 162nn.7–8
Art 2(1), 359n.74
Art 3, 165n.16, 170n.45, 171n.56, 268n.86, 278n.113
Art 3(1)(d), 169n.44
Art 3(2), 15n.57
Art 4, 18–19, 31, 34, 42–43, 44, 61, 80, 84, 93, 95, 143, 163n.11, 257n.18, 298n.204, 349, 354, 355, 360
Art 4(1), 60–61
Art 4(2), 60–61
Art 4A, 31, 31n.11, 42n.54, 53, 54n.14, 62, 101n.20, 132, 135, 160–61n.6, 349, 429–30
Arts 4A(1)–(3), 213–14
Art 4A(1), 32, 54–55, 63, 64, 66–68, 69–70, 74, 78, 101n.17, 351–52
Art 4A(2), 10–11, 16, 18–19, 41–42, 42n.53, 55, 64, 66, 67–68, 69–70, 74, 75–76, 78, 101n.18, 165n.14, 268–70, 269n.91, 350–52
Art 4A(2)(a), 113n.75

Art 4A(2)(b), 54
Art 4A(3), 66–68, 66n.72, 69–70, 74, 269n.90
Arts 4A(4)–(5), 204–5n.134
Art 4A(4), 256n.13
Art 4A(5), 120nn.6–7, 256n.13
Art 4A(6), 104, 104n.39, 106n.46, 110n.64, 114n.82, 165n.14
Art 4(B)(1), 354n.52
Art 4(B)(2), 354n.52
Art 5, 11, 29, 42, 43, 44, 46–47, 116, 116n.89, 142n.3, 167n.33, 222n.41, 257n.21, 332n.33
Art 5(1), 23n.99, 29, 32, 33–34, 34n.19, 35, 38–39, 40–41, 46, 47–49, 208n.150
Art 5(2), 22n.92, 44, 44n.60, 354
Art 7, 167n.32
Arts 8–11, 167n30
Art 8, 390, 405–6
Art 12, 9, 35, 294n.186, 431–32, 431n.131
Art 12(2), 361n.83, 361n.86
Art 12(3), 361n.83, 361n.88
Art 13, 132, 150n.38, 151, 166n.23, 166n.25, 167n.28, 215n.10, 319n.69, 356, 358n.72, 361–62
Art 13(3), 261n.41
Art 14, 166n.24, 356
Art 14(1), 199n.94
Art 14(2), 357n.68
Art 15, 13n.40, 368n.126
Art 16, 146–47, 151, 356, 357–58, 369n.137
Art 17, 63, 142n.3, 360, 433, 434
Art 17(4), 166n.26
Art 18, 360
Art 18(3), 357n.65
Art 19, 149n.36, 202n.119, 360
Art 19(1), 360n.79
Art 20, 14n.49, 149n.36, 202–3, 202n.120, 334n.40, 358n.71, 360
Art 20(1), 360n.80
Art 20(2), 380–82
Art 20(3), 360.81
Arts 21–48, 165–66n22
Arts 21–22, 47–48n69
Art 21, 16n.61, 22n.94, 151, 155, 155n.59, 165–66n.18, 166n.20,

235–36, 244–48, 249, 250–51, 257n.20, 355–56
Art 21(1), 365n.108
Arts 21(2)–(3), 15n.55
Art 21(3), 13n.42
Art 22, 144–45, 144n.14, 147–34, 149, 150, 151n.43, 152
Art 22(1), 359n.76, 365n.107
Art 22(2), 14n.52
Art 23, 13n.45, 145, 198
Art 23(2), 14n.49, 198n.83
Arts 23(3)–(4), 13n.43
Art 23(4), 380–82
Arts 25–32, 151n47
Arts 25–30, 13n40
Art 25, 165–66n.18, 197–98, 358nn.71–73, 360n.77, 366
Art 25(1), 14n.49, 366n.109
Art 26, 198, 358n.72, 366, 367
Art 26(1), 198n.87, 393n.102
Art 26(2), 366n.115
Art 26(4), 14n.52, 367n.117
Art 27, 198–99, 199n.90, 358n.72, 367
Art 28, 165–66n.18, 206, 367n.120
Art 29, 165–66n.18, 358n.72
Art 29(1), 369n.131
Art 29(3), 393n.103
Art 30, 205–6
Art 30(2), 368n.127
Art 33, 14n.48, 223n.45, 256n.13, 358n.71
Art 34, 369n.133
Art 38, 151n.46, 165–66n.18, 369, 369n.133
Art 39, 10–11, 432, 432n.135
Art 39(1), 8n.22
Art 40, 176n.85
Art 42, 213, 213n.5, 216–18, 222–23, 224–25, 226–27, 228, 229, 230–32, 233, 356n.60
Art 43, 22n.94
Art 44, 176n.86, 357n.65
Art 44(2), 14n.52
Arts 46–48, 35, 294–95n188, 361n83
Art 46, 203, 203n.125, 358n.71, 358n.73
Art 46(2), 14n.49, 149n.36
Art 47, 149n.36

Arts 49–57, 167n29
Art 49, 333
Art 49(1), 200n.99
Art 49(2), 200n.99
Art 49(3), 200n.99
Art 50, 199nn.95–96, 358n.73
Art 51, 14n.48, 200, 204n.130
Arts 51(1)–(2), 14n.49
Art 51(1), 200n.102
Art 52, 333, 358n.71
Art 52(2), 14n.49
Art 53, 204n.130, 371n.145
Art 54, 200, 200n.104
Art 56, 223n.45
Art 57(1), 200n.100
Art 58(1), 13n.47
Art 60, 13n.40, 13nn.46–47, 183n.8, 353n.49, 358n.71
Art 60(1), 200–1
Art 61, 13n.47, 22n.94, 345n.7
Art 62, 22n.94, 249, 249n.98, 371
Arts 63–66, 13n47
Art 63, 22n.94
Art 63(3), 13n.42
Art 69, 22n.94
Art 70, 370
Art 71, 22n.94, 370
Art 74, 371n.142
Art 76, 356n.60
Art 78(1), 208n.148
Art 78(2), 208n.149
Art 81(2), 372n.154, 372n.155
Arts 82–108, 93n50, 246–47
Arts 82–88, 11n35
Art 82, 8n.22, 167n.31, 177n.91, 202, 358–59, 358n.71, 358n.73
Art 82(1), 201, 201n.109
Art 83, 373n.156
Art 84, 11n.34, 177n.91, 358n.71, 358n.73
Art 84(1), 8n.22
Art 84(2), 373n.159
Art 85, 167n.31, 179n.99, 351–52
Art 86, 373n.160
Art 87, 48n.70, 177n.87, 178n.95, 199n.98, 202, 203n.124, 358n.71, 358n.73
Arts 87–88, 167n31

Art 87(1), 8n.22, 201, 201n.110, 203n.123
Art 87(2), 201–2, 201n.112
Art 88, 201, 202, 358n.71
Arts 88(1)–88(3), 201n.111
Arts 89–108, 11n35
Art 89, 202, 202n.117, 373n.157
Art 91, 223n.45
Art 92, 223n.45, 356n.60, 387–88
Art 92(1), 387n.72
Art 95, 201–2, 356n.60, 358n.71
Art 95(1), 201–2nn.113–14
Art 96, 202, 202n.118
Arts 97–98, 202n.116
Art 97, 202
Art 98, 202
Arts 99–108, 166n.27
Art 99, 8n.22, 48n.70, 373n.160
Art 99(1), 48n.71
Art 100, 22n.94
Art 102, 8n.22, 201, 203n.124, 358n.71, 358n.73
Art 103, 358n.71, 358n.73
Art 104, 13n.42
Art 105, 175, 175n.82, 177n.91, 373n.159
Art 106, 175n.83, 358n.71
Art 107(2), 13n.42
Art 108, 202, 202n.115, 358n.73
Art 108(1), 8n.22
Art 108(2), 366n.112
Art 109, 246
Art 110, 364n.98
Art 111, 15n.56
Arts 118–119, 35n.27
Art 118, 16n.61, 29, 165–66n.18, 258, 258n.29, 259, 260–62, 274–75, 285, 294n.185, 299, 362–64
Art 118(1), 23n.96, 32–34, 32n.12, 34n.21, 36, 39
Art 119, 261n.44
Art 120(1), 364n.103
Art 120(6), 365n.104
Art 122, 8n.22, 13nn.41–42, 155n.58
Art 123, 22nn.94–95, 349n.26
Art 126, 151n.47, 349n.26, 372
Art 127(1), 359
Art 127(2), 359

Arts 129–131, 168nn.39–40
Art 129, 175n.81
Art 130, 150n.38
Art 133, 345n.9, 402n.154
Annex IV.A, 352–53
Convention (IV) Relative to the Protection of Civilian Persons in Time of War, Aug. 12, 1949 (Fourth Geneva Convention)
generally, 15–16, 20, 40, 90–91, 91n.42, 93, 101n.19, 159n.1, 182–83, 182n.5, 255–56, 255n.9, 257–58, 262–64, 266, 270–71, 274, 280, 282–83, 286–87, 299, 345, 374, 423n.83, 426n.98
Art 3, 268n.86, 278n.113
Art 4, 16n.59, 20n.84, 165n.15, 258n.28, 262n.49
Art 6, 37
Art 9, 390, 405–6
Art 23, 389
Art 27, 279
Art 27(4), 403–4
Art 35, 267–68
Art 42, 262n.51, 264–65, 403–4
Art 43, 263n.55, 355
Art 43(1), 263n.57, 263n.59
Art 45, 267nn.79–80
Art 47, 272n.100
Art 49, 266n.77, 267–68, 269–70
Arts 64–78, 93n51
Art 78, 263n.52, 263n.55, 264–65, 355
Art 78(2), 263n.57, 263n.60
Art 84, 48n.69
Art 85(1), 150n.39
Art 85(3), 393n.103
Art 89(1), 393n.102
Arts 99–104, 93n51
Arts 132–133, 263–64n58
Art 132, 265n.69, 266n.72, 267–68, 294n.185
Art 133, 294n.185
Art 134, 266n.73, 267–68
Art 146, 175n.81
Protocols to the Convention, June 8, 1977
generally, 73, 159, 162–63, 165, 168n.38, 343–44, 388, 391–92, 394–95, 396, 406, 414, 422–23

Protocol Additional to the Geneva
 Conventions of 12 August 1949, and
 Relating to the Protection of Victims
 of International Armed Conflicts,
 June 8, 1977 (Additional Protocol I)
 generally, 10–11, 12, 14–15, 17, 44, 56,
  57–58, 60, 64, 71, 72, 143n.8, 159n.2,
  165, 169, 185n.13, 203–4, 203n.126,
  213n.6, 244, 255–56, 256n.11, 259,
  335, 335n.45, 336, 354, 357–58,
  364–65, 406, 422–23
 Art 1(4), 143, 162n.7, 271n.98
 Art 11(1), 150
 Arts 11(3)–(6), 151n.44
 Art 16, 271n.95
 Art 26(1), 198n.85
 Art 26(4), 198n.88
 Art 34(2)(c), 365n.105
 Art 35, 218, 218n.24, 220n.33
 Art 37, 60n.41
 Art 41, 198n.84, 394–95
 Art 41(2), 223n.44
 Art 41(3), 15n.54
 Arts 43–45, 143
 Art 43, 10n.30, 17n.63, 213–14
 Art 43(2), 167n.31
 Art 44, 57–58, 57n.24, 72, 72nn.95–96, 204n.128
 Art 44(1), 222n.41
 Art 44(2), 57n.24, 58, 58n.31
 Art 44(3), 17n.62, 57, 72–73, 79
 Art 44(4), 72, 72n.97
 Art 44(7), 72, 72n.98
 Art 45, 11n.31, 204n.128, 244n.75
 Art 45(1), 44n.61
 Art 46(1), 59, 59n.37
 Art 49(3), 126n.33, 138
 Art 50(1), 18–19, 18n.74, 46–47
 Art 51(3), 19n.75, 116n.91, 121n.9, 138
 Art 52(2), 126n.33, 394–95
 Art 70, 388n.76, 389
 Art 70(1), 389n.78
 Art 70(2), 389n.78
 Art 75, 15–16, 161, 165n.17, 172–75,
  173n.73, 244n.75, 355, 388n.76
 Art 75(1), 150n.38, 357n.70
 Arts 75(3)–(7), 174n.75
 Art 75(4), 174n.79
 Art 75(5), 366nn.112–13
 Art 77(4), 366n.113
 Art 85, 266n.78, 267–68
 Art 85(4)(b), 259n.31
 Art 91, 6n.8
 Art 96, 271–72
Protocol Additional to the Geneva
 Conventions of 12 August 1949, and
 Relating to the Protection of Victims
 of Non-International Armed Conflicts,
 June 8, 1977 (Additional Protocol II)
 generally, 27–28, 27n.1, 35, 159n.2,
  165, 169, 277, 277n.110, 278, 285,
  286–87, 290, 406, 422–23
 Art 1, 162n.9
 Arts 2–6, 165n17, 173–74n73
 Art 2(2), 24n.101
 Art 4, 278n.114
 Art 5, 278n.115
 Art 5(1)(b), 150n.39
 Art 5(4), 35n.24
 Art 6, 173–74, 174n.76
 Art 6(3), 174n.78
 Art 6(5), 289–90, 289n.168
 Art 10, 271n.95
 Art 13(3), 121n.9
 Arts 75(3)–(4), 174n.77
Protocol Additional to the Geneva
 Conventions of 12 August 1949,
 and Relating to the Adoption of an
 Additional Distinctive Emblem,
 Dec. 8, 2005
 generally, 184–85n.11

Hague Conventions and Regulations

Convention No. II with Respect to the
 Laws and Customs of War on Land,
 July 29, 1899 (Hague II)
 generally, 185n.13, 242, 242n.62
 Arts 10–12, 243n64
 Art 10, 243n.65
 Art 11, 243n.66
 Art 12, 243n.67
Convention No. IV Respecting the Laws
 and Customs of War on Land, Oct.
 18, 1907 (Hague IV)
 generally, 84n.13, 185n.13, 242,
  242n.62, 257n.19

Art 2, 68n.78
Art 3, 6n.8
Arts 10–12, 242n64
Art 10, 243n.65
Art 11, 243n.66
Art 12, 243n.67

Convention No. X for the Adaptation to Maritime Warfare of the Principles of the Geneva Convention, Oct. 18, 1907 (Hague X)
Preamble, 386n.64

Convention No. XI Relative to Certain Restrictions with Regard to the Exercise of the Right of Capture in Naval War, Oct. 18, 1907 (Hague XI)
generally, 120n.3, 133
Art 5, 132–33, 132n.71, 136n.89, 137
Art 8, 133, 136n.89

Convention No. XIII Concerning the Rights and Duties of Neutral Powers in Naval War, Oct. 18, 1907 (Hague XIII)
generally, 119n.2

Regulations Respecting the Laws and Customs of War on Land, annexed to Convention No. II with Respect to the Laws and Customs of War on Land, July 29, 1899 (Hague Regulations of 1899)
generally, 54n.15, 61, 65n.69, 66, 68, 71, 83, 104, 185n.13, 190–94, 198–99, 200–1, 326, 347–48, 347n.15, 354
Art 1, 54, 61n.48, 68n.79
Art 2, 104n.37
Art 6, 191n.49
Art 7(2), 191n.47, 199n.89
Art 13, 83n.12
Art 29, 59n.34

Regulations Respecting the Laws and Customs of War on Land, annexed to Convention No. IV Respecting the Laws and Customs of War on Land, Oct. 18, 1907 (Hague Regulations of 1907)
generally, 54, 54n.16, 59, 61, 65n.69, 68, 71, 185n.13, 190–94, 198–99, 200–1, 243, 243n.64, 255–56, 255n.10, 326, 326n.12
Art 1, 61n.48, 62, 64, 64n.63, 68n.78, 68n.79, 87n.26, 257–58, 258n.25, 269n.87, 326–27
Art 2, 104n.38
Art 4, 326–27
Arts 6–20, 326–27
Art 6, 191n.50
Art 6(3), 191n.50
Art 7(2), 191n.47, 198n.86, 199n.89
Art 8, 192n.52
Art 10, 257n.19
Art 12, 246n.84
Art 13, 83
Art 17, 191n.51
Art 23, 178n.94
Art 23(b), 60, 60n.40
Arts 29–30, 59n35

Declaration Concerning Expanding Bullets, July 29, 1899
generally, 220, 221n.37

Vienna Convention on the Law of Treaties, May 23, 1969

generally, 184–85n.11, 377–78, 379, 380–82, 383, 384, 385, 390, 391–92, 407, 413, 413n.28
Art 26, 415–16
Arts 31–33, 345, 345n8, 379n17, 379, 380, 414
Art 31, 43n.59, 60–61, 205n.139, 379–80, 382–83, 395–96, 397, 399, 402–4, 414, 415, 416–17
Art 31(1), 61n.44, 69, 69n.85, 383n.39, 396, 414, 414n.35, 415–16
Art 31(2), 61n.45, 396, 414, 415n.36, 416
Art 31(3), 350n.33, 388, 414, 415n.37, 416, 416n.45, 420
Art 31(3)(a), 388
Art 31(3)(b), 388n.75, 390–91, 396, 399–400, 407
Art 31(3)(c), 391, 423
Art 31(4), 415n.38
Art 32, 379, 380, 388, 391, 395–96, 399–400, 402–4, 407, 414, 415, 415n.39, 416–18
Art 33, 345n.9, 379, 380, 383–84
Art 33(1), 402–3
Art 33(3), 402–3

Art 33(4), 402-3
Art 61, 14n.50

UNITED NATIONS CHARTER

generally, 293
Art 2(4), 131
Art 51, 428
Art 103, 298

OTHER TREATIES

African Charter on Human and Peoples' Rights, June 27, 1981
  Art 3, 172n.63
  Arts 6-7, 172n63
  Art 6, 285n.148
Agreement between the British and Ottoman Governments respecting Prisoners of War and Civilians, Dec. 1917
  generally, 347n.18
Agreement Between the United States of America and Germany Concerning Prisoners of War, Sanitary Personnel, and Civilians, Nov. 11, 1918
  generally, 187n.23, 193n.59
Agreement Governing the Activities of States on the Moon and Other Celestial Bodies, Dec. 18, 1979
  generally, 152
  Art 10(1), 153n.48
Agreement on the Rescue of Astronauts and the Return of Objects Launched in Outer Space, Apr. 22, 1968 (Rescue Agreement)
  generally, 153-54, 155, 156
  Arts 1-4, 153n50
  Art 1, 153n.50
  Art 2, 153n.51
  Art 3, 153n.52
  Art 4, 142n.3, 153n.54
American Convention on Human Rights, Nov. 22, 1969
  Arts 7-9, 172n63
  Art 7, 285n.148
Convention Against Torture and Other Cruel, Inhuman or Degrading Treatment or Punishment, Dec. 10, 1984
  generally, 172n.63, 422-23, 422n.77
Convention for the Amelioration of the Condition of the Wounded in Armies in the Field, Aug. 22, 1864
  generally, 191n.44, 308n.2, 310
Convention for the Protection of Human Rights and Fundamental Freedoms, Nov. 4, 1950
  generally, 172-73, 279n.119, 285-86, 299-300, 422-23, 422n.79
  Arts 5-7, 172n63
  Art 5, 278-79, 285n.149, 299n.206
  Art 6, 172n.65
  Art 6, §1, 172-73n68
  Art 6, §2, 172-73n67
  Art 6, §3(b), 173n.69
  Art 6, §3(c), 173n.70
  Art 6, §3(d), 173n.71
Convention of Copenhagen IV (1917)
  generally, 192-93
  Ch III, Art 1, 193n.57
Convention on Registration of Objects Launched into Outer Space, Jan 14, 1975 (Registration Convention)
  generally, 153
  Art 1, 153n.54
  Art 1(b), 144n.12
Convention on the Prohibition of the Development, Production, Stockpiling and Use of Chemical Weapons and on their Destruction, Sept. 17, 1997 (Chemical Weapons Convention)
  generally, 219-20, 219n.27
  Art 1(5), 219
  Art II(9)(d), 219, 219n.28
Convention Relating to the Status of Refugees, July 28, 1951
  Art 33, 261n.46
Declaration Concerning the Laws of Maritime War, Feb. 26, 1909 (London Declaration)
  generally, 120n.3, 123, 123n.22, 126, 130
  Art 14, 130n.60
  Arts 22-64, 119-20n4
  Art 37, 131n.61

Art 45(2), 131n.62
Art 46, 124–25, 126
Art 46(1), 131n.66
Art 46(2), 123n.20, 131n.65
Art 46(3), 123n.20, 131n.65
Art 46(4), 131n.67
Art 55, 123
Art 56, 123
Art 57, 121n.11
Art 57(1), 121n.11
Art 57(2), 121n.11
Art 60, 126
Art 63, 124–25, 126

Declaration Renouncing the Use, in Time of War, of Explosive Projectiles Under 400 Grammes Weight, Nov. 29/Dec. 11, 1868
generally, 191n.45, 308, 308n.3, 310

Dix-Hill Cartel on Prisoner Exchanges, July 22, 1862
generally, 239–40
Art 4, 239n.24

International Covenant on Civil and Political Rights, Dec. 16, 1966
generally, 422–23, 422n.78
Art 9, 172n.63, 285n.148
Art 9(4), 208n.151
Art 9(5), 208n.151
Art 12(4), 293n.183
Art 14, 172–73, 172n.64
Art 14, §1, 172n.66
Art 14, §2, 172n.67
Art 14, §3, 173nn.70–71
Art 14, §3(c), 173n.68
Art 14, §3(d), 173n.69
Arts 14–15, 172n.63
Art 15, §1, 173n.72

Peace Treaty between the Holy Roman Emperor and the King of France and their Respective Allies, Oct. 24, 1648
Arts CX–CXI, 238–39, 238n.14, 242

Procés-Verbal: Relating to the Rules of Submarine Warfare Set Forth in Part IV of the Treaty of London of April 22, 1930, Nov. 6, 1936 (London Submarine Protocol)
generally, 126–27, 126n.35

Project of an International Declaration concerning the Laws and Customs of War, Aug. 27, 1874 (Brussels Declaration)
generally, 59, 61, 68, 71, 82n.7, 83, 86, 87, 103, 189–90, 242, 347
Art 9, 61n.48, 68n.79
Art 10, 103, 103n.35, 104
Art 27, 189n.38
Art 28, 190n.40, 215n.12
Arts 31–33, 242n62
Art 34, 83n.11, 86n.21

Responsibility of States for Internationally Wrongful Acts, Jan 28, 2002
Art 30, 270n.92

Rome Statute of the International Criminal Court July 17, 1998
generally, 60, 168n.41, 184–85n.11, 221, 221n.39, 267–68, 268n.82, 422–23, 422n.76
Art 8(2)(b)(xi), 60n.42

Stabilization Force, Framework Agreement
Annex 1A, 168n.38
Annex 6, 168n.38

Statute of the International Court of Justice, June 26, 1946
generally, 401–2
Art 38(1)(d), 400n.141, 402n.152

Treaty of Addis Ababa, 1896
generally, 347n.13

Treaty of Amity and Commerce Between His Majesty the King of Prussia and the United States of America, Sept. 10, 1785 (Treaty of Amity)
generally, 187, 187n.22
Art XXIV, 187n.24

Treaty on Principles Governing the Activities of States in the Exploration and Use of Outer Space, Including the Moon and Other Celestial Bodies, Jan 27, 1967 (Outer Space Treaty)
Art I, 141–42n.2
Art III, 141–42n.2
Art IV, 149
Art IV(2), 149n.37
Art V, 142n.3, 152
Art VI, 141–42n.2
Art VIII, 152

CONTRIBUTORS

Jemma Arman is a regional legal adviser of the International Committee of the Red Cross based in Nairobi. In her previous assignment, she was a legal adviser in the Commentaries Update Unit.

Laurie R. Blank is a Clinical Professor of Law and the Director of the International Humanitarian Law Clinic at the Emory University School of Law.

Fred L. Borch III is the Professor of Legal History & Leadership at The Judge Advocate General's Legal Center & School and the Regimental Historian & Archivist for the U.S. Army Judge Advocate General's Corps. He retired from the U.S. Army's Judge Advocate General's Corps at the rank of Colonel.

Emily Crawford is an Associate Professor at the University of Sydney Law School.

Eugénie Duss is a doctoral candidate at the University of Geneva, Switzerland.

Gloria Gaggioli is the Director of the Geneva Academy of International Humanitarian Law and Human Rights and an Associate and Swiss National Science Foundation Professor at the Law Faculty of the University of Geneva.

Chris Hanna is a former Director-General of the Australian Defence Force Legal Services and currently a legal practitioner in the Australian Capital Territory. He transferred to the Royal Australian Air Force Reserve at the rank of Air Commodore.

Wolff Heintschel von Heinegg holds the Chair of Public Law, in particular public international law, European law, and foreign constitutional law, at the Europa-Universitat Viadrina in Frankfurt (Oder), Germany. He is also the President of the International Society for Military Law and the Law of War.

Jean-Marie Henckaerts is head of the Commentaries Update Unit of the International Committee of the Red Cross.

Heleen Hiemstra is a legal adviser in the Commentaries Update Unit of the International Committee of the Red Cross.

Eric Talbot Jensen is a Professor of Law at Brigham Young University Law School.

Derek Jinks is the A.W. Walker Centennial Chair at the University of Texas School of Law.

Pavle Kilibarda is a Postdoctoral Researcher at the Faculty of Law of the University of Geneva.

Christopher J. Koschnitzky, Major, U.S. Army, is a Judge Advocate and Military Professor at the Stockton Center for International Law, United States Naval War College.

Kvitoslava Krotiuk is an adviser in the Office of the President of the International Committee of the Red Cross. In her previous assignment, she was a legal adviser in the Commentaries Update Unit.

Robert Lawless is an Assistant Professor in the Department of Law and the Research Director of the Lieber Institute for Law and Warfare at the United States Military Academy at West Point.

Kubo Mačák is a legal adviser jointly assigned to the Commentaries Update Unit and the Arms and Conduct of Hostilities Unit of the International Committee of the Red Cross.

Rob McLaughlin is a Professor at the Australian National Centre for Oceans Resources and Security and a Senior Fellow at the Stockton Center for International Law, United States Naval War College.

Michael W. Meier is the Special Assistant to the Judge Advocate General for Law of War Matters at the Department of the Army.

Mikhail Orkin is a legal adviser in the Commentaries Update Unit of the International Committee of the Red Cross.

Bruce "Ossie" Oswald is a Professor at Melbourne Law School.

Ellen Policinski is a legal adviser in the Commentaries Update Unit of the International Committee of the Red Cross.

Shane Reeves, Brigadier General, U.S. Army, is the Dean of the Academic Board for the United States Military Academy at West Point. General Reeves is also the Co-Founder of the Lieber Series.

Stuart W. Risch, Lieutenant General, U.S. Army, is the Judge Advocate General of the United States Army.

Marco Sassòli is a Professor of International Law at the University of Geneva.

Michael N. Schmitt is the G. Norman Lieber Distinguished Scholar at the U.S. Military Academy, Professor of International Law at the University of Reading, Strauss Center Distinguished Scholar at the University of Texas, and the Charles H. Stockton Distinguished Scholar-in-Residence at the U.S. Naval War College.

David Wallace, Brigadier General (Retired), United States Army, is the United States Naval Academy's Class of 1971 Distinguished Military Professor of Law & Leadership.

Sean Watts is a Professor of Law and Co-Director of the Lieber Institute for Law and Warfare at the United States Military Academy at West Point. He is also a Visiting Professor at the University of Reading.

Winston S. Williams, Colonel, U.S. Army, is a Judge Advocate and the Head of the Department of Law at the United States Military Academy at West Point.

PART ONE

Prisoner of War Status

PART ONE

Prisoner of War Status

1

Prisoners of War (POWs) in Proxy Warfare: The Application of Geneva Convention III to Organized Armed Groups Detaining POWs of Territorial States or Detained as POWs by Territorial States

MARCO SASSÒLI[*] AND EUGÉNIE DUSS[**] ■

INTRODUCTION

As clearly determined by the International Criminal Tribunal for the former Yugoslavia (ICTY) in the *Tadić* case, an armed conflict between a State and an armed group is subject to the international humanitarian law (IHL) of

---

[*]. Marco Sassòli is a Professor of International Law at the University of Geneva, Switzerland.

[**]. Eugénie Duss is a teaching assistant and doctoral candidate at the University of Geneva, Switzerland. Parts III–V of this contribution are based upon the results of her research in view of her PhD thesis on international humanitarian law applicable in proxy warfare. We thank Mr. Joshua Niyo, LLM and doctoral candidate at the Graduate Institute of International and Development Studies for having revised this text.

international armed conflict (IAC) if a foreign State controls that group.[1] For the purposes of this contribution, we will call the first State involved the "territorial State," although hostilities could occur on the territory of another State—which could raise additional legal difficulties that we will ignore here. The armed group controlled by another State will be called the "proxy-armed group" and the State sponsoring the proxy will be called the "controlling State."

Good ideas developed in a courtroom or in academic writings have to withstand the test of reality.[2] This is even more so in IHL, which is a profoundly pragmatic endeavor and meaningful only if it can work on the battlefield. One such idea, which totally conforms to legal logic, is the aforementioned "*Tadić*-theory," which, as explained, applies IAC IHL to hostilities between the territorial State and a proxy-armed group. Geneva Convention (III) Relative to the Treatment of Prisoners of War is an essential part of IAC IHL. The rules contained in that instrument concerning prisoners of war (POWs) differ significantly from the IHL rules of non-international armed conflicts (NIACs) governing detention of enemy fighters; only very rarely can they be applied by analogy to a NIAC. In this chapter, we attempt to apply the Third Geneva Convention to a proxy-armed group—which, as an armed group, would normally be addressed by NIAC IHL.

Part II examines why armed conflicts conducted by a proxy-armed group are subject to IAC IHL. We will explain the controversies surrounding the *Tadić* theory and explain why the correct test for the applicability of IAC IHL in these situations is that the proxy is under overall control of the controlling State. Yet, as we will discuss, the *Tadić* theory raises particular problems for the application of the Third Geneva Convention. The rest of the chapter will attempt to solve those problems.

In Part III, we will inquire whether soldiers of the territorial State who have fallen into the power of the proxy are POWs and, a more complicated issue, how the Third Geneva Convention has to be interpreted to allow the proxy to respect it. In Part IV, we will inquire whether members of the proxy-armed group who have fallen into the power of the territorial State are POWs, a much more delicate question, and, if so, how they can be treated in conformity with the Third Geneva Convention. In Part V, we will deal with the release and repatriation of POWs held under the circumstances described in Parts III and IV. The conclusion will then address a number of questions concerning our very flexible interpretation of the Third Geneva Convention, particularly whether the *Tadić* theory is justified or whether it should rather be abandoned.

---

1. Prosecutor v. Tadić, Case No. IT-94-1-A, Appeals Chamber Judgment, ¶¶ 88–145 (Int'l Crim. Trib. for the former Yugoslavia July 15, 1999). *See* Military and Paramilitary Activities in and against Nicaragua (Nicar. v. U.S.), Judgment, 1986 I.C.J. Rep. 14, ¶¶ 115, 219 (June 27) (the ICJ dealt exclusively with the attribution for State responsibility purposes and left open the question whether IAC IHL or NIAC IHL applied).

2. Notably, the main judge involved in the Tadić case, Antonio Cassese, was an eminent academic.

II. ARMED CONFLICTS CONDUCTED BY A PROXY-ARMED GROUP ARE SUBJECT TO IAC IHL

A. The *Tadić* Theory and Controversies Surrounding It

IACs are armed conflicts between States. However, States as abstract entities cannot engage in violence, which triggers an IAC. Only human beings can. It is therefore logical to apply IAC IHL, if the use of force by a human being against a State is attributable to another State. Such attribution is equally possible in cases in which one State uses force against another State through an armed group fighting the latter State on its territory.

This was the situation the ICTY confronted in its first case, *Tadić*. Duško Tadić committed his crimes during a conflict between the Bosnian Serb forces (VRS) and the government of Bosnia and Herzegovina. However, the VRS was found to be linked to another State, the (then) Federal Republic of Yugoslavia, in such a way that VRS conduct was attributable to that State. This enabled the ICTY to convict Tadić for grave breaches of the Geneva Conventions, which apply only in IACs. Such IAC IHL applicability where a proxy-armed group is fighting governmental forces may occur in two ways: the foreign State either has had the necessary control over the armed group from the beginning of the conflict, or the foreign State gains control at a later point during a NIAC between the armed group and the (territorial) State, which transforms the NIAC into an IAC. Both situations occur frequently.

The International Criminal Court (ICC),[3] the International Committee of the Red Cross (ICRC),[4] and most scholars have espoused this *Tadić* theory, which has led to major debates both in scholarly writings and between the International Court of Justice (ICJ) and the ICTY. Its idea is that once an armed group is linked in a particular way to a controlling State, its conduct is attributable to that State and the armed conflict between the proxy-armed group and the territorial State is governed by the IAC IHL.

Some (including the ICJ) object, insisting that State responsibility and the classification of armed conflicts as IACs are distinct issues that are governed by different tests.[5] We agree with the

---

3. Prosecutor v. Thomas Lubanga Dyilo, Case No. ICC-01/04-01/06-2842, Judgment, ¶ 541 (Mar. 14, 2012).

4. INTERNATIONAL COMMITTEE OF THE RED CROSS, COMMENTARY ON THE THIRD GENEVA CONVENTION: CONVENTION (III) RELATIVE TO THE TREATMENT OF PRISONERS OF WAR ¶¶ 298–306 (2020), https://ihl-databases.icrc.org/applic/ihl/ihl.nsf/Comment.xsp?action=openDocument&documentId=0B46B7ADFC9E8219C125858400464543 [hereinafter 2020 GC III Commentary].

5. Application of the Convention on the Prevention and Punishment of the Crime of Genocide (Bosn. & Herz. v. Serb. & Montenegro), Judgment, 2007 I.C.J. Rep. 43, ¶ 405 (Feb. 26); Theodor Meron, *Classification of Armed Conflict in the Former Yugoslavia: Nicaragua's Fallout*, 92 AMERICAN JOURNAL OF INTERNATIONAL LAW 236, 237–42 (1998); Marko Milanovic & Vidan Hadzi-Vidanovic, *A Taxonomy of Armed Conflict*, *in* RESEARCH HANDBOOK ON INTERNATIONAL

ICTY,[6] the ICRC,[7] and the majority of scholars that the underlying test must be the same. Even though only human beings can act in the real world, many rules of international law, including those on whether an armed conflict is international, refer to States. Therefore, one must attribute the actions of those who acted to a State to determine whether one State has used force against another. The rules on attribution in the law of State responsibility determine whether certain conduct is attributable to a State and, therefore, subject to the rules of international law addressing States. Indeed, the law of State responsibility provides the only solution because international law contains no other general rules to determine what actions constitute the conduct of a State. IHL contains special rules to attribute human conduct to a State, but only to a very limited extent—that is, when it makes all acts of members of its armed forces attributable to a State.[8]

B. Overall Control as the Correct Test

The second controversial issue concerning the *Tadić* theory is the degree of control necessary to make IAC IHL applicable. The ICJ and a majority of scholars insist that an armed group's conduct is only attributable to a State if that State had "effective control of the military or paramilitary operations in the course of which the alleged violations were committed,"[9] or if the armed group was "completely dependent" on the foreign State.[10] In the *Tadić* case, by contrast, the ICTY observed that the ICJ's reasoning was not "consonant with the logic of the law

---

Conflict and Security Law 256, 272–73 (Nigel D. White & Christian Henderson eds., 2013); Djemila Carron, *When Is a Conflict International? Time for New Control Tests in IHL*, 98 International Review of the Red Cross 1019, 1026–28 (2016)and the authors to whom she refers.

6. Prosecutor v. Tadić, Case No. IT-94-1-A, Appeals Chamber Judgment, ¶ 104 (Int'l Crim. Trib. for the former Yugoslavia July 15, 1999); Antonio Cassese, *The Nicaragua and Tadić Tests Revisited in Light of the ICJ Judgment on Genocide in Bosnia*, 18 European Journal of International Law 649 (2007).

7. 2020 GC III Commentary, *supra* note 4, ¶ 306.

8. Convention No. IV Respecting the Laws and Customs of War on Land art. 3, Oct. 18, 1907, 36 Stat. 2227, T.S. No. 539; Protocol Additional to the Geneva Conventions of 12 August 1949, and Relating to the Protection of Victims of International Armed Conflicts art. 91, June 8, 1977, 1125 U.N.T.S. 3 [hereinafter Additional Protocol I].

9. Military and Paramilitary Activities in and against Nicaragua (Nicar. v. U.S.), Judgment, 1986 I.C.J. Rep. 14, ¶ 115 (June 27); reaffirmed by Application of the Convention on the Prevention and Punishment of the Crime of Genocide (Bosn. & Herz. v. Serb. & Montenegro) Judgment, 2007 I.C.J. Rep. 43, ¶¶ 404–07 (Feb. 26).

10. Application of the Convention on the Prevention and Punishment of the Crime of Genocide (Bosn. & Herz. v. Serb. & Montenegro) Judgment, 2007 I.C.J. Rep. 43, ¶¶ 391–95 (Feb. 26).

of State responsibility" and was "at variance with judicial and State practice."[11] Indeed, for both attribution under the law of State responsibility and the classification of a conflict as an IAC, the ICTY found that it is sufficient that the external State has "overall control going beyond the mere financing and equipping of such forces and involving also participation in the planning and supervision of military operations."[12]

Today, the ICRC follows the ICTY's position,[13] while the ICC does so at least for classification purposes.[14] As for the ICJ, it determined that the "overall control test" might be appropriate to classify a conflict, but not to attribute State responsibility.[15] The majority of scholars and the ILC (at least implicitly) agree with the ICJ.[16]

We believe that the two tests must be the same, not only for the logical reasons mentioned above, but also for practical reasons.[17] Indeed, the ICJ's approach would leave a serious responsibility gap because an intervening State with overall but not effective control would be party to an IAC, but not responsible for the actions of those fighting on its behalf. In addition, the responsibility of the armed group itself for IHL violations is a completely uncharted area. Furthermore, the effective control test is inappropriate for classification purposes, as the conflict's classification would frequently change depending on whether the outside State has (or does not have) effective control over a particular operation. For these reasons, while insisting that the test must be the same, we agree with the ICRC that the overall control test applies both for attribution of State responsibility and for classification purposes.

Even so, we must mention one scholar's new approach to these controversial issues. Djemila Carron follows the effective control test for the attribution of State responsibility,[18] but with regard to classification, she suggests a test of "general and strict control" when the question is whether an existing NIAC becomes an IAC because an outside State gains control over the armed group involved.[19]

---

11. Prosecutor v. Tadić, Case No. IT-94-1-A, Appeals Chamber Judgment, ¶¶ 115–44 (Int'l Crim. Trib. for the former Yugoslavia July 15, 1999).

12. *Id.*, ¶¶ 131, 145.

13. 2020 GC III Commentary, *supra* note 4, ¶ 306.

14. Prosecutor v. Thomas Lubanga Dyilo, Case No. ICC-01/04-01/06-2842, Judgment, ¶ 541 (Mar. 14, 2012).

15. Application of the Convention on the Prevention and Punishment of the Crime of Genocide (Bosn. & Herz. v. Serb. & Montenegro), Judgment, 2007 I.C.J. Rep. 43, ¶ 405 (Feb. 26).

16. International Law Commission, Report on the Work of its Fifty-Third Session, U.N. Doc. A/56/10, at 48, ¶ 5 (2001).

17. 2020 GC III Commentary, *supra* note 4, ¶¶ 304–06.

18. Carron, *supra* note 5, at 1025–26; DJEMILA CARRON, L'ACTE DÉCLENCHEUR D'UN CONFLIT ARMÉ INTERNATIONAL 273–77 (2016).

19. CARRON, *supra* note 18, at 422–33; Carron, *supra* note 5, at 1031–37.

According to Carron, it is sufficient that the control of the State over the group is "general"; it is not necessary that the State have control over each of the group's actions for them to be governed by IAC IHL. The requirement that the control be "strict" refers to the intensity of State control over the group. When there is no preexisting NIAC, however, she suggests a test of "specific (scope) and strict (intensity) control" to determine whether violent acts by an armed group controlled by a foreign State trigger an IAC.[20]

C. Difficulties in Actually Applying IAC IHL

Whichever is the correct test, the internationalization of an armed conflict through State control conforms to legal logic. However, it does not correspond to State practice. In addition, it is not easy to apply in the field. Except for Georgia's 2008 hostilities with South Ossetia, States have never considered that IAC IHL governs their fight against a rebellious armed group, even when they denounce such rebels as mere agents of foreign powers.[21] Furthermore, from a political point of view, it is difficult to imagine that an armed group would comply with IAC IHL based on the argument that it is subject to the overall control by an outside State. This is because both the group and the foreign State will always deny such control. Additionally, as only the State and not the armed group is a party to the IAC, it will be difficult for organizations like the ICRC to either engage the armed group, or offer their services with a view to fostering the respect of IHL.

As we will demonstrate for the Third Geneva Convention, an armed group would have great practical difficulty in complying with many IAC IHL rules because they were drafted for States.[22] Some commentators have suggested solving this problem by holding only the controlling State to the standards of IAC IHL; in contrast, the proxy-armed group and the territorial State would be held to NIAC IHL standards in their relations.[23] This solution, however, makes the entire construction of internationalization through proxy nearly meaningless because IAC IHL would not apply to most conduct in the conflict. Nonetheless, we may revert to it if it is too difficult or unrealistic to apply the Third Geneva Convention to the proxy-armed group.

---

20. Carron, *supra* note 5, at 1028–31.

21. *See* Noam Zamir, Classification of Conflicts in International Humanitarian Law: The Legal Impact of Foreign Intervention in Civil Wars 129–34 (2017).

22. Convention (III) Relative to the Treatment of Prisoners of War arts. 39(1), 82, 84(1), 87(1), 99, 102, 108(1), 122, Aug. 12, 1949, 6 U.S.T. 3316, 75 U.N.T.S. 135 [hereinafter Third Geneva Convention].

23. Andrew Clapham, *The Concept of International Armed Conflict, in* The 1949 Geneva Conventions: A Commentary, ¶¶ 25–26 (Andrew Clapham, Paola Gaeta & Marco Sassòli eds., 2015).

The alternative is to adapt, as far as both the conduct of the armed group (not effectively controlled by the State with overall control) and that of the territorial State toward the armed group are concerned, IAC IHL functionally to what the group is actually able to comply with and to its non-State nature.[24] Our attempt to do so is the focus of the remainder of this contribution.

III. TREATMENT OF SOLDIERS OF THE TERRITORIAL STATE AS POWS

A. POW Status: Are They in the Power of the Controlling State?

POWs are members of the armed forces of one State who have fallen into the power of the enemy during an IAC. To fit with reality and facilitate implementation, it would be tempting to consider the proxy-armed group as the detaining power of soldiers of the territorial State. This is, in particular, the case if the controlling State has no effective control over the capture and internment, and such conduct is therefore not attributable to it according to the ICJ.

Yet IAC IHL, including the Third Geneva Convention, nevertheless applies because that State has overall control over the group. However, the proxy-armed group would not be a party to the conflict, and therefore would not be bound by the Third Geneva Convention. Indeed, we will see that many rules of the Third Geneva Convention are typically addressed to States and parties to an IAC (which is, in our case, the controlling State) and not to its armed forces. One has therefore to consider the controlling State as the detaining power. Under Article 12 of the Third Geneva Convention, POWs are in the hands of the controlling State and not in those of individuals or military units who have captured them; the controlling State is responsible for their treatment. Should it not have the necessary effective control to ensure their proper treatment, the controlling State must establish it. If one considers overall control sufficient for attribution purposes, it would also be contrary to the very idea of attribution not to consider the controlling State as the detaining power. A State can never detain anyone, other than through human beings whose conduct is attributable to that State.

Although the controlling State is legally the detaining power, the proxy-armed group and its members are addressees of the Third Geneva Convention based upon the principle of effectiveness (which requires rules to be interpreted in a way that makes them have a practical effect), and because their conduct is attributable to the controlling

---

24. See Tom Gal, *Unexplored Outcomes of Tadić: Applicability of the Law of Occupation to War by Proxy*, 12 JOURNAL OF INTERNATIONAL CRIMINAL JUSTICE 59, in particular 73–75 (2014). See Henri Meyrowitz, *Le droit de la guerre dans le conflit vietnamien*, 13 ANNUAIRE FRANÇAIS DE DROIT INTERNATIONAL 153, 168–82 (1967).

State.[25] We will also suggest below that a proxy-armed group may be considered to be part of the controlling State's armed forces. A State's armed forces are obviously bound by IHL.[26] All this means that members of the proxy-armed group may also exercise the prerogatives of a detaining power, such as the right to intern POWs, without any further justification or procedure for the duration of active hostilities.[27]

B. POW Treatment

When it comes to the treatment of POWs required by the Third Geneva Convention, the premise that the POWs held by the proxy-armed group are detained by the controlling State encounters some conceptual and practical problems. Those problems could obviously be avoided if the proxy-armed group transferred such POWs immediately to the controlling State. But such a requirement would be unrealistic, as the controlling State would not engage in proxy warfare if it was ready to assume its responsibilities as a party to the conflict. We will deal here mainly with the conceptual problems, while the practical challenges depend on both the human and the financial resources, as well as the territorial control, of each proxy-armed group.[28]

1. COMMANDER OF POW CAMP

A first difficulty arises from Article 39 of the Third Geneva Convention, prescribing that "[e]very [POW] camp shall be put under the immediate authority of a responsible commissioned officer belonging to the regular armed forces of the Detaining Power." This provision must, however, be interpreted today, contrary to its wording, as allowing all armed forces under overall control of a party to an IAC to run POW camps.[29] In any event, the distinction between regular and irregular armed forces has been abandoned by Additional Protocol I.[30] Already

---

25. For the proposition that organs of a State are bound by its international obligations. *See, e.g.*, LaGrand (Ger. v. U.S.), Provisional Measures, Order, 1999 I.C.J. Rep. 9, ¶ 28 (Mar. 3); Difference Relating to Immunity from Legal Process of a Special Rapporteur of the Commission on Human Rights, Advisory Opinion, 1999 I.C.J. Rep. 62, ¶ 67 (Apr. 29); Prosecutor v. Blaškić, Case No. IT-95-14, Decision on the objection of the Republic of Croatia to the issuance of *subpoeanae duces tecum*, ¶¶ 67, 91 (Int'l Crim. Trib. for the former Yugoslavia July 18, 1997); Ward Ferdinandusse, *Out of the Black-Box? The International Obligation of State Organs*, 29 BROOKLYN JOURNAL OF INTERNATIONAL LAW 45, in particular 109ff (2003).

26. LINDSEY CAMERON & VINCENT CHETAIL, PRIVATIZING WAR 307–13 (2013).

27. Third Geneva Convention, *supra* note 22, art. 21.

28. Silvia Sanna, *Treatment of Prisoners of War*, *in* THE 1949 GENEVA CONVENTIONS, *supra* note 23, ¶ 116.

29. 2020 GC III Commentary, *supra* note 4, ¶ 2483.

30. Additional Protocol I, *supra* note 8, art. 43.

under the Third Geneva Convention, it would have been inconceivable and very dangerous from a humanitarian point of view to consider that resistance groups falling under its Article 4A(2) could not hold such POWs.

2. Article 5 Tribunals

According to Article 5 of the Third Geneva Convention, when doubt exists regarding the status of persons who "committed a belligerent act," they must be treated as POWs "until such time as their status has been determined by a competent tribunal." The *travaux préparatoires* of the more demanding provision of Additional Protocol I[31] and State practice both indicate that such a competent tribunal does not have to comply with the requirements of an independent and impartial tribunal capable of conducting a criminal trial.[32] Theoretically, it may be argued that a proxy-armed group is able to constitute such a tribunal in the name of the controlling State. Such a tribunal must, however, function according to rules[33] and the theoretical detaining power—the controlling State—will never adopt domestic rules foreseeing that, and how, the proxy-armed group could make such decisions. We, therefore, consider that the proxy-armed group may adopt such rules, which is easier to accept than for criminal tribunals discussed below. This is because the substantive criterion governing the decision—that is, the question whether the person belongs to the armed forces of the territorial State—is set forth in the Third Geneva Convention itself.

3. Trials

The issue is much more delicate for criminal trials by the proxy-armed group because they require that the proxy establish a (military) court offering the essential guarantees of independence and impartiality.[34] They, furthermore, require that the detaining power comply with a detailed regime on judicial guarantees, applicable law, competent courts, and admissible punishment and treatment while serving a sentence. The regime combines specific minimum guarantees and the principle of assimilation.[35] That principle requires that POWs be afforded, depending on the rule, the same treatment as members of the armed forces of the detaining power or, in some cases, as the local civilian population.

Without intervention of the controlling State, which is unrealistic to require, a proxy-armed group will not be able to comply because the regime frequently refers to the legislation of the detaining power, and to the rules, courts, and procedures applicable to members of the armed forces of the detaining power.[36]

---

31. Additional Protocol I, *supra* note 8, art. 45.

32. Commentary on the Additional Protocols of 8 June 1977 to the Geneva Conventions of 12 August 1949, ¶ 1745 n.29 (Yves Sandoz, Christophe Swinarski & Bruno Zimmermann eds., 1987)[hereinafter ICRC APs Commentary].

33. 2020 GC III Commentary, *supra* note 4, ¶ 1125.

34. Third Geneva Convention, *supra* note 22, art. 84.

35. *Id.*, arts. 82–88, 89–108; 2020 GC III Commentary, *supra* note 4, ¶ 3601.

36. 2020 GC III Commentary, *supra* note 4, ¶ 3566.

One may object that a proxy-armed group does not need to try POWs it holds, because it may keep them interned without trial. Nevertheless, a detaining power has an obligation to prosecute POWs for war crimes. It also has to maintain order in the POW camp and protect POWs from fellow POWs, which is only possible if it is able to try them as appropriate.

The only realistic solution, therefore, is to accept that members of the proxy-armed group serve as a reference for the principle of assimilation. In addition, the group may, despite the text of the Third Geneva Convention, which refers to the detaining power, establish a court and adopt the necessary rules of procedure. Scholarly writings and some judgments affirm that armed groups have the necessary legislative capacity;[37] they discuss how they can do this—and actually do it—in NIACs.[38]

Much remains, however, controversial. This is due to the tension between the desire to make it possible for armed groups to comply with IHL and the fear of opening a Pandora's box of unfair trials. In addition, we have to solve a problem created by the *Tadić* theory, which prescribes that IAC IHL binds proxy-armed groups, by applying IHL of NIACs and related controversies by analogy. As for the applicable substantive law, it is not unfair to judge acts committed by POWs during their captivity under the rules of the group that controlled the POWs when they committed their acts. Under the principle of legality, acts committed prior to capture could, however, only be prosecuted if they constituted international crimes.

---

37. Ilaşcu and Others v. Moldova and Russia, 2004-VII Eur. Ct. H.R. 179, ¶ 460; 2020 GC III Commentary, *supra* note 4, ¶ 728; KUBO MAČÁK, INTERNATIONALIZED ARMED CONFLICTS IN INTERNATIONAL LAW 210–12 (2018); DARAGH MURRAY, HUMAN RIGHTS OBLIGATIONS OF NON-STATE ARMED GROUPS 197, 209 (2016).

38. Stockholms tingsrätt [TR] [district courts, courts of first instance in civil and criminal matters] 2017 B 3787-16 (Swed.) with a partial translation *in* 16 JOURNAL OF INTERNATIONAL CRIMINAL JUSTICE 403 (2018); confirmed by Svea Hovrätt [HovR] [Court of Appeals] 2017 B 2259-17 (Swed.); leave to appeal was denied by Högsta Domstole, https://ihl-databases.icrc.org/applic/ihl/ihl.nsf/Comment.xsp?action=openDocument&documentId=31FCB9705FF00261C1258585002FB096; Tom Ginsburg, *Rebel Use of Law and Courts*, 15 ANNUAL REVIEW OF LAW AND SOCIAL SCIENCE 495 (2019); Ezequiel Heffes, *Generating Respect for International Humanitarian Law: The Establishment of Courts by Organized Non-State Armed Groups in Light of the Principle of Equality of Belligerents*, 18 YEARBOOK OF INTERNATIONAL HUMANITARIAN LAW 181, 194–97 (2016); Mark Klamberg, *The Legality of Rebel Courts During Non-International Armed Conflicts*, 16 JOURNAL OF INTERNATIONAL CRIMINAL JUSTICE 235, 243–54, 256–58 (2018); RENÉ PROVOST, REBEL COURTS (2021); Sandesh Sivakumaran, *Courts of Armed Opposition Groups: Fair Trials or Summary Justice?*, 7 JOURNAL OF INTERNATIONAL CRIMINAL JUSTICE 489, 498–506 (2009); Jonathan Somer, *Jungle Justice: Passing Sentence on the Equality of Belligerents in Non-International Armed Conflict*, 89 INTERNATIONAL REVIEW OF THE RED CROSS 655, 671–76, 687–89 (2007).

4. OTHER RULES ON THE TREATMENT OF POWs

The Third Geneva Convention foresees a very detailed protection regime for POWs. It addresses such issues as humane treatment; the obligation to provide for their maintenance free of charge; questioning; property; evacuation from the battlefield; security; quarters; food, clothing, and canteens; hygiene and medical attention; religious, intellectual, and physical activities; discipline; respect of rank; work; financial resources; relations with the detaining authorities; POW representatives; and death. Many of these obligations raise difficulties for certain States as detaining powers.[39] This is even more the case for various proxy-armed groups that have more limited financial and personal resources, as well as international relations, than a State.

Such groups may also find it challenging to fulfill positive obligations to maintain and protect POWs;[40] to establish a national information bureau;[41] and to notify the power of origin with the considerable detail that must be provided from capture to release.[42] However, the ICRC can assist in this respect if it is given (as it must be) access to the POWs. In many cases, an armed group will also be reluctant to provide notice, as it must under the Third Geneva Convention, of the geographic location of POW camps and to mark them. This is likely because it fears that the territorial State will try to liberate them or at least will know where the group is deployed.[43] These obligations are, however, not absolute under the very text of the Third Geneva Convention if one considers the *travaux préparatoires* carefully.[44] For an armed group with only limited and oscillating control of territory, it will also be more difficult to intern POWs away from its forces, which are legitimate targets of attacks, as it should under the Third Geneva Convention.[45]

The rates of the pay advances POWs must receive are low under the text of the Third Geneva Convention, and may even be more limited if they "seriously embarrass the Detaining Power." Thus, a proxy-armed group certainly can pay them.[46] However, the rules on POWs' accounts and possible transfers from and to such accounts will be impossible to respect for an armed group, having no access to the international banking system.[47] This obstacle may theoretically

---

39. Prisoners of War—Eritrea's Claim 17, XXVI R.I.A.A. 23, Partial Award, ¶¶ 77, 96–101, 128–38 (Eri.-Eth. Claims Comm'n, July 1, 2003); Prisoners of War—Ethiopia's Claim 4, XXVI R.I.A.A. 73, Partial Award, ¶¶ 116–25 (Eri.-Eth. Claims Comm'n, July 1, 2003).

40. Third Geneva Convention, *supra* note 22, arts. 15, 25–30, 60.

41. *Id.*, art. 122.

42. *Id.*, arts. 21(3), 63(3), 104, 107(2), 122.

43. *Id.*, art. 23(3)–(4).

44. 2020 GC III Commentary, *supra* note 4, ¶¶ 2042, 2050.

45. Geneva Convention, *supra* note 22, art. 23.

46. *Id.*, art. 60.

47. *Id.*, arts. 58(1), 60, 61, 63–66.

be overcome through current alternative methods of money transfer requiring only access to the internet. Finally, even beyond judicial guarantees, some Third Geneva Convention rules refer to the legislation of the detaining power, directly[48] or indirectly, through the principle of assimilation.[49] We suggest that in those cases this can be understood to refer to rules of the proxy-armed group or, if no such legislation exists, to the legislation of the territorial State.

Generally, there are different ways to adapt the obligations of the proxy-armed group to what the armed group can actually deliver. Normally, impossibility of execution,[50] or the circumstance precluding unlawfulness of force majeure,[51] cannot be invoked because they presuppose a material impossibility for the State bound by the obligation, which is the controlling State. That State, however, could comply with its obligations if it had the necessary will. Compliance that is politically unrealistic to expect is not materially impossible. Nevertheless, if the armed group is bound by IHL rules, it should also be able to invoke circumstances precluding unlawfulness to justify its non-respect.

A number of points relativize these challenges. First, many obligations under the Third Geneva Convention are obligations of means,[52] which require only best efforts. Second, as has been suggested with respect to adapting NIAC IHL to the capacity of a non-State armed group,[53] a sliding scale of obligations could equally be applied to a proxy-armed group. An armed group that is better organized and has more stable control over territory would be obliged to comply with the full panoply of rules of the Third Geneva Convention, while less organized proxy-armed groups would have to comply only with those for which they are able to deliver. This would allow distinguishing a lack of will from an inability to comply.

Third, if the proxy-armed group is unable to respect even the minimum guarantees of humane treatment, it must release its POWs. Additional Protocol

---

48. *Id.*, arts. 33, 51.

49. *Id.*, arts. 20, 23(2), 25(1), 46(2), 52(2), 53(1)–(2); 2020 GC III Commentary, *supra* note 4, ¶ 34.

50. Vienna Convention on the Law of Treaties art. 61, May 23, 1969, 1155 U.N.T.S. 331.

51. International Law Commission, Report on the Work of its Fifty-Third Session, art. 23, U.N. Doc. A/56/83 as corrected by U.N. Doc. A/56/49(Vol. I)/Corr.4 (2001).

52. *See, e.g.*, Third Geneva Convention, *supra* note 22, arts. 22(2), 26(4), 44(2).

53. International Committee of the Red Cross, Strengthening International Humanitarian Law Protecting Persons Deprived of Their Liberty: Synthesis Report from Regional Consultations of Government Experts 27–28 (Nov. 2013); Geoffrey Corn & Eric Talbot Jensen, *Transnational Armed Conflict: A "Principled" Approach of the Regulation of Counter-Terror Combat Operations*, 42 Israel Law Review 46, 56ff (2009); Marco Sassòli, *Introducing a Sliding-Scale of Obligations to Address the Fundamental Inequality Between Armed Groups and States?*, 93 International Review of the Red Cross 426, 430 (2011); Roy S. Schöndorf, *Extra-State Armed Conflicts: Is There a Need for a New Legal Regime?*, 37 New York University Journal of International Law and Politics 1, 31–33, 56–59 (2005).

I requires this even outside proxy warfare.[54] Alternatives could be to resuscitate the concept of release on parole,[55] which would, however, require a minimum of cooperation from the territorial State, or a transfer of the POWs to a neutral State according to the rules of the Third Geneva Convention on internment in neutral countries.[56] These rules, however, presuppose an agreement between the three parties concerned. Fourth, another alternative for a proxy-armed group unable to fulfill its positive obligations is to ask for, and accept, an offer of services by an impartial humanitarian body such as the ICRC to assist the POWs and in ensuring humane treatment. This would not even oblige the armed group to recognize its proxy status and the applicability of IAC. Indeed, the rules on such offers of services in IACs and NIACs are very similar,[57] and the ICRC delivers the same services in both situations. Finally, wherever the Third Geneva Convention applies the principle of assimilation discussed above, one could refer to the situation of the proxy-armed group's members (with a continuous combat function), instead of that of members of the controlling State's regular forces. It is indeed those members who actually detain the POWs and also know best how they themselves are treated.

IV. THE TREATMENT OF MEMBERS OF THE PROXY-ARMED GROUP AS POWS

Compared with the treatment of captured members of the territorial State's armed forces by the proxy-armed group, the reverse situation—the respect of the Third Geneva Convention by the territorial State toward members of the proxy-armed group—raises fewer practical difficulties, although legal ones remain.

A. POW Status of the Members of the Proxy-Armed Group

From a policy perspective, it appears to be a fundamental requirement of fairness that members of the proxy-armed group who must comply under the *Tadić* theory with IAC IHL, including the Third Geneva Convention, should also benefit from that law. This also leads to an equality of belligerents, which is important in order to obtain respect for IHL (although technically that equality exists in the

---

54. Additional Protocol I, *supra* note 8, art. 41(3).

55. Third Geneva Convention, *supra* note 22, art. 21(2)–(3).

56. *Id.*, art. 111. For a recent example in Afghanistan in the 1980s, a situation that was classified as a NIAC, but could possibly also have been an IAC by proxy. *See External Activities: May–June 1984*, 24 INTERNATIONAL REVIEW OF THE RED CROSS 230, 239–40 (1984).

57. *Compare* Third Geneva Convention, *supra* note 22, art. 3(2), *with id.*, art. 9.

IAC between the two States parties to the IAC and not between those fighting for each side).[58] In addition, if the members of the proxy-armed group are not POWs, they are—according to the letter of the Fourth Geneva Convention—not protected civilians; this status is reserved for "[p]ersons . . . who . . . find themselves . . . in the hands of a Party to the conflict or Occupying Power of which they are not nationals."[59] They would therefore only benefit from the fundamental guarantees of Article 75 of Additional Protocol I. If one followed the suggestion of the ICTY that nationality must be replaced by allegiance,[60] they would benefit from the full protection of the Fourth Geneva Convention. However, this would put the territorial State in a disadvantageous situation, because it could intern members of the proxy-armed group only for individually assessed and periodically reassessed imperative security reasons. Meanwhile, the proxy-armed group could intern members of the territorial State's armed forces, without any individual reason, until the end of active hostilities.[61]

Legally, the conclusion that members of the proxy-armed group interned by the territorial State must be POWs is not obvious. There are three main legal obstacles.

1. Do Members of the Proxy-Armed Group "Belong" to the Controlling State?

In the categories of the Third Geneva Convention, members of the proxy-armed group do not form part of the controlling State's (regular) armed forces. They could be "[m]embers of other militias and members of other volunteer corps, including those of organized resistance movements, belonging to a Party to the conflict and operating in or outside their own territory," who benefit from POW status under Article 4A(2) subject to certain conditions. First, the group must thus "belong" to a State party to the IAC. Second, it must comply with the famous four conditions:

> (a) that of being commanded by a person responsible for his subordinates;
> (b) that of having a fixed distinctive sign recognizable at a distance;
> (c) that of carrying arms openly; [and]
> (d) that of conducting their operations in accordance with the laws and customs of war.

---

58. MAČÁK, *supra* note 37, at 146–48.

59. Convention (IV) Relative to the Protection of Civilian Persons in Time of War art. 4, Aug. 12, 1949, 6 U.S.T. 3516, 75 U.N.T.S. 287 [hereinafter Fourth Geneva Convention].

60. *See* Prosecutor v. Tadić, Case No. IT-94-1-A, Appeals Chamber Judgment, ¶¶ 163–69 (Int'l Crim. Trib. for the former Yugoslavia July 15, 1999).

61. Third Geneva Convention, *supra* note 22, arts. 21, 118.

Third, as with all other combatants, the member must individually distinguish himself or herself from the civilian population in a way and during a time that differs under customary law and under Additional Protocol I.[62]

Additional Protocol I does not distinguish between regular and irregular armed forces but adopts a broad and unified concept of armed forces that comprises all organized armed groups under a command responsible to a party to the IAC. It adds that such forces shall be subject to an internal disciplinary system enforcing, among other things, compliance with IHL.[63] Although the concept of "command responsible to a party" seems to be narrower than that of "belonging" to a party, there are good reasons to consider that it comprises, at least, all those who belong to a party.[64]

What the requirement of "belonging" under the Third Geneva Convention implies is a controversial issue.[65] Some argue that it corresponds to control under the law of State responsibility.[66] However, we agree with others who contend that the concept is wider.[67] Indeed, the purpose of Article 4A(2) was to confer

---

62. Additional Protocol I, *supra* note 8, art. 44(3); 1 CUSTOMARY INTERNATIONAL HUMANITARIAN LAW, r 106 (Jean-Marie Henckaerts & Louise Doswald-Beck eds., 2005)[hereinafter ICRC CIHL Study].

63. Additional Protocol I, *supra* note 8, art. 43. According to the ICRC CIHL Study, this wide definition of armed forces and combatants corresponds to customary international law. See ICRC CIHL Study, *supra* note 62, r 4, at 16.

64. ICRC APs Commentary, *supra* note 32, ¶ 1662; ICRC CIHL Study, *supra* note 62, r 4, at 14, 16; INTERNATIONAL COMMITTEE OF THE RED CROSS, INTERPRETIVE GUIDANCE ON THE NOTION OF DIRECT PARTICIPATION IN HOSTILITIES UNDER INTERNATIONAL HUMANITARIAN LAW 22 (2009)[hereinafter ICRC Interpretive Guidance]; Geoffrey Corn & Chris Jenks, *Two Sides of the Combatant Coin: Untangling Direct Participation in Hostilities from Belligerent Status in Non-International Armed Conflicts*, 33 UNIVERSITY OF PENNSYLVANIA JOURNAL OF INTERNATIONAL LAW 313, 326 (2011); ALLAN ROSAS, THE LEGAL STATUS OF PRISONERS OF WAR: A STUDY OF INTERNATIONAL HUMANITARIAN LAW APPLICABLE IN ARMED CONFLICTS 262 (2005); Siobhan Wills, *The Legal Characterization of the Armed Conflicts in Afghanistan and Iraq: Implications for Protection*, 58 NETHERLANDS INTERNATIONAL LAW REVIEW 173, 191 (2011). See 2020 GC III Commentary, *supra* note 4, ¶ 1009 (the ICRC rather disagrees but admits that at least everyone who is belonging to an armed group under overall control is also under a command responsible to that State).

65. Katherine Del Mar, *The Requirement of "Belonging" Under International Humanitarian Law*, 21 EUROPEAN JOURNAL OF INTERNATIONAL LAW 105, 111–21 (2010); ZAMIR, *supra* note 21, at 137–42.

66. Prosecutor v. Tadić, Case No. IT-94-1-A, Appeals Chamber Judgment, ¶¶ 91–95 (Int'l Crim. Trib. for the former Yugoslavia July 15, 1999); Prosecutor v. Thomas Lubanga Dyilo, ICC-01/04-01/06, Decision on Confirmation of Charges, ¶¶ 209–11 (Jan. 29, 2007); 2020 GC III Commentary, *supra* note 4, ¶¶ 299–300, 304; Tristan Ferraro, *The ICRC's Legal Position on the Notion of Armed Conflict Involving Foreign Intervention and on Determining the IHL Applicable to This Type of Conflict*, 97 INTERNATIONAL REVIEW OF THE RED CROSS 1227, 1249–50 (2015); ICRC Interpretive Guidance, *supra* note 64, at 23. See also Sean Watts, *Who Is a Prisoner of War*, in THE 1949 GENEVA CONVENTIONS, *supra* note 23, ¶ 30.

67. *See, e.g.*, Del Mar, *supra* note 65, at 111–12, 115–17; MAČÁK, *supra* note 37, at 173–74.

POW status upon resistance movements, such as those that were active in France, Italy, Yugoslavia, Belarus, and Ukraine during the Second World War. Those movements were not subject to "overall control," and even less to "effective control," by the States for whom they were fighting.

Tacit agreement must therefore be sufficient;[68] and that tacit agreement exists so long as the State's government does not reject an armed group's claim that it is fighting on the State's behalf.[69] If the overall control test is correct for attribution purposes, a proxy-armed group belongs to the controlling State under the first understanding of what "belonging" means. However, overall control that leads to internationalization clearly also includes tacit agreement required by the second understanding.

Still, many commentators suggest that the State must acknowledge the group as fighting for it.[70] We agree. Indeed, members of secret services or staff of private military and security companies do not have POW status even if they comply with all other conditions. For this reason, members of a proxy-armed group would normally not have POW status because the controlling State, nearly by definition, denies that the proxy-armed group is fighting for it.[71]

However, one may object that a facade refusal to recognize the real overall control should not count. A State cannot deprive persons, by statements, from the protection they benefit from according to the actual situation.[72] Such an interpretation is in conformity with the purpose of Article 4A(2), which was to extend POW status to increase the interest of irregular forces in complying with IHL.[73] As Article 4 of the Third Geneva Convention defines not only POW status but also combatant status in an IAC, such an interpretation would also avoid difficulties for the territorial State in its conduct of hostilities. Indeed, if members of the proxy-armed group are not combatants, they are civilians.[74] As such, they could

---

68. COMMENTARY TO GENEVA CONVENTION III RELATIVE TO THE TREATMENT OF PRISONERS OF WAR, 57 (Jean Pictet ed., 1960).

69. CAMERON & CHETAIL, *supra* note 26, at 395–97.

70. *Id.* at 396–97, 400–01; ZAMIR, *supra* note 21, at 140–41; 2020 GC III Commentary, *supra* note 4, ¶ 1005.

71. CAMERON & CHETAIL, *supra* note 26, at 397; ZAMIR, *supra* note 21, at 125, 129–34, 140–42. *See also* Military Prosecutor v. Omar Mahmud Kassem, Judgment, Israeli Military Court sitting in Ramallah (Apr. 13, 1969), published in English *in* 42 INTERNATIONAL LAW REPORTS 470, 477–78 (1971).

72. The controlling State's claim that the proxy-armed group does not belong to it and the territorial State's subsequent denial of POW status could be considered as implicit agreement to restrict the rights that the Third Geneva Convention confers upon POWs, without legal effect according to Article 6 of the Third Geneva Convention.

73. For how granting combatants privilege encourages compliance with IHL, *see* EMILY CRAWFORD, THE TREATMENT OF COMBATANTS AND INSURGENTS UNDER THE LAW OF ARMED CONFLICT 157–58 (2010); Del Mar, *supra* note 65, at 113; MAČÁK, *supra* note 37, at 142–45, 157–58.

74. Additional Protocol I, *supra* note 8, art. 50(1).

only be targeted if, and for such time, as they directly participate in hostilities.[75] This result could be avoided if the concept of members of an armed group with a continuous combat function created by the ICRC for NIACs[76] was also applied in IACs,[77] at least for members of proxy-armed groups. Such a result would be contrary to the letter of Article 50(1) of Additional Protocol I. The ICRC rejects it when the group does not belong to a party to the conflict.[78] It would lead once more to the absurd result under the *Tadić* theory that the applicability of IHL of IACs is diluted through the reintroduction of elements of NIAC IHL.

2. An Exception for Nationals of the Detaining Power from POW Status?

Under the text of the Third Geneva Convention, nationality does not matter for POW status. What counts is the power on which they depend, and this must be the adverse party in the IAC. As we have just discussed, the proxy-armed group belongs to the controlling State and its members, therefore, depend upon that State. A different issue is to determine who belongs to the proxy-armed group or who is its member, an issue we will discuss later. However, it is widely argued that a detaining power—in our case, the territorial State—does not have to give full POW privileges to its own nationals, even if they belong to the armed forces of the enemy. The majority view in military manuals, a judicial precedent, and scholarly writings is that such persons do not have POW status.[79] In our opinion, this nevertheless implies that they must be treated in accordance with the Third Geneva Convention. An alternative view asserts that they have POW status, but may, nevertheless, be prosecuted for treason.[80]

---

75. *Id.*, art. 51(3).

76. ICRC Interpretive Guidance, *supra* note 64, at 33–35.

77. Sabrina Henry, *Exploring the "Continuous Combat Function" Concept in Armed Conflicts: Time for an Extended Application?*, 100 International Review of the Red Cross 267, 275–79 (2018).

78. ICRC Interpretive Guidance, *supra* note 64, at 23–25.

79. Office of the General Counsel, U.S. Department of Defense, Law of War Manual § 4.4.4.2 (rev. ed. 2016); Public Prosecutor v. Oie Hee Koi [1968] AC 829 (PC); Yoram Dinstein, *Unlawful Combatancy*, in International Law and the War on Terrorism 152, 163–64 (Fred L. Borch & Paul S. Wilson eds., 2003) (Vol. 79, U.S. Naval War College International Law Studies); Tamás Hoffmann, *Squaring the Circle?—International Humanitarian Law and Transnational Armed Conflicts*, in Les règles et institutions du droit international humanitaire à l'épreuve des conflits armés récents 234 n.67 (Michael J. Matheson & Djamchid Momtaz eds., 2010); Rosas, *supra* note 64, at 247. For this view with some nuances, see Zamir, *supra* note 21, at 142–47.

80. Roberta Arnold, *Training with the Opposition: The Status of the "Free Iraqi Forces" in the US' War Against Saddam Hussein*, 63 Heidelberg Journal of International Law 631, 646–50 (2003); Howard S. Levie, Prisoners of War in International Armed Conflict, 74–76 (1978); Ka Ho Tse, *The Relevancy of Nationality to the Right to Prisoner of War Status*, 8 Chinese Journal of International Law 395, 399 (2009); Watts, *supra* note 66, ¶ 58; René-Jean

If this "nationality exception" were applied, most members of the proxy-armed group would be deprived of POW status, as they are nationals of the territorial State. This would again be contrary to the aforementioned arguments of fairness, equality of the belligerents, and encouragement to comply with IHL.[81]

There are a number of ways to overcome this problem. First, nationality could be replaced by allegiance, as the ICTY did for the definition of protected civilians in the very same *Tadić* case,[82] which the ICC later reaffirmed.[83] This was done in spite of the fact that the criterion of nationality appears in the Fourth Geneva Convention's definition of "protected civilians."[84] However, as we have explained elsewhere, the ICTY's reinterpretation of the protected civilian concept is doubtful because of the method of interpretation it applied.[85] From the point of view of the principle *nullum crimen sine lege*, it is also astonishing that the ICTY reinterpreted—contrary to clear treaty provisions—an essential element of a crime after its commission to the detriment of the accused.

Practically, the ICTY's allegiance approach is also very difficult to apply during a conflict. Allegiance is more difficult to determine than nationality, and it may change more easily in the heat of a conflict. We would not recommend that detainees claim protected person status on the basis that they have severed allegiance from the detaining authority, as this might further undermine their chance to be respected. However, such policy objections are weaker for the Third Geneva Convention, where the term "nationality" does not appear in the definition of protected persons, and where allegiance is more manifest through belonging to the proxy-armed group. Some scholars consider that while individual allegiance does not normally reinstitute POW status, particular circumstances may do so. Those circumstances include proxy-armed groups representing either large parts of the territorial State's population (or parts of territory) that have been hindered in changing the government through a democratic process.[86] The problem with this suggestion is that, like the *Tadić* theory's conditions for the applicability

---

Wilhelm, *Peut-on modifier le statut des prisonniers de guerre?*, 35 INTERNATIONAL REVIEW OF THE RED CROSS 681, 682 (1953). *See* MAČÁK, *supra* note 37, at 175–76 (completely rejects that nationality matters for POW status or treatment).

81. CRAWFORD, *supra* note 73, at 157–58; MAČÁK, *supra* note 37, at 142–48, 156–58.

82. Prosecutor v. Tadić, Case No. IT-94-1-A, Appeals Chamber Judgment, ¶¶ 163–66, 168–69 (Int'l Crim. Trib. for the former Yugoslavia, July 15, 1999).

83. Prosecutor v. Katanga, ICC-01/04–01/07, Decision on Confirmation of Charges, ¶¶ 289–93 (Sept. 30, 2008).

84. Fourth Geneva Convention, *supra* note 59, art. 4.

85. Marco Sassòli & Laura M. Olson, *The Judgment of the ICTY Appeals Chamber on the Merits in the Tadić Case—New Horizons for International Humanitarian and Criminal Law?*, 82 INTERNATIONAL REVIEW OF THE RED CROSS 733, 743–44 (2000).

86. ROSAS, *supra* note 64, at 387–88; ZAMIR, *supra* note 21, at 146–47.

of IAC IHL, the State concerned will never recognize that those conditions for applying the allegiance criterion are fulfilled.

Second, one may object to the very idea that nationality of the detaining power deprives an individual of POW status. It may be correct that a national joining enemy armed forces who falls again into the power of his or her State of nationality is deprived of POW status. However, in case of proxy warfare, this would be contrary to the *Tadić* theory's logic, which leads to the classification of an armed conflict between a State and a proxy-armed group on its territory as an IAC. To replace nationality of the territorial State with adversity to that State demonstrated through fighting for another State is a logical consequence of the classification of such a conflict as international.[87]

3. Who Belongs to the Proxy-Armed Group?

We have seen that the proxy-armed group may be considered as belonging to the controlling State. This raises the question of who belongs to the armed group. Technically, the answer is to be found in IAC IHL, in which formal incorporation is decisive. But the reality is that armed groups are—even when a State has overall control over them—organized differently from State armed forces. It is much more difficult to determine who belongs to an armed group than to identify who belongs to governmental armed forces. Persons join and quit armed groups in an informal way, while members of governmental armed forces are formally incorporated and dismissed. As armed groups are inevitably illegal under the law of the territorial State, which will never accept an exception for those under the overall control of a controlling State, their members will do their best not to appear as belonging to the group.

It is, therefore, suggested to draw, even for POW status determination purposes, an analogy to the criterion suggested by the ICRC for determining who is targetable in a NIAC. This would include as members (benefiting for our purposes from POW status) only those who have a continuous combat function.[88] This is equally what the ICRC suggests for targeting purposes for armed groups that belong to a party to the IAC.[89] Such a limitation of POW status to those having a continuous combat function is justified by the fact that overall control is derived from the participation of the controlling State in the organization, coordination, and planning of the *military* operations of an armed group.[90] Other members of the proxy-armed group are therefore civilians who typically do not have protected civilian status, unless nationality is replaced by allegiance as suggested by the ICTY.

87. Mačák, *supra* note 37, at 148, 175.

88. ICRC Interpretive Guidance, *supra* note 64, at 33–35.

89. *Id.* at 25, 39.

90. Prosecutor v. Tadić, Case No. IT-94-1-A, Appeals Chamber Judgment, ¶¶ 137, 145 (Int'l Crim. Trib. for the Former Yugoslavia July 15, 1999). *See also* Prosecutor v. Thomas Lubanga Dyilo, ICC-01/04-01/06, Decision on Confirmation of Charges, ¶ 211 (Jan. 29, 2007).

To identify members of a proxy-armed group with a continuous combat function in an IAC is easier than in a NIAC.[91] As discussed earlier, this is because the proxy-armed group must collectively distinguish itself from the civilian population under IAC IHL, and a member must do so individually to retain POW status. In case of doubt, a competent tribunal has to determine the status of a member of a proxy-armed group who has committed a belligerent act.[92] Such doubts may be raised not only by the conduct and function of the individual, but also by the classification of the armed group to which he or she belongs.[93] This includes whether the group is actually a proxy, or whether it fulfills the collective conditions for POW status.

B. The Treatment of Members of the Proxy-Armed Group

Once it is determined that members of a proxy-armed group are POWs, their treatment according to the Third Geneva Convention raises fewer problems than is the case with respect to proxy-armed groups respecting the rules applicable to soldiers of the territorial State. Admittedly, many Third Geneva Convention rules refer to the consent of, decisions of, agreements with, or transmission of (information) to the power on which the POW depends.[94] It may seem inappropriate to impose those functions on the controlling State, which will necessarily deny that the POWs depend on it. However, it is also unrealistic, and contrary to the idea of an IAC, that the territorial State must relate itself to the proxy-armed group. In any case, if the power on which the POWs depend does not consent or conclude an agreement, the Third Geneva Convention offers a default regime. The notifications it receives will reach the families of the persons concerned through the ICRC Central Tracing Agency in parallel.[95] The controlling State will simply not react to the notifications it receives or will consider them as propaganda or provocation.

---

91. *But see* Jody M. Prescott, *The Convergence of Violence Around a Norm: Direct Participation in Hostilities and Its Significance for Detention Standards in Non-International Armed Conflict*, in DETENTION OF NON-STATE ACTORS ENGAGED IN HOSTILITIES: THE FUTURE LAW 68–70 (Gregory Rose & Bruce Oswald eds., 2016).

92. Third Geneva Convention, *supra* note 22, art. 5(2).

93. ICRC APs Commentary, *supra* note 32, ¶ 1743.

94. Third Geneva Convention, *supra* note 22, arts. 21, 43, 61, 62, 63, 69, 71, 100, 123.

95. *Id.*, art. 123 refers to *id.*, art. 122(4), which prescribes: "This information shall make it possible quickly to advise the next of kin concerned."

V. RELEASE AND REPATRIATION OF POWS

A question common to POW members of the territorial State's armed forces and proxy-armed group is when and where do they have to be repatriated. Members of a proxy-armed group interned as POWs by the territorial State must be released and repatriated without delay after the cessation of active hostilities in the IAC.[96] The IAC between the controlling State and the territorial State (involving in reality mainly the proxy-armed group) may end when the controlling State loses (voluntarily or involuntarily) overall control over the armed group.

In a textual interpretation of the Third Geneva Convention, this could be seen as the end of active hostilities in the IAC. Nevertheless, if hostilities between the armed group that is no longer a proxy and the territorial State continue, it is reasonable, and conforms to the object and purpose of POW internment, to allow the territorial State not to release those POWs until the hostilities with the armed group actually end.[97] An alternative interpretation is that the continuing internment of the POW in this case must be justified under NIAC IHL.[98] In both cases, it may be argued that the POWs should continue to benefit from POW treatment pending release. A State that lawfully or unlawfully fails to repatriate POWs at the end of an IAC must continue to treat them as POWs.[99] Others consider that in case of such "internalization," NIAC IHL and domestic law govern the treatment of the former POW.[100]

The repatriation of POW members of the proxy-armed group also raises the question of where they should be repatriated. Technically, this would be to the controlling State. If that State accepts and the POW so wishes, this may be the appropriate conclusion. However, as most members of the proxy-armed group may never have lived on the territory of the controlling State, it would be improper to call such a transfer "repatriation" and to require it.

An actual repatriation may occur if the armed group to which the POW belongs still controls territory after the cessation of active hostilities. Otherwise, the POW

---

96. *Id.*, art. 118(1).

97. *See, e.g.*, Hamdi v. Rumsfeld, 542 U.S. 507, 519–21 (2004); *id.* at 588 (Thomas, J., dissenting); Al-Alwi v. Trump, 236 F. Supp. 3d 417 (D.D.C. 2017); *aff'd*, Al-Alwi v. Trump, No. 17-5067 (D.C. Cir. 2018), *available at* https://law.justia.com/cases/federal/appellate-courts/cadc/17-5067/17-5067-2018-08-07.html. *See also* John B. Bellinger III, *Legal Issues in the War on Terrorism—A Reply to Silja N. U. Vöneky*, 8 German Law Journal 871, 872 n.7 (2007); Mačák, *supra* note 37, at 109–10; 2020 GC III Commentary, *supra* note 4, ¶ 1111.

98. Marco Sassòli, *Release, Accommodation in Neutral Countries, and Repatriation of Prisoners of War, in* The 1949 Geneva Conventions, *supra* note 23, ¶ 24.

99. Third Geneva Convention, *supra* note 22, art. 5(1); Sassòli, *supra* note 98; 2020 GC III Commentary, *supra* note 4, ¶ 1112.

100. In relation to the 2003–11 Iraq War, *see* Knut Dörmann & Laurent Colassis, *International Humanitarian Law in the Iraq Conflict*, 47 German Yearbook of International Law 293, 328 (2004).

can only be released to his or her former place of residence. Once released, the member of the proxy-armed group obviously loses POW status and IAC IHL no longer governs his or her treatment. The POW's fate is instead governed by the agreement between the proxy-armed group and the territorial State, which ended active hostilities between them, and by any NIAC IHL rules that continue to apply after the end of the NIAC.[101] Indeed, once the controlling State no longer has overall control, the conflict between the armed group and the territorial State turns into a NIAC. However, we would argue that the previous POW status of the member of the proxy-armed group has one aftereffect. On account of combatant and POW immunity, he or she may not be punished for participation in hostilities during such time as he or she had combatant status because IAC IHL applied at the time.

As with POW members of the proxy-armed group, the obligation to release and repatriate POWs held by the proxy-armed group might also not be triggered when overall control ends (and IAC IHL no longer applies) but hostilities between the armed group and the territorial state continue. It may only be triggered when the NIAC between the territorial State and the armed group ends because it is unrealistic to require the armed group to repatriate the territorial State's soldiers while it is still fighting against that State.

If we consider that such POWs may continue to be interned—or if they are retained unlawfully, although they should have been released—the question arises as to whether the group is still an addressee of IAC IHL and therefore of the Third Geneva Convention. We might consider that it remains so by virtue of the principle of effectiveness, in which case the group must either continue to treat the POWs in accordance with Convention or release them. Conversely, we might assume that, unlike the States that hold individuals as POWs after the conflict has ended, the armed group is not required to continue to treat them in accordance with the Third Geneva Convention simply because the conflict is no longer an IAC.

VI. CONCLUSION

The *Tadić* approach, according to which IAC IHL applies to an armed conflict between the territorial State and a proxy controlled by another State, corresponds to legal logic. There are strong arguments in favor of overall control as the decisive test. However, when applied in practice during an armed conflict to the actual protection of persons affected by the conflict, this raises serious legal and practical problems.

---

101. Protocol Additional to the Geneva Conventions of 12 August 1949, and Relating to the Protection of Victims of Non-International Armed Conflicts art. 2(2), June 8, 1977 1125 U.N.T.S. 609.

These challenges are particularly acute when requiring the territorial State and (even much more so) the proxy to comply with the Third Geneva Convention. The fact that the proxy and the controlling State deny control is only part of the problem. Even a proxy willing to apply the Convention will confront serious difficulties. We have shown that through a sometimes very innovative interpretation of its provisions, it is possible to respect most requirements (although not its letter). This involves, however, general controversies in the interpretation of the Third Geneva Convention, such as those regarding the concept of belonging and the importance of nationality for POW status. IHL can require neither the proxy to do the impossible, nor the controlling State to directly intervene or establish effective control.

Nevertheless, one may also wonder whether the applicability of IAC IHL is unrealistic and, therefore, erroneous in this situation—at least as far as the rights and obligations of members of the proxy are concerned. However, the premise lies at the heart of the *Tadić* decision. Is this not a further example of a theory developed by an international tribunal *after the facts* on IHL issues to facilitate conviction of an accused?[102] Can such standards be applied *during* the conflict, as they must if those standards derive from IHL? If this is not the case, such theories not only should make criminal lawyers pause because of their implicit ex post facto character, but also should be abandoned for IHL. Indeed, unrealistic rules do not protect anyone; they undermine the credibility and, therefore, the protective force of the entire IHL regime with the fighting parties.

We will let the readers decide whether our attempts to interpret the Third Geneva Convention very freely to render it realistic for the proxy situation are convincing and lead to realistic results. In the meantime, whether the Third Geneva Convention should be applied according to its letter, or whether the *Tadić* theory should be abandoned in an essential part—leaving NIAC IHL to govern the rights and obligations of (members of) the proxy—remains an open question. We only appeal to the reader not to answer that proxies should not exist and be discouraged. Indeed, it is the very essence of IHL that it applies to a situation—namely, armed conflict—which should not exist and should be discouraged.

---

102. Note that Tadić could have been held accountable for what he did, even if he was only involved in a NIAC.

2

The Application of the Third Geneva Convention in Fluid Conflicts

LAURIE R. BLANK* ∎

The four Geneva Conventions of 1949 set forth a clear framework for the identification and classification of armed conflicts and the applicable law. Conflicts are either international armed conflicts (IACs), governed by the full panoply of the four Geneva Conventions, or non-international armed conflicts (NIACs), governed by Common Article 3 and, eventually, Additional Protocol II[1] where applicable. As customary international law has continued to develop, the applicable legal rules governing the use of force and targeting in IACs and NIACs have continued to merge, such that few gaps remain.[2] However, the legal rules for detention—and the accompanying issues of treatment and prosecution—have not seen the same type of convergence. Detention and prosecution rights, protections, and obligations rest on status,[3] which

---

*. Laurie R. Blank is a Clinical Professor of Law and Director, International Humanitarian Law Clinic, Emory University School of Law.

1. Protocol Additional to the Geneva Conventions of 12 August 1949, and Relating to the Protection of Victims of Non-International Armed Conflicts, June 8, 1977, 1125 U.N.T.S. 609 [hereinafter Additional Protocol II].

2. Prosecutor v. Tadić, Case No. IT-94-1-AR-72, Decision on Defence Motion for Interlocutory Appeal on Jurisdiction, ¶¶ 96–127 (Int'l Crim. Trib. for the former Yugoslavia Oct. 2, 1995).

3. Convention (III) Relative to the Treatment of Prisoners of War art. 4, Aug. 12, 1949, 6 U.S.T. 3316, 75 U.N.T.S. 135 [hereinafter Third Geneva Convention].

remains the most significant distinction between the law of IACs and that of NIACs.[4]

Where conflicts are distinguishable as either international or non-international, parties to a conflict, judicial bodies, other States, advocacy groups, and other actors can readily identify the law applicable to a given situation or issue, even if the specific application or implementation of that legal rule may be complicated. However, where conflicts fluctuate between international and non-international based on the changing character of the parties involved or the involvement of additional parties, significant complexities arise. The usually straightforward determination during IAC that a captured enemy soldier is a prisoner of war (POW) becomes the much more difficult question of what authority the detaining party has and what treatment and disposition that soldier is owed when the conflict becomes a NIAC. These "fluid conflicts," that is, conflicts that morph from international to non-international or vice versa, perhaps even more than once, present a range of interesting questions of both law and policy.

This chapter examines the application of the Third Geneva Convention in fluid conflicts, specifically with respect to the status of detainees and the obligation to release and repatriate. The 2020 Commentary to the Third Geneva Convention raises the question of the application of the Convention in situations where IAC transitions to NIAC, but does so only in a minor way and presents the issue as open for debate and perhaps unresolved by the text of the Convention itself. On the question of how the Convention applies where a NIAC becomes an IAC, the Commentary is silent. Although few if any adjudications or other formal pronouncements on these issues exist, understanding how the transitions in a fluid conflict can and should affect the status and treatment of persons is essential for effective operational planning and preparation. A deeper examination of the Convention, including the basis for the key applicable provisions, suggests that although the meaning and intent of the Third Geneva Convention are readily decipherable, if not explicit, the debate rests on the underlying "storyline" or theme that could or should drive interpretation in such situations.

As a starting point, the instant analysis focuses only on conflicts that switch from one classification to the other and does not address situations of parallel conflicts, where one or more IACs and NIACs are ongoing in the same location at the same time.[5] The parallel conflicts scenario is more common and raises different and equally interesting questions about the application of the law of armed

---

4. *See, e.g.,* Yoram Dinstein, *Concluding Remarks on Non-International Armed Conflicts, in* NON-INTERNATIONAL ARMED CONFLICT IN THE TWENTY-FIRST CENTURY 399, 407 (Kenneth Watkin & Andrew J. Norris eds., 2012) (Vol. 88, U.S. Naval War College International Law Studies).

5. The conflicts in Syria, Libya, and the Democratic Republic of the Congo include parallel conflicts, for example. *See, e.g.,* U.N. Human Rights Council, *Report of the International Commission of Inquiry to Investigate All Alleged Violations of International Human Rights Law in the Libyan Arab Jamahiriya,* ¶¶ 62–66, U.N. Doc. A/HRC/17/44 (June 1, 2011) (coexisting non-international and international armed conflicts in Libya); Prosecutor v. Thomas Lubanga Dyilo, Case No. ICC-01/04-01/06-2842, Judgment, ¶¶ 524–67 (Mar. 14, 2012) (coexisting international

conflict (LOAC) and the Geneva Conventions but is outside the scope of this chapter. Rather, the chapter addresses two situations: an IAC that becomes a NIAC when one of the parties to the conflict switches from being a State actor to a non-State actor; and a NIAC that becomes an IAC when the non-State armed group becomes a State. Examples of the former include the transition from an IAC between the United States and Afghanistan in the fall of 2001 to a NIAC in which the United States and several other States were fighting alongside Afghanistan against the Taliban after the Taliban fell from power but continued to fight as an insurgent group against the new government.[6] Examples of the latter are less common but include the conflict in the former Yugoslavia or that between Sudan and South Sudan, which began as a long-running NIAC within Sudan and transitioned to an IAC between the two countries when South Sudan became an independent State in 2011.[7]

Part I of this chapter examines status determinations of persons in fluid conflicts under the Third Geneva Convention, whether in an IAC that becomes a NIAC or in a NIAC that transitions to an IAC. The analysis focuses on the meaning of specific key terms in the Third Geneva Convention and how, in the circumstance of a fluid conflict, the meaning and interpretation of those provisions should determine the appropriate status of individuals. In the IAC transitioning to NIAC context, the first subpart thus examines the meaning and the object and purpose of "final release and repatriation" in Article 5(1) and "cessation of active hostilities" in Article 118. The plain meaning and historical underpinning for these provisions demonstrate strong support for the proposition that persons captured and detained as POWs in an IAC continue, as a matter of law, to enjoy that status and the accompanying protections and privileges even after the transition to a NIAC.

The second subpart assesses the appropriate interpretation of two phrases from Article 5 in the context of a NIAC that becomes an IAC: "fall into the power of the enemy" and "should any doubt arise." Applying the meaning ascribed to these terms and the purpose for their inclusion in the treaty to this situation presents a challenging contrast between a reasonable interpretation of the treaty that supports POW status for now-qualifying persons originally detained during the NIAC, and the expected approach of States in rejecting POW status for such persons based on the essence of the distinction between IAC and NIAC.

---

armed conflict, occupation, and non-international armed conflict in the Democratic Republic of the Congo).

6. *See, e.g.*, Françoise J. Hampson, *Afghanistan 2001–2010*, *in* INTERNATIONAL LAW AND THE CLASSIFICATION OF CONFLICTS 242 (Elizabeth Wilmshurst ed., 2012).

7. *See, e.g.*, News Release, International Committee of the Red Cross, South Sudan: ICRC Facilitates Repatriation of Sudanese Prisoners of War, News Release 12/90 (Apr. 26, 2012), *available at* https://www.icrc.org/en/doc/resources/documents/news-release/2012/south-sudan-news-2012-04-26.htm (noting the international armed conflict between the two States).

This dilemma highlights the underlying questions at the heart of the application of the Third Geneva Convention in fluid conflicts, which are explored in greater detail in Part II. A first key question is whether, when conflicting interpretations are possible, the analysis should rest on a broader theme or approach—a guiding principle of sorts—rather than a more iterative approach. If so, the second key question is which mantra should drive status determinations in fluid conflicts: a "most protected status" approach or a "you are where you started" maxim.

I. STATUS DETERMINATIONS IN FLUID CONFLICTS

Consider a conflict between two States that, due to changes in the governing entity of one, becomes a conflict between a State and a non-State armed group. For example, one State defeats the other State's army, deposes its government, disbands its military, and supports the emergence of a new government. The new government and the State supporting it then face an insurgency by members of the disbanded military and other forces. Alternatively, one State initiates an armed conflict against another State in which the governing entity is already fighting an internal conflict. After defeating the governing entity, it helps install the opposition as the new government and supports it militarily against the now-insurgent (former State armed forces) group. In both cases, what was an IAC is now a NIAC. In either the former conflict (that is, Iraq) or the latter conflict (that is, Afghanistan), if the first State has detained military personnel of the original enemy State as POWs, it will then face the question of how to classify and treat those persons once the conflict transitions to a NIAC and they no longer belong to the regular armed forces of a State. In the starkest sense, the question is whether the change to NIAC allows the detaining power "to effectively strip by force the protections granted in [IAC] to the remaining combatants of the defeated State, turning them into unprivileged belligerents."[8]

In the opposite type of fluid conflict, a NIAC can become an IAC in two primary ways. One possibility is that a foreign State's involvement in the existing NIAC "internationalizes" the conflict, as in the case of the former Federal Republic of Yugoslavia's involvement on behalf of the Republika Srpska in Bosnia.[9] Another option is that a State engaged in a NIAC on its own territory breaks apart such that the opposition force is now the military of a new independent State and the continuing conflict is now an IAC between two States. Examples include some aspects of the conflict in the former Yugoslavia and, perhaps, the conflict in and

---

8. Marko Milanovic, *The Applicability of the Conventions to "Transnational" and "Mixed" Conflicts*, in THE 1949 GENEVA CONVENTIONS: A COMMENTARY 27, 33 (Andrew Clapham, Paola Gaeta & Marco Sassòli eds., 2015).

9. Prosecutor v. Tadić, Case No. IT-94-1-A, Appeals Chamber Judgment, ¶¶ 88–162 (Int'l Crim. Trib. for the former Yugoslavia July 15, 1999).

between Sudan and South Sudan.[10] Both scenarios present the possibility of persons detained during the NIAC who, if they were captured and detained after the conflict became an IAC, could or would qualify as POWs.

The analysis in this part applies only to the status, treatment, and disposition of persons who were captured and detained as POWs in an IAC that then becomes a NIAC, or persons detained in a NIAC that transitions to an IAC and who fall within one of the categories of POWs in Article 4 of the Third Geneva Convention. The former could be soldiers of the former State who are held by the other State, or they could be soldiers of the State who are held by the former State that is now an opposition group. The latter could be fighters for an organized armed group that becomes the regular armed forces of a State and are declared members as such, or they could be soldiers in the original State military detained by the organized armed group that is now a State. The instant discussion primarily addresses the obligations of the State that is holding persons who were or could be POWs, but these questions can also be relevant for the status and rights of persons who were POWs but are now detained by an organized armed group after the transition to a NIAC. As noted earlier, this discussion does not address individuals detained in parallel conflicts or those who did not originally or would not qualify for POW status in fluid conflicts and thus never benefited from the protections of the Third Geneva Convention when the conflict was originally an IAC, or would not benefit even if detained after a transition to an IAC.

A. International Armed Conflict Becomes Non-International Armed Conflict

The Third Geneva Convention sets forth detailed protections for POWs in IACs, protections that rest on two key determinations: the existence of an IAC and the satisfaction of the criteria in Article 4A of the Third Geneva Convention with respect to those persons. Article 4A provides that certain categories of persons are entitled to POW status in an IAC, including members of the regular armed forces of a State, members of volunteer militia belonging to the State and meeting certain criteria, and participants in a *levée en masse*, among others.[11] Once that status is determined, the rights and obligations flow from there: authority to detain, protections for POWs, combatant immunity, release and repatriation at the end of the conflict, and many others. In NIAC, by contrast, the law does not provide for any specific status determinations or classes of persons; the authority to detain is uncertain or at least contested; and the protections and obligations are, while equally essential, less comprehensive.

---

10. *See* Dapo Akande, *Classification of Armed Conflicts: Relevant Legal Concepts*, in INTERNATIONAL LAW AND THE CLASSIFICATION OF CONFLICTS 43, *supra* note 6; Milanovic, *supra* note 8, at 35.

11. Third Geneva Convention, *supra* note 3, art. 4A.

In the case of fluid conflicts, once an IAC transitions to a NIAC, the first element—the existence of an IAC—no longer exists. The second, meeting the criteria for POW status in Article 4A(1), also appears to be in doubt: if the persons belong to the organized armed group that formerly was the armed forces of a State, then they are no longer members of the regular armed forces of a State. At first glance then, POW status would not apply and, indeed, it would not apply to persons captured and detained after the conflict became a NIAC. However, this situation of POWs captured and detained before the change in characterization of the conflict isolates the specific question of whether and how the Third Geneva Convention's rules and protections for POWs continue if the two parties are still fighting against each other but the conflict is no longer an IAC.

The 2020 Commentary to the Third Geneva Convention presents two possible approaches to this question. Under the first, the obligation to release and repatriate at the "cessation of active hostilities"[12] is not triggered if "hostilities between the same actors continue, even if the legal characterization of the armed conflict has changed."[13] As a result, the "Third Convention remains the legal basis for [the prisoners'] internment, and, pursuant to Article 5(1), the prisoners remain protected by the Convention until their final release and repatriation."[14]

The second approach mandates that the persons detained as POWs when the conflict was international in character must be released because "active hostilities in the international armed conflict are deemed to have ceased, thus triggering the Article 118(1) obligation to release and repatriate prisoners of war."[15] As a result, the authority to detain no longer derives from the Third Geneva Convention because there is no longer an IAC between the two parties, so any further internment must rest on "another legal basis ... and an individualized assessment of the security threat posed by each prisoner should be undertaken."[16] The Commentary then notes two options for the relevant legal protections. The first is that such persons would then be protected by Common Article 3 of the four 1949 Geneva Conventions and other law applicable in NIAC. In the alternative, based on a strict reading of the text, they should continue to benefit from the protections of the Third Geneva Convention.[17] Although the second option hews much more

---

12. Third Geneva Convention, *supra* note 3, art. 118(1).

13. INTERNATIONAL COMMITTEE OF THE RED CROSS, COMMENTARY ON THE THIRD GENEVA CONVENTION: CONVENTION (III) RELATIVE TO THE TREATMENT OF PRISONERS OF WAR ¶ 1111 (2020), https://ihl-databases.icrc.org/applic/ihl/ihl.nsf/Comment.xsp?action=openDocument&documentId=0837F01F5B0DBC5BC125858500469047 [hereinafter 2020 GC III COMMENTARY].

14. *Id.*

15. *Id.*, ¶ 1112.

16. *Id.*

17. *Id.*, ¶ 1113.

closely to continued POW status, either option is a downgrading, to a lesser or greater degree, of status and protection.

The legal and operational difference between these two perspectives is stark. The Commentary, however, does not analyze the merits of the two perspectives, leaving an open question for States facing such a scenario. Nonetheless, the text, the underlying history, and the core tenets and goals of the LOAC strongly suggest that the first approach—the continued protection of the Third Geneva Convention and continued status as a POW as a matter of law—is the proper application of the law in such situations. Furthermore, the second approach, mandating a fresh start for detention and detention authority without continued full application of the Third Geneva Convention, disadvantages such persons or leaves a gap in protection, which the law ordinarily disfavors.

On an initial read, the Third Geneva Convention appears to have been written based on the assumption that when an IAC ends, the conflict ends overall. Understandably, given the nascent concept of non-international armed conflict at the time of the drafting, the Third Geneva Convention does not seem to contemplate an IAC that ends, not because the fighting has stopped, but because the conflict has changed character to a NIAC. Given the nature of conflicts like Afghanistan and Iraq, which continued for many years as NIACs after "de-internationalization," it is particularly useful to note that "the drafters of the Conventions did not foresee the possibility of a conflict mutating from an international armed conflict to an indefinitely lengthy 'internationalised internal armed conflict,' in which the former occupants [or State adversaries] become allies of the State's new government."[18] As a result, one can see the perhaps instinctive reaction that once an IAC becomes non-international, the Third Geneva Convention ceases to apply and to provide the requisite framework for detention. However, both the text of the treaty itself and the historical and prospective concerns that motivated the drafters demonstrate that such a narrow reading of the treaty is not only unsupported but also undermines the very goals of the treaty itself.

The textual provisions that bear on the question of the proper status, treatment, and disposition of persons previously classified as POWs and now held by an opposition group in a NIAC create a web of protection for such persons precisely to prevent the detaining power from taking advantage of a loss of or gap in protection. Although Common Article 2 sets the initial conditions for application of the Convention upon a declaration of war or other armed conflict between two States, the specific temporal application of the Convention and its protections for persons is set forth in Articles 5(1) and 118(1). A look at the text of these two articles and the core objectives of the drafters demonstrates that the Convention's protections are not limited solely to the period of IAC when the conflict itself continues in another form.

---

18. Siobhan Wills, *The Obligations Due to Former "Protected Persons" in Conflicts That Have Ceased to Be International: The People's Mujahedin Organization of Iran*, 15 JOURNAL OF CONFLICT & SECURITY LAW 117, 138 (2010).

Article 5(1) states that the Convention "shall apply to the persons referred to in Article 4 [that is, persons classified as POWs during an IAC] from the time they fall into the power of the enemy and until their final release and repatriation."[19] Individuals who were already detained as POWs during the original IAC have clearly already fallen into the power of the enemy, understood to be "any adversary during an [international] armed conflict."[20] Importantly, the text of Article 5(1) does not state that the Convention applies to persons protected under the Convention until the end of the conflict or until the two States are no longer fighting against each other—or any other criteria; rather, it links the protection to the duration of the detention of the individual, thus ensuring that protection lasts until the person is no longer in a situation demanding such protection. Article 118(1) then provides the relevant guidance for release and repatriation, the endpoint of the Convention's application to such persons, stating that POWs "shall be released and repatriated without delay after the cessation of active hostilities."[21]

When read in conjunction, Articles 5(1) and 118(1) therefore establish a temporal scope of protection in which the Third Geneva Convention applies to POWs from the time they fall into the power of the enemy in an IAC until their final release and repatriation, which, at the latest, must be without delay after the end of active hostilities. The protection of the Convention is linked not to the end of IAC per se, but rather to the end of "hostilities." The key concepts for understanding how the Third Geneva Convention applies in the specific context of fluid conflicts are, therefore, "final," "release and repatriation," and "end of active hostilities."

1. "Release and Repatriation"

"Release and repatriation" is generally understood to mean returning POWs to the "situation which they enjoyed when they were captured"[22] or "to the Power on which they depended before falling into [the detaining power's] hands."[23] Fulfilling this obligation requires more than simply setting persons free from detention; it requires affirmative steps to help them return to their home country or other appropriate location. As a starting point, therefore, if POWs detained in the course of the original IAC are still in the custody of the power that originally detained them, then, at a minimum, they have not yet been released and repatriated and the Third Geneva Convention's protections still apply. However, the fact that they now—once the conflict transitions to a NIAC—either are in the

---

19. Third Geneva Convention, *supra* note 3, art. 5(1).

20. COMMENTARY TO GENEVA CONVENTION III RELATIVE TO THE TREATMENT OF PRISONERS OF WAR 50 (Jean Pictet ed., 1960) [hereinafter 1960 GC III COMMENTARY]. *See also* 2020 GC III COMMENTARY, *supra* note 13, ¶ 964 (enemy refers to "the adversary State during an international armed conflict").

21. Third Geneva Convention, *supra* note 3, art. 118(1).

22. 1960 GC III COMMENTARY, *supra* note 20, at 547.

23. 2020 GC III COMMENTARY, *supra* note 13, ¶ 4447.

hands of a non-State armed group or are members of a non-State armed group introduces complications that question whether the Convention still applies, because the Third Geneva Convention as a whole does not apply in a NIAC.

Notably, treaty law applicable during NIAC does not include any specific obligation to release persons who are detained in the course of the conflict. Additional Protocol II recognizes that measures to ensure the safety of such detainees must be taken if the detaining power "decide[s] to release persons deprived of their liberty,"[24] but does not mandate release at any particular point during or at the end of the conflict. As a matter of customary international law, it is generally accepted, based on the practice and official statements of numerous States, that persons detained in a NIAC "must be released as soon as the reasons for the deprivation of their liberty cease to exist."[25] However, the customary law rule lacks granularity regarding when reasons for detention cease to exist and how such determinations should be made.

The rules regarding release and repatriation of POWs in the Third Geneva Convention are thus central both to understanding the continued status of POWs held in what is now a NIAC and to ensuring their continued protection as POWs. The obligation to release and repatriate at the cessation of active hostilities not only forms the endpoint of internment of POWs, as noted above, but also provides a critical link mandating the continued POW status and treatment for such persons. Even if one were to follow the approach that the transition from IAC to NIAC constitutes the end of active hostilities—as a legal matter—such as to require release of POWs under Article 5(1), the continuation of hostilities as a matter of fact would be a strong reason to refrain from repatriation due to security concerns alone. Although the obligation to release and repatriate "'without delay' is strict . . ., the action to be taken is limited to what is feasible in the specific circumstances and may depend on [various] factors . . ., as well as the security situation and the ability of a State to receive the repatriated prisoners."[26] The very nature of the release and repatriation obligation effectively leads to the continuation of POW status during some or all of the NIAC because of the security threat those continued hostilities posed. Throughout this time, the detailed and comprehensive rules for how release and repatriation occur, such as the provisions for POWs' personal effects and the apportioning of the costs of repatriation, will apply.[27] So too will the provisions for the transfer of POWs, from the logistical obligations in Articles 46–48 of the Third Geneva Convention to the continued responsibility to correct any failure to protect the rights of POWs who have been transferred in accordance with Article 12.

---

24. Additional Protocol II, *supra* note 1, art. 5(4).

25. 1 CUSTOMARY INTERNATIONAL HUMANITARIAN LAW 451, rule 128 (Jean-Marie Henckaerts & Louise Doswald-Beck eds., 2005).

26. *See* 2020 GC III COMMENTARY, *supra* note 13, ¶ 4462.

27. Third Geneva Convention, *supra* note 3, arts. 118–19.

This analysis, however, addresses only the status and treatment of such persons until they are repatriated. It does not address when such repatriation must, or even may not, take place. Two qualifiers for "release and repatriation" ultimately drive that analysis: "final" and "the cessation of active hostilities."

2. "Cessation of Active Hostilities"

The "cessation of active hostilities" is the trigger for the obligation to release and repatriate. One approach presented in the 2020 Commentary is that the transition from IAC to NIAC marks an end of sorts to the IAC, thus triggering the obligation to release and repatriate any detainees. This argument rests on the notion that "the hostilities related to the [IAC] and the [NIAC] are considered to be distinct," such that "active hostilities in the [IAC] are deemed to have ceased"[28] even if fighting between the two parties continues. Accordingly, any detainees must be released and repatriated or, more likely, released and then immediately re-detained in the context of the NIAC due to the threat they pose. As a pragmatic matter, however, this "interpretation . . . would lead to manifestly impractical or even absurd outcomes."[29] Beyond the practical unreality of releasing and re-detaining individuals as a conflict changes character, neither the treaty text nor the reasoning underpinning the text supports this interpretation of the "cessation of active hostilities" as a matter of law. Indeed, imposing a firm but false "break" between the international and non-international phases of an armed conflict detracts from the very purpose of using the end of hostilities concept as the trigger for release and repatriation. Detention and internment during armed conflict are based on the "legitimate concern [of] prevent[ing] military personnel from taking up arms once more against the captor State."[30] Although that justification for detention no longer exists once the hostilities end, it does exist for the entire time until the fighting is over, regardless of the characterization of the conflict.

In accordance with the commonly understood meaning of "hostilities" and "cessation of hostilities," the mere switch in characterization from international to non-international does not constitute a "cessation of hostilities." Hostilities generally can be described as "equivalent to the sum of all conduct regulated by the law of hostilities, namely the choice and use by the parties to an armed conflict of means and methods of injuring the enemy."[31] Such conduct and actions occur across any transition between types of conflict. As Lauterpacht explained, the phrase "cessation of hostilities" in Article 118(1),

---

28. 2020 GC III Commentary, *supra* note 13, ¶ 1112. See also Marco Sassòli, *Release, Accommodation in Neutral Countries, and Repatriation of Prisoners of War*, in The 1949 Geneva Conventions, *supra* note 8, 1039, 1048.

29. Kubo Mačák, Internationalized Armed Conflicts in International Law 109 (2018).

30. 1960 GC III Commentary, *supra* note 20, at 547; In re Territo, 156 F.2d 14 (9th Cir. 1946).

31. Nils Melzer, Targeted Killing in International Law 269 (2008).

refers not to suspension of hostilities in pursuance of an ordinary armistice which leaves open the possibility of a resumption of the struggle, but to a cessation of hostilities as the result of total surrender or of such circumstances or conditions of an armistice as render it out of the question for the defeated party to resume hostilities.[32]

Furthermore, the historical basis for the treaty provision in the aftermath of the Second World War shows that the end of active hostilities was not a "flexible [concept] to take account of situations where the pattern has been an alternation of military operations and peaceful periods" but rather referred to "the end of military operations," situations in which "active hostilities have definitely stopped and will not be resumed."[33]

The comparable provision in Article 6 of the Fourth Geneva Convention refers to the "general close of military operations," which is commonly understood to be "the final end of all fighting between all those concerned."[34] International jurisprudence takes a similar approach, with the International Criminal Tribunal for the former Yugoslavia considering "whether at any point ... the international armed conflict had found a sufficiently general, definitive and effective termination so as to end the applicability of the law of armed conflict ... in particular whether there was a general close of military operations."[35] Each of these understandings of the concept of cessation of active hostilities relies on the facts on the ground. "Whether hostilities survive [the de-internationalization of a conflict] is a question of fact,"[36] therefore, and is not tethered to the legal characterization of the conflict as either international or non-international. Insisting that a legal transition means an end of hostilities when fighting is still ongoing is merely a fiction and does a disservice to the law. As a result, a transition from IAC to NIAC alone does not trigger the obligation to release and repatriate or, therefore, mark an end to POW status and protections.

---

32. 2 Lassa Oppenheim, International Law: A Treatise 613, § 275 (Hersh Lauterpacht ed., 7th ed. 1952) (1905). *See also* Office of the General Counsel, U.S. Department of Defense, Law of War Manual § 9.37.2 (rev. ed., Dec. 2016) [hereinafter DoD Law of War Manual] ("it is the complete end of the fighting with clearly no probability of resumption of hostilities in the near future").

33. Christiane Shields Delessert, Release and Repatriation of Prisoners of War at the End of Active Hostilities: A Study of Article 118, Paragraph 1 of the Third Geneva Convention Relative to the Treatment of Prisoners of War 71–72 (1977). *See also* Sassòli, *supra* note 28, at 1047 ("there must be a reasonable expectation that hostilities will not resume").

34. Oscar M. Uhler et al., Commentary to Geneva Convention IV Relative to the Protection of Civilian Persons in Time of War 62 (1958).

35. Prosecutor v. Gotovina and Marc, Case No. IT-06-90-T, Judgment, ¶ 1694 (Int'l Crim. Trib. for the former Yugoslavia Apr. 15, 2011).

36. Mačák, *supra* note 29, at 109.

3. "Final"

The meaning of "final" in Article 5(1) provides a key component for assessing the application of the Third Geneva Convention when a conflict has transitioned from international to non-international and, in so doing, also adds further texture to the meaning of "end of active hostilities." As the Commentary explains, the inclusion of the word "final" in characterizing release and repatriation is "the essential provision which prevents the 'transformation' of prisoners of war."[37] The purpose was to prevent detaining powers from releasing POWs and then returning them to captivity under another framework or using them as civilian workers. Such "transformation" was unfortunately a common practice during the Second World War. Faced with a shortage of labor to manufacture weapons and ammunition and constrained by the prohibition in the 1929 Geneva Convention on Prisoners of War against using POWs in the manufacture of armaments,[38] the German government offered POWs bonus compensation, civilian clothing, mail access, and other advantages to take "captivity leave"—and then "required [them] to relinquish the status defined by the 1929 Convention."[39] In areas under Allied occupation, German POWs were "discharged as prisoners and interned as civilian detainees because of their connection with the National-Socialist Party."[40] Both categories of persons "lost their rights under the Convention"[41] and "were left unreservedly to the mercy of the Detaining Power."[42] The drafters of the 1949 Geneva Conventions specifically sought to prevent any such "transformation" or recharacterization of POWs, as a direct response to the loss of protection such persons faced during the Second World War.[43] The word "final" plays a central role in this reaffirmation of protection, serving to "prevent the Detaining Power from returning 'released' prisoners of war to captivity under some other guise."[44]

---

37. 1960 GC III COMMENTARY, *supra* note 20, at 75.

38. Convention Relative to the Treatment of Prisoners of War art. 31, July 27, 1929, 47 Stat. 2021, 118 L.N.T.S. 343 ("Work done by prisoners of war shall have no direct connection with the operations of the war. In particular, it is forbidden to employ prisoners in the manufacture or transport of arms or munitions of any kind, or on the transport of material destined for combatant units.").

39. Reports and Documents Submitted by the ICRC to the Preliminary Conference of National Societies of 1946, Vol. II, p. 546.

40. *Id.* at 551.

41. *Id.*

42. *Id.* at 546.

43. 2020 GC III COMMENTARY, *supra* note 13, ¶ 1098 (Article 5 "was designed to counter the practice by some States of discharging prisoners of war and then immediately apprehending them again and interning them as 'civilian detainees'"); Final Record of the Diplomatic Conference of Geneva of 1949, Vol. II-A, at 245 (noting that Article 5 was "introduced in order to make the situation clear beyond all manner of doubt").

44. 2020 GC III COMMENTARY, *supra* note 13, ¶ 1105.

The historical backdrop and foundation for the framework set forth in Article 5(1) demonstrate that viewing the transition from IAC to NIAC as a distinct moment at which release and repatriation is obligatory risks undermining the object and purpose of the law. If, as is obvious in this specific context, fighting between the two parties continues in the NIAC, then the party detaining the POWs will see no legal or operational basis to release them: the ongoing hostilities mean that Article 118(1)'s obligation to release and repatriate has not been triggered and no party to a conflict would release able-bodied fighters for the other side to return to the battlefield.[45] Indeed, as the updated Commentary notes, "in light of the continuing armed confrontations, ... it is unlikely to be willing to release and repatriate them at the moment when the classification of the conflict changes because of an expectation that they may rejoin hostilities in the now [NIAC]."[46] Recognizing that there is little to no likelihood of release, given the realities of the facts on the ground, an interpretation that nonetheless leads to a "release and re-detain" description of their internment leads directly to the "transformation" against which the drafters deliberately sought to protect. The suggestion, offered as one possibility in the updated Commentary and by other scholars, that persons captured as POWs during the prior IAC are subsequently "protected by Common Article 3 ..., customary international humanitarian law [of] non-international armed conflicts" and, therefore, subject to "the same [legal regime] as that applicable to persons who fall into the power of the enemy after the change of the classification of the conflict"[47] simply does not comport with the letter or spirit of the Third Geneva Convention.

More common, however, is the assertion that "even though a new legal basis must be sought for the prisoners' continued internment, they continue to benefit from the protections of the Third Convention for as long as they are not in fact released and repatriated."[48] This approach ensures the continued application of the

---

45. As an example, Amnesty International argued that when the "international armed conflict in Afghanistan ended in June 2002[,] those who were captured by the USA during hostilities—and who the USA was obliged to treat as prisoners of war in the absence of a determination 'by a competent tribunal' that they were not—were required to be released, unless charged with criminal offences." Amnesty International, *Guantanámo and Beyond: The Continuing Pursuit of Unchecked Executive Power* 12 (May 13, 2005), *available at* https://www.amnesty.org/download/Documents/84000/amr510632005en.pdf. From the U.S. perspective, "such a rule [would be] an unduly formalistic and impractical interpretation of [the law]." John Bellinger, *Legal Issues in the War on Terrorism—A Reply to Silja N.U. Vonelay*, 8 GERMAN LAW JOURNAL 871, 872 n.7 (2007).

46. 2020 GC III COMMENTARY, *supra* note 13, ¶ 4460.

47. *Id.*, ¶ 1113, https://ihl-databases.icrc.org/applic/ihl/ihl.nsf/Comment.xsp?action=openDocument&documentId=0837F01F5B0DBC5BC125858500469047. *See also* Knut Dörmann & Laurent Colassis, *International Humanitarian Law in the Iraq Conflict*, 47 GERMAN YEARBOOK OF INTERNATIONAL LAW 293, 334 (2004)("a more appropriate approach would be to consider that these persons are now protected by common Article 3 to the four GCs, customary rules applicable to non-international armed conflicts, relevant rules of human rights law and Iraqi law, as their deprivation of liberty is no longer linked to the former international armed conflict but rather to one of the current non-international ones").

48. 2020 GC III COMMENTARY, *supra* note 13, ¶ 1113.

protections of POW status but mandates that the detaining power have or put in place another legal justification for detention to substitute for the authority found in the Geneva Convention during IAC. For example, in response to a query by the United Kingdom House of Commons, the International Committee of the Red Cross (ICRC) replied as follows regarding the status of detainees following the transition of the conflict in Afghanistan from international to non-international:

> Some important legal consequences of the re-qualification of the conflict concern persons arrested by the United States or allied forces in Afghanistan or elsewhere in connection with the conflict and are still held in detention: First, those persons should have their legal status determined on an individualized basis. . . . Secondly, the Third and Fourth Geneva Conventions no longer provide a legal basis for continuing to hold without charge persons captured in Afghanistan between 7 October 2001 and 19 June 2002. . . . Persons captured in Afghanistan before 19 June 2002 meanwhile continue to benefit from the protection of the Third and Fourth Geneva Conventions until their release and repatriation.[49]

The ICRC took a similar position regarding comparably placed detainees in the conflict in Iraq after the transition from the U.S. and U.K. occupation to Iraqi government control in late June 2004. Noting that most persons detained in connection with the hostilities were "now no longer protected by the whole of the Third or Fourth Geneva Convention but by Common Article 3 of the Geneva Conventions and by customary rules applicable in non-international armed conflicts," the ICRC explained that Iraqi POWs detained before the transition of authority and still interned by the multinational forces

> should either be released, charged and tried or placed within another legal framework that regulates their continued internment. They remain protected by the Third Geneva Convention—for prisoners of war . . . until they are released or handed over to Iraqi authorities.[50]

This interpretation appears to strike a balance between the mandate in Article 5(1) that the Convention continue to apply to persons detained under its protection until their final release and repatriation and the absence of any provision for POW detention or status in NIAC. It ensures that POWs from a prior IAC benefit

---

49. Letter from the Clerk of the Committee to Philip Spoerri, Legal Advisor, International Committee of the Red Cross and reply, Select Committee on International Development, Appendices to the Minutes of Evidence, app. 8 (Dec. 20, 2002), *available at* https://publications.parliament.uk/pa/cm200203/cmselect/cmintdev/84/84ap09.htm.

50. International Committee of the Red Cross, *Iraq Post 28 June 2004: Protecting Persons Deprived of Freedom Remains a Priority* (Aug. 5, 2004), https://www.icrc.org/en/doc/resources/documents/misc/63kkj8.htm.

from the protections of that status throughout the entirety of their internment, as the Third Geneva Convention requires. However, separating out the legal authority for detention and requiring a new basis or legal framework for detention risks subjecting detained persons to the very "transformation" the Convention sought to prohibit and protect against by reframing the internment even in a partial manner and requiring a different legal basis for the detention.

B. Non-international Armed Conflict Becomes International Armed Conflict

Although there are many complex issues regarding detention in NIAC, internationalized NIAC, and mixed conflicts, the instant analysis focuses solely on if and how the Third Geneva Convention applies in the context of a NIAC that becomes an IAC. To that end, the only persons at issue in this analysis are those who qualify for POW status—that is, protection under the Third Geneva Convention—once it is an IAC but who were captured earlier in the conflict when it was a NIAC. For example, consider members of a non-State armed group captured and detained by the State during a NIAC. The Third Geneva Convention does not apply to the conflict and those detained persons are not eligible for POW status, which does not exist during a NIAC. Subsequently, after the non-State armed group becomes the government of a newly independent State on some portion of the original State's original territory and during the continued but now IAC between those same two parties, the original State detains members of the new State's armed forces. Those detained persons are, of course, entitled to POW status as the members of the regular armed forces of a State. Analyzing the application of the Third Geneva Convention in such fluid conflicts then raises the question of whether the earlier group of detainees, who fight for the very same entity and are detained by the same detaining power, are now also covered by the Third Geneva Convention's protections for POWs.

Alternatively, consider an internationalized NIAC, when a foreign State intervenes in a NIAC in another State[51] or when the foreign State exercises overall control over the non-State armed group fighting in that NIAC.[52] Here, the category of persons for whom these questions about the application of the Third Geneva Convention arise is quite limited. Those who could qualify for POW status in such situations would be persons falling within Article 4A(2) of the Third Geneva Convention: "Members of . . . militias . . . belonging to a Party to the

---

51. *See, e.g.,* U.N. Human Rights Council, *supra* note 5, ¶ 66 (noting that the intervention of NATO states in the conflict in Libya internationalized the conflict by triggering a parallel international armed conflict).

52. Prosecutor v. Tadić, Case No. IT-94-1-A, Appeals Chamber Judgment, ¶ 162 (Int'l Crim. Trib. for the former Yugoslavia July 15, 1999); Prosecutor v. Thomas Lubanga Dyilo, Case No. ICC-01/04-01/06, Decision on Confirmation of Charges, ¶ 211 (Jan. 29, 2007).

conflict"[53] who fulfill the four relevant conditions of operating under responsible command, having a fixed distinctive sign, carrying arms openly, and abiding by the LOAC. Members of other non-State armed groups—that is, groups that either do not belong to the State within the meaning of Article 4A(2) or do not fulfill the four conditions—fighting in the now mixed conflict or IAC would not be eligible for consideration as POWs. As a result, the analysis in this section remains limited solely to persons who, if captured after the internationalization of the conflict, would be eligible for POW status under Article 4A(2) and were captured and detained during the NIAC and remain in detention.

Neither the Third Geneva Convention nor the Commentary offers specific guidance regarding the status of persons detained in a NIAC that transitions to an IAC. On first glance, a reasonable approach would be to apply the detention and status rules of NIAC to persons captured and detained before the transition and apply the detention and status rules of IAC to those captured and detained after the transition. In essence, the timing of the start of a person's detention would be the determining factor in which body of law applies.

Key language in both Article 4 and Article 5 of the Third Geneva Convention challenges this presumption, however, raising two potential issues regarding the Convention's application: the meaning of "fallen into the power of the enemy" and the trigger for the obligation to hold an Article 5 tribunal. The first is the initial descriptive language regarding persons who may be entitled to POW status. The second introduces the requirement to provide a competent tribunal to determine the status of any persons for whom "any doubt arise[s]" regarding whether they qualify for POW status. Although the existing law and Commentary offer little if any guidance on how to interpret these specific provisions in the context of persons detained in an IAC that began as a NIAC, their relevance is clear. No less, once the conflict becomes an IAC, the Third Geneva Convention applies, necessitating inquiry into how it applies to such persons.

1. "Fallen into the Power of the Enemy"

Article 4 states that POWs "are persons belonging to one of the [stated] categories, who have fallen into the power of the enemy."[54] In 1949, the drafters of the Geneva Convention deliberately chose that language rather than the term "captured" used in the 1929 Geneva Convention. As the 2020 Commentary explains, "the new term was introduced to make it clear that the Third Geneva Convention protects not only 'captured' prisoners of war, but also those who have fallen into the power of the enemy by other means, such as surrender or mass capitulation."[55] Although it is inherent in the notion of falling into the power of the enemy that there is an armed conflict because a State only has enemies during an armed conflict,

---

53. Third Geneva Convention, *supra* note 3, art. 4A(2).

54. *Id.*, art. 4A.

55. 2020 GC III Commentary, *supra* note 13, ¶ 960.

nothing in the treaty or its commentaries provides guidance on when during that conflict any such persons must have been taken into custody.[56] Thus, although the notion of having fallen into the power of the enemy "implies that the Detaining Power exercises some level of physical control or restraint over the person, and that the person is no longer willing or able to participate in hostilities or defend themselves,"[57] the consequence of such persons having ended up in the detaining power's custody after the conflict began but before it became an IAC is unaddressed. In any other situation, the issue of persons already detained at the beginning of application of the Third Geneva Convention would not apply, because the fact of one State's military personnel detained by another State would trigger the Convention. One could therefore argue that by the plain meaning of Article 4's text and the explanations in the Commentary,[58] persons detained during the NIAC phase of the conflict could constitute persons who have fallen into the power of the detaining power. Alternatively, if the words "fallen into" connote a particular timing, such that the "falling into" must happen while the conflict is an IAC, then persons detained during the NIAC would not fit within that definition.

The meaning of "the enemy" in Article 4 is also relevant. The commentaries explain that it "refers to the enemy State, namely the adversary State during an [IAC]."[59] Again, the question of timing arises—does the meaning of "adversary State during an [international] armed conflict" refer to any time when the determination of status is being made or to the moment when the person first was taken into custody? If the latter, the fact that the person was captured or surrendered during the NIAC phase of the conflict would seem to preclude him or her from meeting the definition of falling into the power of *the enemy*, because the detaining power was not, at that time, an adversary State in an IAC. In contrast, under the former meaning, once the conflict becomes an IAC, any persons captured and still detained after the transition are in the power of the enemy.

2. Doubt and the Article 5 Tribunal

The absence of any clear guidance regarding the status of persons captured and detained before the transition from NIAC to IAC also implicates Article 5 of the Third Geneva Convention, which provides:

> Should any doubt arise as to whether persons, having committed a belligerent act and having fallen into the hands of the enemy, [are entitled to POW

---

56. Sean Watts, *Who Is a Prisoner of War?*, in The 1949 Geneva Conventions, *supra* note 8, 889, 893 ("No provision of Article 4 explicitly addresses the possibility of a change in the character of a conflict affecting the status of detained persons.").

57. 2020 GC III Commentary, *supra* note 13, ¶ 961.

58. *See* Vienna Convention on the Law of Treaties art. 31, May 23, 1969, 1155 U.N.T.S. 331.

59. 2020 GC III Commentary, *supra* note 13, ¶ 964. *See also* 1960 GC III Commentary, *supra* note 20, at 50 ("the term 'enemy' covers any adversary during an 'armed conflict which may arise between two or more of the High Contracting Parties'").

status], such persons shall enjoy the protection of the present Convention until such time as their status has been determined by a competent tribunal.[60]

This rule appears in Additional Protocol I and in numerous military manuals as well.[61] It is designed to protect persons whose status is unclear by ensuring that a tribunal determines their status and that they are protected under the Third Geneva Convention until such determination is made. As a result, a detaining power cannot evade its obligations to such persons under the Convention by either rejecting assertions of POW status or indefinitely delaying a determination of their status—"Article 5(2) was expressly drafted to ensure that there is no gap in protection and to remove any incentive to delay a decision on status."[62] Although the Third Geneva Convention does not include persons already detained in the earlier NIAC in the categories of persons eligible for POW status during an IAC, nor does it deny POW status to such persons. As a result, the doubt regarding their status[63] mandates a determination by a competent tribunal and, at a minimum, such persons are entitled to POW status until that determination is made.

Articles 4 and 5 therefore offer no definitive guidance regarding the inclusion or exclusion of those who were previously detained in a NIAC but otherwise qualify as persons entitled to POW status within the framework of the Third Geneva Convention. In the absence of such guidance, one approach to resolving this uncertainty is to look to a thematic guide or story—a connective tissue of interpretation, as it were, as a source of answers. In essence, is there an overarching mantra that should guide the application of the Third Geneva Convention in fluid conflicts?

II. SEEKING THE UNDERLYING STORYLINE

The status of persons, and therefore their rights and protections, rests without fail on the nature of the conflict and the persons' membership or lack thereof in

---

60. Third Geneva Convention, *supra* note 3, art. 5(2).

61. Protocol Additional to the Geneva Conventions of 12 August 1949, and Relating to the Protection of Victims of International Armed Conflicts art. 45(1), June 8, 1977, 1125 U.N.T.S. 3 [hereinafter Additional Protocol I]; DoD LAW OF WAR MANUAL, *supra* note 32, § 4.27.

62. 2020 GC III COMMENTARY, *supra* note 13, ¶ 1122.

63. Examples in the Commentary of situations raising doubt about whether a person is entitled to POW status include "when it is not clear whether the person in fact belongs to any of the categories enumerated in Article 4," when a person or the Power on which they depend asserts prisoner-of-war status and this is not immediately accepted by the Detaining Power," or if "a Detaining Power considers a person to be a prisoner of war and that person, or the Power on which they depend, contests it." *Id.*, ¶ 1119–21, https://ihl-databases.icrc.org/applic/ihl/ihl.nsf/Comment.xsp?action=openDocument&documentId=0837F01F5B0DBC5BC125858500469047. Any of these—or similar—examples could apply to individuals detained during the earlier non-international armed conflict phase of the conflict.

specified groups. Accordingly, the difference between the direction of change in a fluid conflict—starting as an IAC and becoming a NIAC versus starting as a NIAC and becoming an IAC—appears at first glance to be the key determinant for application of the Third Geneva Convention. This starting point of the conflict as the driving criterion seems to hold true with regard to the status of POWs in what becomes an IAC or even for the more restrictive view of the status of such persons after a transition to a NIAC. Such a result is, of course, not surprising. However, a closer textual read of key provisions of the Third Geneva Convention suggests that the law is more nuanced and more protective, as discussed above, leading to questions about the proper approach.

Although the law does not require an overarching theme, it is axiomatic that predictability and clarity are critical in ensuring its fair and consistent application and protecting against gaps in implementation that leave persons unprotected or underprotected. To that end, the legal analysis above suggests two possible thematic conceptions for the application of the Third Geneva Convention in fluid conflicts. In effect, there are two stories that could explain how the Convention applies—and why. One is that the characterization of the conflict at the starting point of detention will determine a person's status throughout, no matter if, how, or when the conflict changes. Alternatively, the second possible theme is that a person should benefit from the most protected status to which he or she is entitled at any point across the transformation in the conflict. These two "storylines," or themes, rest on differing conceptions of the LOAC, the Third Geneva Convention, and the distinction between international and non-international armed conflict.

A. "You Are Where You Started"

The distinction between international and non-international conflict is foundational, even existential, in determining the application and implementation of the LOAC. A first possible "storyline" reflects this fundamental tenet of the LOAC and rests the application of the Third Geneva Convention in fluid conflicts on the type of conflict in place when the detention of the relevant persons at issue began. Under this approach, which can be described as "you are where you started," once a person is detained and his or her status is determined, a change in the characterization of the conflict does not change that status as a legal matter.

In the context of an IAC that becomes a NIAC, the Articles 5 and 118 analysis above supports this approach as the better reading of the text and the sounder understanding of its historical and purposive goals. Maintaining initial POW status matches with the guarantees intended by the "final release and repatriation" language and protects against a detaining power ratcheting down a person's protection for its own convenience or for more nefarious purposes. The storyline thus tracks the textual interpretation and broader context: you are where you started because the law specifically rejects any downgrading of status.

When a NIAC becomes an IAC, this theme affirms a classical or conservative approach that rejects the option of POW status for persons otherwise qualifying during the IAC except for the fact that they were originally detained while the conflict was a NIAC. Indeed, this conclusion follows directly from the fact that the core distinction between the two types of conflict is the status of persons and the corresponding applicable rules. The firm prohibition on "transformation" of POWs in Article 5(1), discussed in Part I above, also offers support for the "you are where you started" theme, even though some textual interpretations of Articles 4 and 5 could support either temporary protection or full status as POWs. Although that prohibition is designed specifically to prevent any downgrading of POWs to a less protected status before their final release and repatriation, it also could apply more broadly to discourage or prevent any change in status due to new circumstances after the start of detention. To this end, some argue that "permitting post-capture events to alter determinations of status appears a dangerous course of action, too susceptible to manipulation by Detaining Powers, and therefore deliberately rejected by the drafters of the GC III."[64] Parties to an IAC may in fact choose to grant POW protections to such persons as a matter of policy, but requiring them to do so as a matter of law would, by this argument, undermine the stability of the Third Geneva Convention's protection regime and open too much maneuver space for States to determine the status and protection of vulnerable persons. In light of the specific, and historically based, concerns about States recategorizing POWs in order to exploit their loss of protection, this concern is well founded.

However, such an approach means that persons captured and detained across this transition in conflict classification who would qualify for POW status in IAC would nonetheless not have access to such status and the accompanying privileges and treatment simply because they were captured and detained before the transition in conflict classification offered the opportunity for such status. In contrast, similarly situated persons captured and detained after the transition to IAC would, solely by dint of the different timing, have access to POW status where appropriate. The result is that the same types of persons would receive different status and treatment during the same conflict, a problematic result, at least on first impression—but one that could perhaps be forestalled by finding a different theme or storyline to navigate the uncertainties of status in fluid conflicts.

B. "Most Protected Status"

An alternative storyline is one that focuses on the most protected status for which a person qualifies during the permutations of a fluid conflict. Indeed, the presumption that uncertainty about a person's status should always be resolved in favor of greater protections is a foundational theme in the LOAC. Article 50(1) of Additional Protocol I requires that any person be considered a civilian in case of

---

64. Watts, *supra* note 56, at 893.

doubt[65] and Article 5 of the Third Geneva Convention similarly mandates a presumption of POW status. With respect to the latter, the Commentary reaffirms the relevant underlying purpose of the LOAC, explaining that the presumption "recognizes the special vulnerability of persons in the power of the enemy" and seeks to ensure that a person's protection "does not depend solely on the subjective belief of the Detaining Power."[66]

Uncertainty and vulnerability are sources of great danger in any armed conflict—and are only exacerbated in fluid conflicts when both the facts on ground and unresolved questions of law leave the door open for fewer protections and opportunities to assert the right to better status. The "you are where you started" theme above may affirm the classical dichotomy between IAC and NIAC, but it fails to live up to LOAC's mandate of meeting the highest presumption of status and protection. A different story of the Third Geneva Convention in fluid conflicts, however, can do so. Rather than an interpretation of the Third Geneva Convention's application in the NIAC-to-IAC scenario that prevents a change *to* POW status in order to affirm the explicitly stated prohibition against a change *from* POW status,[67] a "most protected status" approach enables persons to benefit from the most protective status to which they are or have been entitled in situations of changing or changed circumstances. Such an approach appears ideally suited to fluid conflicts, in which the same parties are fighting against each other across the change in conflict classification.

The LOAC already mandates this "most protected status" interpretation in the case of IACs that become NIACs. POWs detained beyond the transition to a NIAC retain the protections of POW status, as fixed by the plain text of Article 5(1) of the Third Geneva Convention. Thus, for example, POW camps established during the IAC phase of the conflict must remain in operation. Not only must these persons continue to have the same types of internment facilities, which are clearly distinct from facilities used for penal or disciplinary measures,[68] but they

---

65. Although the precise extent of the rule of doubt with regard to civilian status remains subject to debate, it is widely accepted that "persons who have not committed hostile acts, but whose status seems doubtful because of the circumstances . . . should be considered to be civilians until further information is available." INTERNATIONAL COMMITTEE OF THE RED CROSS, COMMENTARY ON PROTOCOL ADDITIONAL TO THE GENEVA CONVENTIONS OF 12 AUGUST 1949, AND RELATING TO THE PROTECTION OF VICTIMS OF INTERNATIONAL ARMED CONFLICTS (PROTOCOL I) ¶ 1920 (1987), https://ihl-databases.icrc.org/applic/ihl/ihl.nsf/Comment.xsp?action=openDocument&documentId=F387522EE8A5C20FC12563CD004346D4. The United States does not accept a "legal presumption of civilian status . . . for persons or objects" under customary international law. DoD LAW OF WAR MANUAL, *supra* note 32, § 5.4.3.2. The United Kingdom modifies the rule in Additional Protocol I, art. 50(1) by referring to "substantial doubt." UNITED KINGDOM MINISTRY OF DEFENCE, THE MANUAL OF THE LAW OF ARMED CONFLICT ¶ 5.3.4 (2004).

66. 2020 GC III COMMENTARY, *supra* note 13, ¶ 1120.

67. *See supra* text accompanying notes 37–44.

68. As the Commentary to Article 21 of the Third Geneva Convention explains, "The concept of internment should not be confused with that of detention. Internment involves the obligation not to leave the town, village, or piece of land, whether or not fenced in, on which the camp installations are situated, but it does not necessarily mean that a prisoner of war may be

also cannot be interned with other security detainees or criminal detainees.[69] Similarly, any POWs captured and detained during an IAC retain combatant immunity for all lawful belligerent acts committed during the IAC, even if they continue to be detained after the transition to a NIAC.[70] Clearly, a retroactive loss of combatant immunity would violate the core objectives of Article 5(1)'s mandate of continued protection. It would also run counter to the principle of *nullum crimen sine lege*—the principle of legality—according to which no one may face criminal responsibility for an act that was not a criminal offense at the time it was committed.[71] On a broader level, without this continued application of combatant immunity, combatants in any IAC would face enormous unpredictability and uncertainty about the legality of their actions during that conflict. In the same manner, any disciplinary or judicial proceedings against POWs detained after the transition to a NIAC must remain in the same system the detaining power uses for its own military personnel. Thus, even if the detaining power now engaged in a NIAC establishes special military or civilian tribunals to investigate and prosecute offenses by persons captured and detained in the course of that NIAC, it

---

confined to a cell or a room. Such confinement may only be imposed in execution of penal or disciplinary sanctions...." 1960 GC III COMMENTARY, *supra* note 20, at 178.

69. Articles 21 and 22 of the Third Geneva Convention prohibit POWs from being held in penitentiaries or other prison facilities, or with criminal offenders, and Article 84 of the Fourth Geneva Convention prohibits civilian internees from being interned with either POWs or criminal defendants. Third Geneva Convention, *supra* note 3, arts. 21–22; Convention (IV) Relative to the Protection of Civilian Persons in Time of War art. 84, Aug. 12, 1949, 6 U.S.T. 3516, 75 U.N.T.S. 287 ("internees shall be accommodated and administered separately from prisoners of war and from persons deprived of liberty for any other reason"). *See also* 2020 GC III COMMENTARY, *supra* note 13, ¶ 1996, ("housing prisoners of war with persons convicted of a criminal offence might compromise the security of the prisoners of war.... Especially in the case of an international armed conflict, there are risks of violence, intimidation or discrimination against prisoners of war in penitentiaries housing ordinary convicts, since the prisoners of war are usually foreigners belonging to the armed forces of a State with which the Detaining Power is in conflict").

70. Third Geneva Convention, *supra* note 3, arts. 87, 99. *See also* DOD LAW OF WAR MANUAL, *supra* note 32, § 4.4.3 ("International law affords combatants a special legal immunity from the domestic law of the enemy State for their actions done in accordance with the law of war"); United States v. List et al. (The Hostage Case), 11 TRIALS OF WAR CRIMINALS BEFORE THE NUREMBERG MILITARY TRIBUNALS UNDER CONTROL COUNCIL LAW NO. 10, at 1236 (1950)("acts done in time of war under the military authority of an enemy cannot involve criminal liability on the part of officers or soldiers if the acts are not prohibited by the conventional or customary rules of war.").

71. Third Geneva Convention, *supra* note 3, art. 99(1); G.A. Res. 217 (III) A, Universal Declaration of Human Rights, art. 11(2) (Dec. 10, 1948); *see also, e.g.*, Prosecutor v. Milutinović, Case No. IT-99-37-AR72, Decision on Dragoljub Ojdanić's Motion Challenging Jurisdiction—Joint Criminal Enterprise, ¶ 37 (Int'l Crim. Trib. for the former Yugoslavia May 21, 2003); 1 INTERNATIONAL MILITARY TRIBUNAL, TRIAL OF THE MAJOR WAR CRIMINALS BEFORE THE INTERNATIONAL MILITARY TRIBUNAL, NUREMBERG, 14 NOVEMBER 1945–1 OCTOBER 1946 219 (1947).

may not use those tribunals for disciplinary or judicial proceedings against the POWs carried over from the IAC. These protections are of particular importance in protecting against the transformation of POWs into other detainees in practice, even if not as a matter of law. These rules only serve to reinforce the importance of the "most protected status" theme as a guiding framework for the LOAC.

The more challenging question is whether this "more protected status" approach should apply as well to determining the status and protections of persons originally detained in a NIAC who then would qualify for protection under the Third Geneva Convention if they continue to be detained after the conflict is internationalized. As a policy matter, the operational needs and constraints of a detaining power may well produce this result—for example, to avoid operating two different detention facilities, to enable mixing of different populations of detainees who otherwise would be required to be held separately,[72] or as a way to claim greater legitimacy based on enhanced compliance with the law. The broader question, however, is whether such status and treatment can be considered required by the law, as opposed to motivated by policy, strategic, and operational considerations. Doing so would uphold Article 5(1)'s admonition against any transformation of POWs and provide the POW status that one might pragmatically assume would attach to persons who become eligible for such status when a conflict becomes international because the entity for which they fight now is or belongs to a State.

III. CONCLUSION

Fluid conflicts present a particular set of operational challenges as parties to an armed conflict address the changing status of their adversaries or their own change in status in the midst of ongoing hostilities. Beyond these pragmatic considerations lie legal issues regarding the precise interpretation of key provisions of the Third Geneva Convention—provisions that then drive the application of the Convention's protections. The distinction between international and non-international armed conflict and the firm difference between the applicable rules is axiomatic in the LOAC and yet fluid conflicts strain this clear differentiation in multiple ways, from a blurring of the lines between the types of conflict to uncertainty regarding how and when the law applies to given situations throughout the conflict. With regard to the latter concern, the text and underlying purpose and history of key provisions of the Third Geneva Convention provide a means to alleviate uncertainty. Given the importance of clarity and predictability

---

72. During the Vietnam War, for example, the United States employed an expanded definition of POW that encompassed members of the Vietcong—who would not qualify under a plain reading of the Third Geneva Convention—for multiple reasons, including the desire to avoid transferring such individuals to South Vietnamese domestic facilities and the hope of promoting reciprocal treatment for U.S. aviators captured by the Vietnamese. *See* GEORGE S. PRUGH, LAW AT WAR: VIETNAM 1964–1973 66 (1991) (Vietnam Studies).

in enhancing the implementation of the LOAC and, as a result, the protection of persons and the effectiveness of military operations during armed conflict, analytical tools and methodologies to help reduce uncertainty in the law are critically important.

To that end, this analysis of the application of the Third Geneva Convention in fluid conflicts—which does not enjoy any firm guidance in the Commentary or other sources—suggests two possible thematic approaches to guide legal and operational decision-making, minimize unpredictability, and enhance consistency. One option is that the status of persons who are or would be entitled to POW status at one or more points in a fluid conflict is determined based on the nature of the conflict when such persons were captured and detained. Therefore, whatever status they have—or lack—at the moment of detention is the status they retain throughout the fluid conflict, even if a change in the classification of the conflict might present an opportunity for a "better" status. The second option is to grant such persons the "most protected status" to which they are entitled at any point across a fluid conflict, meaning that their status can never be "downgraded" if the conflict changes but can be "upgraded" in such situations. Under this view, individuals captured and detained as POWs would remain POWs even if the conflict transitions to a NIAC, and persons captured and detained during a NIAC who would qualify as POWs when that conflict becomes an IAC would enjoy a status boost commensurate with the change in classification of the conflict.

The first option tracks the traditional path according to which the classification of a conflict drives all other questions, particularly related to the status of persons—an approach that may seem irrefutable given the structure of the LOAC.[73] But the law also affirms the equal application of the law and requires that persons for whom there is any doubt regarding their status—whether as a POW or a civilian—benefit from the more protected status, a fundamental posture that bolsters the second possible methodology. In considering these two possibilities, the idea of defaulting to the more protected status in situations of doubt then argues in favor of the "most protected status" approach as a broader theme or storyline for the application of the Third Geneva Convention in fluid conflicts.

---

73. *See, e.g.,* NILS MELZER, INTERNATIONAL HUMANITARIAN LAW: A COMPREHENSIVE INTRODUCTION 53 (2016).

3

The Regular Armed Forces, Uniforms, and Prisoner of War Status

MICHAEL N. SCHMITT* AND
CHRISTOPHER J. KOSCHNITZKY**

INTRODUCTION

During the ongoing conflict in Ukraine, Russian forces have at times failed to wear uniforms.[1] The failure of regular armed forces to wear uniforms during armed conflict is not a new phenomenon. For instance, during the international armed conflict phases of operations in Afghanistan and Iraq, Coalition forces faced adversaries who had shed their uniforms, wore nontraditional uniforms, or regularly dressed in civilian clothes. And, at times, U.S. special forces personnel have donned indigenous attire. These practices drew the attention of the international humanitarian law (IHL) community, especially with respect to the consequences

---

*. Michael N. Schmitt is the G. Norman Lieber Distinguished Scholar at the United States Military Academy. He is also Professor of Public International Law at the University of Reading, Strauss Center Distinguished Scholar and Visiting Professor of Law at the University of Texas, and the Charles H. Stockton Distinguished Scholar-in-Residence at the U.S. Naval War College.

**. Major Christopher J. Koschnitzky is a Judge Advocate in the United States Army. Major Koschnitzky co-wrote this piece while assigned as a Military Professor at the Stockton Center for International Law, U.S. Naval War College.

1. *See* Chris Koschnitzky & Michael N. Schmitt, *Russians Troops Out of Uniform and Prisoner of War Status*, ARTICLES OF WAR (Mar. 4, 2022), https://lieber.westpoint.edu/russian-troops-out-of-uniform-pow-status/.

should the individuals concerned be captured "out of uniform."[2] Of particular concern was whether failure to be in uniform at the time of capture would result in denial of prisoner of war (POW) status.

Debate over the matter subsided when those conflicts evolved from international into non-international armed conflicts, during which POW status does not exist. However, as the conflicts wound down, attention turned back to those between States. In 2014, for instance, an international armed conflict broke out between Ukraine and Russia, during which the uniform issue arose in the guise of "little green men."[3] Today, peer and near-peer conflicts between the United States and its partners on the one hand, and Russia, China, Iran, or North Korea on the other, are greater concerns for policy makers, the armed forces, and their lawyers than has been the case for decades.[4]

Should hostilities erupt between States, IHL issues, especially on detention, will inevitably surface quickly. This is so for several reasons. First, most IHL—and there is a lot of it—deals with armed conflicts qualifying as international. The 1949 Geneva Convention Relative to the Treatment of Prisoners of War (Third Geneva Convention) alone, for instance, has 121 articles.[5]

Second, IHL is a target-rich environment for normative controversy and exploitation. China, for instance, has incorporated a "lawfare" campaign into its overall theater strategy.[6] The Guantánamo experience demonstrates that detention law can be a lucrative lawfare battlespace.

Third, and perhaps most important, the number of troops likely to be captured during State-on-State hostilities could be huge. Recall that during the first Gulf

---

2. Confusion and disagreement on the issue of wearing uniforms led the late Hays Parks to write his seminal article, *Special Forces' Wear of Non-Standard Uniforms*. Parks felt the need to take on the issue because disagreement existed even among U.S. judge advocates regarding the rules and the cost of noncompliance. W. Hays Parks, *Special Forces' Wear of Non-Standard Uniforms*, 4 CHICAGO JOURNAL OF INTERNATIONAL LAW 493 (2003).

3. *See, e.g.*, Shane R. Reeves & David Wallace, *The Combatant Status of the "Little Green Men" and Other Participants in the Ukraine Conflict*, 91 INTERNATIONAL LAW STUDIES 361 (2015).

4. *See, e.g.*, Todd Huntley, *Special Operations Forces Wear of Non-Standard Uniforms*, ARTICLES OF WAR (Oct. 13, 2021), https://lieber.westpoint.edu/hays-parks-sof-non-standard-uniforms/ . Huntley notes that forces will likely find it necessary to wear nonstandard uniforms during missions in "gray zone" operations. *Id.*

5. Convention (III) Relative to the Treatment of Prisoners of War, Aug. 12, 1949, 6 U.S.T. 3316, 75 U.N.T.S. 135 [hereinafter Third Geneva Convention].

6. The People's Republic of China "has explicitly adopted lawfare (the synonymous term in Chinese is *falu zhan* or 'legal warfare') as a major component of its strategic doctrine." ORDE F. KITTRIE, LAWFARE: LAW AS A WEAPON OF WAR 162 (2016). Lawfare is one of the "Three Warfares" approved by the Chinese Central Military Commission, which defines the term as the "use of international and domestic laws to gain international support and manage possible political repercussions of China's military actions." *Id.* (quoting Central Military Commission, People's Liberation Army, China Regulation on Political Work, art. 14(18) (Dec. 2003).

War, Coalition forces captured over 71,000 Iraqi soldiers in a matter of days.[7] Looking forward, a Russian move into Eastern Europe or a conflict between the Koreas would have the potential for captures far exceeding that figure. Clarity in the criteria for qualification of POW status is essential if only because of the potential numbers of troops who might be captured.

Fortunately, despite being engaged in *non*-international armed conflicts for most of the past two decades, the United States has continued to address POWs in legal guidance for its armed forces. In particular, the Department of Defense published its *Law of War Manual* in 2015 (updated the following year),[8] while the U.S. Army replaced its 1956 *The Law of Land Warfare*[9] in 2019 with a joint Army and Marine Corps publication, *The Commander's Handbook on the Law of Land Warfare*.[10] Both deal with the subject in depth. Then, in 2021, the International Committee of the Red Cross (ICRC) released its updated *Commentary* on the Third Geneva Convention.[11] That product has returned the topic of POW status and treatment to the forefront of discussion among IHL experts.

In this chapter, we zero in on the issue of whether a member of the armed forces captured out of uniform or wearing a nontraditional uniform benefits from the extensive protections POWs enjoy under the Third Geneva Convention, most of which are considered to reflect customary international law.[12] The key provision in this regard is Article 4A, which lays out who is entitled to POW status.[13] It provides:

---

7. Jon F. Bilbo, *Enemy Prisoners of War (EPW) Operations During Operation Desert Storm* 3 (U.S. Army War College Military Studies Program Paper, Apr. 15, 1992), https://apps.dtic.mil/sti/pdfs/ADA251209.pdf.

8. OFFICE OF THE GENERAL COUNSEL, U.S. DEPARTMENT OF DEFENSE, LAW OF WAR MANUAL (rev. ed., Dec. 2016) [hereinafter DoD LAW OF WAR MANUAL].

9. Department of the Army, FM 27-10, The Law of Land Warfare (1956), https://tile.loc.gov/storage-services/service/ll/llmlp/law_warfare-1956/law_warfare-1956.pdf [hereinafter FM 27-10].

10. DEPARTMENT OF THE ARMY AND HEADQUARTERS, U.S. MARINE CORPS, FIELD MANUAL (FM)/MARINE CORPS TACTICAL PUBLICATION (MCTP) 11-10C, COMMANDER'S HANDBOOK ON THE LAW OF LAND WARFARE (2019) [hereinafter COMMANDER'S HANDBOOK].

11. INTERNATIONAL COMMITTEE OF THE RED CROSS, COMMENTARY ON THE THIRD GENEVA CONVENTION: CONVENTION (III) RELATIVE TO THE TREATMENT OF PRISONERS OF WAR (2020), https://ihl-databases.icrc.org/ihl/full/GCIII-commentary [hereinafter 2020 GC III COMMENTARY].

12. *See, e.g.*, discussion in Frédéric Mégret, *The Universality of the Geneva Conventions*, in THE 1949 GENEVA CONVENTIONS: A COMMENTARY 669 (Andrew Clapham, Paola Gaeta & Marco Sassòli eds., 2015); Theodor Meron, *The Geneva Conventions as Customary Law*, 81 AMERICAN JOURNAL OF INTERNATIONAL LAW 348 (1987).

13. Third Geneva Convention, *supra* note 5, art. 4A. The list of individuals in Article 4A also appears in the two Geneva Conventions on the wounded, sick, and shipwrecked: Convention (I) for the Amelioration of the Condition of the Wounded and Sick in the Armed Forces in the Field art. 13, Aug. 12, 1949, 6 U.S.T. 3114, 75 U.N.T.S. 31; Convention (II) for the Amelioration

A. Prisoners of war, in the sense of the present Convention, are persons belonging to one of the following categories, who have fallen into the power of the enemy:
  (1) Members of the armed forces of a Party to the conflict, as well as members of militias or volunteer corps forming part of such armed forces.
  (2) Members of other militias and members of other volunteer corps, including those of organized resistance movements, belonging to a Party to the conflict and operating in or outside their own territory, even if this territory is occupied, provided that such militias or volunteer corps, including such organized resistance movements, fulfil the following conditions:
    (a) that of being commanded by a person responsible for his subordinates;
    (b) that of having a fixed distinctive sign recognizable at a distance;
    (c) that of carrying arms openly;
    (d) that of conducting their operations in accordance with the laws and customs of war.
  (3) Members of regular armed forces who profess allegiance to a government or an authority not recognized by the Detaining Power.
... [14]

Note Article 4A(2)(b)'s requirement that irregular groups that are not part of the armed forces seeking to benefit from POW status must have a fixed distinctive sign, usually satisfied by wearing a uniform. It is a criterion that had appeared earlier in Article 1 of the Regulations Respecting the Laws and Customs of War on Land that were annexed to Hague Convention (II) of 1899[15] and Hague Convention (IV) of 1907.[16] The question we address is whether this requirement is implicit in Article 4A(1) for members of the regular armed forces or groups incorporated into the armed forces, such that their failure to distinguish themselves results in forfeiture of POW status.

---

of the Condition of the Wounded, Sick, and Shipwrecked Members of Armed Forces at Sea art. 13, Aug. 12, 1949, 6 U.S.T. 3217, 75 U.N.T.S. 85.

14. Third Geneva Convention, *supra* note 5, art. 4A.

15. Regulations Respecting the Laws and Customs of War on Land, annexed to Convention No. II with Respect to the Laws and Customs of War on Land, July 29, 1899, 32 Stat. 1803, T.S. No. 403 [hereinafter 1899 Hague Regulations].

16. Regulations Respecting the Laws and Customs of War on Land, annexed to Convention No. IV Respecting the Laws and Customs of War on Land, Oct. 18, 1907, 36 Stat. 2227, T.S. No. 539 [hereinafter 1907 Hague Regulations]. *See also* COMMENTARY TO GENEVA CONVENTION III RELATIVE TO THE TREATMENT OF PRISONERS OF WAR 51–52 (Jean Pictet ed., 1960) [hereinafter 1960 GC III COMMENTARY] (stating that "certain countries still had militias and volunteer corps which, although part of the armed forces, were quite distinct from the army as such. . . . The mention of militias and volunteer corps was therefore maintained as it appears in the Hague Regulations, although strictly speaking it was probably not essential.").

There are two views. By the first, the wearing of the uniform or other distinguishing attire at the time of capture has no bearing upon status as a POW; it is the captured soldier's inclusion in the enemy armed forces that accords that status. Accordingly, the requirement is absent from Article 4A(1) but present in the provision covering members of "other militias" and "other volunteer corps" that are not part of the armed forces of a party to the conflict. This view, which relies on the plain text of Article 4A(1), shall be examined first.

By the contrary view, those captured out of uniform are unprivileged combatants. As such, they forfeit POW status and its attendant protections, as well as combatant immunity. Proponents of the position argue that Article 4A(2)'s four conditions are those that already implicitly characterize members of the regular armed forces; absent satisfaction of the conditions, individuals cannot be considered as members of the regular armed forces, at least for the purpose of the article's grant of POW status. A related question is what sort of uniform or other distinguishing attire satisfies the requirement. We examine this approach next.

Before turning to these competing positions, however, several related issues must be dispensed with to avoid confusion with the issue at hand here.

I. DISPENSING WITH THE SIDE ISSUES

A number of matters tend to surface in discussions of the relationship between wearing uniforms and POW status. To focus consideration on the narrow issue of if, and if so when, the failure of members of a State's armed forces to wear uniforms or other distinctive indicia precludes POW status, they merit brief mention.

Obligation to Distinguish Oneself from the Civilian Population

The wearing of distinctive indicia by the armed forces is a practice stretching back to the earliest days of warfare, although the original and primary purpose for doing so was not for distinction from the civilian population.[17] This practice evolved into the wearing of uniforms in the sixteenth and seventeenth centuries.[18] Today, the soldiers of all States wear them.

However, a degree of disagreement exists over whether such a requirement resides in IHL. For instance, Hays Parks, the U.S. Army's and later the Department of Defense's Law of War Adviser, argued that "[w]earing a partial uniform, or

---

17. *See* Toni Pfanner, *Military Uniforms and the Law of War*, 86 INTERNATIONAL REVIEW OF THE RED CROSS 93, 95–97, 105 (2004) (noting that "distinctive elements were intended to reflect the military traditions of armies or regiments rather than to distinguish the force from other armies, and even less to distinguish it from the civilian population").

18. *Id.* at 98–101.

even civilian clothing, is illegal only if it involves perfidy."[19] Parks was not alone in this view. Referring to the requirement of distinction between combatants and civilians, Toni Pfanner, the former editor-in-chief of the *International Review of the Red Cross*, likewise contended that the "general use of military uniforms on the battlefield doubtless helps to achieve this overall goal [of distinction]. There is, however, no general obligation for soldiers to wear uniforms."[20] Pfanner makes this claim recognizing that it is at odds with Knut Ipsen's assertion of a "'self-evident' (*selbstverständlich*) obligation enshrined in customary law to wear uniforms in hostilities."[21]

Similarly, Waldemar Solf, Karl Partch, and Michael Bothe's commentary on the Additional Protocols claimed that it was only with Additional Protocol I that a failure to distinguish oneself from the civilian population became an IHL violation for States parties, as distinct from being "merely a condition affecting loss of the combatants' privilege and entitlement to prisoner of war status."[22] And Yoram Dinstein asserts:

> Since—under customary law—the removal of a fixed distinctive emblem (such as uniform) by a combatant during military operations is a matter of loss of privileged status, and not a breach of the *jus in bello* (let alone a war crime), it follows that each belligerent party is at liberty to factor in a cost/benefit calculus as to whether or not circumstances militate in favor of retaining the fixed distinctive emblem or removing it. If members of Special Forces units are fighting behind enemy lines, and if the enemy has a demonstrably poor track record in observing the *jus in bello* norms concerning the protection of *hors de combat* enemy personnel, the conclusion may be arrived at that on the whole it is well worth assuming the risk of (potential) loss of prisoner of war status upon capture while benefiting from the (actual) advantage of disguise.[23]

The opposing view is that the wearing of a uniform or some other means of distinguishing combatants from civilians is implicitly required by the principle of distinction, which the International Court of Justice labeled as one of the two "cardinal principles" of IHL, both of which were "intransgressible" under customary international

19. Parks, *supra* note 2, at 512–13.

20. Pfanner, *supra* note 17, at 123.

21. *Id.* at 104 n.31.

22. NEW RULES FOR VICTIMS OF ARMED CONFLICTS: COMMENTARY ON THE TWO 1977 PROTOCOLS ADDITIONAL TO THE GENEVA CONVENTIONS OF 1949, at 285 (2d ed. revision by Michael Bothe, 2013).

23. Yoram Dinstein, *Jus in Bello Issues Arising in the Hostilities in Iraq in 2003*, 80 INTERNATIONAL LAW STUDIES 43, 45 (2006).

law.²⁴ Distinction not only operates with regard to the conduct of attacks but also requires doing what is feasible under the circumstances to avoid endangering the civilian population unnecessarily. As has been noted, "the adversary is obliged at all times to make a distinction between the civilian population and combatants, in order to ensure respect for and protection of the civilian population."²⁵ The ICRC's IHL database has collected extensive State practice to support characterization of the requirement as a matter of customary IHL.²⁶

Article 44(3) of the 1977 Additional Protocol I, a treaty law reflection of the distinction principle, provides: "In order to promote the protection of the civilian population from the effects of hostilities, combatants are obliged to distinguish themselves from the civilian population while they are engaged in an attack or in a military operation preparatory to an attack." The ICRC commentary to the article explains: "This provision imposes the fundamental rule that combatants are obliged to distinguish themselves from the civilian population while they are engaged in an attack or in a military operation preparatory to an attack, or in any action carried out with a view to combat."²⁷

As treaty law, the Protocol binds only parties to the instrument. Yet, the status of the provision as reflective of international law is bolstered by the United States' long-standing objection to the following sentence, which goes on to remove the requirement to wear a uniform or display distinctive indicia in certain circumstances in which "an armed combatant cannot so distinguish himself."²⁸

---

24. Legality of the Threat or Use of Nuclear Weapons, Advisory Opinion, 1996 I.C.J. Rep. 226, ¶ 78 (July 8). In some cases, it can be argued that the fourth criterion—that of "carrying arms openly"—could meet the distinction requirement itself. *See, e.g.*, ALLAN ROSAS, THE LEGAL STATUS OF PRISONERS OF WAR: A STUDY IN INTERNATIONAL HUMANITARIAN LAW APPLICABLE IN ARMED CONFLICTS 341 (1976) (stating that these two criteria are intended to "protect the civilian population from attack and to ensure a certain fairness in fighting"). Indeed, Article 44 of Additional Protocol I recognizes that in certain circumstances where a combatant cannot wear a uniform, the combatant "need only carry his arms openly." Protocol Additional to the Geneva Conventions of 12 August 1949, and Relating to the Protection of Victims of International Armed Conflicts art. 44(2), June 8, 1977, 1125 U.N.T.S. 3 [hereinafter Additional Protocol I]. The gravamen of this argument is beyond the scope of this chapter.

25. COMMENTARY ON THE ADDITIONAL PROTOCOLS OF 8 JUNE 1977 TO THE GENEVA CONVENTIONS OF 12 AUGUST 1949, ¶ 1695 (Yves Sandoz, Christophe Swinarski & Bruno Zimmermann eds., 1987)[hereinafter 1987 AP Commentary].

26. 2 CUSTOMARY INTERNATIONAL HUMANITARIAN LAW, rule 106 (Jean-Marie Henckaerts & Louise Doswald-Beck eds., 2005) [hereinafter CIHL Study].

27. 1987 AP Commentary, *supra* note 25, ¶ 1692.

28. *See* Letter of Transmittal from Ronald Reagan, President of the United States, to United States Senate (Jan. 29, 1987), https://www.loc.gov/rr/frd/Military_Law/pdf/protocol-II-100-2.pdf. ("Another provision [of Additional Protocol I] would grant combatant status to irregular forces even if they do not satisfy the traditional requirements to distinguish themselves from the civilian population and otherwise comply with the laws of war. This would endanger civilians among whom terrorists and other irregulars attempt to conceal themselves."). *See also* DoD LAW OF WAR MANUAL, *supra* note 8, §§ 4.6.1.2, 5.4.8.2, 19.20.1.5.

Although Article 44 was primarily designed to adjust the law with respect to guerrilla operations, its text is not so limited, and the logic of the first sentence (and the U.S. objection to the second) would apply equally to members of the regular armed forces.

The Department of Defense's *Law of War Manual* is in accord. It provides: "Parties to a conflict must . . . take certain measures to help ensure that military forces and civilians can be visually distinguished from one another."[29] The U.S. Army and Marine Corps Commander's *Handbook on the Law of Land Warfare* similarly provides: "Soldiers and Marines who fall within Article 4A(1) of the [Third Geneva Convention], including special operations forces, are expected to carry out their operations in standard uniform."[30] Although it is a close case, this is, in our estimation, the correct understanding of the law; States have a legal obligation to distinguish members of their armed forces from civilians.

But the question of whether the failure to wear uniforms violates IHL is a red herring vis-à-vis that of POW status. As noted above, the fact that a member of the armed forces may have committed IHL violations before capture does not deprive that individual of the right to be a POW. Article 44(2) of Additional Protocol I makes the same point: "While all combatants are obliged to comply with the rules of international law applicable in armed conflict, violations of these rules shall not deprive a combatant of his right to be a combatant or, if he falls into the power of an adverse Party, of his right to be a prisoner of war. . . ."[31] Accordingly, the question is the consequences of the behavior irrespective of whether failure to wear a uniform or other distinctive indicia constitutes an "internationally wrongful act."[32]

Spies and Saboteurs

There are distinct IHL rules regarding spying or sabotage without distinguishing oneself from the civilian population. The Department of Defense (DoD) *Law of War Manual* provides that "spies, saboteurs, and other persons engaged in secretive hostile activities behind enemy lines" forfeit the "privileges of combatant status, including POW status."[33] The feature common to both spying and sabotage

---

29. DoD Law of War Manual, *supra* note 8, § 2.5.3.

30. Commander's Handbook, *supra* note 10, ¶ 3-18.

31. Additional Protocol I, *supra* note 24, art. 44(2).

32. International Law Commission, Draft Articles on Responsibility of States for Internationally Wrongful Acts, with Commentaries, [2001] 2(2) Yearbook of the International Law Commission, art. 2 [hereinafter Articles on Responsibility of States].

33. DoD Law of War Manual, *supra* note 8, § 4.17.5; *see also id.*, § 9.3.2.1; Richard Baxter, *So-Called Unprivileged Belligerency: Spies, Guerrillas, and Saboteurs*, 28 British Yearbook of International Law 323, 329 (1951) (quoting 2 De Jure Belli Libri Tres 282–83 (1612) ("This also is a reason why you should be unwilling to assume that role [of spy], because it is denied the privileges attaching to military service. And therefore the law against spies seems

is the need to conceal identity, which invariably means a purposeful attempt at blending in with the civilian population.[34] Thus, if individuals gather intelligence or conduct hostile action behind enemy lines while in uniform or wearing other distinctive indicia that confirm combatant status, they do not forfeit POW status.

As the 2020 ICRC *Commentary* to the Third Geneva Convention observes, this is a "longstanding rule of customary international law" that before 1949 had appeared in the Lieber Code, the Brussels Declaration, the *Oxford Manual*, and, most importantly, the 1907 Hague Regulations.[35] In addition, the U.S. Army included the rule in its 1956 manual, *The Law of Land Warfare* (FM 27-10).[36] The rule also appears in Additional Protocol I, Article 46(1), for parties to that instrument.[37] While some of these sources, such as Article 46(1), cite only spies, "there is a well-established practice that saboteurs are treated in the same way as spies with regard to prisoner-of-war status."[38] This explains the DoD Manual's reference to both activities.

This chapter deals with the separate issue of individuals captured while not wearing uniforms or other distinctive indicia who are neither spying nor engaging in sabotage behind enemy lines, as in the case of capture when a position is overrun. In other words, does the non-wearing of a uniform or other distinctive indicia, standing alone, result in a loss of POW entitlement?

---

just, since they have divested themselves of the character which would prevent their being treated in that cruel and degrading fashion.")). If they return to their lines, subsequent capture will not merit denial of POW status. 2020 GC III COMMENTARY, *supra* note 11, ¶ 988. *See* CIHL STUDY, *supra* note 26, rule 107 ("The Brussels Declaration and the Hague Regulations recognize that a spy who rejoins his or her armed forces and who is subsequently captured must be treated as a prisoner of war and incurs no responsibility for previous acts of espionage").

34. "A person may be considered a spy when, (1) acting clandestinely or under false pretenses, (2) in the zone of operations of a belligerent, (3) he or she obtains, or endeavors to obtain, information, (4) with the intention of communicating it to a hostile party." 1899 Hague Regulations, *supra* note 15, art. 29. *See also* Uniform Code of Military Justice (10 U.S.C. §§ 801–946) art. 106; COMMANDER'S HANDBOOK, *supra* note 10, ¶ 1-76 ("During war, any person—military or civilian—whose actions meet all of these elements may be considered a spy under LOAC.").

35. 2020 GC III COMMENTARY, *supra* note 11, ¶ 988; U.S. Department of War, Instructions for the Government of Armies of the United States in the Field, General Orders No. 100, art. 88, Apr. 24, 1863 [hereinafter Lieber Code]; Institute of International Law, The Laws of War on Land arts. 23–25 (1880) (Oxford Manual), *reprinted in* THE LAWS OF ARMED CONFLICTS 29 (Dietrich Schindler & Jiří Toman eds., 4th ed. 2004); Project of an International Declaration concerning the Laws and Customs of War, Brussels, arts. 19–20, Aug. 27, 1874, *reprinted in* THE LAWS OF ARMED CONFLICTS 23 (Dietrich Schindler & Jiří Toman eds., 4th ed. 2004) [hereinafter Brussels Declaration]; 1907 Hague Regulations, *supra* note 16, arts. 29–30.

36. FM 27-10, *supra* note 9, at A-20.

37. Additional Protocol I, *supra* note 24, art. 46(1).

38. 2020 GC III COMMENTARY, *supra* note 11, ¶ 990.

C. Perfidy

Acts of unlawful perfidy involve feigning a protected status under international law in order to kill or wound the enemy.[39] The prohibition is of long lineage, appearing in Article 23(b) of the 1907 Hague Regulations in the guise of treachery.[40] For parties to Additional Protocol I, the prohibition also includes resort to perfidy to capture an adversary.[41] The Statute of the International Criminal Court brands perfidious attacks as war crimes.[42] Its delineation of offenses is a generally reliable source for identifying war crimes under customary law that applies to all States, including those, such as the United States, that are not party to the instrument.

A perfidious attack can be carried out by feigning civilian status in order to cause enemy forces not to know they are about to be attacked. One must be careful to distinguish a perfidious attack from one in which the attacker is merely wearing civilian clothes but carrying arms openly. The latter would not be an unlawful attack because there is no intent to deceive in order to attack.

The important point—one that is often misunderstood—is that the fact of perfidious attack does not on that basis alone deprive an attacker of POW status upon capture. As noted in the *DoD Law of War Manual*, "persons who are alleged to have committed war crimes" are "not necessarily excluded from POW status."[43] Whether members of the armed forces who are alleged to have engaged in perfidy by wearing civilian attire enjoy POW status (and combatant immunity), therefore, depends on the resolution of the central issue under consideration in this chapter.

These side issues dispensed with, analysis turns to the topic at hand: whether the failure of members of the regular armed forces to wear uniforms or other distinctive indicia leads to forfeiture of POW status upon capture.

II. THE ARGUMENT THAT THE ARTICLE 4A(2) CRITERIA DO NOT APPLY TO A STATE'S ARMED FORCES

For those who argue that the members of the regular armed forces need not wear uniforms or other distinctive indicia to benefit from POW status, the starting point is the text itself. Article 31 of the Vienna Convention on the Law of Treaties, which reflects customary law, provides that "[a] treaty shall be interpreted in good faith in accordance with the ordinary meaning to be given to the terms of the treaty in

---

39. *See* DoD Law of War Manual, *supra* note 8, § 5.22.

40. 1907 Hague Regulations, *supra* note 16, art. 23(b).

41. Additional Protocol I, *supra* note 24, art. 37.

42. Rome Statute of the International Criminal Court art. 8(2)(b)(xi), July 17, 1998, 2187 U.N.T.S. 90.

43. DoD Law of War Manual, *supra* note 8, § 9.3.2.2.

their context and in the light of its object and purpose."⁴⁴ Context includes the text itself.⁴⁵ Therefore, for advocates of this view, the presence of the criteria in Article 4A(2) but not in Article 4A(1) can be understood as indicating the drafters' intent to limit their applicability to members of militia or volunteer corps, including organized resistance movements, that are not part of the armed forces.⁴⁶

Accordingly, at least from a textual point of view, the ICRC is correct when it notes in its 2020 *Commentary* that the "difference in wording between subparagraph 4A(1) and 4A(2) seems to indicate clearly" that the conditions apply only to irregular forces, and not to members of the regular military or other groups forming part of the armed forces.⁴⁷ The *Commentary* also points out that the language was modeled after the 1874 Brussels Declaration and the 1899 and 1907 Hague Conventions. In those cases, the drafters set forth the criteria to encompass non-State armed groups and not to define criteria for a State's armed forces.⁴⁸

The Third Geneva Convention's travaux provide a degree of support for the position. During the Diplomatic Conference that drafted the Convention, delegates discussed the matter. One of the working texts of draft Article 4 had imposed the four Article 4A(2) conditions on regular forces; there was no differentiation between the regular armed forces or groups forming part of the armed forces on the one hand, and other militias or volunteer groups on the other.⁴⁹

The Soviet representative, Lieutenant General Nikolai Slavin, expressed concerns about text that might suggest the existence of criteria that members of the regular armed forces would need to satisfy for POW status. Major General René Devijver of Belgium replied that the intent was that only militia or volunteer corps members be required to fulfill the four conditions.⁵⁰ He indicated that the two categories were listed to "avoid any possibility of misunderstanding."⁵¹ For

---

44. Vienna Convention on the Law of Treaties art. 31(1), May 23, 1969, 1155 U.N.T.S. 331 [hereinafter Vienna Convention]. Although the United States is not a party to the Convention, the rules of interpretation reflect customary international law. RICHARD GARDINER, TREATY INTERPRETATION 162 (2d ed. 2015)("[I]t it is now beyond question that the Vienna rules (i.e., articles 31–33) are rules of customary international law").

45. Vienna Convention, *supra* note 44, art. 31(2).

46. *See, e.g.*, Sean Watts, *Who Is a Prisoner of War?*, *in* THE 1949 GENEVA CONVENTIONS: A COMMENTARY 889, ¶ 14 (Andrew Clapham, Paola Gaeta & Marco Sassòli eds., 2015).

47. 2020 GC III COMMENTARY, *supra* note 11, ¶ 1028.

48. Brussels Declaration, *supra* note 35, art. 9; 1899 Hague Regulations, *supra* note 15, art. 1; 1907 Hague Regulations, *supra* note 16, art. 1.

49. ROSAS, *supra* note 24, at 327.

50. II-A FINAL RECORD OF THE DIPLOMATIC CONFERENCE OF GENEVA OF 1949, 466–67 (1949) [hereinafter 1949 GENEVA CONFERENCE FINAL RECORD]; *see also* DoD LAW OF WAR MANUAL, *supra* note 8, at 119 n.150.

51. II-A FINAL RECORD OF THE DIPLOMATIC CONFERENCE OF GENEVA OF 1949, 466–67 (1949).

Devijver, the text was clear (or, at least, good enough): the four conditions did not apply to regular military forces. Ultimately, the Chairman suggested that the topic of the wording should be referred to a Working Group, but the travaux are devoid of any further evidence of resolution of Slavin's concerns.[52]

Slavin's position that status alone entitled a captured soldier to combatant status was shared by one of the few courts to address the matter at the time. On December 19, 1949, a British Military Court at Hamburg considered the question (recall that the Third Geneva Convention was adopted on December 8, 1949 and went into force on October 21, 1950).[53] German Field Marshal Erich von Manstein was accused of war crimes stemming from his treatment of Russian civilians and POWs while he was the ranking officer of German forces in portions of occupied Russia. He argued that some of the Russians were not entitled to POW status, though the facts did not require him to attempt to extend this argument to members of the regular Red Army.[54]

Nonetheless, this triggered the court's consideration of the applicability of Article 1 of the 1907 Hague Regulations, which, as noted above, was the model for Article 4A of the Third Geneva Convention. It found:

> With regard to ... the regular armed forces, the position is clear ... Regular soldiers are so entitled [to POW status] without any of the 4 requirements set out in Article 1; they are requisite in order to give the Militia and the Volunteer Corps the same privileges as the Army.[55]

In explanation, the court provided examples of a detaining power attempting to impose conditions on a belligerent's regular military for POW status. It rejected them all.[56]

The record is incomplete as to Lieutenant General Slavin's substantive concern or the full reasoning underlying the British Military Court's rejection of the application of the four criteria to the regular armed forces. However, Pfanner has advanced one possible justification:

> Captured members of regular forces automatically have prisoner-of-war status because of their link with their *de jure* or *de facto* government and the

---

52. *See also* ROSAS, *supra* note 24, at 327 (describing the same exchange as indicating that Lieutenant General Slavin was insisting on two points: (1) that they must differentiate between the regular military and militia and volunteer groups, and (2) that the criteria could only apply to the latter).

53. 16 ANNUAL DIGEST AND REPORTS OF PUBLIC INTERNATIONAL LAW CASES 509 (Hersch Lauterpacht ed., 1955).

54. *Id.* at 514.

55. *Id.* at 515.

56. *Id.* at 516.

armed forces to which they belong. That status reflects the relationship between the State as a subject of international law, the armed forces as organs of the State and the members of the armed forces as combatants. The very spirit of the Third Geneva Convention is contingent on this relationship which entails that members of the armed forces of a State engaged in an international armed conflict are lawfully participating in hostilities and must not be punished for their mere participation in the conflict.[57]

In other words, it appears that Pfanner is arguing that regular forces enjoy a status that differs from that of militias and volunteer corps that do not form part of the armed forces, or the *levée en masse*. If this is the case, then it arguably would make sense to use general characteristics of the regular forces to assess which independent forces should be entitled to POW status. But to take criteria developed to increase the scope of who among "independent forces" qualifies for POW status only to use them to limit who among the regular armed forces is entitled to POW status would be counterintuitive.

Supportive of this position is the ICRC's 1960 Pictet *Commentary*. Regarding Article 4, it observed that in the event of doubt about whether individuals are "members of the armed forces" under Article 4(A)(1), they may prove their status by presenting an identification card meeting the requirements of Article 17 of the Convention.[58] Of course, such doubt could arise because captured individuals who are not members of the regular armed forces might don military uniforms hoping to benefit from POW treatment. But the more likely scenario is that members of the armed forces would be captured out of uniform and thus need a means to demonstrate entitlement to POW status. The *Commentary* suggests that the card alone would suffice to confirm POW status eligibility.

There is also State practice supporting the position. As Hays Parks observed in 2003, "[h]istorically, regular military forces' entitlement to prisoner of war status has been absolute and unqualified."[59] The ICRC, in its 2020 *Commentary* to the Third Geneva Convention, confirms that "[i]n terms of practice, virtually no State has denied prisoner-of-war status to members of the regular armed forces

---

57. Pfanner, *supra* note 17, at 115.

58. 1960 GC III COMMENTARY, *supra* note 16, at 52. *See also* 1949 GENEVA CONFERENCE FINAL RECORD, *supra* note 50, at 416–17. When Lieutenant General Slavin enquired what would occur if a member of the regular military did not have an identification card in possession at the time of capture, General Dillion, the representative for the United States, replied:

> [A] captured person need not necessarily hold a card at the time of capture. It would suffice for the person to have received a card, and to be able to give proof of the fact. That is to say, the determining factor should be the status of the person concerned, and not the possession of a document.

1960 GC III COMMENTARY, *supra* note 16, at 52.

59. Parks, *supra* note 2, at 509 n.29 (*citing* the Lieber Code, *supra* note 35).

of a State on the grounds that those forces had not fulfilled the conditions."[60] It continues, "notwithstanding the widespread accusations of non-compliance [with the obligation to wear uniforms] made between Parties to the conflict, prisoner-of-war status was not denied on this basis to members of the regular armed forces as a whole during the Second World War nor in most international armed conflicts since."[61]

It appears that this is the position of the U.S. armed forces. Citing Article 4A(1) of the Third Geneva Convention, Article 57 of the Lieber Code,[62] and Article 1 of the Regulations annexed to the 1907 Hague Convention,[63] the *DoD Law of War Manual* endorses the view that membership in a State's armed forces is sufficient for its members to enjoy "combatant" status under the Third Geneva Convention,[64] though it recognizes the four criteria of Article 4A(2) as being "intended to reflect attributes of States' armed forces."[65] Likewise, the U.S. Army and Marine Corps Commander's *Handbook on the Law of Land Warfare* asserts that "[m]embers of the armed forces of a State party to a conflict ... are entitled to POW status based on their membership in the armed forces."[66] In neither instrument is this conclusion conditioned on wearing uniforms or other distinctive indicia. Rather, the sole situations the manuals proffer for loss of POW status are spying and sabotage, points discussed earlier.

There is scholarly support for the position, including from individuals with extensive practitioner experience. For instance, the late Major General (ret.) A.P.V. Rogers, former Director of the United Kingdom's Army Legal Services, has argued that under customary international law and the Third Geneva Convention, the requirements applied only to the unincorporated militia or volunteer corps addressed in Article 4A(2). Special rules existed for members of the regular armed forces who spied or carried out sabotage while in civilian clothes, but it was only with the 1977 Additional Protocol I that the requirement applied to all persons, a point discussed in the next part.[67]

Toni Pfanner has similarly opined:

---

60. 2020 GC III COMMENTARY, *supra* note 11, ¶ 1035.

61. *Id.*

62. Lieber Code, *supra* note 35, art. 57 ("So soon as a man is armed by a sovereign government and takes the soldier's oath of fidelity, he is a belligerent").

63. 1907 Hague Regulations, *supra* note 16, art. 1 ("The laws, rights, and duties of war apply ... to armies").

64. <DoD LAW OF WAR MANUAL, *supra* note 8, § 4.5.

65. *Id.*, § 4.6.1.3.

66. COMMANDER'S HANDBOOK, *supra* note10, ¶ 3-16.

67. Anthony Rogers, *Combatant Status*, in PERSPECTIVES ON THE ICRC STUDY ON CUSTOMARY INTERNATIONAL HUMANITARIAN LAW 101, 114 (Elizabeth Wilmshurst & Susan Breau eds., 2009).

The wording, legal history and the teleological interpretation of the Third Geneva Convention shows, furthermore, that members of regular armed forces—as opposed to irregular armed forces—are combatants owing to their affiliation with a party to an international armed conflict and do not have to fulfil specific constitutive criteria—including a distinctive sign and in particular the wearing of a military uniform—to qualify as prisoners of war in case of capture.[68]

And Hays Parks, responding to the U.S. Justice Department 2002 position discussed in the next part, has offered what is perhaps the most stringent argument against the requirement:

> A common mistake by lay persons, non-international law lawyers, some international law lawyers and, in the case at hand, by senior legal advisers and policymakers in the Bush administration is to recite the four criteria in (a) through (d) of Article 4A(2) as the criteria for any armed group to be eligible for combatant and prisoner of war status. This is a fundamental misunderstanding of the law of war and, in particular, of Article 4A(2), [Third Geneva Convention], and the rationale and history behind it. Extension of combatant and prisoner of war status in Article 4A(2) is intentionally and expressly narrower.
>
> ...
>
> Had governments in 1899, 1907, 1929 or 1949 regarded the wearing of a uniform a prerequisite for captured regular forces' entitlement to prisoner of war status, it would not have been difficult to have said so. They did not.[69]

Sean Watts has summarized the position of its advocates concisely:

> [T]he plainest reading of Article 4(A)(1) is the soundest. Members of regular armed forces qualify for POW status under [the Third Geneva Convention] simply by virtue of their membership in such organizations. Determinations of status under Article 4(A)(1) should require only reliable indicia of status, such as an identification card, leave and earnings statement, or similar documentary, physical, or testimonial evidence indicating membership in a state party's regular armed forces as determined by domestic law.[70]

---

68. Pfanner, *supra* note 17, at 123.

69. W. Hays Parks, *Combatants*, 85 INTERNATIONAL LAW STUDIES 247, 268, 276 (2009). The years 1899, 1907, 1929, and 1949 refer to the 1899 Hague Regulations, *supra* note 15; 1907 Hague Regulations, *supra* note 16; Convention Relative to the Treatment of Prisoners of War, July 27, 1929, 47 Stat. 2021, 118 L.N.T.S. 343 (which was in effect during the Second World War [hereinafter 1929 Geneva Convention]; and Third Geneva Convention, *supra* note 5.

70. Watts, *supra* note 46, ¶ 21.

Thus, by the approach outlined in this part, reliance on membership in the armed forces secures the protections of POW status. Yet while the Third Geneva Convention is concerned with that status, the treaty is equally (if not more so) concerned with protecting the civilian population. This objective forms the foundation for the alternative position supporting the applicability of Article 4A(2) criteria to members of the regular armed forces.

III. THE ARGUMENT THAT THE ARTICLE 4A(2) CRITERIA APPLY TO A STATE'S ARMED FORCES

The competing interpretation of Article 4(A)(1), and in our view the better one, is that the conditions outlined in Article 4A(2) are implicit in the concept "members of the armed forces." There was, therefore, no need for the drafters of the Third Geneva Convention to add that regular armed forces have to wear a "fixed distinctive sign recognizable at a distance" (or meet the other criteria). Exemplifying this position, Yoram Dinstein argued in 2006:

> One of the hallmarks of the hostilities in Iraq, in 2003, was that much of the fighting on the Iraqi side was conducted by "fedayeen" who fought Coalition forces out of uniform. These "fedayeen" were unlawful combatants. But so were any members of US Special Forces (or other Coalition military units) who fought out of uniform.[71]

Numerous points support this interpretation. Perhaps most significantly, there is near-universal State practice over centuries of States' armed forces wearing uniforms or distinctive insignia. While, as noted earlier, distinction from the civilian population may not have been the original and primary purpose for the wearing of uniforms, this secondary benefit is likewise a long-standing purpose. By the time the 1899 Hague Regulations were drafted (and therefore when the Third Geneva Convention was being negotiated a half-century later), members of the armed forces were those fighters who wore uniforms or otherwise distinguished themselves from civilians. This being so, adding a uniform or other distinctive indicia condition to Article 4A(1) would have been to state the obvious.

The ICRC's 1960 Pictet *Commentary* makes precisely this point regarding Article 4A(3). That article extends POW status to "[m]embers of regular armed forces who profess allegiance to an authority not recognized by the Detaining Power."[72] The Free French forces during the Second World War exemplify the

---

71. Dinstein, *supra* note 23, at 44. As Parks writes in the related debate over whether Special Forces were complying with the principle of distinction in Afghanistan, the facts about what Special Forces wore early on in the wars were hard to gather except for those very close to the operations. Parks, *supra* note 2, at 493 n.1.

72. Third Geneva Convention, *supra* note 5, art. 4A(3).

category.⁷³ Like Article 4A(1), Article 4A(3) does not mention the criteria. In this regard, the *Commentary* notes:

> The expression "members of regular armed forces" denotes armed forces which differ from those referred to in sub-paragraph (1) of this paragraph in *one respect only*: the authority to which they profess allegiance is not recognized by the adversary as a Party to the conflict. These "regular armed forces" have all the material characteristics and all the attributes of armed forces in the sense of sub-paragraph (1): they wear uniform, they have an organized hierarchy and they know and respect the laws and customs of war. The delegates to the 1949 Diplomatic Conference were therefore fully justified in considering that *there was no need to specify for such armed forces the requirements stated in sub-paragraph (2) (a), (b), (c) and (d)*.⁷⁴

In other words, the *Commentary* justifies omitting the criteria vis-à-vis Article 4A(3) by referring to Article 4A(1). For that reason, there would equally be no reason to set forth the requirements in the latter.⁷⁵

Taking a slightly different approach while acknowledging the requirements that characterize the armed forces, the *DoD Law of War Manual* focuses on their purpose:

> The conditions set forth in Article 4A(2) of the [Third Geneva Convention] were derived from conditions found in the Regulations annexed to the 1899 Hague II and the 1907 Hague IV. These conditions reflect the attributes common to regular armed forces of a State. By seeking to ensure that participants in hostilities are sufficiently disciplined, law-abiding, and distinguishable from the civilian population, these conditions help protect the civilian population from the hardships of war. In addition, these conditions contribute to the military effectiveness of the force that satisfies the conditions.
>
> These conditions may be understood to reflect a burdens-benefits principle, *i.e.*, the receipt of certain benefits in the law of war (*e.g.*, privileges of combatant status) requires the assumption of certain obligations.⁷⁶

This is an excellent point. However, it would seem counterintuitive to argue that to secure POW status, militia and other volunteer groups not forming part of the

---

73. 1960 GC III COMMENTARY, *supra* note 16, at 62.

74. *Id.* at 62–63 (emphasis added).

75. *See* ROSAS, *supra* note 24, at 328 ("The reason for making an explicit reference to the four conditions in connection with independent forces only at the Brussels Conference of 1874 and the Hague Conferences of 1899 and 1907 was probably that regular armed forces were assumed to fulfil these conditions anyway.").

76. DOD LAW OF WAR MANUAL, *supra* note 8, § 4.6.1 (emphasis added).

armed forces (Article 4A(2)) have to be in uniform or display other distinctive indicia, but members of a State's armed forces (Article 4A(1)) and members of regular armed forces of an authority that the capturing force does not recognize (Article 4A(3)) are relieved from the obligation. Why would members of an unincorporated militia or volunteer corps assume the obligation to secure the benefits of combatant status, but not members of the regular armed forces, if the intent of the conditions is to "help protect the civilian population from the hardships of war" and "contribute to the military effectiveness"? That intent would apply equally to the regular armed forces.

The motivation of the drafters in addressing "[m]embers of the armed forces of a Party" and "members of militias or volunteer corps forming part of such armed forces" separately from "[m]embers of other militias and members of other volunteer corps" was not to impose more stringent criteria for POW status on the latter. Instead, it was to secure protection for "partisans" captured by their adversaries, an objective that the ICRC had long pursued[77] and which had been highlighted by widespread partisan activity during the Second World War.[78]

To achieve this objective, the drafters chose language that flowed from the 1874 Brussels Declaration,[79] and was later included in the 1899[80] and 1907[81] Hague Regulations, to identify the types of "militia."[82] As the *Pictet Commentary* observes:

> [T]he intention of the authors, and the final solution adopted, was to return to the concept of the Hague Regulations. It is true that the phrase "organized resistance movements" was added to "militias" and "volunteer corps." The Conference of Government Experts had generally agreed that the first condition preliminary to granting prisoner-of-war status to partisans was their

---

77. 1960 GC III COMMENTARY, *supra* note 16, at 52–53.

78. Members of militia groups meeting the conditions were already encompassed in Article 1 of the 1907 Hague Regulations, but that treaty had an all-participation clause that meant that it only applied when all States participating in the conflict were party to the instrument. Convention No. IV Respecting the Laws and Customs of War on Land art. 2, Oct. 18, 1907, 36 Stat. 2227, T.S. No. 539. In 1946, the International Military Tribunal at Nuremberg noted: "The rules of land warfare expressed in the Convention undoubtedly represented an advance over existing International Law at the time of their adoption . . . but by 1939 these rules . . . were recognized by all civilized nations, and were regarded as being declaratory of the laws and customs of war." Judgment of the Nuremburg International Military Tribunal 1946, *reprinted in* 41 AMERICAN JOURNAL OF INTERNATIONAL LAW 248–49 (Jan. 1947). The International Military Tribunal for the Far East came to the same conclusion in 1948. Judgment of the International Military Tribunal for the Far East, 22 THE TOKYO WAR CRIMES TRIAL 42–66 (John Pritchard & Sonia M. Zaide eds., 1981).

79. Brussels Declaration, *supra* note 35, art. 9.

80. 1899 Hague Regulations, *supra* note 15, art. 1.

81. 1907 Hague Regulations, *supra* note 16, art. 1.

82. 2020 GC III COMMENTARY, *supra* note 11, ¶ 1010.

forming a body having a military organization. The implication was that *such an organization must have the principal characteristics generally found in armed forces throughout the world*, particularly in regard to discipline, hierarchy, responsibility and honour.[83]

Again, from the beginning, the criteria were based upon characteristics of regular armed forces. They were meant to scope the entitlement of militia and other volunteer corps to POW status so that only those analogous to a State's military forces would qualify, not the other way around.

Moreover, the logic of incentive supports the interpretation. The possibility (an unsettled matter, as discussed earlier) that the failure to wear uniforms might qualify as an internationally wrongful act by the State because members of the armed forces are its organs provides the *State* an incentive for compliance.[84] However, because violations of international law do not preclude POW status for the individuals involved, only the loss of combatant status and the attendant denial of combatant immunity and POW status would motivate *individuals* to wear distinctive indicia.

Most importantly, in our view, teleological interpretation of Article 4A(1) supports the view. Article 31(1) of the Vienna Convention on the Law of Treaties provides that treaties are to be interpreted "in good faith in accordance with the ordinary meaning to be given to the terms of the treaty in their context and in light of its object and purpose."[85] As noted in the 2020 ICRC *Commentary*, the primary object and purpose of the Third Geneva Convention is to "ensure that prisoners of war are humanely treated at all times, while allowing belligerents to intern captured enemy combatants to prevent them from returning to the battlefield."[86]

However, interpretive note should also be taken of the "intransgressible" principle of distinction, the object and purpose of which is to protect civilians from

---

83. 1960 GC III COMMENTARY, *supra* note 16, at 58.

84. Articles on Responsibility of States, *supra* note 32, art. 4.

85. Vienna Convention, *supra* note 44, art. 31(1). *See also* ROSAS, *supra* note 24, at 328 ("Both in view of the wording and legislative history of article 4 it cannot be *a priori* concluded that the four requirements are constructive conditions for prisoner-of-war status with respect to regular forces. . . . The question of what conditions, if any, regular forces have to fulfil in order to benefit from the status of prisoners of war must be decided on the basis of a comprehensive analysis of the Third Convention as a whole, and of the Hague Regulations and customary international law.").

86. 2020 GC III COMMENTARY, *supra* note 11, ¶ 89. Later in the Commentary, it states a more generalized object and purpose, that being to "'mitigate as far as possible, the inevitable rigours [of a war] and to alleviate the condition of prisoners of war.'" *Id.* ¶ 144 (*quoting* 1929 Geneva Convention, *supra* note 69, at the Preamble); *cf.* Michael W. Meier, *A Perspective on the Updated Third Geneva Convention Commentary from a United States Practitioner*, *infra* at C17P40–C17P48 (criticizing the 2020 Commentary's methodology for formulating the "object and purpose" of the Third Geneva Convention, but not with the formulation itself).

the risks of armed conflict to the extent possible. This is a key goal of wearing uniforms and other distinctive indicia, which, as noted, is characterized as a legal requirement by many—including the United States. It would seem incongruent if the principle loomed large in Article 4A(2), but not Article 4A(1) or (3).

The requirement for uniforms as a condition for POW status was a position taken in a 2002 U.S. Department of Justice Office of Legal Counsel opinion on the status of captured Taliban:

> Article 4(A)'s use of the phrase "armed force," we believe, incorporated by reference the four conditions for militia, which originally derived from the Hague Convention IV. There was no need to list the four Hague conditions in Article 4(A)(1) because it was well understood under preexisting international law that all armed forces were already required to meet those conditions. As would have been understood by the [Third Geneva Convention's] drafters, use of the term "armed forces" incorporated the four criteria, repeated in the definition of militia, that were first used in the Hague Convention IV.[87]

According to the opinion:

> [I]t would be utterly illogical to read "armed forces" in Article 4(A)(1) and (3) as somehow relieving members of armed forces from the same POW requirements imposed on members of a militia. There is no evidence that any of the [Third Geneva Convention's] drafters or ratifiers believed that members of the regular armed forces ought to be governed by *lower standards* in their conduct of warfare than those applicable to militia and volunteer forces. Otherwise, a sovereign could evade the Hague requirements altogether simply by designating all combatants as members of the sovereign's regular armed forces.... Further, it would make little sense to construe [the Third Geneva Convention] to deny some members of militias or volunteer corps POW protection for failure to satisfy the Hague conditions (under Article 4(A)(2)), while conferring such status upon other members simply because they have become part of the regular armed forces of a party (under Article 4(A)(1)).[88]

---

87. Memorandum from Assistant Attorney General Jay S. Bybee to Counsel to the President Alberto R. Gonzales, Status of Taliban Forces under Article 4 of the Third Geneva Convention 4 (Feb. 7, 2002), http://www.gwu.edu/~nsarchiv/NSAEBB/NSAEBB127/020207.pdf [hereinafter Office of Legal Counsel opinion]. For support, the opinion cites Major Geoffrey S. Corn & Major Michael L. Smidt, *To Be Or Not to Be, That Is the Question: Contemporary Military Operations and the Status of Captured Personnel*, ARMY LAWYER, June 1999, at 1, 14 n.127; Gregory M. Travalio, *Terrorism, International Law, and the Use of Military Force*, 18 WISCONSIN INTERNATIONAL LAW JOURNAL 145, 184 n.140 (2000); and Michael N. Schmitt, *Bellum Americanum: The U.S. View of Twenty-First Century War and Its Possible Implications for the Law of Armed Conflict*, 19 MICHIGAN JOURNAL OF INTERNATIONAL LAW 1051, 1078 (1998).

88. Office of Legal Counsel opinion, *supra* note 87, at 5.

Unlike a number of other opinions issued by the Office of Legal Counsel during that period, most notably the so-called torture memos,[89] this opinion was never withdrawn.[90] And Justice Department opinions are the authoritative positions of the executive branch of the United States.[91]

The ICRC has taken the same position as the Justice Department. Rule 106 of its Customary International Humanitarian Law Study provides that "[c]ombatants must distinguish themselves from the civilian population while they are engaged in an attack or in a military operation preparatory to an attack. If they fail to do so, they do not have the right to prisoner-of-war status."[92] It cites the Brussels Declaration, the *Oxford Manual*, the Hague Regulations, the Third Geneva Convention, and Additional Protocol I as support, together with numerous cases, military manuals, and State practice.[93]

The ICRC reiterated this stance in its 2020 *Commentary* to the Third Geneva Convention. Regarding Article 4, it observed:

> To enhance the protection of civilians, members of the armed forces must distinguish themselves from the civilian population during military operations. Under customary international humanitarian law, the failure of individual combatants to distinguish themselves while engaged in an attack or in a military operation preparatory to an attack means they forfeit the right to prisoner-of-war status. The purpose of such a requirement is to maximize the distinction between civilians and combatants and thereby enhance the

---

89. In response to Executive Order 13491, the Attorney General reviewed its legal opinions issued between September 11, 2001, and January 20, 2009, pertaining to interrogations and withdrew five of them. Memorandum Opinion from David J. Barron, Acting Assistant Attorney General, Office of Legal Counsel, to the Attorney General, Withdrawal of Opinion on CIA Interrogations (June 11, 2009), https://www.justice.gov/olc/file/2009-06-11-wd-cia-interr-01/download.

90. The Office of Legal Counsel's legal reasoning was soon thereafter attacked by Hays Parks. Parks, *supra* note 69, at 278–83.

91. Principles to Guide the Office of Legal Counsel, *reprinted in* 81 Indiana Law Journal 1345, 1348 (2006) ("OLC's legal determinations are considered binding on the executive branch, subject to the supervision of the Attorney General and the ultimate authority of the President"); but compare Trevor W. Morrison, *Stare Decisis in the Office of Legal Counsel*, 110 Columbia Law Review 1448, 1456 n.31("[T]here is actually some uncertainty whether OLC's opinions are truly binding within the Executive Branch as a technical matter. But there is a longstanding practice of *treating* them as binding.").

92. CIHL Study, *supra* note 26, rule 106. *See* Marco Sassòli et al., How Does Law Protect in War? (online version), glossary entries for "prisoners of war," https://casebook.icrc.org/glossary/prisoners-war; and "uniform," https://casebook.icrc.org/glossary/uniform.

93. CIHL Study, *supra* note 26, rule 106.

protection of the civilian population. Traditionally, this requirement poses no problem for State armed forces, as they normally wear uniforms.[94]

Additional Protocol I is likewise telling. Recall that for States parties, Article 44 of Additional Protocol I provides that combatants are entitled to POW status. It then notes that individuals who qualify as combatants retain that status even if they violate IHL, "except as provided for in paragraphs 3 and 4" of Article 44.[95] Paragraph 3 imposes an obligation on combatants to "distinguish themselves from the civilian population while they are engaged in an attack or in a military operation preparatory to an attack," but then provides that individuals retain combatant status, and, therefore, entitlement to POW status, if unable to distinguish themselves so long as arms are carried openly in military engagements and while visible to the enemy during deployments to the engagement.[96]

In other words, Article 44(3) carves out an exception to the requirement of wearing a uniform for combatant status—one that, as noted above, the United States strongly, and correctly so, opposes. Article 44(4) goes further than the obligation itself and holds that a combatant who fails to distinguish himself as required by Article 44(3) "shall forfeit his right to be a prisoner of war." Curiously, while the individual does not have POW status, he is to receive "protections equivalent in all respects to those accorded to prisoners of war."[97] Finally, Article 44(7) states that "[t]his Article is not intended to change the generally accepted practice of States with respect to the wearing of the uniform by combatants assigned to the regular, uniformed armed units of a Party to the conflict."[98] Thus, both Article 44 and the U.S. response support a general requirement of wearing a uniform for POW status.

Even Additional Protocol I States are uncomfortable with the truncation of the requirement to wear a uniform, and relatedly the relaxation of the criterion for the purpose of POW status. For example, the *U.K. Law of Armed Conflict Manual*, when discussing the provision (the United Kingdom is party to the Protocol), confirms that an individual who is not complying with the general requirement to distinguish him or herself from the civilian population forfeits the right to be

---

94. 2020 GC III COMMENTARY, *supra* note 11, ¶ 983, (citing CIHL STUDY, *supra* note 26, rule 106). *See also id.*, ¶ 1039 ("[M]embers of the armed forces are under an obligation to distinguish themselves sufficiently from the civilian population and not to conceal their weapons during military operations. If individuals do not do so, they lose their entitlement to prisoner-of-war status on an individual basis.").

95. Additional Protocol I, *supra* note 24, art. 44.

96. *Id.*

97. *Id.*, art. 44(4). The majority view at the Diplomatic Conference that drafted Additional Protocol I was that the individual, having lost combatant status, could now be prosecuted for violation of domestic law. 1987 AP COMMENTARY, *supra* note 25, ¶ 1719.

98. Additional Protocol I, *supra* note 24, art 24, art. 44(7).

treated as a POW.⁹⁹ Furthermore, the Manual emphasizes that exceptions to the rule are strictly limited to those in Article 44(3):

> Wide application of this special rule would reduce the protection of civilians to vanishing point. Members of the opposing armed forces would come to regard every civilian as likely to be a combatant in disguise and, for their own protection, would see them as proper targets for attack. The special rule is thus limited to those exceptional situations where a combatant is truly unable to operate effectively whilst distinguishing himself in accordance with the normal requirements. The United Kingdom, together with other states, made a formal statement on ratifying Additional Protocol I that this exception could only apply in occupied territory or in conflicts to which Additional Protocol I, Article 1(4) apply. Even in those cases, there are many occasions on which combatants can still comply with the general rule of distinction, which remains in force, when the special rule would not apply.¹⁰⁰

At the time the Additional Protocols were being negotiated, the United States was clearly in the "uniforms are required for status" camp. For instance, the Air Force's now rescinded *International Law—The Conduct of Armed Conflict and Air Operations* (AFP 110-31), published while the Additional Protocols negotiations were underway, made clear that the criteria applied to all combatants:

> During World War II confusion arose as to the status of organized resistance movements and other irregular forces. The 1949 Geneva Conventions attempted to resolve this controversy by recognizing the [POW] status of irregular forces meeting certain requirements. *Recognition of combatants as lawful belligerents under the Geneva Conventions depends upon certain objective criteria* being met and the existence of an international armed conflict.¹⁰¹

A decade later, Judge Abraham Sofaer, who was then serving as the Legal Adviser for the U.S. State Department, similarly tied the benefits of combatancy to the wearing of uniforms:

> A fundamental premise of the Geneva Conventions has been that to earn the right to protection as military fighters, soldiers must distinguish themselves from civilians by wearing uniforms and carrying their weapons openly . . . Fighters who attempt to *take advantage of civilians by hiding among them in civilian dress*, with their weapons out of view, *lose their claim*

---

99. United Kingdom Ministry of Defence, The Manual of the Law of Armed Conflict ¶ 4.6 (2004) [hereinafter UK Manual].

100. *Id.*, ¶ 4.5.1.

101. Department of the Air Force, AFP 110-31, International Law—The Conduct of Armed Conflict and Air Operations ¶ 3-2(b)(3) (1976) (emphasis added).

to be treated as soldiers. The law thus attempts to encourage fighters to avoid placing civilians in unconscionable jeopardy.[102]

Other non-party States are in accord. Of particular note, Israel takes an unambiguous stance on the matter in its 2006 *Manual on the Rules of Warfare*: "Soldiers in the regular army who do not wear uniform and do not wear a permanent identification sign will not be considered as legitimate combatants."[103]

Courts have taken a similar view, albeit with less-than-clear reasoning on the issue. For example, in *United States v. Buck*, a 1988 case in the Southern District of New York, the court concluded that the defendants, so-called Republic of New Africa officers, were not entitled to POW status. It began by rejecting the assertion that the situation was an armed conflict. But the court went on to observe that even if it had been an armed conflict, the defendants did not comply with the Article 4A(2) criteria. It further held that "[f]or comparable reasons, Article 4(3)'s [sic, 4A(3)'s] reference to members of 'regular armed forces who profess allegiance to a government or an authority not recognized by the Detaining Power,' also relied upon by defendants, does not apply to the circumstances of this case."[104] As noted above, Article 4A(3) does not include the criteria and, therefore, the court's logic seemingly would apply equally to members of a State's armed forces under Article 4A(1).

An analogous stance was taken earlier by an Israeli Military Court in the 1974 *Swarka* case, though in the context of sabotage and saboteurs. In *Swarka*, the court noted that neither the 1907 Hague Regulations nor the Third Geneva Convention expressly requires the wearing of a uniform to qualify as a combatant entitled to POW status. However, it observed that it would be illogical to impose the requirement on Article 4A(2) units, but not members of the regular armed forces. Ultimately, the court held that the defendants, who had entered Israel from Egypt and conducted a rocket attack against a civilian settlement, were not entitled to POW status and were to be prosecuted as saboteurs.[105]

Similarly, the 1968 *Mohamed Ali* case before the Privy Council involved a member of the Indonesian armed forces who wore civilian clothes while placing a bomb in an office building in Singapore. The Privy Council held even though the wearing of a uniform or other distinctive indicia did not appear as a condition in

---

102. Martin D. Dupuis et al., "The Position of the United States on Current Law of War Agreements: Remarks of Judge Abraham D. Sofaer, Legal Adviser, Department of State, January 22, 1987," in *The Sixth Annual American Red Cross–Washington College of Law Conference on International Humanitarian Law: A Workshop on Customary International Law and the 1977 Protocols Additional to the 1949 Geneva Conventions*, 2 AMERICAN UNIVERSITY JOURNAL OF INTERNATIONAL LAW AND POLICY 415, 466 (1987)(emphasis added).

103. ISRAEL MINISTRY OF DEFENSE, THE MANUAL ON THE RULES OF WARFARE (2006), excerpted in CIHL STUDY, *supra* note 26, rule 106.

104. United States v. Buck, 690 F. Supp. 1291, 1298 (S.D.N.Y. 1988).

105. Swarka Case, Israel Military Court, 1974, discussed in CIHL STUDY, *supra* note 26, rule 106.

the Third Geneva Convention or the Hague Regulations for members of the regular armed forces, they nevertheless had to observe them to benefit from POW status:

> It seems to us clear beyond doubt that under International Law a member of the armed forces of a party to the conflict who, out of uniform and in civilian clothing, sets off explosives in the territory of the other party to the conflict in a non-military building in which civilians are doing work unconnected with any war effort forfeits his right on capture to be treated as a prisoner of war.[106]

In the United States, the Supreme Court came to the same conclusion in *Ex parte Quirin*, which involved members of the German armed forces captured while on a sabotage mission in the United States.[107]

Distinguished scholars agree. Yoram Dinstein, for instance, observes:

> Blurring the lines of division between combatants and civilians is bound to result in civilians suffering the consequences of being suspected as covert combatants. Hence, under customary international law, a sanction (deprivation of the privileges of prisoners of war) is imposed on any combatant masquerading as a civilian in order to mislead the enemy and avoid detection.[108]

Marco Sassòli takes the same position,[109] as did Waldemar Solf, Karl Partsch, and Michael Bothe.[110]

Individual Versus Collective Application

Assuming, for the sake of analysis, that the Article 4A(2) criteria apply implicitly to members of a State's armed forces, the question remains whether application for the purposes of POW status is collective or individual. Of course, by the position that the Article 4A(2) criteria apply to members of the regular armed forces, if a State's armed forces are generally following the four criteria, but a member is captured while not wearing a uniform, the individual is not entitled to POW

---

106. Mohamed Ali v. Public Prosecutor [1969] 1 AC 430, 449.

107. *Ex parte* Quirin, 317 U.S. 1, 35–36 (1942).

108. Yoram Dinstein, *Unlawful Combatancy*, 79 INTERNATIONAL LAW STUDIES 151, 153 (2003). *See also* Dinstein, *supra* note 23, at 43.

109. MARCO SASSÒLI, INTERNATIONAL HUMANITARIAN LAW: RULES, CONTROVERSIES, AND SOLUTIONS TO PROBLEMS ARISING IN WARFARE 251 (2019).

110. NEW RULES FOR VICTIMS OF ARMED CONFLICTS, *supra* note 22, at 285.

status. But what if a member of the regular armed forces falls into the hands of the enemy while complying with the four criteria, but the regular armed force to which the member belongs generally does not adhere to the requirement?

Setting aside the issue of whether the four criteria apply to individual members of the regular armed forces (see earlier discussion), the *DoD Law of War Manual* takes the position that the conditions were chosen because they "were intended to reflect attributes of States' armed forces."[111] Thus, the Manual continues, if an "armed force of a State systematically failed to distinguish itself from the civilian population and to conduct its operations in accordance with the law of war, its members should not expect to receive the privileges afforded lawful combatants."[112] This approach presumably would apply mutatis mutandis to the regular armed forces, assuming the Article 4A(2) criteria govern their entitlement to POW status. It is supported by numerous scholars[113] and some domestic case law.[114] In our view, this is the better position, although the noncompliance should be widespread and systematic for reasons to which the ICRC points.[115]

Acknowledging disagreement over the issue, that organization takes the opposite view in its 2020 *Commentary* to the Third Geneva Convention. It asserts that the four conditions are "obligations" but not "collective *conditions* for prisoner-of-war status." The organization reasons that "the entitlement of regular armed forces to prisoner-of-war status provides an important incentive for combatants to comply with international humanitarian law; collectively denying it removes that incentive and risks increasing the danger of non-compliance." The *Commentary* continues that the "conditions also reflect the usual practice of State armed forces, and armed forces will generally conform to them."[116]

---

111. DoD Law of War Manual, *supra* note 8, § 4.6.1.3. As explained above, the DoD Law of War Manual takes the position that the four criteria do not apply to members of a regular armed forces.

112. *Id.*

113. Yoram Dinstein, *Unlawful Combatancy*, 32 Israel Yearbook on Human Rights 247, 255 (2002); Kenneth Watkin, *Warriors Without Rights? Combatants, Unprivileged Belligerents, and the Struggle Over Legitimacy*, 2 Harvard University Program on Humanitarian Policy and Conflict Research Occasional Paper Series, 40–41 (Winter 2005); Michael N. Schmitt, *Asymmetrical Warfare and International Humanitarian Law*, 62 Air Force Law Review 1, 16 (2008); Ruth Wedgwood, *Al Qaeda, Terrorism, and Military Commissions*, 96 American Journal of International Law 328, 349 (2002); Jens David Ohlin, *The Combatant's Privilege in Asymmetric and Covert Conflicts*, 40 Yale Journal of International Law 337, 349 (2015); Geoffrey S. Corn et al., The Law in War: A Concise Overview 57 (2018).

114. 2020 GC III Commentary, *supra* note 11, ¶ 1032 (*citing* Bin Mohamed Ali v. Public Prosecutor, Judicial Committee of the Privy Council (United Kingdom) 452–53 (1968); United States v. Lindh, 212 F. Supp. 2d 541, 557–58 (E.D. Va. 2002), *Ex parte* Quirin, 317 U.S. 1, 35–36 (1942).

115. 2020 GC III Commentary, *supra* note 11, ¶ 1039.

116. *Id.*

The Distinction Requirement—What and When

Assuming that a uniform or other distinctive indicia is necessary for POW status, what suffices to meet that requirement, and when does it attach? The gist of the requirement is that the individuals concerned must be visually distinguishable from the civilian population. The DoD *Law of War Manual* explains:

> The requirement does not specify a particular sign or emblem that persons must wear. Wearing a military uniform satisfies this condition. However, a full uniform is not required. The sign suffices if it enables the person to be distinguished from the civilian population. For example, a helmet or headdress that makes the silhouette of the individual readily distinguishable from that of a civilian can meet this requirement. Similarly, a partial uniform (such as a uniform jacket or trousers), load bearing vest, armband, or other device could suffice, so long as it served to distinguish the members from the civilian population.[117]

The key is visible distinction from the civilian population because civilians are a protected IHL category. This explains why camouflage, a "ruse" of war, is legitimate. Camouflage makes soldiers blend into their surroundings, and those surroundings (such as foliage) are not protected by IHL.[118] The centrality of distinction also explains why a State's special operations troops who dress in the manner of a local friendly force meet the distinction requirement, as was the case in Afghanistan.[119] In these cases, the special operations troops attempt to blend in with another element of combatants but are still distinguishable from the civilian population.

The ICRC agrees:

---

117. DoD Law of War Manual, *supra* note 8, § 4.6.4.1.

118. *Id.*, § 2.5.4; Commander's Handbook, *supra* note 10, ¶ 1-42. For instance, Hays Parks has explained:

> US and Coalition Special Forces began operations in Afghanistan in late September 2001. At the request—initially insistence—of the leaders of the indigenous forces they supported, they dressed in indigenous attire. For identification purposes within the Northern Alliance, this included the Massoud *pakol* (a round brownish-tan or gray wool cap) and Massoud checkered scarf, each named for former Northern Alliance leader Ahmad Shah Massoud, who was assassinated days before the al Qaeda attacks on the World Trade Center and Pentagon. This attire was not worn to appear as civilians, or to blend in with the civilian population, but rather to lower the visibility of US forces vis-à-vis the forces they supported.

Parks, *supra* note 2, at 496–97.

119. Commander's Handbook, *supra* note 10, ¶¶ 1-42, 2-105.

Some States have expressed the view that part of their regular armed forces may wear a "non-standard uniform" as long as they still distinguish themselves from the civilian population. As long as these persons remain recognizable as members of the enemy armed forces, this practice may be accepted.... If, however, non-standard uniforms do not amount to uniforms at all, i.e. because they lack a fixed, distinctive sign recognizable at a distance, members of armed forces thus clad risk being denied prisoner-of-war status.[120]

A related question is when must members of the regular armed forces distinguish themselves to secure their entitlement to POW status. Although the *DoD Law of War Manual* appears to reject a condition precedent of a uniform or other distinctive indicia for POW status, it does recognize an obligation to be so attired.

Logically, if a member of the regular armed forces is captured out of uniform at a time when obligated to wear a uniform or other distinctive indicia, the individual would not be entitled to POW status by the approach that applies the Article 4A(2) criteria to Article 4A(1) personnel. The Manual appears to take the position that "military operations" require uniforms or other distinctive indicia but notes that the requirement is subject to a rule of reason:

> Although military operations generally are conducted while wearing a uniform or other distinctive emblems, there may be occasions, such as a surprise attack by enemy forces, when military personnel are unable to dress in their uniforms before resisting the enemy's assault.
>
> Military personnel not in uniform may resist an attack, so long as they are not wearing the enemy's uniform and do not kill or wound treacherously. For example, military personnel not in uniform who resist an attack, and who do not purposefully seek to conceal their status as combatants, commit no violation of the law of war and remain entitled to the privileges of combatant status. The normal wearing of uniforms or other distinctive emblems, however, should resume as soon as practicable because such wear helps protect the civilian population from erroneous attack by helping to distinguish military forces from the civilian population.[121]

The *DoD Law of War Manual* continues by making the related common-sense observation that "measures such as wearing insignia or other distinctive emblems may be of less practical significance during an attack. During an attack, combatants are likely to be distinguishable based on their activities more than any insignia or devices they are wearing."[122] Notwithstanding this logic, the Manual concludes

---

120. 2020 GC III COMMENTARY, *supra* note 11, ¶ 985.

121. DOD LAW OF WAR MANUAL, *supra* note 8, § 5.4.8.1. *See also* 2020 GC III COMMENTARY, *supra* note 11, ¶ 986.

122. DOD LAW OF WAR MANUAL, *supra* note 8, § 5.4.8.2.

that "[u]nder customary international law, the obligation of combatants to distinguish themselves is a general obligation that the armed forces have as a group and is not limited to times when they are engaged in an attack or in a military operation preparatory to an attack."[123]

For parties to the instrument, Article 44(3) of Additional Protocol I provides: "In order to promote the protection of the civilian population from the effects of hostilities, combatants are obliged to distinguish themselves from the civilian population while they are engaged in an attack or in a military operation preparatory to an attack." It goes on to controversially relax the requirement where an "armed combatant cannot so distinguish himself," a relaxation opposed, as noted earlier, by the United States. Additional Protocol I parties generally restate the Article 44(3) requirement. For instance, the *U.K. Law of Armed Conflict Manual* states:

> The general rule is that all combatants are required to distinguish themselves from the civilian population when engaged in an attack or military operation preparatory to an attack.
>
> In the case of members of the regular armed forces, the generally accepted practice of States is that they do this by wearing uniform.[124]

Although the period appears shorter than the reference to "military operations" in the *DoD Law of War Manual* might suggest, recall that the ICRC's 2020 commentary on Article 4 extracted above likewise uses the term "military operations" as the activity necessitating the wearing of a uniform or distinctive indicia.

In our view, the explanation that has been offered by Yoram Dinstein is sound:

> Still, even regular armies do not require that uniforms be worn at all times. Combatants do not have to wear uniforms either when they are off-duty or when they are working in a back-office. In particular, they do not have to be in uniform if they are operating in a rear-guard location, remote from the contact zone (defined as the frontline area on land where the forward elements of the opposing forces are in contact with each other). The main point is that uniforms are expected to be worn during combat. Even in this respect, there may be exceptional situations. If uniformed soldiers, sent on a combat mission, bivouac overnight, they may remove their uniforms in their tents. Should the encampment be subjected to a surprise raid by the enemy, the aroused defenders may instantaneously use their weapons to repel the attack without being concerned about their semi-clad state.[125]

---

123. *Id.*

124. UK MANUAL, *supra* note 99, ¶ 8.5.

125. YORAM DINSTEIN, THE CONDUCT OF HOSTILITIES UNDER THE LAW OF INTERNATIONAL ARMED CONFLICT 53–54 (3d ed. 2016). *See also* NEW RULES FOR VICTIMS OF ARMED CONFLICTS, *supra* note 22, at 241, 252.

IV. CONCLUSION

The record is not clear. Since the drafting of the Third Geneva Convention, there has been an ongoing debate over whether the failure to wear a uniform when engaging in military operations results in forfeiture of POW status upon capture. Both sides of the debate have mustered strong arguments based on textual analysis, the negotiating record of the treaty, State practice, *opinio juris*, and the object and purpose of the Third Geneva Convention generally and Article 4 specifically.

Ultimately, although reasonable minds may differ, we find the requirement that a uniform or other distinctive indicia be worn in order to qualify for POW status to be the better position—not only one that is defensible in law, but also an approach that makes operational good sense. Those in the field must be able to distinguish combatants from civilians if they are to respect the principle of distinction. They must know whom they can attack and whom they cannot. Uniforms have been, and remain, the key means of making that determination. Failure to distinguish oneself places civilians at risk, and it is a sensible sanction to deny POW status to those who do so. In all likelihood, the debate will only be settled definitively through State practice during future conflicts in which a State party claims that it cannot, or simply does not, clothe its regular armed forces in uniforms, and there is a significant capture of those forces.

4

"Accompanying the Force" in Modern Armed Conflict

ERIC TALBOT JENSEN[*] ■

I. INTRODUCTION

Throughout history, non-military personnel have routinely accompanied fighting forces on the battlefield for purposes of providing their goods or services to the forces. Others would simply want to take advantage of opportunities to scavenge or loot.[1] By the middle of the nineteenth century, the professional army was well established as the mainstay of State armed forces. The 1863 Lieber Code codified many rules concerning the interaction of the armed forces, but it also addressed civilians accompanying such professional forces, including both those "who are attached to the army for its efficiency and promote directly the object of the war"[2] and those "citizens who accompany an army for whatever purpose, such as sutlers, editors, or reporters of journals, or contractors."[3]

---

[*] Professor of Law, Brigham Young University Law School. The author would like to thank Carolyn Sharp for her superb research and other assistance on this chapter.

[1] THE OXFORD COMPANION TO MILITARY HISTORY 170 (Richard Holmes et al. eds., 2001). *See also* Shannon Selin, *How Were Napoleonic Battlefields Cleaned Up?*, IMAGINING THE BOUNDS OF HISTORY (Jul. 8, 2016), https://shannonselin.com/2016/07/napoleonic-battlefield-cleanup/ (noting that some civilians were known to accompany the forces simply to take advantage of opportunities to scavenge or loot).

[2] U.S. Department of War, Instructions for the Government of Armies of the United States in the Field, General Orders No. 100, Apr. 24, 1863 [hereinafter Lieber Code].

[3] *Id.*, art. 50.

Because of their proximity to the fight, it was inevitable that some of these civilians would be captured by the enemy.[4] And, based on their importance to the armed forces, they were given protected status upon capture, which included "'at least' the same treatment as prisoners of war, provided they can prove that they are attached to an army."[5] In other words, while these civilians were not considered combatants, they were given the status and protections of prisoners of war.[6] These protections were authorized by the armed forces under the assumption that the services were provided "in the vicinity of armies."[7]

With the evolution of modern technology and its impact on the conduct of warfare, many civilians[8] who provide goods and services no longer need to be on the battlefield or "in the vicinity" of the armed forces they support. For example, logisticians, weapons maintainers, communications supporters, and cyber technicians can accomplish analogous tasks performed by civilians accompanying the armed forces but can now do so from a distance. Indeed, this trend will only increase as technology continues to evolve. This chapter argues that while a "proximity" test continues to be applicable, there are cases where functionality, or a civilian's importance to the armed forces, might also need to be considered. In other words, there are and will continue to be some civilians who "accompany" the armed forces based on their function only, rather than their proximity, and these civilians should also be afforded the treatment of civilians accompanying the armed forces upon capture.

---

4. *See generally* Major Charlotte M. Liegl-Paul, *Civilian Prisoners of War: A Proposed Citizen Code of Conduct*, 182 MILITARY LAW REVIEW 106 (2004), where the author details the risks of capture to civilians who accompany the armed forces and argues that they should be given instructions on a code of conduct to prevent malfeasance during capture.

5. COMMENTARY TO GENEVA CONVENTION III RELATIVE TO THE TREATMENT OF PRISONERS OF WAR 48–49 (Jean Pictet ed., 1960) [hereinafter 1960 GC III COMMENTARY].

6. Lieutenant Commander Stephen R. Sarnoski, *The Status Under International Law of Civilian Persons Serving with or Accompanying Armed Forces in the Field*, THE ARMY LAWYER, July 1994, at 29, 31.

7. Project of an International Declaration concerning the Laws and Customs of War, Brussels, art. 34, Aug. 27, 1874, *reprinted in* THE LAWS OF ARMED CONFLICTS 1425 (Dietrich Schindler & Jiri Toman eds., 4th ed. 2004) [hereinafter Brussels Declaration]. *See further* the 1960 GC III COMMENTARY, where, reflecting on earlier provisions concerning civilians accompanying the armed forces, the Commentary states: "Article 13 of the [Hague] Regulations refers to individuals who follow an army without directly belonging to it, but whom the combatant Powers have the right to detain for reasons of security. All such persons have the right to 'at least' the same treatment as prisoners of war, provided they can prove that they are attached to an army." 1960 GC III COMMENTARY, *supra* note 5, at 48–49.

8. The term "civilian" will be used in this chapter to describe both civilian employees and contractors. The LOAC makes no distinction between the two for the purposes of this analysis. *See* Michael N. Schmitt, *Humanitarian Law and Direct Participation in Hostilities by Private Contractors or Civilian Employees*, 5 CHICAGO JOURNAL OF INTERNATIONAL LAW 511, 532 (2005).

Part II of this chapter will briefly outline the law that established the protections for civilians who accompany the armed forces, noting the historical primacy of proximity as the key factor in allocating status and protections. Part III will discuss the evolution of proximity, noting its diminished applicability to civilians who are conducting similar tasks to those on the battlefield, but are doing so from great distances. Part IV will contend that the functional aspect of being a civilian who accompanies the force is becoming more important in modern armed conflict, given the progression of technology. Part V will then argue that States should embrace this functional component in allocating prisoner of war status and will propose some criteria for States to consider if accepting this approach. Part VI will conclude.

A caveat is important at this point. This chapter acknowledges that the civilians accompanying the armed forces may also be considered targetable under the law of armed conflict (LOAC). In fact, many contracted personnel who serve in these positions are clearly notified that they may be considered targetable by an enemy, based on their direct participation in hostilities.[9] This chapter will not engage in a discussion of targetability but concentrate on treatment upon capture. These two concepts are both very important but not coterminous.

II. CIVILIANS ACCOMPANYING THE ARMED FORCES

As referenced above, recognition of civilians who accompany the force was codified as early as 1863 with the Lieber Code.[10] Subsequent treaties reinforced this recognition and have also provided individuals and groups who accompany the force with prisoner of war protection. In 1874, the Brussels Declaration stated, "Individuals in the vicinity of armies but not directly forming part of them, such as correspondents, newspaper reporters, sutlers, contractors, etc., can also be made prisoners. These prisoners should however be in possession of a permit issued by the competent authority and of a certificate of identity."[11] Such a permit could be used as proof of a civilian's recognized status as non-military personnel entitled to prisoner of war protection.

This provision was repeated in the 1899[12] and 1907 Hague Declarations. Article 13 of the 1907 Hague IV states:

---

9. U.S. Department of Army, Reg. 715-9, Army Command Policy para. 4-2 (Mar. 24, 2017).

10. Lieber Code, *supra* note 2, arts. 49–50.

11. Brussels Declaration, *supra* note 7, art. 34.

12. Article 13 of the 1899 Convention No. II states: "Individuals who follow an army without directly belonging to it, such as newspaper correspondents and reporters, sutlers, contractors, who fall into the enemy's hands, and whom the latter think fit to detain, have a right to be treated as prisoners of war, provided they can produce a certificate from the military authorities of the army they were accompanying." Convention No. II with Respect to the Laws and Customs of War on Land, July 29, 1899, 32 Stat. 1803, T.S. No. 403.

Individuals who follow an army without directly belonging to it, such as newspaper correspondents and reporters, sutlers and contractors, who fall into the enemy's hands and whom the latter thinks expedient to detain, are entitled to be treated as prisoners of war, provided they are in possession of a certificate from the military authorities of the army which they were accompanying.[13]

These LOAC codifications provided the means for an adversary to verify the official role of civilians via an identification certificate, which would set them apart from those who might be scavenging or otherwise hoping to independently profit in dealings with the armed forces during military operations.

The same protections were echoed in Article 81 of the 1929 Geneva Convention on Prisoners of War, which states:

> Persons who follow the armed forces without directly belonging thereto, such as correspondents, newspaper reporters, sutlers, or contractors, who fall into the hands of the enemy, and whom the latter think fit to detain, shall be entitled to be treated as prisoners of war, provided they are in possession of an authorization from the military authorities of the armed forces which they were following.[14]

Shortly after these provisions were enacted, they were put to test in the Second World War. While the experience of the Second World War reinforced the importance of providing protective measures for civilians who accompany the armed forces, it also highlighted the need for some revisions.[15]

In the postwar 1949 Convention (III) Relative to the Treatment of Prisoners of War (Third Geneva Convention), civilians who accompany the armed forces are dealt with in Article 4. This revised provision states:

> A. Prisoners of war, in the sense of the present Convention, are persons belonging to one of the following categories, who have fallen into the power of the enemy:
>
> ...

---

13. Convention No. IV Respecting the Laws and Customs of War on Land, Oct. 18, 1907, 36 Stat. 2227, T.S. No. 539.

14. Convention Relative to the Treatment of Prisoners of War, July 27, 1929, 47 Stat. 2021, 118 L.N.T.S. 343.

15. *See* 1960 GC III COMMENTARY, where it states: "This provision is an up-to-date version of Article 81 of the 1929 Convention, which in turn was based on Article 13 of the Hague Regulations. The Conference of Government Experts considered that the text of Article 81 of the 1929 Convention had become obsolete (in particular the word 'sutlers' is no longer appropriate) and should include a reference to certain other classes of persons who were more or less part of the armed forces and whose position when captured had given rise to difficulties during the Second World War." 1960 GC III COMMENTARY, *supra* note 5, at 64.

(4) Persons who accompany the armed forces without actually being members thereof, such as civilian members of military aircraft crews, war correspondents, supply contractors, members of labour units or of services responsible for the welfare of the armed forces, provided that they have received authorization from the armed forces which they accompany, who shall provide them for that purpose with an identity card similar to the annexed model.[16]

The "persons" in this article are presumed to be civilians, not combatants.[17] It is also important to note that this list of civilians who qualify for protection is meant to be illustrative, rather than conclusive.[18] This means that the listed categories could expand and evolve. However, the qualifying criteria would remain the same, including the key criterion, which states that in order for civilians to be eligible for the listed protections, they must have "received authorization from the armed forces which they accompany."[19]

The historical development of persons who "accompany the armed forces" and their treatment under prisoner of war status is uncontroverted. Those civilians who are "authorized" by the representative government to accompany the armed forces receive prisoner of war status upon capture. States have taken, and continue to take, a decidedly geographic approach toward those civilians they authorize as accompanying their forces. But this approach may need to change, given the emerging technologies of warfare. It is to this issue that this chapter now turns.

16. Convention (III) Relative to the Treatment of Prisoners of War, Aug. 12, 1949, 6 U.S.T. 3316, 75 U.N.T.S. 135 [hereinafter Third Geneva Convention].

17. For examples of persons who would fit into this provision, *see* Leslie C. Green, The Contemporary Law of Armed Conflict 133 nn.37–40 (3d ed., 2008).

18. *See* the 1960 GC III Commentary, where it states: "The list given is only by way of indication, however, and the text could therefore cover other categories of persons or services who might be called upon, in similar conditions, to follow the armed forces during any future conflict." 1960 GC III Commentary, *supra* 5, at 64. *See also* International Committee of the Red Cross, Commentary on the Third Geneva Convention: Convention (III) Relative to the Treatment of Prisoners of War ¶ 1048 (2020), https://ihl-databases.icrc.org/applic/ihl/ihl.nsf/Comment.xsp?action=openDocument&documentId=1796813618ABDA06C12585850057AB95 [hereinafter 2020 GC III Commentary]; Emanuela-Chiara Gillard, *Business Goes to War: Private Military/Security Companies and International Humanitarian Law*, 88 International Review of the Red Cross 525, 537 (2006) (where the author states: "What is not so clear is precisely who comes within this exception. The above list of possible services provided is indicative, not exhaustive. Neither the *travaux préparatoires* for this provision nor the *Commentary* shed light on the limits of the activities that may be carried out by this category of persons.").

19. *See* Major Brian H. Brady, *Notice Provisions for United States Citizen Contractor Employees Serving with the Armed Forces of the United States in the Field: Time to Reflect Their Assimilated Status in Government Contracts?* 147 Military Law Review 1 (1995) (arguing that the term "assimilation" is a more appropriate description of what is necessary to attain full legal status as a civilian contractor).

III. GEOGRAPHY OR FUNCTION

The historical development and current application of the law seem to argue that the protections provided to civilians accompanying the armed forces are based on both geographic proximity and function. For example, the Lieber Code indicates that civilians who receive these protections would be in the proximity of armed forces *and* serving particular functions.[20] This idea is echoed by the Brussels Declaration, stating that protection is warranted for civilians serving "in the vicinity" of the armies, and also serving those armies in particular ways.[21] Nevertheless, while both elements would be the basis for a State's authorization, proximity seems to have become the threshold consideration.

This approach is confirmed by both governments and scholars. For example, in Article 4A(4) (quoted above) of the ICRC's original Commentary to the 1949 Geneva Convention on Prisoners of War, it is noted:

> These civilians are the only two categories of persons who are entitled to prisoner-of-war status but not entitled to combatant status, immunity or privileges. Their inclusion recognizes that their proximity to the armed forces increases the risk of their being interned with combatants, and makes explicit the protective framework that applies to them.[22]

The preeminence of proximity is also reflected in the writings of military scholars, such as Major Michael Guillory, whose influential article on this topic states:

> Civilians accompanying the armed forces include civilian government employees, civilian members of military aircraft crews, supply contractor personnel, contractor technical representatives, war correspondents, and members of labor units or civilian services responsible for the welfare of armed forces. They are different from other civilians because their proximity to the fighting places them at greater risk of injury, death, and capture. They are also different in that they must receive authorization from the armed forces that they accompany, and have been provided with an identity card.[23]

Here, Guillory relies on proximity as the qualifying condition upon which a State grants its authorization. This approach also aligns with the development of the LOAC. Because nearness to the battlefield increases the risks associated

---

20. Lieber Code, *supra* note 2, arts. 49–50.

21. Brussels Declaration, *supra* note 7, art. 34.

22. 2020 GC III Commentary, *supra* note 18, ¶ 1045.

23. Major Michael E. Guillory, *Civilianizing the Force: Is the United States Crossing the Rubicon?*, 51 Air Force Law Review 111, 115 (2001).

with accompanying the armed forces,[24] it is natural that "conditions [that] expose employees to loss of life or limb as a result of hostile enemy activity"[25] would result in proximity as the primary qualification.

Guillory's mention of the identification card highlights its importance but should not be interpreted as a requirement for receiving prisoner of war status. Beginning with the Brussels Declaration, some form of State-provided identification became the signal that the specific civilian had received authorization to accompany the forces from his or her sponsoring State. This language was carried over in subsequent treaties.[26] However, the importance of the card was minimized in the 1949 Conventions, removing the card as proof of authorization by the sponsoring State.[27] Instead the Convention placed an obligation upon the sponsoring State to "provide [the civilian] for that purpose with an identity card similar to the annexed model," making it conclusive for granting status if such a card was produced but not precluding status if no card was presented.

The Commentary to Article 4 confirms that possession of the card is not determinative of a civilian's status. Rather, the key point remains State authorization. Stated further:

> After some discussion, the Stockholm draft which, in the case of persons accompanying the armed forces, made possession of an identity card an absolute condition of the right to be treated as a prisoner of war, was modified and the resulting text included in the Convention is more flexible.
>
> The application of this provision is therefore dependent on authorization to accompany the armed forces, and the identity card merely serves as proof. The identity card corresponds virtually to a soldier's uniform or a partisan's arm-band; in case of doubt, the question must be settled pursuant to Article 5, paragraph 2, hereafter.[28]

This approach remains predominant today. For example, modern U.S. practice states:

---

24. *See generally* Major Lisa L. Turner & Major Lynn G. Norton, *Civilians at the Tip of the Spear*, 51 AIR FORCE LAW REVIEW 1 (2001)(where the authors discuss the use of civilians and contractors to support the armed forces and the risks associated with such service).

25. Brady, *supra* note 19, at 1, 5.

26. Regulations Concerning the Laws and Customs of War on Land, annex to Convention No IV Respecting the Laws and Customs of War on Land art. 1, Oct. 18, 1907, 36 Stat. 2277, T.S. No. 539. *See also* Convention Relative to the Treatment of Prisoners of War, July 27, 1929, 47 Stat. 2021, 118 L.N.T.S. 343.

27. HOWARD S. LEVIE, PRISONERS OF WAR IN INTERNATIONAL ARMED CONFLICT 62 (1977) (Vol. 59, U.S. Naval War College International Law Studies).

28. 1960 GC III, *supra* note 5, at 65.

> The [contractors authorized to accompany the force] will be issued an official Geneva Conventions identification card (either a DOD Uniformed Services Identification and Privilege Card, common access card (CAC) with Geneva Conventions identifier) . . . The CACs issued to [contractors authorized to accompany the force] are valid only while going through a processing center and while serving in the [area of operations]. The expiration date for CACs issued to CAAF will be the end of the period of employment within the [area of operations].[29]

Here, the direction to remove the "official Geneva Convention identification card" when the civilian leaves the proximity of the armed forces confirms that the current approach for providing "authorization" is primarily based on deference to the geographic proximity of the civilian to the battle space. Indeed, the recently legislated ability of a military commander to assert criminal jurisdiction through the Uniform Code of Military Justice on contractors deployed with the military assumes physical proximity.[30] This change was based at least to some degree on the groundbreaking case *Reid v. Covert*, where the United States Supreme Court argued that "[f]rom a time prior to the adoption of the Constitution the extraordinary circumstances present in an area of actual fighting have been considered sufficient to permit punishment of some civilians in that area by military courts under military rules."[31]

However, proximity should not be understood as a guarantee of authorization. In addition, the proximate civilian must also serve a facilitating function. The United States, for example, acknowledges that some civilians will not be authorized to accompany the armed forces, even if they are working in proximity to deployed armed forces. U.S. Department of Defense Joint Publication 4-10, Operational Contract Support, states:

> [Civilians authorized to accompany the force] generally includes all US civilian and [third-country national] employees not normally residing within the operational area whose area of performance is in the direct vicinity of US forces and who are routinely collocated with US forces (especially in uncertain or hostile environments) . . . [Civilians authorized to accompany the force] status only applies to selected contractor personnel in foreign operations and is not applicable in operations within the US. During international armed conflicts, [civilians authorized to accompany the force] are protected

---

29. Reg. 715-9, Army Command Policy, *supra* note 9, para. 3-2e, f(2).

30. Pub. L. No. 111-84, § 1803(a)(1), 123 Stat. 2612 (2009).

31. Reid v. Covert, 354 U.S. 1, 33 (1957). *See also* Geoffrey S. Corn & Victor M. Hansen, *Even If It Ain't Broke, Why Not Fix It? Three Proposed Improvements to the Uniform Code of Military Justice* 6 Journal of National Security Law & Policy 447, 473–82 (2013), where the authors discuss the assertion of jurisdiction over civilians "accompanying the armed forces" under the 2006 Uniform Code of Military Justice amendment.

as prisoners of war [in accordance with] the Geneva Convention Relative to the Treatment of Prisoners of War.[32]

Here, the preeminence of proximity to active hostilities plays a key role in determining whether a civilian fits into the privileged category. In this case, civilians operating from within the United States are excluded from qualifying as "accompanying" civilians because of their lack of proximity to the conflict. However, the following paragraph describes instances when proximity is insufficient to guarantee authorized status, despite proximity. As opposed to civilians who *are* authorized to accompany the armed forces and receive the applicable status,

> [local national] and some non-[local national] employees working on a DOD contract in the operational area . . . are not afforded [civilians authorized to accompany the force] status [in accordance with] the nature of the contract. These include DOD contractor prime and associated subcontractor employees whose area of performance is not in the direct vicinity of US forces. Non-[qualified civilians authorized to accompany the force] are usually non-mission-essential personnel (e.g., day laborers, delivery personnel, and cleaning service personnel) who neither reside with US forces nor receive AGS such as billeting and subsistence. During international armed conflict, non-[qualified civilians authorized to accompany the force] contractor employees are not entitled to protection under the *Geneva Convention Relative to the Treatment of Prisoners of War* but may still be afforded protected status under the *Geneva Convention Relative to the Protection of Civilian Persons in Time of War*.[33]

In other words, some functions, such as day laborers and delivery personnel, simply do not warrant the status of civilians accompanying the force. Civilians performing these functions are not "authorized," despite their proximity, because their function is not of the kind that would cause them to be granted prisoner of war status. Thus, even though these civilians would be in harm's way, they are nevertheless ineligible for "accompanying" status. So, while proximity is certainly a critical element, it seems to be applied on a case-by-case basis, depending on the facilitating function the contractor serves.

This coupling of proximity and function may be historically important, but it is losing its utility in modern armed conflict. As will be discussed below, many civilians perform tasks that are analogous to those traditionally performed by civilians "accompanying the armed forces," but do so from immense distances, sometimes thousands of miles from the "area of actual fighting." The technological

---

32. Joint Chiefs of Staff, Joint Publication 4-10, Operational Contract Support I-10 (Mar. 4, 2019).

33. *Id.* at I-10 to I-11.

developments of modern armed conflicts call for a reassessment of the "proximity" requirement as the primary consideration for granting civilians prisoner of war status upon capture. Instead, "accompanying" status should be evaluated on a case-by-case basis depending on the function, or role, of the civilian.

IV. MODERN ARMED CONFLICT AND "ACCOMPANYING"

Throughout history, technological innovations have tended to lengthen the battlefield, increasing the distance between fighting parties. The employment of the longbow was the key to the English victory at Agincourt in 1415.[34] The use of gunpowder and eventual rifling of barrels increased the distance at which forces could engage each other and the destructive force they could bring to the fight.[35] The use of hot air balloons[36] and eventually of flight for reconnaissance and then attack further extended the range of offensive strikes in combat.[37] The development of rocketry not only added great distance and standoff to attacks,[38] but eventually opened space to exploration and militarization.[39] Most recently, the development of the internet and the world's entrance into the digital age has facilitated cyber operations that have already impacted the conduct of modern armed conflict.[40]

As the law developed, it made no distinction for members of the State armed forces who were not engaged on the field of battle. In other words, whether on the battlefield or not, members of the armed forces were subject to engagement and also eligible for the LOAC-mandated prisoner of war status if captured.[41] Similarly, the 1949 Convention Relative to the Protection of Civilian Persons in

---

34. ANNE CURRY, THE BATTLE OF AGINCOURT (2015).

35. Roger Crowley, *The Guns of Constantinople: History's First Great Artillery Barrage, in 1453, Shattered the Byzantine Capital and Changed Warfare Forever*, 24 MILITARY HISTORY 44 (2007).

36. *Balloon Evolution*, SCIENTIFIC AMERICAN (Mar. 29, 1999), https://www.scientificamerican.com/article/balloon-evolution/.

37. *Zeppelin Raids: How Did First World War Zeppelin Raids Affect British Civilians?*, THE NATIONAL ARCHIVES, https://www.nationalarchives.gov.uk/education/resources/zeppelin-raids/ (last visited Oct. 30, 2021). See also Ari Unikoski, *The War in the Air—Bombers: Germany, Zeppelins* (Aug. 22, 2009), FIRSTWORLDWAR.COM, https://www.firstworldwar.com/airwar/bombers_zeppelins.htm.

38. Benjamin Brimelow, *How the Nazis Developed a "Wonder Weapon" That the Allies Couldn't Stop and Changed the Face of Future Wars*, BUSINESS INSIDER (Sept. 8, 2020), https://www.businessinsider.com/nazi-v2-rocket-couldnt-stop-allies-but-influence-future-missiles-2020-8.

39. Adam G. Quinn, *The New Age of Space Law: The Outer Space Treaty and the Weaponization of Space*, 17 MINNESOTA JOURNAL OF INTERNATIONAL LAW 475 (2008).

40. Stephen W. Korns & Joshua E. Kastenberg, *Georgia's Cyber Left Hook*, U.S. ARMY (Apr. 7, 2009), https://www.army.mil/article/19351/georgias_cyber_left_hook.

41. *See* Hamdi v. Rumsfeld, 542 U.S. 507 (2004).

Time of War (Fourth Geneva Convention) establishes a regime where protected persons receive specific status and treatment, even if they fall into the hands of an adversary while located away from the battlefield.[42]

Similar status and treatment protections have not been codified with respect to civilians who accompany the force. The narrow language of the LOAC, combined with the apparent practice of States, seems to still allocate prisoner of war protections for supporting civilians only when they are "in the vicinity" of armed forces on the battlefield. The innovations of modern-day combat now allow for a dramatically increased distance in which a fighter can engage an enemy. By extension, civilians who accompany the armed forces have similarly been distanced from the battlefield.

Several examples will aptly illustrate this point. First, the earliest articulations of protections for civilians included those who were "contractors." While contractors at that time performed mostly logistics functions, such as providing food and supplies,[43] the continuing complexity of modern weapons and communications systems eventually required contractors to not only provide but also maintain such systems. Oftentimes, these contractors have been located "in the vicinity" of the armed conflict, but there are also times where they have not been. For example, aircraft that are based sometimes thousands of miles from the battlefield require contractors to maintain their flight systems and their ordnance.[44] These contractors perform the very same functions as other contractors who operate "in the vicinity" of armed forces in conflict. The only difference is that they are not similarly geographically located.

Contractors who maintain nuclear weapons and their delivery systems are in a comparable position. Nuclear weapons and those who trigger them are targetable during armed conflict, despite their distance from the battlefield. If captured, these members of the military would be given combatant status. However, because the civilian contractors who maintain these weapon systems are not in the vicinity of the conflict, it is unclear whether they would be given prisoner of war status if subsequently captured. Despite being able to produce a government-issued identification card, they would likely be treated as civilians under the Fourth Geneva Convention.

This incongruity is most obvious in the cyber realm.[45] Many cyber systems, including those used for both offensive and defensive military actions, are maintained by civilian contractors. In fact, the United States National Security Agency, a Department of Defense organization, is almost completely manned by

---

42. Convention (IV) Relative to the Protection of Civilian Persons in Time of War, Aug. 12, 1949, 6 U.S.T. 3516, 75 U.N.T.S. 287 [hereinafter Fourth Geneva Convention].

43. *See* Brady, *supra* note19.

44. Turner & Norton, *supra* note 24, at 9.

45. J. Ricou Heaton, *Civilians at War: Reexamining the Status of Civilians Accompanying the Armed Forces*, 57 AIR FORCE LAW REVIEW 155, 159–60 (2005).

civilians.[46] As cyber tools continue to play an increased role in military operations, civilian contractors who build and maintain those systems will continue to play a critical role as well. While some of these contractors will be on the battlefield, many others will not, but both will perform exactly the same functions.[47] And, if both groups are performing equally important functions, then they should both be granted the same prisoner of war status if captured.

As a final example, the newly organized United States Space Force[48] will also be heavily dependent on civilian contractors. Civilian organizations are playing an increasing role in both commercial and government space operations.[49] While space operations will have dramatic impacts on the battlefield, both combatants and the civilians who "accompany" them will remain at great distances from the actual geographic fight. Nevertheless, those combatants will be afforded prisoner of war status upon capture, and the contractors in direct support of those military space operations should receive the same benefit.

These examples clearly illustrate how emerging technologies have increased the geographic distance between belligerent forces and the civilians who accompany them. Combatants continue to maintain their status as members of the armed forces and no doubt exists as to their prisoner of war status upon capture. However, it is less clear that States will also continue to treat civilians who perform the traditional services of those who accompany the force, but do so at great geographic distances from the actual conflict, as prisoners of war. The most obvious way to solve this question is by placing greater emphasis on the functional aspect of "accompanying the force," as opposed to the geographic aspect. Indeed, it is time for proximity to be discontinued as the threshold criteria for geographically distanced civilians accompanying the force. Instead, States should rely mostly on function as the qualifying criteria for such civilians who perform identical services as their geographically proximate counterparts who receive the "accompanying" status.

---

46. Ellen Nakashima & Aaron Gregg, *NSA's Top Talent Is Leaving Because of Low Pay, Slumping Morale and Unpopular Reorganization*, WASHINGTON POST (Jan. 2, 2018), https://www.washingtonpost.com/world/national-security/the-nsas-top-talent-is-leaving-because-of-low-pay-and-battered-morale/2018/01/02/ff19f0c6-ec04-11e7-9f92-10a2203f6c8d_story.html (noting that "the NSA employs a civilian workforce of about 21,000").

47. *See* Christopher E. Bailey, *Cyber Civilians as Combatants*, 8 CREIGHTON INTERNATIONAL AND COMPARATIVE LAW JOURNAL 4, 11–12 (2016)(where the author argues that civilian cyber practitioners who work at Department of Defense agencies such as the National Security Agency would qualify as civilians accompanying the force).

48. *About the United States Space Force*, UNITED STATES SPACE FORCE, *available at* https://www.spaceforce.mil/About-Us/About-Space-Force/ (last visited May 11, 2021).

49. Kate Duffy, *Elon Musk's SpaceX Wins 2 Pentagon Contracts for Nearly $160 Million to Launch Missions with Its Falcon 9 Rockets*, BUSINESS INSIDER (Mar. 11, 2021), https://www.businessinsider.com/elon-musk-spacex-won-two-pentagon-contracts-launch-military-rockets-2021-3.

V. EMBRACING A "FUNCTION" APPROACH

The above examples illustrate that, as emerging technologies play an increased role in modern warfare, "accompanying the force" has less and less to do with proximity to the armed forces. Rather, determinations as to whether a particular civilian warrants the protections afforded by Article 4 of the Third Geneva Convention should be based on the function the civilian performs, particularly with regard to those civilians who are geographically separated from the actual conflict. This "function" approach to status determinations would allow States to "authorize" geographically separated civilians as accompanying the forces in order for them to claim the appropriate LOAC protections.

Before advocating in more detail for increased attention on the functions performed by geographically separated civilians, it is important to clarify why extending this protection is necessary. If these civilians are geographically separated from the fight, what are the chances that they will ever be captured? And if they will never be captured, is this an argument with little meaning?

Though this lack of geographic proximity will decrease the likelihood of capture, it will not extinguish it. There are various ways that a geographically separated civilian might come under the power of an enemy. For example, a civilian who supports forces in conflict from a distance but later is captured as part of a subsequent occupation or annexation of territory would be treated as a civilian unless otherwise "authorized" to come under the protections of Article 4 of the Third Geneva Convention. Similarly, a civilian who might be "accompanying the force" in one geographic location, and then travels to another geographic location where he or she is captured, would also benefit from being able to claim prisoner of war status.

These determinations would almost certainly have a great impact on the treatment given at and after the point of capture. Being classified as a prisoner of war would generate a different set of rights for the captured individual. These rights have broader protections than the ones available to civilians. Perhaps the most noteworthy protection is that a civilian prisoner of war would not be triable or punishable for his or her assistance to the war effort,[50] whereas this might not be the case if treated as a civilian under the Fourth Geneva Convention.[51]

Although the potential for a geographically distanced (but functionally important) civilian to come under the power of an enemy is somewhat limited, States should begin to consider under what conditions they might "authorize" such civilians as "persons who accompany the armed forces" for the purposes of Article 4 of the Third Geneva Convention. Central to this consideration should be the function performed by the civilian.

As demonstrated above, not all civilians who are proximate to the armed conflict will be authorized as "persons who accompany the armed forces." There are

---

50. Third Geneva Convention, *supra* note 16, arts. 82–108.

51. Fourth Geneva Convention, *supra* note 42, arts. 64–78, 99–104.

roles of certain civilians whose support, though proximate to the armed forces, does not warrant prisoner of war status upon capture. Their function, such as day laborers, is not the type of support that States choose to recognize as deserving that special treatment. In contrast, the recognition of the importance of certain functions provides the key to the extension of protections to geographically distanced civilians.

States should adopt an approach where civilians outside the area of operations who serve the same or similar functions as those located within the area of operations receive similar authorization and subsequent prisoner of war status upon capture. Technology that allows an aircraft to deliver lethal force while stationed thousands of miles from the actual fight should not prevent a civilian who maintains that aircraft and ordnance from receiving similar treatment upon capture as a civilian who does the exact same job in the area of operations. Similarly, there is no logical reason that a cyber technician who performs vital cyber tasks outside the geographic conflict area, similar to those performed by technicians located in the area of conflict, should not receive the same prisoner of war status upon capture. Because advancing technologies now allow civilians to have a vital function in support of the armed forces who are not proximate to the armed conflict, protections should logically extend to these geographically distanced civilians as well.

Analyzing each civilian's function on a case-by-case basis, including those performed at great distances from the battlefield, will more accurately reflect the protections that are warranted. Importantly, States can simply extend their "authorization" to geographically separated civilians if they determine that their function is analogous to those performed by civilians who are proximate. States can signal this authorization by issuing Geneva identification cards to these civilians. While not determinative with respect to the denial of status,[52] issuing an identification card would secure this protection for persons who are later captured. In support of these changes, States should modify their manuals to reflect this extended coverage, noting that lack of proximity is not a disqualifier in cases where civilians serve the same or very similar functions to those close to combat. Official statements would also cement this new approach.

This transition from heavy reliance on proximity to increased emphasis on function with geographically distanced civilians will allow States to more accurately reflect the realities of modern warfare and will extend protections in accordance with those realities. Because the LOAC allows for the extension of such authorization, States should accordingly provide protections for these geographically distanced essential civilian workers.

---

52. LEVIE, *supra* note 27, at 62.

VI. CONCLUSION

The history of warfare has recognized the reality of a warring army's need for civilian support. In order to facilitate that support, the LOAC extends the protections of prisoner of war status to those civilians who have been designated by their sponsoring State as "authorized" to "accompany the armed forces."

The emergence of new technologies that create the need for civilians to support military operations from distant locations ought not to prevent such civilians from receiving the same protections upon capture as their colleagues who perform the same or similar functions on the battlefield. States can provide coverage for non-geographically proximate civilians by simply changing their doctrine and "authorizing" these civilians as meeting the requirements of Article 4 of the Third Geneva Convention. Making this change will more clearly reflect the realities of modern warfare and extend protections to individuals who deserve no less.

5

Levée en Masse in Twenty-First-Century Armed Conflict

WINSTON S. WILLIAMS* AND ROBERT LAWLESS**

I. INTRODUCTION

It is the year 2035. After issuing a series of threats and massing significant combat power in the border region, State A invades State B. During the invasion, State A's conventional ground troops and formations of semiautonomous combat drones approach Town X in State B. With State B's armed forces engaged elsewhere, the local populace in Town X engages in armed resistance against State A's invading forces. The local resistance has some success initially against State A's conventional forces, but they are overpowered by the combat drones. Realizing the asymmetry in the land battle, some technologically savvy residents of Town X begin hacking the combat drones remotely by infiltrating State A's tactical networks. These efforts prove remarkably effective—the hackers disrupt the drones and enable the local ground fighters to prolong the battle in Town X. Ultimately, State A's combat power overcomes the local fighters and State A gains control of Town X. In securing Town X, State A's forces locate and detain some of the hackers. Assuming this scenario constitutes an international armed conflict between States A and B,

---

*. Colonel Winston Williams is an Associate Professor and the Department Head of the Department of Law at the United States Military Academy, West Point. The views expressed here are those of the authors and do not necessarily represent the views of the United States Military Academy, the United States Army, or the United States government.Professor of Law, Brigham Young University Law School. The author would like to thank Carolyn Sharp for her superb research and other assistance on this chapter.

**. Robert Lawless is an Assistant Professor in the Department of Law and the Research Director of the Lieber Institute for Law and Warfare at the United States Military Academy, West Point. The views expressed here are those of the authors and do not necessarily represent the views of the United States Military Academy, the United States Army, or the United States government.

Winston S. Williams and Robert Lawless, *Levée en Masse in Twenty-First-Century Armed Conflict* In: *Prisoners of War in Contemporary Conflict*. Edited by: Michael N. Schmitt and Christopher J. Koschnitzky, Oxford University Press.
© Oxford University Press 2023. DOI: 10.1093/oso/9780197663288.003.0005

what is the legal status of the detained hackers? Do they qualify as members of a *levée en masse*?

Given the likely proliferation of these systems and capabilities, the changing character of warfare risks significantly outpacing the law that regulates it. What would this mean for *levée en masse* and the accompanying requirement to afford prisoner of war (POW) status to members of such a group? Specifically, how could the challenges related to civilians leveraging cyber capabilities to thwart an invasion potentially impact their status upon capture? While to some, *levée en masse* may appear to be an obsolete concept in modern warfare, the International Committee of the Red Cross (ICRC) asserted, in its 2020 Commentary to the Third Geneva Convention, that it should not be discarded. The Commentary states that "practice has suggested that even in circumstances where the invading force employs advanced military technology, the approach of an invading army could still prompt civilians to take up arms against it."[1] This chapter examines these questions and how they may be answered in future armed conflict situations. While this topic has been addressed to some extent,[2] this chapter approaches the subject "from the ground up" with a tactical perspective. Thus, the chapter's aim is to examine how the concept of *levée en masse* under the current law of armed conflict (LOAC) may apply to future war characterized by the employment of cyber-related capabilities by the military and, potentially, civilians.

In some respects, the scenario above is a classic fact pattern for a *levée en masse*—an invading enemy force approaching unoccupied territory encountering an armed resistance consisting of local civilian fighters.[3] As we will explain, under the LOAC, the Town X residents engaged in conventional land battle against State A's forces who carry arms openly and comply with the LOAC likely are entitled to POW status upon capture.[4] However, it is less clear whether and how the civilian hackers meet the criteria of a *levée en masse*. After examining this question, we ultimately conclude that civilians such as those in the scenario above do not meet the legal criteria required for a *levée en masse*.

---

1. INTERNATIONAL COMMITTEE OF THE RED CROSS, COMMENTARY ON THE THIRD GENEVA CONVENTION: CONVENTION (III) RELATIVE TO THE TREATMENT OF PRISONERS OF WAR ¶ 1063 (2020), https://ihl-databases.icrc.org/applic/ihl/ihl.nsf/Comment.xsp?action=openDocument&documentId=1796813618ABDA06C12585850057AB95 [hereinafter 2020 GC III COMMENTARY].

2. *See, e.g.*, David Wallace & Shane R. Reeves, *The Law of Armed Conflict's "Wicked" Problem: Levée en Masse in Cyber Warfare*, 89 INTERNATIONAL LAW STUDIES 646 (2013); Christopher Waters, *New Hacktivists and the Old Concept of Levée en Masse*, 37 DALHOUSIE LAW JOURNAL 771 (2014).

3. COMMENTARY TO GENEVA CONVENTION III RELATIVE TO THE TREATMENT OF PRISONERS OF WAR 67–68 (Jean Pictet ed., 1960) [hereinafter 1960 GC III COMMENTARY].

4. *See* Convention (III) Relative to the Treatment of Prisoners of War art. 4, Aug. 12, 1949, 6 U.S.T. 3316, 75 U.N.T.S. 135 [hereinafter Third Geneva Convention]. For this discussion, see *infra* note 51 and accompanying text.

This introduction will be followed by an examination of the role that autonomous systems, robots, and cyber capabilities are expected to play in future armed conflict. In Part III, we assess the LOAC status of *levée en masse*, including its history and current state. In Part IV, we analyze the hypothetical scenario set forth above to determine whether and how *levée en masse* may apply in such a conflict. We conclude the chapter in Part V.

II. AUTONOMOUS ROBOTS AND CYBER OPERATIONS IN FUTURE ARMED CONFLICT

The armed conflict scenario set forth above, although set in the future, seems more like an informed prediction than science fiction. Indeed, it is difficult to imagine future warfare without the employment of autonomous weapons, robots, and the kind of cyber capabilities deployed in the scenario. There has been a significant amount of research and money expended to develop these emerging technologies for use in future wars. In fact, China is pursuing the development of "new types of combat forces, including AI and unmanned—in other words autonomous or near-autonomous—combat systems."[5] The United States, with its renewed focus on peer and near-peer competitors, views autonomous weapons and cyber capabilities as a critical component of keeping pace with these competitors.[6] These changes have expanded beyond strategic planning down to the tactical level. For example, the U.S. Army lists its Cyber Branch as a "combat arms branch" akin to Infantry, Armor, and Field Artillery.[7] This decision by the U.S. Army foreshadows the contributions that cyber operators will make to the front lines of tomorrow's wars.

With respect to autonomous robots of war, the future is coming perhaps more quickly than we may imagine. Early versions of the kind of autonomous robot system involved in the example scenario above currently exist. For example, the Tracked Hybrid Modular Infantry System (THeMIS), created by an Estonian company, "consists of a mobile body mounted on small tank treads, topped with a remote-weapon turret that can be equipped with small or large-caliber machine guns."[8] For their part, States are working on "autonomous platforms that

---

5. Melissa Chan, *China and the U.S. Are Fighting a Major Battle over Killer Robots and the Future of AI*, Time (Sept. 13, 2019), https://time.com/5673240/china-killer-robots-weapons.

6. *See* U.S. Department of Defense, Summary: Department of Defense Cyber Strategy (2018).

7. Brandon O'Connor, *West Point Class of 2020 Receives Branches Through New Market Model Branching System*, DVIDS (Nov. 14, 2019), https://www.dvidshub.net/news/351701/west-point-class-2020-receives-branches-through-new-market-model-branching-system.

8. Kelsey D. Atherton, *Are Killer Robots the Future of War? Parsing the Facts on Autonomous Weapons*, New York Times Magazine (Nov. 15, 2018), https://www.nytimes.com/2018/11/15/magazine/autonomous-robots-weapons.html.

pair weapons with sensors and targeting computers,"[9] just the sort of platform that might be implemented in the THeMIS. As another example, a U.S. Marine Corps project called Sea Mob involves the development of water vessels that operate autonomously and without humans on board to navigate and potentially fire .50-caliber machine guns.[10] In fact, in May and June 2021, it was widely reported that "the age of autonomous killer robots may already be here."[11] The incident occurred in Libya in March 2020. According to a UN report, during hostilities in the Libyan Civil War, Turkey deployed the STM *Kargu-2*, a "lethal autonomous weapons system," to "hunt down" and "remotely engage" enemy logistics convoys and retreating fighters.[12] The UN Panel of Experts on Libya, which wrote the report, referred to the STM *Kargu-2* as a "fire, forget and find" system capable of attacking targets "without requiring data connectivity between the operator and the munition."[13] The report's assertions in this regard were controversial and debated.[14] However, the point remains that legal, ethical, and operational issues surrounding the deployment of autonomous robots during armed conflict are increasingly relevant.

The deployment of autonomous robots in future armed conflict will inevitably be accompanied by efforts to hack, disrupt, and manipulate such systems. In theory, autonomous robots will be capable of operating free from any networked link to human operators. But such systems will still require networked connectivity. For example, swarms of robots will communicate among themselves to engage in complex and coordinated operations during hostilities.[15] Such networked connectivity opens the door to hacking and infiltration efforts through the cyber domain. This is particularly relevant in situations similar to that presented in the

---

9. *Id.*

10. Zachary Fryer-Biggs, *Coming Soon to a Battlefield: Robots That Can Kill*, THE ATLANTIC (Sept. 3, 2019), https://www.theatlantic.com/technology/archive/2019/09/killer-robots-and-new-era-machine-driven-warfare/597130.

11. Alyse Stanley, *The Age of Autonomous Killer Robots May Already Be Here*, GIZMODO (May 30, 2021), https://gizmodo.com/flying-killer-robot-hunted-down-a-human-target-without-1847001471.

12. Rep. of the Panel of Experts on Libya, transmitted by Letter Dated 8 March 2021 from the Panel of Experts on Libya Established Pursuant to Resolution 1973 (2011) Addressed to the President of the Security Council, ¶ 63, U.N. Doc. S/2021/229 (Mar. 8, 2021).

13. *Id.*

14. James Vincent, *Have Autonomous Robots Started Killing in War?*, THE VERGE (June 3, 2021), https://www.theverge.com/2021/6/3/22462840/killer-robot-autonomous-drone-attack-libya-un-report-context.

15. Jules Hurst, *Robotic Swarms in Offensive Maneuver*, NATIONAL DEFENSE UNIVERSITY PRESS (Oct. 1, 2017), https://ndupress.ndu.edu/Publications/Article/1326017/robotic-swarms-in-offensive-maneuver; Courtney Linder, *The Government Wants to Use Your Brainwaves to Train Swarms of Military Robots*, POPULAR MECHANICS (Feb. 10, 2020), https://www.popularmechanics.com/technology/robots/a30855506/darpa-swarm-robots-video-game).

example scenario above: armed resistance movements conducted by irregular forces and civilians against a disproportionately powerful invading enemy force. In such situations, civilians such as the resistance hackers in the example are likely to exploit opportunities in the cyber domain to counter their disadvantageous asymmetry.[16]

III. *LEVÉE EN MASSE*: HISTORY AND OVERVIEW

POW status during an international armed conflict is most commonly applicable to persons who have fallen into the power of the enemy and who are (1) members of the armed forces of a belligerent party[17] or (2) members of militias and volunteer corps that belong to a belligerent party and fulfill the following four criteria:

(a) that of being commanded by a person responsible for his subordinates;
(b) that of having a fixed distinctive sign recognizable at a distance;
(c) that of carrying arms openly; and
(d) that of conducting their operations in accordance with the laws and customs of war.[18]

Most persons who fall into the power of a belligerent party and do not satisfy the criteria under (1) or (2) above are not entitled to POW status.[19] But there is an exception for members of a *levée en masse*.[20]

Levée en masse refers to a specific kind of armed resistance during armed conflict—the civilian population's spontaneous and collective uprising in response to and during a territorial invasion.[21] The notion of a *levée en masse* stands for a rather remarkable proposition: "that at the point of invasion—and in order to forestall occupation—the civilian population can take up arms spontaneously."[22]

---

16. Andrew Phillips, *The Asymmetric Nature of Cyber Warfare*, USNI News (Oct. 14, 2012), https://news.usni.org/2012/10/14/asymmetric-nature-cyber-warfare.

17. Third Geneva Convention, *supra* note 4, art. 4(A)(1).

18. *Id.*, art. 4(A)(2).

19. At most, these individuals are considered protected persons and must be handled by the detaining force in accordance with the provisions of the Fourth Geneva Convention. *See* Convention (IV) Relative to the Protection of Civilian Persons in Time of War, Aug. 12, 1949, 6 U.S.T. 3516, 75 U.N.T.S. 287.

20. There are other exceptions—for example, civilian aircraft crew members, war correspondents, and supply contractors who accompany the armed forces. *See* Third Geneva Convention, *supra* note 4, art. 4(A).

21. Wallace & Reeves, *supra* note 2, at 649.

22. Yoram Dinstein, The Conduct of Hostilities Under the Law of International Armed Conflict 57 (3rd ed. 2016).

Thus, *levée en masse* is in tension with the general law-of-war concept of distinction, according to which combatants—that is, members of the armed forces of the belligerent parties—must distinguish themselves from civilians and in engaging in hostilities must distinguish between enemy combatants and civilians.[23] *Levée en masse*, in contrast, represents a hybrid status of sorts by affording POW status and protections to certain civilians who engage in armed conflict hostilities.[24] As William Hall wrote in 1880:

> It is impossible to push the doctrine that combatants and noncombatants must remain separate to its logical results when the duty and sentiment of patriotism, and the injury, which even in modern warfare is always suffered in private persons, combine to provoke outbursts of popular resistance. Persons must sometimes be admitted to the privileges of soldiers who are not included in the regular army. At the same time the interests of invading belligerents lead them to reduce the range of privilege as much as possible.[25]

In this passage, Hall highlights the tension between the interest in maintaining a clear line between combatants and civilians and the interest in recognizing the legitimacy of popular resistance based on patriotism, valor, and duty.[26]

The notion of *levée en masse* dates back to the French Revolution.[27] In 1793, the French National Convention decreed: "From this moment until that in which every enemy has been driven from the territory of the Republic, every Frenchman is permanently requisitioned for service with the armies."[28] From this point onward, States began to accept the legitimacy of the *levée en masse* in armed conflict. In 1963, Francis Lieber included an article on *levée en masse* in his seminal and influential codification of the customary LOAC. Article 51 of the Lieber Code states:

> If the people of that portion of an invaded country which is not yet occupied by the enemy, or of the whole country, at the approach of a hostile army, rise,

---

23. OFFICE OF THE GENERAL COUNSEL, U.S. DEPARTMENT OF DEFENSE, LAW OF WAR MANUAL 62–63 (Dec. 2016) [hereinafter DoD LAW OF WAR MANUAL].

24. In fact, many take the view that the LOAC considers such individuals to be not civilians but rather combatants. *See, e.g., id.* at 104.

25. WILLIAMS EDWARD HALL, A TREATISE ON INTERNATIONAL LAW 549–50 (1880).

26. *Id.*

27. During the French Revolution, "the Montagnard Committee on Public Safety decreed the *levée en masse* on 23 August 1793, subjecting to conscription for war all national resources, human and material." Theda Skocpol & Meyer Kestnbaum, *Mars Unshackled: The French Revolution in World-Historical Perspective*, *in* THE FRENCH REVOLUTION AND THE BIRTH OF MODERNITY 21 (Ferenc Fehér ed., 1990).

28. Emily Crawford, *Levée en Masse—A Nineteenth Century Concept in a Twenty-First Century World* 3 (Sydney Law School, Legal Studies Research Paper No. 11/31, May 2011).

under a duly authorized levy, *en masse* to resist the invader, they are now treated as public enemies, and, if captured, are prisoners of war.[29]

Article 51 represents one of the first codifications of *levée en masse* and became the foundation for subsequent treaties to build upon.[30]

The issue of *levée en masse*, and irregular warfare more generally, was debated during the Brussels Conference of 1874.[31] The conference was convened by Tsar Alexander II of Russia and included delegates from Germany, France, Austria-Hungary, the Ottoman Empire, Russia, and Great Britain.[32] The fundamental debate concerned sovereign authorization as the basis for belligerent qualification. For example, during the Franco-Prussian War, irregular French fighters called *franc-tireurs* engaged in armed resistance against German forces after French regular forces had been largely defeated.[33] *Franc-tireurs* frustrated German forces and prolonged the defeat of France.[34] Thus, States that found themselves in the position of Germany sought to restrict who could engage in warfare to regular forces. In contrast, States such as France advocated for the legal legitimacy of irregular resistance fighters such as the *franc-tireurs*.

While the resulting Brussels Declaration was not ratified, it did provide the foundation for subsequent treaties on combatant status and *levée en masse*. The latter was codified in Article 10 of the Declaration, which states:

> The population of a territory which has not been occupied, who, on the approach of the enemy, spontaneously take up arms to resist the invading troops without having had time to organize themselves in accordance with Article 9, [which sets forth the criteria for the laws, rights, and duties of war to apply to armed conflict participants,] shall be regarded as belligerents if they respect the laws and customs of war.[35]

---

29. U.S. Department of War, Instructions for the Government of Armies of the United States in the Field, General Orders No. 100, art. 51, Apr. 24, 1863 [hereinafter Lieber Code].

30. The phrase "duly authorized *levée en masse*" was dropped in subsequent LOAC codifications.

31. Tracey L. Dowdeswell, *The Brussels Peace Conference of 1874 and the Modern Laws of Belligerent Qualification*, 54 OSGOODE HALL LAW JOURNAL 805, 825 (2017).

32. *Id.*

33. Bastian M. Scianna, *A Predisposition to Brutality?*, 30 SMALL WARS & INSURGENCIES 968, 974 (2019), *available at* https://publishup.uni-potsdam.de/opus4-ubp/frontdoor/deliver/index/docId/43421/file/ppr165.pdf.

34. *Id.* at 970 (citing Paul B. Buchanan, Prolonging the Inevitable: The Franc-Tireur and the German Army in the Franco-German War of 1870–1871 (1997) (PhD diss., Kansas State University)).

35. Project of an International Declaration concerning the Laws and Customs of War art. 10, Brussels, Aug. 27, 1874, *reprinted in* THE LAWS OF ARMED CONFLICTS 23 (Dietrich Schindler & Jiří Toman eds., 4th ed. 2004).

It is worth pausing to note the differences between Article 10 of the Brussels Declaration and Article 51 of the Lieber Code. First, Article 10 does not rely on State authorization and is rather conditions-based in its definition of *levée en masse*. In other words, under Article 10, State authorization is irrelevant to the determination of what constitutes a *levée en masse*. Second, Article 10 includes the additional requirement to respect the laws and customs of war. Consequently, the Brussels Declaration clarified the definition of *levée en masse* and sought to impose regulation upon the conduct of civilian participants of such groups. Yet the States present at the conference could not come to a consensus and Article 10 did not become law.

More than two decades after the Brussels Conference, the 1899 Hague Peace Conference was convened to "consider a possible reduction of the excessive armaments" and to limit "the progressive development of existing weapons."[36] Although no consensus could be reached on the issue of limiting or reducing armaments, the Conference did agree on numerous provisions related to the laws and customs of warfare. One of these provisions covered *levée en masse*, stating:

> The population of territory which has not been occupied who, on the enemy's approach, spontaneously take up arms to resist the invading troops without having time to organize themselves in accordance with Article I, [which, like Article 9 of the Brussels Declaration, sets forth the criteria for the laws, rights, and duties of war to apply to armed conflict participants,] shall be regarded as belligerents, if they respect the laws and customs of war.[37]

The language is almost identical to the language from the Brussels Declaration and gathered the consensus of the States present at the 1899 Convention. Surprisingly, the 1899 Convention fully adopted the language from the contentious Brussels Conference despite the disagreement over combatant qualification. Eight years later, during the 1907 Hague Peace Conference, the 1899 language was modified to add the requirement that participants of a *levée en masse* "carry arms openly."[38] This addition was the last major modification to the law governing *levée en masse*.

In 1949, the Third Geneva Convention adopted almost verbatim the language of the 1907 Hague Regulations.[39] Article 4(A)(6) of the Convention provides for

---

36. James Brown Scott, The Hague Conventions and Declarations of 1899 and 1907 v (1915).

37. Regulations Respecting the Laws and Customs of War on Land art. 2, annexed to Convention (II) with Respect to the Laws and Customs of War on Land, July 29, 1899, 32 Stat. 1803, T.S. No. 403.

38. Regulations Respecting the Laws and Customs of War on Land art. 2, annexed to Convention No. IV Respecting the Laws and Customs of War on Land, Oct. 18, 1907, 36 Stat. 2227, T.S. No. 539. In full, Article 2 states: "The inhabitants of a territory which has not been occupied, who, on the approach of the enemy, spontaneously take up arms to resist the invading troops without having had time to organize themselves in accordance with Article 1, shall be regarded as belligerents if they carry arms openly and if they respect the laws and customs of war."

39. Third Geneva Convention, *supra* note 4, art. 4(A)(6.

POW status for persons who fall into the power of the enemy and meet the following conditions:

> Inhabitants of a non-occupied territory, who on the approach of the enemy spontaneously take up arms to resist the invading forces, without having had time to form themselves into regular armed units, provided they carry arms openly and respect the laws and customs of war.[40]

The similarity between the language adopted in the Third Geneva Convention and that of the 1907 Hague Regulations reflects the strong resistance within the 1949 Diplomatic Conference to any deviation from the conditions set forth in the Regulations.[41] Thus, the Hague definition had become permanently enshrined into international law by the time of the drafting of the 1949 Geneva Conventions.

The historical roots of *levée en masse* are deep, but this legal concept remains relevant and has been implicated in recent armed conflicts. For example, the Trial Chamber of the International Criminal Tribunal for the former Yugoslavia determined that, for a brief period in 1992, certain Bosnian Muslim resistance fighters in and around Srebrenica constituted a *levée en masse*.[42] Additionally, it was reported that, during the 2008 international armed conflict between Russia and Georgia, "it was not only the army that rose [in defense of Georgia] but also regular citizens," groups of which wore camouflage, carried military equipment, and "said they were there to defend the city from Russian attack."[43]

The legal evolution of *levée en masse* detailed above is informative to its application to modern armed conflict situations for three reasons. First, history shows that States felt compelled to recognize the legitimacy of inhabitants of unoccupied territory who resisted invasion. As William Hall suggested in 1880, inhabitants of territory that is being invaded have a legitimate interest in defending themselves.[44] It would be unreasonable and unrealistic to expect or require inhabitants of unoccupied territory to capitulate during an invasion, and there is no reason to think that this will be any different in contemporary or future armed conflicts. Second, history also shows that States are simultaneously resistant to affording legal legitimacy to civilians to participate in hostilities in broad terms. For example, the tension between Germany and France over the *franc-tireurs* underscores this reluctance, which likely influenced the temporal restriction included in the

---

40. *Id.*

41. 1960 GC III COMMENTARY, *supra* note 3, at 67.

42. Prosecutor v. Orić, Case No. IT-03-68-T, Judgment, ¶¶ 135–36 (Int'l Crim. Trib. for the former Yugoslavia June 30, 2006).

43. GARY D. SOLIS, THE LAW OF ARMED CONFLICT: INTERNATIONAL HUMANITARIAN LAW IN WAR 216 (2nd ed. 2016) (quoting Nicholas Kulish & Michael Schwirtz, *Sons Missing in Action, If Indeed They Found It*, NEW YORK TIMES, Aug. 12, 2008, at A10).

44. HALL, *supra* note 25, at 549–50.

requirements for *levée en masse*—it is limited to the initial invasion of unoccupied territory.[45] Third, the broader law-of-war concept of distinction highlights a need for participants in a *levée en masse* to set themselves apart somehow from the civilian population. Thus, the requirement to carry arms openly could be viewed as a way to facilitate compliance with the principle of distinction. As we will see, the historical interests underlying the development of the *levée en masse* doctrine remain relevant today. Furthermore, the changing character of warfare places pressure on the doctrine and tests its relevance for contemporary and future armed conflicts.

IV. *LEVÉE EN MASSE* IN FUTURE ARMED CONFLICT: A SCENARIO-BASED ANALYSIS

The discussion in the previous part yields the following distilled list of elements for the existence of a *levée en masse* under the LOAC. First, the group of persons must be inhabitants of unoccupied territory.[46] Second, the individuals in the group "must spontaneously take up arms to resist an invading force" of the unoccupied territory with insufficient time "to form themselves into regular armed units."[47] Third, the individuals must respect the laws and customs of war.[48] Fourth, they must carry arms openly.[49] Upon capture of a person belonging to a group that meets these criteria, he or should would be entitled to POW status, including all of the rights and protections thus entailed.[50]

Returning to the scenario presented in the introduction,[51] do the civilian residents of Town X in State B engaged in armed resistance against State A's invading forces—including the hackers—constitute a *levée en masse*? Those Town X residents engaged in conventional ground combat against State B's armed forces likely qualify as members of a *levée en masse*. The scenario establishes that they are local residents of Town X, which is unoccupied and into which State A's forces invaded. Furthermore, the Town X residents appear to have formed their armed

---

45. The 2020 Commentary to the Third Geneva Convention of 1949 reinforced this limitation. 2020 GC III COMMENTARY, *supra* note 1, ¶ 1064. The 2020 Commentary states that "Article 4A(6) provides for the recognition of prisoner-of-war status for people who take up arms within a narrow window of time, namely during the actual invasion period. If the resistance continues after this window, when the inhabitants have had time to organize into regular armed units, Article 4A(6) loses its relevance." *Id.*

46. Third Geneva Convention, *supra* note 4, art. 4(A)(6).

47. *Id.*

48. *Id.*

49. *Id.*

50. *See generally* Third Geneva Convention, *supra* note 4.

51. *See supra* Part I.

resistance movement spontaneously in response to the absence of State B forces to counter the invasion. The scenario does not expressly state whether the residents carry arms openly, but it may be presumed for the sake of argument that the apparent speed and intensity of combat would require the residents to engage in persistent and open combat, which would entail the open carrying of arms. Similarly, we may assume for the sake of argument that the residents conform with the LOAC, including the requirement to direct their combat operations against State B forces and other lawful targets. Accordingly, we may assume that any such Town X residents captured by State B during the hostilities would be entitled to POW status and receive the attendant rights and protections.

The analysis of the legal status of the hackers is more complicated and much less clear. Before discussing the four elements of a *levée en masse*, some observations are in order about the general characteristics of a group of individuals comprising a *levée en masse*. A *levée en masse* is by nature an unstable group and likely is dynamic in its organizational structure and membership. The urgency of the armed conflict situation and the ensuing spontaneous formation of the armed resistance make it practically impossible for such a group to conform with the organizational and structural requirements of the LOAC for irregular groups of armed fighters. Thus, even in the context of conventional ground combat, there may be ambiguity about who qualifies as a member of a *levée en masse*. For example, one can imagine gray areas when it comes to the residency of the group members. For some members, of course, it will be clear that they are inhabitants of the territory subject to invasion. But, in other cases, it may be difficult to draw a clear line between those fighters who qualify as inhabitants because they are sufficiently connected—geographically or culturally, for example—with the invaded territory and those fighters who do not qualify as inhabitants and thus are not members of the *levée en masse*.

Such questions about membership of a *levée en masse* are compounded when discussing individuals engaged in cyber operations. As will be discussed below,[52] cyber operations are largely free of the geographical and temporal restraints naturally imposed on fighters in conventional ground combat. As a result, the factual circumstances traditionally used to identify members of a *levée en masse* are absent in the cyber domain. Thus, the cyber domain presents an especially sharp threshold challenge in determining which cyber operators, including the resistance hackers in the example scenario under consideration, constitute members of the *levée en masse*.

Turning now to the four elements of a *levée en masse*, we must first determine whether the individuals engaged in armed resistance are inhabitants of unoccupied territory. According to the scenario, the hackers resisting State A's invading forces are residents of unoccupied Town X. Thus, it appears that the hackers satisfy the first element. That said, one may reasonably "fight the facts" of the hypothetical scenario on this point and question the likelihood that resistance hackers

---

52. *See infra* notes 53–73 and accompanying text.

in a future conflict would be limited to residents of Town X. There are several reasons suggesting that this may not be the case.

First, cyberspace generally, and cyber armed conflict specifically, de-emphasizes the importance of factors such as residency and geographical habitation. Cyberspace has been defined as a "global domain within the information environment consisting of the interdependent networks of information technological infrastructures and resident data, including the Internet, telecommunications networks, computer systems, and embedded processors and controllers."[53] The global and interconnected character of cyberspace make it possible for cyber operators physically located far from one another to engage in coordinated action. This holds true for hackers engaged in cyber resistance movements of the kind under examination here. Indeed, hackers and other cyber operators typically form tight-knit communities that span borders and other physical geographic limitations. Such communities are highly integrated and based on subject matter interests and (in some cases) other philosophical positions rather than on geographical or even national ties. As such, it would seem that resistance hackers would be unlikely to come from Town X, but rather would come from various locations within or even beyond State B.

Second, hostile invasions in future armed conflict—for example, State A's invasion of State B—almost certainly will not occur as they have in the past. Operation Overlord, the famous invasion on the Normandy coast of France by Allied forces during the Second World War, consisted of more than 4,000 ships and landing craft carrying 176,000 armed forces members and their accompanying military equipment and weaponry.[54] Cyber capabilities available to both invading forces and resistance forces may limit belligerent parties' reliance on large military formations and increase the importance of information operations, espionage, and other efforts largely focused on the cyber domain of warfare.[55] Thus, in planning an invasion of State B, State A's military forces likely will leverage cyber operations to engage in information operations designed, for example, to confuse State B's armed forces or to undermine the civilian population's trust in its own government.[56] Such operations likely would precede (or even replace, in some cases) any large-scale ground invasion of State B.

As a result, perhaps the most important part of a future land invasion will occur without respect to physical boundaries, such as those designating Town X in State

---

53. Chairman, Joint Chiefs of Staff, Joint Publication 3-12, Cyberspace Operations GL-4 (2018).

54. R. Ernest Dupuy & Trevor N. Dupoy, The Encyclopedia of Military History: From 3,500 B.C. to the Present 1106 (revised ed. 1977).

55. Raphael S. Cohen et al., The Future of Warfare in 2030: Project Overview and Conclusions 24 (2020), *available at* https://www.rand.org/content/dam/rand/pubs/research_reports/RR2800/RR2849z1/RAND_RR2849z1.pdf.

56. *See, e.g.*, Chaveso Cook & Liam Collins, *Psyop, Cyber, and Infowar: Combating the New Age IED*, Modern War Institute (Apr. 6, 2021), https://mwi.usma.edu/psyop-cyber-and-infowar-combating-the-new-age-ied.

B. Cyber operations and their effects will be perceived not in geographical but rather in virtual space. This further decreases the likelihood that any hacker resistance, such as that envisioned in the example scenario, would arise and organize in accordance with geographical limitations.[57] Rather, hacker resistance movements are much more likely to consist of individuals operating throughout and, in many cases, beyond State B's physical territory.[58]

For these reasons, while the resistance hackers in the example scenario appear to meet the habitation requirement of the first element, it is unlikely that such civilians engaged in cyber operations in future armed conflict will reside in the geographical area in which the invasion is resisted; rather, they will participate in such operations from diverse geographical regions and will be organized based on virtual rather than physical, geographical relationships.

The second element of a *levée en masse* requires that the resistance fighters coalesce spontaneously and without sufficient time to form into regular armed forces units. As with geography, the temporal aspects of future armed conflict will surely be impacted by other characteristics of future warfare—including the increased prevalence of and reliance upon cyber capabilities. Historically, armed conflict has occurred at speeds that tax human cognition and capabilities. Indeed, States have sought to exploit the element of speed in armed conflict. For example, the U.S. Army recognizes in its military doctrine the importance of operational initiative—"the setting of tempo and terms of action throughout an operation."[59] By increasing the speed of military operations during armed conflict, the U.S. Army seeks to present the "enemy force with multiple dilemmas," "force that enemy to react continuously until driven into an untenable position," and "abandon their preferred options, reactive to friendly actions, and make mistakes."[60] In short, States use speed and tempo to overwhelm and create urgency in the enemy.

The LOAC acknowledges the often-overwhelming speed and urgency of warfare. For example, States have insisted that in applying law-of-war rules during the conduct of hostilities, "[d]ecisions by military commanders or other persons responsible for planning, authorizing, or executing military action must be made in good faith and based on their assessment of the information available to them

---

57. See P. W. Singer & Allan Friedman, Cybersecurity and Cyberwar: What Everyone Needs to Know 13 (2014). (The authors emphasize the virtual nature of cyberspace, thus that it "is made up of digitized data that is created, stored, and, most importantly, shared. This means that it is not merely a physical place and thus defies measurement in any kind of physical dimension.").

58. Nicholas A. Bredenkamp & Mark Grzegorzewski, *Supporting Resistance Movements in Cyberspace*, 7 Special Operations Journal 17, 20 (2021) (suggesting that the nature of cyberspace facilitates the creation of geographically dispersed resistance movements, including allowing "the resistance movement to essentially 'crowd source' worldwide support for their cause, creating a support base far greater than what is possible in traditional movements").

59. Headquarters, Department of the Army, ADP 3-0, Operations 1-11 (2019).

60. *Id.*

at the time."[61] In other words, States reject the notion that reasonable decisions made by combatants during hostilities may be "second-guess[ed] . . . with the benefit of hindsight."[62] One reason for States' insistence in this regard is the speed at which warfare occurs.

The second element of *levée en masse*—the requirement that resistance movements form spontaneously without time to form regular armed units—likewise constitutes, at least in part, an acknowledgment of the speed and urgency of warfare. The lawfulness of the *levée en masse* reflects the understanding that enemy invasions often catch States and populations off guard—for example, when the civilian population of an unoccupied territory is unaware of an invasion or when their States' armed forces are unexpectedly unable to mobilize in a timely or effective manner to resist the invasion. When the speed and tempo of warfare foster urgency in this manner, belligerent parties are afforded the legal space to address the threat posed by the enemy—including by forming a *levée en masse* made up of civilian resistance fighters.

In the example scenario under consideration, the spontaneity requirement for a *levée en masse* must be evaluated with due regard to the fact that the resistance hackers are operating in the cyber domain. It one sense, the high speed at which cyber operations occur suggests that the spontaneity requirement should be relaxed in favor of resistance hackers such as those in Town X.[63] If cyber operations typically occur at speeds beyond or close to the limits of human cognition—and if, as discussed above, cyber operations lack the geographic limitations that accompany conventional means and methods of warfare—then perhaps this operational reality would (or should) support a finding that resistance hackers often will meet the spontaneity requirement. On this view, the largely unpredictable character of cyber operations—they may occur anywhere at any time—and the urgency generated by such operations in some sense may often render *any* civilian resistance spontaneous.[64]

However, in another sense, the spontaneity requirement seems ill-suited for resistance fighters operating in the cyber domain. The virtual nature of cyber

---

61. DoD LAW OF WAR MANUAL, *supra* note 23, at 196; *see also id.* at 196 n.67 (citing and quoting the military doctrinal publications of other States, in which they express support for this interpretation of combatants' law-of-war duties).

62. *Id.* at 196.

63. James Johnson & Eleanor Krabill, *AI, Cyberspace, and Nuclear Weapons*, WAR ON THE ROCKS (Jan. 31, 2020), https://warontherocks.com/2020/01/ai-cyberspace-and-nuclear-weapons.

64. It should be noted here that, as Pictet argues, for a *levée en masse* to form in accordance with Article 4(A)(6) of the Third Geneva Convention, "it is not necessary for the inhabitants who take up arms to have been surprised by the invasion." 1960 GC III COMMENTARY, *supra* note 3, at 67. Thus, the "spontaneity" requirement may be met, for example, when the inhabitants "have been warned" about the invasion, but "did not have sufficient time to organize themselves." *Id.* The ICRC's 2020 Commentary concurs with this view. *See* 2020 GC III COMMENTARY, *supra* note 1, ¶ 1066.

operations creates a physical distance between the armed conflict hostilities and the participants. This physical distance offers a buffer between the destruction of warfare and the individuals engaged in cyber operations. For example, the resistance hackers in Town X may be less likely to feel the immediate impact of the destructive effects of the hostilities occurring in the town. This physical distance thus may offer a psychological distance. Cyber operators may be afforded the time and space to reflect on the hostilities—including by applying reasoning to the armed conflict situation and responding in a measured and operationally sound manner—that those engaged in conventional ground combat do not receive. This is not to suggest that cyber warfare entails no psychological—or physical, for that matter—consequences for cyber operators.[65] Rather, we argue only that cyber operators may be afforded the time and space to plan, organize, execute, and react during hostilities, which often would cut against a finding of spontaneity of action. The more space and time an individual has to conduct hostilities, the less urgent the situation and thus, perhaps, the less need there is for spontaneous action.[66]

Furthermore, the relative safety of cyber operators—compared with individuals engaged in conventional ground combat—also undercuts the spontaneity requirement of a *levée en masse*. Underlying the notion of *levée en masse* is an unmistakable acknowledgment of valor and heroism. In other words, "[u]nderpinning the revolutionary mobilization of a *levée en masse* is patriotic zeal coupled with the initiative of the citizen-soldier under emergency circumstances."[67] While the

---

65. *See, e.g.*, Craig Hinkley, *Preventing PTSD and Burnout for Cybersecurity Professionals*, DARKREADING (Sept. 16, 2019), https://www.darkreading.com/risk/preventing-ptsd-and-burnout-for-cybersecurity-professionals.

66. Another aspect of the tension between cyber operations and the *levée en masse* legal notion is that the latter is envisioned as of exceedingly short duration. As Pictet put it in his Commentary to the Third Geneva Convention, "It should, however, be emphasized that a mass levy can only be considered to exist during a very short period, i.e. during the actual invasion period. If resistance continues, the authority commanding the inhabitants who have taken up arms, or the authority to which they profess allegiance, must either replace them by sending regular units, or must incorporate them in its regular forces. Otherwise, the mass levy could not survive the total occupation of the territory which it has tried in vain to defend." 1960 GC III COMMENTARY, *supra* note 3, at 68. It is hard to say how the nature of operations in the cyber domain would impact this aspect of *levée en masse*. On the one hand, cyber operations often occur at speeds that far exceed that of ground combat. On the other hand, the remoteness, anonymity, and relative safety of cyber operations could conceivably prolong a resistance movements' fight against an invasion.

67. Wallace & Reeves, *supra* note 2, at 650. Similarly, Greenspan said that the lawfulness of a *levée en masse* reflected the belief that "[t]he first duty of a citizen is to defend his country, and provided he does so loyally he should not be treated as a marauder or criminal." MORRIS GREENSPAN, THE MODERN LAW OF LAND WARFARE 62 (1959); *see also* DoD LAW OF WAR MANUAL, *supra* note 23, at 160 ("In discussions of the status of private acts of hostility under international law, the point is often made that international law does not require States to prevent what they may regard as acts of patriotism and heroism"); Richard R. Baxter, *So-Called Unprivileged Belligerency: Spies, Guerrillas, and Saboteurs*, 28 BRITISH YEARBOOK OF

LOAC does not expressly refer to these considerations, they underpin the *levée en masse* notion—both historically and conceptually. But resistance hackers engaged in cyber operations, including those in Town X in the example scenario, operate largely anonymously[68] and from a point of relative safety. The geographical and temporal distance between such operators and the physical effects of the hostilities thus sits uneasily with the conceptual and historical bases of the *levée en masse*.

Somewhat relatedly, the LOAC incorporates notions of honor[69] and chivalry.[70] These notions stand for, among other things, the proposition that the LOAC "demands a certain amount of fairness in offense and defense and a certain mutual respect between opposing military forces."[71] In particular, combatants must not "resort to means, expedients, or conduct that would constitute a breach of trust with the enemy."[72] Others have explored the relationship between law-of-war honor (as well as concrete law-of-war rules that emanate from it, such as perfidy) and cyber operations.[73] It is sufficient here to note that the blurring between military and civilian persons and objects prevalent in cyber armed conflict raises serious issues about how the LOAC applies in the cyber domain. More importantly for present purposes, notions of honor and fair play also seem relevant to the justification for the lawfulness of *levée en masse*. As already noted, States' acceptance of the *levée en masse* as a lawful status in armed conflict is based largely on the dire urgency of the resistance movement.[74] It is this urgency that justifies the relaxation of normal rules governing combatant status, including the requirements of organization and distinction. But if, as suggested above, that urgency is generally eased in the cyber realm—thus permitted reflection and measured response in ways not possible in conventional ground combat—then notions of honor and fair play within the LOAC suggest that the relaxed standards afforded to a *levée en masse* may not be appropriate.

INTERNATIONAL LAW 323, 342 (1951) ("In both occupied and unoccupied areas, resistance activities, guerilla warfare, and sabotage by private persons may be expected to continue on at least as widespread a basis in future warfare as they have in the past. More often than not, patriotism or some sort of political allegiance lies at the room of such activities.").

68. *See infra* note 88 and accompanying text.

69. *See* DoD LAW OF WAR MANUAL, *supra* note 23, at 65–69.

70. *Id.* at 66.

71. *Id.* at 65–66 (citing several persuasive sources of State doctrine and prominent publicists).

72. *Id.* at 66–67.

73. *See, e.g.*, Colonel Gary P. Corn & Commander Peter P. Pascucci, *The Law of Armed Conflict Implications of Covered or Concealed Cyber Operations: Perfidy, Ruses, and the Principle of Passive Distinction*, *in* THE IMPACT OF EMERGING TECHNOLOGIES ON THE LAW OF ARMED CONFLICT 273 (Eric Talbot Jensen & Ronald T. P. Alcala eds., 2019).

74. *See supra* note 63 and accompanying text.

The third element of a *levée en masse* is that its members respect the laws and customs of war. It is an interesting feature of *levée en masse*—and one not confined to cyber operations but rather generally applicable—that such groups are relieved of the requirement to be "commanded by a person responsible for his subordinates,"[75] which is applicable to other irregular groups engaged in the conduct of hostilities. On the one hand, this seems inevitable: the reactive and spontaneous character of the *levée en masse* in the face of an enemy invasion makes it practically impossible for the group to organize itself sufficiently, including identifying and coalescing around a commander.

On the other hand, there is an important connection between the command requirement and the compliance requirement for POW status. The command requirement "is designed to exclude individuals . . . acting on their own in wartime."[76] There are many reasons to limit the conduct of hostilities to armed groups rather than individuals. One reason is that an armed group commanded by an effective leader is more capable of acting in coordination and in conformity with shared norms, including the LOAC. Indeed, as the U.S. Department of Defense states in its Law of War Manual, the command requirement for POW status "helps ensure that the armed group has sufficient discipline and organization to conduct its operations in accordance with the law of war."[77]

The connection between the command requirement and the requirement to conform with the LOAC seems especially important in the cyber domain. Cyber operations, as discussed above, are dispersed geographically and temporally. As such, cyber operators—even those coordinating their efforts to achieve operational effects against the enemy—may be unlikely to have the means and opportunity to disseminate LOAC rules. More fundamentally, it is unclear whether cyber operators are in a position to appreciate the existence and content of LOAC norms. In conventional ground combat, *levée en masse* members at least have the benefit of observing the enemy's regular troops and discerning what military operations that conform with the LOAC look like. The virtual realm does not afford this opportunity to cyber fighters. Furthermore, ground fighters—even civilians taking part in a *levée en masse*—are likely to have at least some of the skills and knowledge relevant to the conduct of hostilities, such as how to use weaponry and other basic combat equipment. Intuitively, it seems that such individuals are likely to have some sense of the ethics that accompany the use of such equipment, which often tracks roughly the LOAC's requirements. Cyber operators, however, operate in a realm that does not necessarily incorporate the ethics and legal considerations related to military combat operations. Thus, it seems that cyber operators' ability

---

75. Third Geneva Convention, *supra* note 4, art. 4(A)(2)(a); *see also* DoD Law of War Manual, *supra* note 23, at 117; Marco Sassòli, International Humanitarian Law: Rules, Controversies, and Solutions to Problems Arising in Warfare 252 (2019).

76. Dinstein, *supra* note 22, at 52.

77. DoD Law of War Manual, *supra* note 23, at 121.

to conform to LOAC requirements would be significantly impacted by the norm dissemination that naturally accompanies a command structure.

The fourth and final element of a *levée en masse* is the requirement to carry arms openly. Members of a *levée en masse* are relieved of the requirement to wear a fixed distinctive sign recognizable at a distance, which is normally a condition for the members of an irregular armed group to qualify for POW status. This is probably due to the coordination problems inherent in a spontaneously formed resistance to an invasion. But the requirement to carry arms openly remains as a link to the fundamental LOAC concept of distinction. Even during the chaos of an invasion into unoccupied territory, the belligerent parties are required to meet the requirements of distinction, including distinguishing themselves from civilians and conducting their operations against lawful targets.[78] The ICRC's 2020 Commentary to the Third Geneva Convention reinforce the purpose of this requirement, stating that "[c]arrying arms openly helps to ensure that persons involved in a *levée en masse* are accorded the protections of prisoner-of-war status."[79]

Unsurprisingly, cyber operators engaged in resistance hacking against an invading enemy force are unlikely to meet this requirement. The tools of cyber military operations are the same computer systems, networks, and infrastructure used in all cyber activity, including purely civilian activity.[80] One might argue that the prevalence of cyber operations in contemporary and future warfare justifies the inclusion of these systems, networks, and infrastructure within the definition of "arms." For example, the experts behind the Tallinn Manual concluded that "[c]yber means of warfare . . . include any cyber device, materiel, instrument, mechanism, equipment, or software used, designed, or intended to be used to conduct a cyber attack."[81]

Notwithstanding the likelihood that terms such as "arms" and "means of warfare" may be interpreted progressively to include cyber systems and tools increasingly used in armed conflict, the fourth element of *levée en masse* requires not only that group members carry "arms" but that they do so "openly."[82] While this requirement must be interpreted reasonably, "depending on the nature of the weapon and the prevailing circumstances,"[83] it must be kept in mind that the

---

78. *Id.* at 62.

79. 2020 GC III COMMENTARY, *supra* note 1, ¶ 1067.

80. *See, e.g.*, Michelle Nichols, *Tech-Savvy Taliban Fights War in Cyberspace*, REUTERS (July 20, 2011), https://www.reuters.com/article/us-afghanistan-taliban-technology/tech-savvy-taliban-fights-war-in-cyberspace-idUSTRE76J1IL20110720.

81. TALLINN MANUAL 2.0 ON THE INTERNATIONAL LAW APPLICABLE TO CYBER WARFARE 452–53 (Michael N. Schmitt ed., 2017). This is not to say that the International Group of Experts that prepared the Tallinn Manual considered the terms "arms" and "means of warfare" equivalent, as they certainly are not.

82. Third Geneva Convention, *supra* note 4, art. 4(A)(6).

83. DINSTEIN, *supra* note 22, at 54.

"carry openly" requirement is "linked to the cardinal principle of distinction between combatants and civilians."[84] Certain requirements for POW status—the requirement of a commander responsible for subordinates and that of wearing a fixed distinctive sign recognizable at a distance—are relaxed for the *levée en masse*, even at the costs of undermining the distinction concept to some degree. But the drafters of the Third Geneva Convention were unwilling to forgo the "carry arms openly" requirement. Undoubtedly, the costs to the principle of distinction would be too high if this requirement were forgone. As Pictet put it in his Commentary to the Third Geneva Convention, "[i]n the absence of any distinctive sign, the requirement of carrying arms 'openly' is of special significance and has a more precise implication . . .; this requirement is in the interest of combatants themselves who must be recognizable in order to qualify for treatment as prisoners of war. They must therefore carry arms visibly."[85]

Thus, once again, the character of cyber operations comes into sharp tension with the assumptions underlying the LOAC generally and the notion of *levée en masse* in particular. Cyber operations necessarily implicate ambiguity between the legal status of the operators and the means through which such operations are carried out. "Over 90 percent of the physical and virtual layers of cyberspace are civilian owned and controlled"—thus, "nearly all cyber operations occur on, in, or through civilian cyberspace infrastructure."[86] Cyber operations during armed conflict often heavily rely on elements of deception and surprise and thus often exploit this ambiguity.[87] As a result, and as was the case with respect to other elements of *levée en masse*, the "carry arms openly" requirement seems ill-suited to resistance hacking operations of the kind involved in the scenario.

In sum, the resistance hackers in the example scenario would not constitute a *levée en masse* according to the elements required currently under the LOAC. Accordingly, if captured by State A, the hackers would not be entitled to POW status and the ensuing protections. As detailed throughout this part, this conclusion is due in large part to the difficulty of resolving the tension between the realities of contemporary and future cyber operations in armed conflict and the *levée en masse* concept, which was developed in light of armed conflict conditions that are outdated in several important ways.

Even if States ultimately insist on maintaining the possibility of a cyber *levée en masse*, such as the resistance hackers' combat operations in the scenario at the beginning of this chapter, other aspects of operations in the cyber domain likely will undermine the utility of the *levée en masse* status in future warfare. Most notably, cyber operations are notoriously difficult to attribute accurately to those individuals carrying them out. Determining the source of cyber operations

---

84. *Id.* at 52.

85. 1960 GC III Commentary, *supra* note 3, at 67.

86. Corn & Pascucci, *supra* note 73, at 277.

87. *Id.* at 287–88.

is extraordinarily time and resource consuming. It is not uncommon that attribution processes take "several weeks or months of analyzing intelligence and forensics."[88] This is time that belligerent parties simply do not have in the midst of high-intensity armed hostilities. As a result, unless we see remarkable gains in the ability of States to attribute cyber operations reliably and accurately, cyber operators—including the resistance hackers in our example scenario—likely will remain cloaked in anonymity. At the very least, it seems unlikely that belligerent parties will find themselves in control of such individuals such that they must conduct a POW status determination.

Two final notes about the legal status of State B's resistance hackers in the example scenario are worth making. First, if State A captures the hackers during the invasion, State A's capturing forces are required to determine the hackers' legal status. This is essential for State A to satisfy the requirement to afford protection to such individuals "from the time they fall into the power of the enemy."[89] If State A has any doubt about whether the resistance hackers qualify as POWs, State A forces would be required to conduct an Article 5 tribunal to determine their status.[90] However, such a tribunal would be tasked with making a factual determination about whether the hackers satisfied the requirements of a *levée en masse*, rather than a legal analysis of the sort explored throughout this part. In other words, the members of the Article 5 tribunal would be provided by State A with legal guidance as to whether such acts by groups within the cyber domain could in any case meet the requirements of a *levée en masse*. They would not be free to make such a determination themselves. Thus, it is all the more important that States examine this legal question in anticipation of potential applications in future armed conflict.

Second, while they would not be entitled to POW status upon capture, it is a separate question whether the resistance hackers would be subject to lethal targeting during State A's invasion of Town X. This is because the failure of the resistance hackers to qualify for POW status does not necessarily imply that they retain the protections to which they normally would be entitled as civilians. Indeed, if the hackers are directly participating in hostilities, they will lose such protection against attack for as long as they are directly participating.[91] If the hackers were captured rather than attacked during hostilities, their direct participation in hostilities would make them liable to criminal prosecution, including potentially for murder or attempted murder.[92]

---

88. OFFICE OF THE DIRECTOR OF NATIONAL INTELLIGENCE, A GUIDE TO CYBER ATTRIBUTION 2 (2018).

89. Third Geneva Convention, *supra* note 4, art. 5.

90. *Id.*

91. Protocol Additional to the Geneva Conventions of 12 August 1949, and Relating to the Protection of Victims of International Armed Conflicts art. 51(3), June 8, 1977, 1125 U.N.T.S. 3.

92. 1960 GC III COMMENTARY, *supra* note 3, at 77.

V. CONCLUSION

The example scenario presented in the introductory part of this chapter offers an opportunity to reconsider the notion of *levée en masse* in light of the changing characteristics of warfare, including the potential deployment of autonomous combat robots and the hacking of such robots. In exploring these matters, it became clear that many of the characteristics of future armed conflict will likely undermine the utility and practical applicability of the *levée en masse* doctrine.

This is not to suggest that the *levée en masse* will or should be abandoned as a legal status in international armed conflict. Indeed, as noted in the introduction to this chapter, in its influential 2020 Commentary to the Third Geneva Convention, the ICRC argues that the possibility of a "civilian uprising" as envisioned by the rules respecting a *levée en masse* "should not be discarded."[93] History suggests that notions of patriotism, nationalism, and valor will continue to compel civilian resistance fighters to engage in hostilities on behalf of their State when the State's regular forces are incapable of doing so. It further seems likely that States facing hostile invasion will in many instances encourage such conduct. Thus, the notions underlying *levée en masse* may well remain an aspect of the conduct of hostilities in future armed conflict.

The issue in such circumstances—and the central question of this chapter—is the legal status of civilians who fall into the power of the enemy after engaging in hostilities as part of a resistance movement. The LOAC requires belligerent parties who detain such individuals to determine their legal status. In doing so, if States wish to retain the international legal notion of *levée en masse*, they will have to reconcile the unique characteristics of hostile cyber operations and the elements of a *levée en masse* as they exist under current international law.

---

93. 2020 GC III COMMENTARY, *supra* note 1, ¶ 1063.

6

Prisoner of War Status in the Context of Naval Warfare: On the Status of Masters and Crews of Neutral Merchant Vessels

WOLFF HEINTSCHEL VON HEINEGG* ■

I. INTRODUCTION

The law of naval warfare is a rather special sub-branch of the law of armed conflict[1] in that its provisions are not limited to the protection of victims of armed conflict and the regulation of the conduct of hostilities. It also provides rules on the relationship between the parties to an international armed conflict at sea and neutral States under the law of maritime neutrality.[2] Moreover, under prize law,

---

*. Professor Heintschel von Heinegg holds the Chair of Public Law, in particular public international law, European law, and foreign constitutional law, at the Europa-Universitat Viadrina in Frankfurt (Oder), Germany. He is also the President of the International Society for Military Law and the Law of War.

1. For the distinction between land and sea warfare, see C.J. COLOMBOS, THE INTERNATIONAL LAW OF THE SEA 548ff. (6th rev. ed. 1967); LASSA OPPENHEIM, 2 INTERNATIONAL LAW: A TREATISE 457ff. (H. Lauterpacht ed., 7th ed. 1952).

2. The law of maritime neutrality, which is not dealt with in the present chapter, is the subject of one treaty only: Convention No. XIII Concerning the Rights and Duties of Neutral Powers in Naval War, Oct. 18, 1907, Stat. 2415, T.S. No. 545. This chapter focuses on neutral merchant vessels and their masters and crews. Neutral civil aircraft and their personnel have been excluded in order to avoid unnecessary duplications. However, with some minor modifications, the rules identified, and the conclusions drawn, apply to neutral civil aircraft and their personnel *mutatis mutandis*.

Wolff Heintschel von Heinegg, *Prisoner of War Status in the Context of Naval Warfare: On the Status of Masters and Crews of Neutral Merchant Vessels* In: *Prisoners of War in Contemporary Conflict*. Edited by: Michael N. Schmitt and Christopher J. Koschnitzky, Oxford University Press. © Oxford University Press 2023. DOI: 10.1093/oso/9780197663288.003.0006

belligerents are permitted to visit, search, divert, and capture enemy and, if certain conditions are met, neutral merchant vessels.[3] Accordingly, the law of naval warfare is characterized by a strong economic element. The effects of the exercise of prize measures by the parties to an international armed conflict on international shipping and maritime trade can be considerable.[4]

While the conditions under which neutral merchant vessels are liable to be captured as prize are well established,[5] the status of the masters and crews of such vessels who are not enemy nationals is less clear than one may assume. Other than the personnel of enemy merchant vessels, they do not enjoy prisoner of war (POW) status under the 1949 Convention (III) Relative to the Treatment of Prisoners of War (Third Geneva Convention) if they have fallen into the hands of a belligerent.[6] Nor are they included in the categories of protected persons under the 1949 Convention (II) for the Amelioration of the Condition of the Wounded, Sick, and Shipwrecked Members of Armed Forces at Sea (Second Geneva Convention).[7] Against the background that neutral merchant vessels may, under certain conditions, also be liable to be attacked as lawful military objectives,[8] it is quite surprising that the consequences for their masters and crews are regulated only in some (national) manuals and marginally, if at all.

---

3. Some aspects of prize law are regulated in Convention No. XI Relative to Certain Restrictions with Regard to the Exercise of the Right of Capture in Naval War, Oct. 18, 1907, 36 Stat. 2396, T.S. No. 544 [hereinafter Hague Convention XI]. For prize law, see also the following three non-binding documents: Declaration Concerning the Laws of Maritime War arts. 22–64, Feb. 26, 1909, *reprinted in* THE DECLARATION OF LONDON, FEBRUARY 26, 1909, at 112 (James B. Scott ed., 1919) [hereinafter London Declaration]; Institute of International Law, The Law of Naval Warfare Governing the Relations between Belligerents (1913) (Oxford Manual of Naval Warfare), *reprinted in* THE LAWS OF ARMED CONFLICTS 1123 (Dietrich Schindler & Jiří Toman eds., 4th ed. 2004) [hereinafter 1913 Oxford Manual]; SAN REMO MANUAL ON INTERNATIONAL LAW APPLICABLE TO ARMED CONFLICTS AT SEA ¶¶ 112–58 (Louise Doswald-Beck ed., 1995) [hereinafter SAN REMO MANUAL].

4. *See* Ahmed S. Rahman, *Fighting the Forces of Gravity—Seapower and Maritime Trade Between the 18th and 20th Centuries*, 47 EXPLORATIONS IN ECONOMIC HISTORY 28 (2010).

5. *See infra* Part III.B.

6. Convention (III) Relative to the Treatment of Prisoners of War, Aug. 12, 1949, 6 U.S.T. 3316, 75 U.N.T.S. 135 [hereinafter Third Geneva Convention]. Article 4A(5) of the Third Geneva Convention includes in the categories of POWs "members of crews, including masters, pilots and apprentices, of the merchant marine and the crews of civil aircraft of the Parties to the conflict."

7. Convention (II) for the Amelioration of the Condition of the Wounded, Sick, and Shipwrecked Members of Armed Forces at Sea, Aug. 12, 1949, 6 U.S.T. 3217, 75 U.N.T.S. 85 [hereinafter Second Geneva Convention]. Article 13(5) of the Second Geneva Convention includes in the categories of protected persons the same persons as included in Article 4A(5) of the Third Geneva Convention.

8. *See infra* Part III.A.

In that context, another question arises. In land warfare, it is generally recognized that civilians taking a direct part in the hostilities lose their protection against attack, are not entitled to POW status, and may be held criminally responsible under the applicable domestic criminal law.[9] It is, however, far from settled whether and to what extent the concept of direct participation in the hostilities is applicable in naval warfare or whether such participation results in the obligation of the belligerent into whose hands such civilians have fallen to accord to them POW status.[10]

The present chapter, in Part II, discusses the conditions for a vessel qualifying as a neutral as distinct from an enemy merchant vessel. It will be shown that such classification is both dependent on a variety of factors and comparatively difficult, considering the various approaches taken by States and developments regarding so-called flags of convenience. Still, such classification is of overall importance because it may be indicative of the status of the personnel of merchant vessels. Part III provides a brief overview of the rules of the law of naval warfare according to which neutral merchant vessels become liable to be attacked or to be captured as prize. The legal status of the masters and crews of captured neutral merchant vessels is the focus of Part IV, which also deals with the applicability of the concept of direct participation in the hostilities and the ensuing consequences.

II. NEUTRAL MERCHANT VESSELS DISTINGUISHED FROM ENEMY MERCHANT VESSELS

The "governing criterion applicable to vessels is that the enemy or neutral character of a vessel is determined by the flag which she is entitled to fly."[11] Nevertheless, regarding the exceptions to this rule, the "views of different States have varied and still vary considerably."[12] It is, therefore, not sufficient to determine the enemy

---

9. Protocol Additional to the Geneva Conventions of 12 August 1949, and Relating to the Protection of Victims of International Armed Conflicts art. 51(3), June 8, 1977, 1125 U.N.T.S. 3 [hereinafter Additional Protocol I]; Protocol Additional to the Geneva Conventions of 12 August 1949, and Relating to the Protection of Victims of Non-International Armed Conflicts art. 13(3), June 8, 1977, 1125 U.N.T.S. 609. For a discussion of the concept, see, inter alia, NILS MELZER, INTERNATIONAL COMMITTEE OF THE RED CROSS, INTERPRETIVE GUIDANCE ON THE NOTION OF DIRECT PARTICIPATION UNDER INTERNATIONAL HUMANITARIAN LAW (2009).

10. *See infra* Part IV.C.

11. COLOMBOS, *supra* note 1, at 559. *See also* London Declaration, *supra* note 3, art. 57(1); 1913 Oxford Manual, *supra* note 3, art. 51(1). At the 1909 London Conference, the delegates were not prepared to take a decision on the so-called Rule of 1756. Accordingly, Article 57(2) of the London Declaration excludes from Article 57 the "case where a neutral vessel is engaged in a trade which is closed in time of peace." For the Rule of 1756, see COLOMBOS, *supra* note 1, 678ff. Today, no such monopoly as envisaged in the Rule of 1756 exists; therefore, the Rule has fallen into desuetude.

12. ERIK CASTRÉN, THE PRESENT LAW OF WAR AND NEUTRALITY 325–26 (1954).

or neutral character by reference to the flag alone. Today, with the considerable number of merchant vessels flying so-called flags of convenience,[13] the parties to the conflict will be even more reluctant than in the nineteenth and first half of the twentieth centuries to classify a vessel as a neutral merchant ship for the sole reason that she is flying the flag of a State that is not party to the conflict.

A. Enemy Flag

There is, however, agreement that "prima facie" a vessel flying the enemy's flag "bears enemy character . . . whatever may be the nationality of her owner—whether a subject of a neutral State, or of either belligerent."[14] It continues to be the generally accepted approach taken by States[15] that the "fact that a merchant vessel is flying the flag of an enemy State . . . is conclusive evidence of its enemy character."[16]

B. Neutral Flag Not Conclusive Evidence

The fact that a vessel is flying the flag of a neutral State is, if at all, "prima facie evidence of its neutral character"[17] only. According to a long-standing principle, the

---

13. According to UNCTAD, the leading flags of registration in 2020 were Panama (329 million deadweight tons), Liberia (275 deadweight tons), and Marshall Islands (262 million deadweight tons). "For example, at the beginning of 2020, more than half of all ships owned by Japanese entities were registered in Panama; more than a fifth of the ships owned by Greek entities were registered in Liberia and another fifth in Marshall Islands." These and further data are available at *e-Handbook of Statistics 2021*, UNCTAD (2021), https://stats.unctad.org/handbook/MaritimeTransport/MerchantFleet.html.

14. OPPENHEIM, *supra* note 1, at 277–78. For a discussion of the relevant decisions of British and U.S. prize courts, see COLOMBOS, *supra* note 1, at 560.

15. U.S. NAVY, U.S. MARINE CORPS & U.S. COAST GUARD, NWP 1-14M/MCTP 11-10B/COMDTPUB P5800.7A, THE COMMANDER'S HANDBOOK ON THE LAW OF NAVAL OPERATIONS § 7.5 (2022) [hereinafter 2022 NWP 1-14M]; UNITED KINGDOM MINISTRY OF DEFENCE, THE MANUAL OF THE LAW OF ARMED CONFLICT ¶ 13.84 (2004) [hereinafter UK MANUAL]; FEDERAL MINISTRY OF DEFENCE (Germany), ZDv 15/2, LAW OF ARMED CONFLICT MANUAL ¶ 1026 (2013) [hereinafter GERMAN MANUAL]; CHIEF OF THE GENERAL STAFF (CANADA), B-GJ-005-104/FP-021, LAW OF ARMED CONFLICT AT THE OPERATIONAL AND TACTICAL LEVELS, ¶ 858(1) (2001) [hereinafter CANADIAN MANUAL]; DANISH MINISTRY OF DEFENCE, MILITARY MANUAL ON INTERNATIONAL LAW RELEVANT TO DANISH ARMED FORCES IN INTERNATIONAL OPERATIONS ¶ 4.5.2.1 (2016) [hereinafter DANISH MANUAL]; NORWEGIAN MINISTRY OF DEFENCE, MANUAL OF THE LAW OF ARMED CONFLICT ¶ 10.6a3 (2013/2018) [hereinafter NORWEGIAN MANUAL].

16. SAN REMO MANUAL, *supra* note 3, ¶ at 112.

17. *Id.*, ¶ 113.

nationality of a ship is determined by the flag she is entitled to fly.[18] Such entitlement depends on a decision of the flag State in accordance with its domestic law. Accordingly, a vessel flying the flag of a neutral State bears enemy character if she has, "under the Municipal Law of such State, no right to fly the flag she showed."[19] Further exceptions apply if the vessel "is under the orders or control of an agent placed on board by the enemy Government" or "if she is in the exclusive employment of the enemy Government."[20] Accordingly, merchant vessels flying a neutral flag bear enemy character if they operate "directly under enemy control, orders, charter, employment, or direction."[21]

Contrary to the 1909 London Declaration,[22] enemy character of a vessel can, according to customary international law, also be determined by ownership.[23] As rightly held by Tucker, the "neutral flag cannot serve as a device to protect vessels from seizure whose actual status indicates either continued ownership or control by individuals who themselves possess enemy character."[24] It is, however, still unsettled whether the nationality of the owner depends on citizenship and/or on residence in enemy or enemy-controlled territory.[25] As regards corporations, there seems to be general agreement, however, that their nationality is determined not only by the country of registration or their seat, but also, in times of armed conflict, by the so-called control test.[26] Accordingly, a corporation, while not registered or located in enemy territory but under the effective control of a majority of enemy nationals, qualifies as an enemy owner.

The provisions of Articles 55 and 56 of the 1909 London Declaration on the validity of a transfer of an enemy to a neutral flag before or after the outbreak of hostilities[27] have to be understood as:

> an obvious attempt to compromise differences in State practice. However, the manner in which they were formulated was such as to allow a considerable latitude in interpretation, and during World War I belligerents—or at

---

18. COLOMBOS, *supra* note 1, at 559. *See also* United Nations Convention on the Law of the Sea art. 91, Dec. 10, 1982, 1833 U.N.T.S. 397.

19. OPPENHEIM, *supra* note 1, at 278.

20. London Declaration, *supra* note 1, art. 46(2), (3), which is declaratory of customary international law. *See* OPPENHEIM, *supra* note 1, at 278.

21. 2022 NWP 1-14M, *supra* note 15, § 7.5.2.

22. London Declaration, *supra* note 3.

23. SAN REMO MANUAL, *supra* note 3, ¶ at 117.

24. ROBERT W. TUCKER, THE LAW OF WAR AND NEUTRALITY AT SEA 76 (1955)(Vol. 50, U.S. Naval War College International Law Studies).

25. *See also* SAN REMO MANUAL, *supra* note 3, at 193, Explanation of ¶ 117.

26. TUCKER, *supra* note 24, at 76.

27. *See also* Article 52 of the 1913 Oxford Manual, *supra* note 3.

least those belligerents professing to follow the Declaration of London—did not hesitate to resort to that interpretation most nearly in accord with their traditional practice.[28]

Whereas contemporary national manuals do not address the validity of a transfer from an enemy to a neutral flag, it is safe to hold that such "transfers effected either immediately prior to or following the outbreak of war will be—in principle—recognized as valid if made in good faith by the purchaser and resulting in the complete divestiture of enemy ownership or control."[29]

C. Acquisition of the Character of, or Assimilation to, an Enemy Warship or Enemy Merchant Vessel?

According to Anglo-American doctrine, neutral merchant vessels "acquire" enemy character if they are engaged in any of the following activities:

- taking a direct part in the hostilities;
- acting in any capacity as a naval or military auxiliary; or
- (forcible) resistance to the legitimate exercise of the right of visit and search.[30]

This approach is also partly reflected in Article 46 of the 1909 London Declaration, which provides:

> A neutral vessel will be condemned and, in a general way, receive the same treatment as would be applicable to her if she were an enemy merchant vessel:
> (1) if she takes a direct part in the hostilities;
> ...
> (4) if she is exclusively engaged at the time either in the transport of enemy troops or in the transmission of intelligence in the interest of the enemy.

The concept of "acquiring" the character of an enemy warship or enemy merchant vessel may not be confused with the legal effects of the grounds according to which the flying of a neutral flag is inconclusive as to the true nationality of a merchant vessel. Unfortunately, Article 46 of the 1909 London Declaration and, to a certain extent, Navy Warfare Publication (NWP) 1-

---

28. TUCKER, *supra* note 24, at 80.

29. *Id.*, at 81. *See also* SAN REMO MANUAL, *supra* note 3, at 194, Explanation of ¶ 117.

30. OPPENHEIM, *supra* note 1, at 278–79; TUCKER, *supra* note 24, at 78, 318ff.; 2022 NWP 1-14M, *supra* note 15, § 7.5.

14M[31] deal with them in the same context. It may be added that, according to Article 63 of the 1909 London Declaration, forcible resistance to the legitimate exercise of the right of visit, search, and capture merely involves the condemnation of the vessel, without assimilating it to an enemy merchant vessel.

The preferable approach should, therefore, be to clearly distinguish between the factors that have a bearing on the (true) nationality of merchant vessels and those activities resulting in the liability of neutral merchant vessels to the same treatment as enemy warships or enemy merchant vessels and those rendering them liable to be captured.[32] The latter activities do not have a bearing on their status as neutral merchant vessels; they merely deprive them of their principal protection from attack or capture and condemnation. These activities will be summarized in Part III.

D. Preliminary Conclusions

In accordance with the above findings, and for the purposes of the present chapter, vessels qualify as neutral merchant vessels if:

- they are entitled to fly the flag of a neutral State under the applicable domestic law of that State;
- they are not under the orders or control of an agent placed on board by the enemy government;
- they are not in the exclusive employment of the enemy government;
- they are not owned by enemy nationals or enemy corporations; and
- the transfer from an enemy to a neutral flag effected prior to or after the outbreak of hostilities is valid.

Merchant vessels that qualify, according to the preceding elements, as neutral merchant vessels retain their neutral status even if they take a direct part in the hostilities, act as auxiliaries, or forcibly resist the legitimate exercise of the belligerent right of visit, search, and capture.

Vessels flying the flag of the enemy or that do not fulfill the above conditions are enemy merchant vessels. These findings are without prejudice to the legality of attacks against merchant vessels, whether enemy or neutral, or their liability to be captured as prize.

---

31. U.S. Navy, U.S. Marine Corps & U.S. Coast Guard, NWP 1-14M MCWP 5-12/COMDTPUB P5800.7A, The Commander's Handbook on the Law of Naval Operations, § 7.5 (2007) [hereinafter 2007 NWP 1-14M]; 2022 NWP 1-14M, *supra* note 15.

32. For a similar approach, see Tucker, *supra* note 24, at 318ff.

III. NEUTRAL MERCHANT VESSELS LIABLE TO ATTACK OR CAPTURE

In times of armed conflict at sea, neutral merchant vessels continue to enjoy the right to freely navigate at sea and to engage in innocent trade. Accordingly, attacks against such vessels will be lawful only if they engage in activities that qualify as an effective contribution to the enemy's military action and if their destruction offers a definite military advantage.[33] In that context, it is important to note that most States do not recognize the approach taken, in particular, by the United States. Under the U.S. approach, a contribution to the enemy's war-sustaining effort will also render a vessel a lawful military objective.[34] Here, however, is not the appropriate occasion to enter into an in-depth discussion on that issue. As in the case of attack, the capture of neutral merchant vessels is lawful only if such capture is in compliance with the recognized rules of prize law.

A. Neutral Merchant Vessels as Lawful Military Objectives

Neither the 1909 London Declaration nor the 1913 Oxford Manual addresses the conditions under which neutral merchant vessels qualify as lawful military objectives. While Articles 46 and 63 of the 1909 London Declaration deal with direct participation in hostilities, transportation of enemy troops, transmission of intelligence in the interest of the enemy, and forcible resistance to the exercise of visit, search, and capture, such acts are considered to merely "involve ... the condemnation of the vessel" and not her sinking. Of course, Article 60 deals with the status of the personnel when the vessel "has directly or indirectly taken part in the hostilities," but the consequences of such participation for the vessel are not addressed.

The 1913 Oxford Manual is silent on that matter. However, the 1936 London Submarine Protocol[35] has added some clarity insofar as merchant vessels, whether enemy or neutral, do not enjoy the protection afforded by the Protocol "in case

---

33. These elements are generally recognized as reflective of customary international law and, therefore, applicable in naval warfare. *See* 2022 NWP 1-14M, *supra* note 15, § 5.3.1; CANADIAN MANUAL, *supra* note 15, ¶ 406(2); GERMAN MANUAL, *supra* note 15, ¶ 1029; NORWEGIAN MANUAL, *supra* note 15, ¶ 7.2; DANISH MANUAL, *supra* note 15, ¶¶ 2.3, 4.5.2; SAN REMO MANUAL, *supra* note 3, ¶ 40. In that context, it must be borne in mind that, according to Article 49(3) of Additional Protocol I, *supra* note 9, the definition of military objectives in Article 52(2) of Additional Protocol I does not apply to warfare at sea if attacks are not directed against targets on land or if they may not "affect the civilian population, individual civilians or civilian objects on land."

34. 2022 NWP 1-14M, *supra* note 15, §§ 5.3.1, 7.4, 8.2, 8.6.2, 8.7.1.

35. Procés-Verbal: Relating to the Rules of Submarine Warfare Set Forth in Part IV of the Treaty of London of April 22, 1930, Nov. 6, 1936, 173 L.N.T.S. 353, 3 Bevans 298, *reprinted in* 31 AMERICAN JOURNAL OF INTERNATIONAL LAW SUPPLEMENT 137 (1939).

of persistent refusal to stop on being duly summoned, or of active resistance to visit and search." Moreover, in its judgment on Admiral Dönitz, the Nuremberg Tribunal was "not prepared to hold Dönitz guilty for his conduct of submarine warfare against British armed merchant ships."[36] The Tribunal also excluded from the protective scope of the Protocol merchant vessels under convoy of enemy warships, those integrated "into the warning network of naval intelligence," and "British merchant ships [that] had been ordered to ram U-boats if possible."[37] While those parts of the judgment have shed some light on the legal consequences of activities rendering a merchant vessel a lawful target at sea, they merely relate to enemy and not neutral merchant vessels.

For a long time, the classification of neutral merchant vessels as lawful military objectives that make them liable to be attacked was, therefore, left to national manuals, the most important and influential being the U.S. Manuals of 1955,[38] 1997,[39] 2007,[40] and 2022.[41] As seen, the United States has adopted the approach that neutral merchant vessels acquire the character of enemy warship or enemy merchant vessel through certain activities. According to the 1955 U.S. Naval Manual:

> Neutral merchant vessels . . . acquire enemy character and are liable to the same treatment as enemy warships . . . when engaging in the following acts:
> 1. Taking a direct part in the hostilities on the side of an enemy;
> 2. Acting in any capacity as a naval or military auxiliary to an enemy's armed force.[42]

The "same treatment as enemy warships" implies that neutral merchant vessels may be attacked and destroyed or captured without prize procedures.[43]

The U.S. Manual further states:

---

36. United States v. Dönitz, 1 TRIALS OF WAR CRIMINALS BEFORE THE NUREMBERG MILITARY TRIBUNALS UNDER CONTROL COUNCIL LAW NO. 10, at 312 (1947).

37. *Id.*

38. U.S. DEPARTMENT OF THE NAVY, NWIP 10-2, LAW OF NAVAL WARFARE (1955)[hereinafter NWIP 10-2].

39. Annotated Supplement to the Commander's Handbook on the Law of Naval Operations (1997) [hereinafter NWP 9 Annotated Supplement].

40. 2007 NWP 1-14M, *supra* note 31.

41. 2022 NWP 1-14M, *supra* note 15.

42. NWIP 10-2, *supra* note 38, § 501a. *See also* TUCKER, *supra* note 24, at 319–20.

43. NWIP 10-2, *supra* note 38, § 503a.

Neutral merchant vessels ... acquire enemy character and are liable to the same treatment as enemy merchant vessels ... when engaging in the following acts:
1. Operating directly under enemy control, orders, charter, employment, or direction;
2. Resisting an attempt to establish identity, including visit and search.[44]

The phrase "same treatment as enemy merchant vessels" certainly implies that, under the said conditions, neutral merchant vessels are liable to be captured. It is, however, not entirely clear whether the acts rendering enemy merchant vessels liable to attack and destruction[45] also apply to neutral merchant vessels engaging in such activities, because the assimilation of neutral merchant vessels with enemy merchant vessels may be understood as being limited to the two acts referred to above. However, the acts rendering enemy merchant vessels liable to attack may be subsumed under the concept of "[t]aking a direct part in the hostilities." There is no indication in the U.S. Manual that neutral merchant vessels acting in that manner are not considered lawful targets.

Subsequent versions of the U.S. Manual adopt the same approach as the 1955 Manual.[46] In the 2022 version, the provision according to which a neutral merchant vessel acquires the character of an enemy merchant vessel contains an explicit reference to the provision on actions that may be taken against enemy merchant vessels. It provides that enemy merchant vessel and, thus, neutral merchant vessels:

> may be attacked and destroyed by surface warships, either with or without prior warning, in any of the following circumstances:
> 1. If persistently refusing to stop upon being duly summoned to do so
> 2. If actively resisting visit and search or capture
> 3. If sailing under convoy of enemy warships or enemy military aircraft
> 4. If armed with systems or weapons beyond that required for self-defense against terrorist, piracy, or like threats

---

44. *Id.*, § 501b.

45. *Id.*, § 503b(3) provides: "Enemy merchant vessels may be attacked and destroyed, either with or without prior warning, in any of the following circumstances:

1. Actively resisting visit and search or capture.
2. Refusing to stop upon being duly summoned.
3. Sailing under convoy of enemy warships or enemy military aircraft.
4. If armed, and there is reason to believe that such armament has been used, or is intended for use, offensively against an enemy.
5. If incorporated into, or assisting in any way, the intelligence system of an enemy's armed forces.
6. If acting in any capacity as a naval or military auxiliary to an enemy's armed forces."

46. NWP 9 Annotated Supplement, *supra* note 39, ¶ 7.5; 2007 NWP 1-14M, *supra* note 31, § 7.5; 2022 NWP 1-14M, *supra* note 15, § 7.5.

5. If incorporated into, or assisting in any way, the intelligence system of the enemy's armed forces
6. If acting in any capacity as a naval or military auxiliary to an enemy's armed forces
7. If integrated into the enemy's war-fighting/war-sustaining effort and compliance with the rules of the 1936 London Protocol would, under the circumstances of the specific encounter, subject the surface warship to imminent danger or would otherwise preclude mission accomplishment.[47]

With the adoption of the San Remo Manual in 1994, the circumstances rendering a neutral merchant vessel liable to be attacked as a lawful military objective have been identified as follows:

Merchant vessels flying the flag of neutral States may not be attacked unless they:
(a) are believed on reasonable grounds to be carrying contraband or breaching a blockade, and after prior warning they intentionally and clearly refuse to stop, or intentionally and clearly resist visit, search or capture;
(b) engage in belligerent acts on behalf of the enemy;
(c) act as auxiliaries to the enemy's armed forces;
(d) are incorporated into or assist the enemy's intelligence system;
(e) sail under convoy of enemy warships or military aircraft; *or*
(f) otherwise make an effective contribution to the enemy's military action, e.g., by carrying military materials, and it is not feasible for the attacking force to first place passengers and crew in a place of safety. Unless circumstances do not permit, they are to be given a warning, so that they can re-route, off-load, or take other precautions.[48]

The provisions of the San Remo Manual have been either adopted verbatim[49] or recognized as reflective of customary international law[50] in national manuals that have been published by States after the adoption of the San Remo Manual. Irrespective of the more liberal approach underlying the U.S. Manuals,[51] the San Remo Manual's provision on neutral merchant vessels qualifying as lawful targets

---

47. 2022 NWP 1-14M, *supra* note 15, § 8.6.2.2.

48. SAN REMO MANUAL, *supra* note 3, at ¶ 67.

49. UK MANUAL, *supra* note 15, ¶ 13.47; CANADIAN MANUAL, *supra* note 15, ¶¶ 719(3), 835; NORWEGIAN MANUAL, *supra* note 15, ¶ 10.36.

50. DANISH MANUAL, *supra* note 15, ¶ 4.5.2.4; GERMAN MANUAL, *supra* note 15, ¶ 1236.

51. Note that, according to the U.S. position, a contribution to the enemy's war-sustaining effort also renders merchant vessels, enemy or neutral, liable to attack.

is, therefore, generally accepted as correctly reflecting the law of naval warfare as it stands today.[52]

Finally, it is important to point to a key difference between enemy and neutral merchant vessels liable to be attacked. The former become lawful targets if they are "armed to an extent that they could inflict damage to a warship."[53] This rule must be understood against the background of the two World Wars and the widely held view that enemy merchant vessels are under no obligation to submit to visit and capture and that they "may defend themselves, may return the attack, and eventually seize the attacking men-of-war."[54] However, "they must not commit hostilities."[55] Of course, it is not easy "to draw a clear line between defensive and offensive action."[56] Nevertheless, the distinction between defensively and offensively armed enemy merchant vessels[57] seems to have survived. Be that as it may, insofar as neutral merchant vessels are concerned, they may be armed, and a distinction between offensive and defensive arming is not necessary.[58] It must be borne in mind, however, that neutral merchant vessels are under a positive obligation to submit to visit, search, and capture; and they are not entitled to render resistance or to use force against a belligerent warship. Their arming is permissible only for defending themselves "against pirates and similar threats."[59]

B. Neutral Merchant Vessels Liable to Capture

Although neutral merchant vessels are not as such liable to be captured as prize, it has since the adoption of the 1909 London Declaration been recognized that they may be captured if they are:

- breaching, or attempting to breach, a blockade;[60]

---

52. See, however, MINISTÈRE DE LA DÉFENSE, MANUEL DE DROIT DES CONFLITS ARMÉS 42 (2012), which adopts a considerably cautious position vis-à-vis the San Remo Manual: "les dispositions figurant dans le manuel ne constituent pas encore à proprement parler des règles de droit positif; . . . Il convient donc de rester prudent dans l'appréciation de la valeur de ce texte, et de comparer ses dispositions avec le droit antérieur."

53. SAN REMO MANUAL, *supra* note 3, ¶ at 60(f).

54. OPPENHEIM, *supra* note 1, at 266.

55. *Id.*

56. TUCKER, *supra* note 24, at 61.

57. *See also* COLOMBOS, *supra* note 1, at 521ff.

58. CANADIAN MANUAL, *supra* note 15,, ¶ 835(2); NORWEGIAN MANUAL, *supra* note 15, ¶ 10.37; DANISH MANUAL, *supra* note 15, ¶ 4.5.2.4

59. NORWEGIAN MANUAL, *supra* note 15, ¶ 10.37.

60. London Declaration, *supra* note 3, art. 14.

- carrying contraband;[61] or
- on a voyage especially undertaken with a view to the transport of individual passengers who are embodied in the armed forces of the enemy.[62]

That list of activities rendering neutral merchant vessels liable to be captured as prize has been adopted in the San Remo Manual[63] and in national manuals,[64] and it has been amended by the following acts:

- the presentation of irregular or fraudulent documents, the lack of necessary documents, or the destruction, defacement, or concealment of documents;
- violation of regulations established by a belligerent within the immediate area of naval operations.

In this context, it is important to note that, according to the position taken by the United States and the present author, a merchant vessel operating directly under enemy control, orders, charter, or direction[65] bears enemy character and no longer qualifies as a neutral merchant vessel. Moreover, if the vessel "takes a direct part in the hostilities,"[66] or if she "is exclusively engaged at the time either in the transport of enemy troops or in the transmission of intelligence in the interest of the enemy,"[67] she becomes a lawful military objective and, thus, liable to be attacked.

The rules on the capture of neutral merchant vessels are reflective of customary international law, even though the legality of the exercise of prize measures has sometimes been criticized as outdated and incompatible with contemporary international law.[68] This position is, however, incompatible with the positions taken by States and, thus, with customary international law. It is based on an erroneous interpretation of the prohibition of the use of force under Article 2(4) of the U.N. Charter because a use of force directed against an individual non-State vessel cannot be considered a use of force against the respective flag State.

---

61. *Id.*, art. 37.

62. *Id.*, art. 45(2). *See also* TUCKER, *supra* note 24, at 325–26.

63. SAN REMO MANUAL, *supra* note 3, ¶ at 146.

64. UK MANUAL, *supra* note 15, ¶ 13.106; CANADIAN MANUAL, *supra* note 15, ¶¶ 719(1), (2), 869(1), (2); NORWEGIAN MANUAL, *supra* note 15, ¶ 10.79; DANISH MANUAL, *supra* note 15, ch. 14 ¶ 4.7, at 604; GERMAN MANUAL, *supra* note 15, ¶ 240.

65. London Declaration, *supra* note 3, art. 46(2), (3); SAN REMO MANUAL, *supra* note 3, ¶ 146(c).

66. London Declaration, *supra* note 3, art. 46(1).

67. *Id.*, art. 46(4).

68. *See* Andrew Clapham, *Booty, Bounty, Blockade, and Prize: Time to Reevaluate the Law*, 97 INTERNATIONAL LAW STUDIES 1200 (2021), https://digital-commons.usnwc.edu/cgi/viewcontent.cgi?article=2984&context=ils.

IV. LEGAL STATUS OF MASTERS AND CREWS OF CAPTURED NEUTRAL MERCHANT VESSELS

Whereas neutral merchant vessels may be liable to attack or capture if they engage in any of the activities identified in the preceding part, the status of their masters and crews has not been dealt with in any treaty in force. As mentioned above, they are not included in the categories of protected persons under either Article 13 of the Second Geneva Convention or Article 4A of the Third Geneva Convention. Of course, it has been generally understood that "those not included in this enumeration [of Article 13 of the Third Geneva Convention] still remain protected, either by other Conventions, or simply by the general principles of International Law."[69] In its Commentary on Article 4A(5) of the Third Geneva Convention, the International Committee of the Red Cross (ICRC) merely states:

> Article 4A(5) does not apply to persons of enemy or neutral nationality serving as crew of neutral vessels or aircraft. Contemporary economic realities in the shipping industry are such that a vessel may be, and frequently will be, flagged in a neutral State. These individuals may not be taken as prisoners of war.[70]

Article 5 of the 1907 Convention No. XI Relative to Certain Restrictions with Regard to the Exercise of the Right of Capture in Naval War (Hague Convention XI)[71] deals only with the masters, officers, and members of the crews of captured enemy merchant vessels who "are not made prisoners of war" if they are nationals of a neutral State. Whereas neutral crew members may never be made POWs, the "captain and officers" may be made POWs, unless "they promise formally in writing not to serve on an enemy ship while the war lasts." The different treatment

---

69. II-A FINAL RECORD OF THE DIPLOMATIC CONFERENCE OF GENEVA OF 1949, 191 (1949). This has been re-emphasized in the ICRC Commentary on Article 13 of the Second Geneva Convention. *See* INTERNATIONAL COMMITTEE OF THE RED CROSS, COMMENTARY ON THE SECOND GENEVA CONVENTION: CONVENTION (II) FOR THE AMELIORATION OF THE CONDITION OF THE WOUNDED, SICK AND SHIPWRECKED MEMBERS OF ARMED FORCES AT SEA ¶ 1503 (2017), https://ihl-databases.icrc.org/applic/ihl/ihl.nsf/Comment.xsp?action=openDocument&documentId=52711B8A67F20D11C1258115003BE318.

70. INTERNATIONAL COMMITTEE OF THE RED CROSS, COMMENTARY ON THE THIRD GENEVA CONVENTION: CONVENTION (III) RELATIVE TO THE TREATMENT OF PRISONERS OF WAR ¶ 1056 (2020), https://ihl-databases.icrc.org/applic/ihl/ihl.nsf/Comment.xsp?action=openDocument&documentId=1796813618ABDA06C12585850057AB95. *See also* H.S. LEVIE, Prisoners of War in International Armed Conflict 63 (1977) (Vol. 59, U.S. Naval War College International Law Studies): "It should . . . be noted that for the members of the crew to be entitled to prisoner-of-war status upon capture, the merchant vessel or civilian aircraft must fly the flag of a Party to the conflict."

71. Hague Convention XI, *supra* note 3.

of captains and officers, on the one hand, and members of the crew, on the other hand, were explained as follows:

> [I]t appeared that to exact a promise from sailors, the scope of which they would hardly understand and the execution of which it might at times be very difficult to control, would impose a hardship frequently impossible to enforce. Hence the distinction established by the text. The sailors are purely and simply free; the captain and officers are set free only if they promise formally and in writing not to serve on an enemy ship as long as the war lasts.[72]

According to Article 8 of Hague Convention XI, these provisions "do not apply to ships taking a direct part in the hostilities." In that case, neutral personnel of enemy merchant vessels may be made POWs.[73]

One might be inclined to interpret the provisions of Hague Convention XI such that they have an indirect bearing on the status of the neutral personnel of captured neutral vessels. Accordingly, as a general rule, the personnel of neutral merchant vessels captured as prize will have to be released without requiring the master and officers to provide a formal promise. As an exception, they could be made POWs if the vessel qualifies as a lawful military objective—that is, if she has "directly participated in the hostilities." However, the wording is clear, and any interpretation of Hague Convention XI to that effect will have to be based on additional arguments.[74]

A. Personnel of Neutral Merchant Vessels Captured as Prize

The masters, officers, and members of the crews of neutral merchant vessels that have been captured as prize may not be made POWs if they are nationals of a neutral State. In principle, they must be released and allowed to return to their home country or to any other destination to which they wish to go. These are the general rules that have been adopted by States and by scholars.

According to Article 76(3) of the German Prize Ordinance of 1939,[75] the masters, officers, and crews of captured neutral vessels must be released if they provide

---

72. Extracts from the General Report of the Fourth Commission, Actes et documents, vol. I, 266; *reprinted in* THE REPORTS TO THE HAGUE CONFERENCES OF 1899 AND 1907, 735ff., 737 (J. Brown Scott ed., 1917).

73. For a discussion of Articles 5 and 8 of Hague Convention XI, see COLOMBOS, *supra* note 1, at 566; OPPENHEIM, *supra* note 1, at 266–67; TUCKER, *supra* note 24, at 112; D.P. O'CONNELL, 2 THE INTERNATIONAL LAW OF THE SEA 1117 (I.A. Shearer ed. 1984).

74. SAN REMO MANUAL, *supra* note 3, ¶ at 60(f).

75. Prisenordnung vom 28. August 1939, Reichsgesetzblatt (Imperial Law Gazette) 1939 Teil (Part) I, 1585 [hereinafter German Prize Ordinance].

evidence of their neutral nationality.[76] This is also the position that has consistently been taken in the U.S. Manuals. According to Naval Warfare Information Publication (NWIP) 10-2, the "officers and crews of captured neutral merchant vessels . . . who are nationals of a neutral State should not be made prisoners of war."[77] This general rule:

> is applicable as well to the officers and crews, nationals of a neutral State, of captured neutral merchant vessels . . . which have acquired enemy character and which are liable to the same treatment as enemy merchant vessels . . . Hence, a distinction must be made between the treatment accorded to the personnel of such vessels.[78]

Accordingly, the acquisition of the character of an enemy merchant vessel does not imply that the personnel of a captured neutral merchant vessel would have to be treated in the same manner as the personnel of enemy merchant vessels. Provisions to the same effect are provided in the U.S. Manuals of 1997,[79] 2007,[80] and 2017.[81] The Manuals of Canada, Denmark, France, Germany, and Norway do not address the issue.

The general rule has also been recognized by scholars. Castrén holds:

> The crew (and the officers) of a neutral merchant ship may generally not be made POWs even though the vessel is captured and the crew will not give any kind of promise to refrain from participation in war operations or from serving in the enemy navy during the war (although, as we have seen, a promise of this kind may be demanded in the more serious cases of unneutral service).[82]

According to Tucker:

---

76. The original German version reads: "Kapitän, Offiziere und Mannschaften aufgebrachter neutraler Fahrzeuge sind freizulassen, wenn sie eine neutrale Staatsangehörigkeit nachweisen."

77. NWIP 10-2, *supra* note 38, § 513.

78. *Id.*, at 5–14 n.41.

79. NWP 9 Annotated Supplement, *supra* note 39, ¶ 7.10.2: "The officers and crews of captured neutral merchant vessels and civil aircraft who are nationals of a neutral nation do not become prisoners of war and must be repatriated as soon as circumstances reasonably permit. This rule applies equally to the officers and crews of neutral vessels and aircraft which have assumed the character of enemy merchant vessels or aircraft by operating under enemy control or resisting visit and search."

80. 2007 NWP 1-14M, *supra* note 31, § 7.10.2.

81. 2022 NWP 1-14M, *supra* note 15, § 7.10.2.

82. Castrén, *supra* note 12, at 578.

[T]he neutral nationals serving as officers and crew of neutral vessels... may not be treated as prisoners of war. Nor is there any justification for placing the personnel of neutral prizes under any special restraint, unless this is shown to be necessary for the security of the prize crew.[83]

Today, Tucker's view is even more valid because prize crews (that is, boarding teams) may not be sufficiently trained in operating a merchant vessel and navigating it to a safe port. Interestingly, other scholars do not address the issue.

However, this is immaterial because the general rule, according to which the neutral personnel of captured neutral merchant vessels are to be released and not made POWs, that has found its way into the San Remo Manual provides, inter alia, that "[n]ationals of a neutral State... who are members of the crew of enemy or neutral merchant vessels... are to be released and may not be made prisoners of war."[84]

A rule identical to the San Remo provision has been included in the UK Manual.[85]

B. Personnel of Neutral Merchant Vessels Qualifying as Lawful Military Objectives

The fact that the personnel of neutral merchant vessels have not been included in the categories of persons protected under Article 13 of the Second Geneva Convention and Article 4A of the Third Geneva Convention, although such vessels may qualify as lawful military objectives, might be understood as a confirmation of the general rule identified above. Consequently, the rule would not be subject to any exceptions. However, such a conclusion would not correctly reflect customary international law. In other words, there may be exceptional circumstances that would justify holding the masters, officers, and crews of neutral merchant vessels as POWs.

Seemingly, one exception to the general rule is provided for in Article 60 of the 1913 Oxford Manual:

When a public or a private ship has directly or indirectly taken part in the hostilities, the enemy may retain as prisoners of war the whole personnel of the ship, without prejudice to the penalties he might otherwise incur.[86]

---

83. TUCKER, *supra* note 24, at 347.

84. SAN REMO MANUAL, *supra* note 3, ¶ at 166.

85. UK MANUAL, *supra* note 15, ¶ 13.120c.

86. 1913 Oxford Manual, *supra* note 3, art. 60.

Indeed, since the provision does not, like Articles 56–58, explicitly use the phrase "enemy ship, public or private," it might be argued that Article 60 also applies to neutral merchant vessels and their personnel.[87] However, the use of the term "enemy" suggests that the provision exclusively applies to the personnel of enemy merchant vessels.

The 1939 German Prize Ordinance, in Article 76(4), provides that the general obligation to release the neutral personnel of captured neutral merchant vessels does not apply if the captured vehicle has rendered violent resistance or taken part in the hostilities.[88] However, the German Prize Ordinance does not accord POW status to them. Arguably, neutral personnel may then be detained and subjected to criminal prosecution.

According to the U.S. position, "there is a clear exception . . . in the case of personnel of neutral merchant vessels . . . which take a direct part in the hostilities on the side of the enemy, or which serve in any way as a naval or military auxiliary for an enemy."[89]

This view has been explained by Tucker as follows:

> It has already been observed that neutral merchant vessels may acquire enemy character by undertaking to perform any one of several services on behalf of a belligerent. In the more serious forms of unneutral service, where the neutral takes a direct part in the hostilities or acts in a manner as a naval auxiliary to an enemy's forces, it may be assimilated to an enemy warship and rendered liable to attack on sight. There can be little question that if the personnel of such vessels fall into the hands of the other belligerent they are subject to detention as prisoners of war.[90]

However, the same author also holds that "the imputation of enemy character to neutral merchant vessels is not to be taken as an indication that the officers and crews of such vessels, when captured, may therefore be made prisoners of war."[91]

Castrén, however, is not prepared to accord POW status to the neutral personnel of neutral merchant vessels having directly participated in the hostilities: "If the

---

87. *Id.*, arts. 56–58.

88. German Prize Ordinance, *supra* note 75: "Die Bestimmungen der Abs. 1 bis 3 finden keine Anwendung, wenn das aufgebrachte Fahrzeug gewaltsamen Widerstand geleistet oder an Kampfhandlungen teilgenommen hat."

89. NWIP 10-2, *supra* note 38, § 513 n.40; 2007 NWP 1-14M, *supra* note 31, § 7.10.2; 2022 NWP 1-14M, *supra* note 15, § 7.10.2. *See also* NWP 9 Annotated Supplement, *supra* note 39, ¶ 7.10.2, which, in footnote 165, cites as authority Articles 5 and 8 of Hague Convention XI, which, however, only apply to the neutral personnel of enemy merchant vessels.

90. Tucker, *supra* note 24, at 115.

91. *Id.*, at 115 n.63.

crew have forcibly resisted visitation or capture, or if they have taken a direct part in hostilities, the result may even be a court-martial."[92]

While there seems to be no general agreement on the POW status of the neutral personnel of neutral merchant vessels qualifying as lawful military objectives, in particular because most of the other national manuals, with the exception of the UK Manual,[93] do not address the issue at all, it is quite surprising that the San Remo Manual provides:

> Neutral nationals . . . who are members of the crew of enemy or neutral merchant vessels . . . are to be released and may not be made prisoners of war unless the vessel . . . has committed an act covered by paragraphs 60, 63, 67 or 70, or the member of the crew has personally committed an act of hostility against the captor.[94]

This provision has certainly been inspired by the U.S. position. The only authority quoted in the Explanations to the San Remo Manual is NWP 9, paragraph 7.9.2 [sic].[95] It may, therefore, be doubted whether the San Remo Manual is in that regard reflective of customary international law.

It must be borne in mind, however, that the U.S. Manuals have been adopted by other States, in particular in South America and Asia. The San Remo Manual, despite some deficits, has generally been considered a restatement of customary international law. Therefore, the treatment as POWs of the neutral personnel of a neutral merchant vessels that is liable to be attacked because of its conduct may, in principle, be the correct approach. However, in view of the importance of the issue, it would be desirable if the matter were also included in other national manuals and taken into due consideration by institutions such as the ICRC.

Still, the matter is addressed in a rather undifferentiated manner and in disregard of the realities of (modern) merchant shipping. Even if direct participation in the hostilities—or rather, an effective contribution to the enemy's military action by use of a neutral merchant vessel—can result in the acquisition of the character of an enemy warship, this does not justify as such the detention of all neutral personnel as POWs. As in the case of Article 5 of Hague Convention XI, the members of the crew must be distinguished from the master and the officers.

While the explanation for such distinction given in 1907[96] is no longer acceptable, it remains common practice. It is provided for under the domestic law of

---

92. CASTRÉN, *supra* note 12, at 578.

93. UK MANUAL, *supra* note 15, ¶ 13.120c. Of course, the UK Manual has adopted the San Remo Manual almost entirely. It is, however, far from clear whether the decision to closely follow the San Remo Manual has been based on a thorough assessment of the ensuing consequences for the Royal Navy.

94. SAN REMO MANUAL, *supra* note 3, ¶ 166(c).

95. *Id.*, at 231, Explanation of ¶ 166(c).

96. See discussion *supra* at C675–C6P76.

flag States that the members of the crew are obliged to obey and follow the orders of the master and officers. Accordingly, neutral crew members may not be made POWs and must be released without undue delay even if their vessel has become a lawful target by use. Regularly, the crew will have no opportunity to prevent the master and the officers from taking a certain course of action. And, quite often, they do not have the same nationality. Accordingly, only the master and the officers may be made POWs in such circumstances.

C. Criminal Liability of the Personnel of Neutral Merchant Vessels

The final issue to be discussed is whether the neutral members of a neutral merchant vessel's personnel may be held criminally responsible if they have taken a direct part in the hostilities.

Before elaborating on this, it is important to clarify whether and to what extent the concept of direct participation in hostilities applies to naval warfare at all. In that context, it may be recalled that, according to Articles 49(3) and 51(3) of Protocol Additional to the Geneva Conventions of 12 August 1949, and Relating to the Protection of Victims of International Armed Conflicts, the loss of protection in case and for such time as civilians take a direct part in the hostilities does not apply to naval warfare if no attacks are launched against targets on land, or if it "may not affect the civilian population, individual civilians or civilian objects on land."[97] Moreover, enemy merchant vessels are said to be entitled to actively or forcibly resist the exercise visit and capture or to defend themselves against attacks.[98] Arguably, therefore, the concept of direct participation in the hostilities would not be applicable in such situations and the master and officers of an enemy merchant vessel could not be held criminally responsible for their conduct.

It may be recalled, however, that this only holds true for defensive actions taken by enemy merchant vessels. It has been stressed that the crews of such vessels "must not commit hostilities, and if they do so they are liable to be treated as criminals... The [opposing] opinion is without foundation nowadays."[99] The case of Captain Fryatt, who was executed by Germany as a *franc-tireur* because he had attempted to ram a German U-boat[100]—which may well be perceived of as an offensive act of hostility—does not provide evidence against the applicability of the concept of direct participation in the hostilities and against the criminal responsibility of those having committed such an act. Captain Fryatt's execution

---

97. Additional Protocol I, *supra* note 9.

98. See discussion *supra* at C6P62.

99. OPPENHEIM, *supra* note 1, at 266.

100. For the Fryatt case, see COLOMBOS, *supra* note 1, at 521ff.; OPPENHEIM, *supra* note 1, at 467–68.

was condemned as illegal because of the unlawful submarine warfare Germany resorted to during the First World War:

> Moreover, if merchantmen must expect to be attacked without warning by a lawless enemy, they need not wait to be attacked before they themselves resort to hostilities. Thus, when in 1915, during the First World War, Germany resorted to her nefarious submarine practice, and merchantmen were torpedoed without warning, or, if they were warned, their crews were endangered in their lives by being put in lifeboats on the high seas, it was perfectly legitimate for merchantmen of the Allies to attempt to ram German submarines, even if signaled to stop and submit to visitation.[101]

Therefore, the concept of direct participation applies to offensive acts by the personnel of enemy merchant vessels and, a fortiori, to offensive and defensive acts of hostility by the personnel of neutral merchant vessels that, other than enemy merchant vessels, are under a positive obligation to comply with belligerent orders.

As seen in the preceding part, international instruments, as well as national manuals, make use of the concept of "direct participation in the hostilities" in the context of the use of vessels as distinguished from the conduct of individuals. For the latter, the term "act of hostility" is used.[102] Accordingly, an act of "direct participation in the hostilities" rendering a vessel liable to be attacked does not as such justify the conclusion that the members of the vessel's personnel have committed an "act of hostility" or that they have individually taken a direct part in the hostilities. Moreover, they may be held criminally responsible only if they "are personally guilty of an act of hostility."[103] For instance, if a member of the personnel of a neutral merchant vessel that has been summoned to stop and to submit to visit and search commits an act of violence against members of the boarding team, this will qualify as an act of hostility and will result in individual criminal responsibility under the applicable domestic criminal law of the captor State.

V. CONCLUDING REMARKS

Under the law of naval warfare, the status of the neutral personnel of neutral merchant vessels is clear if such vessels have been captured as prize. As soon as the vessels have been taken to a safe port, the masters, officers, and crews must be released without undue delay and they may be detained only if that proves necessary for the ensuing procedures before a prize court. If such vessels have become lawful targets because of an effective contribution to the enemy's military

---

101. OPPENHEIM, *supra* note 1, at 467. *See also* TUCKER, *supra* note 24, at 59 n.34.

102. *See* 1913 Oxford Manual, *supra* note 3, art. 61; SAN REMO MANUAL, *supra* note 3, ¶ 166(c).

103. 1913 Oxford Manual, *supra* note 3, art. 60.

action (that is, if the vessels have directly participated in the hostilities), their neutral personnel may be made POWs. This, however, is limited to the master and the officers. The general rule with regard to crew members is that they must be released without undue delay. These rules are without prejudice to the individual criminal responsibility of those who have committed individual "acts of hostilities" against the intercepting warship. Committing an "act of hostility" qualifies as a "direct participation in the hostilities" by a civilian.

While these conclusions may be considered to reflect customary international law, it would add clarity and enhance protection of the neutral personnel of captured neutral merchant vessels if States other than the United States included them in their national military manuals. Legal clarity would also benefit considerably if the concept of acquiring the character of an enemy warship or of an enemy merchant vessel was abandoned. That would allow a less confusing determination of the neutral character of merchant vessels and, thus, of their neutral personnel.

7

Prisoners of War in Space?

ROB MCLAUGHLIN* ■

I. INTRODUCTION

Any analysis of the application of the international armed conflict (IAC) prisoner of war (POW) regime in outer space is an exercise in interpretive prediction. That said, there are two reasons to assess that this task is, as a matter of law, not merely a speculative exercise of *lex ferenda*. The first reason is that there is little doubt that international law (including the law of armed conflict[1]) applies in outer space.[2]

---

*. Professor, Australian National Centre for Oceans Resources and Security; Senior Fellow, Stockton Centre for International Law, U.S. Naval War College; Honorary Professor, Australian National University.

1. Michael N. Schmitt, *International Law and Military Operations in Space*, 10 MAX PLANCK YEARBOOK OF UNITED NATIONS LAW 89 (2006); Dale Stephens & Cassandra Steer, *Conflicts in Space: International Humanitarian Law and Its Application to Space Warfare*, 40 MCGILL ANNALS OF AIR AND SPACE LAW 1 (2015); Jack M. Beard, *Soft Law's Failure on the Horizon: The International Code of Conduct for Outer Space Activities*, 38 UNIVERSITY OF PENNSYLVANIA JOURNAL OF INTERNATIONAL LAW 335 (2016); Dale Stephens, *The International Legal Implications of Military Space Operations: Examining the Interplay Between International Humanitarian Law and the Outer Space Legal Regime*, 94 INTERNATIONAL LAW STUDIES 75 (2018); Caitlyn Georgeson & Matthew T. Stubbs, *Targeting in Outer Space: An Exploration of Regime Interactions in the Final Frontier*, 85 JOURNAL OF AIR LAW AND COMMERCE 609 (2020).

2. Indeed, this point is fundamental to the Treaty on Principles Governing the Activities of States in the Exploration and Use of Outer Space, Including the Moon and Other Celestial Bodies, Jan. 27, 1967, 18 U.S.T. 2410, T.I.A.S. No. 6347, 610 U.N.T.S. 205 [hereinafter Outer Space Treaty], Article I: "Outer space, including the Moon and other celestial bodies, shall be free for exploration and use by all States without discrimination of any kind, on a basis of equality and in accordance with international law, and there shall be free access to all areas of celestial bodies"; Article III: "States Parties to the Treaty shall carry on activities in the exploration and use of outer space, including the Moon and other celestial bodies, in accordance with international law, including the Charter of the United Nations, in the interest of maintaining international peace and security and promoting international co-operation and

This is not to say that there is agreement regarding the application and intersection of general international law, outer space law, and the IAC POW regime. The intersection between the law on the return of astronauts[3] and the POW regime for military personnel (in or from space) is a case in point. The second reason is that there is nothing glaringly obvious (to date) that would make it legally impossible for the POW regime to be applied to personnel who fall into the power of the enemy in space. Indeed, there will undoubtedly be practical limitations to how the POW regime is applied. For example, it is unlikely that current appreciations of the regime would countenance a long-term POW "camp" in a space object or on a celestial body. But these practical constraints do not rule out the application of other components of the POW regime, such as initial assessment and treatment,[4] and transport,[5] in outer space.

---

understanding"; Article VI: "States Parties to the Treaty shall bear international responsibility for national activities in outer space, including the Moon and other celestial bodies, whether such activities are carried on by governmental agencies or by non-governmental entities, and for assuring that national activities are carried out in conformity with the provisions set forth in the present Treaty."

3. Outer Space Treaty, *supra* note 2, Article V: "States Parties to the Treaty shall regard astronauts as envoys of mankind in outer space and shall render to them all possible assistance in the event of accident, distress, or emergency landing on the territory of another State Party or on the high seas. When astronauts make such a landing, they shall be safely and promptly returned to the State of registry of their space vehicle. . . . In carrying on activities in outer space and on celestial bodies, the astronauts of one State Party shall render all possible assistance to the astronauts of other States Parties. . . . States Parties to the Treaty shall immediately inform the other States Parties to the Treaty or the Secretary-General of the United Nations of any phenomena they discover in outer space, including the Moon and other celestial bodies, which could constitute a danger to the life or health of astronauts"; Agreement on the Rescue of Astronauts and the Return of Objects Launched in Outer Space, Apr. 22, 1968, 19 U.S.T. 7570, 672 U.N.T.S. 119 [hereinafter Rescue Agreement], Article 4: "If, owing to accident, distress, emergency or unintended landing, the personnel of a spacecraft land in territory under the jurisdiction of a Contracting Party or have been found on the high seas or in any other place not under the jurisdiction of any State, they shall be safely and promptly returned to representatives of the launching authority."

4. For example, Convention (III) Relative to the Treatment of Prisoners of War, Aug. 12, 1949, 6 U.S.T. 3316, 75 U.N.T.S. 135 [hereinafter Third Geneva Convention], Article 5: "Should any doubt arise as to whether persons having committed a belligerent act and having fallen into the hands of the enemy belong to any of the categories enumerated in Article 4, such persons shall enjoy the protection of the present Convention until such time as their status has been determined by a competent tribunal"; Article 17: "Every prisoner of war, when questioned on the subject, is bound to give only his surname, first names and rank, date of birth, and army, regimental, personal or serial number, or failing this, equivalent information."

5. *Id.*, Article 19: "Prisoners of war shall be evacuated, as soon as possible after their capture, to camps situated in an area far enough from the combat zone for them to be out of danger"; Article 20: "The evacuation of prisoners of war shall always be effected humanely and in conditions similar to those for the forces of the Detaining Power in their changes of station."

This chapter will deal only with the issue of POWs in IAC situations. Absent State concession,[6] recognition of belligerency,[7] or the application of Article 1(4) of the 1977 Additional Protocol I,[8] the IAC-focused POW regime established across the four 1949 Geneva Conventions does not apply in non-international armed conflict. Additionally, the focus of this chapter is upon POWs as defined in Article 4 of the Third Geneva Convention and Articles 43–45 of Additional Protocol I.[9] It does not deal with the issues of civilian internees or security detainees (that is, "[o]thers deprived of their liberty for reasons related to an armed conflict").[10]

Consequently, the chapter proceeds as follows. In Part II, the issue of "place of internment" is addressed. This part will focus on habitable space objects and celestial bodies (including the Moon). In Part III, the matter of "conditions of detention" is explored. Here, the focus is on the limitations inherent in the space environment and on habitable space objects. Finally, in Part IV, the situation of military astronauts and "personnel of spacecraft" is analyzed. For this part, the issue of where two ostensibly *lex specialis* regimes intersect is most acute.

II. THE PLACE OF INTERNMENT: THE LAW DOES NOT ALLOW FOR CONTINUED INTERNMENT ON HABITABLE SPACE OBJECTS OR CELESTIAL BODIES LIKE THE MOON

A. Habitable Space Objects

In general, a spacecraft might be defined as "any man-made craft capable of being used in outer space activity."[11] In legal terms, however, spacecraft are a species

---

6. OFFICE OF THE GENERAL COUNSEL, U.S. DEPARTMENT OF DEFENSE, LAW OF WAR MANUAL (rev. ed., Dec. 2016) [hereinafter DoD LAW OF WAR MANUAL], § 9.3.1: "In some cases, the policy of the United States has been to afford detainees certain POW protections even when they may not apply as a matter of law. Certain POW protections may be afforded to an individual without affecting the legal status of that individual or the legal status of a group to which that person belongs."

7. ROB MCLAUGHLIN, RECOGNITION OF BELLIGERENCY AND THE LAW OF ARMED CONFLICT 145–50 (2020).

8. Protocol Additional to the Geneva Conventions of 12 August 1949, and Relating to the Protection of Victims of International Armed Conflicts, June 8, 1977, 1125 U.N.T.S. 3 [hereinafter Additional Protocol I].

9. As elaborated in other chapters of this book.

10. *Cf.* COMMENTARY ON THE ADDITIONAL PROTOCOLS OF 8 JUNE 1977 TO THE GENEVA CONVENTIONS OF 12 AUGUST 1949 (Yves Sandoz, Christophe Swinarski & Bruno Zimmermann eds., 1987) at 1386, ¶ 4568: "The term 'deprived of their liberty for reasons related to the armed conflict' . . . covers both persons being penally prosecuted and those deprived of their liberty for security reasons, without being prosecuted under penal law. However, there must be a link between the situation of conflict and the deprivation of liberty; consequently prisoners held under normal rules of criminal law are not covered by this provision."

11. Julian G. Verplaetse, *On the Definition and Legal Status of Spacecraft*, 29 JOURNAL OF AIR LAW AND COMMERCE 131, 132 (1963).

of "space object" that is defined in the Convention on Registration of Objects Launched into Outer Space as including "component parts of a space object as well as its launch vehicle and parts thereof."[12] More precise definitions of spacecraft have been proposed, such as that spacecraft "should be capable of moving in outer space (either orbital or suborbital) without any support from the air, and should have a power source not dependent upon external oxygen."[13] However, currently, the legally correct approach is to understand the possible locations of internment on human-made objects in space as being habitable "space objects" and thus subject to the rules applicable to space objects. Thus, while it would prima facie seem logical and appropriate to refer to internment in "spacecraft," the term "habitable space object" is used to remain as close as possible to the relevant texts.

1. Ongoing Internment

No person may lawfully be interned within a habitable space object in outer space. With respect to combatants in IACs, the applicable rule is Article 22 of the Third Geneva Convention. This article expressly provides that POWs "may be interned only in premises located *on land*."[14] The U.S. Department of Defense Law of War Manual explains:

> This rule is intended to ensure that POWs are interned in a relatively safe and healthy environment. For example, in prior conflicts, POWs interned on ships were not held in hygienic and humane conditions. Similarly, POWs held on ships faced increased risk from the dangers of war.[15]

Three points are of immediate relevance. First, on the face of the text, there is no reason why this provision should not, and does not, apply equally to military space operations involving the capture of POWs, and the rule is unequivocal. Consequently, long-term internment in a habitable space object would breach Article 22 because it is not internment "on land." Indeed, the 2020 Commentary on the Third Geneva Convention by the International Committee of the Red

---

12. Convention on Registration of Objects Launched into Outer Space art. I(b), Jan. 14, 1975, 28 U.S.T. 695, 1023 U.N.T.S. 15 [hereinafter Registration Convention].

13. Paul Stephen Dempsey & Maria Manoli, *Suborbital Flights and the Delimitation of Air Space Vis-à-Vis Outer Space: Functionalism, Spatialism and State Sovereignty* 16 (Submission to the United Nations Office of Outer Space Affairs by the Space Safety Law & Regulation Committee of International Association for the Advancement of Space Safety, Sept. 2017), http://iaass.space-safety.org/wp-content/uploads/sites/24/2018/03/Definition-Delimitation-Air-Outer-PSDMM-16Jan2018.pdf.

14. Third Geneva Convention, *supra* note 4, Article 22 (emphasis added): "Prisoners of war may be interned only in premises located *on land* and affording every guarantee of hygiene and healthfulness."

15. DoD Law of War Manual, *supra* note 6, § 9.11.3.1.

Cross (ICRC) is explicit in this regard: "The requirement to intern prisoners of war 'on land' also prohibits the potential internment of prisoners in outer space."[16]

Second, the POW regime is clear that "[n]o POW may at any time be sent to or detained in areas where he or she may be exposed to the fire of the combat zone."[17] It is improbable that an enemy habitable space object used for military purposes would not be a priority target in military space operations, thus rendering the ongoing detention of POWs in such a place impermissible. Additionally, in the expectation that POW camps are located outside of combat zones, Article 23 mandates that "all useful information regarding the geographical location of prisoner of war camps" will be shared with, inter alia, the enemy State whose personnel are interned in the camp. Ongoing internment in a habitable space object would clearly be inadvisable as it would require communicating the location of that space object with the enemy. Practically, this requirement could not be properly fulfilled.

Third, while accepting the occasional shortcomings of analogies from sea to space, it is difficult to see why the injunction against interning POWs on vessels at sea would not provide an operative analogy to internment in a habitable space object.[18] As the 2020 Commentary explains, the rationale for the limitation is as follows:

> The purpose of this provision is "to avoid the permanent off-shore confinement of prisoners in warships which do not guarantee appropriate conditions of treatment and control over the correct application of [international humanitarian law]." Internment of prisoners aboard ships would render access to essential services more difficult. Moreover, the right of delegates of the Protecting Power, if one is appointed, and of the ICRC to visit prisoners of war pursuant to Article 126 is made substantially more difficult. It may also prove more difficult to guarantee the minimum requirements set by the Convention in terms of, for example, hygiene and space for recreational and physical activities.[19]

This does not mean that temporary detention in a ship (and, by analogy, a habitable space object) is impermissible. Temporary detention in a ship is allowed for transportation, evacuation, when an adequate facility ashore is still being identified, or when medical treatment is being provided on the ship and continued care on the ship is advisable.[20]

---

16. INTERNATIONAL COMMITTEE OF THE RED CROSS, COMMENTARY ON THE THIRD GENEVA CONVENTION: CONVENTION (III) RELATIVE TO THE TREATMENT OF PRISONERS OF WAR ¶ 1987 (2020), https://ihl-databases.icrc.org/applic/ihl/ihl.nsf/Comment.xsp?action=openDocument&documentId=3AF43403A399F1C4C1258584004651EB [hereinafter 2020 GC III COMMENTARY].

17. DoD LAW OF WAR MANUAL, *supra* note 6, § 9.5.2.3.

18. There are exceptions to this provision that allow for temporary internment, such as for transportation to a proper place of internment.

19. 2020 GC III COMMENTARY, *supra* note 16, ¶ 1984.

20. DoD LAW OF WAR MANUAL, *supra* note 6, § 9.10.4.

Such stays are to be "as brief as possible."[21] The *Altmark* incident on February 16, 1940 is an example of the misfortune that falls upon POWs when that does not occur. During this incident, HMS *Cossack* entered Norwegian territorial waters to free 299 Allied POWs (primarily captured merchant vessel crews) taken by *Graf Spee* and other German naval units during operations in the Atlantic Ocean.[22] Many of the POWs in *Altmark* had been held on-board for months. As a contemporary report observed, "300 British seamen had been kept for weeks and months in close confinement" and "had for long been living under intolerable conditions."[23] Indeed, "the British prisoners . . . were found locked in shell rooms and store rooms and in an empty oil tank."[24] Unlike the POWs on the *Altmark*, Iraqi sailors captured at sea during the Second Gulf War in 2003, as well as some Iraqi personnel who were captured or surrendered ashore in the Al Faw peninsula area, were held only for a very short period on coalition warships pending transport to shore and internment in a POW camp. This option was carefully considered, and as was observed at the time:

> [A]rrangements were made by senior UK commanders for [POWs] and casualties to be transported to and temporarily held in Royal Navy warships until [POW] facilities were available ashore. While not an ideal scenario for naval commanders, and not a measure to be taken lightly in view of the existing law, this was deemed a prudent contingency to provide a realistic and reasonably safe temporary option in view of the relatively low risk to the warships in the northern Arabian Gulf.[25]

Furthermore, the expectation in the Second Geneva Convention[26] is that POWs will be initially be covered by the First Geneva Convention,[27] and also the Second and Third Geneva Conventions, from the time at which the POWs fall into the

---

21. 2020 GC III COMMENTARY, *supra* note 16, ¶ 1985.

22. *See generally* D.P. O'CONNELL, THE INFLUENCE OF LAW ON SEA POWER 41 (1975); James Farrant, *Altmark and Belligerent Use of Neutral Territorial Waters*, *in* MARITIME OPERATIONS LAW IN PRACTICE (David Letts & Rob McLaughlin eds., forthcoming 2022). This incident is primarily cited as an example of the misuse of neutral waters, and the nature of neutral obligations, but it is also instructive as to the hazards of long-term internment in ships.

23. *The "Altmark" Incident*, 17 BULLETIN OF INTERNATIONAL NEWS 225 (1940).

24. *Id.* at 226.

25. Neil Brown, *Legal Considerations in Relation to Maritime Operations against Iraq*, 86 INTERNATIONAL LAW STUDIES 128, 134 (2010).

26. Convention (II) for the Amelioration of the Condition of the Wounded, Sick, and Shipwrecked Members of Armed Forces at Sea, Aug. 12, 1949, 6 U.S.T. 3217, 75 U.N.T.S. 85 [hereinafter Second Geneva Convention].

27. Convention (I) for the Amelioration of the Condition of the Wounded and Sick in the Armed Forces in the Field, Aug. 12, 1949, 6 U.S.T. 3114, 75 U.N.T.S. 31.

belligerent's hands.[28] Therefore, POWs must be transferred to shore internment at the first available opportunity, as the Third Geneva Convention requires. Article 16 of the Third Geneva Convention specifically provides that "the wounded, sick and shipwrecked of a belligerent who fall into enemy hands shall be prisoners of war, and the provisions of international law concerning prisoners of war shall apply to them."[29]

At the point of landing, the bare regime established in the Second Geneva Convention then yields almost completely to the more elaborated POW regime established in the Third Geneva Convention. In particular, the Third Geneva Convention establishes clear requirements in terms of the ongoing treatment, obligations, and liabilities of the interning state and the POWs themselves.[30] To quote the ICRC's 2017 Commentary on the Second Geneva Convention:

> Thus, on a ship, the obligations set out in the Second Convention will predominate. Where possible, and as soon as necessary, however, the more detailed provisions of the Third Convention will apply. In any event, as soon as wounded, sick or shipwrecked persons are transferred to land, the First and Third Conventions will apply.[31]

It must, however, be observed that the second sentence of Article 16 states: "The captor may decide, according to circumstances, whether it is expedient to hold them, or to convey them to a port in the captor's own country, to a neutral port or even to a port in enemy territory." This is not to be read as an option to intern at sea; rather, this is understood to refer to "[t]he type of circumstances that may be invoked" to *temporarily* hold POWs in a ship, such as "operational reasons that do not permit the ship to change its course immediately, or possibly where holding the persons on board ship, temporarily, is safer and the conditions more suitable than the alternative."[32] Nevertheless, given the parallel application (at sea) of both Conventions, and the need to comply as soon as possible with the more elaborated POW scheme established in the Third Geneva Convention, Article 22 of that Convention continues to operate: "Accordingly, persons may only be held

---

28. *See, e.g.*, Second Geneva Convention, *supra* note 26, art. 4.

29. *Id.*, arts. 12, 16; INTERNATIONAL COMMITTEE OF THE RED CROSS, COMMENTARY ON THE SECOND GENEVA CONVENTION: CONVENTION (II) FOR THE AMELIORATION OF THE CONDITION OF THE WOUNDED, SICK AND SHIPWRECKED MEMBERS OF ARMED FORCES AT SEA ¶ 1576 (2017), https://ihl-databases.icrc.org/applic/ihl/ihl.nsf/Comment.xsp?action=openDocument&documentId=52C11AB40D938DE4C1258115003BFC3F [hereinafter 2017 GC II COMMENTARY]; COMMENTARY TO GENEVA CONVENTION III RELATIVE TO THE TREATMENT OF PRISONERS OF WAR 182 (Jean Pictet ed., 1960): "The use of boats, rafts or 'pontoons' is ... absolutely forbidden."

30. *See*, inter alia, Second Geneva Convention, *supra* note 26, art. 16.

31. 2017 GC II COMMENTARY, *supra* note 29, ¶ 1577 (2017).

32. *Id.*, ¶ 1579.

on board a ship as a temporary measure, pending transfer to land. If the ship is a warship, it is especially important that the time a person is held on board is limited to the absolutely necessary."[33]

Given the clear and unambiguous text of Article 22 of the Third Geneva Convention, buttressed by the view of the ICRC in its 2020 Commentary, it is textually clear that the use of habitable space objects for ongoing internment of POWs is impermissible in space. Additionally, taking account of issues that already arise in the context of the close situational analogy of on ongoing internment at sea—such as identifying operational factors that might legitimize a delay in transfer to shore—an analogy to the legal framework for internment at sea provides a ready set of detailed potential touchpoints to inform this assessment.

2. Transport of POWs from Outer Space to Earth

As noted above, for the purposes of delivery to an appropriate place of internment on (Earthly) land, a distinction must be made between the ongoing internment of POWs in habitable space objects, and moving people around in space, and from space to Earth. It is conceivable that, in the future, military personnel could fall into the hands of a belligerent party while in outer space. This may occur as a result of rescue, surrender, or deliberate action to capture those personnel.

For example, consider an IAC between States A and B in which State A seizes State B's space station by docking with that station under a "false flag" and then takes control of the station. State A could then deny State B access to the capabilities managed from that space object and collect essential intelligence from the systems in that space object. In this situation, State A must treat the State B military crew of that space station as POWs. The challenge now confronting State A is how to transfer these State B POWs back to Earth to deliver them to an appropriate place of ongoing internment. This will necessarily involve transfer to a space object capable of returning to Earth. One may not be immediately available. Reasoning by analogy to the situation of combatants who fall into enemy hands at sea, there is consequently no reason why these POWs might not be held on board a habitable space object as a temporary measure, and only for the time that is absolutely necessary until they can be safely returned to Earth.[34]

When considering what is "necessary" in this context, legal, operational, and humanitarian considerations must be assessed in light of the intensely practical challenges of returning POWs from outer space to Earth. To this point, consider another example where an orbital space station is crewed by military personnel from States A and B. Upon outbreak of an IAC between these two States in the

---

33. *Id.*

34. *Id.*: "[P]ersons may only be held on board a ship as a temporary measure, pending transfer to land. If the ship is a warship, it is especially important that the time a person is held on board is limited to that absolutely necessary." *See also* DoD Law of War Manual, *supra* note 6, § 9.10.4; United Kingdom Ministry of Defence, The Manual of the Law of Armed Conflict ¶ 8.37.1 (2004).

terrestrial environment, crew from State A surrender to their colleagues (now enemy) from State B. Although State B is now under an obligation to return these POWs to Earth for appropriate internment on land, it is not precluded from holding them temporarily aboard the space station while doing so is the safer course of action and until such time as a reasonable opportunity to transfer them back to Earth arises.[35] The transfer back to Earth must be effected humanely and in conditions no less favorable than those under which the astronauts of State B are ordinarily transferred, and might be delayed for medical reasons if the transfer of a wounded or sick POW may endanger their recovery.[36] However, as noted previously, the obligation to remove the POW from an area of probable ongoing combat operations must inform any assessment of the duration of a temporary internment pending evacuation to Earth.

B. Internment of POWs on the Moon or Other Celestial Objects

Article IV of the 1966 Treaty on Principles Governing the Activities of States in the Exploration and Use of Outer Space, Including the Moon and Other Celestial Bodies (Outer Space Treaty) supports the prohibition against interning POWs on the Moon or other celestial bodies. Article IV prohibits "[t]he establishment of military bases, installations and fortifications . . . on celestial bodies." A POW internment facility—which would by definition be an installation of a military nature—would thus also be prohibited.[37] Article IV may not unequivocally prohibit all forms of (non-POW-related) detention on the Moon and other celestial bodies, but it is thus clear that POW internment facilities are prohibited. Additionally, concerning habitable space objects, ongoing internment of POWs on a celestial object (that is, not "land") would also be a clear breach of the POW regime applicable in an IAC in light of Article 22 of the Third Geneva Convention.

C. Conclusions

In the future, there may be long-term established facilities in the form of large habitable space objects, or on the Moon or other celestial objects, that are capable of paralleling the size, scope, and function of POW internment facilities on land on Earth. It is also possible that, in the future, a period of internment in a

---

35. *See, e.g.*, United States, Army Regulation 190-8 on Enemy Prisoners, Retained Personnel, Civilian Internees and Other Detainees, Oct. 1, 1997, 5, ¶ 2-1*b*(2): "[POWs] recovered at sea may be temporarily held on board as operational needs dictate, pending a reasonable opportunity to transfer them to a shore facility, or to another vessel for transfer to a shore facility."

36. Third Geneva Convention, *supra* note 4, arts. 19, 20, 46(2), 47.

37. Outer Space Treaty, *supra* note 2, art. IV(2).

relatively permanent fixed installation adapted for long-term human habitation may be a more humanitarian outcome than immediate space transportation back to Earth. But that is not the current state of the law. As the law presently stands, internment on a habitable space object or a celestial body would be a clear breach of the obligation to intern on land. Such ongoing internment would also be very difficult to reconcile with the general prohibition of inhuman treatment[38] and with the general duty to provide sufficient safeguards as regards health and hygiene.[39] It would also be difficult to reconcile internment in space with the other specific conditions of detention provided for in the Third Geneva Convention. It is to these matters that the chapter now turns.

III. THE CONDITIONS OF DETENTION: THE DIFFICULTY OF COMPLYING WITH CERTAIN REQUIREMENTS IN THE SPACE ENVIRONMENT

A. The Third Geneva Convention (and Additional Protocol I) Requirements and the Practicalities of the Space Environment

In the context of IACs, the prohibition of internment of POWs on habitable space objects and celestial bodies follows from the clear text of Article 22 of the Third Geneva Convention because these premises must be located on land. Additionally, the specific and detailed accommodation, activity, facilities, and hygiene requirements stipulated in the POW regime are in any event predominantly incompatible with ongoing internment in habitable space objects, or on celestial bodies. The same can be said in relation to Article 11(1) of Additional Protocol I.[40] The entire edifice of the POW regime—as is stated in the Department of Defense Law of War Manual—is that these "provisions should be interpreted in light of the principles that underlie POW detention and, in particular, in light of the goal of advancing the humane treatment of POWs."[41] Four issues of note therefore arise.

38. Common Article 3 to the four Geneva Conventions; Third Geneva Convention, *supra* note 4, arts. 13, 130; Additional Protocol I, *supra* note 8, art. 75(1); 1 CUSTOMARY INTERNATIONAL HUMANITARIAN LAW Rules 87, 90 (Jean-Marie Henckaerts & Louise Doswald-Beck eds., 2005) [hereinafter 1 CUSTOMARY IHL].

39. Convention (IV) Relative to the Protection of Civilian Persons in Time of War art. 85(1), Aug. 12, 1949, 6 U.S.T. 3516, 75 U.N.T.S. 287; Protocol Additional to the Geneva Conventions of 12 August 1949, and Relating to the Protection of Victims of Non-international Armed Conflicts art. 5(1)(b), June 8, 1977, 1125 U.N.T.S. 609 1977; 1 CUSTOMARY IHL, *supra* note 38, Rule 121.

40. "The physical or mental health and integrity of persons who are in the power of the adverse Party or who are interned, detained or otherwise deprived of liberty as a result of a situation referred to in Article 1 shall not be endangered by any unjustified act or omission."

41. DoD LAW OF WAR MANUAL, *supra* note 6, § 9.1.2; *see also* § 9.2.4: "Moreover, interpretations of the GPW that provide for humane treatment should be favored over rigid interpretations of the GPW that lead to results that would be detrimental to the welfare of POWs."

First, as noted above, Article 13 of the Third Geneva Convention requires that all POWs be "humanely treated." This obligation is both broad and contextual, but requires the "provision of adequate food and drinking water; provision of adequate clothing; safeguards for health and hygiene; provision of suitable medical care; protection from violence and against the dangers of the armed conflict; entitlement to sleep; and the right to maintain appropriate contacts with the outside world."[42] The space environment, coupled with the technical challenges and expense of space flight, indicates that these would be difficult obligations to fulfill to a level equivalent to their potential and expected fulfillment on land. Indeed, it is difficult to see how the unforgiving and dangerous environment of outer space could be conceived of as other than an "unhealthy area, or where the climate is injurious for them," which obliges the interning power to remove the POWs "as soon as possible to a more favourable climate."[43]

Second, Article 16 of the Third Geneva Convention states that POWs must have access to "the medical attention required by their state of health."[44] As the Law of War Manual observes of this obligation, "POWs suffering from serious disease, or whose condition necessitates special treatment, a surgical operation, or hospital care, *must* be admitted to any military or civilian medical unit where such treatment can be given."[45] It is unlikely that this obligation will be as readily able to be fulfilled in outer space with limited access to medical equipment and personnel.

Third, the "land-contextualized" application of the requirements for natural light, access to items of habitual diet, permitted use of tobacco, access to a canteen, mandated minimum level of hygiene and medical attention, and provision of facilities and equipment for "intellectual, educational, and recreational pursuits, sports and games"[46] would all be difficult to replicate in a habitable space object or on a celestial body. There is no room within the current POW regime for adopting an "outer-space-contextualized" application of these obligations because the regime is absolutely clear that ongoing POW internment facilities must be on land, and thus the only acceptable interpretation of these conditions can be with a land-based facility as the context.

Finally, internment of POWs in outer space would effectively foreclose any possibility that the ICRC could gain regular access to POWs as required during an IAC.[47] It would also make offering the option of parole—as per Article 21 of the Third Geneva Convention—a practical impossibility.

---

42. 2020 GC III COMMENTARY, *supra* note 16, ¶ 1575.

43. Third Geneva Convention, *supra* note 4, art. 22.

44. *See also* Additional Protocol I, *supra* note 8, art. 11(3)–(6).

45. DoD LAW OF WAR MANUAL, *supra* note 6, § 9.14.2.1 (emphasis added).

46. Third Geneva Convention, *supra* note 4, arts. 25–32, 38.

47. *Id.*, art. 126.

B. Conclusions

As with the question of "place" of internment, the detailed treatment requirements fundamental to the POW regime encapsulated in the Third Geneva Convention would be difficult to parallel adequately in outer space. This is especially the case when the Article 22 minimum baseline for the furnishing of these treatment obligations is as available on land.

IV. THE SITUATION OF MILITARY ASTRONAUTS AND SPACECRAFT PERSONNEL

A. The Applicable Law in Relation to Astronauts Generally

To understand the applicable law in relation to astronauts, one must first determine who exactly is an "astronaut," who has "personnel" status, and whether the distinction matters. Article V of the Outer Space Treaty relevantly provides:

> States Parties to the Treaty shall regard astronauts as envoys of mankind in outer space and shall render to them all possible assistance in the event of accident, distress, or emergency landing on the territory of another State Party or on the high seas. When astronauts make such a landing, they shall be safely and promptly returned to the State of registry of their space vehicle.
>
> In carrying on activities in outer space and on celestial bodies, the astronauts of one State Party shall render all possible assistance to the astronauts of other States Parties.

Article VIII of the Outer Space Treaty then refers to "personnel" in space in terms that indicate a distinction from astronauts.

This apparent distinction is *potentially* relevant in the context of the application of the POW regime insofar as non-astronaut military personnel in outer space would clearly be subject to the POW regime without any need to consider the special status of astronauts. However, this conclusion is challenged by two additional provisions of outer space law. The first is from the sparsely ratified 1979 Agreement Governing the Activities of States on the Moon and Other Celestial Bodies, which complicates this distinction by asserting that:

> States Parties shall adopt all practicable measures to safeguard the life and health of *persons on the moon*. For this purpose *they shall regard any person on the moon as an astronaut within the meaning of article V* of the Treaty on Principles Governing the Activities of States in the Exploration and Use of Outer Space, including the Moon and Other Celestial Bodies and as part of the personnel of a spacecraft within the meaning of the Agreement on the

Rescue of Astronauts, the Return of Astronauts and the Return of Objects Launched into Outer Space.[48]

The second relevant—and potentially ameliorating—provision is from the 1967 Agreement on the Rescue of Astronauts, the Return of Astronauts and the Return of Objects Launched into Outer Space (Rescue Agreement), which concerns "personnel of a spacecraft [who] have suffered accident or are experiencing conditions of distress or have made an emergency or unintended landing."[49] The obligations that follow from this status and situation are that:

(1) States must "inform other States and the UN" whenever a relevant State "receives information or discovers that the personnel of a spacecraft have suffered accident or are experiencing conditions of distress or have made an emergency or unintended landing in territory under its jurisdiction or on the high seas or in any other place not under the jurisdiction of any State";[50]
(2) States must "rescue... and render... all necessary assistance" to any "personnel of a spacecraft [who] land in territory under the jurisdiction" of the relevant State;[51]
(3) States must "extend assistance in search and rescue operations... to assure... [the] speedy rescue" of "personnel of a spacecraft [who] have alighted on the high seas or in any other place not under the jurisdiction of any State";[52] and
(4) any such personnel in the power of a relevant State through rescue or landing shall be "safely and promptly returned to representatives of the launching authority" [which, for our current purposes, is perhaps better characterized as the "launching State,"[53] as defined in the Registration Convention].[54]

Of significance, the clear intent of the Rescue Agreement is to ensure that all people in distress in outer space, or who have been rescued, are equally safeguarded and returned—regardless of whether they were an astronaut, a military mission

---

48. Agreement Governing the Activities of States on the Moon and Other Celestial Bodies art. 10(1), Dec. 18, 1979, 1363 U.N.T.S. 3 (emphasis added).

49. Rescue Agreement, *supra* note 3, arts. 1–4.

50. *Id.*, art. 1.

51. *Id.*, art. 2.

52. *Id.*, art. 3.

53. Registration Convention, *supra* note 12, art. 1: "For the purposes of this Convention: (a) The term 'launching State' means: (i) A State which launches or procures the launching of a space object; (ii) A State from whose territory or facility a space object is launched."

54. Rescue Agreement, *supra* note 3, art. 4.

specialist, or a space tourist. Increasingly, commentary has tended to distinguish between "professional" and "highly trained" mission specialists as "astronauts" and "personnel," and other people who are in space for private or non-mission related purposes.[55] This is an ongoing discussion among States and space law specialists. However, for the purposes of this analysis, all military personnel of a belligerent who are involved in military operations in, from, or through space will be either astronauts or personnel of a spacecraft for the purposes of the parallel application of the law of armed conflict and space law. Accordingly, there is no material consequence to astronauts being "envoys of mankind in outer space" in relation to the application of the POW regime; rather, their relevant status when considering the intersection of the POW regime and the Rescue Agreement is as personnel of a spacecraft. This is especially the case when an astronaut for any reason returns to Earth, because at that point they are no longer acting as an envoy "in outer space."

B. Military Astronauts and Personnel in Outer Space as POWs

Assuming that the military personnel of a belligerent State who are in outer space are capable of falling into the hands of the enemy State during an IAC, two situations arise. First, it is possible that these military personnel are captured by or surrender to enemy forces in outer space. This may, to all intents and purposes, look like a rescue—just as there is an obligation to rescue the shipwrecked after engagements at sea.[56] But in this situation, there is arguably no issue of rescue or return as described in the Rescue Agreement beyond the already addressed requirements of the POW regime. This same assessment would apply to enemy military personnel located on the Moon or a celestial body who fall into the enemy's hands, given the correlation of personnel on the Moon with astronauts. The Rescue Agreement generally does not speak to return obligations arisings in situations only in outer space, with no "landing" component. There is an exception for the potential situation of a space object crewed by State A military personnel crashing on the Moon or a celestial body, and then being rescued/captured by military personnel of enemy State B who are already on, or who then land on, the Moon or that celestial object (as a place beyond the jurisdiction of any State).

The second situation is that military personnel who were until recently in space, have landed in the enemy State's territory, or are rescued from a place outside the

---

55. *See, e.g.*, Frans G. von der Dunk, *International Space Law*, in HANDBOOK OF SPACE LAW 80 (2015); Irmgard Marboe, Julia Neumann & Kai-Uwe Schrogl, *The 1968 Agreement on the Rescue of Astronauts, the Return of Astronauts and the Return of Objects Launched into Outer Space*, in 2 COLOGNE COMMENTARY ON SPACE LAW 1, 33–42 (Stephan Hobe, Bernhard Schmidt-Tedd, Kai-Uwe Schrogl & Gérardine Meishan Goh eds., 2013).

56. Second Geneva Convention, *supra* note 26, art.18.

jurisdiction of any State, by that enemy State—which may include, as noted above, where that unanticipated or emergency landing is on the Moon or a celestial object. The options that arise in this situation are the following:

(1) prioritize the Rescue Agreement obligation and return the military space personnel to their "launching State"—which is, in this scenario, also the enemy State; or
(2) prioritize the application of the Third Geneva Convention regime and classify those rescued enemy military space personnel as POWs, and then intern them in an appropriate POW facility on land for the duration of the conflict.

There is, to date, no State practice that speaks to this conundrum. Nor has any State made an explicit statement as to this interpretive challenge. It seems that States will likely prioritize their right to treat the landed/rescued military space personnel as POWs in the same way as rescued military personnel at sea are made POWs. As has been said, the purpose of the POW regime is "to disable the POW and to prevent him or her from further participation in hostilities."[57] It would be contrary to this purpose that a State seeking to degrade its enemy's capabilities by refusing it access to the skills of highly trained military personnel who have come into the power of that State would elevate obligations under the Rescue Agreement to return the personnel of a spacecraft above its rights and obligations in line with the POW regime. This is not to say that the notification obligations that attend the rescuing State under the Rescue Agreement should not be fulfilled. Clearly, the notification obligations can and should be fulfilled, and this is neither contrary to, nor would it undermine, similar obligations in the POW regime.[58]

The likelihood that a belligerent State would return highly trained and specialized military space personnel to its adversary in the midst of an IAC is unlikely. However, it is possible that this situation could be ripe for the use of the parole scheme countenanced in Article 21 of the Third Geneva Convention as a means of achieving the ultimate "return" outcome envisaged in the Rescue Agreement:

> Prisoners of war may be partially or wholly released on parole or promise . . .
> Prisoners of war who are paroled or who have given their promise . . . are bound on their personal honour scrupulously to fulfil, both towards the Power on which they depend and towards the Power which has captured them, the engagements of their paroles or promises. In such cases, the Power on which they depend is bound neither to require nor to accept from them any service incompatible with the parole or promise given.[59]

---

57. DoD Law of War Manual, *supra* note 6, § 9.2.1.

58. *See, e.g.*, Third Geneva Convention, *supra* note 4, art. 122.

59. *Id.*, art. 21.

But, once again, this would likely be understood by States primarily as an option under the law of armed conflict, rather than an obligation under the Rescue Agreement.

V. CONCLUSION

In one respect, assessing the law applicable to POW operations in space is quite simple. This is because there are clear and long-standing rules around the treatment and conditions of internment; the requirement for internment on shore; and the transport of POWs, which should be considered as equally applicable to space as to other physical domains of operations. Furthermore, these rules tend to indicate that the scope for POW operations in space will be quite limited, and in this regard the analogy from POW operations at sea is informative. In other respects, there may be more scope for uncertainty—for example, with deconflicting the competing rights and expectations encompassed by the POW regime with the specific rules around astronauts and the personnel of spacecraft as found in instruments such as the Rescue Agreement. Ultimately, it seems reasonably clear that there is little reason to doubt, as a matter of law, that the regime applicable to POWs in situations of IAC can and does apply in space. The key vulnerability attending any assessment of this subject is the absence of current State practice.

PART TWO

Prisoner of War Protections and Transfers and Release

8

Protecting Prisoners of War in Contemporary Conflicts

DEREK JINKS*

What protection must be accorded prisoners of war (POWs) in international humanitarian law (IHL)? How might this protection scheme shed light on the role of personal status categories in IHL? Without question, the 1949 Geneva Conventions[1] and the 1977 Additional Protocols thereto[2] guarantee POWs several important rights and privileges. It is a mistake, however, to infer from this proposition that the denial of POW status carries significant detrimental consequences for the scope and content of detainee rights. As I have argued elsewhere, careful analysis of the text, structure, and history of the Geneva Conventions demonstrates that the Conventions provide a similarly robust rights regime for all detainees in time of armed conflict.[3]

---

*. A.W. Walker Centennial Chair, University of Texas School of Law.

1. *See* Convention (I) for the Amelioration of the Condition of the Wounded and Sick in the Armed Forces in the Field, Aug. 12, 1949, 6 U.S.T. 3114, 75 U.N.T.S. 31 [hereinafter First Geneva Convention]; Convention (II) for the Amelioration of the Condition of the Wounded, Sick, and Shipwrecked Members of Armed Forces at Sea, Aug. 12, 1949, 6 U.S.T. 3217, 75 U.N.T.S. 85 [hereinafter Second Geneva Convention]; Convention (III) Relative to the Treatment of Prisoners of War, Aug. 12, 1949, 6 U.S.T. 3316, 75 U.N.T.S. 135 [hereinafter Third Geneva Convention]; Convention (IV) Relative to the Protection of Civilian Persons in Time of War, Aug. 12, 1949, 6 U.S.T. 3516, 75 U.N.T.S. 287 [hereinafter Fourth Geneva Convention].

2. *See* Protocol Additional to the Geneva Conventions of 12 August 1949, and Relating to the Protection of Victims of International Armed Conflicts, June 8, 1977, 1125 U.N.T.S. 3 [hereinafter Additional Protocol I]; Protocol Additional to the Geneva Conventions of 12 August 1949, and relating to the Protection of Victims of Non-International Armed Conflicts, June 8, 1977, 1125 U.N.T.S. 609 [hereinafter Additional Protocol II].

3. *See* Derek Jinks, *The Declining Significance of POW Status*, 45 HARVARD INTERNATIONAL LAW JOURNAL 367 (2004).

Irrespective of whether detainees are assigned POW status, IHL accords protections that approximate, in many important respects, the protection accorded POWs.[4] Moreover, several recent developments in humanitarian law and policy suggest that the gap in protection is closing. The trajectory of IHL reflects what I have called an emerging "protective parity" across status categories.[5] The fundamental driver of this protective parity is the idea that some non-derogable floor of fundamentally fair and humane treatment ought to be accorded all persons in all circumstances. Of course, this strong commitment to an intransgressible minimum standard of treatment for detainees has a flattening effect for IHL across conflict types and personal status categories. Indeed, in many ways, the broadly applicable, fundamental guarantees of the Geneva Conventions have overtaken their once-more-fulsome analogs in the protection schemes codified for more narrowly defined status categories, such as POWs.[6]

---

4. This chapter analyzes the protection owed POWs under IHL. The role of international human rights law is not analyzed as such. In some crucial respects explained in Section II, international human rights law informs the interpretation of IHL. And there are good reasons to think that international human rights law confers some meaningful protection on POWs—providing an important supplement to IHL. The applicability of human rights law in time of armed conflict, though, is a matter of some complexity and controversy. The content of IHL is arguably both more detailed and more narrowly tailored to the realities of armed conflict. *See, e.g.*, G.I.A.D. Draper, *Humanitarian Law and Human Rights*, in REFLECTIONS ON LAW AND ARMED CONFLICTS (Michael A. Meyer & Hilaire McCoubrey eds., 1998). In addition, the applicability of human rights law, particularly in international armed conflict, may be limited by "derogability, territorial scope, or 'jurisdiction.'" Gerald L. Neuman, *Humanitarian Law and Counterterrorist Force*, 14 EUROPEAN JOURNAL OF INTERNATIONAL LAW 283, 292 (2003). The chapter does not attempt to resolve these issues, offering only an account of the protection scheme of IHL. I have elsewhere argued that human rights law is broadly applicable, even if only in a qualified way on some issues. *See* Derek Jinks, *International Human Rights Law in Time of Armed Conflict*, in THE OXFORD HANDBOOK ON INTERNATIONAL LAW IN ARMED CONFLICT (Andrew Clapham & Paola Gaeta eds., 2014).

5. *See* Derek Jinks, *Protective Parity and the Laws of War*, 79 NOTRE DAME LAW REVIEW 1493 (2004).

6. The Third Geneva Convention defines the status category, in part, as follows:

Prisoners of war, in the sense of the present Convention, are persons belonging to one of the following categories, who have fallen into the power of the enemy:

(1) Members of the armed forces of a Party to the conflict as well as members of militias or volunteer corps forming part of such armed forces.
(2) Members of other militias and members of other volunteer corps, including those of organized resistance movements, belonging to a Party to the conflict and operating in or outside their own territory, even if this territory is occupied, provided that such militias or volunteer corps, including such organized resistance movements, fulfil the following conditions:
   (a) that of being commanded by a person responsible for his subordinates;
   (b) that of having a fixed distinctive sign recognizable at a distance;
   (c) that of carrying arms openly;

This is not to say, though, that status categories (or conflict types) are wholly irrelevant. The claim is not that residual status categories—such as persons rendered *hors de combat* within the meaning of Common Article 3 of the 1949 Conventions or persons detained in connection with the conflict within the meaning of Article 75 of Additional Protocol I—enjoy *greater* protection than POWs. POWs, after all, are also protected by these fundamental guarantees. Nor is the claim that all detainees in all conflicts are entitled to the same standard of treatment in all respects. Some categories of detainees, including POWs, are entitled to specific protections that exceed the minimum requirements of fundamental fairness and humanity. Although there is a baseline of treatment that must be accorded all detainees, POWs—owing to their circumstances and the larger normative commitments of IHL—enjoy greater protection.

The upshot is that conflict classifications and personal status categories largely no longer matter with respect to fundamental humanitarian guarantees. These considerations continue to matter, however, for several context-specific and status-specific protections. The objective of this chapter is to analyze the protection scheme for POWs. In Section I, I explain the role of status categories in IHL—and how and why the law governing them has changed over time. The fundamental guarantees enshrined in the Conventions are analyzed in Section II. The generally applicable rules requiring fundamentally fair and humane treatment are canvassed in this part. I also analyze several rules specific to POWs reflecting these general principles. The bottom line in Section II is that POWs must be treated in accordance with the fundamental requirements of humanity and fairness—as is the case for all detainees in time of conflict. In Section III, I analyze several POW protections that go beyond these fundamental guarantees. These protections reflect considerations and normative commitments only loosely connected to

---

(d) that of conducting their operations in accordance with the laws and customs of war.

(3) Members of regular armed forces who profess allegiance to a government or an authority not recognized by the Detaining Power.

...

(6) Inhabitants of a non-occupied territory, who on the approach of the enemy spontaneously take up arms to resist the invading forces, without having had time to form themselves into regular armed units, provided they carry arms openly and respect the laws and customs of war.

Third Geneva Convention, *supra* note 1, art. 4A. The Third Geneva Convention also applies to civilians authorized to accompany the armed forces, and crew members of the merchant marine and civil aircraft performing tasks related to the conflict. See Third Geneva Convention, *supra* note 1, art. 4A(4)–(5); INTERNATIONAL COMMITTEE OF THE RED CROSS, COMMENTARY ON THE THIRD GENEVA CONVENTION: CONVENTION (III) RELATIVE TO THE TREATMENT OF PRISONERS OF WAR ¶ 1058 (2020), https://ihl-databases.icrc.org/applic/ihl/ihl.nsf/Comment.xsp?action=openDocument&documentId=1796813618ABDA06C12585850057AB95 [hereinafter 2020 GC III COMMENTARY] ("[P]ersons entitled to prisoner-of-war status on the basis of Article 4A(5) are only those members of the crew whose professional activities are directly linked to the military activities of the armed forces.").

concerns about the inhumanity and barbarity of war. They are grounded, instead, in the idea that POWs are entitled to a special measure of respect, honor, dignity, and fairness because they are members of armed forces sanctioned to fight on behalf of a sovereign State.

I. PERSONAL STATUS CATEGORIES AND IHL

Personal status categories are a crucial regime element in IHL. The overall structure of the regime makes clear how this is so. In the detention context, the conceptual structure of the Geneva Conventions is simple: (1) at certain times (2) certain categories of persons (3) are entitled to a certain standard of treatment. Each structural feature of the regime plays an important role in promoting humanitarian outcomes.

First, IHL has a limited material field of application. That is, the circumstances in which the rules apply are limited. The 1949 Geneva Conventions and the 1977 Additional Protocols thereto include important rules defining when the rules apply. Some rules apply in international armed conflicts (IACs),[7] some apply in instances of belligerent occupation incident to an IAC,[8] and some apply in non-international armed conflicts (NIACs).[9] Second, IHL has a limited, varied, and overlapping personal field of application. The rules are designed to protect persons placed in particularly vulnerable circumstances in time of war. Broadly, two kinds of vulnerabilities are addressed: (1) persons made vulnerable because they have been subjected to the authority of the enemy (for example, detainees or prisoners); and (2) persons made vulnerable because they have been subjected to the lethality of the enemy (for example, targetable persons). The categories of vulnerable persons covered by IHL—commonly referred to as "protected persons"—are carefully defined in IHL. Third, IHL establishes a bundle of guarantees for each category of protected persons. At bottom, these rules require a standard of treatment designed to address the vulnerabilities associated with the relevant material and personal fields of application. The upshot is that contemporary IHL is a specialized regime. It addresses the need for specific rules in the context of organized, intense hostilities because such situations pose a high risk of radically inhumane and unfair treatment. Within this context, specific categories of persons face a particularly high risk of mistreatment—and are likely to be deprived of any other meaningful legal status at the hands of the enemy. Finally, the baseline protections accorded such persons are modest, but important. The idea is that protection accorded persons in armed hostilities must balance the competing

---

7. *See, e.g.,* Third Geneva Convention, *supra* note 1, art. 2; Additional Protocol I, *supra* note 2, art. 1(4).

8. *See, e.g.,* Third Geneva Convention, *supra* note 1, art. 2.

9. *See, e.g., id.,* art. 3; Additional Protocol II, *supra* note 2, art. 1.

imperatives of humanitarianism and human rights, on the one hand, and legitimate military aims, on the other.

Personal status categories in IHL, therefore, describe persons entitled to some specific bundle of protections in a specific context. The contours of the status categories are influenced by a few crucial ideas. First, these categories seek to describe those persons subjected to the authority or lethality of the enemy—and hence placed in a uniquely vulnerable situation requiring special humanitarian protection. Such persons are most likely to be subjected to inhumane treatment because of their actual or perceived affiliation with the "enemy" in time of armed conflict. Second, imposing harmful measures against such persons is not typically crucial to the pursuit of any legitimate military objective. The categories of persons protected are often persons who pose no ongoing threat to the military operations of the enemy. The most prominent examples include persons captured and detained, and civilians not participating in the fight. Third, special considerations might require that some status categories receive protections that go beyond fundamentally humane treatment. Hence, the bundle of protections accorded some categories influences the scope of the status category in these cases.

These structural considerations make clear the kind of work that the concept of POW is designed to do in IHL. Indeed, the predicament of, and protection accorded, POWs nicely illustrate each of the three features of IHL status categories. When captured, members of the opposing armed forces are plainly placed in an extremely vulnerable position. They face heightened risk of various forms of aggravated mistreatment, including torture, cruel and degrading treatment, imprisonment in inhumane conditions, punishment based on a standardless trial, and even summary execution.[10] Moreover, the mistreatment of POWs is largely unrelated to the pursuit of any legitimate military objective. Only persons who have "fallen into the power of the enemy" are classified as POWs.[11] The category, after all, includes only persons who are prisoners—that is, they have been placed *hors de combat*. Any possible military advantage that might result from mistreatment of enemy persons no longer participating in the fight is, on the conventional view, clearly outweighed by the humanitarian costs of that mistreatment. The protection accorded POWs also nicely illustrates the third and final point about status categories—that is, POWs, owing to special considerations, are entitled to something more than the baseline of humane treatment. Recall that POWs are members of armed forces associated with a sovereign State. Context-specific considerations of fairness, honor, and dignity suggest that such persons ought not be punished for their very participation in the fight and that they ought to be treated with the respect and honor befitting their professional military status. As I will discuss more fully in Section III of this chapter, POWs are, therefore, accorded additional protections—including so-called assimilation rights and combatant immunity—which, in turn, suggest that the category of "prisoner of

---

10. *See generally* PRISONERS IN WAR (Sibylle Scheipers ed., 2010).

11. Third Geneva Convention, *supra* note 1, art. 4.

war" be defined in a sufficiently narrow way to align with these special concerns. The critical point is that special characteristics of POWs support their overprotection relative to the baseline required by the principle of humanity. The point is not that they are entitled to fundamentally fair and humane treatment only because of these special considerations.

Before outlining the protection accorded POWs, it is important to note the trajectory of IHL. Doing so will help situate our discussion of POWs in broader debates about the role of status categories in IHL. Prior to the mid-twentieth century, the law of war, in the main, applied only to formally recognized wars between sovereign States.[12] This law protected only narrowly defined classes of "privileged" members of national militaries or, less commonly, "innocent" civilians. Persons falling outside these status categories were formally unprotected.[13]

The POW status category, considered in isolation, reflects the classical approach in many respects. The POW category applies only in an IAC and belligerent occupation incident to such conflict. The POW category is defined in great detail—and it clearly excludes many persons participating in the organized hostilities. As several of the other chapters in this volume make clear, there are important, difficult debates about who qualifies for POW status and who might not. Moreover, POW status seems to turn, in at least some cases, on compliance with reciprocity

---

12. *See, e.g.*, LINDSAY MOIR, LAW OF INTERNATIONAL ARMED CONFLICT (2002); EDWARD KWAKWA, THE INTERNATIONAL LAW OF ARMED CONFLICT: PERSONAL AND MATERIAL FIELDS OF APPLICATION (1992).

13. G.I.A.D. Draper articulates the conventional view in the classical law of war:

Civilians participating in combat ceased to be immune from attack. They might be killed in combat, and, on capture, were liable to be treated as marauders and executed summarily at the discretion of the captor commander. [T]heir very participation, however conducted, was in itself a violation of the law of war, or, alternatively, conduct that put them outside its protection and left them at the mercy of the enemy.

G.I.A.D. Draper, *The Status of Combatants and the Question of Guerrilla Warfare, in* REFLECTIONS ON LAW AND ARMED CONFLICTS, *supra* note 4, at 206, 208; Richard R. Baxter, *The Duties of Combatants and the Conduct of Hostilities (Law of the Hague), in* INTERNATIONAL DIMENSIONS OF HUMANITARIAN LAW 93, 106 (UNESCO ed., 1988) (arguing that unlawful combatants "upon capture were not entitled to be treated either as prisoners of war or as peaceful civilians" and that they "fell outside the protected categories"); *see also* 2 LASSA OPPENHEIM, INTERNATIONAL LAW: A TREATISE 257 (Hersh Lauterpacht ed., 7th ed. 1952) (1905) (arguing that persons qualifying as neither lawful combatants nor innocent civilians were "liable to be treated as war criminals and shot."); J.M. SPAIGHT, WAR RIGHTS ON LAND 37 (1911)("[W]ar law has a short shrift for the non-combatant who violates its principles by taking up arms."); *id.* at 35–72 (outlining the long history of summary treatment accorded unlawful combatants). EMMERICH DE VATTEL, THE LAW OF NATIONS 481 (Luke White trans., 1792)(1758) ("A nation attacked by such sort of [unlawful combatants] is not under any obligation to observe towards them the rules of wars in form.").

constraints—suggesting that denial of POW protection might be contemplated by regime architects as an inducement to compliance.[14]

But much has changed in the law surrounding the definition of POWs. The 1949 Conventions and the later Additional Protocols expanded the material and personal fields of application of IHL. Some rules now apply in the context of NIACs—that is, armed conflicts between States and non-State groups or conflicts between non-State groups. Affiliation with a sovereign party to the armed conflict is no longer a precondition for international legal protection. Status categories have also been broadened. The concept of "civilian" is defined very broadly in the 1949 Conventions—and such persons are accorded a detailed inventory of humanitarian protections similar in most critical respects to those accorded POWs.[15] Most importantly, contemporary IHL includes residual, gap-filling status categories designed to protect all detained persons. These provisions have exceptionally broad material and personal fields of application—and they accord all persons in such circumstances the fundamental guarantees required by the principle of humanity. The provisions include Common Article 3[16] of the 1949 Conventions and the "fundamental guarantees" provisions of Additional Protocols I and II.[17] These changes help illustrate the declining role of status categories with respect to the core mission of IHL. They also clarify with precision the distinctive protections accorded POWs—as well as the fact that those protections are de-linked from more fundamental concerns about the principle of humanity.

II. GENERALLY APPLICABLE PROTECTIONS: THE PRINCIPLE OF HUMANITY

A. Third Geneva Convention Standard of Treatment

The Third Geneva Convention establishes a detailed standard of treatment for POWs. Although POWs may be interned for the duration of the hostilities, their detention is not punitive.[18] Detention is authorized instead only to prevent POWs from contributing to the military action of the party for which they

---

14. The most obvious examples are the preconditions for POW status stipulated in Article 4A(2) and (6). *See* Third Geneva Convention, *supra* note 1, art. 4A(2) (requiring inter alia compliance with the laws and customs of war to qualify for POW status); art. 4A(6) (same).

15. *See* Fourth Geneva Convention, *supra* note 1, art. 4; *see also* Jinks, *supra* note 3.

16. *See, e.g.*, Third Geneva Convention, *supra* note 1, art. 3.

17. *See* Additional Protocol I, *supra* note 2, art. 75; Additional Protocol II, *supra* note 2, arts. 2–6.

18. *See* Third Geneva Convention, *supra* note 1, arts. 21, 118. The non-punitive character of the detention dictates several specific features of the regime governing conditions of confinement. *See* 2020 GC III COMMENTARY, *supra* note NOTEREF _Ref85233717 \h * MERGEFORMAT 6, ¶ 1934, ("The fact that internment has no punitive character informs the regime of internment set out in the subsequent chapters of the Third Convention: living conditions in prisoner-of-war

fought.[19] The scheme, therefore, is designed to afford the detaining State a mechanism for disabling members of the opposing armed forces short of killing or wounding them. In other words, the authority to intern is itself a humanitarian measure—one that provides the detaining State a tactically, operationally, and strategically viable alternative to harsher, more summary measures. "Internment" is authorized, but "close confinement" of POWs is prohibited.[20] Close confinement in this context is defined as "uninterrupted detention in a room, barrack or cell."[21] Mandatory minimum conditions of confinement are prescribed in detail.[22] POWs have a right to release and repatriation at the end of the conflict.

POWs shall in all circumstances be treated humanely and protected against any cruel, inhumane, or degrading treatment.[23] POWs are entitled in all circumstances to be respected for their persons and their honor. They must be protected against "insults and public curiosity."[24] No acts of violence or intimidation may be directed against POWs.[25] Interrogational abuse is also broadly prohibited by the Third Geneva Convention.[26] The Third Geneva Convention includes a detailed inventory of fair trial rights—prescribing as a default that POWs be tried via the same procedure utilized for the armed forces of the detaining State.[27]

---

camps are not like prison settings but offer access, for example, to canteens, sanitary facilities, common or recreation areas and to open air, as required by the Convention."); *see also, e.g.,* Third Geneva Convention, *supra* note 1, arts. 25, 28, 29, 38.

19. *See* 2020 GC III COMMENTARY *supra* note 6, ¶ 1921 ("It is a longstanding custom that Parties to an armed conflict may capture combatants and intern them as prisoners of war to prevent them from returning to the battlefield.").

20. Third Geneva Convention, *supra* note 1, art. 21 (providing that "prisoners of war may not be held in close confinement except where necessary to safeguard their health and then only during the continuation of the circumstances which make such confinement necessary"); *see also* 2020 GC III COMMENTARY, *supra* note 6, ¶ 1923 ("The drafters of the 1949 Geneva Conventions restated that close confinement is acceptable only where it is imposed to safeguard health, but specifically declined to include security measures as another exception.").

21. 2020 GC III COMMENTARY, *supra* note 6, ¶ 1945.

22. Third Geneva Convention, *supra* note 1, arts. 21–48.

23. *Id.*, art. 13.

24. *Id.*, art. 14; *see also* OFFICE OF THE GENERAL COUNSEL, U.S. DEPARTMENT OF DEFENSE, LAW OF WAR MANUAL 549 (rev. ed., Dec. 2016) [hereinafter DoD LAW OF WAR MANUAL] ("[O]rganizing a parade of POWs through the civilian population, thereby exposing them to assault, ridicule, and insults, would be prohibited. Displaying POWs in a humiliating fashion on television or on the internet would be prohibited.")

25. Third Geneva Convention, *supra* note 1, art. 13.

26. *Id.*, art. 17(4) ("No physical or mental torture, nor any other form of coercion, may be inflicted on prisoners of war to secure from them information of any kind whatever."); *id.* ("Prisoners of war who refuse to answer may not be threatened, insulted, or exposed to unpleasant or disadvantageous treatment of any kind.").

27. *Id.*, arts. 99–108.

The Third Geneva Convention also prohibits reprisals against POWs[28] and precludes the use of POWs as slave labor.[29] POWs have the right to communicate with protective agencies.[30] In addition, they may not be prosecuted for their simple participation in the hostilities—that is, they are entitled to "combatant immunity."[31] Moreover, the Third Geneva Convention makes clear that POW rights are inalienable[32] and non-derogable.[33]

All States have now ratified this treaty,[34] and many have incorporated its protections directly into domestic law.[35] Several influential national military

---

28. *Id.*, art. 13.

29. *Id.*, arts. 49–57.

30. *Id.*, arts. 8–11.

31. The 1949 Geneva Conventions do not expressly accord any such privilege. It is nevertheless universally recognized. *See, e.g.*, Waldemar A. Solf & Edward R. Cummings, *A Survey of Penal Sanctions Under Protocol I to the Geneva Conventions of August 12, 1949*, 9 CASE WESTERN RESERVE JOURNAL OF INTERNATIONAL LAW 205, 212 (1977)("[T]hose who are entitled to the juridical status of 'privileged combatant' are immune from criminal prosecution for those warlike acts which do not violate the laws and customs of war but which might otherwise be common crimes under municipal law."); Major Geoffrey S. Corn & Major Michael L. Smidt, *"To Be or Not To Be, That Is the Question": Contemporary Military Operations and the Status of Captured Personnel*, ARMY LAWYER, June 1999, at 14 (arguing that combatants, as privileged belligerents, are entitled to "a blanket of immunity for their pre-capture warlike acts"); United States v. List et al. (The Hostage Case), 11 TRIALS OF WAR CRIMINALS BEFORE THE NUREMBERG MILITARY TRIBUNALS UNDER CONTROL COUNCIL LAW NO. 10, at 759, 1228–29 (1950). Moreover, the privilege may be inferred from several provisions of the Third Geneva Convention. *See* Third Geneva Convention, *supra* note 1, arts. 82, 85, 87–88. Additional Protocol I makes the privilege explicit. See Additional Protocol I, *supra* note 2, art. 43(2) ("Members of the armed forces of a Party to a conflict are combatants, that is to say, they have the right to participate directly in hostilities.").

32. Third Geneva Convention, *supra* note 1, art. 7 (providing that "[p]risoners of war may in no circumstances renounce in part or in entirety the rights secured to them by the present Convention, and by the special agreements referred to in the foregoing Article, if such there be").

33. *Id.*, art. 5 (providing that the Convention "shall apply to the persons referred to in Article 4 from the time they fall into the power of the enemy and until their final release and repatriation").

34. *See States Parties, Convention (III) Relative to the Treatment of Prisoners of War. Geneva, 12 August 1949*, INTERNATIONAL COMMITTEE OF THE RED CROSS, https://ihl-databases.icrc.org/applic/ihl/ihl.nsf/States.xsp?xp_viewStates=XPages_NORMStatesParties&xp_treatySelected=375 (last visited May 14, 2021) (documenting 196 ratifications). *See also* ANNOTATED SUPPLEMENT TO THE COMMANDER'S HANDBOOK ON THE LAW OF NAVAL OPERATIONS 490 n.47 (A.R. Thomas & James C. Duncan eds., 1999)(Vol. 73, U.S. Naval War College International Law Studies) ("[The Third Geneva Convention] is the universally accepted standard for treatment of [POWs]; virtually all nations are parties to it and it is now regarded as reflecting customary law.").

35. *See* INTERNATIONAL COMMITTEE OF THE RED CROSS, INTERNATIONAL HUMANITARIAN LAW, NATIONAL IMPLEMENTATION DATABASE, https://ihl-databases.icrc.org/ (last visited May 14, 2021)(providing excerpts of implementing national legislation from over 50 countries).

manuals direct their armed forces to observe unconditionally the obligations embodied in the Third Geneva Convention.[36] They are now also formally accepted by several international organizations supervising multinational force deployments, including the United Nations[37] and NATO.[38] These rules are accompanied by an elaborate criminal enforcement regime. Under the Third Geneva Convention, for example, the mistreatment of persons entitled to POW status constitutes a "grave breach" of IHL,[39] giving rise to individual criminal liability and so-called universal jurisdiction over perpetrators.[40] The criminalization of violations of POW rules has also been recognized in several important international agreements concerning the scope of international criminal law—including the International Criminal Court[41] and the International Criminal Tribunal for the former Yugoslavia.[42]

---

36. *See, e.g.*, Department of the Army, FM 27-10, The Law of Land Warfare ch. 3 (1956); CHIEF OF THE GENERAL STAFF (CANADA), B-GJ-005-104/FP-021, LAW OF ARMED CONFLICT AT THE OPERATIONAL AND TACTICAL LEVELS (2001); UNITED KINGDOM WAR OFFICE, MANUAL OF MILITARY LAW, PART III: THE LAW OF WAR ON LAND (1958); THE HANDBOOK OF HUMANITARIAN LAW IN ARMED CONFLICTS (Dieter Fleck ed., 1999).

37. *See* United Nations Secretariat, Secretary General's Bulletin, Observance by United Nations Forces of International Humanitarian Law, U.N. Doc. ST/SGB/1999/13 (Aug. 6, 1999), https://digitallibrary.un.org/record/277660?ln=en.

38. As part of the IFOR/SFOR mandate under the Dayton Accords, NATO agreed to enforce the substantive commitments of the parties, including the commitment to observe the 1949 Geneva Conventions. *See* Stabilization Force, Framework Agreement, Annex 1A (authorizing forces to enforce the agreement), Annex 6 (outlining human rights obligations of the parties and enumerating the 1949 Geneva Conventions as part of the applicable law), *available at* http://www.nato.int/sfor/basic/gfap.htm (last visited May 14, 2021). This institutional commitment to the Geneva Conventions is not surprising, given that all NATO States are party to the four 1949 Conventions. Indeed, the only real difficulty regards the applicability of the 1977 Protocols to the Conventions in NATO operations.

39. *See* Third Geneva Convention, *supra* note 1, arts. 129–131.

40. The "grave breach" regime of the Geneva Conventions does not formally confer "universal jurisdiction." Rather, the Conventions require States to prosecute or extradite persons accused of grave breaches. *See* Third Geneva Convention, *supra* note 1, arts. 129–31; *see also* Edward M. Wise, *Aut Dedere aut Judicare: The Duty to Prosecute or Extradite*, *in* 2 INTERNATIONAL CRIMINAL LAW: PROCEDURAL AND ENFORCEMENT MECHANISMS 15 (M. Cherif Bassiouni ed., 2d ed. 1999). These provisions do not purport to confer on States jurisdictional authority they would not otherwise enjoy. Rather, the "prosecute or extradite" obligation is aimed at securing international cooperation in the suppression of serious violations of the Conventions. *Id.* at 17–19.

41. *See* Rome Statute of the International Criminal Court art. 8, July 17, 1998, 2187 U.N.T.S. 90.

42. *See* S.C. Res. 808 (Feb. 22, 1993), U.N. Doc. S/RES/808 *annexed to* The Secretary-General, *Aspects of Establishing an International Tribunal for the Prosecution of Persons Responsible for the Serious Violations of International Humanitarian Law Committed in the Territory of the Former Yugoslavia*, U.N. Doc. S/25704, art. 2 (May 3, 1993), *reprinted in* 32 I.L.M. 1159 (1993).

In summary, POWs are entitled to a detailed, highly legitimated standard of treatment. Much of this scheme aims to ensure that POWs are accorded fundamentally fair and humane treatment for the duration of their war-related captivity. In other words, much of the Third Geneva Convention addresses the horrors often associated with "war victims" that make a specialized IHL necessary in the first place.

B. Fundamental Guarantees Provisions

The Third Geneva Convention scheme outlined above provides substantial humanitarian protection to all POWs. Many of its important protections, though, are also recognized in generally applicable fundamental guarantees provisions of IHL. That is, POWs are guaranteed many of the same legal protections itemized above simply in virtue of their status as a conflict-related detainee. These entitlements flow not from the specific preconditions for POW status, but instead from the fact that they have been made subject to the authority of the enemy in time of armed conflict. This section details these protections—highlighting the significant overlap with the core commitments of the Geneva Conventions. Three clusters of fundamental guarantees are addressed: Common Article 3, the fundamental guarantees provisions of Additional Protocols I and II, and the fair trial rights of the penal repression regime established by the Geneva Conventions. These schemes protect POWs. They supplement the specific provisions of the Third Geneva Convention canvased in the previous section. And, in some respects, the protection described here eclipses that contemplated in the specific provisions of the Third Geneva Convention. The picture that emerges clarifies the role of status categories in IHL. It also helps isolate, with some precision, the protections that follow from POW status proper and why this is so.

1. COMMON ARTICLE 3

The Geneva Conventions also specify fundamental humanitarian protections applicable to *all* persons subject to the authority of a party to the conflict. These principles, first codified in Common Article 3 of the Conventions, govern the treatment of persons no longer taking active part in the hostilities.[43] All such persons are entitled to humane treatment and, in the case of criminal charges, fair trial by "a regularly constituted court, affording all the judicial guarantees which are recognized as indispensable by civilized peoples."[44] The provision obligates States to apply, at a minimum, the following principles in armed conflicts "not of an international character":

---

43. It is important to note that the provision expressly covers persons who take up arms against the State and applies even to persons who do not lay down their arms voluntarily. Plainly, this would include all persons who might qualify for POW status.

44. Third Geneva Convention, *supra* note 1, art. 3(1)(d).

(1) Persons taking no active part in the hostilities, including members of armed forces who have laid down their arms and those placed "hors de combat" by sickness, wounds, detention, or any other cause, shall in all circumstances be treated humanely, without any adverse distinction founded on race, colour, religion or faith, sex, birth or wealth, or any other similar criteria. To this end, the following acts are and shall remain prohibited at any time and in any place whatsoever with respect to the above-mentioned persons:

   (a) violence to life and person, in particular murder of all kinds, mutilation, cruel treatment and torture;
   (b) taking of hostages;
   (c) outrages upon personal dignity, in particular humiliating and degrading treatment;
   (d) the passing of sentences and the carrying out of executions without previous judgment pronounced by a regularly constituted court, affording all the judicial guarantees which are recognized as indispensable by civilized peoples.

(2) The wounded and sick shall be collected and cared for.[45]

Common Article 3, therefore, seemingly necessitates humane treatment and fair trial rights for all persons rendered *hors de combat* in NIACs.

By its terms, though, the provision applies only to armed conflicts "not of an international character."[46] The structure and history of the Conventions, however, make clear that the provision applies in *all armed conflicts*. Utilizing language originally proposed as text for the preamble to the four Conventions, the drafters of the provision sought to invoke the core principles of the treaty that should pierce the veil of sovereignty and apply even in the absence of an IAC. Indeed, the character of Common Article 3 was well understood by the drafters of the Conventions, as evidenced by the ICRC Commentary:

This minimum requirement in the case of a non-international armed conflict, is *a fortiori* applicable in international conflicts. It proclaims the guiding principle common to all four Geneva Conventions, and from it each of them derives the essential provision around which it is built.[47]

The purpose of Common Article 3 was to "ensur[e] respect for the few essential rules of humanity which all civilised nations consider as valid everywhere and under all circumstances and as being above and outside war itself."[48] In short, "[i]t is both legally and morally untenable that the rules contained in Common Article 3,

---

45. *Id.*, art. 3.

46. *Id.*

47. Oscar M. Uhler et al., Commentary to Geneva Convention IV Relative to the Protection of Civilian Persons in Time of War (1958).

48. *Id.* at 44.

which constitute mandatory minimum rules applicable to internal conflicts, in which rules are less developed than in respect of international conflicts, would not be applicable to conflicts of an international character."[49] Indeed, the applicability of Common Article 3 to IACs is now recognized in the jurisprudence of the International Court of Justice,[50] the International Criminal Tribunal for the former Yugoslavia,[51] the International Criminal Tribunal for Rwanda,[52] and the Inter-American Commission for Human Rights.[53] The United States Supreme Court has also endorsed this view.[54] It is U.S. military policy to apply Common Article 3 in all armed conflicts.[55]

Common Article 3 mandates that all persons protected by the provision "shall in all circumstances be treated humanely."[56] In general, this requirement directs the detaining authority to extend the protections of the Conventions' broad "humane treatment" provisions to all persons not taking active part in hostilities. Similar to the protections accorded POWs, Common Article 3 expressly prohibits: (1) "violence to life and person," including torture and cruel treatment; and (2) "outrages upon personal dignity," including humiliating and degrading treatment.[57]

With respect to due process rights, Common Article 3 prohibits "the passing of sentences and the carrying out of executions without previous judgment pronounced by a regularly constituted court, affording all the judicial guarantees which are recognized as indispensable by civilized peoples."[58] This rule prohibits

---

49. Prosecutor v. Delalic et al., Case No. IT-96-21-A, Appeals Chamber Judgment, ¶ 150 (Int'l Crim. Trib. for the former Yugoslavia Feb. 20, 2001).

50. *See* Military and Paramilitary Activities in and against Nicaragua (Nicar. v. U.S.), Judgment, 1986 I.C.J. Rep. 14, ¶ 114 (June 27).

51. *See* Prosecutor v. Tadić, Case No. IT-94-1-I, Decision on Defense Motion for Interlocutory Appeal on Jurisdiction, ¶ 87 (Int'l Crim. Trib. for the former Yugoslavia Oct. 2, 1995).

52. *See* Prosecutor v. Akayesu, Case No. ICTR 96-4-T, Judgment, ¶ 601 (Sept. 2, 1998).

53. *See* Abella v. Argentina, Case 11.137, Inter-Amer. Comm'n H.R., Report No. 55/97, OEA/Ser.L/V/II.98, doc 6 rev. ¶¶ 155–56 (1997).

54. *See* Hamdan v. Rumsfeld, 548 U.S. 557, 630–31 (2006) (explaining that Common Article 3 provides "some minimal protection" in all armed conflicts).

55. *See* DoD Law of War Manual, *supra* note 24, at 511 ("Although Common Article 3 of the 1949 Geneva Conventions provides that it applies '[i]n the case of armed conflict not of an international character occurring in the territory of one of the High Contracting Parties,' Common Article 3 reflects minimum standards for humane treatment that apply to all military operations. Thus, during both international and non-international armed conflict, Common Article 3 reflects a minimum yardstick of humane treatment protections for 'all persons taking no active part in hostilities, including members of armed forces who have laid down their arms and those placed hors de combat by sickness, wounds, detention, or any other cause.'").

56. Third Geneva Convention, *supra* note 1, art. 3.

57. *Id.*

58. *Id.*

punishment without a "previous judgment"—suggesting that a formal adjudication is required.⁵⁹ Moreover, the body pronouncing this judgment must be "regularly constituted," suggesting that it must be established in law and must not be convened especially for the punishment of the adversary.⁶⁰ Furthermore, this body must be a "regularly constituted *court*," (emphasis added) suggesting that there must be adequate safeguards in place to ensure the impartiality, independence, and fairness of the institution issuing the judgment.⁶¹

Moreover, the text of Common Article 3—specifically, the reference to the opinions of "judicial guarantees which are recognized as indispensable by civilized peoples"—establishes an evolving standard that, *by design*, tracks customary international law in this area.⁶² In addition to the developments embodied in Article 75 of Additional Protocol I (referenced above and detailed below), international human rights law has, in the past fifty years, elaborated a detailed body of due process norms that now arguably define the minimum requirements of procedural fairness. Several international human rights treaties establish minimum procedural protections for all individuals deprived of their personal liberty.⁶³ International human rights law also has established an extensive inventory of procedural rights for individuals facing criminal charges. The International Covenant on Civil and Political Rights (ICCPR)⁶⁴ and the European Convention for the Protection of Human Rights and Fundamental Freedoms⁶⁵ also include detailed fair trial provisions. Specifically, Article 14 of the ICCPR recognizes the right to "a fair and public hearing by a competent, independent and impartial tribunal established by law."⁶⁶ This provision enumerates the minimum procedural requirements of a "fair trial," including the right to be presumed innocent,⁶⁷ the

---

59. *Id.*

60. *Id.*

61. *Id.*

62. *See, e.g.*, Moir, *supra* note 12, at 203–08 (arguing that the judicial guarantees of Common Article 3 must be understood in light of international human rights treaties); Jordan Paust, *Judicial Power to Determine the Status and Rights of Persons Detained*, 44 Harvard International Law Journal 503, 511–12 n.27, 514 (2003).

63. *See, e.g.*, Convention Against Torture and Other Cruel, Inhuman or Degrading Treatment or Punishment, Dec. 10, 1984, 1465 U.N.T.S. 85; Convention for the Protection of Human Rights and Fundamental Freedoms arts. 5–7, Nov. 4, 1950, 213 U.N.T.S. 222 [hereinafter ECHR]; International Covenant on Civil and Political Rights arts. 9, 14–15, Dec. 16, 1966, 999 U.N.T.S. 171 [hereinafter ICCPR]; African Charter on Human and Peoples' Rights arts. 3, 6–7, June 27, 1981, 21 I.L.M. 59; American Convention on Human Rights arts. 7–9, Nov. 22, 1969, 1144 U.N.T.S. 123.

64. *See* ICCPR, *supra* note 63, art. 14.

65. *See* ECHR, *supra* note 63, art. 6.

66. ICCPR, *supra* note 63, art. 14, ¶ 1.

67. *See id.*, art. 14, ¶ 2; ECHR, *supra* note 63, art. 6, ¶ 2.

right to be tried without undue delay,[68] the right to prepare a defense,[69] the right to defend oneself in person or through counsel,[70] the right to call and examine witnesses,[71] and the right to protection from retroactive criminal laws.[72] Because these principles are recognized in numerous widely ratified human rights treaties, several unanimously supported international resolutions, and nearly all national constitutions, they arguably reflect the "judicial guarantees which are recognized as indispensable by civilized peoples." In short, Common Article 3 confers due process rights equivalent to, if not greater than, those accorded specifically to POWs in the Third Geneva Convention.

2. ADDITIONAL PROTOCOL I AND II FUNDAMENTAL GUARANTEES

The fundamental guarantees provisions of Additional Protocols I and II also provide substantial humanitarian protection to all conflict-related detainees, including POWs.[73] Similar to the 1949 Conventions, the Additional Protocols have been broadly endorsed in the international community.[74]

---

68. See ICCPR, *supra* note 63, art. 14, ¶ 3(c); ECHR, *supra* note 63, art. 6, ¶ 1.

69. See ICCPR, *supra* note 63, ¶ 3(d); ECHR, *supra* note 63, art. 6, ¶ 3(b).

70. ICCPR, *supra* note 63, art. 14, ¶ 3:

In the determination of any criminal charge against him, everyone shall be entitled to the following minimum guarantees, in full equality . . . (d) To be tried in his presence, and to defend himself in person or through legal assistance of his own choosing; to be informed, if he does not have legal assistance, of this right; and to have legal assistance assigned to him, in any case where the interests of justice so require, and without payment by him in any such case if he does not have sufficient means to pay for it.

ECHR, *supra* note 63, art. 6, ¶ 3(c).

71. See ICCPR, *supra* note 63, art. 14, ¶ 3 ("In the determination of any criminal charge against him, everyone shall be entitled to the following minimum guarantees, in full equality: . . . (e) To examine, or have examined, the witnesses against him and to obtain the attendance and examination of witnesses on his behalf under the same conditions as witnesses against him"); ECHR, *supra* note 63, art. 6, ¶ 3(d).

72. See ICCPR, *supra* note 63, art. 15, ¶ 1 ("No one shall be held guilty of any criminal offence on account of any act or omission which did not constitute a criminal offence, under national or international law, at the time when it was committed.").

73. See Additional Protocol I, *supra* note 2, art. 75; Additional Protocol II, *supra* note 2, arts. 2–6. By its terms, Article 75 of Protocol I applies to all "persons who are in the power of a Party to the conflict and who do not benefit from more favourable treatment under the Conventions or this Protocol."

74. Over 170 States have ratified Additional Protocol I. *See States Parties, Protocol Additional to the Geneva Conventions of 12 August 1949, and Relating to the Protection of Victims of International Armed Conflicts (Protocol I), 8 June 1977*, INTERNATIONAL COMMITTEE OF THE RED CROSS, https://ihl-databases.icrc.org/applic/ihl/ihl.nsf/Treaty.xsp?action=openDocument&documentId=D9E6B6264D7723C3C12563CD002D6CE4 (reporting 174 State parties)

The substance of these rules tracks closely the substance of Common Article 3 of the 1949 Conventions. By its terms, Article 75 requires humane treatment in all circumstances and requires that its protections be provided without any adverse distinction based on "race, colour, sex, language, religion, or belief, political or other opinion, or on any similar category." It also prohibits violence to the life, health, or well-being of all covered persons (including murder, torture, corporal punishment, and all "outrages upon personal dignity"), the taking of hostages, and collective punishments. Moreover, the provision requires several fundamental judicial guarantees in cases of arrest and detention.[75] Article 6 of Additional Protocol II makes this scheme formally applicable in NIACs as defined in that treaty.[76] Second, Article 75 elaborates the "judicial guarantees" clause of Common Article 3 by enumerating several specific fair trial rights.[77] Article 6 of Additional Protocol II does the same for NIACs.[78] Echoing the language of Common Article 3, Article 75 provides:

No sentence may be passed and no penalty may be executed on a person found guilty of a penal offence related to the armed conflict except pursuant to a conviction pronounced by an impartial and regularly constituted court respecting the generally recognized principles of regular judicial procedure. . . .[79]

Unlike Common Article 3, Article 75 of Additional Protocol I specifies many of these principles. They include (1) the provision of "all necessary rights and means of defence" (which almost certainly includes the right to counsel, the right to be present at the hearing, the right to compel process, the right to be informed of pending charges, the right to be accorded sufficient time and resources

---

(last visited May 14, 2021). And 169 States have ratified Additional Protocol II. *See States Parties, Protocol Additional to the Geneva Conventions of 12 August 1949, and Relating to the Protection of Victims of Non-International Armed Conflicts (Protocol II), 8 June 1977,* INTERNATIONAL COMMITTEE OF THE RED CROSS, https://ihl-databases.icrc.org/applic/ihl/ihl.nsf/States.xsp?xp_viewStates=XPages_NORMStatesParties&xp_treatySelected=475 (reporting 169 State parties) (last visited May 14, 2021). Although the United States has not ratified either Protocol, it accepts that the fundamental guarantees provisions reflect customary international law. *See* DOD LAW OF WAR MANUAL, *supra* note 24, at 512 ("Article 75 of [Additional Protocol I] and Relevant [Additional Protocol II] Provisions. Article 75 of [Additional Protocol I] reflects fundamental guarantees for the treatment of persons detained during international armed conflict. Although not a Party to [Additional Protocol I], the United States has stated that the U.S. Government will choose out of a sense of legal obligation to treat the principles set forth in Article 75 as applicable to any individual it detains in an international armed conflict, and expects all other nations to adhere to these principles as well. This statement was intended to contribute to the crystallization of the principles contained in Article 75 as rules of customary international law applicable in international armed conflict.").

75. Additional Protocol I, *supra* note 2, art. 75(3)–(7).

76. Additional Protocol II, *supra* note 2, art. 6.

77. *Id.*, art. 75(3)–(4).

78. *Id.*, art. 6(3).

79. Additional Protocol I, *supra* note 2, art. 75(4).

to formulate a defense, and the right to challenge alleged unfairness in the proceedings on appeal); (2) the right to be presumed innocent; (3) freedom from compelled self-incrimination; (4) the right to be advised of rights and available post-conviction remedies; (5) freedom from ex post facto application of the criminal law; and (6) recognition of the principle of *non bis in idem*.[80]

In summary, Article 75 of Additional Protocol I protects all persons subject to the power of the enemy, including POWs, and provides detailed, substantial protection, particularly to persons detained and persons facing criminal charges.

3. Penal Repression Regime Protections

In addition to the protections discussed above, the Geneva Conventions extend much of the Third Geneva Convention fair trial regime to *all persons facing trial for war crimes*. Indeed, the Conventions prescribe a detailed inventory of procedural rights guarantees for prosecutions brought under their substantive provisions. That is, the Geneva Conventions provide for minimum procedural rights for any person charged with serious violations of their substantive rules irrespective of the detainee's status under the Geneva Conventions. Individuals prosecuted for violations of the Geneva Conventions, regardless of their status as "protected persons," must be provided with "safeguards of proper trial and defence, which shall not be less favourable than" those outlined in Articles 105 and following of the Third Geneva Convention.[81] Article 105 specifically provides for basic fair trial rights, including the right to counsel of the defendant's choice, the right to confer privately with counsel, the right to call witnesses, and the right to an interpreter.[82] These provisions also require, for example, that accused persons be granted the same right of appeal as that accorded members of the armed forces of the detaining power.[83]

III. POW-SPECIFIC PROTECTIONS: BEYOND THE PRINCIPLE OF HUMANITY

The analysis so far makes clear that POWs must be accorded substantial protection in IHL. The most fundamental guarantees of fair and humane treatment, however, apply to POWs not only because they satisfy the stringent requirements for POW status in connection with an IAC, but also simply because they are detained in connection with an armed conflict by an entity that classifies them as the enemy. The material and personal fields of application of IHL have clearly expanded over time—hence,

---

80. *See id.*

81. *See* First Geneva Convention, *supra* note 1, art. 49; Second Geneva Convention, *supra* note 1, art. 50; Third Geneva Convention, *supra* note 1, art. 129; Fourth Geneva Convention, *supra* note 1, art. 146.

82. Third Geneva Convention, *supra* note 1, art. 105.

83. *Id.*, art. 106.

the role of status categories has changed in IHL. There are special vulnerabilities associated with being made a prisoner by enemy forces in time of armed conflict. In the main, the nature and extent of these vulnerabilities do not meaningfully vary depending on whether the detainee was a member of the regular armed forces of the opposing forces, a civilian who took up arms, or a member of a partisan terrorist organization. Status categories have, therefore, become generalized—and the protections accorded them flattened. For this increasingly robust core of humanitarian protection, conflict classification and personal status matter less and less. In addition, the scope and content of these fundamental guarantees have been extended over time in ways that now arguably exceed the level of protection accorded POWs in some contexts. The most obvious example here, documented at some length in Section II, is fair trial rights. The most critical point, though, is that much of the protection accorded POWs is not tightly linked to the specific requirements for POW status. POWs must be protected in most crucial respects not because they are members of the armed forces of a State (or members of a sufficiently regularized, private force belonging to a State), but because they are now-vulnerable human beings who no longer pose an immediate military threat to the detaining power.

Even so, some protections accorded POWs go beyond this humanitarian baseline. These protections reflect considerations and normative commitments only loosely connected to general concerns about inhumanity in time of conflict. They are grounded, instead, in the idea that POWs are entitled to a special measure of respect, honor, dignity, and fairness because they are members of armed forces sanctioned to fight on behalf of a sovereign State. In other words, these protections are tightly linked to the specific requirements for POW status. Many of them are relatively modest in the grand scheme of IHL—and the larger regime of atrocity prevention. In any case, they reflect a discernible moral logic. Understanding these protections helps isolate, with some precision, what is at stake in POW status determinations. They also help illustrate the kind of work that status categories do in contemporary IHL. Two distinct kinds of protections, with distinct rationales, merit discussion.

First, some POW protections are designed to accord members of the opposing armed forces the honor and respect befitting a professional soldier. For example, officer POWs may be bound to salute only detaining power officers of higher rank and the camp commander.[84] POWs must also be permitted to wear "badges of rank and nationality, as well as decorations."[85] More generally, POWs are entitled "to be treated with the regard due their rank."[86] The Third Geneva Convention

---

84. *See id.*, art. 39. Moreover, the ICRC recommends, and some States embrace, the policy that detaining power officers return salute POWs. *See, e.g.*, DoD LAW OF WAR MANUAL, *supra* note 24, at 601 ("Although not required by the [Third Geneva Convention], Detaining Power officers should return salutes as a matter of courtesy.").

85. Third Geneva Convention, *supra* note 1, art. 40.

86. Third Geneva Convention, *supra* note 1, art. 44 ("Officers and prisoners of equivalent status shall be treated with the regard due to their rank and age."); art. 45 ("Prisoners of war other than officers and prisoners of equivalent status shall be treated with the regard due to their rank and age.").

also explicitly prohibits deprivation of rank as a disciplinary or judicial punishment.[87] And POWs may not be assigned to labor that would be looked upon as humiliating for a member of the detaining power's own forces.[88]

The most important example of this kind of protection is the right to "assimilation." The Third Geneva Convention requires that POWs be assimilated along a few axes to the legal regime governing the armed forces of the detaining State. That is, POWs are subject to the same rules and procedures governing the armed forces of their captors.[89] Note that this POW right to trial by regular military court is, in many instances, a legal disability. It is well understood that trial procedures utilized by military courts often fall short of international due process standards, and typically fall short of the rights recognized in the parallel civilian system.[90] In other words, the "same procedures, same courts" right accorded POWs has ambiguous protective consequences. Of course, the criminal procedural rights otherwise recognized in the Geneva Conventions establish a protective floor—no war detainee may be tried by procedures that fall short of the requirements outlined in the fundamental guarantees provisions of the Conventions.[91] The important point is that several specific protections in the Third Geneva Convention entitle POWs to be treated like members of the opposing armed forces—a suite of protections clearly linked to the specific requirements of POW status. But the humanitarian value of these protections is unclear—and the content of POW fair trial rights in this context has arguably been overtaken by the legal developments associated with fundamental guarantees.

---

87. *See* Third Geneva Convention, art. 87 ("No prisoner of war may be deprived of his rank by the Detaining Power, or prevented from wearing his badges.").

88. *See id.*, art. 52.

89. *See id.*, art. 82 ("A prisoner of war shall be subject to the laws, regulations and orders in force in the armed forces of the Detaining Power; the Detaining Power shall be justified in taking judicial or disciplinary measures in respect of any offence committed by a prisoner of war against such laws, regulations or orders."); *id.*, art. 84 ("A prisoner of war shall be tried only by a military court, unless the existing laws of the Detaining Power expressly permit the civil courts to try a member of the armed forces of the Detaining Power in respect of the particular offence alleged to have been committed by the prisoner of war.").

90. *See, e.g.*, 2020 GC III COMMENTARY, *supra* note 6, ¶¶ 3564–77 (cautioning against assimilation for some categories of POWs because of concerns related to the standards of treatment accorded armed forces of detaining power); U.N. Sub-Committee on the Promotion and Protection of Human Rights, *Issue of the Administration of Justice Through Military Tribunals*, U.N. Doc. E/CN.4/Sub.2/2002/4 (July 9, 2002) (prepared by Louis Joinet) (summarizing poor human rights record of military courts).

91. The Third Geneva Convention also requires that the procedures used to try POWs satisfy the minimum requirements of Chapter III of the Third Geneva Convention. These include the important trial rights established in Article 105. These protections, though, fall well short of what is otherwise required by the fundamental guarantees provisions of the Conventions and their Protocols. *See* Third Geneva Convention, *supra* note 1, arts. 82, 84, 105.

Second, some protections are designed to guard against mistreatment of POWs for their loyalty, obedience, and allegiance to the State for which they fight. For example, POWs cannot be compelled to accept a parole agreement forbidden by the laws and regulations of the party to which they belong.[92] POWs may not be punished for escaping captivity, if recaptured.[93] More generally, POWs may not be compelled to take direct part in war efforts against the State of which they are nationals.[94] If POWs face judicial punishment following criminal conviction, the sentencing authority must take into account that they owe allegiance to another sovereign and their predicament is due to circumstances beyond their control.[95]

The most important example of this kind of protection is "combatant immunity."[96] As discussed in Section II, POWs may not be punished for their simple participation in the fight.[97] Although POWs are entitled to engage in combat, they

---

92. *See id.*, art. 21.

93. *See id.*, art. 91 ("Prisoners of war who have made good their escape in the sense of this Article and who are recaptured, shall not be liable to any punishment in respect of their previous escape."); 2020 GC III COMMENTARY, *supra* note 6, ¶ 3780 ("[A]ttempts to escape may be viewed as a demonstration of patriotism and of the most honourable intentions, and not as a crime. According to this precept, prisoners of war have a right, a moral duty, and sometimes, under the law of the Power on which they depend, even a legal obligation to escape").

94. *See* Regulations Respecting the Laws and Customs of War on Land, annexed to Convention No. IV Respecting the Laws and Customs of War on Land, Oct. 18, 1907, 36 Stat. 2227, T.S. No. 539, art. 23 ("A belligerent is likewise forbidden to compel the nationals of the hostile party to take part in the operations of war directed against their own country, even if they were in the belligerent's service before the commencement of the war."); DoD LAW OF WAR MANUAL, *supra* note 24, at 334 ("During international armed conflict, it is prohibited to compel the nationals of the hostile party to take part in the operations of war directed against their own country, even if they were in the belligerent's service before the commencement of the war. Underlying this prohibition is the principle that States must not compel foreign nationals to commit treason or otherwise to violate their allegiance to their country.").

95. *See* Third Geneva Convention, *supra* note 1, art. 87.

96. In many respects, combatant immunity straddles the two kinds of protections analyzed in Section III. In one sense, the protection reflects the sense that it would be unfair to punish POWs for their simple participation in the conflict on behalf of, and at the behest of, a sovereign party to which they belong. Hence, it provides a good example of the second kind of special POW rule. On the other hand, the immunity might be thought to flow from the more general commitment to assimilation. The otherwise lawful, warlike acts of the armed forces of the detaining power are not criminalized—therefore, assimilation would preclude prosecuting POWs for the same acts. *See, e.g.*, Geoffrey S. Corn, *Thinking the Unthinkable: Has the Time Come to Offer Combatant Immunity to Non-State Actors?*, 22 STANFORD LAW & POLICY REVIEW 253, 264 (2011) (implying that Article 82 of the Third Geneva Convention provides a legal basis for combatant immunity). Hence, we might conclude that combatant immunity is a good example of the first kind of special POW protection—because it relates to the POW's right to be accorded the respect and honor due a professional warrior. In my view, the immunity is best classified as suggested in the main text above because it must often be understood as an excusing condition—most notably, where the POW fights on behalf of a party acting in violation of the *jus ad bellum*.

97. *See supra* note 96 (explaining the legal basis for "combatant immunity").

must comply with IHL.[98] Accordingly, POWs may be prosecuted for pre-capture offenses if their actions (1) rise to the level of a "war crime;"[99] or (2) are unrelated to the state of hostilities (that is, are common crimes).[100] Moreover, combatant immunity does not preclude prosecution for any internationally recognized offense. For example, POWs could be prosecuted for "crimes against humanity"[101] or acts of terrorism in the context of an armed conflict.[102] The important point, though, is that combatant immunity is a special POW protection that is tightly linked to the prerequisites for POW status. Its rationale is delinked from more fundamental appeals to the principle of humanity.

* * * *

IHL accords substantial legal protection to POWs. Many of these protections closely track the increasingly robust fundamental guarantees accorded all conflict-related detainees. Some POW protections, though, reflect a different protective

---

98. For example, McDougal has stated that:

> [A]cts committed in war by enemy civilians and members of armed forces may be punished as crimes under a belligerent's municipal law only to the extent that such acts are violative of the international law on the conduct of hostilities. Clearly the rules of warfare would be pointless if every single act of war may by unilateral municipal fiat be made a common crime and every prisoner of war executed as a murderer. International law delineates the outer limits of the liability of supposed war criminals; and conformity with that law affords a complete defense for the violent acts charged.

MYRES S. McDOUGAL & FLORENTINO P. FELICIANO, THE INTERNATIONAL LAW OF WAR: TRANSNATIONAL COERCION AND WORLD PUBLIC ORDER 712 (1994) (citations omitted). *See also* Annotated Supplement to the Commander's Handbook, *supra* note 34, at 490 n.47 ("The [Third Geneva Convention's] underlying philosophy is that POWs should not be punished merely for having engaged in armed conflict."); *id.* at 492 ("Prisoners of war may not be punished for hostile acts directed against opposing forces prior to capture, unless those acts constituted violations of the law of armed conflict.")

99. Even if convicted for pre-capture offenses, enemy combatants retain the benefits of the POW regime of the Third Geneva Convention according to Article 85 of that treaty: "Prisoners of war prosecuted under the laws of the Detaining Power for acts committed prior to capture shall retain, even if convicted, the benefits of the present Convention." Third Geneva Convention, *supra* note 1, art. 85.

100. *See, e.g.*, United States v. Noriega, 746 F. Supp. 1506, 1526 (S.D. Fla. 1990), *aff'd*, 117 F.3d 1206 (11th Cir. 1997), *cert. denied*, 523 U.S. 1060 (1998) (prosecuting prisoner of war for drug trafficking).

101. *See* 2020 GC III COMMENTARY, *supra* note 6, at ¶¶ 3620–46 (Commentary to Article 85 identifies "crimes against humanity" as crime that pierces combatant immunity).

102. *See, e.g.*, Hans-Peter Gasser, *Acts of Terror, "Terrorism," and International Humanitarian Law*, 84 INTERNATIONAL REVIEW OF THE RED CROSS 547 (2002)(cataloging various war crimes provisions implicated by acts of terrorism).

logic. Indeed, POWs are overprotected with respect to the humanitarian baseline because of special considerations of fairness, honor, and respect tightly linked to the specific requirements for POW status. The analysis in this chapter provides (1) a detailed catalog and assessment of the protections accorded POWs; (2) an account of the role of personal status categories in contemporary IHL; and (3) a qualified normative defense of special protections accorded to POWs.

Military Assimilation and the 1949 Third Geneva Convention on Prisoners of War

SEAN WATTS* ■

I. INTRODUCTION

Nearly seventy-five years after its adoption, the 1949 Third Geneva Convention Relative to the Treatment of Prisoners of War remains one of the most significant regulatory achievements of the law of war.[1] It is a signal installment of the long-running Geneva legal regime dedicated to the protection of victims of war.[2] As a

---

*. Professor of Law and Co-Director, United States Military Academy at West Point, Department of Law & Lieber Institute for Law and Warfare; Visiting Professor, Reading University, United Kingdom. I am very grateful to Dustin Lewis, Research Director, Harvard Law School Program on International Law and Armed Conflict, for a helpful research consultation.

1. Convention (III) Relative to the Treatment of Prisoners of War, Aug. 12, 1949, 6 U.S.T. 3316, 75 U.N.T.S. 135 [hereinafter Third Geneva Convention]. International law regulates force and armed conflict in at least two respects. The so-called *jus ad bellum* regulates States' resort to force in their international relations. The *jus in bello* regulates the conduct of hostilities during armed conflict. The Third Geneva Convention falls squarely in the latter category of regulation. Although, as adopted, the articles of the Convention do not consistently use numbered subparagraphs, this chapter will use such numbering to clarify citations and assist readers who wish to consult the Convention.

2. The *jus in bello*, also known as the law of war, the law of armed conflict, or international humanitarian law, can be organized into two genres or traditions. A Geneva tradition regulates the treatment of victims of war and has included treaties dating to 1864, 1906, 1929, and 1949. A Hague tradition regulates the conduct of hostilities, including especially targeting operations. *See, e.g.*, LESLIE C. GREEN, THE CONTEMPORARY LAW OF ARMED CONFLICT 31 (2d ed. 2000). Though the treaties adopted in neither Geneva nor The Hague conform perfectly to this subject matter bifurcation, the traditions remain a useful way to organize the law of war. *See* GARY D.

regulation of conduct in war, perhaps only the First Geneva Convention for the Amelioration of the Condition of the Wounded and Sick rivals the Third Geneva Convention in terms of recognition.[3] It is not only universally ratified or acceded to by the community of States; the Third Convention is also deeply integrated into the military legal doctrine and training programs of its States Parties' armed forces.[4]

At 143 articles, however, the Third Geneva Convention is also an imposing and difficult instrument. Only the Fourth Geneva Convention Relative to the Protection of Civilian Persons,[5] at 158 articles, exceeds it in length. It is not surprising that efforts to distill the Third Convention into a digestible form often involve substantial simplifications. For instance, U.S. military doctrine has long reduced prisoner of war treatment obligations at points of capture to "Five Ss," including orders to "search, segregate, silence, speed, and safeguard."[6] Other sources

---

SOLIS, THE LAW OF ARMED CONFLICT: INTERNATIONAL HUMANITARIAN LAW IN WAR 89 (2d ed. 2016).

3. Convention (I) for the Amelioration of the Condition of the Wounded and Sick in the Armed Forces in the Field, Aug. 12, 1949, 6 U.S.T. 3114, 75 U.N.T.S. 31.

4. *See, e.g.*, UNITED KINGDOM MINISTRY OF DEFENCE, JOINT DOCTRINE PUBLICATION 1-10, CAPTURED PERSONS (4th ed., Sept. 2020) (featuring Third Geneva Convention treatment obligations throughout); CHIEF OF DEFENCE STAFF (CANADA), B-GJ-005-110/FP-020, PRISONER OF WAR HANDLING DETAINEES AND INTERROGATION & TACTICAL QUESTIONING IN INTERNATIONAL OPERATIONS (2004); United States, Army Regulation 190-8 on Enemy Prisoners of War, Retained Personnel, Civilian Internees and Other Detainees, Oct. 1, 1997 (integrating Third Geneva Convention obligations into U.S. military detention doctrine).

5. Convention (IV) Relative to the Protection of Civilian Persons in Time of War, Aug. 12, 1949, 6 U.S.T. 3516, 75 U.N.T.S. 287.

6. DEPARTMENT OF THE ARMY, FM 71-1, TANK AND MECHANIZED INFANTRY COMPANY TEAM 7-25 (Jan. 26, 1998). Military detention doctrine that followed U.S. signature but preceded U.S. ratification of the 1949 Third Geneva Convention also sought to simplify treatment obligations. For instance, a U.S. Army publication identified five principles for handling POWs, including search, speed of evacuation, segregation, method of handling, and skill in interrogation. DEPARTMENT OF THE ARMY, FM 19-40, HANDLING PRISONERS OF WAR 19–20 (1952). More detailed instructions directed units detailed to escort POWs:

(1) Prevent escapes. (2) Maintain segregation at all times. (3) Prevent prisoners from discarding or destroying any insignia or documents not taken, or overlooked by the capturing unit, to include collection by rear guards of any documents dropped by prisoners. (4) Prevent anyone, other than authorized interrogators, from talking to prisoners. (5) Prevent anyone from giving prisoners food, drink, or cigarettes prior to interrogation in so far as such act does not violate any requirement concerning the treatment of prisoners of war. (6) Enforce silence among prisoners at all times. (7) Deliver prisoners to the division or equivalent collecting point as soon as possible.

Id. at 27–28.

find identifying principles associated with the Third Convention, as opposed to belaboring specific rules, a useful approach to understanding it.[7]

But notoriety and reduction have also given rise to myth and mischaracterization. Alongside the myth that prisoners of war must be paid in Swiss francs,[8] military assimilation—the notion that, for overarching purposes of treatment, POWs are effectively integrated into the armed forces of a detaining power—is a prominent mischaracterization of the Third Geneva Convention. Although billed by respected sources as a central or general principle of POW treatment, military assimilation features neither universally nor uniformly in the Third Geneva Convention.[9] Instead, text and records of the debates that produced the Third Geneva Convention paint military assimilation only as an occasional regulatory technique used to secure compromise rather than as a wider organizing formula or overarching principle of the Convention. Assimilation of detaining-power military treatment standards to POWs proved a convenient approach to identify and secure agreement on select conditions of treatment without articulating specific conduct or absolute standards of treatment.

It is certainly true that several articles of the Third Geneva Convention resort to military assimilation. It is also true that military assimilation was not an innovation of the Convention. Long-standing customs regulating land warfare, as

---

7. *See, e.g.*, JONATHAN CROWE & KYLIE WESTON-SCHEUBER, PRINCIPLES OF INTERNATIONAL HUMANITARIAN LAW 101–02 (2013) (identifying "a number of principles governing the treatment of prisoners of war"). Crowe and Weston-Scheuber include, among POW principles, "humane treatment," "respect for persons and their honour," "equal treatment," and a prohibition on punishment for taking part in combat. *Id.* at 102.

8. *See, e.g.*, Liliane Stadler, *The Transfer of Soviet Prisoners of War from Afghanistan to Switzerland, 1982–1984* 4 (Woodrow Wilson International Center for Scholars, Working Paper No. 94, Dec. 2020) (recounting a Soviet soldier's demand to be paid 700 Swiss francs in cash). The Third Geneva Convention does not require that POWs receive Swiss francs as payment. Rather, Article 60 of the Convention requires a detaining power to provide monthly advances of pay in its own currency. Third Geneva Convention, *supra* note 1, art. 60. The article's reference to Swiss francs merely serves as a basis for conversion of amounts owed to five categories of POW by military rank into the detaining power's currency. The requirement that advances of pay be made in the detaining power's currency accords with the expectation that POWs will spend the currency while interned to "improve their lot during captivity." COMMENTARY TO GENEVA CONVENTION III RELATIVE TO THE TREATMENT OF PRISONERS OF WAR 305 (Jean Pictet ed., 1960) [hereinafter 1960 GC III COMMENTARY].

9. INTERNATIONAL COMMITTEE OF THE RED CROSS, COMMENTARY ON THE THIRD GENEVA CONVENTION: CONVENTION (III) RELATIVE TO THE TREATMENT OF PRISONERS OF WAR ¶ 30 (2020), https://ihl-databases.icrc.org/applic/ihl/ihl.nsf/Comment.xsp?action=openDocument&documentId=1B9A4ABF10E7EAD2C1258585004E7F19 [hereinafter 2020 GC III COMMENTARY] (identifying a principle of assimilation in the regulation of POW treatment); MARCO SASSÒLI, INTERNATIONAL HUMANITARIAN LAW 264 (2019). Professor Sassòli summarizes POW protection as "a combination between the obligation to offer them the same conditions given to members of the armed forces of the Detaining Power and minimum guarantees defined in Convention III." *Id.* He later expressly identifies assimilation as a principle of POW treatment that operates in conjunction with specified minimums. *Id.* at 265, 267.

well as preceding treaties, had resorted to military assimilation to regulate treatment of POWs with respect to quarters, rations, and clothing. Yet military assimilation is not a predominant or pervasive feature of the protections afforded to POWs under the Third Geneva Convention or current customary international law.[10] The Convention resorts to assimilation selectively and, in some cases, it even rejects or repeals resorts to assimilation by preceding law of war treaties. By the time of the 1949 diplomatic conference that produced the Convention, repeated experience with wartime internment revealed that military assimilation was in some cases detrimental to POW health. Experience often showed that independent or enumerated standards or even assimilation of civilian standards of treatment better protected POWs or were less susceptible to manipulation. Thus, while military assimilation persists as a treatment standard in the Third Geneva Convention, it features only selectively and robustly so only with respect to penal measures.

A correct understanding of how the Third Geneva Convention features military assimilation is not only important to rigorous and faithful application of the Convention's carefully codified code of treatment. It is also an essential bulwark against unfounded and unsanctioned restraints on States' internment of enemy prisoners in armed conflict. Assimilation has, of late, been the basis for extraordinarily broad claims concerning obligations of treatment toward POWs. A proper conception of the Third Geneva Convention guards against such overreach, reserving resort to military assimilation to the more rigorous and legitimate amendment procedures employed by States Parties under the law of treaties.[11]

---

10. Courts and commentators often regard the four 1949 Geneva Conventions as reflective of customary international law. Ethiopia-Eritrea Claims Commission, Partial Award, Prisoners of War, Ethiopia's Claim 4, ¶¶ 30–32, Jul. 1, 2003 [hereinafter Ethiopia Claim Partial Award]; Ethiopia-Eritrea Claims Commission, Partial Award, Prisoners of War, Eritrea's Claim 4, ¶¶ 39–41, Jul. 1, 2003; Theodor Meron, *The Geneva Conventions as Customary Law*, 81 AMERICAN JOURNAL OF INTERNATIONAL LAW 348 (1987). Perhaps more importantly than the views of courts and commentators, select States themselves have expressed this view. *See, e.g.*, Ethiopia Claim Partial Award, *supra*, ¶ 31 (indicating that the filings of the governments of both Ethiopia and Eritrea to the Claims Commission viewed the 1949 Third Geneva Convention as reflective of customary international law). These views would likely equate the extent to which the Third Geneva Convention resorts and does not resort to military assimilation with customary international law.

11. Vienna Convention on the Law of Treaties, May 23, 1969, 1155 U.N.T.S. 331 [hereinafter Vienna Convention]. The Vienna Convention includes a widely ratified collection of default rules and procedures for negotiation, formation, adoption, ratification, amendment, suspension, and termination of treaties. Many treaties, however, include their own measures for amendment. *See, e.g.*, Rome Statute of the International Criminal Court art. 121(1), July 17, 1998, 2187 U.N.T.S. 90. The 1949 Geneva Conventions include no such general amendment provisions. Historically, diplomatic conferences have been convened to adopt either replacement conventions or supplemental protocols that States may ratify, accede to, or reject at their discretion. The most recent major supplement to the 1949 Conventions was proposed at a United Nations-sponsored conference in Tehran in 1969. *See* International Conference on Human Rights, Teheran, Iran, 22 April to 13 May 1968, Resolution XXIII, *Human Rights in*

II. MILITARY ASSIMILATION IN HISTORICAL PRACTICE

As with so much of the law of war, international regulation of POW treatment has been both reactive and iterative.[12] Perhaps more than any subject of the law of war, POW rules have been systematically revisited, refined, and adopted by States.[13] By the early twentieth century, a sort of trial-and-error approach to developing POW treatment standards emerged at the international legal conferences that produced law of war treaties. Assimilation of treatment standards that already applied to States' own armed forces proved a convenient technique to record and loosely express treatment obligations for captured enemy forces. As a historical matter, military assimilation evolved from literal enlistment to general equivalence of treatment standards and finally to selective incorporation of military treatment standards. Early assimilative approaches drew exclusively from military classes of the detaining power. Later instruments, however, selectively incorporated conditions and treatment applicable to the civilian populations of captors.

A. Early Instruments and Custom

Absorption—the practice of forced enlistment of POWs into armed forces—was perhaps the earliest and most severe form of military assimilation. Describing ancient Asian practices, Professor Levie noted "[a]bsorption into one's own army, enslavement, or ransom were the

---

Armed Conflicts, Final Act of the International Conference on Human Rights, pmbl., ¶ 2, UN Doc. A/ CONF.32/41 (May 12, 1968). States supplemented the 1949 Conventions further in 2005 respecting a new protective emblem. Protocol Additional to the Geneva Conventions of 12 August 1949, and Relating to the Adoption of an Additional Distinctive Emblem, Dec. 8, 2005, 2404 U.N.T.S. 261.

12. *See* Gerald I.A.D. Draper, *The Historical Background and General Principles of the Geneva Conventions of 1949, reprinted in* REFLECTIONS ON LAW AND ARMED CONFLICTS: THE SELECTED WORKS ON THE LAWS OF WAR BY THE LATE PROFESSOR COLONEL G.I.A.D. DRAPER, OBE 54 (Michael A. Meyer & Hilaire McCoubrey eds., 1998)(relating law of war reactions to major events in warfare).

13. Multilateral treaties that have regulated POW status or treatment include Protocol Additional to the Geneva Conventions of August 12, 1949, and Relating to the Protection of Victims of International Armed Conflicts, June 8, 1977, 1125 U.N.T.S. 3 [hereinafter Additional Protocol I]; Third Geneva Convention, *supra* note 1; Convention Relative to the Treatment of Prisoners of War, July 27, 1929, 47 Stat. 2021, 118 L.N.T.S. 343 [hereinafter 1929 Geneva Convention]; Convention No. IV Respecting the Laws and Customs of War on Land, Oct. 18, 1907, 36 Stat. 2227, T.S. No. 539; Regulations Respecting the Laws and Customs of War on Land, annexed to Convention No. IV Respecting the Laws and Customs of War on Land, Oct. 18, 1907, 36 Stat. 2227, T.S. No. 539 [hereinafter 1907 Hague Regulations]; Convention No. II with Respect to the Laws and Customs of War on Land, July 29, 1899, 32 Stat. 1803, T.S. No. 403 and its annex, Regulations concerning the Laws and Customs of War on Land [hereinafter 1899 Hague Regulations].

alternatives."[14] Absorption later yielded to detention for ransom and, later still, internment under conditions of marginally improved treatment followed by unconditional repatriation.[15] Nonetheless, researchers report difficulty identifying standards of treatment owed between belligerents prior to the last quarter of the eighteenth century.[16] Lack of expressed or agreed-on standards in that period is likely attributable to the expectation that prisoners' home States or States of origin would be primarily responsible for their maintenance.[17] The ready availability of existing or previously acquired military rations and uniforms often made supporting prisoners with such supplies an efficient option—in theory, that is.

In practice, however, this system of support proved inadequate. Detaining powers often prevented prisoners' States of origin from delivering humanitarian goods or from purchasing supplies for their POWs from the local economy. Early in the American Revolutionary War, General George Washington informed the Continental Congress that European and British powers confined POWs in public jails and on prison ships where supplies could not reach them.[18] He also noted the refusal of British authorities to permit American representatives to purchase and deliver supplies for their interned comrades.[19] In hopes of reciprocally improved treatment for its own forces held prisoner, and as an especially early resort to military assimilation, the American Continental Congress legislated a standard for prisoner rations based on rations provided to American forces.[20] Reports indicate

---

14. HOWARD S. LEVIE, PRISONERS OF WAR IN INTERNATIONAL ARMED CONFLICT 1, 4 (1977) (Vol. 59, U.S. Naval War College International Law Studies) [hereinafter LEVIE, PRISONERS OF WAR]. POWs were perhaps more frequently made slaves, a practice banned by one of the earliest recorded Western European regulations of warfare. Decree of the Third Lateran Council, 1139 *in* HOWARD S. LEVIE, DOCUMENTS ON PRISONERS OF WAR 4 (1979)(Vol. 60, U.S. Naval War College International Law Studies) [hereinafter LEVIE, DOCUMENTS]. Important to an accurate conception of how law regulated conflict in that period, the Decree only protected "prisoners of war of the Catholic faith." *Id.*

15. *See* RÉMY AMBÜHL, PRISONERS OF WAR IN THE HUNDRED YEARS WAR: RANSOM CULTURE IN THE LATE MIDDLE AGES 1 (2015) (describing POW fate as "intimately connected" with ransom during the Middle Ages); MORRIS GREENSPAN, THE MODERN LAW OF LAND WARFARE 95 (1959) (describing "protective custody" as the general principle of treatment of POWs since the eighteenth century).

16. WILLIAM FLORY, PRISONERS OF WAR: A STUDY IN THE DEVELOPMENT OF INTERNATIONAL LAW 18 (1942). The practice of ransoming POWs began to fall into disfavor by the seventeenth century, though sporadic practice persisted long after. *See, e.g.*, Treaty of Peace between Spain and the Netherlands, Jan. 30, 1648 *in* LEVIE, DOCUMENTS, *supra* note 14, at 5.

17. FLORY, *supra* note 16, at 53–54 (describing varied treatment and maintenance provided to American, Dutch, and French prisoners held by British forces during the American Revolution).

18. *Id.* at 55 (citing 4 JOURNALS OF CONGRESS 361–62 (May 11, 1776)).

19. FLORY, *supra* note 16, at 55.

20. *Id.* at 54 (citing 3 JOURNALS OF CONGRESS 4000 (Dec. 2, 1775)).

that the military assimilation standard gradually developed into a customary practice with respect to clothing and lodging, as well as food.[21]

From custom, military assimilation soon matured into convention. It made an early codified international appearance in the 1785 Treaty of Amity between the United States and Prussia. A provision of the Treaty addressing POWs pledged that:

> common men be disposed in cantonments open and extensive enough for air and exercise, and lodged in barracks as roomy and good as are provided by the party in whose power they are for their own troops; that the officers shall also be daily furnished by the party in whose power they are, with as many rations, and of the same articles and quality as are allowed by them . . . to officers of equal rank in their own army.[22]

A later 1828 renewal of the Treaty of Amity, which included the prior provisions on POWs, applied as recently as relations between the United States and Germany during the First World War.[23] The Treaty of Amity also advanced standards for POW treatment by foreswearing the practice of imprisonment and resort to irons or shackles.[24] Permitting POWs to move about camps unshackled reinforced their military and honorable character. In this respect, the Treaty of Amity likened them more to their captor military counterparts rather than to civilian convicts.

Despite early codification, military assimilation in this period did not extend to all matters that it might have. The extent to which POWs were subject to courts of the detaining power did not result from military assimilation in any significant respect. For instance, Flory reports that British and American law, dating to the middle eighteenth century, subjected POWs fully to the civilian courts of the

---

21. FLORY, *supra* note 16, at 54 (providing, however, no specific citations to authority or examples).

22. Treaty of Amity and Commerce Between His Majesty the King of Prussia and the United States of America, Sept. 10, 1785, 8 U.S. Stat. 84 [hereinafter Treaty of Amity]. Prussia and the United States renewed this treaty in 1799 and again in 1828. As late as 1902, German military legal doctrine referred to the Treaty of Amity favorably. GERMAN GENERAL STAFF, KRIEGSBRAUCH IM LANDKRIEGE 89 (J.H. Morgan trans., McBride, Nast & Co. 1915) (1902).

23. FLORY, *supra* note 16, at 48 n.59 (citing UNITED STATES, STATE DEPARTMENT, FOREIGN RELATIONS, SUPP II 51–53, 55, 57–59 (1918)). A bilateral supplemental agreement on POWs between the United States and Germany replaced the former treaties with respect to wartime detention matters in 1918. Agreement Between the United States of America and Germany Concerning Prisoners of War, Sanitary Personnel, and Civilians, 11 Nov. 1918, UNITED STATES, STATE DEPARTMENT, FOREIGN RELATIONS SUPP. II, 103 (1918) *reproduced in* LEVIE, DOCUMENTS, *supra* note 14, at 115–57.

24. Treaty of Amity, *supra* note 22, art. XXIV.

detaining power for criminal acts rather than to specialized military courts.[25] The basis for this grant of jurisdiction appears to have been not jurisdictional schemes applicable to the armed forces of the detaining power but rather the fact of governmental control of prisoners and the "general jurisdiction" of these courts.

In the mid-to-late nineteenth century, like many customs and usages of war, military assimilation received renewed scholarly and political attention. Early in the American Civil War, Union Army regulations prescribed that POWs should "receive for subsistence one ration each, without regard to rank."[26] The designation presumably referred to the unit of rations provided to Union troops. The later and now renowned United States Army General Orders 100—known as the Lieber Code—also resorted to military assimilation for treatment of POWs held by Union forces.[27] The Code most clearly assimilated POWs to Union troops for purposes of labor. It acknowledged that prisoners may be required to work "according to their rank and condition," equating the corresponding ranks of enemy forces to ranks of the detaining power.[28] Also, a variant of assimilation that might be called "POW assimilation" regulated treatment of religious and medical personnel, as well as messengers. Although the Lieber Code made clear that these noncombatants and couriers were not POWs, it assimilated POW treatment standards to them.[29]

However, the Lieber Code also featured departures from strict military assimilation. For example, it strayed from the previously issued U.S. order respecting rations, merely requiring that POWs receive "plain and wholesome food."[30] And although it called for the application of martial law, including "dictation of general laws," to occupied territory,[31] the Lieber Code indicated that martial law should be "less stringent" than that applied to armed forces, particularly in "fully occupied and conquered" places.[32]

---

25. FLORY, *supra* note 16, at 8 (citing Government and People v. M'Gregory, *in* U.S. WAR DEPARTMENT, A DIGEST OF OPINIONS OF THE JUDGE ADVOCATES GENERAL OF THE ARMY 1075 (1912)).

26. FLORY, *supra* note 16, at 63, n. 171 (citing U.S. WAR DEPARTMENT, REVISED REGULATIONS FOR THE ARMY OF THE UNITED STATES 107, art. 764 (1861)).

27. U.S. Department of War, Instructions for the Government of Armies of the United States in the Field, General Orders No. 100, Apr. 24, 1863) [hereinafter Lieber Code]. *See also* David Wallace and Shane Reeves's chapter, "The Lieber Code and Prisoners of War: A Legacy of Practical Humanitarianism."

28. *Id.*, art. LXXVI.

29. *Id.*, arts. LIII, XCIX. The Code prescribed POW assimilation likewise for so-called hostages, persons presented to an enemy force "as a pledge for the fulfillment of an agreement." *Id.*, arts. LIV–LV.

30. *Id.*, art. LXXVI.

31. *Id.*, art. III. *See generally id.*, arts. I–III.

32. *Id.*, art. V.

Meanwhile, early Confederate legislation on POWs resorted directly to military assimilation. Confederate statutes commanded that "the rations furnished [POWs] shall be the same in quantity and quality as those furnished to enlisted men in the army of the Confederacy."[33] Despite rampant accounts of poor treatment of Union POWs,[34] other reports indicate that the Confederacy recognized and generally applied the Union's original order of assimilation of military rations in its own camps.[35] The same reports suggest that Union forces frequently did not observe the assimilative standard as expressed by the Lieber Code.[36] Neither did the assimilative standard operate with respect to criminal or disciplinary jurisdiction during the American Civil War. The Confederate side subjected POWs to a variety of jurisdictional schemes that did not always coincide with those applicable to members of the belligerents' armed forces.[37] No open or express resort to military assimilation established or obliged these practices, it seems.

Late nineteenth-century European instruments inspired by the Lieber Code made similarly spotty use of military assimilation. The 1874 Brussels Declaration—which never entered into force but surfaced in substantially similar form in later international legal instruments—required, in the absence of agreement otherwise, that detaining powers provide clothing and food to prisoners of war "on the same footing as" that supplied to their own armed forces.[38] Meanwhile, the 1880

---

33. FLORY, *supra* note 16, at 63 n.171 (citing CONFEDERATE STATES OF AMERICA, THE STATUTES AT LARGE OF THE PROVISIONAL GOVERNMENT OF THE CONFEDERATE STATES OF AMERICA 154 (May 21, 1861)).

34. *See* Aaron Sheehan-Dean, Lex Talionis *in the U.S. Civil War: Retaliation and the Limits of Atrocity*, *in* THE CIVIL WAR AS GLOBAL CONFLICT: TRANSNATIONAL MEANINGS OF THE AMERICAN CIVIL WAR 175–76 (David T. Gleeson & Simon Lewis eds., 2014) (relating Confederate practices of murdering captured Union troops, particularly black soldiers). *See also* Cadet Paul Lawless, The Development of American POW Treatment and Its Relevance in the Modern Era of War (Apr. 19, 2021) (Honors thesis, United States Military Academy, West Point) (on file with author) (citing BENJAMIN G. CLOYD, HAUNTED BY ATROCITY: CIVIL WAR PRISONS IN AMERICAN MEMORY 27 (2010) (recounting Confederate reduction of rations for Union POWs); CHARLES W. SANDERS, WHILE IN THE HANDS OF THE ENEMY: MILITARY PRISONS OF THE CIVIL WAR 41 (2005)(relating Union reprisals undertaken in response to Confederate abuse of POWs)).

35. FLORY, *supra* note 16, at 18. Flory indicates that in some circumstances the Confederates exceeded the standard of military assimilation, feeding Union prisoners better rations than those provided to their own forces. *Id.*

36. *Id.* at 64 (citing 40th Cong., 3d Sess., House Rep. No. 45, 780–84). *See* SANDERS, *supra* note 34, at 41.

37. UNITED STATES, WAR DEPARTMENT, A DIGEST OF OPINIONS OF THE JUDGE ADVOCATE GENERAL OF THE ARMY 1075 (1912) (relating advice in 1865 that "the Government might in its discretion turn [a POW] over for trial to the State authorities").

38. Project of an International Declaration concerning the Laws and Customs of War art. 27, Brussels, Aug. 27, 1874, *reprinted in* THE LAWS OF ARMED CONFLICTS 23 (Dietrich Schindler & Jiří Toman eds., 4th ed. 2004)[hereinafter Brussels Declaration].

Oxford Manual, assembled and published by the Institute of International Law, repeated the Brussels Declaration provisions.[39] The 1880 Manual, like the Brussels Declaration, resorted to military assimilation for trials of military offenses, stating that POWs "are subject to the laws and regulations in force in the army of the enemy."[40]

These instruments saw resort to military assimilation for POW treatment standards at its zenith, proving a convenient tool for consensus in these early, though inchoate, efforts to secure multilateral agreement on the regulation of hostilities. In the wake of early industrialized wars, including the American Civil War, the Second Italian War of Independence, the Franco-Prussian War, and the Russo-Turkish War, attitudes toward POWs shifted decidedly away from ancient conceptions.[41] Traces of assimilation, though broader in approach, can even be found in moral and philosophical theories of wartime detention. Considering the status of POWs, James Lorimer observed:

> Combatants who throw down their arms are entitled to claim from humanity, as a whole, that protection which their own State is unable to afford them. By abandoning their own State they become citizens of the world. As such they are non-combatants; and, apart from such precautions as may be necessary to prevent their resuming their combatant character in the existing war, they are entitled to be treated like other non-combatants.[42]

B. Early Twentieth-Century Codification and Experience

Inspired by revolutionary changes in the character of warfare, and especially by industrialization's increases in the scale of battlefield suffering, The Hague Peace Conferences of 1899 and 1907 revolutionized the international regulation of war.[43] The Hague Conferences transposed the law of war from a loose collection of vague

---

39. Institute of International Law, THE LAWS OF WAR ON LAND (1880) (Oxford Manual), *reprinted in* THE LAWS OF ARMED CONFLICTS 29 (Dietrich Schindler & Jiří Toman eds., 4th ed. 2004).

40. *Id.*, art. 62 (repeating the work of the Brussels Declaration, *supra* note 38, art. 28).

41. *See* PIERRE BOISSIER, 1 HISTORY OF THE INTERNATIONAL COMMITTEE OF THE RED CROSS: FROM SOLFERINO TO TSUSHIMA 265 (1985)(noting expansion of the work of humanitarian relief societies from the wounded and sick exclusively to protection of healthy POWs).

42. JAMES LORIMER, 2 INSTITUTES OF THE LAW OF NATIONS 72 (1884). *See also* JULIUS STONE, 1 LEGAL CONTROLS OF INTERNATIONAL CONFLICT 651 (1954) (noting law of war responsiveness to "the attitudes and mental outlook of the peoples of the world," particularly with respect to rules for POW treatment).

43. *See* DIETRICH SCHINDLER & JIŘÍ TOMAN, THE LAWS OF ARMED CONFLICTS: A COLLECTION OF CONVENTIONS, RESOLUTIONS AND OTHER DOCUMENTS v–vi (4th ed. 2004)(recounting compulsory military service, numbers of victims, and technological improvements as revolutionizing late-nineteenth-century warfare).

customs and brief treaties dedicated to discreet subjects, such as the wounded[44] or exploding projectiles,[45] to a widely ratified collection of conventions that codified nearly the full extent of existing regulations on hostilities.[46] The Regulations annexed to Hague Conventions II and IV of 1899 and 1907 respectively added housing to the military assimilative standards for food and clothing provided to POWs.[47] During the First World War, consistent with the Hague Regulations, the United States and other powers reportedly housed POWs in military barracks or in buildings "similar to the regulation barracks."[48] The 1899 Hague Regulations also resorted to military assimilation to compensate POWs on projects of public service.[49]

With very few exceptions, the Regulations annexed to Hague Conventions II and IV are identical. However, the 1907 IV Hague Regulations, in a rare amendment to their 1899 predecessor, relaxed military assimilation as a measure for POW compensation, instead accounting for the nature of work done by POWs to determine pay.[50] In a further departure from their 1899 predecessor, the 1907 Regulations required that officer POWs be paid according to the scales applicable to officers of the armed forces of the detaining power, rather than according to those of their State of origin.[51] Concerning discipline, both the 1899 and 1907 Hague Regulations adopted the 1874 Brussels Declaration and the 1880 Oxford

---

44. Convention for the Amelioration of the Condition of the Wounded in Armies in the Field, Aug. 22, 1864, 22 Stat. 940, 129 Consol. T.S. 361 (comprising ten brief articles devoted exclusively to the protection of wounded persons).

45. Declaration Renouncing the Use, in Time of War, of Explosive Projectiles Under 400 Grammes Weight, Nov. 29/Dec. 11, 1868, 138 Consol. T.S. 297, 18 MARTENS NOUVEAU RECUEIL (ser. 1) 474, http://www.icrc.org/applic/ihl/ihl.nsf/Article.xsp?action=openDocument&documentId=568842C2B90F4A29C12563CD0051547C.

46. *See generally* A. PIERCE HIGGINS, THE HAGUE PEACE CONFERENCES AND OTHER INTERNATIONAL CONFERENCES CONCERNING THE LAWS AND USAGES OF WAR: TEXTS OF THE CONVENTIONS WITH COMMENTARIES (1909)(relating summaries of proceedings at the Hague Peace Conferences and drafts of instruments referred to at the Conferences).

47. 1899 Hague Regulations, *supra* note 13, art. 7(2). The 1907 Hague Regulations reproduced their predecessor's assimilative standards for food, quarters, and clothing. 1907 Hague Regulations, *supra* note 13, art. 7(2).

48. FLORY, *supra* note 16, at 58 (citing UNITED STATES, WAR DEPARTMENT, 1 ANNUAL REP. 183 (1917); United States, War Department, General Order No. 54, 1917).

49. 1899 Hague Regulations, *supra* note 13, art. 6 (stating: "Work done for the state shall be paid according to the tariffs in force for soldiers of the national army employed on similar tasks.").

50. 1907 Hague Regulations, *supra* note 13, art. 6. Where the 1899 Regulations had referred only to rates in force for soldiers of the detaining power, the 1907 Regulations abandoned military assimilation in cases where no military rates of pay existed for the specific work executed by POWs. *Id.*, art. 6(3).

51. *Id.*, art. 17. Article 17 states: "Officers taken prisoners shall receive the same rate of pay as officers of corresponding rank in the country where they are detained...."

Manual scheme of full military assimilation for offenses by prisoners.[52] However, that arrangement attracted apt criticism. Preferring fixed rather than assimilated punishments, Professor Hyde observed:

> [T]he [Hague] standard is believed to be an unsafe one, exposing the captive to cruel treatment if guilty of slight and technical offenses against a captor eager for excuse to impose a harsh penalty, and habitually severe in disciplining its own forces. As a safeguard, it would seem essential to fix by general agreement the nature and extent of penalties to be imposed for certain specified offenses known to be of common occurrence.[53]

Criticism notwithstanding, it appears that some States Parties to the Hague Regulations incorporated the military assimilative regime for discipline into domestic law. During the First World War, the military assimilative standard found early expression in the British Parliament, though with modification. Edward Grey observed:

> His Majesty's Government consider that all prisoners of war, other than officers on full pay at time of capture, are entitled to be treated only as soldiers, that is, to be fed, clothed, and housed on a scale similar to that provided for British soldiers. In view of the social position of many of the prisoners, His Majesty's Government, have, however, decided that prisoners approved by the local military authorities who are able and willing to pay for a superior diet, may be given diet and accommodation on a scale similar to that provided for officers.[54]

Yet, on a broader scale, detaining powers found themselves overwhelmed by the number of enemy captives and often unprepared to house, feed, or clothe them consistently with the Hague Regulations.[55] The belligerents of the First World War later resorted to supplemental bilateral agreements to address the conditions

---

52. *Id.*, art. 8.

53. CHARLES CHENEY HYDE, 2 INTERNATIONAL LAW, CHIEFLY AS APPLIED AND INTERPRETED BY THE UNITED STATES 337 (1922)(crediting Lieutenant Colonel George V. Strong, Judge Advocate, United States Army, with the idea of adopting a fixed system of available disciplinary measures and punishments for POWs).

54. FLORY, *supra* note 16, at 65–66 (quoting GREAT BRITAIN, PARLIAMENTARY PAPERS, CD., 7817, at 6 (1914)).

55. FLORY, *supra* note 16, at 59 (citing ERNST HECHT, LES PRISONNIERS DE GUERRE 47–49 (1915); GREAT BRITAIN, 80 PARLIAMENTARY DEBATES 5th ser., c. 1871 (House of Commons, Mar. 10, 1915); GREAT BRITAIN, PARLIAMENTARY PAPERS, CD. 7817 at 11 (1914)).

and treatment of POWs.⁵⁶ Some of these agreements plainly abandoned military assimilation. The 1917 Convention of Copenhagen, for instance, required that POWs receive rations commensurate with those allowed to the detaining powers' *civilian* populations.⁵⁷ The 1917 Convention resorted to further civilian assimilation for prisoners employed at heavy labor, requiring the detaining power to serve rations provided to civilian workers in the same professions.⁵⁸ Other bilateral agreements, however, resorted to flat caloric amounts rather than military assimilation to regulate rations and regulated working hours of prisoners by assimilation of civilian labor standards.⁵⁹ And, although supported universally at the diplomatic conferences in The Hague, the assimilated pay standard of the 1907 Regulations proved difficult to implement, considering the variance in States' military rank structures. Resentment roiled from the possibility that some prisoners might receive higher or lower pay during captivity than during their active service.⁶⁰ These and other difficulties led some First World War belligerent States to mutually abandon the military assimilative standard on a bilateral basis in favor of fixed salaries.⁶¹

Identified during the latter stages of the First World War, the need for bilateral and multilateral agreements to supplement the 1907 Hague Convention's POW treatment regime inspired the first peacetime multilateral treaty dedicated exclusively to POWs. The 1929 Geneva Convention on Prisoners of War supplemented the 1899 and 1907 Hague regimes but also represented an expansion of the law-of-war Geneva tradition from its prior focus on the wounded and sick.⁶² Discussions at the diplomatic conference that formed the 1929 Geneva Prisoner

---

56. CHARLES H. MURPHY, CONG. RESEARCH SERV., 71-161 F, PRISONERS OF WAR: REPATRIATION OR INTERNMENT IN WARTIME: AMERICAN AND ALLIED EXPERIENCE 1775–PRESENT 7–10 (1971).

57. FLORY, *supra* note 16, at 66 (citing Convention of Copenhagen IV, Ch. III, art. 1 (1917)). Professor Levie indicates that the Convention of Copenhagen can be found in the archives of the Ministry of Foreign Affairs, Copenhagen. LEVIE, DOCUMENTS, *supra* note 14, at 86.

58. FLORY, *supra* note 16, at 66.

59. *Agreement Between the United States of America and Germany Concerning Prisoners of War, Sanitary Personnel, and Civilians, Berne, Nov. 11, 1918*, 13 AMERICAN JOURNAL OF INTERNATIONAL LAW SUPPLEMENT 1 (1918), *in* LEVIE, DOCUMENTS, *supra* note14, at 115, 125. The American–German Agreement included a reference to military assimilation to regulate rations generally but also established specific minimum caloric intakes and minimum weights of bread rations. *Id.*

60. FLORY, *supra* note 16, at 83.

61. *Id.* at 84 n.75 (citing UNITED STATES, DEPARTMENT OF STATE, FOREIGN RELATIONS, SUPP. II 39, 41 (1918); FRANCE, JOURNAL OFFICIEL 590 (1916)).

62. Convention Relative to the Treatment of Prisoners of War, July 27, 1929, 2 Bevans 932 [hereinafter 1929 Geneva Convention]. For discussion of the Geneva tradition of the law of war, see *supra* note 2.

of War Convention included concern that assimilation of standards for detaining powers' armed forces to POWs would prove inadequate in many respects.[63]

Yet the 1929 Convention did not abandon military assimilation entirely. It committed standards for hygiene, dampness, heat, and light to objective feasibility-based standards while regulating living area, air, and bedding according to conditions provided to "troops at base camps" of the detaining power.[64] The 1929 Convention also required the detaining power to provide food rations "equal in quantity and quality to that of troops at base camps."[65] Addressing the issue of pay, States abandoned the 1907 Regulations' resort to military assimilation. Instead, the Convention assimilated the detaining power's pay scheme for officers but capped officer pay at the amount prisoners would have received from their State of origin.[66] Soldiers detailed to labor received pay "in accordance with the rates in force for soldiers of the national army doing the same work."[67] Meanwhile, indicating its comparatively expansive coverage, the 1929 Convention prescribed maximum working hours and benefits for POWs injured while on labor details or detachments.[68] To do so, the Convention reached beyond military assimilation, incorporating instead "provisions applicable to laborers of the same class according to the legislation of the detaining Power," another early resort to civilian assimilation for POWs.[69] Finally, and in perhaps its clearest resort to military assimilation, the 1929 Convention subjected POWs to the "laws, regulations, and orders in force in the armies of the Detaining Power" as well as the punishments corresponding to violations of each.[70]

---

63. FLORY, *supra* note16, at 55.

64. 1929 Geneva Convention, *supra* note 13, art. 10. The reporter of the diplomatic conference indicates that the phrase "troops at base camps" referred to soldiers outside zones of hostilities, including in "barracks, depots or instruction camps." FLORY, *supra* note 16, 60, n.150 (citing CONSEIL FÉDÉRAL SUISSE, ACTES DE LA CONFÉRENCE DIPLOMATIQUE RÉUNIE À GEVÈVE DU 1ER AU 27 JUILLET 1929 476–77 (1930)).

65. 1929 Geneva Convention, *supra* note13, art. 11.

66. *Id.*, art. 23.

67. *Id.*, art. 34.

68. *Id.*, arts. 30, 27.

69. *Id.*, art. 27. The 1929 Geneva Convention anticipated that the domestic legal regimes of some States Parties might not include injured worker compensation schemes. Such Parties undertook an obligation, however, to recommend adoption of "all proper measures" of indemnification by their national legislatures. *Id.*, art. 27.

70. *Id.*, arts. 45, 46. At the 1929 diplomatic conference, the International Committee of the Red Cross (ICRC) had proposed an enumerated list of sanctions in lieu of the military assimilative approach to disciplinary punishment. *See* Code de Prisonniers de Guerre, Avant-Projet de Convention Élaboré par le Comité International de la Croix-Rouge, art. 50, 1929, *in* ACTES DE LA CONFÉRENCE DIPLOMATIQUE, *supra* note 64, at 27. States did not adopt the proposal, but the Committee would have its way later. *See infra* text accompanying note 117.

Despite the encouraging signs of an exclusive focus on POWs and significant expansion of legal protections, the 1929 Geneva Convention failed in many respects.[71] First, neither Japan nor the Soviet Union ratified the Convention, greatly limiting the number of POWs who would enjoy its protection as a matter of treaty law during the Second World War.[72] Second, the 1929 Convention did not include effective measures for enforcement. Finally, diplomatic negotiations and academic research indicate that the 1929 Convention's military assimilative provisions accounted for a substantial portion of its failings.[73] Many of these provisions proved either impractical or ill-suited to the actual needs of POWs held in unfamiliar climates or by armed forces from vastly different military and cultural traditions. The aftermath of the Second World War, particularly the persistent suffering and abuse of POWs, made clear the need to replace the 1929 Convention with more comprehensive and effective legal protections that included a further reworking of military assimilation.[74]

---

71. *See* LEVIE, DOCUMENTS, *supra* note 14, at 178 (assessing that the 1929 Convention "failed to provide solutions to many of the problems which had surfaced during World War I").

72. Japan signed but did not ratify the 1929 Convention; the Soviet Union did not sign or accede to it. *See* SCHINDLER & TOMAN, *supra* note 43, at 443. During the Second World War, both Japan and the Soviet Union made commitments to apply the 1929 Conventions as non-State Parties that in many cases proved disingenuous. *See* Trial of General Tanaka Hisakasu, 6 LAW REPORTS OF TRIALS OF WAR CRIMINALS 66 (1946) (United Nations War Crimes Commission) (noting a Japanese telegram sent to the ICRC indicating that Japan would apply the 1929 Convention subject to reciprocity and "*mutatis mutandis*"). *See also* Stephen Connor, *Side-Stepping Geneva: Japanese Troops Under British Control, 1945-47*, 45 JOURNAL OF CONTEMPORARY HISTORY 389 (2010) (recounting postwar difficulty classifying Japanese POWs in British hands). *Contra* Walton K. Richardson, *Prisoners of War as Instruments of Foreign Policy*, *in* 2 READINGS IN INTERNATIONAL LAW FROM THE NAVAL WAR COLLEGE REVIEW 1947–1977 325, 327 (Richard B. Lillich & John Norton Moore eds., 1980) (Vol. 62, U.S. Naval War College International Law Studies) (asserting that "Japan never did announce adherence to the Geneva Convention of 1929") (citing UNITED STATES, DEPARTMENT OF THE ARMY, OFFICE OF THE ASSISTANT CHIEF OF STAFF, INTELLIGENCE, EUGENE T. OLSON, PRISONER OF WAR POLICY OF THE SOVIET UNION 35–37 (1953)). Later, a post-Second World War U.S. military commission determined that the 1929 Geneva Convention on Prisoners of War had reflected customary international law with respect to select articles. United States v. von Leeb et al., 11 TRIALS OF WAR CRIMINALS BEFORE THE NUREMBERG MILITARY TRIBUNALS UNDER CONTROL COUNCIL LAW NO. 10 462, 535–38 (1950). *See also* Richard R. Baxter, *Multilateral Treaties as Evidence of Customary International Law*, 41 BRITISH YEAR BOOK OF INTERNATIONAL LAW 275, 286 (1965)(discussing details of the von Leeb et al. military commission's findings on customary international laws of war).

73. Joseph V. Dillon, *The Genesis of the 1949 Conventions Relative to the Treatment of Prisoners of War*, 5 MIAMI LAW QUARTERLY 40, 44 (1950). Major General Dillon notes that "[o]ne of [the 1929 Convention's] fundamental faults was its adoption of national standards rather than absolutes." *Id.* (citing 1929 Geneva Convention, *supra* note 13, art. 11).

74. *See* GERALD I.A.D. DRAPER, THE RED CROSS CONVENTIONS OF 1949 (1958) (recounting that at the German Sachsenhausen camp alone, sixty thousand Soviet POWs died in the winter of 1941–42). Colonel Professor Draper indicates, however, that the 1929 Convention was applied

III. THE 1949 THIRD GENEVA CONVENTION

Preceded by preliminary expert and governmental meetings that produced a series of working drafts, a diplomatic conference convened in Geneva in 1949 adopted a new generation of Geneva Conventions.[75] The result for purposes of POW treatment was a significantly expanded catalog of obligations, including selective resorts to military assimilation. Commentators, eager to lend a degree of accessibility, have seized on assimilation as an important tool and even a distinguishing feature of the Third Geneva Convention.[76] A recent and comprehensive International Committee of the Red Cross (ICRC) analysis concludes that assimilation "runs through the Convention as a whole."[77] Commentators have also seized on military assimilation as a distinguishing feature of POW status, setting it apart from that of interned civilians.[78] It has been observed that "only [POWs] enjoy so-called 'assimilation rights'—the rule requiring that lawful combatants be accorded the same rights as members of the detaining state's armed forces."[79]

Across a range of subjects—including quarters, food, clothing, labor, and discipline—the Third Geneva Convention employs treatment standards assimilated from armed forces. Yet, like preceding efforts, the Third Geneva Convention makes only limited and sporadic use of military assimilation. In fact, the records of the diplomatic conference that finalized and adopted the Convention include very few references to

"in varying degrees" in the Western European and African theaters of the Second World War. *Id.* at 50.

75. Text of Draft International Conventions for the Protection of War Victims as Approved by the XVIIth International Red Cross Conference at Stockholm in August 1948, *in* SWITZERLAND, FEDERAL POLITICAL DEPARTMENT, 1 FINAL RECORD OF THE DIPLOMATIC CONFERENCE OF GENEVA OF 1949 45 (1949). Another account credits genesis of the 1949 Conventions to the Second World War United States Provost Marshal General of the European Theater of Operations. Jan P. Charmatz & Harold M. Wit, *Repatriation of Prisoners of War and the 1949 Geneva Convention*, 62 YALE LAW JOURNAL 391, 400 n.43 (1953) (citing Dillon, *supra* note 73, at 43–44).

76. 2020 GC III COMMENTARY, *supra* note 9, ¶ 30, https://ihl-databases.icrc.org/applic/ihl/ihl.nsf/Comment.xsp?action=openDocument&documentId=1B9A4ABF10E7EAD2C12585850 04E7F19; SASSÒLI, *supra* note 9, at 264; Derek Jinks, *The Declining Significance of POW Status*, 45 HARVARD INTERNATIONAL LAW JOURNAL 367, 368 (2004) (noting the lack of assimilation "into the legal regime governing the armed forces of the detaining state" as a gap in protection between POWs and civilians protected under the Fourth Geneva Convention).

77. 2020 GC III COMMENTARY, *supra* note 9, ¶ 4003.

78. Derek Jinks, *Protective Parity and the Laws of War*, 79 NOTRE DAME LAW REVIEW 1493, 1500 (2004).

79. *Id.*

assimilation.[80] The picture of military assimilation in the Third Geneva Convention is less one of an overarching principle or theme running through the whole of the Convention and more one of an occasional technique to secure compromise on historically fraught issues of POW treatment. Thus, careful study and appreciation of the Convention's selective and limited resort to military assimilation are essential to a correct understanding of the POW treatment obligations of States.

A. Quarters

The Third Geneva Convention regulates POW housing chiefly at Article 25. The article requires that POWs be quartered "under conditions as favorable as forces of the Detaining Power who are billeted in the same area."[81] In this respect, the article employs a sort of localized military assimilation. The frame of reference for housing equivalence is troops of the detaining power who are generally co-located with the POWs in question. Considering the Convention's obligation to evacuate POWs from zones of hostilities, the likely assumption is that such troops would be housed in relatively stable and comparatively comfortable quarters also suitable for the potentially lengthy internments served by POWs. The article is understood to mean that POW quarters need not be identical but must compare favorably to those of the detaining power's armed forces.

Article 25 immediately indicates, however, that even localized military assimilation is not fully adequate and that detaining powers must depart from—or, in the words of the article, "shall make allowance for"—the habits and customs of POWs for purposes of housing. Thus, military assimilation is not fully descriptive of the Convention's approach to POW quarters. Preparatory work at a 1947 Conference of Experts convened in advance of the 1949 diplomatic conference concluded that "[p]ure, formal equality with the living conditions of the Detaining Power's armed forces as the sole standard was thus seen as potentially problematic."[82] This aspect of negotiating history explains the Convention's departure from strict military assimilation in this case. Article 25 and its negotiating history illustrate well the

---

80. To the author's knowledge, the term appears prominently in two passages. *See* SWITZERLAND, FEDERAL POLITICAL DEPARTMENT, 2-A FINAL RECORD OF THE DIPLOMATIC CONFERENCE OF GENEVA OF 1949 518, 532 (1949) [hereinafter 2-A FINAL RECORD].

81. Third Geneva Convention, *supra* note 1, art. 25(1).

82. 2020 GC III COMMENTARY, *supra* note 9, ¶ 2073 (citing Report on the Work of the Conference of Government Experts for the Study of the Conventions for the Protection of War Victims 134–38 (Apr. 14–26, 1947)). Still, the ICRC comment reports that Article 25 resorts to "the principle of assimilation." 2020 GC III COMMENTARY, *supra* note 9, ¶ 2074. Here is an example of the Commentary ascribing assimilation in a very broad and somewhat imprecise fashion. Later, however, a comment notes "the Convention's approach of adopting a nuanced principle of assimilation." *Id.*, ¶ 2091. This reference to "a nuanced principle of assimilation" may be a better articulation of what the Convention does in this and many other cases.

need to clarify what assimilation means and how it should be used to best understand and implement the Convention.

Additionally, with respect to quarters and specifically concerning civil defense and protection, Article 23 of the Third Geneva Convention resorts to civilian rather than military assimilation. It requires that POWs have access to bomb shelters and protection from the hazards of war to the same extent as the local civilian population, and that they are afforded all other measures of protection enjoyed by the local population.[83] Here, military assimilation is abandoned in favor of civilian assimilation, a wise concession to the distinction between the troops of detaining powers as lawful targets of attack and POWs as persons *hors de combat*.[84]

B. Food and Clothing

Article 26 of the Third Geneva Convention addresses the historically challenging issue of feeding POWs. The article requires that rations "keep prisoners of war in good health and . . . prevent loss of weight or the development of nutritional deficiencies."[85] Thus, rather than resort to the prior military assimilation standards of the 1907 Hague and 1929 Geneva Conventions, or even the caloric tables used by First World War supplemental agreements, the Third Geneva Convention imposes a results-based standard based on objectively measurable effects of diet on POWs.[86] Further, in light of poor historical experience with prisoners adjusting to the tastes, nutritional qualities, and portions of the foods of foreign cultures, the Convention requires that the detaining power take account "of the habitual diet of the prisoners."[87] In this respect, the Convention again expressly rejects military assimilation, particularly when there is great dietary or nutritional variance between captors and captives. The Convention further insulates the issue of food from assimilation of detaining power military standards and influence by requiring, to the extent possible, that POWs be involved in preparation of their own meals.[88]

Turning to clothing, another subject that States had occasionally regulated through military assimilation, Article 27 of the Third Geneva Convention rejects the approach of the 1899 and 1907 Hague Conventions, which required that

---

83. Third Geneva Convention, *supra* note 1, art. 23(2).

84. *See* Additional Protocol I, *supra* note 13, art. 41 (addressing the notion of persons *hors de combat*, including those in the hands of an enemy).

85. *Id.*, art. 26(1).

86. *Compare id.* with 1907 Hague Regulations, *supra* note 13, art. 7(2) and 1929 Geneva Convention, *supra* note 13, art. 11.

87. Third Geneva Convention, *supra* note 1, art. 26(1).

88. *Id.*, art. 26(4).

POWs receive clothing "on the same footing as the troops of the Government."[89] The Third Geneva Convention largely reaffirmed the 1929 Geneva Convention approach of merely requiring the detaining power to furnish adequate clothing. However, the 1949 Convention improved on the 1929 Convention by emphasizing that POWs must receive "sufficient quantities" and that clothing must be appropriate to "the climate of the region where the prisoners are detained."[90]

A further clause of Article 27 indicates that captured enemy uniforms (presumably those of the POWs in question) "should . . . be made available to clothe prisoners of war."[91] Jean Pictet, the editor of influential and nearly contemporaneous commentaries to the 1949 Geneva Conventions, related that production of clothing specifically intended for prisoners in wartime had presented considerable difficulties for detaining powers.[92] He concluded that, contrary to Article 27, the best practical arrangement may be for prisoners' power of origin to send uniforms through relief organizations.[93] More interesting, perhaps, Pictet concluded that requiring POWs to wear the uniform of the detaining power is forbidden as a violation of the Convention's guarantee of honor, a stark rejection of strict military assimilation.[94]

C. Labor and Pay

The Convention's limited resort to military assimilation is reflected most simply in its prohibition on compelling service in the war effort.[95] POWs, unlike their counterparts in the captor's armed forces, may not be assigned or compelled to perform tasks that support the war effort of the detaining power.[96] As much as any provision for POW protection, this prohibition emphasizes rejection of the ancient practice of prisoner absorption.[97] The absence of a duty of loyalty on the part of POWs to the detaining power further reflects States' rejection of military assimilation.[98]

---

89. 1907 Hague Regulations, *supra* note 13, art. 7; 1899 Hague Regulations, *supra* note 13, art. 7.

90. Third Geneva Convention, *supra* note 1, art. 27.

91. *Id.*

92. 1960 GC III Commentary, *supra* note 8, at 201.

93. *Id.*

94. *Id.* (citing Third Geneva Convention, *supra* note 1, art. 14(1)).

95. Third Geneva Convention, *supra* note 1, art. 50.

96. *Id.* Article 50 enumerates authorized classes of work for POWs, many of which include a qualifier that they may not have a "military character or purpose."

97. *See supra* text accompanying note 14.

98. Third Geneva Convention, *supra* note 1, art. 87.

While POWs may not be made to work in support of the detaining power's war effort, they may more generally be put to labor.[99] They may even work for private employers.[100] Historically, including during the Second World War, POW labor had been abused.[101] Considering this experience, the Third Geneva Convention regulates the conditions of POW labor closely. Article 51 resorts to assimilation to regulate working conditions, including accommodation, food, clothing, and equipment.[102] However, the article assimilates conditions applicable to "nationals of the Detaining Power employed in similar work," rather than to military conditions.

Article 54 reflects a significant change from the scheme for occupational injuries to POWs under Article 27(4) of the preceding 1929 Geneva Convention. The 1929 Convention had assigned responsibility for injury payments and compensation to the detaining power, including, by some interpretations, an obligation that extended to the period following final repatriation. The 1929 Convention also made injury claims subject to the domestic legal regime of the detaining power.[103] The 1947 Experts Conference and, ultimately, the 1949 Convention abandoned this scheme and shifted responsibility to the power on which the injured POW depends.[104] In this case, States abandoned assimilation in favor of a context-specific rule for compensation of injuries that accounts for the realities of the usually temporary relationship between a POW and a detaining power.

Finally, with respect to labor, Article 60(1) of the Third Geneva Convention largely eliminates the "practice of tying the amount of the advance of pay to the pay scale of the armed forces of either the Detaining Power or the Power of Origin."[105] This provision seems at odds with—and even designed to avoid—military assimilation, which had been the approach to POW pay of the 1899 and 1907 Hague

---

99. *Id.*, art. 49(1). Non-commissioned officer POWs may only be assigned to supervisory tasks. *Id.*, art. 49(2). Meanwhile, officers may not be compelled to work. *Id.*, art. 49(3).

100. *Id.*, art. 57(1).

101. *See* Kinue Tokudome, *Troubling Legacy: World War II Forced Labor by American POWs of the Japanese*, 4 THE ASIA-PACIFIC JOURNAL (Mar. 29, 2006), *available at* https://apjjf.org/-Kinue-TOKUDOME/1920/article.html (relating Japanese as well as German forced labor abuses). *Cf.* GEORGE G. LEWIS & JOHN MEWHA, UNITED STATES, DEPARTMENT OF THE ARMY, PAM. NO. 20-213, HISTORY OF PRISONER OF WAR UTILIZATION BY THE UNITED STATES ARMY (June 1955)(providing a detailed account of U.S. efforts to comply with international law conventions and customs with respect to POW labor).

102. Third Geneva Convention, *supra* note 1, art. 51(1).

103. 1929 Geneva Convention, *supra* note 13, art. 27(4).

104. Third Geneva Convention, *supra* note 1, art. 54.

105. LEVIE, PRISONERS OF WAR, *supra* note 14, at 198. *See* 2020 GC III COMMENTARY, *supra* note 9, ¶ 2897.

Regulations. The decision with respect to military assimilation for pay was, however, contested.[106]

D. Penal and Disciplinary Matters

During the Second World War, the ICRC collected evidence of severe penal and disciplinary practices against POWs.[107] In many cases, abuse illustrated the dangers of then-prevailing unfettered military assimilation standards for discipline.[108] In response, States made mixed use of military assimilation in their designs for the penal and disciplinary sections of the Third Geneva Convention. They altered the pre-existing framework to relax application or mitigate operation of detaining power standards of discipline and penal law.

Addressing penal and disciplinary sanctions generally, Article 82(1) of the Third Geneva Convention retains full military assimilation. Like its predecessors, the article indicates that POWs are "subject to the laws, regulations and orders in force in the armed forces of the Detaining Power."[109] Article 102 also requires that POWs be tried and sentenced only by "the same courts according to the same procedure" as the detaining power's armed forces. Similarly, Article 87(1) limits punitive sentences to penalties applicable to "members of the armed forces of the [Detaining] Power who have committed the same acts," effectively assimilating military penal schemes.[110] Meanwhile, Article 88 resorts to an unfiltered form of military assimilation, insisting that punishments of non-commissioned officers, officers, and women POWs accord with the treatment of their detaining power counterparts.[111]

Yet Article 87(2) softens military assimilation somewhat by directing States, when fixing punishments, to account for the fact that POWs owe no allegiance to the detaining power.[112] Article 95, addressing pretrial confinement, includes a similarly qualified resort to military assimilation. Under the article, a detaining power may only subject a POW to close pretrial confinement when "a member of the armed forces of the Detaining Power would be so kept."[113] Yet the article also

---

106. 2-A FINAL RECORD, *supra* note 80, at 279–80, 532. A delegate from Canada stated that "the principle of assimilation to the pay of troops of the Detaining Powers would not be acceptable to his country since in many cases it would be far too low." *Id.*

107. International Committee of the Red Cross, *Report of the International Committee of the Red Cross on Its Activities During the Second World War (September 1, 1939–June 30, 1947)*, 2 THE CENTRAL AGENCY FOR PRISONERS OF WAR 439–40 (1948).

108. *See supra* text accompanying note 70.

109. Third Geneva Convention, *supra* note 1, art. 82(1).

110. *Id.*, art. 87(1).

111. *Id.*, art. 88(1)–(3).

112. *Id.*, art. 87(2).

113. *Id.*, art. 95(1).

permits close pretrial confinement of POWs "if it is essential in the interests of camp order and discipline," even if such confinement would not be available for members of the armed forces of the detaining power.[114]

Concerning execution of punishments, the Third Geneva Convention again presents a mixed bag. Article 108 insists that POWs serve sentences "in the same establishments and under the same conditions as members of the armed forces of the Detaining Power" for penal offenses resulting in conviction and confinement.[115] Meanwhile, Articles 97 and 98 explicitly enumerate standards of confinement for mere disciplinary offenses, rather than assimilate or guarantee equivalence to armed forces of the detaining power.[116]

Article 89 and other disciplinary articles complicate the Convention's scheme for maintaining order somewhat by qualifying or abandoning military assimilation of disciplinary standards. Where Articles 82 and 88 resort to military assimilation and Articles 87 and 95 to qualified military assimilation, Article 89 enumerates exclusive disciplinary, as opposed to penal, sanctions applicable to POWs.[117] Article 96 is likewise an illustration of poor prior experience with the principle of assimilation. In fact, the article's text bears no indicia of assimilation, instead enumerating procedural safeguards applicable to disciplinary measures against POWs.[118] Subsequent articles on disciplinary procedures lack resorts to military assimilation as well. Overall, military assimilation with respect to disciplinary sanctions under the Third Geneva Convention proves either a misnomer or a gross oversimplification.

E. Miscellaneous Protections

Finally, the Third Geneva Convention includes dispersed provisions that resort to military assimilation to regulate POW treatment on miscellaneous subjects. Two of these address movement of POWs.

First, the Third Geneva Convention obliges States to evacuate POWs sufficiently far from areas of combat to place them out of danger.[119] Addressing the conduct of POW evacuations, Article 20 requires humane circumstances and "conditions similar to those for the forces of the Detaining Power in their changes of station."[120]

---

114. *Id.*

115. *Id.*, art. 108.

116. *See id.*, arts. 97–98.

117. *Id.*, art. 89. Recall that the ICRC had earlier proposed an exclusive list of disciplinary punishments applicable to POWs, which States declined to adopt in 1929. *See supra* note 70.

118. Third Geneva Convention, *supra* note 1, art. 96.

119. *Id.*, art. 19.

120. *Id.*, art. 20.

This nearly assimilative approach of Article 20 resulted from "lengthy discussions" at the Diplomatic Conference of 1949.[121] The ICRC has recently concluded that, during evacuation, "the conditions for POWs must, as far are [sic] possible, be similar to those for the forces of the Detaining Power when they are moved."[122] The phrase "as far are possible" may not be an ideal characterization. It certainly reflects a sentiment of assimilation but seems not to reflect the language of the article. Article 20 presents instead a diluted brand of assimilation. Compared with other fully assimilative articles of the Convention, such as those addressing penal punishments[123] or criminal trial forum and procedure,[124] Article 20 requires only similarity. Moreover, the article further conditions military assimilation with specific obligations with respect to food, water, clothing, and medical attention that apply regardless of the conditions under which detaining power forces move. Additionally, and wisely, Article 20 requires precautions to ensure POW safety that in many cases are not enjoyed by members of the detaining power's armed forces.

Second, Article 46 of the Convention addresses transfers of POWs between camps. An assimilative approach is apparent in the article's requirement that conditions of transfer are "not less favourable than those under which the forces of the Detaining Power are transferred."[125] Yet, like its counterpart respecting evacuations, Article 46 includes specific requirements for food, water, clothing, and medical attention that prevent POWs from suffering the deprivations that their captor counterparts may endure during long wartime movements or transfers. Like so many of the Third Geneva Convention's provisions, military assimilation does not render a complete understanding of the Convention's requirements applicable to POW transfer and is, in many respects, a misnomer for its carefully considered and historically aware approach.

IV. CURRENT AND FUTURE MILITARY ASSIMILATION DOCTRINE

The 1949 Third Geneva Convention does not reflect in any sense a completion of States' centuries-long project to regulate internment of POWs. Additional Protocol I of 1977 altered select POW provisions in significant respects.[126] Objections to these amendments formed the basis of both reservations by States Parties and

---

121. 1960 GC III COMMENTARY, *supra* note 8, at 173.

122. 2020 GC III COMMENTARY, *supra* note 9, ¶ 1884.

123. Third Geneva Convention, *supra* note 1, art. 87(1).

124. *Id.*, art. 102. Articles 87 and 102 refer specifically and exclusively to standards applicable to members of armed forces of the detaining power.

125. *Id.*, art. 46.

126. Additional Protocol I, *supra* note 13.

refusals by major military powers, including the United States, to ratify.[127] These amendments, however, related chiefly to qualification standards for POW status and to assumptions made with respect to claims of POW status, rather than to treatment standards or conditions of internment.[128] In fact, the diplomatic conference that adopted Additional Protocol I made no significant alternations to the Third Geneva Convention's various and selective resorts to military assimilation.

Still, as recently as 2020, the ICRC asserted that "over the course of modern history, prisoners of war have thus been for the most part 'assimilated' into the armed forces of the Detaining Power."[129] The Committee explains that "the term 'assimilation' reflects an understanding that prisoners of war will be treated on the same terms as members of the armed forces of the Detaining Power."[130] Later, the Committee adds that assimilation "runs through the Convention as a whole."[131] As the preceding sections have made clear, the Committee's assessments in these instances are overbroad and mischaracterize significantly both the general theme and specific articles of the Third Geneva Convention.[132] A more precise characterization by the Committee may be found in a later passage that indicates "the principle of assimilation requires that prisoners of war be treated in the same way as members of the Detaining Power's own forces *in relation to a given issue*."[133]

The Committee further concedes that resorts to assimilation are not without difficulty. It acknowledges that applying assimilation to civilian categories of POWs, including persons authorized to accompany armed forces and merchant ship and air crews, "raises particular challenges."[134] Nonetheless, the identification

---

127. *See, e.g.*, Canada, Statement of Understanding to Additional Protocol I, Article 44(3), *in* SCHINDLER & TOMAN, *supra* note 43, at 797 (stating that Canada will only apply Additional Protocol I relaxed criteria for POW status in occupied territory or armed conflict against colonial, occupying, or racist regimes). *See also* United States, The White House, Letter of Transmittal (Jan. 29, 1987), *reproduced in* Thomas M. Franck, *Agora: The U.S. Decision Not to Ratify Protocol I to the Geneva Conventions on the Protection of War Victims*, 81 AMERICAN JOURNAL OF INTERNATIONAL LAW 910 (1987) (objecting that Additional Protocol I "would grant combatant status to irregular forces even if they do not satisfy the traditional requirements to distinguish themselves from the civilian population and otherwise comply with the laws of war").

128. Additional Protocol I, *supra* note 13, arts. 44, 45.

129. 2020 GC III COMMENTARY, *supra* note 9, ¶ 30 (citing Third Geneva Convention, *supra* note 1, arts. 51, 53).

130. *Id.*, ¶ 30. The updated Commentary recites Articles 51 and 53 as examples of such assimilation. Yet careful inspection reveals that these articles resort not to military assimilation but rather to civilian assimilation. *See* Third Geneva Convention, *supra* note 1, arts. 51, 53. *See also supra* text accompanying note 102.

131. 2020 GC III COMMENTARY, *supra* note 9, ¶ 4003.

132. *See generally supra* Part III.

133. 2020 GC III COMMENTARY, *supra* note 9, ¶ 33 (emphasis added).

134. *Id.*, ¶ 37. It is not widely appreciated that POW status has long extended beyond members of armed forces to civilians accompanying armed forces and crews of certain aircraft and ships

of military assimilation as a principle of the Convention and as reflecting a quantitative majority of treatment standards (for example, "for the most part"[135]) of POW treatment tempts misunderstanding and misapplication of the Third Geneva Convention.

Other sources have dabbled with military assimilation, though seemingly with comparatively greater fidelity. A U.S. federal district court also noted the role of assimilation in the Third Geneva Convention, although in a more modest form.[136] Coining assimilation as the "principle of 'equivalency,'" the court noted the Convention's rules for prosecution of criminal conduct of POWs and "other Articles of the Convention."[137] The court did not, however, perceive equivalency as an overarching feature of the Convention. Instead, it appropriately restricted its discussion of equivalency to the subject of criminal procedure.

Whether the federal district court and the ICRC correctly attributed the status of principle to military assimilation (or equivalency) is worth consideration. Principles are attractive for setting patterns of meaning that enhance general understanding, predictability, and certainty.[138] Principles may in this sense perform some of the interpretive work often assigned to the objects and purposes of treaties.[139] Principles are regarded as distinct from the latter in that a treaty may express or be guided by multiple principles, whereas treaties are generally regarded to have a single object and purpose.[140] Principles also form the foundations or bases for rules.[141]

The ICRC employs the principle of assimilation in precisely this fashion with respect to the Third Geneva Convention.[142] For example, the Committee's analysis

in enemy hands. Third Geneva Convention, *supra* note 1, art. 4A(4)–(5); Sean Watts, *Who Is a Prisoner of War?*, *in* THE 1949 GENEVA CONVENTIONS: A COMMENTARY 890, 906–07 (Andrew Clapham et al. eds., 2015)(analyzing sections of the Third Geneva Convention relative to persons accompanying armed forces and crew members of merchant marine and civil aircraft).

135. 2020 GC III COMMENTARY, *supra* note 9, ¶ 30.

136. United States v. Noriega, 746 F. Supp. 1506, 1526 (S.D. Fla. 1990).

137. *Id.* at 1526.

138. Rüdiger Wolfrum, *General International Law (Principles, Rules, and Standards)*, *in* MAX PLANCK ENCYCLOPEDIA OF PUBLIC INTERNATIONAL LAW ¶ 7 (Anne Peters ed., 2010) (indicating that principles may "serve as a tool in the interpretation, application, and in particular, in progressive development of international law").

139. Vienna Convention, *supra* note 11, art. 31; Jan Klabbers, *Treaties, Object and Purpose*, *in* MAX PLANCK ENCYCLOPEDIA OF PUBLIC INTERNATIONAL LAW ¶ 11 (Anne Peters ed., 2006) (describing an object and purpose as "'the essential provisions of the treaty, which constitute its raison d'être'" (quoting Special Rapporteur, *Tenth Report on Reservations to Treaties*, International Law Commission, 14–15, U.N. Doc. A/CN.4/588 & Add.1-2 (June 1, 14, and 30, 2005) (by Alain Pellet)).

140. Klabbers, *supra* note 139, ¶ 6.

141. Wolfrum, *supra* note 138, ¶¶ 64–73 (defining the concept of rules in general international law).

142. 2020 GC III COMMENTARY, *supra* note 9, ¶ 32.

of Article 30 concerning medical attention concludes, "[a]s for the level of medical care that an infirmary must be able to provide to be considered adequate, it is generally accepted that the Detaining Power should apply the same standards as it would to a similar infirmary for its own armed forces."[143] Yet military assimilation proves problematic, even in this reportedly uncontroversial circumstance. Full military assimilation does not in fact guide medical attention given to POWs. The Committee itself acknowledges as much when it later backtracks on military assimilation to POW medical care. The Committee does not, for example, endorse medical evacuation to the territory of the detaining power, as would often be the case for treatment of that power's own gravely wounded or sick armed forces.[144] Rather than resort to military assimilation as a principle in the first place, only to qualify it selectively and unpredictably, the Committee may have been better served to avoid military assimilation with respect to Article 30 altogether, as did the drafters of the article in 1949.

Others who have not explicitly recognized a principle of military assimilation have resorted to it to fill apparent gaps in the Third Geneva Convention as well. For instance, Professor Levie addresses the possibility of shortages of items normally stocked in the canteens or stores for POWs that Article 28 of the Convention requires the detaining power to install. He resorts to assimilation to the civilian population to fill an apparent gap in the Convention:

> Of course, the stock available at prisoner-of-war canteens will depend largely upon the availability of canteen-type items in the territory of the Detaining Power. If there is, for example, a shortage of tobacco or soap or candy in the territory of the Detaining Power, there will likewise be a shortage of this item in the prisoner-of-war canteens. As in the case of food shortages, to expect any Detaining Power to maintain prisoners of war at a higher standard than that of its own civilian population is an excess of naivete. Unfortunately, the Convention does not contain any provision covering this situation. Presumably, if any such item is rationed to the civilian population, prisoners of war should, by analogy to other Convention provisions, receive a comparable ration.[145]

More concerning than imprecision with or overstating the extent of military assimilation, however, are resorts to military assimilation to springboard more ambitious revisions to the Convention's universally agreed POW treatment regime. The alleged principle of military assimilation has been cited, for instance, to extend human rights law protections applicable to members of armed forces to

---

143. *Id.*, ¶ 2231.

144. *Id.*

145. Levie, Prisoners of War, *supra* note 14, at 144.

POWs.[146] This argument alleges that because POWs are effectively assimilated as soldiers of the detaining power, they, like members of armed forces, enjoy human rights vis-à-vis the detaining power.

The ICRC, for example, envisions through military assimilation an incorporation of human rights law to POWs. It observes:

> Through the principle of assimilation, developments in international law since 1949, including human rights law, as far as they have been incorporated into the domestic legal system governing military personnel, will become applicable to prisoners of war, for example in terms of the relevant procedures for placement in and release from confinement awaiting trial.[147]

To the extent that the Committee means merely to remark that POWs will coincidentally (and, in all likelihood, collaterally) benefit from States' application of international human rights law standards to their armed forces, the observation is not particularly concerning. The human rights assimilation argument may be reasonable to the extent to which military assimilation actually features in the Convention—that is, the extent to which standards applicable to members of the detaining power's armed forces reflect implementation of that State's human rights obligations.

However, understood in conjunction with the overbroad claim that military assimilation is a pervasive or universal aspect of POW treatment more generally, human rights incorporation proves disconcertingly disruptive. That is, if military assimilation is to inform POW treatment "as a whole," human rights law standards might be understood to displace the carefully crafted and selective resorts by the Third Geneva Convention to assimilation. Worse, unrestrained military assimilation might be understood to undo the considered repeals and amendments made to POW protection through assimilation. In cases where the Convention abandons assimilation, the extension of human rights obligations would undermine the Convention's evolved and selective scheme of protection.

To illustrate the disruption of an unfettered claim of human rights incorporation through military assimilation, consider the issue of detention review. Neither the Third Geneva Convention nor any preceding instrument regulating POW treatment includes particularly refined opportunities for POWs to challenge the legality of their internment. The Third Geneva Convention affords POWs opportunities to communicate requests concerning conditions to a camp

---

146. Eden Lapidor, *New Developments in ICRC Commentaries to the POW Convention*, Just Security (June 18, 2020), https://www.justsecurity.org/70863/pow-geneva-convention-commentary-highlights-of-new-developments (relating comments by a panelist explaining that "GC III demands that prisoners of war be treated the same as soldiers of the detaining power (an 'assimilation' principle), it is important to note that the soldiers of the detaining power receive the protections of human rights law").

147. 2020 GC III Commentary, *supra* note 9, ¶ 4022 (citing its own analysis of Article 82 at ¶ 3557 and its introduction at ¶ 34).

commander.¹⁴⁸ Additionally, POWs are permitted to communicate complaints to prisoners' representatives and in the extraordinarily rare instance when they are appointed protecting powers.¹⁴⁹ Finally, the Convention requires detaining powers to convene a "competent tribunal" to resolve doubt concerning POW status.¹⁵⁰ But otherwise, the Third Geneva Convention does not include significant opportunities to review the fact of detention. The Convention largely assumes from a person's qualification for POW status that internment is lawful. Although out of step with prevailing notions of due process in other contexts, the Convention's system is a reflection of operational experience, limited resources, the pressing need for security in conditions of armed conflict, and the military necessity of depriving enemies of fighting forces.

An understanding of military assimilation that includes human rights enjoyed by the members of a detaining power's armed forces would disrupt the Convention's limited but deliberately designed system. International human rights law is broadly understood to include significant individual rights to challenge detention.¹⁵¹ And, although as applied to members of a State's armed forces, some human rights may be modified in scope or substance, the right to challenge detention is generally retained. A rich assortment of administrative and even judicial remedies is available to challenge detention, including time-consuming, resource intensive, and searching standards of review. While perhaps laudable from a purely humanitarian perspective, extension of these standards to the armed conflict context is neither envisioned by States nor in many cases feasible in the stark context of POW camps.

At present, such broad claims respecting military assimilation and human rights law are not accompanied by widespread supporting practice of States. In fact, some detaining powers, confronted with expectations of applying human rights law to wartime detention, have scaled back detention operations, outsourcing them to allied partners who operate free from such restraints.¹⁵² Yet the reach and

---

148. Third Geneva Convention, *supra* note 1, art. 78(1).

149. *Id.*, art. 78(2).

150. *Id.*, art. 5(1).

151. International Covenant on Civil and Political Rights art. 9(4), Dec. 16, 1966, 999 U.N.T.S. 171. The Covenant further guarantees compensation to persons unlawfully detained. *Id.*, art. 9(5).

152. *See* Stephen Pomper, *Human Rights Obligations, Armed Conflict, and Afghanistan: Looking Back Before Looking Ahead*, in THE WAR IN AFGHANISTAN: A LEGAL ANALYSIS 525, 535 (Michael N. Schmitt ed., 2009) (Vol. 85, U.S. Naval War College International Law Studies). Pomper notes a discrepancy between U.S. and European approaches to human rights and armed conflict detention policies. He observes: "The discrepancy between US and European approaches to detention may be partly responsible for having impaired the ability of NATO/ISAF to conduct effective detention operations. Under a rule that applies to all NATO/ISAF forces (including US components under NATO/ISAF command), forces are generally prohibited from holding detainees for longer than ninety-six hours before transferring them to Afghan authorities. This system avoids legal and other complications that might arise out of medium- or long-term

influence of the advocates of human rights incorporation by military assimilation portend future misunderstandings in this respect.

To be sure, military assimilation offers potential humanitarian benefits. States have confirmed as much by retaining military assimilation in some aspects of the Third Geneva Convention. Military assimilation still offers potential to improve the lot of POWs as vulnerable victims of armed conflict. First, as has long been noted, military assimilation offers valuable economy to detention operations, permitting a detaining power to resort to supplies, procedures, and protections that it already has on hand and with which it has facility and experience. Second, military assimilation also amounts to a very practical form of differential obligations, inherently matched to the existing resources and capabilities of various States.[153] Last, as the ICRC and others urge, military assimilation can involve an updating function that is difficult to secure through other means of revision, such as treaty amendment. As States improve and modernize treatment and regulation of their armed forces, POWs enjoy similar improvements and modernizations to the extent that military assimilation applies.[154]

V. CONCLUSION

Efforts to capture and convey the spirit or essence of the Third Geneva Convention are, in abstract, admirable. Correctly applied, the Convention offers perhaps unparalleled practical potential to reduce suffering in war. Yet these efforts must always involve careful examination of the history, text, and subsequent practice of States to avoid mischaracterization. Characterizations of the Convention's resort to military assimilation are no exception. To be sure, military assimilation presents an attractively simple account of or general principle of POW protection. Yet reality indicates the shortcomings and even misconceptions of such an approach. Rather than an overarching principle applicable to the Convention "as a whole" or "for the most part," military assimilation is, at best, an occasional means of compromise and protection of the Third Geneva Convention.

States have resorted only selectively to military assimilation for good reason. Despite its ancient roots, military assimilation has not proved a fail-safe. In the

---

detention, particularly for States that might face challenges under the European Convention on Human Rights, but it has its costs." *Id.*

153. *See* Gabriella Blum, *On a Differential Law of War*, 52 HARVARD INTERNATIONAL LAW JOURNAL 163 (2011) (offering a qualified assessment of the expected effects of differential obligations—obligations linked to capabilities—under the laws of war and concluding that desirability is a function of whether abuse or propensity to resort to force is likely to result). *See also* Adam Roberts, *The Equal Application of the Law of War: A Principle Under Pressure*, 90 INTERNATIONAL REVIEW OF THE RED CROSS 931 (2008)(exploring the related question whether the law of war should operate identically to all types of conflicts).

154. Of course, were a State to regress or reduce protections or treatment of its armed forces, POWs would suffer similarly to the extent that full unmitigated military assimilation applied.

wake of the mixed and even negative experience with military assimilation during the two World Wars, commentary contemporaneous to the 1949 Third Geneva Convention included an important caution. Jean Pictet observed: "The experience of the 1914–1918 war showed, however, that abuses might result from any strict assimilation of prisoners of war with the armed forces of the Detaining Power."[155]

Therefore, accounts of military assimilation as a means of protecting POWs should hew as closely as possible to the careful bargains struck by States over centuries of experimentation and legal development. It is important to understand that the law of war has never taken military assimilation to its full logical or semantic limits. Historical and textual evidence indicates instead a selective and even waning resort to military assimilation. If it has ever been a principle of POW protection at all, military assimilation has always been a principle that is executed selectively. Efforts to expand or revive military assimilation should be undertaken cautiously and, as always, through the time-tested means of international law development that involves the deliberate and open participation of States and their armed forces.

---

155. 1960 GC III COMMENTARY, *supra* note 8, at 406.

10

The Use of Force Against Prisoners of War: Operationalizing Article 42

CHRIS HANNA* AND BRUCE "OSSIE" OSWALD** ∎

On August 5, 1944, a mass Japanese prisoner of war (POW) breakout occurred at the Cowra POW Camp in New South Wales, Australia. Groups of approximately two to three hundred POWs rushed to the wire in four places. They carried baseball bats, staves, improvised clubs, and dining and kitchen knives, some of which had been sharpened or serrated.

Outside the perimeter fences were two machine gunners. They opened fire. The Japanese killed one of the gunners and swarmed the other. In the meantime, guards sought to stem escapes from other areas of the camp. At one point, an armed party located prisoners crawling through the grass and, on receiving no reply to an order to halt, opened fire. The sentry located in "F" tower was armed with an Owen gun,[1] a rifle, and grenades. All the rifle and Owen gun ammunition issued was used by this sentry.

---

*. Chris Hanna is a former Director-General of Australian Defence Force Legal Services and is a legal practitioner in the Australian Capital Territory. This chapter was written in the author's personal capacity and does not necessarily represent the views of the Australian Government, the Australian Department of Defence, or the Australian Defence Force.

**. Bruce "Ossie" Oswald is a Professorial Fellow at Melbourne Law School.

1. The Owen gun was an Australian designed and made submachine gun.

Chris Hanna and Bruce "Ossie" Oswald, *The Use of Force Against Prisoners of War: Operationalizing Article 42* In: *Prisoners of War in Contemporary Conflict*. Edited by: Michael N. Schmitt and Christopher J. Koschnitzky, Oxford University Press.
© Oxford University Press 2023. DOI: 10.1093/oso/9780197663288.003.0010

An order had been given to fire on anyone moving in the Japanese officers' compound, but to avoid hitting the buildings. Of the 1,104 Japanese POWs who occupied the camp, 378 escaped through the wire; 530 reached other parts of the camp but did not manage to break out.

Patrols of Australian military personnel armed with bayonets and commanded by unarmed officers searched the surrounding countryside for escapees. One officer was surprised by eight to twelve Japanese on a hill. They killed him.

Large groups of escapees surrendered to the Australians. However, on August 6 at 0430 hours, an Australian patrol was rushed by six escapees armed with baseball bats, axe handles, and sticks. One was seen to be in the possession of a bayonet. When shots were fired at their feet, the escapees dived for cover. They were then ordered to come with their hands up, which they did. When the escapees were about fifteen yards off, they held their elbows close to their bodies. When the Australians realized that they still had possession of their weapons, the escapees were ordered to halt and drop them. They did so reluctantly.

The Italian, Korean, and Formosan POWs who were also held at the camp did not participate in the riot or breakout and suffered no casualties. One hundred and thirty-eight Japanese POWs were found in the camp and either did not attempt to escape or were unsuccessful.

A Court of Inquiry was convened to inquire into and report on the circumstances surrounding this incident, including the conduct of any person or persons involved. The main findings of the Court can be summarized as follows:

- the use of arms was necessary and was stopped at the earliest possible moment having regard to the circumstances; and
- the discipline and general conduct of guards were highly satisfactory, and there was no evidence of wrongful acts or omissions towards the POWs or of the illegitimate use of force during the recapture of escapees.[2]

On the night of the breakout, three Australian soldiers were killed and another three were wounded. In the following nine days, 334 prisoners were retaken. During the incident, 234 Japanese POWs were killed and 108 wounded.[3] Australian Privates B.G. Hardy and R. Jones, who were overwhelmed while manning a machine gun post, were posthumously awarded the George Cross.

---

2. *See* NAA A7711, VOLUME 1—History: Report on the Directorate of Prisoners of War and Internees at Army Headquarters, Melbourne, 1939–1951: Volume 1 [pages 1–279] and Volume 2 [pages 280–476] [includes matters relating to internees, prisoners of war, war crimes, Prisoners of War Information Bureau in Australia, and a report on the Cowra Breakout escape attempt by Japanese Prisoners of War in August 1944]; Australian National Archives at 175–83.

3. *Cowra Breakout*, AUSTRALIAN WAR MEMORIAL (Dec. 7, 2020), https://www.awm.gov.au/articles/encyclopedia/cowra.

I. INTRODUCTION

The lengthy epigraph to this chapter serves several purposes. First, it draws attention to the fact that POW riots and escapes are a reality that planners and commanders must consider.[4] Second, it reaffirms that such riots and escapes may be extremely violent. Third, it is a reminder that not everyone in the POW camp might want to riot or escape; therefore, the planning for the use of weapons must be carefully considered. Fourth, it also indicates that notwithstanding the violent nature of the escape, the response to those POWs who made it to the surrounding countryside focused on recapture rather than attacking escapees on sight. Finally, it is a reminder that the use of force against POWs will be subject to measures of accountability.

With the above points in mind, this chapter has a narrow aim: it examines how to best operationalize the use of weapons against POWs to ensure that planners and commanders maintain the required levels of security in POW camps, while ensuring that the protective status to which POWs are entitled is maintained. The chapter achieves this aim by relying on Article 42 of the 1949 Convention (III) Relative to the Treatment of Prisoners of War (Third Geneva Convention) as the benchmark against which to assess the use of weapons against escaping POWs.[5]

The focus is on POWs as defined in Article 4(A)(1)–(3) of the Third Geneva Convention and Article 43 of the Protocol Additional to the Geneva Conventions of 12 August 1949, and Relating to the Protection of Victims of International Armed Conflicts (Additional Protocol I).[6] It does not address the use of weapons against civilian POWs (such as journalists or members of the merchant marines), internees, or those detained in a non-international armed conflict. It is hoped, however, that in those situations some of the discussion will prove useful by analogy. It is also hoped that the brief discussion on the use of a "law enforcement

---

4. For a brief description of the treatment of POWs during the Second World War, see GARY SOLIS, THE LAW OF ARMED CONFLICT: INTERNATIONAL HUMANITARIAN LAW IN WAR 314–16 (2010). For many States, the last POW escape cases to which the Third Geneva Convention applied occurred in Korea in 1952. *See* COMMENTARY TO GENEVA CONVENTION III RELATIVE TO THE TREATMENT OF PRISONERS OF WAR 247 (Jean Pictet ed., 1960)[hereinafter 1960 GC III Commentary].

5. Convention (III) Relative to the Treatment of Prisoners of War, Aug. 12, 1949, 6 U.S.T. 3316, 75 U.N.T.S. 135 [hereinafter Third Geneva Convention]. Article 42 provides: "The use of weapons against prisoners of war, especially against those who are escaping or attempting to escape, shall constitute an extreme measure, which shall always be preceded by warnings appropriate to the circumstances." There are no reservations to this article.

6. Protocol Additional to the Geneva Conventions of 12 August 1949, and Relating to the Protection of Victims of International Armed Conflicts, June 8, 1977, 1125 U.N.T.S. 3 [hereinafter Additional Protocol I].

paradigm" to deal with POWs will provide a foundation for further research and analysis.

Following this introductory Part I, the chapter has four substantive parts. Part II outlines the broad context in which the use of weapons against POWs should be considered. Part III deconstructs Article 42 of the Third Geneva Convention by examining key terms in the provision: (1) "use of weapons," (2) "escaping or attempting to escape," and (3) "extreme measures" and "warnings." Part IV discusses whether a law enforcement paradigm is useful when considering the use of lethal force against POWs. Part V suggests how to operationalize Article 42.

II. CONTEXT: LAW AND PRAGMATISM

Understanding the context in which weapons may be used against POWs is important because it sharpens some of the operational concerns that might arise and provides a benchmark against which doctrine development and planning may be undertaken. What follows is an overview of some of the legal and pragmatic concerns that arise when considering the use of weapons against POWs.

The framework for the treatment of POWs is founded on two general legal principles. First, POWs must not be the "object of attack."[7] This is to say, the use of force against POWs cannot be considered pursuant to the conduct of hostilities paradigm.[8] The International Committee of the Red Cross (ICRC) has reinforced this approach in its 2020 Commentary on the Third Geneva Convention:

> This is because persons deprived of their liberty are clearly *hors de combat* and "have fallen into the power of the enemy" in the sense of Article 4 of the Convention. Thus, they cannot be engaged under the rules governing the conduct of hostilities, regardless of the fact that they were lawful targets before their capture.[9]

---

7. UNITED KINGDOM MINISTRY OF DEFENCE, THE MANUAL OF THE LAW OF ARMED CONFLICT ¶ 5.6 (2004).

8. For a more detailed discussion of the conduct of hostilities paradigm, see, for example, *id.* at ch. 5.

9. INTERNATIONAL COMMITTEE OF THE RED CROSS, COMMENTARY ON THE THIRD GENEVA CONVENTION: CONVENTION (III) RELATIVE TO THE TREATMENT OF PRISONERS OF WAR ¶ 2539 (2020) [hereinafter 2020 GC III Commentary], https://ihl-databases.icrc.org/applic/ihl/ihl.nsf/Comment.xsp?action=openDocument&documentId=261C96F149E8E094C1258585003A9CCB.

The second principle flows from the first. POWs must be treated humanely and protected against acts of violence or intimidation.[10] This principle repudiates an older view by which POWs "could be killed . . . butchered or offered as sacrifices to the gods."[11]

Notwithstanding these two principles, historically there was a broad view that weapons could be used against escaping POWs. For example, in both the 1870 Declaration and the 1880 Oxford Manual, it was accepted that "[a]rms may be used, after summoning, against prisoner of war attempting to escape."[12] This acceptance that weapons may be used against escaping POWs appears to reflect a pragmatic concern about POWs rejoining their own forces or other enemy forces and thereby returning to the fight. However, the principle of humanity was not totally ignored because the use of arms would only be justified if a POW was first called upon to surrender.

Acknowledging that weapons may be used against escaping POWs sat uncomfortably with States. As explained in the 2020 Commentary:

> This was not because its relevance was disputed, but because "it was felt that this was a delicate matter to express in a Convention." Drafters feared that stating in a humanitarian convention that weapons may be used against prisoners of war would be understood as an invitation to employ lethal force rather than as a reminder of the associated limits on such use of force.[13]

By the end of the Second World War, however, it appears that States remained reluctant to prohibit the use of arms against POWs. This is notwithstanding:

> [t]he experience of the Second World War, which included excessive use of force against and murder of prisoners of war, notably after escape attempts, as well as the establishment of "death lines" in camps or "death zones" outside camps, which prisoners of war were absolutely forbidden to cross or enter under penalty of being fired upon by guards or sentries.[14]

---

10. *See* Third Geneva Convention, *supra* note 5, art. 13.

11. H. Lauterpacht, 2 Oppenheim's International Law 291 (6th ed. 1940).

12. Project of an International Declaration concerning the Laws and Customs of War art. 28, Brussels, Aug. 27, 1874, *reprinted in* The Laws of Armed Conflicts 23 (Dietrich Schindler & Jiří Toman eds., 4th ed. 2004). These words are replicated in Institute of International Law, The Laws of War on Land art. 68 (1880) (Oxford Manual), *reprinted in* The Laws of Armed Conflicts 29 (Dietrich Schindler & Jiří Toman eds., 4th ed. 2004).

13. 2020 GC III Commentary, *supra* note 9, ¶ 2521, https://ihl-databases.icrc.org/applic/ihl/ihl.nsf/Comment.xsp?action=openDocument&documentId=261C96F149E8E094C1258585003A9CCB.

14. *Id.*, ¶ 2522.

During the April 1947 negotiations over the Third Geneva Convention, the ICRC proposed that "if the use of arms against [POWs] attempting to escape could not be prohibited, it should at least be subject to regulations."[15] States working on the provision also recommended that a "more extensive ruling should be made regarding the use of arms against [POWs], in view of the many deaths caused by abuses in this respect."[16] This endorsement led to the insertion of a clause within the general heading of escapes by POWs, providing that "[a]rms shall not be used against [POWs] except to prevent escape or enforce discipline. Such use shall only serve as a last resort; and shall always be preceded by appropriate warning."[17]

By May 1948, it was generally accepted by the delegates that because the April 1947 amendment dealt with the use of arms in relation to discipline, it was appropriate to shift it to the section entitled "Discipline," rather than leaving it in the stipulations concerning escapes.[18] The shift was accepted and the draft article now read:

> The use of arms against prisoners of war, especially against those who are escaping or attempting to escape, shall only constitute a last resort, which must always be preceded by warnings appropriate to the circumstances.[19]

There are two observations concerning discussions between April 1947 and May 1948 about the use of arms against POWs. First, their use was not prohibited outright. This is important because it seems that States generally accepted that the use of arms might be required at the very least to maintain discipline and to prevent escapes. The ICRC's 1960 Commentary, in addressing this matter, reaffirmed that "[c]aptivity is based on force, and although there can be no doubt on the matter, it is recognized in international customary law that the detaining power has the right to resort to force in order to keep prisoners captive."[20] This acknowledges the broad general principle that the detaining power has the right to hold POWs in order to stop them from rejoining the fight.

Moreover, acceptance of the need to enforce discipline reflects the broad obligation of detaining powers to maintain law and order among POWs for their benefit and for the safety of others. In relation to discipline, it is noteworthy that the May 1948 draft removed the reference to "enforcing discipline." Perhaps the reason for this was an understanding that if the use of arms appeared under the section heading of "Discipline," it would be reasonable to conclude that arms may be used

---

15. Report on the Work of the Conference of Government Experts for the Study of the Conventions for the Protection of War Victims 213 (Apr. 14–26, 1947).

16. *Id.*

17. *Id.* at 212.

18. XVIIth International Red Cross Conference, Stockholm, August 1948: Report 77 (May 1947).

19. *Id.*

20. 1960 GC III Commentary, *supra* note 4.

to enforce discipline. It is also reasonable to assume that the mention to discipline is related to serious offenses because Article 42's reference to the use of weapons was qualified throughout the drafting process and into the final provision.

Second, the use of arms was further limited to *in extremis* situations and only permissible after warnings appropriate to the circumstances had been given. These limitations perhaps reflect the importance that States placed on the protective status of POWs as *hors de combat*. They also reflect the pragmatic recognition that violent treatment, such as the excessive use of force against POWs, might also be meted out to the detaining power's military personnel held by the enemy. This concern reaffirms the broad general principle of reciprocity.

During the October 1948 meeting, a further change was made to the draft article: the word "arms" was replaced with the word "weapons." While there is no explanation in the records for this change, it is arguable that the word "arms" refers specifically to firearms, whereas the word "weapons" has a broader meaning, as it includes any object that can be used to cause harm. Thus, the word "arms" would not include a pickaxe handle, whereas the word "weapons" would.

By the October meeting, States had settled on the wording of what would become Article 42 of the Third Geneva Convention:

> The use of weapons against prisoners of war, especially against those who are escaping or attempting to escape, shall constitute an extreme measure, which shall always be preceded by warnings appropriate to the circumstances.[21]

In summary, Article 42 may be understood by acknowledging the broad general principle that POWs cannot be the objects of attack, but also that states have legitimate concerns about escaping POWs. First, POWs must be sufficiently cognizant of the risks associated with escaping or serious breaches of discipline. As put bluntly in the 1960 Commentary, "[o]ne cannot require the Detaining Power to reinforce the sentry units indefinitely at the expense of its active combat forces. The only remaining alternative is therefore to adopt very strict measures in order to intimidate prisoners of war."[22] Second, guards and sentries of POWS must be reminded that the general principle of not using violence against POWs may only be overridden in extreme circumstances.

III. DECONSTRUCTING ARTICLE 42

To better understand how to operationalize Article 42, it is helpful to deconstruct it by focusing on key text, particularly (1) "use of weapons," (2) "escaping or attempting to escape," and (3) "extreme measures" and "warnings."

---

21. International Committee of the Red Cross, Draft Revised or New Conventions for the Protection of War Victims art. 35 (May 1948) (emphasis added).

22. 1960 GC III Commentary, *supra* note 4, at 247.

A. Use of Weapons

As stated in the 2020 Commentary, Article 42 governs the use of all weapons.[23] However, does it govern the use of all weapons pursuant to international humanitarian law (IHL)? This question is not answered in the *travaux preparatoires*. If one assumes, however, that because Article 42 is found in the Third Geneva Convention, it follows that the term "weapons" is to be interpreted pursuant to IHL, then two further questions arise. First, may a detaining power use all generally IHL-compliant weapons against POWs? Second, are there any IHL rules that prohibit the use of specific weapons against POWs?

1. Use of Certain Weapons on General Principles

The answer to the first question is relatively straightforward. If the weapon is lawful pursuant to Article 35 of Additional Protocol I, it may be assumed that the weapon is lawful under IHL for use against POWs even though its use is not during combat operations.[24]

The answer to the second question depends on whether it can also be assumed that if the use of a weapon is unlawful on general principles, it cannot be used against POWs. The preferred answer is that it cannot be so used, but an unqualified response would be inadequate. First, there is a question regarding whether the use of force (and weapons) in the management of POWs involves the employment of a "method of warfare" to which the principles and rules applicable to combat operations should be applied. Second, not all "unlawful weapons" are prohibited merely on the basis of "general principles." Both issues are discussed below.

2. Specifically Unlawful Weapons

States that have ratified treaties that unequivocally prohibit the use of certain weapons in an armed conflict, such as anti-personnel land mines,[25] would also be prohibited from using them against POWs. However, there are two instances where it is less clear whether weapons and ammunition that are banned for use in

---

23. 2020 GC III Commentary, *supra* note 9, ¶ 2527.

24. Additional Protocol I, *supra* note 6, art. 35:

> 1. In any armed conflict, the right of the Parties to the conflict to choose methods or means of warfare is not unlimited.
> 2. It is prohibited to employ weapons, projectiles and material and methods of warfare of a nature to cause superfluous injury or unnecessary suffering.
> 3. It is prohibited to employ methods or means of warfare which are intended, or may be expected to, cause widespread, long-term and severe damage to the natural environment.

25. Other weapons that are subject to specific use during armed conflict include mines, booby traps and other devices, cluster munitions, incendiary weapons, blinding lasers, herbicides, and nuclear weapons. *See, e.g.*, Office of the General Counsel, U.S. Department of Defense, Law of War Manual 343 (rev. ed., Dec. 2016) [hereinafter DoD Law of War Manual] and subsequent discussion.

armed conflict are permitted if used against POWs. These instances are the use of riot control agents and expanding rounds.

(a) Riot Control Agents

The ICRC's Customary International Humanitarian Law study states that "[t]he use of riot-control agents as a method of warfare is prohibited."[26] This conclusion is based on Article 1(5) of the Chemical Weapons Convention.[27] This article provides that each "State Party undertakes not to use riot control agents as a method of warfare." However, Article II(9)(d) of the Convention permits the use of riot control agents for "law enforcement including domestic riot control purposes."[28]

According to the study, several States interpret the Chemical Weapons Convention as permitting the use of riot control agents against rioting POWs. For example, Australia's position is that riot control agents are permitted during times of conflict to deal with situations such as rioting POWs or civilians.[29] The United States also takes this view by arguing that the use of riot control agents is permitted in areas under "direct and distinct U.S. military control, to include controlling rioting prisoners of war."[30] New Zealand, while not permitting the use of riot control agents, does not prohibit their use either. Although not explicit in the context of use with POWS, the New Zealand Defense Force *Manual of Armed Forces Law* provides, "Subject to orders, members of the [New Zealand Defense Force] may use riot control agents that have been issued for their use to suppress riots, rescue hostages, perform law enforcement tasks or assist the civil authorities. Because factual situations may overlap, NZDF commanders are to exercise care in the decision to use riot control agents during armed conflict, even though their use may not obviously be a 'method of warfare.'"[31] There are several

---

26. CUSTOMARY INTERNATIONAL HUMANITARIAN LAW Rule 75 (Jean-Marie Henckaerts & Louise Doswald-Beck eds., 2005), https://ihl-databases.icrc.org/customary-ihl/eng/docs/v1_rul_rule75.

27. Officially known as the Convention on the Prohibition of the Development, Production, Stockpiling and Use of Chemical Weapons and on their Destruction, Sept. 17, 1997, 2056 U.N.T.S. 211.

28. *Id.*, art. II(9)(d).

29. *See* CUSTOMARY INTERNATIONAL HUMANITARIAN LAW, *supra* note 26, Rule 75, https://ihl-databases.icrc.org/customary-ihl/eng/docs/v2_rul_rule75.

30. Executive Order 11850—Renunciation of certain uses in war of chemical herbicides and riot control agents (Apr. 8, 1975), https://www.archives.gov/federal-register/codification/executive-order/11850.html. *See also* DoD LAW OF WAR MANUAL, *supra* note 25, § 6.16.

31. NEW ZEALAND DEFENCE FORCE, MANUAL OF ARMED FORCES LAW: VOLUME 4 LAW OF ARMED CONFLICT DM 69 ¶ 7.6.37 (2d ed. 2017), https://usnwc.libguides.com/ld.php?content_id=47364407.

countries that prohibit the use of riot control agents in armed conflict without providing a caveat as to their use against POWs.[32]

One interpretation of the permissive approach is that it is based on the belief that the use of riot control agents should not be considered a "method of warfare" when used in the context of rioting POWs (who are not being engaged as combatants during the conduct of hostilities). Therefore, it is legitimate to apply a different approach. This permissive approach acknowledges that such agents are widely used by States for law enforcement purposes, which might be applied by clear analogy to the management of rioting POWs.

It is also arguable that the use of these agents in POW camps does not give rise to any superfluous injury and unnecessary suffering concerns, at least as far as such uses are confined to where riot control agents would be legitimately used in analogous civilian circumstances and in a similar manner and quantity.[33] This point is reinforced by the 1960 Commentary, which acknowledges that weapons that do not cause fatal injuries, such as tear gas and truncheons, may be used in situations such as mutinies by POWs (before resorting to "weapons of war").[34]

It is also important to note that the prohibition on the use of riot control agents as a method of warfare is primarily based on the desire to keep chemical weapons, in all forms, off the battlefield to avoid provoking an escalation to the use of other more deadly chemicals.[35] In this sense, the prohibition of the use of riot control agents as a method of warfare is not strictly or directly an application of the general IHL principles, but rather a precautionary device to support the application of a specific prohibition. Accordingly, the use of riot control agents in the limited and quite different circumstances of managing POWs does not compromise the purpose of the prohibition.

(b) Expanding Ammunition

The Customary International Humanitarian Law study states that expanding bullets are prohibited.[36] This view draws on the 1899 Hague Declaration Concerning Expanding Bullets, as a statement of customary international law:

---

32. *See* CUSTOMARY INTERNATIONAL HUMANITARIAN LAW, *supra* note 26, Rule 75, https://ihl-databases.icrc.org/customary-ihl/eng/docs/v2_rul_rule75.

33. *See* Additional Protocol I, *supra* note 6, art. 35.

34. 1960 GC III Commentary, *supra* note 4, at 247.

35. *See, e.g.*, the Netherlands position as stated in CUSTOMARY INTERNATIONAL HUMANITARIAN LAW, *supra* note 26, Rule 75, https://ihl-databases.icrc.org/customary-ihl/eng/docs/v2_rul_rule75.

36. CUSTOMARY INTERNATIONAL HUMANITARIAN LAW, *supra* note 26, Rule 77, https://ihl-databases.icrc.org/customary-ihl/eng/docs/v1_rul_rule77.

> The Contracting Parties agree to abstain from the use of bullets which expand or flatten easily in the human body, such as bullets with a hard envelope which does not entirely cover the core or is pierced with incisions.[37]

However, the U.S. Department of Defense Law of War Manual provides:

> The law of war does not prohibit the use of bullets that expand or flatten easily in the human body. Like other weapons, such bullets are only prohibited if they are calculated to cause superfluous injury. The U.S. armed forces have used expanding bullets in various counterterrorism and hostage rescue operations, some of which have been conducted in the context of armed conflict.[38]

It might further be argued that the U.S. view is supported by the Elements of Crimes under the Rome Statute of the International Criminal Court,[39] which has a cumulative test in relation to the use of hollow point ammunition. The relevant elements of that test include:

> The bullets were such that their use violates the international law of armed conflict because they expand or flatten easily in the human body.
> The perpetrator was aware that the nature of the bullets was such that their employment would uselessly aggravate suffering or the wounding effect.[40]

Based on these elements, it is reasonable to consider whether the ICRC's insistence regarding the customary IHL prohibition still applies to all bullets with these physical characteristics, whatever their actual military utility in the specific circumstances. In any event, there is perhaps no reason to recommend a dogmatic prioritization of technical specifications if this means that a bullet that may cause fewer collateral effects than a "standard" bullet (by preventing over-penetration and/or limiting ricochet effects) should be automatically excluded across all operational scenarios, including when dealing with rioting POWs or hostage situations in a POW camp.

A differential approach might be grounded on the proposition that the use of force within a POW camp is not a "method of warfare." Alternatively, whatever approach is taken for combat operations, it might be safe to adopt a circumstance-specific approach within the limited and relatively controlled environment of a

---

37. Declaration (IV, 3) Concerning Expanding Bullets, July 29, 1899, 187 Consol. T.S. 459, 26 Martens Nouveau Recueil.

38. DoD Law of War Manual, *supra* note 25, § 6.5.4.4.

39. Rome Statute of the International Criminal Court, July 17, 1998, 2187 U.N.T.S. 90.

40. International Criminal Court, Elements of Crimes (2011), art. 8(2)(b)(xix) (War crime of employing prohibited bullets).

POW camp, provided the use of expanding rounds is confined to those analogous circumstances where such rounds would be used by civilian authorities for law enforcement (for example, hostage rescue). As with riot control agents, the adoption of a different approach within a POW camp would not compromise the underlying purposes of any wider prohibitions applicable to the battlefield.

B. Escaping or Attempting to Escape and Other Situations

It is generally accepted that POW status commences from the moment a combatant falls "into the power of the enemy"[41] or, put another way, is in the control of the enemy. This restraint on liberty may arise from "surrender, surprise capture, desertion, or having become overcome by active force."[42] Furthermore, because Article 42 falls under the provisions relating to discipline in the Third Geneva Convention, it may be assumed that any use of weapons is in the context of preventing escapes and harm rather than punishing POWs.[43]

1. Escaping or Attempting to Escape

Two issues arise in relation to the reference to "escaping or attempting to escape." First, when considering the use of weapons, does it matter where or when the escape is occurring? For example, does it matter that the escape occurs at the time of capture as opposed to when the POW is moved to a POW camp that may be in another country? This is a matter that the 1960 and 2020 commentaries fail to address in detail. Yet, it is an important pragmatic issue concerning the level of threat posed to the detaining power. Prima facie, escape at the point of capture is going to be more "threatening" to the detaining power than escape in another country. Accordingly, what qualifies within the scope of an extreme but legitimate measure might be tied to the chances that escapees can rejoin their own forces or otherwise recommence hostilities.

For instance, it would be reasonable for a guard to immediately use lethal force without warning if a POW escape will reveal a concealed captor's presence and position. It might also be the case that the act of escape in certain circumstances (such as when in the close presence of the enemy) might be regarded as rejoining the fight, at which point the escapee would no longer be a POW entitled to the

---

41. Third Geneva Convention, *supra* note 5, art. 5. This trigger for POW status is also reflected in Additional Protocol I, *supra* note 6, art. 44(1).

42. Sean Watts, *Who Is a Prisoner of War*, *in* THE 1949 GENEVA CONVENTIONS: A COMMENTARY 890, 892 (Andrew Clapham, Paola Gaeta & Marco Sassòli eds., 2015). *See also* MARCO SASSÒLI, INTERNATIONAL HUMANITARIAN LAW: RULES, CONTROVERSIES, AND SOLUTIONS TO PROBLEMS ARISING IN WARFARE (2019), ¶¶ 8.80–8.85 for combatants who lose POW status.

43. 2020 GC III Commentary, *supra* note 9, ¶ 2529.

protection of Article 42. In these situations, the paramount concern for the detaining power is the immediate threat to security posed by the escaping POW.[44]

The second issue involves identifying when a POW's actions related to an escape have developed to a point where it is legitimate to even consider using lethal force. Relevant to this discussion is the question of "control," a term that appears elsewhere in the Third Geneva Convention[45] but not in Article 42 itself. That is, the legitimacy of the use of force is inextricably linked to and limited by the detaining power's right to retain and regain control over POWs (whether as individuals or in a group). Consequently, it is only when, by the actions of the POW, this control is placed at immediate and substantive risk, or has already been lost and needs to be regained, that lethal force can be considered. Relatedly, the 1960 Commentary notes that it is "important . . . to make a distinction between escape proper and acts or phases preparatory thereto."[46] The 1960 Commentary then cites an example of when a POW is caught making preparations to escape within the camp limits. In that case, lethal force is not authorized because there was no immediate and substantive risk of loss of control.[47]

In a POW camp situation, this issue is tied to a much broader question: Does Article 42 remain the controlling provision once a POW has escaped the boundaries of the camp? That is, at what point for the purposes of the use of force is the POW no longer considered to be an escapee (the escape has ended), but rather has reverted to their previous status as a combatant?

The starting point for this discussion is to consider whether there are any preparatory acts related to escaping or attempting to escape that might warrant the use of weapons. For example, do acts such as acquiring "tools, maps, plans or other aids facilitating flight" or starting "to dig a tunnel or stock food supplies"[48] justify the use of weapons? It is difficult to see why such acts would, in any circumstances, place the detaining power's control at immediate risk. Of course, once the construction of the tunnel reaches outside the boundaries of the camp, different considerations might surface. However, even then there would be many variables to consider in determining whether the actions of the POWs had progressed beyond mere preparation. Such a conclusion might be readily reached if a tunnel had an exit point outside of the camp.

---

44. These comments aside, this paper limits its coverage to the Third Geneva Convention and, primarily, escape from the POW camp environment rather than the field combat environment. Specifically, the paper does not seek to address the application of Additional Protocol I art. 41(2) concerning the position of persons *hors de combat* who attempt to escape from their captor and who may be subject to attack.

45. *See, e.g.*, Third Geneva Convention, *supra* note 5, arts. 33, 56, 91, 92.

46. 1960 GC III Commentary, *supra* note 4, at 246.

47. *Id.*

48. 2020 GC III Commentary, *supra* note 9, ¶ 2529.

The U.S. position is that POWs "should not be fired upon if they are apprehended within the camp limits while preparing to escape and there is no risk of escape or harm to anyone."[49] Implicit in this position is the fact that at this point in an escape plan the detaining power has not lost control of the POW, nor is it about to lose control. Consequently, there is no immediate risk of escape and, objectively, the POW is not yet escaping. Conversely, however, if risk of escape exists, the U.S. view of the situation may be different and the mere fact that the POW is physically still in the camp may not be decisive. For example, might the use of weapons be justified if a POW is seen cutting the wire to an outer perimeter wire (that is, the POW is carrying out the last preparatory act before escaping from the camp)? Does it matter if there are dozens of POWs cutting the wire and the escape appears to involve many POWs? Both scenarios could amount to what the 1960 Commentary envisages as the "escape proper" rather than "acts or phases preparatory thereto."[50]

The 1960 Commentary addresses these types of "advanced" escape attempts by stating that "fire may be opened only when there is no other means of putting an immediate stop to the attempt."[51] This might be characterized as forming part of a "control" test. That is, if firearms are not used at a particular point, control of the POW will be lost or, if it has just been lost, not immediately regained. Nevertheless, the reference to "no other means" is perhaps more relevant to satisfying the requirement that lethal force only be used as an "extreme measure" (discussed later), as opposed to identifying the initial point when control has been or is about to be lost.

The 2020 Commentary has added a significant degree of sophistication and structure to the analysis of this area of law and practice but has only been able to take the discussion to a certain point. A control test is alluded to in the 2020 Commentary when it suggests that the use of weapons against POWs carrying out preparatory acts to escape would not be justified because the POW "is not yet eluding the control of the detaining authority."[52] However, perhaps frustrated by a lack of consistent and/or disclosed State practice or other expert commentary, and having suggested that the loss of control test might determine when weapons may be used against POWs, the 2020 Commentary does not develop the issue of when that loss of control for purposes connected with Article 42 will manifest. Instead, the 2020 Commentary's substantive comments relate to the separate subject of when an escape is to be considered "successful" and, hence, when the escaping POW will have lost any Article 42 protection and can be re-engaged as a combatant. In this sense, the 2020 Commentary shifts its argument by stating

---

49. DoD Law of War Manual, *supra* note 25, § 9.22.6.

50. 1960 GC III Commentary, *supra* note 4, at 246.

51. *Id.*

52. 2020 GC III Commentary, *supra* note 9, ¶ 2529.

that the law is unsettled on this point because there are two views concerning the conditions for a successful escape:[53]

> According to one view, an escape is successful only when the conditions for a successful escape as defined in Article 91 are fulfilled.
>
> According to the second view, if escaping prisoners of war have made their way outside the camp or are otherwise no longer under immediate pursuit, the escape is already successful for the purpose of targeting and they can be targeted under the rules on the conduct of hostilities, under which the restrictions on the use of force in Article 42 do not apply (and no further warnings are required).[54]

Without resolving the differences between the two views, the 2020 Commentary then suggests that the conduct of hostilities rules, rather than the constraints of Article 42, apply to targeting escaped prisoners when they:

> can no longer be considered *hors de combat*, either because a) they are about to rejoin their armed forces or the armed forces of an allied Power and thus targetable again under the rules on the conduct of hostilities based on their combatant status, or b) they are otherwise directly engaged in a hostile act (not including the escape itself) after having made their way outside the camp and escaped the control of the Detaining Power; and this regardless of whether their escape has been successful in the sense of Article 91. This is because, as indicated above, the reason for the special restrictions on the use of force in Article 42 are based on the fact that the person is *hors de combat*, under the control of the Detaining Power. When this is no longer the case, there is no further need to apply Article 42.[55]

The references to "control" in this part of the 2020 ICRC discussion do not advance an understanding of how the concept of control relates to the application of force under Article 42 itself. Nor does it, more precisely, assist in identifying when the risk to control is such that it can be said that the POW is escaping rather than just preparing to escape.

In contrast, perhaps, the 1960 Commentary addresses the notion of control in a more direct manner by arguing that "fire may be opened only when there is no other means of putting an immediate stop to the attempt. From the moment the person attempting to escape comes to a halt, he again places himself under the protection of the Detaining Power. . . ."[56] This interpretation suggests that control

---

53. *Id.*, ¶ 2554.

54. 2020 GC III Commentary, *supra* note 9, ¶¶ 2552–53.

55. *Id.*, ¶ 2554.

56. 1960 GC III Commentary, *supra* note 4, at 246.

refers to the moment when a POW would no longer be able to be controlled by the guard, and it would not be possible for the guard to immediately regain control.

If this interpretation of Article 42 is correct, it follows that lethal force can be used in at least some circumstances against POWs before they have left the camp, although those circumstances remain opaque. Conversely, if it is not correct, the earliest point at which an escape attempt has progressed sufficiently to warrant the use of lethal force (albeit with other factors to be considered, including the issuing of warnings and consideration of alternative means) remains unsettled.

It might be suspected that States, on grounds of potential reciprocity with an adversary, would tend toward a position (perhaps as a matter of policy) that favored restraint and moderation. That is, States may decide to continue to apply an Article 42-based approach to those POWs who have reached outside of the camp, at least in the context where an immediate reacquisition of control is reasonably achievable (for example, the escapees can be readily pursued and captured or they are within the range where warnings can still be heard—essentially, where control was lost but can be immediately regained). This is not to say, however, that they will not be shot at. Rather, any firing will be preceded by warning, will be a last resort, and, overall, will be an extreme measure.

There are circumstances where the mere loss of control arguably should immediately end the application of Article 42 and permit the targeting of the escapees within the context of the law of armed conflict. This would be a particularly reasonable approach in situations where the ability to regain control would be difficult because of the prevailing operational conditions—such as a POW escaping during a firefight with the enemy. Moreover, a detaining power would be entirely justified in differentiating its approaches between scenarios while remaining within the law. That is, even if a State considered the 'second' view referred to in the 2020 Commentary (that is, having "made their way outside the camp or are otherwise no longer under immediate pursuit" this is sufficient for a "successful" escape) to be legally sound, it might reserve taking action based upon it for a more operationally pressing scenario and instead adopt a more restrained, if not graduated, approach to POWs who are on the run from a camp.

In this context, it might also be noted that it appears that in the Cowra example, the actions of the Australian forces when sweeping the countryside for escaped Japanese POWs, even while under threat, were generally consistent with an Article 42 approach to the use of force. That is, predating the adoption of Article 42, the substantive approach was more in line with the first rather than second view. Perhaps this supports an observation that in many (but not necessarily all) circumstances, POWs who have taken the precipitous step of escaping will find themselves in a highly vulnerable, rather than a genuinely combative, position. This observation might deter a blanket or dogmatic adoption of the second view, whether on a legal or merely policy basis. Instead, it might suggest that the application of Article 42, at least as a matter of policy, should extend as long as feasible, if only to avoid potentially unnecessary killings (which, among other things, may have adverse effects on the detaining power's guard personnel) and perhaps a sense of unease if a State has expressly encouraged its vulnerable personnel to escape if captured. Finally, if the loss of control test is applied to when the use of weapons may be justified against POWs, it cannot be said that just because a loss of control has occurred, guards may use weapons. The Article 42 caveat of "extreme measure" (discussed below) will still apply.

2. OTHER SITUATIONS

While it is true that Article 42 makes no reference to other situations in which the use of weapons might be justified, it is clear because of the word "especially" in Article 42 that the use of force might be justified in other situations. These situations include POWs rioting, looting, committing arson, or committing serious assaults. Such serious offenses might also occur in the context of POWs escaping or attempting escape. One way of imagining these serious offenses is to consider them as common criminal offenses. If they are common criminal offenses, then it follows that the means and methods used to deal with POWs who commit them are those that would be applicable pursuant to the domestic criminal law of the detaining power.

The 2020 Commentary states that when a POW is "posing an imminent threat to life or limb, either to the guards or to fellow prisoners, . . . the guards may use force to defend themselves or others as a last resort, in accordance also with applicable rules and principles under domestic law and international human rights law."[57]

The 2020 Commentary's reference above to guards using "force to defend themselves" suggests that guards who do use force will rely on the doctrine of self-defense to justify their acts.[58] The practical effect of this reliance means that unlike combatant immunity, which is available to all combatants, the guards may be subjected to prosecution for using force unlawfully. Furthermore, in relying on individual self-defense, which is firmly entrenched in domestic law doctrine, they would be arguing that their use of force was justified under the circumstances. Consequently, what will matter in examining the guard's justification for using a weapon will be the criminal law and procedure of the detaining power. For example, if the detaining power is Australia, the doctrine of self-defense that an Australian Defence Force guard would apply is found in the Australian Commonwealth Criminal Code Act 1995.

It might, however, be the case that the detaining power has passed specific legislation to deal with the rights and responsibilities of POW guards. For example, it may enact a specific law of self-defense rule for POW guards that is broader than the self-defense law that is generally imagined in peacetime. Furthermore, it may be that other defenses are recognized that are context specific, such as a defense of superior orders.

---

57. 2020 GC III Commentary, *supra* note 9, ¶ 2531.

58. The 1960 GC III Commentary states that guards and sentries may act in "legitimate self-defence" when, for example, they are about to be overwhelmed: *supra* note 4, at 247.

One assumes that in situations where other serious crimes are being committed—such as rioting, arson, and serious assaults—the doctrine of self-defense would also apply. However, would the doctrine apply where there is no threat to life and limb, such as when POWs are looting the camp? The answer would depend on the domestic law of the detaining power. In Australia, for example, lethal force in such circumstances would not be permitted to protect property.[59] Such is the case in many other jurisdictions.

C. Extreme Measures Preceded by Warnings

An important aspect of the use of weapons under Article 42 is the strict limitation placed on their use—it is "an extreme measure." Two matters arise when considering how this clause interacts with Article 42. First, is the use of all weapons an extreme measure or only the use of firearms? Second, what test should be applied to determine whether a guard's use of weapons was within the scope of a legitimate extreme measure?

It is reasonable to assume that the use of lethal force would fall within the limitation of an extreme measure. However, would the use of non-lethal weapons also be an extreme measure? This is a more difficult question because of the competing aims of protecting the status of POWs and maintaining discipline. Perhaps it is because of these competing aims that the 1960 Commentary states (as cited earlier): "One cannot require the Detaining Power to reinforce the sentry units indefinitely at the expense of its active combat forces. The only remaining alternative is to adopt very strict measures in order to intimidate prisoners of war."[60] This form of intimidation must still be within the construct of Article 42 as an extreme measure.

The definition of what is meant by the term "extreme measure" is addressed in the 1960 Commentary: "'An extreme measure' means that fire may be opened only when there is no other means of putting an immediate stop to the attempt [to escape]."[61] Determining when there is "no other means" suggests that the test is subjective. This is to say that the POW guard must believe that they have no other option but to use their weapon. It would also be reasonable to assume that the POW guard's belief must be reasonable. Thus, there is also an objective element to the test.

This does not mean that a guard must embark on a protracted consideration of all their options, or even take significant risks where delay in using force may improve the chances of effective escape from the camp. Instead, it means that if a guard has reasonably concluded that a POW's escape attempt can be thwarted by,

---

59. *See* Australian Commonwealth Criminal Code Act 1995, s. 10.4(3)(a).

60. 1960 GC III Commentary, *supra* note 4, at 247.

61. *Id.* at 246.

say, dispatching an available ready reaction force (for example, to wait for them on the other side of the fence or wall), or by the guard simply approaching the escapee (for instance, as the POW tries to cut through a wire obstacle), then these options must be taken. What it also means is that the justification for relying on a POW crossing a "line of death" as a basis for using lethal force will be absent if there are readily available alternatives to prevent the escape. Clearly, therefore, a prudent detaining power would devote the necessary resources to ensuring that there are alternative security arrangements in place to prevent escapes, albeit this is not a strict legal requirement.

In relation to warnings, it seems clear from Article 42 that warnings must be given prior to POW guards using weapons. As with all warnings, the person to whom the warning is issued must understand the warning and the warning "must also be followed, where feasible, by sufficient time for it to be observed."[62] Warnings may be verbal, a show of graduated force, or by instrument. What is uncertain is whether warnings are required in every conceivable situation. Further, might in some circumstances warnings be pre-loaded in the sense of notifying POWs that "if you try to escape, I will shoot you"—particularly if the POWs are still on the battlefield, where a further warning may compromise a tactical position. It might be argued that, in keeping with the spirit of Article 42, any verbal or use of graduated warnings must be in the context of what is reasonable under the circumstances.

The use of warning shots as a part of the graduated use of force will depend on the doctrine of the detaining power. The 2020 Commentary makes the point:

> Warning shots are potentially risky, as they may harm bystanders or trigger an escalation in violence. For these reasons, some States have replaced them by a mere "show of force," i.e. the guards showing what weapons they have at their disposal and of their readiness to use them, such as by placing a finger on the trigger or charging a weapon. When not forbidden under domestic law, warning shots should only be fired with due caution.[63]

In keeping with the protective status of POWs, there is, of course, no justification as a matter of law for using weapons indiscriminately.

It is true that Article 42 makes it clear that the use of weapons is not a "first resort, but a last resort."[64] Nevertheless, "[i]f the facts require the use of lethal force, there is no legal requirement to use non-lethal force first."[65] Consequently, it would be reasonable to assume that there is no reason to issue warnings or to use graduated force if such facts existed.

---

62. 2020 GC III Commentary, *supra* note 9, ¶ 2545.

63. *Id.*, ¶ 2547.

64. *Id.*, ¶ 2538.

65. *Id.*, ¶ 2549.

IV. LAW ENFORCEMENT PARADIGM

The term "law enforcement" is not referred to in the Third Geneva Convention or in the 1960 Commentary. However, the 2020 Commentary states:

> Since 1949, under international human rights law, international legal standards have developed pertaining to the use of force in law enforcement operations, including the circumstances under which individuals may lawfully be deprived of their lives by State agents in the performance of their duties. Furthermore, law enforcement rules and principles exist in virtually all domestic legal orders. In practice, these legal frameworks seek to achieve a similar type of protective result in terms of their imposing a graduated response and escalation of the use of force when it comes to the use of weapons.[66]

Care is required in associating, let alone promoting, the term "law enforcement" in the context of the use of force against POWs. First, while Article 42 provides a legal framework for the treatment of POWs, the contents of a law enforcement regime will vary from jurisdiction to jurisdiction (if not within the same jurisdiction). Accordingly, a blanket, imprecise reference to "law enforcement" is unhelpful. Second, the underlying reasons for using force against POWs to maintain discipline or to prevent escape differ from those related to civilian law enforcement.

These are differences that may cut multiple ways as to whether the comparative approach between POWs and domestic criminal prisoners should be more or less severe. For instance, notions of preserving community safety or simply the need to uphold the law are quite different from the drivers concerning the treatment of POWs. Moreover, the urge to moderate the level of force used against POWs on the grounds of reciprocity is unlikely to be present in a domestic prison scenario. Most importantly, it may be doubted that the incorporation of (or deference to) a law enforcement paradigm substantially improves the framework that is already presumed to exist under Article 42, particularly as it relates to escaping prisoners.

One way to understand the relevance of applying a law enforcement paradigm to escaping prisoners is to examine how domestic jurisdictions deal with such situations. For example, in the Australian State of Victoria, there is specific statutory authority to use firearms against an escaped criminal inmate. Victoria's legislation only authorizes the discharge of a firearm by an "escort officer" when it "is the only practicable way to prevent the escape of the prisoner from custody."[67] Additionally, the relevant officer must "if it is practicable to do so, give an oral warning to that person to the effect that the person will be shot at if that person does not stop escaping [etc.]."[68] If anything, by referring to practicalities, this latter

---

66. *Id.*, ¶ 2535.

67. Corrections Act 1986 (Vic), s. 55EB(1)(b).

68. *Id.*, s. 55EB(4)(a).

requirement is less stringent than the black letter requirement in Article 42. The relevant officer must also be satisfied that "discharging a firearm at the person does not create an unnecessary risk to any other person."[69] This is not, however, a blanket prohibition on incurring risk. Upon analysis, these tenets within the Victorian legislation are already reflected one way or another in Article 42 itself or in the commentary on it. This would raise the question of whether there is anything substantive to be drawn from this domestic law enforcement paradigm. Moreover, with this particular example, it may (unwittingly) be that the domestic law enforcement framework is catching up to IHL, noting that the specific relevant domestic law provisions were only introduced in 2014.[70]

It must also be recognized that a law enforcement paradigm does not necessarily present a safer or more protective outcome for the domestic prisoner in comparison to that enjoyed by a POW. For instance, the underlying U.S. constitutional position is undeniably permissive with respect to the use of force against convicted prisoners, including escaping prisoners. The U.S. constitutional limits on the use of force against convicted prisoners are drawn from the Eighth Amendment, under which deadly force is only prohibited if it amounts to a "cruel and unusual punishment."[71]

The U.S. Supreme Court confirmed this as the legal standard governing the use of force in prison contexts in *Whitley v. Albers*.[72] In that case, the Court stated that the conduct prohibited by the Eighth Amendment was characterized by "obduracy and wantonness," rather than inadvertency or an error made "in good faith."[73] The question of whether measures taken by officers "inflicted unnecessary and wanton pain and suffering" was dependent upon a finding that the force applied was not applied in a "good-faith effort to maintain or restore discipline" but rather was applied "maliciously and sadistically for the purpose of causing harm."[74] While various U.S. jurisdictions (state and federal) may have incorporated limitations on the use of deadly force against escaping prisoners (including, through express references to what is reasonable and necessary),[75] this appears in many cases to remain a revocable choice. It might be presumed that the protections understood to be incorporated into Article 42 are on firmer ground.

If the focus shifts away from "correctional" to a more general law enforcement conception, there is increased scope for divergence from the principles applicable

---

69. *Id.*, s. 55EB(4)(b).

70. Corrections Legislation Amendment Act 2014 (Vic), s. 8.

71. U.S. CONST. amend VIII.

72. Whitley v. Albers, 475 U.S. 312 (1986). *See also* Graham v. Connor et al., 490 U.S. 386 (1989).

73. *Whitley*, 475 U.S. at 318–326. *See also* Hudson v. McMillian, 503 U.S. 1 (1992); Sims v. Artuz, 230 F.3d 14, 21 (2nd Cir., 2000).

74. *See Hudson*, 503 U.S. at 6; *Sims*, 230 F.3d at 21.

75. *See, e.g.*, ALA. CODE § 13A-3-27(h)(1) (2018).

via Article 42. For instance, in Victoria, it is permitted for a police officer or citizen to:

> use such force not disproportionate to the objective as he believes on reasonable grounds to be necessary to prevent the commission, continuance or completion of an indictable offence or to effect or assist in effecting the lawful arrest of a person committing or suspected of committing any offence.[76]

The Victorian courts have interpreted what is reasonable by considering two factors:

> [1] He is entitled to use such a degree of force as in the circumstances he believes is necessary to effect his purpose, [2] provided that the means adopted by him are such as a reasonable man placed as he was placed would not consider to be disproportionate to the evil to be prevented (i.e., the commission of the felony or the escape of the felon).[77]

This is not a replication of Article 42 in any form and does not point toward the central requirements of that article in a meaningful way. Most importantly, this provides a clear example of where it is necessary to precisely examine the term "law enforcement" to understand what is being referred to.

Overall, a fair conclusion to draw from the various domestic law enforcement paradigms is that, while they should not be discounted as having relevance to the discussion of the use of force against POWs, the lack of uniformity and the potential for outcomes for prisoners who do not meet the express and implicit standards of Article 42 suggest that caution and nuance are required.

V. OPERATIONALIZING THE LAW

In view of the above analysis of matters that need to be considered, the following proposal is offered as to how States may wish to interpret and apply Article 42 (either in doctrine or as orders).

A. Discipline

1. The use of force is permitted against POWs who are committing or about to commit serious breaches of discipline.

---

76. Crimes Act 1958 (Vic), s. 462A.

77. R v. Turner [1962] VR 30, 36.

a. In circumstances where there is a serious breach of discipline which threatens life, such as rioting, arson, hostage taking, serious assaults, the use of force, including lethal force, is permitted. In such circumstances, the use of weapons, including riot control agents and expanding bullets, is permitted.
b. In circumstances where the breach of discipline does not threaten life, the use of lethal force is prohibited.
c. Unless acting in self-defense where it would be unreasonable to give a warning, warnings must be given prior to the use of force.

B. Escape — In the Field

1. The use of force, including lethal force, is permitted to stop a POW who is being held in the field from escaping if it is reasonably believed that the POW is likely to pose a threat to the Detaining Power, Coalition Forces, or Partnered Forces.

   a. A warning is to be given if lethal force is to be used unless the circumstances of the escape or operational conditions make it unreasonable to do so.
   b. Riot control agents and expanding bullets shall not be used to stop an escape or attempted escape.

C. Escape — From POW Camps

1. The use of force, including lethal force, is permitted to stop a POW from escaping where it is reasonably believed that unless lethal force is used, the Detaining Power will lose control over the POW or, in self-defense.
2. A warning is to be given if force is to be used unless the circumstances of the escape or operational conditions make it unreasonable to do so.
3. Weapons, including riot control agents and expanding bullets, are permitted to stop an escape or attempted escape.

Of course, this list is not a substitute for further discussion of the unresolved and uncertain issues identified in this chapter. These issues include articulating a philosophical approach to the question of when lethal force can be used against escaping POWs (potentially adopting a "control" test), resolving when the use of force paradigm shifts from Article 42 back to that which is applicable during the conduct of hostilities, and clarifying which weapons that are specifically regulated on the battlefield may or may not be used against POWs. This discussion is clearly an activity best initiated, if not completed, before rather than during the next conflict in which POWs are taken and held.

11

Parole of Prisoners of War Under Article 21 of the Third Geneva Convention: The Past, Present, and Future

EMILY CRAWFORD* ∎

I. INTRODUCTION

Article 21 of Convention (III) Relative to the Treatment of Prisoners of War (Third Geneva Convention)[1] is, arguably, *the* pivotal provision of that Convention: it provides explicit legal authority for States to detain captured enemy personnel as prisoners of war (POWs). However, despite the centrality of this authorization to the entire legal basis of the Conventions, the bulk of Article 21—177 words out of a total of 265—is not dedicated to the legal justification for detention but is instead focused on affirming that "[p]risoners of war (POWs) may be partially or wholly released on parole or promise." Article 21 goes on to provide guidelines on such parole, including recommendations that it be allowed "where this may contribute to the improvement of [the POW's] state of health" and that no POW should be compelled to accept parole, but that, if they do, parolees "are bound on their personal honour scrupulously to fulfil, both towards the Power on which they depend and towards the power which has captured them, the engagements of their paroles or promises."

---

*. Associate Professor, The University of Sydney Law School.

1. Convention (III) Relative to the Treatment of Prisoners of War, Aug. 12, 1949, 6 U.S.T. 3316, 75 U.N.T.S. 135 [hereinafter Third Geneva Convention].

In essence, parole is an agreement on the part of the captive soldier to refrain from participating in hostilities in return for limited or unrestricted release from POW captivity. Parole—from the French "word" or "promise,"[2] as in "to give one's word"[3]—is a concept grounded in medieval notions of chivalry and honor, underpinned by both pragmatic and humanitarian objectives, traceable as far back as ancient Roman times. By the eighteenth century, it was a given that POWs could be paroled during their captivity, with parole agreements established during conflicts such as the Franco-Prussian War, the Boer War, and the American Civil War. However, by the time of the adoption of Article 21, the practice of parole was far less common, with exceptionally limited employment of parole during the First and Second World Wars.

With this historical background in mind, this chapter will examine the history of parole of POWs—why it was adopted, and why it has fallen into desuetude. The chapter will also examine whether the tradition of parole remains a viable or useful option for States, in light of new technologies and new practices in the conduct of armed conflicts.

II. A BRIEF HISTORY OF PAROLE IN STATE PRACTICE

The earliest records of the treatment of captives in times of armed conflict indicate that prisoners taken during war could, at best, hope to be enslaved, with the more likely outcome being summary execution. Records from ancient civilizations such as Mesopotamia, Egypt, Assyria, Greece, and Rome all indicate that captured enemy soldiers were either executed or taken as spoils of war and enslaved[4]—a practice that was likely followed in Asia as well.[5] The exception was the Carthaginians, who regularly employed a system of parole, most famously with Roman general Marcus Atilius Regulus. Regulus was paroled by the

---

2. Oxford-Hachette French Dictionary: French–English (4th ed., 2012).

3. *Parole*, Oxford English Dictionary, https://www.oed.com/view/Entry/138072?rskey=onAZrP&result=3#eid (last visited May 10, 2021).

4. *See, e.g.*, J.N. Postgate, Early Mesopotamia: Society and Economy at the Dawn of History 254–55 (1996); James Henry Breasted, Ancient Records of Egypt: Historical Documents from the Earliest Times to the Persian Conquest, Vol. 2: The Eighteenth Dynasty 49–50, 165–66 (1988); Daniel Luckenbill, Ancient Records of Assyria and Babylonia, Vol 1: Historical Records of Assyria from the Earliest Times to Sargon 279–84 (1989); Hans van Wees, Greek Warfare: Myths and Realities 146–47 (2004); J.E. Lendon, Soldiers and Ghosts: A History of Battle in Classical Antiquity 235–36 (2005). For a more general overview of the treatment of captives during ancient times, *see* Alexander Gillespie, A History of the Laws of War, Vol.1: The Customs and Laws of War with Regards to Combatants and Captives 104–19 (2011).

5. *See* Howard Levie, Prisoners of War in International Armed Conflicts 1, 3–4 (1977) (Vol. 59, U.S. Naval War College International Law Studies); Gary D. Brown, *Prisoner of War Parole: Ancient Concept, Modern Utility*, 156 Military Law Review 200, 201–03 (1998).

Carthaginians, on the promise that he would return to Rome and advocate in the Senate for peace between Carthage and Rome. On appearing before the Senate, Regulus put forward the case for peace, but, when asked for his own opinion, he advocated continuing the war. Having given his word, Regulus returned to Carthage, where he was tortured to death.[6]

The practice of enslaving or killing captives continued until the Middle Ages, when several developments brought about a change in the treatment of prisoners in wartime. First, in 1179, the Third Lateran Council prohibited the enslavement of Christian POWs.[7] The prohibition was adopted during a period of history—the Middle Ages—that was also witnessing the second development that would change the treatment of prisoners in wartime: the emergence of a code of chivalry. Notions of chivalry changed the ways in which war was fought, at least by a particular class of combatant—that of the knight.[8] Chivalry emerged as, essentially, a military code of conduct adhered to by knights, "the heavily armed and armoured mounted warriors who dominated the military landscape between the eleventh and fifteenth centuries AD."[9] Originally, the status of knight was related to the possession of specific equipment and materiel. However, in time, knighthood became inextricably entwined with hereditary nobility, and with it came the belief that members of the same rank and caste, even of opposing forces,[10] were deserving of honorable treatment in warfare—namely, capture rather than execution.[11]

---

6. *See* M. TULLIUS CICERO, DE OFFICIIS 1.39 (Walter Miller trans., 1913); William R. Nifong, *Promises Past: Marcus Atilius Regulus and the Dialogue of Natural Law*, 49 DUKE LAW JOURNAL 1077 (2000). The poet Horace wrote of Regulus's sacrifice: 'And yet he knew what the barbarian torturer/was preparing for him: nonetheless, he moved/aside the relatives who tried to stop him/and the crowd trying to delay him/as though he were just leaving court after/a long case for clients, the outcome decided,/setting off for the fields of Venafrum/or Spartan Tarentum.' Horace, *Courage and Decadence: The Regulus Ode*, PANTHEON POETS, https://www.pantheonpoets.com/poems/courage-and-decadence-the-regulus-ode/.

7. Canon XXIV, Third Lateran Council, *reprinted in* LEVIE, *supra* note 5, at 4.

8. Though the Second Lateran Council banned the use of the crossbow on the grounds of being an offense to God (*see* Canon XIV, Second Lateran Council, *reprinted in* H.J. SCHROEDER, DISCIPLINARY DECREES OF THE GENERAL COUNCILS: TEXT, TRANSLATION, AND COMMENTARY 204 (1937)), scholars argue that the prohibition was more likely precipitated by the fact that crossbows were able to penetrate the kinds of armor worn only by knights and could be used by anyone without special training, thus undermining the military supremacy of the Christian knight. Chivalry, in this sense, was motivated as much by self-interest as it was by codes of honor. *See* RICHARD SHELLY HARTIGAN, CIVILIAN VICTIMS IN WAR: A POLITICAL HISTORY 74 (1982).

9. PAUL ROBINSON, MILITARY HONOUR AND THE CONDUCT OF WAR 60 (2006).

10. Only if those forces were fellow Christians. *See id.*, at 74.

11. This honorable treatment did not extend to soldiers who were not knights. *See* RAIN LIIVOJA, CHIVALRY WITHOUT A HORSE: MILITARY HONOUR AND THE MODERN LAW (2012). *Honor and the Modern Law of Armed Conflict*, *in* THE LAW OF ARMED CONFLICT: HISTORICAL AND CONTEMPORARY PERSPECTIVES (Rain Liivoja & Andres Saumets eds., 2012).

Honor alone was not, however, the sole motivator for capturing knights. As members of noble, landowning estates, knights were wealthy. Keeping them as captives meant that they could be ransomed for considerable sums of money.[12] The practice of ransoming prisoners in wartime continued for some time, until it gradually transformed into the practice of paroling such prisoners. This was partially driven by changes in the nature of warfare, shifting from an endeavor fought by private armies that were personally loyal to a prince, to endeavors fought by persons answering a call of duty from the State. As Rousseau argued, "war is a relation not between man and man but between state and state, and individuals are enemies only accidentally, not as men nor even as citizens but as soldiers; not as belonging to their country but as defenders of it."[13] Therefore, if soldiers were not the personal enemy of the capturing state, they could not be the personal spoils of war of the enemy and thus they were not able to be ransomed.

By the seventeenth century, parole was a recognized part of international law, included in the Peace of Westphalia,[14] and noted as accepted practice by authors such as Grotius,[15] Gentili,[16] and Vattel.[17] Central to the notion of parole was that the paroled prisoner would be granted liberty so long as they vowed not to take up arms against their captor or attempt escape until an exchange of POWs was completed.[18] By the eighteenth and nineteenth centuries, the practice of parole was at its zenith. Officers and enlisted were regularly paroled during the American Revolution,[19] with both the British and the Americans compelling parolees to "promise and engage, on my word and honor, and on the faith of a gentleman"[20]

---

12. ROBINSON, *supra* note 9, at 75. Prior to the Middle Ages, parole was the exception rather than the rule, except, interestingly, in Islamic cultures, where ransom and POW exchange were more common.

13. JEAN-JACQUES ROUSSEAU, DU CONTRAT SOCIAL OU PRINCIPES DU DROIT POLITIQUE 9–10 (1762).

14. Peace Treaty between the Holy Roman Emperor and the King of France and their respective Allies arts. CX–CXI, Oct. 24, 1648, *available at* https://avalon.law.yale.edu/17th_century/westphal.asp.

15. HUGO GROTIUS, DE JURE BELLI AC PACIS, bk. III, ch. VII, I, 604–05 (1625).

16. ALBERICO GENTILI, DE JURE BELLI, bk. 3, 295–96 (1588).

17. 2 EMER DE VATTEL, LE DROIT DES GENS, bk. III, ch. XVI, sec. 264. *See* WILLIAM FLORY, PRISONERS OF WAR: A STUDY IN THE DEVELOPMENT OF INTERNATIONAL LAW 117 (1942).

18. ALLAN ROSAS, THE LEGAL STATUS OF PRISONERS OF WAR: A STUDY IN INTERNATIONAL HUMANITARIAN LAW APPLICABLE IN ARMED CONFLICTS 47 (1976).

19. CHARLES METZGER, THE PRISONER IN THE AMERICAN REVOLUTION 193 (1971); George Coil, *War Crimes of the American Revolution*, 82 MILITARY LAW REVIEW 171, 187 (1978); DANSKE DANDRIDGE, AMERICAN PRISONERS OF THE REVOLUTION 51 (1967).

20. The Congressionally Mandated Oath, *reprinted in* Brown, *supra* note 5, at 204. Similar wording and provisions were included in British parole agreements. *See* CHARLES METZGER, THE PRISONER IN THE AMERICAN REVOLUTION 192 (1971).

to, inter alia, "not directly or indirectly, give any intelligence whatsoever"[21] to the enemy, or "do or say anything in opposition to, or in prejudice of"[22] the enemy, until discharge or repatriation. Likewise, during the Napoleonic Wars, the War of 1812, and the Mexican War, parole regimes were utilized frequently, though not without abuses of the system.[23]

The American Civil War saw the most widespread use of a system of parole, through the Dix-Hill Cartel. Formally established in July of 1862, the Cartel provided that all POWs were to be discharged on parole ten days after their capture[24] and that while on parole, they were prohibited from serving in the armed forces. This included in the role of "military police or constabulary force in any fort, garrison or field-work held by either of the respective parties, nor as guards of prisoners, depots or stores, nor to discharge any duty usually performed by soldiers"[25] until they were formally exchanged. However, once parolees had been formally exchanged, they were at liberty to rejoin the conflict.

Parole of POWs was, fundamentally, pragmatic—as Stephen Neff puts it, "rationalism and calculation were the order of the day."[26] Parole freed up resources that would otherwise have been spent maintaining POWs in detention facilities, potentially for protracted periods of time. It also benefited the side with fewer overall numbers of fighting-age men; returning such men to the ranks enabled the conflict to continue to be fought.[27] Moreover, the very notion of parole played on concepts of honor and duty for parolees—as Gary Brown notes, "generally, parole was offered only to officers, those 'gentle' members of the educated and upper class. To gentlemen, honor meant a great deal, and parole was a matter of honor."[28]

However, despite the pragmatic benefits of parole, and the centrality of notions of honor,[29] in practice, parole regimes tended not to last long, with violations of

---

21. The Congressionally Mandated Oath, *reprinted in* Brown, *supra* note 5, at 204.

22. *Id.*

23. *See* Brown, *supra* note 5, at 204–05; FLORY, *supra* note 17, at 117; LEVIE, *supra* note 5, at 399; GEORGE G. LEWIS & JOHN MEWHA, HISTORY OF PRISONER OF WAR UTILIZATION BY THE UNITED STATES ARMY 1776-1945 23–26 (1955).

24. Dix-Hill Cartel on Prisoner Exchanges art. 4, July 22, 1862, *reprinted in* AMERICAN CIVIL WAR: INTERPRETING CONFLICT THROUGH PRIMARY DOCUMENTS 233 (Justin D. Murphy ed., 2019).

25. *Id.*

26. Stephen Neff, *Prisoners of War in International Law: The Nineteenth Century, in* PRISONERS IN WAR 57 (Sibylle Scheipers ed., 2010).

27. As Flory noted, "the detaining state may find it advantageous to release prisoners on parole in order to avoid maintaining them during the progress of the war and to liberate prison guards for active duty." FLORY, *supra* note 17, at 119.

28. Brown, *supra* note 5, at 210.

29. *See* Renaud Morieux, *French Prisoners of War, Conflicts of Honour, and Social Inversions in England, 1744-1783*, 56 THE HISTORICAL JOURNAL 55 (2013).

parole common. The American Civil War was the last time in history in which parole was practiced in a systematic way on a large scale.[30] The Dix-Hill Cartel lasted only ten months: both sides frequently failed to observe the requirements of exchange "as soon as practicable," and there were frequent violations of agreements not to return to the fight. In one particularly notable instance, thirty-seven thousand paroled Confederate soldiers were found to have returned to battle in direct violation of the terms of parole.[31] Later examples of limited parole regimes, such as during the Boer War, were also marked by violations, with British POWs paroled by the Boers frequently breaking their parole oaths.[32]

By the time of the Russo-Japanese War of 1904,[33] there were few instances of parole being offered or accepted and, by the outbreak of the First World War in 1914, the practice of parole had essentially fallen into desuetude.[34] During that conflict, German officers were allowed on parole in France,[35] but the practice was quickly terminated when Germany did not extend similar privileges to captured French officers.[36] Likewise, only two instances of parole seem to have been recorded as occurring during the Second World War, with Italian POWs paroled by U.S. forces in Sicily[37] and U.S. forces paroled by the Japanese in the Philippines.[38]

---

30. Neff, *supra* note 26, at 61.

31. *See* JAMES MCPHERSON, BATTLE CRY OF FREEDOM 792 (1988); CHARLES MURPHY, PRISONERS OF WAR: REPATRIATION OR INTERNMENT IN WARTIME—AMERICAN AND ALLIED EXPERIENCE, 1775 TO PRESENT 2–3 (1971).

32. JONATHAN VANCE, OBJECTS OF CONCERN: CANADIAN PRISONERS OF WAR THROUGH THE TWENTIETH CENTURY 18 n.29 (1994).

33. *See* SAKUYÉ TAKAHASHI, INTERNATIONAL LAW APPLIED TO THE RUSSO-JAPANESE WAR WITH THE DECISIONS OF THE JAPANESE PRIZE COURTS 107–08 (1908).

34. Neff, *supra* note 26, at 61. *See also* Neville Wylie & Lindsey Cameron, *The Impact of World War I on the Law Governing the Treatment of Prisoners of War and the Making of a Humanitarian Subject*, 29 EUROPEAN JOURNAL OF INTERNATIONAL LAW 1327 (2019).

35. R.C. HINGORANI, PRISONERS OF WAR 187 n.23 (1963).

36. HERBERT FOOKS, PRISONERS OF WAR 301 (1924).

37. GEORGE G. LEWIS & JOHN MEWHA, HISTORY OF PRISONER OF WAR UTILIZATION BY THE UNITED STATES ARMY 1776–1945 178–79 (1955); Neff, *supra* note 26, at 61.

38. LEVIE, *supra* note 5, at 400. Comments in the report of the Conference of Government Experts for the Study of the Conventions for the Protection of War Victims, convened to consider the draft revised conventions, seem to indicate that the practice of limited parole was far more common than just the two reported cases in Sicily and the Philippines. The report notes that "certain Delegations stated that their countries, though generally speaking adverse to liberty on parole being granted to members of their own armed forces, were led to conclude arrangements with the enemy for temporary liberty on parole of certain PW who required exercise." INTERNATIONAL COMMITTEE OF THE RED CROSS, REPORT ON THE WORK OF THE CONFERENCE OF GOVERNMENT EXPERTS FOR THE STUDY OF THE CONVENTIONS FOR THE PROTECTION OF WAR VICTIMS (GENEVA, APRIL 14–26, 1947) 133–34 (1947) [hereinafter REPORT ON THE CONFERENCE OF GOVERNMENT EXPERTS].

III. THE HISTORY OF PAROLE IN INTERNATIONAL LAW

As described in Part II of this chapter, parole was well-established in State practice for many centuries. With the push toward codification of the international law of war that began in the latter part of the nineteenth century, these practices began to be included in documents on the law of war.

The first significant written iteration of parole was in the Lieber Code,[39] the rules of war adopted by the Union armies during the American Civil War. Parole was extensively covered in fifteen articles in the Code,[40] setting out rules about how parole was to be granted. The Code seemingly foreshadowed the coming demise of the practice of parole, outlining in Article 123 that "[r]elease of prisoners of war by exchange is the general rule; release by parole is the exception." The Code also reaffirmed that parole entailed an oath not to participate in the hostilities[41] unless exchanged,[42] and that a parole breaker was liable to punishment by death for violating their oath.[43] It excluded from parole violations of certain domestic military service, such as "recruiting or drilling the recruits, fortifying places not besieged, quelling civil commotions, [and] fighting against belligerents unconnected with the paroling belligerents," as well as "civil or diplomatic service for which the paroled officer may be employed."[44]

The practice of parole was framed entirely as a matter of choice, rather than obligation, for parties to a conflict: POWs "may be released from captivity by exchange, and, under certain circumstances, also by parole,"[45] but the decision to implement such a system remains at the discretion of the parties.[46] Moreover, no participant in the hostilities is under an obligation to accept an offer of parole[47]—as parole is positioned as "an individual, but not a private act,"[48] no POW "can be forced by the hostile government to parole himself."[49]

---

39. U.S. Department of War, Instructions for the Government of Armies of the United States in the Field, General Orders No. 100, Apr. 24, 1863 [hereinafter Lieber Code].

40. *Id.*, arts. 119–34.

41. *Id.*, art. 120.

42. *Id.*, art. 130.

43. *Id.*, art. 124.

44. *Id.*, art. 130.

45. *Id.*, art. 199.

46. *Id.*, arts. 132–33.

47. *Id.*, art. 133.

48. *Id.*, art. 121.

49. *Id.*, art. 133.

The Lieber Code was "instantly influential":[50] following the Code's adoption during the American Civil War, several States adopted Lieber-style codes for their armed forces, including Prussia,[51] the Netherlands,[52] France,[53] Russia,[54] Serbia,[55] Argentina,[56] the United Kingdom,[57] Portugal,[58] and Spain.[59] The Code was, as Geoffrey Best has put it, "the quarry from which all the subsequent codes were cut."[60] Its formulation of parole was largely followed, though in less detail, in the first attempt to adopt an international instrument on the law of war—the 1874 Project of an International Declaration concerning the Laws and Customs of War,[61] which would come to be known as the Brussels Declaration. Though the Declaration was not adopted as a binding instrument, its formulation of the law of war was itself influential in bringing about the binding 1899 and 1907 Hague Conventions,[62] which likewise adopted similar, if shortened, Lieber-style provisions on parole.[63]

---

50. JOHN FABIAN WITT, LINCOLN'S CODE: THE LAWS OF WAR IN AMERICAN HISTORY 343 (2012).

51. In 1870.

52. In 1871.

53. In 1877.

54. In 1877; revised in 1904.

55. In 1878.

56. In 1881.

57. In 1883; revised in 1904.

58. In 1890.

59. In 1893. For comments on the above-noted military codes, *see* THOMAS ERSKINE HOLLAND, THE LAWS OF WAR ON LAND: WRITTEN AND UNWRITTEN 72–73 (1908).

60. GEOFFREY BEST, HUMANITY IN WARFARE: THE MODERN HISTORY OF THE INTERNATIONAL LAW OF ARMED CONFLICTS 171 (1980).

61. Project of an International Declaration concerning the Laws and Customs of War, Brussels, Aug. 27, 1874, *reprinted in* THE LAWS OF ARMED CONFLICTS 23 (Dietrich Schindler & Jiří Toman eds., 4th ed. 2004). The parole provisions were contained in Articles 31–33. The Russian delegate and President of the Brussels Conference, Baron Jomini, explicitly noted that the Conference had its origins in the Lieber Code. RICHARD SHELLY HARTIGAN, LIEBER'S CODE AND THE LAW OF WAR 22 (1985).

62. Convention No. II with Respect to the Laws and Customs of War on Land, July 29, 1899, 32 Stat. 1803, T.S. No. 403 [hereinafter Hague II]; Convention No. IV Respecting the Laws and Customs of War on Land, Oct. 18, 1907, 36 Stat. 2227, T.S. No. 539 [hereinafter Hague IV].

63. In Hague II and Hague IV, *supra* note 62, arts. 10–12. Parole was also included in Article 75 of the 1880 Oxford Manual, a non-binding instrument published by the Institute of International Law, which provides: "Prisoners of war may be released in accordance with a cartel of exchange, agreed upon by the belligerent parties." Institute of International Law, The Laws of War on Land (1880) (Oxford Manual), *reprinted in* THE LAWS OF ARMED CONFLICTS 29 (Dietrich Schindler & Jiří Toman eds., 4th ed. 2004).

In the Hague Regulations,[64] Lieber's expansive rules on parole were narrowed down to three essential elements. First, "[p]risoners of war may be set at liberty on parole if the laws of their country authorize it, and, in such a case, they are bound, on their personal honour, scrupulously to fulfil, both as regards their own Government and the Government by whom they were made prisoners, the engagements they have contracted";[65] if POWs accept parole, they are not required to provide any service incompatible with the oath of parole (nor can their government accept any offer from the POW to carry out services that would violate the terms of parole).

Second, POWs cannot be compelled to accept parole, nor are governments obligated to assent to a request for parole[66]—parole is a right available to the State, not the captive. The detaining authority is under no obligation to offer parole and the detained combatant is under no obligation to accept it.

Finally, "[a]ny prisoner of war, who is liberated on parole and recaptured, bearing arms against the Government to whom he had pledged his honour, or against the allies of that Government, forfeits his right to be treated as a prisoner of war, and can be brought before the courts."[67]

Parole was not explicitly provided for in the 1929 Geneva Convention on POWs;[68] the conventions of 1929 were designed not to replace the Hague Regulations, but rather to supplement the preexisting rules,[69] which meant there was no need to repeat the established rules on parole in the 1929 instrument. However, reference was made to parole in Article 77, which stated that Bureaux of Relief and Information should be kept informed about POWs who are granted parole and should serve as the depository of any personal effects left behind by paroled POWs in order to transmit such effects to the parolee's home country.

The shortcomings[70] of the 1929 Convention were made apparent during the Second World War. When the International Committee of the Red Cross (ICRC) convened a conference of State experts to consider revising and developing the conventions, it was agreed that provisions on parole should be included in new conventions on the treatment of POWs.[71] The Commission of Government

---

64. Regulations Respecting the Laws and Customs of War on Land, annexed to Convention No. IV Respecting the Laws and Customs of War on Land, Oct. 18, 1907, 36 Stat. 2227, T.S. No. 539 [hereinafter Hague Regulations].

65. Hague II and Hague IV, *supra* note 62, art. 10.

66. Hague II and Hague IV, *supra* note 62, art. 11.

67. Hague II and Hague IV, *supra* note 62, art. 12.

68. Convention Relative to the Treatment of Prisoners of War, July 27, 1929, 47 Stat. 2021, 118 L.N.T.S. 343.

69. THE LAWS OF ARMED CONFLICTS 421 (Dietrich Schindler & Jiří Toman eds., 4th ed. 2004).

70. *See* Wade Mansell and Karen Openshaw, *The History and Status of the Geneva Conventions*, *in* THE GENEVA CONVENTIONS UNDER ASSAULT 18 (Sarah Perrigo & Jim Whitman eds., 2010).

71. Revised and New Draft Conventions for the Protection of War Victims, Remarks and Proposals Submitted by the International Committee of the Red Cross, Document for the

Experts, tasked with reviewing and debating the new draft conventions, "thought useful to take up the question of liberty of [POWs] on parole . . . in order to have a self-contained [POW] Convention"[72]—that is, a document that did not require reference to preexisting instruments, such as the Hague Regulations. As to the question of parole, States experts, "though generally speaking adverse to liberty on parole being granted to members of their own armed forces,"[73] were nonetheless convinced that limited parole, particularly for disabled POWs, "would be particularly valuable"[74] and should therefore be explicitly included in the new POW convention.

Draft Article 19 of the new POW convention reiterated the formulation of parole as contained in the Hague Regulations, but amended the Regulations in a few respects, eliminating certain provisions and including new rules. The article, eventually adopted as Article 21, states:

> Prisoners of war may be partially or wholly released on parole or promise, in so far as is allowed by the laws of the Power on which they depend. Such measures shall be taken particularly in cases where this may contribute to the improvement of their state of health. No prisoner of war shall be compelled to accept liberty on parole or promise.
>
> Upon the outbreak of hostilities, each Party to the conflict shall notify the adverse Party of the laws and regulations allowing or forbidding its own nationals to accept liberty on parole or promise. Prisoners of war who are paroled or who have given their promise in conformity with the laws and regulations so notified, are bound on their personal honour scrupulously to fulfil, both towards the Power on which they depend and towards the power which has captured them, the engagements of their paroles or promises. In such cases, the Power on which they depend is bound neither to require nor to accept from them any service incompatible with the parole or promise given.

Article 21 remains the most recent international law on parole. Though there are provisions on protections for POWs in Additional Protocol I,[75] parole is not mentioned in that instrument.

---

consideration of Governments invited by the Swiss Federal Council to attend the Diplomatic Conference at Geneva 43 (April 21, 1949) (1949), noting that the XVIIth International Red Cross Conference in Stockholm Conference in 1948 had agreed to include parole in the new draft convention.

72. REPORT ON THE CONFERENCE OF GOVERNMENT EXPERTS, *supra* note 38, at 133–34.

73. *Id.*, 134.

74. *Id.*

75. Protocol Additional to the Geneva Conventions of 12 August 1949, and Relating to the Protection of Victims of International Armed Conflicts arts. 45, 75, June 8, 1977, 1125 U.N.T.S. 3.

IV. THE SUBSTANCE OF THE INTERNATIONAL LAW ON PAROLE FOR POWS

Article 21, as adopted, generally repeats the law as outlined in the Hague Regulations. The first paragraph affirms that a POW can accept whole or partial parole, but that no POW may be compelled or coerced into accepting liberty on parole or promise. Partial parole is necessarily limited—it may be granted for the purpose of allowing a POW to "visit a place of worship or to attend a class"[76]—while full parole amounts to total release from captivity, including to the POW parolee's home.

Article 21 also affirms that the POW must abide by the laws and regulations of the State on which they depend—usually their State of nationality. What this means in practice is that a POW may not accept parole if their home State forbids the use of parole, as is the case in the United States,[77] or else places restrictions on the acceptance of parole—this is elaborated in more detail in the following paragraphs of Article 21. Moreover, if a POW *was* coerced into accepting parole, the 2020 Commentary to the Third Geneva Convention makes it clear that the unwilling parolee would not be under an obligation to respect the terms of their parole.[78] The 1960 Commentary on Article 21 rather poetically emphasizes the importance of this obligation:

> The last sentence, which categorically forbids the Detaining Power to compel a prisoner of war to accept liberty on parole or promise, is of the utmost importance. A prisoner who is faced with the choice—either internment or release on parole, with all the consequences entailed thereby—is also faced with a problem of conscience which he must be absolutely free to solve. A person who gives his parole gives a personal undertaking on his honour for which he is in the first place responsible to himself.[79]

In the first notable amendment to the law on parole, Article 21 omitted reference to the section that states that the detaining power is under no obligation to grant parole at the request of a POW, though the option remains for a POW to

---

76. INTERNATIONAL COMMITTEE OF THE RED CROSS, COMMENTARY ON THE THIRD GENEVA CONVENTION: CONVENTION (III) RELATIVE TO THE TREATMENT OF PRISONERS OF WAR ¶ 1953 (2020), https://ihl-databases.icrc.org/applic/ihl/ihl.nsf/Comment.xsp?action=openDocument&documentId=64B426BB4E773EADC12585850044BFC6 [hereinafter 2020 GC III COMMENTARY].

77. *See* Exec. Order No. 10,631, 20 Fed. Reg. 6,057, art. III (Aug. 17, 1955), *amended by* Exec. Order No. 12,017, 42 Fed. Reg. 57,941 (Nov. 3, 1977), *further amended by* Exec. Order No. 12,633, 53 Fed. Reg. 10,355 (Mar. 30, 1988).

78. 2020 GC III COMMENTARY, *supra* note 76, ¶ 1964.

79. COMMENTARY TO GENEVA CONVENTION III RELATIVE TO THE TREATMENT OF PRISONERS OF WAR 181 (Jean Pictet ed., 1960) [hereinafter 1960 GC III COMMENTARY].

request parole. The Hague Regulations had specifically stated that "[a] prisoner of war cannot be compelled to accept his liberty on parole; similarly the hostile Government is not obliged to accede to the request of the prisoner to be set at liberty on parole." This explicit statement was ultimately excluded from Article 21.

Additionally, the inclusion of specific reference to parole for reasons of health or hygiene was a new addition in Geneva in 1949, "inserted as a result of a practice which, if not widespread, was followed during the Second World War."[80] This portion of Article 21 was included to allow instances where POWs could be granted limited release, with the 2020 Commentary noting that such limited release could be for the purpose of attending specialist medical treatment, or for something as quotidian as "parole . . . even for a very short period such as to take a walk outside the camp limits."[81] The 2020 Commentary makes it clear that this provision operates without prejudice to Article 109, which requires repatriation of seriously wounded and sick POWs.[82]

The remainder of Article 21 covers essentially procedural aspects of parole: all parties to the conflict are obligated to notify adverse parties of their domestic laws and regulations regarding parole, so that the detaining authority is aware whether parole is allowed or prohibited. This paragraph also reiterates previous formulations of parole, providing that paroled POWs are honor bound to fulfill their oath, and that the State on which they depend is not obligated to accept from a parolee any work incompatible with the oath of parole, nor may it require such service from parolees. Though the provision does not expressly say so, the Commentary notes that the oath taken regarding parole is the "promise that they will not take flight or will not take up arms again."[83]

Significantly, Article 21 broke with custom and treaty law to explicitly provide that a POW who violated their parole conditions would still be, if recaptured, entitled to POW treatment and status. Historically, a POW who violated parole was "not only subject to judicial punishment but he was also not entitled to prisoner-of-war status";[84] under Article 21, POWs may be subject to prosecution by the detaining power for having violated parole, but must still be afforded POW status and treatment, including the extensive judicial protections outlined

---

80. 2020 GC III COMMENTARY, *supra* note 76, ¶ 1960.

81. *Id.*

82. *Id.*

83. *Id.*, ¶ 1968.

84. LEVIE, *supra* note 5, at 402. Under Article 12 of the Hague Regulations, *supra* note 64, "[p]risoners of war liberated on parole and recaptured bearing arms against the Government to whom they had pledged their honour, or against the allies of that Government, forfeit their right to be treated as prisoners of war, and can be brought before the courts." The Lieber Code, *supra* note 39, was even more strict: under Article 124, "[b]reaking the parole is punished with death when the person breaking the parole is captured again."

in Articles 82–108 of the Third Geneva Convention.[85] However, as noted in the 2020 Commentary, there is no guidance given on what kind of penal or disciplinary action is permissible regarding the breach of parole, noting that:

> The Convention is silent on the attitude, from the penal or disciplinary point of view, to be taken by the Power on which the prisoner depends in regard to a breach of parole by members of its armed forces. This remains for that Power to regulate, if it so wishes, under its national laws and regulations. In particular, if a prisoner who has been paroled breaks their promise, there is nothing in the Convention that would oblige that Power to return the prisoner to the Detaining Power.[86]

The 1960 Commentary adds the flourish that "the 'sanction' for a breach of parole is not necessarily of a disciplinary or penal nature; it is, first of all, a moral sanction by virtue of the consequent dishonor for the person concerned."[87]

V. PAROLE IN THE TWENTY-FIRST CENTURY AND BEYOND: OBSOLETE CONCEPT OR UNTAPPED OPPORTUNITY?

By the time the 1949 Geneva Conventions were adopted, the practice of parole was essentially nonexistent. Both law and practice in relation to POWs had been steadily moving toward better rules regulating conditions of captivity and moving away from release during the conflict, evidence of the "increasingly 'attritional' mindset that took hold in strategic thinking from late 1914 [which] stifled any thought of exchanging able-bodied military prisoners."[88]

Since the adoption of Article 21, there has been little in the way of State practice regarding parole. Indeed, the 1958 U.K. manual on warfare notes this specifically: "The exchange of prisoners of war is nowadays rare. The rule generally observed is to exchange man for man and rank for rank, with due allowance if titles of ranks or grades differ or if there is no exact equivalent. A condition is

---

85. See discussion of draft Article 19 in 2A FINAL RECORD OF THE DIPLOMATIC CONFERENCE OF GENEVA OF 1949, at 252–53, 320, 391, 411, 472–74, 581 (1949).

86. 2020 GC III COMMENTARY, *supra* note 76, ¶ 1972.

87. 1960 GC III COMMENTARY, *supra* note 79, at 180.

88. Neville Wylie & Lindsey Cameron, *The Impact of World War I on the Law Governing the Treatment of Prisoners of War and the Making of a Humanitarian Subject*, 29 EUROPEAN JOURNAL OF INTERNATIONAL LAW 1327, 1333 (2018). Severely invalided POWs were frequently repatriated, or interned in neutral countries. *Id.* at 1333–35.

often made that the men exchanged shall not participate as soldiers in the war—in fact they are paroled."[89]

Given that parole was well established in both practice and law for centuries, how then can we account for its diminution? That several States have prohibited their service personnel from accepting offers of parole is likely the main reason. For example, in the Canadian manual on the law of armed conflict,[90] it is noted that "Canadian law does not permit members of the [Canadian forces] to give their parole."[91] Likewise, the United States prohibits its personnel from "accepting parole or special favors from the enemy"[92] as a matter of policy, as does the United Kingdom.[93]

An additional contributing factor may be that some States, as a matter of policy or law, impose the duty on captured personnel to escape captivity and rejoin their armed forces. For example, New Zealand's manual of the law of armed conflict states:

> It is the duty of every captured member of the [New Zealand Defence Force (NZDF)] to attempt to escape and rejoin the NZDF to continue the fight against the opposing force. Promising not to escape enables the enemy to divert members of its guard force to combat duties and may amount to aiding the enemy. Members of the NZDF are not to give an undertaking not to escape or return to hostilities (parole) and cannot be forced to do so.[94]

---

89. UNITED KINGDOM, WAR OFFICE, THE LAW OF WAR ON LAND BEING PART III OF THE MANUAL OF MILITARY LAW § 249 (1958).

90. CHIEF OF THE GENERAL STAFF (CANADA), B-GJ-005-104/FP-021, LAW OF ARMED CONFLICT AT THE OPERATIONAL AND TACTICAL LEVELS (2001).

91. *Id.*, § 1025.

92. U.S. NAVY & U.S. MARINE CORPS, FM 6-27/MCTP 11-10C, THE COMMANDER'S HANDBOOK ON THE LAW OF LAND WARFARE, § 3.167 (2019). For an overview of U.S. policy on parole, see also Brown, *supra* note 5, at 214–16.

93. U.K. MINISTRY OF DEFENCE, JSP 383, THE JOINT SERVICE MANUAL OF THE LAW OF ARMED CONFLICT § 8.108 (2004).

94. NEW ZEALAND DEFENCE FORCE/TE OPE KAATUA O AOTEAROA, DM 69 (2 ED) MANUAL OF ARMED FORCES LAW, VOLUME 4: LAW OF ARMED CONFLICT § 12.15.6 (2017). *See also* Exec. Order No. 10,631, 20 Fed. Reg. 6,057, art. III (Aug. 17, 1955), *amended by* Exec. Order No. 12,017, 42 Fed. Reg. 57,941 (Nov. 3, 1977), *further amended by* Exec. Order No. 12,633, 53 Fed. Reg. 10,355 (Mar. 30, 1988). Article III states: "If I am captured I will continue to resist by all means available. I will make every effort to escape and aid others to escape. I will accept neither parole nor special favors from the enemy."

Other writers,[95] as well as the ICRC in the updated Commentary to the Third Geneva Convention,[96] have also noted that notions of honor may have played a role in parole falling out of favor—ironic, given the historical centrality of notions of honor to the origins of the system of parole. As argued by the ICRC in its updated Commentary, "[t]he main reason for the decline, in addition to national prohibitions on accepting release, may be mistrust of the opposing Party, as well as mistrust by fellow prisoners of those who accept offers of parole."[97]

Is parole therefore just a quaint historic relic in the Conventions, much like the provision in Article 62 ensuring that, at a minimum, POWs undertaking employment shall be paid a fair working rate no less than "one-fourth of one Swiss franc for a full working day"?[98] Is there any future utility in Article 21's parole provision? Arguably, parole may still serve some purpose, especially if one is mindful of one of the original reasons behind the adoption of parole in practice—that of pragmatism. Eric Talbot Jensen puts it eloquently:

> Collecting large numbers of POWs and/or detainees is always problematic for an armed force, and especially so for an invading force. The required expenditure of resources can be quite burdensome to a force even as well supplied as the United States. Offering parole ... may be a way ... to decrease the significant logistics requirements required for detainees.[99]

Parole may therefore be a way for detaining authorities to avoid the logistical and financial burden of having to maintain detention facilities for large numbers of detainees.

Additionally, parole may offer legal benefits for the detaining powers. Increasingly, State armed forces are becoming involved in more protracted armed conflicts—for example, only in 2021 was the complete withdrawal of U.S. and other allied troops from Afghanistan secured, following a twenty-year-long engagement in that country.[100] By granting parole to detainees captured during protracted armed conflicts, parties to an armed conflict could, in addition to

---

95. *See* WILLIAM P. LYONS, PRISONERS OF WAR AND THE CODE OF CONDUCT 352 (1980) (Vol. 62, U.S. Naval War College International Law Studies); CATHERINE MAIA ET AL. LA PROTECTION DES PRISONNIERS DE GUERRE EN DROIT INTERNATIONAL HUMANITAIRE 467 (2015).

96. 2020 GC III COMMENTARY, *supra* note 76.

97. *Id.*, ¶ 1957.

98. Third Geneva Convention, *supra* note 1, art. 62.

99. Eric Talbot Jensen, *Combatant Status: It Is Time for Intermediate Levels of Recognition for Partial Compliance*, 46 VIRGINIA JOURNAL OF INTERNATIONAL LAW 209, 240 (2005).

100. Nick Niedzwiadek, *Biden Announces Withdrawal from Afghanistan in Speech Heavy on Symbolism*, POLITICO (Apr. 14, 2021), https://www.politico.com/news/2021/04/14/biden-announces-withdrawal-afghanistan-481524. See also similar announcements by Australian and British authorities: (Anthony Galloway, "Australia to Withdraw All Troops from Afghanistan After Biden's Vow to End War," SYDNEY MORNING HERALD (Apr. 15, 2021), https://www.smh.

minimizing or avoiding the costs involved with such protracted detention, circumvent concerns under international human rights law regarding indefinite detention.[101] As Joshua Clover notes:

> First, paroling these detainees would alleviate concerns over the fact that they may otherwise be held indefinitely. Second, although they may appear to be "freed," paroled prisoners of war are prohibited from being employed in active military service against their original captors. Third, if these parolees are later discovered to have "broken" their parole, the original detaining power, in this case the United States, "has extensive options in dealing with the miscreant." Though the laws of war conflict on some of the procedural specifics, the parole breaker could conceivably lose his prisoner of war status.[102]

Offering parole in situations of protracted detention during prolonged armed conflicts would seem to be an obvious solution to a number of problems. For example, in 2020, it was noted that "the detention facility at the U.S. Naval Base in Guantánamo Bay, Cuba will enter its twentieth year. Forty Muslim men remain captive there, at a cost of $540 million per year; $13 million per detainee."[103] Offering some form of parole might be a way to alleviate the burdens that come from such prolonged detention, and the frequent legal challenges that often accompany it.[104]

It must be noted, however, that the detainees in Guantánamo Bay were and are, for the most part, persons detained in relation to a non-international armed conflict—that is, the category of conflict where there is no POW status.[105] This would mean that a grant of parole would be a policy decision, rather than a decision

com.au/politics/federal/australia-to-withdraw-all-troops-from-afghanistan-after-biden-vows-to-end-war-20210415-p57jeb.html; *British Troops to Withdraw from Afghanistan Alongside NATO and the US*, SKY NEWS (Apr. 15, 2021), https://news.sky.com/story/british-troops-to-withdraw-from-afghanistan-alongside-nato-and-the-us-12275659).

101. *See* Alfred de Zayas, *Human Rights and Indefinite Detention*, 87 INTERNATIONAL REVIEW OF THE RED CROSS 15 (2005); Jonathan Hafetz, *Detention Without End: Reexamining the Indefinite Confinement of Terrorism Suspects Through the Lens of Criminal Sentencing*, 61 UCLA LAW REVIEW 326 (2014).

102. Joshua S. Clover, *Remember, We're the Good Guys: The Classification and Trial of the Guantanamo Bay Detainees*, 45 SOUTH TEXAS LAW REVIEW 351, 370 (2004), citing Brown, *supra* note 5, at 212.

103. Hina Shamsi et al., "Toward a New Approach to National and Human Security: Close Guantanamo and End Indefinite Detention," JUST SECURITY (Sept. 11, 2020), https://www.justsecurity.org/72367/toward-a-new-approach-to-national-and-human-security-close-guantanamo-and-end-indefinite-detention/.

104. *See, e.g.*, the challenges to detention raised in the cases R v. Gul [2013] UKSC 64 and Mohammed v. Ministry of Defence [2014] EWHC 1369 (QB).

105. *See* EMILY CRAWFORD, THE TREATMENT OF COMBATANTS AND INSURGENTS UNDER THE LAW OF ARMED CONFLICT 70–77 (2010).

pursuant to Article 21 of the Third Geneva Convention. As most conflicts nowadays are non-international armed conflicts, or operations "other than war,"[106] Article 21 would not, as a matter of law, be applicable to prolonged detentions in non-international armed conflicts.

However, Article 21 parole remains in play in protracted *international* armed conflicts, and, as a matter of policy, the logic behind granting parole for any detainees remains valid, regardless of whether the conflict is international or non-international.[107] As the ICRC has noted, release on parole "may offer an advantage to the Detaining Power, for example if it does not have the means to intern prisoners of war. This might be the case if it lacks the necessary space, facilities and provisions"[108]—this logic is applicable for *any* detaining authority. Moreover, concerns about whether paroled detainees or POWs might rejoin the conflict (though this is comparatively rare recently, according to research[109]) could be potentially circumvented, or at least minimized, through the use of curfew, electronic monitoring, regular reporting to authorities, and other control orders, similar to those imposed on certain domestic criminal law parolees, and "modern technologies, such as electronic monitoring systems, could assist in ensuring compliance with the promise on which a release is based."[110] Indeed, the ICRC makes this very point in its updated Commentary,[111] which suggests that this "ancient concept"[112] does indeed have "modern utility."[113]

VI. CONCLUSION

For centuries, releasing prisoners captured during armed conflict, whether for money or reciprocal exchange, was accepted practice during times of war. However, in the last hundred years, the practice of parole has fallen out of favor

---

106. *See* YORAM DINSTEIN, NON-INTERNATIONAL ARMED CONFLICTS IN INTERNATIONAL LAW 2–3 (2021).

107. Indeed, as noted by Brown, parole has been employed in non-international armed conflicts. *See* Brown, *supra* note 5, at 207–08.

108. 2020 GC III COMMENTARY, *supra* note 76, ¶ 1954.

109. Research by Andrew Silke and John Morrison puts recidivism rates for released terrorists as comparatively low—frequently less than 10 percent. *See* Andrew Silke & John Morrison, *Re-Offending by Released Terrorist Prisoners: Separating Hype from Reality* (International Centre for Counter-Terrorism Policy Brief, Sept. 2020), https://icct.nl/app/uploads/2020/09/Re-Offending-by-Released-Terrorist-Prisoners.pdf.

110. 2020 GC III COMMENTARY, *supra* note 76, ¶ 1957. *See also* Chris Jenks & Eric Talbot Jensen, *Indefinite Detention Under the Laws of War*, 22 STANFORD LAW & POLICY REVIEW 41 (2011).

111. 2020 GC III COMMENTARY, *supra* note 76, ¶ 1957.

112. Brown, *supra* note 5.

113. *Id.*

with States, with the law enunciating rules geared toward captivity rather than release, except in limited circumstances. However, though parole is now seldom practiced, the reasons underlying its adoption remain as true today as when the concept emerged. Moreover, modern technologies may make the practice of parole easier for States that find themselves increasingly caught up in protracted and expensive conflicts. It may be possible, in time, that parole enjoys a resurgence in practice, as a pragmatic and humanitarian option for parties to armed conflicts.

Detention of Suspected Terrorists in Connection with Armed Conflict: A Focus on Release and Repatriation

PAVLE KILIBARDA* AND GLORIA GAGGIOLI** ■

I. INTRODUCTION

The past two decades have seen much scholarly inquiry into detention in times of armed conflict and in the context of counterterrorism, particularly in the United States in the aftermath of 9/11 and the establishment of the detention

---

*. Pavle Kilibarda is a Postdoctoral Researcher at the Faculty of Law of the University of Geneva. He holds a PhD in law from the University of Geneva, an LLM in international humanitarian law and human rights from the Geneva Academy of International Humanitarian Law and Human Rights, and a BA in international relations from the University of Belgrade. He has previously worked as a Teaching Assistant at the Geneva Academy, a Legal Training Associate at the ICRC and as a Researcher at the Belgrade Centre for Human Rights.

**. Gloria Gaggioli is the Director of the Geneva Academy of International Humanitarian Law and Human Rights (Geneva Academy) and an Associate/Swiss National Science Foundation Professor at the Law Faculty of the University of Geneva. Prior to joining the University of Geneva, she served as Legal Adviser in the ICRC Legal Division. This chapter is based on research conducted as part of Gloria Gaggioli's project on "Preventing and Combating Terrorism and Violent Extremism: Towards a Legal-Empirical Approach," funded by the Swiss National Science Foundation. The views expressed here are the authors' own and do not reflect the position of any institutions with which they are affiliated.

Pavle Kilibarda and Gloria Gaggioli, *Detention of Suspected Terrorists in Connection with Armed Conflict: A Focus on Release and Repatriation* In: *Prisoners of War in Contemporary Conflict*. Edited by: Michael N. Schmitt and Christopher J. Koschnitzky, Oxford University Press. © Oxford University Press 2023. DOI: 10.1093/oso/9780197663288.003.0012

center at Guantánamo Bay.¹ A body of literature numbering thousands of pages of legal analysis has been produced in relation to Guantánamo and other facilities maintained by Western States in the context of the "War on Terror," but efforts scrutinizing other situations and contexts have been fairly limited. In fact, armed conflicts with a counterterrorist element may be identified around the world, often posing similar legal and humanitarian challenges in places as diverse as Malaysia,² Syria,³ and Israel⁴ as they did in Guantánamo.

In our view, many doctrinal works on detention in armed conflicts suffer from two deficiencies. First, by focusing on the "big picture" of detention, they either neglect or marginalize the question of release and repatriation. From the perspective of individual detainees, these issues will normally be crucial. Some works that genuinely problematize the matter typically do so from a domestic law perspective or end up taking a position that is heterodox from a mainstream international law perspective.⁵

Our goal is, therefore, to subject the armed conflict regime on the release and repatriation of detainees to a more in-depth analysis, particularly in the context of extraterritorial non-international armed conflicts (NIACs) pitting States against organized armed groups (OAGs) described as "terrorists." Unlike "traditional" armed conflicts, the War on Terror and other counterterrorist NIACs have all the earmarks of a "Forever War"⁶ and, with no end in sight to hostilities, some

---

1. *See, e.g.*, Curtis A. Bradley & Jack L. Goldsmith, *Congressional Authorization and the War on Terrorism*, 118 HARVARD LAW REVIEW 2047 (2005); Marco Sassòli, *The International Legal Framework for Fighting Terrorists According to the Bush and the Obama Administrations: Same or Different, Correct or Incorrect?*, 104 ASIL PROCEEDINGS 277 (2010); William K. Lietzau, *Detention of Terrorists in the Twenty-First Century*, in NON-INTERNATIONAL ARMED CONFLICT IN THE TWENTY-FIRST CENTURY 323 (Kenneth Watkin & Andrew J. Norris eds., 2012) (Vol 88, U.S. Naval War College International Law Studies); John Bellinger III & Vijay M. Padmanabhan, *Detention Operations in Contemporary Conflicts: Four Challenges for the Geneva Conventions and Other Existing Law*, 105 AMERICAN JOURNAL OF INTERNATIONAL LAW 201 (2017).

2. *See Malaysia: New Anti-Terrorism Law a Shocking Onslaught Against Human Rights*, AMNESTY INTERNATIONAL (Apr. 7, 2015), https://www.amnesty.org/en/latest/news/2015/04/malaysia-new-anti-terrorism-law-a-shocking-onslaught-against-human-rights/.

3. For an overview of the indefinite detention of individuals in Northern Syria, *see* RIGHTS & SECURITY INTERNATIONAL, EUROPE'S GUANTANAMO: THE INDEFINITE DETENTION OF EUROPEAN WOMEN AND CHILDREN IN NORTH EAST SYRIA (2021).

4. *See* Emmanuel Gross, *Human Rights, Terrorism and the Problem of Administrative Detention in Israel: Does a Democracy Have the Right to Hold Terrorists as Bargaining Chips?*, 18 ARIZONA JOURNAL OF INTERNATIONAL AND COMPARATIVE LAW 721 (2001).

5. *See, e.g.*, Bradley & Goldsmith, *supra* note 1, who argue for an "individualization" of the concept of the end of active hostilities.

6. This phrase was coined by science fiction writer and Vietnam veteran Joe Haldeman for his eponymous 1974 novel chronicling the dehumanizing conflict between Earth and an extraterrestrial species known as the Taurans. The captivating term and its pertinence in the War on Terror have not been lost on contemporary authors. *See, e.g.*, Jack Goldsmith & Matthew C. Waxman, *The Other Forever War Anniversary*, TIME, Sept. 10, 2016; Boyd van Dijk, *15 Years*

detainees face the prospect of spending the rest of their lives in a detention center with no criminal charges raised against them.

The current chapter is structured as follows. In Part II, we examine the rules on the release and repatriation of persons detained in an international armed conflict (IAC), where the rules of international humanitarian law (IHL) are better developed and more accessible. Although terrorists will usually be detained in the context of NIACs, individuals suspected of terrorism can doubtless be detained in an IAC, as demonstrated by the early stages of the war in Afghanistan.[7] The Afghan context will also allow us to examine the implications of conflict transformation on detention modalities. In Part III, we focus on the release, relocation, and repatriation in NIACs. We will look at the state of treaty and customary law and doctrinal suggestions for filling in the remaining legal lacunae and we will consider the matter of detention by OAGs. This is the heart of our analysis; hence, we will try to frame it as far as possible in terms of actual State practice and needs. In Part IV, we consider the impact of international counterterrorist legislation on detention in armed conflicts. Combined, these discussions will allow us to propose in Part V a realistic and human rights consonant detention regime. Part VI concludes the chapter.

II. RELEASE AND REPATRIATION OF DETAINEES IN IACS

The IAC detention regime is provided in detail in several IHL treaties. These notably include Convention (III) Relative to the Treatment of Prisoners of War (Third Geneva Convention)[8] and Convention (IV) Relative to the Protection of Civilian Persons in Time of War (Fourth Geneva Convention),[9] but also the earlier Regulations Respecting the Laws and Customs of War on Land of 1907 (Hague Regulations)[10] and the Protocol Additional to the Geneva Conventions of 12 August 1949, and Relating to the Protection of Victims of International

---

Later: A History of the Forever War and the Laws of War (Part 1 of 2), OPINIO JURIS (Oct. 7, 2016), http://opiniojuris.org/2016/10/07/15-years-later-a-history-of-the-forever-war-and-the-laws-of-war-part-1-of-2/; Chris Rogers, *The Forever War, in the Hands of Others: Tracing the Real Power of U.S. Law and Policy in the War on Terror*, 47 COLUMBIA HUMAN RIGHTS LAW REVIEW 78 (2016).

7. See Marco Sassòli, *La "guerre contre le terrorisme," le droit international humanitaire et le statut de prisonnier de guerre*, 39 CANADIAN YEARBOOK OF INTERNATIONAL LAW 211 (2001).

8. Convention (III) Relative to the Treatment of Prisoners of War, Aug. 12, 1949, 6 U.S.T. 3316, 75 U.N.T.S. 135 [hereinafter Third Geneva Convention].

9. Convention (IV) Relative to the Protection of Civilian Persons in Time of War, Aug. 12, 1949, 6 U.S.T. 3516, 75 U.N.T.S. 287 [hereinafter Fourth Geneva Convention].

10. Regulations Respecting the Laws and Customs of War on Land, annexed to Convention No. IV Respecting the Laws and Customs of War on Land, Oct. 18, 1907, 36 Stat. 2227, T.S. No. 539 [hereinafter Hague Regulations].

Armed Conflicts (Additional Protocol I).[11] This regime remains legally and practically relevant in the twenty-first century and has not been rendered obsolete by developments in international human rights law (IHRL).[12]

Like so many other aspects of the IAC framework, detention is *status-based*. The Geneva Conventions establish different rules and procedures for persons deprived of liberty based on whether they are combatants or civilians. With a few exceptions, such as noncombatants exceptionally entitled to status or treatment as prisoners of war (POWs) under the Third Geneva Convention,[13] the regime is clear-cut and does not leave a legal black hole. If a person in the power of the enemy is not entitled to POW status or treatment, then that person must be considered a civilian internee and is protected by the Fourth Geneva Convention.[14] Under the Fourth Geneva Convention, security detention is a measure of last resort, necessitating a *threat-based* determination in each case. Both POWs and internees may be detained in relation to criminal charges.[15] Deprivation of liberty in relation to criminal proceedings should be scrutinized considering common domestic and IHRL standards in such cases.

A. Detention, Release, and Repatriation in the Third and Fourth Geneva Conventions

1. POWS

The protection of enemy combatants who have been placed *hors de combat* through capture or injury is a cornerstone of the IAC framework and perhaps one of the oldest principles of IHL.[16] The reasons for this are not purely humanitarian: they are rooted in ancient notions of honor and chivalry, but also reciprocity—detaining powers treating rival forces with humanity could count on their own troops benefiting from the same standards in like circumstances. In the

---

11. Protocol Additional to the Geneva Conventions of 12 August 1949, and Relating to the Protection of Victims of International Armed Conflicts, June 8, 1977, 1125 U.N.T.S. 3 [hereinafter Additional Protocol I].

12. This was confirmed by the European Court in the Hassan case. *See* Hassan v. United Kingdom, 2014-VI Eur. Ct. H.R. 1, ¶¶ 96ff., https://www.echr.coe.int/Documents/Reports_Recueil_2014-VI.pdf.

13. Third Geneva Convention, *supra* note 8: see Article 4A(4), (5) for civilians connected to the armed forces who are entitled to POW status and Article 33 regarding military medical personnel and chaplains who are entitled to treatment as POWs without having that status.

14. Marco Sassòli, International Humanitarian Law: Rules, Controversies, and Solutions to Problems Arising in Warfare 273ff. (2019).

15. Because of combatant immunity, POWs cannot be prosecuted for acts of hostility that are consonant with IHL. However, this immunity notably does not shield individuals from prosecution for war crimes.

16. Sassòli, *supra* note 14, at 248ff.

past, an opponent's misbehavior would be paid for dearly by the opponent's imprisoned comrades, thus disincentivizing ill-treatment through fear of reprisals.[17] As the IAC regime is largely uncontroversial today, we will only recall its major features and draw attention to the most relevant points regarding the release and repatriation of POWs.

Members of the armed forces of a belligerent party to an IAC who fall into the hands of the enemy are considered POWs and entitled to the protection of the Third Geneva Convention.[18] Although POW status is commonly presumed to ipso facto entail deprivation of liberty, this is not the case: the enemy belligerent is, in principle, free to release POWs "unconditionally on territory under its control or . . . on parole if they promise not to leave the territory controlled by the enemy or re-join their armed forces."[19] However, the treaty provides an explicit basis for the internment of POWs that is not qualified by any threat-based assessment or review.[20] Apart from numerous rules on the treatment of POWs, the Third Geneva Convention does not provide any sort of procedural safeguards in relation to detention other than access to a status review tribunal in case of doubt regarding an individual's entitlement to POW status.[21] In cases where an individual's status is unclear and has not yet been decided by such a tribunal, the Third Geneva Convention establishes a presumption in favor of POW status. There have been some attempts to link status review to habeas corpus;[22] however, as status review only concerns determining individual status, it does not seem to us appropriate to refer to it as a form of habeas corpus.[23]

Not all combatants will be entitled to the protection of the Third Geneva Convention. It is not controversial that a failure to distinguish oneself from the

---

17. A notable incident arose during the Second World War, when the Germans started shackling British POWs after German soldiers had been tied up by British forces during the Dieppe Raid in 1942. *See* ALFRED DE ZAYAS, THE WEHRMACHT WAR CRIMES BUREAU, 1939–1945, 108 (1989). Such reprisals are prohibited under contemporary international law.

18. Third Geneva Convention, *supra* note 8, art. 4.

19. Sassòli, *supra* note 14, at 264. *See also* Convention No. IV Respecting the Laws and Customs of War on Land, Oct. 18, 1907, 36 Stat. 2227, T.S. No. 539; Hague Regulations, *supra* note 10, art. 10.

20. "The Detaining Power may subject prisoners of war to internment. It may impose on them the obligation of not leaving, beyond certain limits, the camp where they are interned, or if the said camp is fenced in, of not going outside its perimeter." Third Geneva Convention, *supra* note 8, art. 21.

21. *Id.*, art. 5.

22. U.N. Working Group on Arbitrary Detention, *United Nations Basic Principles and Guidelines on the Right of Anyone Deprived of Their Liberty to Bring Proceedings Before a Court*, Principle 16, WGAD/CRP.1/2015 (May 4, 2015). A similar approach is advocated by LOUISE DOSWALD-BECK, HUMAN RIGHTS IN TIMES OF CONFLICT AND TERRORISM 279 (2011).

23. Conversely, POWs detained for the purposes of a criminal trial may indeed be entitled to habeas corpus in the true sense of the word.

civilian population at the moment of capture may lead to loss of POW status.[24] More problematic is the notion that the commission of war crimes may lead to such status being curtailed from an individual or group. This idea is based on an *a contrario* reading of Article 1 of the Hague Regulations, which foresees that the "laws, rights, and duties of war" apply to armies, militia, and volunteer corps that, inter alia, "conduct their operations in accordance with the laws and customs of war."[25] The mainstream doctrinal view rejects the notion that the commission of war crimes excludes an individual from POW status.[26] However, as we will discuss in the following section, this has been called into question in the context of the War on Terror.[27] In any case, individuals not entitled to POW status are still protected by the Fourth Geneva Convention.[28]

The Third Geneva Convention imposes strict rules regarding the release and repatriation of POWs. According to Article 118, "[p]risoners of war shall be released and repatriated without delay after the cessation of active hostilities."[29] The updated International Committee of the Red Cross (ICRC) Commentary gives these terms a narrow sense:

> The term "release" ordinarily refers to the ending of a person's internment, and the corresponding return of their liberty. . . .
>
> The term "repatriation" generally refers to the returning of individuals to their places of origin, nationality or residence. Where prisoners of war are concerned, account must be taken of the duty of allegiance which binds members of the armed forces to the Power on which they depend.[30]

---

24. Sassòli, *supra* note 14, at 260.

25. Hague Regulations, *supra* note 10, art. 1.

26. *See* INTERNATIONAL COMMITTEE OF THE RED CROSS, COMMENTARY ON THE THIRD GENEVA CONVENTION: CONVENTION (III) RELATIVE TO THE TREATMENT OF PRISONERS OF WAR ¶ 1039 (2020), https://ihl-databases.icrc.org/applic/ihl/ihl.nsf/Comment.xsp?action=openDocument&documentId=1796813618ABDA06C12585850057AB95 [hereinafter 2020 GC III COMMENTARY]; Sassòli, *supra* note 14, at 260. When the Soviet Union and other communist States made reservations to Article 85 of the Third Geneva Convention to the effect that they would not extend POW status to individuals convicted of war crimes or crimes against humanity, a number of States protested. The United States expressly rejected the reservation. *See* FRITS KALSHOVEN & LIESBETH ZEGVELD, CONSTRAINTS ON THE WAGING OF WAR: AN INTRODUCTION TO INTERNATIONAL HUMANITARIAN LAW 57 (2011).

27. *See, e.g.*, Chris Jenks, *Reimagining the Wheel: Detention and Release of Non-State Actors Under the Geneva Conventions*, in DETENTION OF NON-STATE ACTORS ENGAGED IN HOSTILITIES 100 (Gregory Rose & Bruce Oswald eds., 2016); Bellinger & Padmanabhan, *supra* note 1, at 215.

28. Fourth Geneva Convention, *supra* note 9, art. 4.

29. Third Geneva Convention, *supra* note 8, art. 118.

30. 2020 GC III COMMENTARY, *supra* note 26, ¶¶ 4445–46, https://ihl-databases.icrc.org/applic/ihl/ihl.nsf/Comment.xsp?action=openDocument&documentId=2E2384E30078EF5DC125858500426E02.

This means that the obligation to "repatriate" POWs requires sending them back to the State to which they belong as combatants, not to their State of nationality. Normally this will be the same State, but it is important to take note of this aspect, particularly for the counterterrorism context discussed in the present chapter. Additional Protocol I further foresees that an unjustifiable delay in the repatriation of POWs amounts to a grave breach and thus gives rise to individual criminal responsibility of the persons responsible for the delay.[31] Such an unjustifiable delay would also turn the deprivation of liberty into an arbitrary one.[32]

There are three additional considerations to bear in mind regarding the obligation to release and repatriate POWs. First, the obligation is triggered by the "cessation of active hostilities," whereupon POWs must be released and repatriated "without delay." There are two relevant temporal aspects to be analyzed in this regard: first, the point when active hostilities have ceased; and second, the point after the cessation of active hostilities when failure to release and repatriate POWs will amount to a violation of Article 118 of the Third Geneva Convention.

Both points are objective and do not require that any formalities be taken, although the ICRC recalls that they may be context specific.[33] They may be difficult to identify in practice, particularly in the context of counterterrorism. In the ICRC's view, the cessation of active hostilities predates the general close of military operations and when there arises "no reasonable expectation of [the] resumption [of active hostilities]," which always require acts of warfare, namely violence.[34] Sassòli writes that the "mere absence of fighting is insufficient, but one cannot wait until certainty exists that hostilities will not resume . . . . A reasonable expectation that hostilities have ended must be sufficient."[35] Kolb and Hyde add:

> The moment of effective cessation of hostilities may be difficult to define if hostilities continue on a smaller scale after hostilities have generally ceased . . . To the extent that there is still actual fighting, even through cobelligerent states, the applicability of the [law of armed conflict] for IAC (or for NIAC) will continue.[36]

---

31. Additional Protocol 1, *supra* note 11, art. 85(4)(b).

32. 2020 GC III COMMENTARY, *supra* note 26, ¶ 4464, https://ihl-databases.icrc.org/applic/ihl/ihl.nsf/Comment.xsp?action=openDocument&documentId=2E2384E30078EF5DC125858500426E02.

33. *Id.*, ¶ 4455, https://ihl-databases.icrc.org/applic/ihl/ihl.nsf/Comment.xsp?action=openDocument&documentId=2E2384E30078EF5DC125858500426E02.

34. *Id.*, ¶¶ 4453–54, https://ihl-databases.icrc.org/applic/ihl/ihl.nsf/Comment.xsp?action=openDocument&documentId=2E2384E30078EF5DC125858500426E02.

35. Sassòli, *supra* note 14, at 271.

36. ROBERT KOLB & RICHARD HYDE, AN INTRODUCTION TO THE INTERNATIONAL LAW OF ARMED CONFLICTS 102 (2008).

Thus, if the first reference point (the end of active hostilities) can be established in principle, it may be more difficult to ascertain in practice, with potentially grave implications for detainees. Even low-intensity fighting, for example, around a ceasefire line, could delay the obligation under Article 118 for years.

The temporal scope of the obligation triggered by the end of active hostilities can also be difficult to ascertain, and there exists little guidance on how much time may pass before the failure to release and repatriate may be considered "delayed." Kolb and Hyde recall the Pakistani–Indian conflict and the Iran–Iraq War as situations where POWs were detained for years after even the general close of military operations.[37] In principle, belligerent parties should come to an arrangement regarding the return of POWs, but such deals will not exist in all cases. Therefore, Article 118 of the Third Geneva Convention establishes an obligation independently of the existence of any agreements between the parties.[38] For its part, the ICRC describes this obligation as "strict" but accepts that it is limited to "what is feasible in the specific circumstances,"[39] which makes room for a "feasibility test" when determining whether POWs have been released and repatriated in a timely fashion.

This point is supported by an arbitral award between Eritrea and Ethiopia, when the Arbitral Commission found that Ethiopia's release of POWs on November 19, 2002, after active hostilities had ended on December 12, 2000, did not meet the requirements of Article 118, although it was more complicated to determine when exactly the violation had begun. Surprisingly, it was not, as Eritrea raised, in August 2001, when Ethiopia decided to delay further release and repatriation pending Eritrea's clarification of the fate of a number of its own captured troops. Rather, the Commission concluded that this came to pass in August 2002, when Ethiopia was no longer able to explain the reasons for continuing to keep Eritrean POWs.[40] Before that, Ethiopia's retention of POWs was consistently justified on the basis of arrangements for a safe and orderly transfer and reception, particularly for wounded and sick POWs, ensuring that individuals were not returned against their will, and, to a certain extent, expectations of reciprocity from the other side in releasing Ethiopian POWs. In our view, the Commission's approach in this regard is incorrect, as there is nothing in the Third Geneva Convention suggesting that the release and repatriation of POWs depend in any way on reciprocity: to

---

37. *Id.*, at 103.

38. 2020 GC III COMMENTARY, *supra* note 26, ¶¶ 4474ff., https://ihl-databases.icrc.org/applic/ihl/ihl.nsf/Comment.xsp?action=openDocument&documentId=2E2384E30078EF5DC125858500426E02; Sassòli, *supra* note 14, at 271.

39. 2020 GC III COMMENTARY, *supra* note 26, ¶ 4462, https://ihl-databases.icrc.org/applic/ihl/ihl.nsf/Comment.xsp?action=openDocument&documentId=2E2384E30078EF5DC1258585000426E02.

40. Partial Award, Prisoners of War—Ethiopia's Claim 17, between the Federal Democratic Republic of Ethiopia and the State of Eritrea ¶¶ 143ff. (Eritrea-Ethiopia Claims Commission, July 1, 2003) XXVI RIAA 23.

the contrary, predicating the release of POWs by one side on the behavior of another belligerent party has all the characteristics of a reprisal prohibited by IHL.[41] However, "feasibility"—not including reciprocity but covering the logistical requirements of organizing an orderly and safe release and repatriation—may indeed come into play in this regard, albeit with a strict onus on the detaining power to justify any delay involved in the process.

The second additional consideration regarding the obligation to release and repatriate POWs is that the protection of the Third Geneva Convention extends for as long as an individual POW remains in the power of the enemy and until their final release and repatriation (even if this takes place much later than the end of active hostilities). As "release" refers to release from internment and *not* from the "power of the enemy" (a POW may be released on parole in enemy territory),[42] POWs remain protected until both obligations have been met.

The third additional consideration is that the regime of Article 118 is strict and prima facie does not allow any exceptions. After the Second World War, many POWs expressed fear of repatriation, but States decided against allowing the wishes of individual prisoners to be taken into consideration for repatriation. They found that "special cases" could not be made, "owing to the difficulties they would involve, particularly in countries with strict immigration laws."[43] However, there are today at least two situations where the obligation allows for exceptions. First, the release and repatriation of POWs may be delayed because of a pending criminal trial or while they are serving a sentence, in which case they may be retained "until the end of such proceedings, and, if necessary, until the completion of the punishment,"[44] but during such detention POWs remain protected by the Third Geneva Convention.[45] Second, the repatriation of a POW may be impossible due to the application of the principle of *non-refoulement* as developed in IHRL and international refugee law.[46] Specifically, POWs may face persecution or be threatened with ill-treatment in case of return to their country of origin after an armed conflict, in which case the detaining power would be prevented

---

41. Article 13(3) of the Third Geneva Convention prohibits measures of reprisal against POWs.

42. The ICRC Commentary thus recalls that the obligations to release and repatriate may be implemented "simultaneously or consecutively." See 2020 GC III COMMENTARY, *supra* note 26, ¶ 4447, https://ihl-databases.icrc.org/applic/ihl/ihl.nsf/Comment.xsp?action=openDocument&documentId=2E2384E30078EF5DC125858500426E02.

43. *Id.*, ¶ 440, https://ihl-databases.icrc.org/applic/ihl/ihl.nsf/Comment.xsp?action=openDocument&documentId=2E2384E30078EF5DC125858500426E02. See also INTERNATIONAL COMMITTEE OF THE RED CROSS, REPORT ON THE WORK OF THE CONFERENCE OF GOVERNMENT EXPERTS FOR THE STUDY OF THE CONVENTIONS FOR THE PROTECTION OF WAR VICTIMS (GENEVA, APRIL 14–26, 1947) 245 (1947).

44. Third Geneva Convention, *supra* note 8, art. 119.

45. Sassòli, *supra* note 14, at 270.

46. *See, e.g.*, Soering v. United Kingdom 11 Eur. Ct. H.R. (ser. A) 439 (1989); Convention Relating to the Status of Refugees art. 33, July 28, 1951, 189 U.N.T.S. 137.

from repatriating them. Although Article 118 does not provide such an exception explicitly, it is widely accepted today that the absolute and non-derogable nature of the principle of *non-refoulement* (at least as it exists in IHRL) takes precedence over the obligation to repatriate POWs.[47] It is nevertheless logical to conclude that, even if repatriation is delayed in a POW's best interests, the POW remains protected by the Third Geneva Convention until this does come to pass (the obligation under Article 118 might arise once again in case of a change of circumstances in the POW's country of origin). Finally, it is clear that in some "internationalized" armed conflicts, the obligation to repatriate POWs is a moot point: if a State is engaged in a NIAC against rebel forces within its own territory, and those rebel forces come under the "effective/overall control" of a foreign power, the NIAC will transform into an IAC and captured rebels will be entitled to POW status.[48] However, these POWs will still have the nationality of the detaining power and usually reside within its territory: it makes no sense to "repatriate" them abroad, to a country whose nationals they are not, perhaps by their own State of nationality. In this case, nationality, rather than "allegiance," must be the defining factor.

2. Civilian Internees

The other IAC detention "limb" concerns civilians. Unlike members of the enemy armed forces, enemy nationals cannot be presumed to be a threat to national security. Thus, IHL foresees detention/internment only as an exceptional and extreme measure at a belligerent party's disposal.

The Fourth Geneva Convention protects persons "who, at a given moment and in any manner whatsoever, find themselves, in case of a conflict or occupation, in the hands of a Party to the conflict or Occupying Power of which they are not nationals."[49] Criminal tribunals have come up with a concept of "allegiance," whereby even a State's own nationals may be protected under some circumstances.[50]

The Convention envisages two situations for detention: one regarding protected civilians in a State's own territory, and the other for protected civilians in a territory it occupies. In the first situation, it may order "[t]he internment or placing in assigned residence of protected persons . . . if [its] security . . . makes it absolutely necessary."[51] An occupying power may do the same for "imperative reasons of

---

47. 2020 GC III Commentary, *supra* note 26, ¶ 4469, https://ihl-databases.icrc.org/applic/ihl/ihl.nsf/Comment.xsp?action=openDocument&documentId=2E2384E30078EF5DC125858500426E02.

48. Prosecutor v. Tadić, Case No. IT-94-1-A, Appeals Chamber Judgment, ¶¶ 115ff. (Int'l Crim. Trib. for the former Yugoslavia July 15, 1999).

49. Fourth Geneva Convention, *supra* note 9, art. 4.

50. Prosecutor v. Tadić, Case No. IT-94-1-A, Appeals Chamber Judgment, ¶¶ 163–69 (Int'l Crim. Trib. for the former Yugoslavia July 15, 1999).

51. Fourth Geneva Convention, *supra* note 9, art. 42.

security."[52] In the ICRC's view, the difference in the wording signifies only that internment in occupied territory should be more "exceptional" than in a State's own territory,[53] but otherwise the regime appears to be more or less identical. Thus, the Fourth Geneva Convention provides a legal basis for the internment of civilians in an IAC, as recognized by human rights bodies;[54] nevertheless, States must ensure the existence of adequate detention procedures as required by IHL itself.[55] We will now focus more narrowly on the release and repatriation regime for civilian internees. In this regard, there will be slight differences based on whether the internee is situated in a State's own territory or in an occupied territory.

As the decision to intern is threat-based, the detaining power is under an obligation to release internees as soon as the reasons for their internment have ceased to exist, or as soon as possible after the close of hostilities, whichever point comes sooner.[56] The detaining power is obliged to undertake reviews at least twice a year[57] (six-month review).[58] Here, the own/occupied territory distinction comes into play: the Fourth Geneva Convention requires that the initial and periodic reviews in a high contracting party's own territory be undertaken by an "appropriate court or administrative board,"[59] whereas in occupied territory this should be a "competent body."[60] According to the ICRC, "[d]espite these and other textual differences the rules are in essence the same."[61] There is, of course, some controversy about what this "competent body" should be. The U.N. Working Group on Arbitrary Detention has insisted on the continuing validity of the IHRL right of habeas corpus, necessitating that the review be judicial.[62] However, other human rights bodies, such as the European Court of Human Rights, have not insisted that internment in IACs be reviewed by a regular court as would normally be required under peacetime IHRL. Rather, the "competent body" should "provide sufficient guarantees of impartiality and fair procedure to protect against arbitrariness" and "the first review should take place shortly after the person is taken into detention,

---

52. *Id.*, art. 78.

53. International Committee of the Red Cross, *Internment in Armed Conflict: Basic Rules and Challenges* 4–5 (Opinion Paper, 2014).

54. Hassan v. United Kingdom, 2014-VI Eur. Ct. H.R. 1, ¶¶ 96ff., https://www.echr.coe.int/Documents/Reports_Recueil_2014-VI.pdf.

55. This seems to be the case explicitly with Article 78 and implicitly with Article 43 of the Fourth Geneva Convention. *See* Sassòli, *supra* note 14, at 299.

56. Fourth Geneva Convention, arts. 132–33.

57. *Id.*, arts. 43(1), 78(2).

58. Sassòli, *supra* note 14, at 300.

59. Fourth Geneva Convention, *supra* note 9, art. 43(1).

60. *Id.*, art. 78(2).

61. International Committee of the Red Cross, *supra* note 53, at 5.

62. U.N. Working Group on Arbitrary Detention, *supra* note 22, Principle 16.

with subsequent reviews at frequent intervals, to ensure that any person who does not fall into one of the categories subject to internment under international humanitarian law is released without undue delay."[63] The ICRC also does not insist on proper judicial review and recalls that "[t]he purpose of the review process is to enable a determination of whether such information is reliable and whether the person's activity meets the high legal standard that would justify internment and its duration."[64] In our view, if this "habeas corpus light" accorded to civilian internees need not be handled by a regular court, then the "competent body" must resemble a court in its general contours: chiefly, its independence, its impartiality, and of course its power to order release if the reasons for internment do not, or no longer, exist.[65] Although it has been raised that at least the initial review of internment decisions depends on the internee's motion to challenge their deprivation of liberty,[66] the text of the Fourth Geneva Convention points toward an ex officio review that does not require a motion on the part of the internee and thus differs from the habeas corpus regime under IHRL.

The IAC internment regime requires a nexus between the decision to intern and the ongoing armed conflict or occupation. The existence of such a nexus is a general requirement for the application of IHL. Therefore, it would be illogical for a detaining power to apply IHL standards to situations that are unrelated to the armed conflict and, as such, not regulated by IHL. For example, a State could only rely on Article 42 of the Fourth Geneva Convention to detain an enemy national if that national is considered a security risk *in the context* of the ongoing IAC. If the perception of that individual as a security risk is unrelated to the conflict, then only IHRL applies.[67] If a nexus can be established, Articles 42 and 78

---

63. Hassan v. United Kingdom, 2014-VI Eur. Ct. H.R. 1, ¶ 106, https://www.echr.coe.int/Documents/Reports_Recueil_2014-VI.pdf. Compare this with the notion of "quasi-judicial" oversight in an "expeditious judicial or board . . . review process" of the Inter-American Commission of Human Rights in Coard at al. v. United States, Case no 10.951, Inter-Am. Comm'n H.R., Report No. 109/99, OEA/Ser.L/V/II.106 doc. 6 rev. ¶ 58 (1999).

64. International Committee of the Red Cross, *supra* note 53, at 5.

65. In *Delalić*, a Trial Chamber of the International Criminal Tribunal for the former Yugoslavia determined that a Commission that "did not have the necessary power to finally decide on the release of prisoners whose detention could not be considered as being justified for any serious reason" and whose power "was limited to initiating investigations of the prisoners and conducting interviews with prisoners in order to obtain relevant information concerning other individuals suspected of armed rebellion outside the prison-camp" did not meet the requirements of Article 43 of the Fourth Geneva Convention; *see* Prosecutor v. Delalić et al., Case No. IT-96-21-T, Judgment, ¶¶ 1137ff. (Int'l Crim. Trib. for the former Yugoslavia Dec. 10, 1998).

66. Andrea Harrison, *Periodic Review Boards for Law-of-War Detention in Guantanamo: What Next?*, 24 ILSA JOURNAL OF INTERNATIONAL & COMPARATIVE LAW 541, 551 (2018).

67. This is suggested *a contrario* by the ICRC's Commentary to Article 42: "Subversive activity carried on inside the territory of a Party to the conflict or actions which are of direct assistance to an enemy Power both threaten the security of the country; a belligerent may intern people or place them in assigned residence if it has serious and legitimate reason to think that they

provide a legal basis for internment on the grounds of security following a necessity test to determine whether interning the individual genuinely contributes toward the improvement of a belligerent party's security and whether less intrusive means are unavailable to achieve the same result. There appears to be a widespread opinion in doctrine that this necessity test should be ever more stringent the longer a civilian is kept in internment and at each subsequent review.[68] Both the initial and periodic reviews will need to take into consideration the particular circumstances of each individual. The test of necessity will be more demanding for certain categories, such as children, pregnant women and mothers of infants and young children, and the wounded and sick.[69] Additionally, the internment/security detention of civilians in an IAC is a measure of last resort: this means that it is not an alternative to criminal sanctions. Pejić recalls:

> A person who is suspected of having committed a criminal offence, whether in armed conflict or other situations of violence, has the right to benefit from the additional stringent judicial guarantees provided for in humanitarian and/or human rights law for criminal suspects . . . Unless internment/administrative detention and penal repression are organized as strictly separate regimes there is a danger that internment might be used as a substandard system of penal repression in the hands of the executive power, bypassing the one sanctioned by a country's legislature and courts.[70]

It has therefore been correctly suggested that both the initial and periodic reviews ought to consider whether the internee may be transferred to the criminal justice system.[71] Unlike internment under the Geneva Conventions, criminal prosecution and punishment are not considered *ultima ratio*. Therefore, it is reasonable to consider them a less intrusive alternative to security detention when analyzing the necessity of internment.

---

are members of organizations whose object is to cause disturbances, or that they may seriously prejudice its security by other means, such as sabotage or espionage." OSCAR M. UHLER ET AL., COMMENTARY TO GENEVA CONVENTION IV RELATIVE TO THE PROTECTION OF CIVILIAN PERSONS IN TIME OF WAR 258 (1958) [hereinafter 1958 GC IV COMMENTARY].

68. Fiona de Londras, *Can Counter-Terrorist Internment Ever Be Legitimate?*, 33 HUMAN RIGHTS QUARTERLY 593, 612 (2011); LAWRENCE HILL-CAWTHORNE, DETENTION IN NON-INTERNATIONAL ARMED CONFLICT 242 (2016); Bellinger & Padmanabhan, *supra* note 1, at 232. This also flows from Article 132 of the Fourth Geneva Convention, which requires States to endeavor to release, inter alia, internees who have been detained for a long time.

69. Fourth Geneva Convention, *supra* note 9, art. 132.

70. Jelena Pejić, *Procedural Principles and Safeguards for Internment/Administrative Detention in Armed Conflict and Other Situations of Violence*, 87 INTERNATIONAL REVIEW OF THE RED CROSS 375, 381 (2005).

71. Hill-Cawthorne, *supra* note 68, at 240.

Repatriation may be a more complicated matter to resolve. During hostilities, the Fourth Geneva Convention requires belligerent parties to "endeavour" to conclude agreements to release, repatriate, return to their place of residence, or accommodate in the territory of a neutral State "certain classes of internees, in particular children, pregnant women and mothers with infants and young children, wounded and sick, and internees who have been detained for a long time."[72] Upon the close of hostilities or occupation, high contracting parties are also required to endeavor to ensure the return of internees to their last place of residence or their repatriation.[73] A previous draft provision had foreseen that "[t]he High Contracting Parties shall endeavor upon the close of hostilities or occupation, to facilitate the return to their domicile, or the settlement in a new residence, of all persons who, as the result of war or occupation, are unable to live under normal conditions at the place where they may be" and that they shall "ensure that these persons may be able to travel, if they so desire, to other countries and that they are provided for this purpose with passports or equivalent documents." This wording was dropped, a decision the ICRC Commentary describes as "regrettable."[74] Previously, during the Second World War, internees were largely repatriated because of arrangements between belligerent parties.[75] Accordingly, there is no straightforward obligation under IHL to repatriate civilians in the same way as POWs: belligerent parties are, rather, asked to consider this possibility in good faith.[76] The two-pronged structure of the Fourth Geneva Convention distinguishes between the protection of enemy nationals (and other groups of civilians as appropriate) in a State's own territory and in territory that it occupies. In the latter case, most internees will presumably reside in the occupied territory, ergo it does not make sense to repatriate them elsewhere: indeed, IHL strictly prohibits the transfer of civilians from an occupied territory.[77] However, Additional Protocol I treats as a grave breach "unjustifiable delay in the repatriation of prisoners of war or *civilians*" (emphasis added).[78] This means that there must be a way of properly fleshing out the regime on civilian repatriation.

---

72. Fourth Geneva Convention, *supra* note 9, art. 132.

73. *Id.*, art. 134.

74. 1958 GC IV COMMENTARY, *supra* note 67, at 516.

75. *Id.*, at 511ff.

76. "[T]here is an essential difference between prisoners of war and civilians; prisoners of war must be repatriated, except for special cases; civilians are entitled to leave enemy territory subject to certain restrictions, but neither they nor the State in whose territory they are, have an obligation in this respect." COMMENTARY ON THE ADDITIONAL PROTOCOLS OF 8 JUNE 1977 TO THE GENEVA CONVENTIONS OF 12 AUGUST 1949, ¶ 507 (Yves Sandoz, Christophe Swinarski & Bruno Zimmermann eds., 1987) [hereinafter 1987 COMMENTARY ON THE ADDITIONAL PROTOCOLS].

77. Fourth Geneva Convention, *supra* note 9, art. 49.

78. Additional Protocol I, *supra* note 11, art. 85.

It seems that the distinction between protected civilians in an occupied territory and in a State's own territory is the best starting point for this analysis. First, according to Article 35 of the Fourth Geneva Convention, protected civilians who wish to leave a belligerent party's own territory will have the right to do so "unless their departure is contrary to the national interests of the State." Thus, unlike with POWs, there is no *obligation* to repatriate civilians: repatriation under the Fourth Geneva Convention is in fact a *right* (at least to leave the belligerent party's territory). The wording of the Fourth Geneva Convention additionally suggests that repatriation under such circumstances will concern not only the civilians' country of nationality, but also their country of residence.[79] The belligerent party may expel civilians from its territory should it deem this necessary, provided that the principle of *non-refoulement* is respected[80] (this stands in contrast to the regime on occupied territories, where individual or mass forcible transfers or deportations are prohibited). Second, in an occupied territory, there is likewise no obligation to repatriate civilians, which would be contrary to Article 49 of the Fourth Geneva Convention. However, in an occupied territory, the nationals of neutral and co-belligerent States may also be considered protected persons under the Fourth Geneva Convention,[81] and as such they may or may not be residents of the occupied territory. They may, of course, wish to leave that territory, in which case their return or repatriation would not be prohibited by Article 49. Although there is no equivalent in Section III of the Fourth Geneva Convention (concerning occupied territories) to Article 35, in our view, it is sensible to apply it by analogy to protected civilians in an occupied territory who desire to leave it. Third, as a general observation, the obligation to repatriate is closely linked to the obligation to release prisoners, probably under the influence of the wording and functioning of the Third Geneva Convention. However, there is no necessary link between internment and repatriation (other than the fact that repatriation shall be considered as an alternative to internment, in line with Article 132 of the Fourth Geneva Convention and the specific regime of Article 134). Any specific reference to the return or repatriation of internees is made in light of the possibility, whether in a belligerent party's own or an occupied territory, that they have been interned at a location removed from their place of residence. More narrowly, any possible obligation to repatriate exists in relation to protected civilians in a belligerent party's own territory, and not only in relation to internees. Fourth, it is difficult, based on the above, to determine under what conditions a failure to repatriate civilians could amount to a grave breach under Article 85 of Additional Protocol I. The provision could, of course, be relevant to civilians removed from an occupied territory in violation of Article 49. Thus, if Al Qaeda members captured during the IAC phase of the war in Afghanistan in 2001 were to be considered civilians under the Fourth Geneva Convention, their transfer abroad would have

---

79. See *mutatis mutandis,* Fourth Geneva Convention, *supra* note 9, art. 45.

80. This is foreseen explicitly by the Fourth Geneva Convention, *supra* note 9, art. 45.

81. Sassòli, *supra* note 14, at 290.

been unlawful, but the obligation to repatriate them would remain in force regardless of the legality of the transfer. We are not aware of any jurisprudence in relation to the civilian limb of this provision, which was also omitted from the Rome Statute[82] as "not serious enough" to come before the International Criminal Court.[83] As repatriation has historically taken place following agreements between belligerent parties, it may be that a grave breach could ensue from a failure to respect such an agreement. Alternatively, it could stem from an arbitrary denial of the right to leave a belligerent party's own territory.

B. IAC Detention, Release, and Repatriation in the Context of Counterterrorism

Situations where the law of IACs is applied in a counterterrorism context are rare. The early stages of the war in Afghanistan, from early October 2001 until June 2002 (when the U.N. Security Council recognized the Afghan Transitional Authority as that State's government),[84] were governed by the IAC framework. Although unique in many aspects, this armed conflict demonstrates the challenges inherent in a situation where one of the belligerent parties is seen as harboring terrorists.

From the outset, U.S. forces detained a large number of persons associated with the Taliban (which had previously held effective control over Afghanistan and was therefore its government) and Al Qaeda. Although the majority of these individuals were held in Afghanistan or aboard U.S. warships deployed in the region, around twenty prisoners were transferred to Guantánamo Bay as early as January 2002 (while the IAC stage of the conflict was still ongoing).[85] It soon became apparent that captured Taliban and Al Qaeda members would not be treated as POWs, but the rationale for this emerged only gradually. Beyond arguments concerning the inapplicability of the Geneva Conventions to Al Qaeda as a non-State actor and the inapplicability of Common Article 3[86] to extraterritorial NIACs, the main argument was that Al Qaeda members did not comply with

---

82. Rome Statute of the International Criminal Court, July 17, 1998, 2187 U.N.T.S. 90.

83. Yasmin Naqvi, *Amnesty for War Crimes: Defining the Limits of International Recognition*, 85 INTERNATIONAL REVIEW OF THE RED CROSS 598 n.64 (2003).

84. See S.C. Res. 1419, U.N. Doc. S/RES/1419 (June 26, 2002).

85. *Decision Not to Regard Persons Detained in Afghanistan as POWs*, 96 AMERICAN JOURNAL OF INTERNATIONAL LAW 475, 475 (2002).

86. Convention (I) for the Amelioration of the Condition of the Wounded and Sick in the Armed Forces in the Field art. 3, Aug. 12, 1949, 6 U.S.T. 3114, 75 U.N.T.S. 31 [hereinafter First Geneva Convention]; Convention (II) for the Amelioration of the Condition of the Wounded, Sick, and Shipwrecked Members of Armed Forces at Sea art. 3, Aug. 12, 1949, 6 U.S.T. 3217, 75 U.N.T.S. 85 [hereinafter Second Geneva Convention]; Third Geneva Convention, *supra* note 8, art. 3; Fourth Geneva Convention, *supra* note 9, art. 3.

the requirements of Article 4A(2) of the Third Geneva Convention.[87] Regarding captured Taliban, the George W. Bush administration initially explained its refusal to treat them as POWs on the basis that "Afghanistan was not a functioning state during the conflict and the Taliban was not recognized as a legitimate government."[88] This was later revised to the effect that the Third Geneva Convention *was* applicable to the Taliban, but the Taliban had lost the right to POW status by "violating the laws of war and closely associating itself with Al Qaeda."[89]

This approach to POW status, particularly regarding Taliban combatants, may be easily criticized. It could lead to a slippery slope scenario in other cases, both as regards an IAC against an unrecognized "illegitimate" government[90] and also because the failure to respect the laws of war as leading to an exclusion from POW status has largely been rejected in doctrine, as discussed earlier. The idea that consorting with a terrorist group disentitles from POW status does not appear in legal writings at all. Only a failure to distinguish oneself from the civilian population at the moment of an attack/military operation preparatory to an attack can lead to *individual* loss of POW status. Combatants who thus lose protection under the Third Geneva Convention will still be protected as civilians under the Fourth Geneva Convention. As for Al Qaeda members, if the organization "belonged" to Afghanistan as an irregular group, its members would have been considered combatants and thus entitled to the protection of the Third Geneva Convention upon capture if Al Qaeda complied, as a group, with the requirements of Article 4A(2)[91] (which Al Qaeda in reality did not). However, Taliban members were at least *in principle* entitled to POW status unless they individually failed to distinguish themselves at the moment of capture, in which case they were protected by the Fourth Geneva Convention. If they were POWs, they had to be released and repatriated as soon as possible after the end of active hostilities. As civilians, they could only be detained for as long as they were considered a security threat

---

87. *Decision Not to Regard Persons Detained in Afghanistan as POWs*, supra note 85, at 477. This provision spells out the requirements for the POW status of members of militias and volunteer corps belonging to a belligerent party to an IAC along the lines of Article 1 of the Hague Regulations.

88. *Id.*

89. *Id.*

90. The criterion of effectivity, and not recognition, for determining a State's government was confirmed in the classical Tinoco arbitration. *See* Tinoco Claims Arbitration (Great Britain v. Costa Rica), 1 RIAA 369, 381 (1923). The forces of an unrecognized government are at any rate explicitly listed as entitled to POW status under Article 4A(3) of the Third Geneva Convention.

91. The standard of "belonging" is provided for under Article 4A(2) of the Third Geneva Convention. The formal or informal relationship needed for belonging is described by the ICRC in its commentary to Article 4 of the Third Geneva Convention. *See* 2020 GC III COMMENTARY, *supra* note 26, ¶¶ 1001ff., https://ihl-databases.icrc.org/applic/ihl/ihl.nsf/Comment.xsp?action=openDocument&documentId=1796813618ABDA06C12585850057AB95 (the two main requirements for belonging are that the group fight on behalf of the State party and that the party accept both the fighting role of the group and that it is fighting on its behalf).

and had to be released no later than the close of hostilities. They could under no circumstances be transferred out of Afghan territory, which had to be considered occupied until the new Afghan government was in place. As the transfer of civilians from an occupied territory (for example, to Cuba) violates Article 49 of the Fourth Geneva Convention, their "right to repatriation" may additionally be found within the detaining power's obligation of cessation and non-repetition of internationally wrongful acts.[92] If Al Qaeda members did not qualify for POW status, they too would have to be treated as civilians and detained in line with the Fourth Geneva Convention.[93]

A final point needs to be made regarding the interplay between the IHL of IACs and the counterterrorism legal framework. The fact that members of regular or irregular armed forces are labeled terrorists cannot diminish their rights under the Third Geneva Convention or, subsidiarily, the Fourth Geneva Convention. There are only two ways in which a counterterrorism context may interact with the law of IACs. First, if POWs are suspected of having engaged in acts of terrorism, they can be prosecuted by the detaining power under the following circumstances: the impugned act must be prosecuted insofar as it overlaps with a war crime; the act has been committed after their capture and is criminalized by the detaining power's legislation; or the act was committed prior to capture, but fell outside the scope of hostilities and thereby was not covered by the combatant privilege (according to Sassòli, "it is suggested that this is limited only to extraditable crimes"[94]). Terrorist acts may well be considered as amounting to war crimes and/or extraditable crimes not covered by the combatant privilege, although great care must be taken in the latter case to avoid abuse. Second, regarding civilians, the threat of terrorism can certainly be considered when deciding to intern them. A nexus with the armed conflict would still be required. Thus, the provisions of the Fourth Geneva Convention could be relied upon if the individual deprived of liberty were suspected of having perpetrated or planned to commit a terrorist attack against the detaining power for conflict-related reasons, but not if the terrorist attack is completely isolated from the conflict. In any case, internment would remain *ultima ratio*, as criminal prosecution would be preferable. Prosecution of civilians accused of acts of terrorism on the territory of the belligerent party or in an occupied territory is possible unless such acts are explicitly authorized by IHL. For instance, civilians shall not be convicted for having collected and cared for wounded

---

92. G.A. Res. 56/83, Responsibility of States for Internationally Wrongful Acts (Jan. 28, 2002) A/RES/56/83 [Annex] art. 30.

93. *See, e.g.*, Marco Sassòli, *Use and Abuse of the Laws of War in the War on Terrorism*, 22 MINNESOTA JOURNAL OF LAW & INEQUALITY 105 (2004); ÉRIC DAVID, PRINCIPES DE DROIT DES CONFLITS ARMÉS 171–78 (2012).

94. Sassòli, *supra* note 14, at 266.

combatants/fighters, even if these are considered terrorists.[95] Recent practice shows that certain domestic terrorist offenses are problematic in this respect.[96]

C. The Matter of Conflict "Transformation"

There exists significant jurisprudence and practice to support the notion that the character of an armed conflict as either an IAC or a NIAC may change should the requisite circumstances arise. In this regard, it is most common to speak of the "internationalization" of a conflict: if armed group X fighting State A comes within a certain degree of control by State B, then the NIAC between A and X becomes an IAC between A and B. Such a situation was notably identified by the International Criminal Tribunal for the former Yugoslavia in relation to the war in Bosnia and Herzegovina in the *Tadić* case.[97] There are other situations in which a NIAC may become an IAC: when a national liberation movement[98] makes a declaration accepting to implement the Geneva Conventions and Additional Protocol I in line with Article 96 of Additional Protocol I, or when a secessionist movement achieves statehood and/or recognition by its parent State (with the war of secession still ongoing).[99] If an IAC is understood as a situation where the law of IACs is applicable, then even a NIAC in which the parties agree to implement the

---

95. *See, e.g.*, First Geneva Convention, *supra* note 86, art. 18(3); Additional Protocol I, *supra* note 11, art. 16; Protocol Additional to the Geneva Conventions of 12 August 1949, and Relating to the Protection of Victims of Non-international Armed Conflicts art. 10, June 8, 1977, 1125 U.N.T.S. 609 [hereinafter Additional Protocol II] (for NIACs). *See also* Rule 26 of the ICRC Customary IHL Study: 1 CUSTOMARY INTERNATIONAL HUMANITARIAN LAW (Jean-Marie Henckaerts & Louise Doswald-Beck eds., 2005).

96. Dustin A. Lewis, Naz K. Modirzadeh & Gabriella Blum, *Medical Care in Armed Conflict: International Humanitarian Law and State Responses to Terrorism* 111–41 (Harvard Law School Program on International Law and Armed Conflict Legal Briefing 2015); Ekaterina Ortiz Linares & Marisela Silva Chau, *Reflections on the Colombian Case Law on the Protection of Medical Personnel Against Punishment*, 95 INTERNATIONAL REVIEW OF THE RED CROSS 251 (2013); Stuart Casey-Maslen, *The Status, Rights, and Obligations of Medical and Religious Personnel*, in THE 1949 GENEVA CONVENTIONS: A COMMENTARY 820 (Andrew Clapham, Paola Gaeta & Marco Sasòli eds., 2015).

97. Prosecutor v. Tadić, Case No. IT-94-1-A, Appeals Chamber Judgment, ¶¶ 131ff. (Int'l Crim. Trib. for the former Yugoslavia July 15, 1999).

98. *See* Additional Protocol I, *supra* note 11, art. 1(4).

99. For the idea that the NIAC automatically transforms into an IAC at a certain degree of effectivity, see INTERNATIONAL COMMITTEE OF THE RED CROSS, COMMENTARY ON THE FIRST GENEVA CONVENTION: CONVENTION (I) FOR THE AMELIORATION OF THE CONDITION OF THE WOUNDED AND SICK IN THE ARMED FORCES IN THE FIELD ¶ 231 (2016), https://ihl-databases.icrc.org/applic/ihl/ihl.nsf/Comment.xsp?action=openDocument&documentId=BE2D518CF5DE54EAC1257F7D0036B518 [hereinafter 2016 GC I COMMENTARY]; DJEMILA CARRON, L'ACTE DÉCLENCHEUR D'UN CONFLIT ARMÉ INTERNATIONAL 121–22 (2016). For an opposing view, see Kolb & Hyde, *supra* note 36, at 81; Dapo Akande, *Classification of Armed*

Geneva Conventions and Additional Protocol I by special agreement, or where insurgents are recognized as belligerents, could be considered an IAC for practical purposes. It is not necessary to list all the situations where a NIAC could become an IAC: what matters is how such a transformation influences the position of individual protected persons/detainees, specifically pertaining to release and repatriation.

The same may be said of the reverse phenomenon, situations where an IAC "turns into" a NIAC. In truth, there exists only one major case study on this phenomenon: the war in Afghanistan. As *debellatio* is largely a historic concept in IAC terminology, the law of IACs could remain applicable in an occupied territory long after its sovereign authorities have been displaced by the occupying power. Even if a new government were created under the occupation regime, it would normally not be considered a lawful representative of the occupied territory. The only factor that was apparently able to influence this in Afghanistan was that the new democratic government was confirmed by the U.N. Security Council.[100] We will chiefly focus on this example in our IAC-to-NIAC transformation analysis.

1. IAC TO NIAC

In principle, an IAC can only become a NIAC if the nature of the belligerent parties changes. An IAC is fought between two or more States: NIACs may be fought between States and OAGs or simply between OAGs with no State involvement. Therefore, for an IAC to turn into a NIAC, at least one of the State belligerent parties must become a non-State actor.

The mechanism whereby this could happen is not at all obvious in international law, let alone in IHL. It could happen in case of a change of government. A government is always an authority, namely a political organization exercising control over a specific territory, normally all of the territory of a State. It is conceivable that a governmental authority could transform into a non-State territorial authority. This could happen if a State's government were overthrown by rebel forces after the latter had effectively taken over that State's territory, but loyalist forces continued fighting against the new revolutionary government. This is a situation

---

Conflicts: Relevant Legal Aspects, in INTERNATIONAL LAW AND THE CLASSIFICATION OF CONFLICTS 50 (Elizabeth Wilmshurst ed., 2012); KUBO MAČÁK, INTERNATIONALIZED ARMED CONFLICTS IN INTERNATIONAL LAW 61 (2018); MILOŠ HRNJAZ, RASPAD JUGOSLAVIJE PRED SUDOM: PRAVNA KVALIFIKACIJA ORUŽANIH SUKOBA U JUGOSLAVIJI U PRAKSI SUDOVA U SRBIJI (2021).

100. The ICRC claims to have reclassified the conflict "[f]ollowing the establishment of a new Afghan Government in June 2002 through a *loya jirga* (grand assembly)." This comes across as odd, as such developments in an occupied territory would not usually alter its status in line with Article 47 of the Fourth Geneva Convention. See 2016 GC I COMMENTARY, *supra* note 99, ¶ 400, https://ihl-databases.icrc.org/applic/ihl/ihl.nsf/Comment.xsp?action=openDocument&documentId=59F6CDFA490736C1C1257F7D004BA0EC (Commentary to Common Article 3). Sassòli remarks more realistically that the transformation came about as a result of free elections and a Security Council resolution: Sassòli, *supra* note 14, at 185.

where the nature of the belligerent parties changes from State to non-State actor and vice versa, but the classification remains the same as the conflict was a NIAC to begin with.[101]

The conflict in Afghanistan that began in 2001 is also an example of an armed conflict starting out as an IAC and later "transforming" into a NIAC. The example is unique in modern IHL history. In principle, the application of IAC laws cannot be displaced through the military operations of the hostile belligerent, as IHL remains applicable even in case of the total occupation of a State's territory and the effective destruction of its governmental authority. For a transformation to happen, this would have to come about for reasons unrelated to the IAC but synchronous with it: for example, a belligerent party's government could be supplanted by a new one which is amicable toward the old enemy and joins it in fighting the loyalists (now an armed group). Evidently, such situations will be exceedingly rare.

Where does that leave us with conflict transformation? The underlying notion is that the conflict is the same but changes character. In Afghanistan, the nature of the hostilities against the Taliban did not change simply because a new democratic government was formed and/or the Security Council decided that the Taliban was no longer the government—practically, the same continuum of hostilities persisted (and has never ceased since). But what if this premise is false? Why do we presume that an IAC that "transforms" into a NIAC stays the same conflict? Is it not more sensible to regard the IAC as over and the NIAC as starting?

There are two principal reasons why most lawyers tend to speak of conflict transformation rather than conflict "succession." The first reason could be that, according to the International Criminal Tribunal for the former Yugoslavia, an IAC ends when a "general conclusion of peace" has been reached.[102] To say that this has occurred with hostilities still ongoing seems too much of a legal fiction. This interpretation is not shared by a majority of IHL experts.[103] The second reason is that a new classification exercise would have to be undertaken to determine that

---

101. An example of this phenomenon could be the situation in Afghanistan following the 2021 fall of Kabul and the re-establishment of a Taliban government. This raises the question of whether the old NIAC between the former government and the Taliban as an OAG should be presumed to continue, or if the situation should be reclassified with the Taliban now representing Afghanistan in an armed conflict against loyalists gathered in the National Resistance Front if the latter fulfills the criteria of an OAG (either way, the conflict would be a NIAC). See the website of the Rule of Law in Armed Conflicts project (RULAC) of the Geneva Academy of International Humanitarian Law: *Non-International Armed Conflicts in Afghanistan*, RULAC/ GENEVA ACADEMY (updated 2021), https://www.rulac.org/browse/conflicts/non-internatio nal-armed-conflicts-in-afghanistan#collapse2accord (last visited Nov. 10, 2021).

102. Prosecutor v. Tadić, Case No. IT-94-1-AR-72, Decision on Defence Motion for Interlocutory Appeal on Jurisdiction, ¶ 70 (Int'l Crim. Trib. for the former Yugoslavia Oct. 2, 1995).

103. *See* Marko Milanović, *The End of Application of International Humanitarian Law*, 96 INTERNATIONAL REVIEW OF THE RED CROSS 163 (2015); 2016 GC I COMMENTARY, *supra* note 99, ¶¶ 274ff., https://ihl-databases.icrc.org/applic/ihl/ihl.nsf/Comment.xsp?action=openD ocument&documentId=BE2D518CF5DE54EAC1257F7D0036B518; Sassòli, *supra* note 14, at 191–93.

the intensity and organization threshold for a NIAC has been reached after the end of the IAC. This could imply a lack of IHL protection before the intensity threshold has been reached or before the new non-State armed group becomes sufficiently organized.

The above issues do not, however, seem a decisive finding in favor of transformation versus succession. The second reason in particular does not seem very convincing: it does not seem that in order to conclude that the threshold of a NIAC was reached in Afghanistan one had to draw on the previous IAC rather than evaluate organization and intensity de novo. IAC and NIAC are, after all, legal terms that inform belligerent parties which law to apply to hostilities (which, for their part, may be indistinguishable as internal or international). The war in Afghanistan is an excellent example of our point. If we take for our vantage point the question of applicable law, we will find that it is not very counterintuitive to maintain that, by June/July 2002, the IAC between the United States and the Taliban (as the government of Afghanistan) had ended, and a NIAC between the United States and the Taliban (as an OAG) had begun. Although there have been hostilities in Afghanistan since 2001, the IAC hostilities ended when one of the State belligerents *legally* ceased to exist.

Because IHL does not contain a mechanism for conflict transformation, this poses a distinct advantage from an individual rights perspective. All that needs to be done is to determine which body of law (that of IACs or of NIACs) applied to individuals at the moment their protection under IHL was triggered. For a Taliban combatant captured in January 2002, this is the Third Geneva Convention (or the Fourth Geneva Convention, if he had failed to distinguish himself); for a fighter captured in January 2003, this is Common Article 3.[104] Thus, the former needs to be released and repatriated at the end of active hostilities *in the IAC context*. To say that ongoing hostilities in the NIAC in Afghanistan now prevent the release and repatriation of a POW is analogous to the refusal to release POWs belonging to State B because the detaining power A is now engaged in a separate conflict with State C—it would be absurd. So far, mixing between the IAC and NIAC regimes in the context of conflict transformation has led only to extreme confusion among States and lawyers as to the applicable rules, and the worst possible outcome for detainees: a regime that resembles neither that of an IAC nor that of a NIAC, but some mix of the two, retaining mostly the negative aspects.

States may feel compelled to keep potentially dangerous individuals behind bars: this is where the counterterrorism context comes into play. In our view, such concerns are not cogent enough to override the rules of IHL. Nevertheless, States are free and indeed obliged to prosecute suspected terrorists in the same way as they are required to prosecute suspected war criminals. There are several ways in which conflict succession or transformation could have an impact in this regard. First, once the IAC has ended, the detaining power cannot be allowed to continue

---

104. Silvia Borelli, *Casting Light on the Legal Black Hole: International Law and Detentions Abroad in the "War on Terror,"* 87 INTERNATIONAL REVIEW OF THE RED CROSS 39, 47ff. (2005).

to intern hostile combatants as POWs. This is prohibited by Article 118 of the Third Geneva Convention. If a NIAC subsequently erupts, but the hostilities between the IAC and NIAC stage are interrupted, these are two successive conflicts and there is no "transformation." In this case, the POWs captured during the IAC must be either released and repatriated or criminally prosecuted for international crimes. Second, if the hostilities form a continuum between the IAC and NIAC stage, it may still be possible to speak of conflict succession rather than transformation, leading to the same result as in the previous situation. However, such an approach may be construed as too formalistic. Third, if the hostilities are uninterrupted between the IAC and NIAC stages, then we could indeed accept that the conflict has transformed—the nature of the armed conflict has changed, but not its very existence. In such cases, we could accept that the NIAC internment rules allow the continued internment of individuals who had been POWs during the IAC stage if they are still considered a security threat. The underlying rationale for detaining POWs is to prevent them from rejoining their own forces and is thus ultimately predicated on the detaining power's security. However, individuals initially detained as POWs should not receive lower protection standards in the NIAC stage of their detention, and their combatant privilege should continue to apply for the duration of the internment. In addition, all former POWs should now be entitled to an individual review to determine the risk of them rejoining their forces.

2. NIAC TO IAC

Similar conclusions may be drawn regarding the "internationalization" of a NIAC. The most common scenario analyzed in such a context is one where a State assumes control over an insurgent group abroad and uses it to settle its own scores with the territorial State. According to Sassòli:

> This may occur either when the foreign State has the necessary control over the armed group from the very beginning of the conflict or when it gains control over the armed group at a later time during a NIAC between the armed group and the (territorial) State, thereby turning the NIAC into an IAC.[105]

These two situations are *not* identical: only the latter involves conflict transformation, as an existing NIAC is said to become an IAC, whereas the former is an IAC since its inception.

As mentioned earlier, the Appeals Chamber of the International Criminal Tribunal for the former Yugoslavia took the view in the *Tadić* case that an IAC existed between Bosnia and Herzegovina and the Federal Republic of Yugoslavia on the basis of the latter's overall control of the Bosnian Serb forces. The Court explicitly discusses internationalization: "It is nevertheless imperative to *specify*

---

105. Sassòli, *supra* note 14, at 266.

what *degree of authority or control* must be wielded by a foreign State over armed forces fighting on its behalf in order to render international an armed conflict which is *prima facie* internal."[106] And yet, the Chamber found that the conflict was an IAC to begin with:[107] there was no "internationalization" in the *Tadić* case, at least not in the sense discussed here or described by the Chamber earlier in the same judgment.

The question is, of course, whether a NIAC truly can become an IAC later on, whether through the test of overall control or through some other means. Several remarks may be made in this regard. First, the effects of internationalization cannot be retroactive. Even if NIAC-to-IAC transformation is possible in the way this notion is usually applied, the law of IACs can only be applied *ex nunc*, from the moment of internationalization, and not *ex tunc*, from the start of the NIAC. This means that the law of NIACs will cover situations up to a certain point, after which the law of IACs must apply. Second, this raises many complex issues related to the treatment of detainees captured during the NIAC stage, specifically members of the former OAG with a continuous combat function. According to the *Tadić* approach, fighting members of an OAG that comes under the overall control of a State would have to be considered combatants and entitled to POW treatment. But what of those who are already in the hands of the enemy? Clearly, the treatment prior to internationalization, which cannot have retroactive effects, cannot be scrutinized according to the law of IACs, but it is legitimate to wonder whether captured fighters may now be considered members of a State's armed forces and henceforth entitled to POW status (as a *prospective* effect of internationalization). Alternatively, the former fighters could be entitled to treatment under the Fourth Geneva Convention. Although this question deserves a more extensive legal analysis, it does not seem realistic that a detaining power could be forced to treat as POWs former rebels who may even be undergoing criminal proceedings for rebellion/secession under domestic law (which would now be prevented by the combatant privilege). It is all the more difficult to conceive that States would abide by such rules if the detainee (likely their own national) tried to invoke overall control by, or allegiance to, a hostile State belligerent in order to have their POW status recognized.[108] We might conclude that the detaining power may nevertheless apply IAC standards ex gratia, but, as it is not always easy to determine whether the IAC or NIAC framework is a priori more protective,

---

106. Prosecutor v. Tadić, Case No. IT-94-1-A, Appeals Chamber Judgment, ¶ 162 (Int'l Crim. Trib. for the former Yugoslavia July 15, 1999); *cf.* Prosecutor v. Bemba Gombo, Case No. ICC-01/05-01/08, Judgment, ¶ 130 (Mar. 21, 2016).

107. Prosecutor v. Tadić, Case No. IT-94-1-A, Appeals Chamber Judgment, ¶ 162 (Int'l Crim. Trib. for the former Yugoslavia July 15, 1999).

108. In this regard, we fully agree with Sassòli, who writes: "I would not recommend to any detainee to claim protected person status on the basis that they have severed allegiance with detaining authority as this might further undermine their chance to be respected, and the ICRC would never make this claim on a detainee's behalf": Sassòli, *supra* note 14, at 292.

one should be wary of raising such a possibility. It is therefore best, in our view, to follow the approach we described for IAC-to-NIAC succession and treat detainees according to the rules in force at the time of their capture.[109]

III. Release and Repatriation of Detainees in NIACs

Unlike the detailed regime of detention developed for IACs, the law of NIACs is frustratingly vague on the matter. This is understandable, as States did not wish to give the right to rebel forces to detain their own troops, and drafting Common Article 3 or the Protocol Additional to the Geneva Conventions of 12 August 1949, and Relating to the Protection of Victims of Non-international Armed Conflicts (Additional Protocol II)[110] in a way that distinguished between the obligations/rights of State and non-State belligerent parties to a NIAC would have undermined the principle of belligerent equality.[111] There is no doubt that, in the ICRC's words, "internment is a form of deprivation of liberty which is a common occurrence in armed conflict, not prohibited by Common Article 3,"[112] and that the IHL of NIACs deals with detention. However, to what extent it does so is another matter entirely.

As a majority of armed conflicts pitting States against OAGs described as "terrorists" will be of a non-international character, we now turn to the NIAC detention framework, with a focus on release and repatriation. The requirements for lawful deprivation of liberty may roughly be broken down into the three elements of legal basis, grounds for detention, and judicial/procedural safeguards. This basis–grounds–safeguards triptych thus constitutes the basis of our analysis. As we will see, the lack of explicit provisions has generated considerable controversy around this regime, with numerous scholars attempting to fill the gaps in various ways.

A. The NIAC Detention Regime, Release, and Return/Repatriation

Common Article 3 deals with detention only in passing. As one of the minimal standards to apply in a NIAC, the provision foresees, inter alia, the humane treatment of "[p]ersons taking no active part in the hostilities, including

---

109. This might speak in favor of the second option for IAC-to-NIAC transformation regarding internment discussed in the previous part.

110. Additional Protocol II, *supra* note 95.

111. This view was expressed by the British Court of Appeal in Mohammed v. Secretary of State for Defence [2015] EWCA Civ 843, ¶ 178.

112. International Committee of the Red Cross, *supra* note 53, at 7.

members of armed forces who have laid down their arms and those placed 'hors de combat' by ... *detention,* or any other cause."[113] Additional Protocol II is more explicit: it establishes certain fundamental guarantees for all persons not directly participating in hostilities "whether or not their liberty has been restricted,"[114] as well as specific guarantees for internees and detainees, including on detention conditions, access to relief, religious freedoms, safety guarantees in case of release, and so on.[115] But there is nothing in either Common Article 3 or Additional Protocol II explicitly *authorizing* detention or describing its grounds, let alone regarding release and repatriation (although it is evident that Article 5 of Additional Protocol II covers not only persons subjected to internment but also other persons deprived of their liberty in relation to the armed conflict, such as persons against whom there are criminal proceedings).[116]

The ICRC's view of the NIAC provisions is somewhat ambiguous. In its 2014 position paper on internment in armed conflict, the organization distinguished between the role of IHL in "traditional" and "extraterritorial" NIACs. In the former, it is maintained, "domestic law, informed by the State's human rights obligations, and IHL, constitutes the legal framework for the possible internment by States of persons whose activity is deemed to pose a serious security threat."[117] In the latter, the matter is more complicated because of possible domestic law limitations to a State's detention of foreigners abroad. The ICRC maintains that "both customary and treaty IHL contain an inherent power to intern and may in this respect be said to provide a legal basis for internment in NIAC," but that, nevertheless, "in the absence of specific provisions in common Article 3 or Additional Protocol II, additional authority related to the grounds for internment and the process to be followed needs to be obtained, in keeping with the principle of legality."[118] Such "additional authority" could be found, for example, in the host or detaining State's domestic law, a Security Council resolution, an international agreement, or other sources. It is not clear, however, what the consequences of IHL-based detention should be if there were no additional grounds or procedures for internment in an extraterritorial NIAC, specifically whether IHL and/or IHRL would thereby be violated.

Two well-known cases dealing with internment in armed conflicts emerged concurrently and just after the ICRC's position paper. The first is the abovementioned *Hassan* case at the European Court of Human Rights, in which the Court accepted

---

113. First Geneva Convention, *supra* note 86, art. 3; Second Geneva Convention, *supra* note 86, art. 3; Third Geneva Convention, *supra* note 8, art. 3; Fourth Geneva Convention, *supra* note 9, art. 3.

114. Additional Protocol II, *supra* note 95, art. 4.

115. *Id.*, art. 5.

116. 1987 COMMENTARY ON THE ADDITIONAL PROTOCOLS, *supra* note 76, ¶ 4568.

117. International Committee of the Red Cross, *supra* note 53, at 7.

118. *Id.*, at 7–8.

that it had to apply the Convention for the Protection of Human Rights and Fundamental Freedoms (European Convention on Human Rights)[119] in light of the IAC rules on detention even without a derogation,[120] but noted quite prominently that "[i]t can only be in cases of international armed conflict, where the taking of prisoners of war and the detention of civilians who pose a threat to security are accepted features of international humanitarian law, that Article 5 could be interpreted as permitting the exercise of such broad powers."[121] The Court seems to imply that its analysis in *Hassan* could not simply be transposed into the context of a NIAC. Afterward, the *Serdar Mohammed* case engaged the same issue in relation to NIACs and was discussed by several instances of the British judiciary. The Supreme Court ultimately confirmed that "[c]ommon article 3 does not in terms confer a right of detention" and also that such a right could not be inferred from customary law.[122]

In light of the above, it is useful to recall the basis–grounds–safeguards triad and consider Common Article 3 and Additional Protocol II in that context. Such an exercise is conducted by Hill-Cawthorne, who finds that neither source provides a legal basis for internment, whether explicit or implicit,[123] but that Common Article 3 "in principle" prohibits arbitrary detention by requiring humane treatment (this, according to Hill-Cawthorne, is inferred from Article 27 of the Fourth Geneva Convention, which he finds to prohibit arbitrary detention of protected civilians and whose analogous application in a NIAC may be "self-evident").[124] Others may, and do, provide a different interpretation. In our view, all detention requires an explicit and formal basis in the law and it is thus unclear why internment in NIACs should be an exception: we draw the same conclusion regarding grounds and procedures. Therefore, either IHL does not regulate internment in NIACs, necessitating the establishment or identification of an alternative legal regime, or IHL somehow regulates it "in principle" but its content is unclear, which leads to the same result—namely, the search for a detention framework.

Even if one accepted, as does the ICRC, that IHL provides an adequate legal basis "inherently," it is still necessary to come up with a way to fill in the gaps—including, notably, with respect to release and repatriation. There are different ways in which this may be done. We present here and reflect upon the most interesting theories.

---

119. Convention for the Protection of Human Rights and Fundamental Freedoms, Nov. 4, 1950, 213 U.N.T.S. 222 [hereinafter European Convention on Human Rights, or ECHR].

120. Hassan v. United Kingdom, 2014-VI Eur. Ct. H.R. 1, ¶¶ 102ff., https://www.echr.coe.int/Documents/Reports_Recueil_2014-VI.pdf.

121. *Id.*, ¶ 104.

122. *Id.*, ¶ 12–17.

123. Hill-Cawthorne, *supra* note 68, at 66ff.

124. *Id.*, at 82. The author further notes with disappointment that Additional Protocol II "adds nothing to the procedural regulation of internment": *id.*, at 85.

B. Debates: Filling the NIAC Gap

Several avenues have been proposed for filling the NIAC gap in doctrine; some of them are also explicitly or implicitly present in State practice and in domestic jurisprudence, particularly in the United States. One of the earliest doctrinal approaches to emerge in the aftermath of 9/11 was to apply the Third Geneva Convention regime on POWs by analogy, in which case security detention would be "status-based"—as far as this term may be made in a NIAC. A major alternative suggestion was to apply the threat-based mechanism of the Fourth Geneva Convention. Several other IHL-based theories have also been proposed, as has the idea that one should simply apply IHRL and disregard IHL. In what follows, we will examine the main and most interesting points under these approaches.

1. STATUS-BASED DETENTION: THE THIRD GENEVA CONVENTION ANALOGY

Many prominent decisions on writs for habeas corpus by Guantánamo inmates rely on an analogy with the Third Geneva Convention to determine whether the petitioners were entitled to challenge the lawfulness of their detention. For example, in *Al Adahi*, the District of Columbia Court of Appeals found that the petitioner was "more likely than not" an Al Qaeda member and thus quashed the District Court's habeas writ.[125] In *Al-Warafi v. Obama*, the Court found that an inmate claiming to have been a Taliban medic did not manage to prove as a matter of fact that he had been "medical personnel" in the sense of the Geneva Conventions and thus denied his petition (throughout the judgment, the Court's analysis is based on the Third Geneva Convention).[126] This approach is based on status or membership, as the decisions whether to order release were predicated not on any threat to national security by an individual petitioner but on the petitioner's membership in Al Qaeda or the Taliban.

As Pearlstein points out,[127] the U.S. judicial approach has been primarily based not on IHL directly but rather on the Authorization for Use of Military Force (AUMF) as a domestic law source *referring* to IHL. This has been interpreted as requiring Third Geneva Convention standards for release from detention since the Supreme Court's judgment in the *Hamdi* case.[128] In doctrine, some authors— such as Bradley and Goldsmith[129] or Strauch and Walton[130]—also seem to take for

---

125. Al Adahi v. Obama, Nos. 09-5333, 09-5339 (July 13, 2010).

126. Al-Warafi v. Obama, No. 11-5276 (May 24, 2013).

127. Deborah Pearlstein, Al Warafi's Active Hostilities, JUST SECURITY (May 28, 2015), https://www.justsecurity.org/23271/al-warafis-active-hostilities/.

128. *See* Hamdi v. Rumsfeld, 542 U.S. 507 (2004).

129. *See* Bradley & Goldsmith, *supra* note 1, at 2121ff.

130. Paul Strauch & Beatrice Walton, *Active Hostilities and International Law Limits to Trump's Executive Order on Guantanamo*, EJIL:TALK! (Mar. 13, 2018), https://www.ejiltalk.org/active-hostilities-and-international-law-limits-to-trumps-executive-order-on-guantanamo/.

granted the relevance of the Third Geneva Convention for Guantánamo inmates, in spite of the initial controversy surrounding their status and treatment. But these authors typically neglect to classify the conflict in Afghanistan at its different stages and thus do not actually propose a NIAC regime.

Conversely, a more elaborate and largely status-based framework adapted for NIACs is suggested by Jenks. Criticizing aspects of U.S. practice in relation to Guantánamo, Jenks instead proposes a process that is "status-based" (in relation to membership in an OAG) and takes place every six months to review the need for continued detention. There would be a rebuttable presumption in favor of release at the hearings, where the detainee would have a right to counsel and the ability to present evidence and witnesses. The reviewing body would be administrative, but its decision to release would be final, whereas a decision for continued detention could be reversed by "higher level government officials."[131] Clearly, this approach mixes different legal frameworks. First, it is status-based and fashioned only for OAG members in a manner analogous to the Third Geneva Convention. However, detained OAG members would then undergo a periodic threat-based review (modeled after the Fourth Geneva Convention) rather than be kept until the end of active hostilities as POWs, and would enjoy a number of procedural guarantees imported from IHRL. The most intriguing aspect here is, perhaps, Jenks's vision of the review body, which would be administrative. Its decisions to release would apparently be binding, but the review body would otherwise not have the qualities of a court of law or other "competent body," as discussed earlier. The fact that this body's decisions would be subjected to review by the executive, even if it is only in favor of the accused, does not conform to the notion of independence even in the broadest sense contemplated by international law. Therefore, a human rights body—were it to scrutinize the mechanism—would almost certainly not regard it as an effective remedy to challenge the lawfulness of deprivation of liberty.

In our view, an approach based entirely on the Third Geneva Convention, or mixing the Third and Fourth Geneva Conventions, is inadequate to regulate detention in NIACs. First, as we discuss further below, the end of a NIAC is not as easy to determine as the end of an IAC, and this is all the more problematic when the OAG is considered a terrorist group. Therefore, suspected fighters/OAG members could be subjected to potentially indefinite detention (to make matters worse, a full Third Geneva Convention analogy would establish a presumption in favor of being a fighter rather than civilian). Second, there are other categories of individuals regarding whom the functioning of such a regime remains a mystery. Applying Third Geneva Convention standards to civilians is the same as trying to square the circle (in truth, authorship favoring this solution foresees it only for fighters). However, the categories of population concerned are not exhausted in the fighter–civilian dichotomy, and it is quite uncertain under which regime the detention of, for example, OAG medical and religious personnel should be

---

131. Jenks, *supra* note 27, at 112–13.

reviewed. Lastly, the concept of status is foreign to the IHL of NIACs, so it is doubtful that any status-based mechanism would work. In our view, only a threat-based assessment ought to be considered for contemporary NIACs and the War on Terror.[132]

2. Threat-Based Detention: The Fourth Geneva Convention Analogy

Although U.S. judicial practice largely relies on the AUMF and employs Third Geneva Convention terminology, the Courts' consistency has not been absolute and there exists practice favoring a threat-based approach as well. In *Basardh v. Obama*, the Columbia District Court found that "the AUMF does not authorize the detention of individuals beyond that which is necessary to prevent those individuals from rejoining the battle, and it certainly cannot be read to authorize detention where its purpose can no longer be attained." The Court granted a Guantánamo detainee's writ of habeas corpus on the basis that "the government has failed to meet its burden of establishing that Basardh's continued detention is authorized ... [A]ny ties with the enemy have been severed, and any realistic risk that he could rejoin the enemy has been foreclosed."[133] This approach was later explicitly rejected by the Court of Appeals in another case,[134] but remains illustrative of an alternative IAC-based approach: namely, one that mirrors the Fourth Geneva Convention in its major aspects.

Such a framework is suggested for counterterrorist NIACs by Bellinger and Padmanabhan, who argue that "the most promising approach" is to "terminate detention authority over individual fighters when they no longer pose a threat to the security of the state."[135] The authors explicitly refer to the Fourth Geneva Convention and credit Bradley and Goldsmith for the "intellectual architecture" of the approach. In our view, Bellinger and Padmanabhan's approach shares only the "end of active hostilities" aspect with the Bradley–Goldsmith theory, which is otherwise status-based and which we will discuss momentarily. Bellinger and Padmanabhan also argue for a Fourth Geneva Convention review regime that would take place twice a year, with the initial review subjected to a fairly low

---

132. For a critique of the status-based approach to NIACs and an overview of the position of the ICRC and some States, see Bettina Scholdan, "*The End of Active Hostilities*": *The Obligation to Release Conflict Internees Under International Law*, 38 Houston Journal of International Law 99, 130ff. (2016).

133. Basardh v. Obama, 612 F. Supp. 2d 30, 35 (2009).

134. "Petitioner relies heavily on *Basardh v. Obama* ... where the District Court ordered the release of Basardh, a Yemeni national, when the prospects that he would take up arms '[was], at best, a remote possibility.' ... *Basardh* was decided over a year before *Awad*. Second, and more significantly, with all due respect to the fine District Court Judge who wrote that Opinion, our controlling authority is the Court of Appeals decision in *Awad*, rather than a District Court decision." Al-Adahi v. Obama, 187 F. Supp. 3d 74, 76 (2014).

135. Bellinger & Padmanabhan, *supra* note 1, at 231.

"some-evidence" standard. In subsequent reviews taking place "over a period of years," the standard of proof would evolve to "beyond a reasonable doubt."[136] In the view of these authors, the review itself need not be judicial, as periodic review before a court may put a State's judiciary under great strain and judges may not be well equipped to make decisions better left to military and intelligence experts.[137]

In our view, a threat-based assessment is certainly better than a status-based assessment for NIAC detainees. However, the regime suggested by Bellinger and Padmanabhan is still too restrictive of individual rights. Especially in the context of counterterrorism, criminal prosecution must remain the norm: security detention, if it is even possible under international law, ought to be a measure of last resort (this is, after all, the way it is envisaged by the Fourth Geneva Convention). Any review, whether initial or periodic, therefore must take place often and must scrutinize the concerned individual's position with a very high standard of proof (if that standard can be met, it remains at any rate unclear why States should be allowed to resort to security detention rather than criminal justice). We present our view in Part III.C.

3. "End of Active Hostilities" Approaches

A major issue that appears in any framework based on an IAC analogy is the notion of "end of active hostilities." We have already discussed this issue in relation to the Fourth Geneva Convention, but doctrine on Guantánamo understandably casts it in a different light than what would normally apply to POWs. After all, if IHL is applicable to counterterrorist operations, then it is usually the law of NIACs that applies. But a NIAC may not end in the same way as an IAC does, especially if one of the belligerents is a terrorist group. Several authors—including Bellinger and Padmanabhan,[138] Hathaway et al.,[139] and Pearlstein[140]—propose solutions, but the original analysis was undertaken by Bradley and Goldsmith.

The Bradley–Goldsmith theory was developed for a status-based framework but may also be applied in the context of the Fourth Geneva Convention. Basing their discussion on the AUMF, these authors argue that it is difficult to conceive an end to the War on Terror:

> The traditional concept of "enemy alien" is inapplicable in this conflict; instead of being affiliated with particular states that are at war with the United States, terrorist enemies are predominantly citizens and residents of friendly

---

136. *Id.*, at 232.

137. *Id.*

138. *Id.*, at 231.

139. Oona Hathaway, Samuel Adelsberg, Spencer Amdur, Philip Levitz, Freya Pitts & Sirine Shebayat, *The Power to Detain: Detention of Terrorism Suspects After 9/11*, 38 Yale Journal of International Law 123, 158–59 (2013).

140. Pearlstein, *supra* note 127.

states or even the United States. The battlefield lacks a precise geographic location and arguably includes the United States. It is unclear how to conceptualize the defeat of terrorist organizations, and thus unclear how to conceptualize the end of the conflict.[141]

Under the circumstances, Bradley and Goldsmith argue that the "traditional" IHL solution of detaining enemy combatants until the end of hostilities makes little sense when applied to members of terrorist organizations. They thus propose an alternative, namely that the end of hostilities analysis be *individualized*: "Under this approach, the question is not whether hostilities have ceased with al Qaeda and related terrorist organizations, but rather whether hostilities have, in essence, ceased with the individual because he no longer poses a substantial danger of rejoining hostilities."[142] Whether a "conflict" with an individual Al Qaeda member has ended could be determined, they argue, according to their past conduct, their level of authority in Al Qaeda, their statements and actions during confinement, their age and health, and their psychological profile.[143] Bradley and Goldsmith further recall that the Third Geneva Convention itself calls for the release and repatriation of wounded and sick POWs prior to the end of hostilities and that States have recourse to measures short of detention to contain the threat from suspected terrorists.[144]

In our view, the Bradley–Goldsmith theory is theoretically interesting, but of limited practical value. It is status-based but relies on standards otherwise used in threat-based assessment to effect the early release of internees. As an individualized approach to conflict (de-)classification seems rather unorthodox, we see no value in arguing for such a concept rather than the more traditional threat-based assessment mechanism.

Several other theories revolve around the "end of active hostilities" notion. For example, Hathaway et al. argue that hostilities in the War on Terror should be broken down according to the group involved:

> Another option is to define "hostilities" based on status of conflict between the United States and the particular armed group of which the individual was a part or substantially supported at the time he was detained. Hence, if the Afghan Taliban was no longer involved in armed conflict with the United States, then members of that group who have not been convicted of crimes would be released from detention.[145]

---

141. Bradley & Goldsmith, *supra* note 1, at 2049.

142. *Id.*, at 2125.

143. *Id.*

144. *Id.*, at 2126.

145. Hathaway et al., *supra* note 139, at 159.

(This is preferable to regarding hostilities as ongoing because the United States or other States may still be fighting other members of the "terrorist coalition.") Pearlstein suggests reconceptualizing the end of active hostilities by excluding low-intensity violence. She writes: "The 'active hostilities' term is better read as embodying a pragmatic standard, with a finger on the scale of release."[146] Article 118 of the Third Geneva Convention, Pearlstein argues, is intended to protect POWs, not authorize their detention after hostilities have ended. Therefore, POWs should be released and repatriated as soon as possible even before the armed conflict has ended; a situation of "zero violence" is not necessary to determine that active hostilities have ended. Like the Bradley–Goldsmith theory, these ideas give much food for thought, but they do not constitute a good alternative for detaining terrorists in NIAC situations.

4. IHRL-Based Approaches

An important strain of thought on NIAC internment in doctrine draws the focus away from IHL standards and focuses on IHRL. The authors[147] may interpret Common Article 3 and Additional Protocol II in light of IHRL or simply disregard IHL altogether—the result is essentially the same in both cases. There are good reasons for doing so: because the wording of Common Article 3 and Additional Protocol II is so limited, but also because NIACs usually take place within a State's own territory and often involve fighting against its own nationals, it is not evident why IAC rules should be preferred over IHRL standards that the State is already bound to apply anyway.

The IHRL regime on detention is quite broad and cannot be reproduced here in detail. We will instead recall the general outlines of the IHRL regime on administrative/security detention.

Security detention is possible under most IHRL treaties.[148] Only the European Convention on Human Rights, which contains an exhaustive list of grounds for deprivation of liberty (which does not involve internment), prohibits it outright.[149] European States in principle need to derogate from the Convention to be able to subject individuals to internment; so far, the European Court has only made an exception to this rule for IAC-related detention in the well-known *Hassan* case.[150] Even under the treaties that do not prohibit security detention altogether, the possibilities for its use are extremely narrow. The Human Rights Committee,

---

146. Pearlstein, *supra* note 127.

147. *See, e.g.*, Sassòli, *supra* note 1; Scholdan, *supra* note 132; Hill-Cawthorne, *supra* note 68.

148. *See* International Covenant on Civil and Political Rights art. 9, Dec. 16, 1966, 999 U.N.T.S. 171; American Convention on Human Rights art. 7, Nov. 22, 1969, 1144 U.N.T.S. 123; African Charter on Human and Peoples' Rights art. 6, June 27, 1981, 1520 U.N.T.S. 217.

149. *See* ECHR, *supra* note 119, art. 5.

150. See Hassan v. United Kingdom, 2014-VI Eur. Ct. H.R. 1, https://www.echr.coe.int/Documents/Reports_Recueil_2014-VI.pdf.

examining Article 9 of the International Covenant on Civil and Political Rights, has taken the view that security detention places individuals at a severe risk of arbitrary deprivation of liberty and adds:

> Such detention would normally amount to arbitrary detention as other effective measures addressing the threat, including the criminal justice system, would be available. If, under the most exceptional circumstances, a present, direct and imperative threat is invoked to justify the detention of persons considered to present such a threat, the burden of proof lies on States parties to show that the individual poses such a threat and that it cannot be addressed by alternative measures, and that burden increases with the length of the detention. States parties also need to show that detention does not last longer than absolutely necessary, that the overall length of possible detention is limited and that they fully respect the guarantees provided for by article 9 in all cases. Prompt and regular review by a court or other tribunal possessing the same attributes of independence and impartiality as the judiciary is a necessary guarantee for those conditions, as is access to independent legal advice, preferably selected by the detainee, and disclosure to the detainee of, at least, the essence of the evidence on which the decision is taken.[151]

Thus, in order for security detention to be lawful, it must have an accessible and foreseeable legal basis (preferably in domestic law); be based on grounds that are not arbitrary; be necessary and proportionate; and be subjected to *judicial* review in all cases (habeas corpus).

Several scholars have argued for a direct application of the relevant IHRL standards in situations of NIAC, particularly in relation to the War on Terror. Sassòli has argued against approaches based on an analogy with IACs and for a full application of IHRL as the *lex specialis* in such cases.[152] Scholdan argues that both Common Article 3 and Additional Protocol II draw on due process guarantees that were already present in domestic law and later incorporated into human rights law. Accordingly, IHRL governs detention in NIACs, although it may modify its scope to allow military necessity as grounds of deprivation of liberty for the armed conflict's duration (insofar as this is foreseen by the domestic law of a given State).[153]

Hill-Cawthorne offers a more elaborate framework. He finds that internment in NIACs must meet certain minimum standards to be compliant with the IHRL treaties; sometimes, derogation will be necessary, specifically from the European Convention on Human Rights, in order for this to be possible (derogation is

---

151. U.N. Human Rights Comm., *General Comment No. 35: Article 9 (Liberty and Security of Person)*, ¶ 15, U.N. Doc. CCPR/GC/35 (Dec. 16, 2014).

152. *See, e.g.*, Sassòli, *supra* note 1; *cf.* Els Debuf, Captured in War: Lawful Internment in Armed Conflict (2013).

153. Scholdan, *supra* note 132, at 149.

important not only for the grounds of deprivation of liberty, but also for habeas corpus if States need to deviate from the requirement of having judicial review).[154] Comparing the standard of necessity under the Fourth Geneva Convention with that under IHRL, he finds the former to be too broad as the "security prong" for detention leaves too much discretion to the detaining power.[155] Yet a human-rights-compliant regime in NIACs should certainly take into consideration the threats of the ongoing armed conflict.[156] As per standard IHRL requirements, a legal basis will need to be found: for States, this should be domestic law (Common Article 3 or Additional Protocol II are insufficient in this regard).[157] Otherwise, many IHRL safeguards, including giving the reasons for internment to the internee, are considered non-derogable and thus apply in NIACs as well.[158] As for review, Hill-Cawthorne finds that States can derogate to a certain extent from habeas corpus to allow for nonjudicial review, but the reviewing body must nevertheless meet the criterion of independence and have the power to order release as a court of law. In terms of its composition, there should be at least one member who is a "lawyer with expertise in humanitarian or human rights law or a judge," and the standard of proof should work against internment.[159] The work of the body, including the periodicity of the review, may otherwise follow the contours of the Fourth Geneva Convention, but with great caution so as to not strain what is permissible under IHRL.[160]

---

154. Hill-Cawthorne, *supra* note 68, at 228ff.

155. This is, according to the author, because the grounds for security detention under IHL are not sufficiently clear. See the analysis in *id.*, at 39ff.

156. *Id.*, at 235.

157. *Id.*, at 237. Under IHRL, the legal basis for detention needs to be accessible, clear, precise, and foreseeable, which is manifestly not the case with an "implicit" basis.

158. *Id.*, at 239.

159. *Id.*, at 239–40. Note, however, that this may not be regarded as acceptable by some human rights bodies, such as the Inter-American Court of Human Rights, which has taken a more uncompromising stance on access to judicial review of detention. See, for example, the Court's discussion in Goiburú et al. v. Paraguay, Inter-Amer. Ct. H.R. (ser. C) No. 153, Merits, Reparations and Costs (Sept. 22, 2006), where "access to justice"—seemingly including habeas corpus—is described as a peremptory norm of international law; see more in Hélène Tigroudja, *La Cour interaméricaine des droits de l'homme au service de « l'humanisation du droit international public. » Propos autour des récents arrêts et avis*, 52 ANNUAIRE FRANÇAIS DE DROIT INTERNATIONAL 617 (2006).

160. It should be borne in mind that this aspect of Hill-Cawthorne's proposal does not conform to the strict IHRL notion of habeas corpus as judicial review (reasonably) conducted at the detainee's demand.

C. The Pertinence of Doctrinal Solutions and the Theory—Practice Dichotomy

The various approaches to security detention in situations of armed conflict involving counterterrorism operations are a testament to the importance of this question from an international law perspective. There are, however, two reasons why all of the doctrine raised above ultimately does not provide a full picture of this complex matter. First, although internment is certainly an important piece of the puzzle, it is a subsidiary and not primary means of combating terrorism (in fact, the focus should be on criminal detention, not security detention). Second, the question of repatriation largely remains neglected.[161] We therefore provide our own view of that issue in Part V below. For now, we briefly turn to the matter of criminal prosecution of terrorists in the context of NIAC prosecutions.

The vast majority of suspected terrorists are detained in relation to criminal charges, not for security reasons. As recalled by Hathaway et al.:

> The least contested bases for detention authority in any context are post-conviction criminal detention and pre-verdict detention for those who pose a risk of flight. It is often assumed that such criminal detention is ill-suited to terrorists. However, with very little fanfare, federal district court dockets have been flush with terrorism cases over the past decade. Strikingly, efforts to measure the conviction rate in these cases place it between 86 and 91 percent. Far from being ineffective, then, trying suspected terrorists in criminal courts is remarkably effective.[162]

There are numerous examples of insurgent fighters prosecuted under domestic law, which may treat as "terrorism" the acts of both bona fide terrorist groups and more traditional rebel forces. After the fall of the "Islamic State" group, thousands of captured fighters were prosecuted in Iraq on charges of terrorism.[163] Earlier, Turkey had put hundreds of individuals on trial for alleged links with Kurdish

---

161. One reason for this could be the relative reluctance of many States to resort to internment during contemporary NIACs. For example, in Syria, internment is today largely conducted by non-State armed groups (for example, Kurdish forces) and, in extraterritorial NIACs, foreign detaining powers have typically preferred to transfer their detainees to local authorities.

162. Hathaway et al., *supra* note 139, at 163. We may add to this that there is a visible trend today, in the context of counterterrorism, to expand the list of terrorism-related offenses such as membership in a terrorist group, becoming a "foreign fighter," financing terrorism, and so on—all of these bring the issue more firmly within the scope of criminal justice than risk-based detention regimes.

163. *See, e.g.*, Yolande Knell, *Inside the Iraqi Courts Sentencing IS Suspects to Death*, BBC (Sept. 2, 2017), https://www.bbc.com/news/world-middle-east-41110412.

rebels.[164] In Afghanistan, when the United States transferred control of the Bagram detention facility to the Afghan government in 2009, U.S. officials were concerned that the internment of detainees it considered dangerous would be discontinued and they would be either released or placed in the criminal justice track, which was President Karzai's own preference.[165] The practice of local governments involved in NIACs thus demonstrates a strong preference for the criminal justice path, even in a very difficult context.

Theorists have long advocated criminal prosecution for "atrocity crimes" as a means of achieving positive peace in a post-conflict society and deterring future violations.[166] This is, of course, of great relevance in a counterterrorism context, but the value of prosecution is not merely normative or utilitarian. The fact that it is preferred (even for rebels not labeled as terrorists) demonstrates its practical feasibility, at least in internal NIACs. According to data presented by Dancy and Wiebelhaus-Brahm, the increasing number of NIACs in recent years has also entailed an increase in the number of armed-conflict-related prosecutions (whether for atrocity crimes or in what the authors call "security trials" for acts against the State).[167]

Of course, we are not advocating that insurgents be tried for domestic law violations; this is a matter of every State's domestic policy. IHL itself foresees the possibility of amnesties and, while it does not oblige States to provide them, it requires that the possibility at least be considered.[168] During the *travaux préparatoires* on Additional Protocol II, several States expressed concern that the wording of what is now Article 6(5) might hamper their sovereign right to give amnesties, while admitting that amnesties could be a useful tool for restoring peace in a post-conflict society.[169] Ultimately, the decision to grant amnesties to

---

164. News Wires, *Turkey Puts 205 on Trial Over Alleged Links to Kurdish Rebels*, FRANCE24 (July 2, 2012), https://www.france24.com/en/20120702-turkey-mass-trial-over-links-kurds-rebels-pkk.

165. Deb Riechmann, *U.S. Completes Formal Handover of Bagram Prison to Afghans*, HUFFINGTON POST (Sept. 10, 2012), https://web.archive.org/web/20120913225753/http://www.huffingtonpost.com/2012/09/10/us-hands-over-bagram-prison-afghanistan_n_1869671.html. The Afghan government reportedly provided assurances that the "most dangerous" detainees would not be released.

166. *See, e.g.*, M. Cherif Bassiouni, *Searching for Peace and Achieving Justice: The Need for Accountability*, 59 LAW AND CONTEMPORARY PROBLEMS 9 (1996); Hunjoon Kim & Kathryn Sikkink, *Explaining the Deterrence Effect of Human Rights Prosecutions for Transitional Countries*, 54 INTERNATIONAL STUDIES QUARTERLY 939 (2010).

167. Geoff Dancy & Eric Wiebelhaus-Brahm, *The Impact of Criminal Prosecutions During Intrastate Conflict*, 55 JOURNAL OF PEACE RESEARCH 47, 50ff. (2018).

168. Additional Protocol II, *supra* note 95, art. 6(5).

169. *See Official Records of the Diplomatic Conference on the Reaffirmation and Development of International Humanitarian Law Applicable in Armed Conflicts: Geneva (1974–1977): Volume VIII* 361ff. (1978).

rebels/insurgents remains a sovereign State matter. However, it should undoubtedly be taken into consideration when deciding the lawfulness of internment as well. If internment is subsidiary to criminal prosecution, and the latter possibility is rendered moot because of an amnesty, then clearly security detention will also be impossible in relation to the same acts.

The matter is, of course, different for suspected terrorists, whose acts—insofar as they are criminalized under international law—may not be subjected to amnesties. To the contrary, international law often *obliges* States to prosecute or extradite persons accused of terrorism (but not to subject them to security detention). Criminal justice thus not only becomes an alternative for lawful internment but is an obligation in itself.

D. Detention of Terrorists by Non-State Armed Groups

An important point regarding the NIAC detention regime that we have not reflected upon so far concerns detention by OAGs. In NIACs, individuals may also find themselves detained by a non-State belligerent party. This raises the question not only of what rules an OAG should apply in respect of detainees but even whether they can lawfully detain in the first place.[170] Insofar as IHL is concerned, the regime of Common Article 3 and Additional Protocol II does not distinguish between State and non-State belligerent parties, with the same rules applicable regardless of who is detaining individuals. Nevertheless, the necessity of "importing" IHRL rules to flesh out the NIAC detention framework poses the challenge of explaining whether and how OAGs may be held bound by IHRL standards.[171] The equation becomes even more complex if one were to introduce a counterterrorism perspective, which is normally discussed in relation to State obligations and not those of non-State actors.

OAGs undeniably engage in detention in practice and sometimes detain individuals belonging to designated terrorist groups. A prominent recent example may be found in the large-scale detention of ISIS members by Kurdish forces in Northern Syria. According to media reports, there were as many as eleven thousand ISIS fighters and thousands of their family members detained in Kurdish detention camps in late 2019.[172] The majority of these detainees were "locals," namely

---

170. See, in this regard, the discussion in Andrew Clapham, *Detention by Armed Groups Under International Law*, 93 INTERNATIONAL LAW STUDIES 1 (2017).

171. The question of human rights obligations of non-State actors has proven particularly controversial in recent years. See in this regard ANDREW CLAPHAM, HUMAN RIGHTS OBLIGATIONS OF NON-STATE ACTORS (2006); KATHARINE FORTIN, THE ACCOUNTABILITY OF ARMED GROUPS UNDER HUMAN RIGHTS LAW (2017).

172. *See, e.g.*, Charlie Savage, *The Kurds' Prisons and Detention Camps for ISIS Members, Explained*, NEW YORK TIMES (Oct. 19, 2019), https://www.nytimes.com/2019/10/13/us/politics/isis-prisoners-kurds.html.

nationals of Syria or Iraq, whereas "about 2,000 come from 50 other nations whose home governments have been reluctant to repatriate them."[173] According to reports, there were fears that Kurdish forces might release ISIS detainees en masse in "retaliation" for the failure of their Western allies to confront Turkey over its incursion in Northern Syria.[174] Thus, this single example demonstrates the need to elaborate the OAG detention regime in light of IHL, IHRL, *and* counterterrorism law in relation to all of its key elements: whether and how OAGs may resort to detention (specifically, whether detention should be status-based or threat-based and what role criminal sanctions play in this regard); how release and repatriation may be effected in this context; and what conditions and principles should govern the release, repatriation, and possible transfer of detainees.

Although this problem warrants a much more detailed analysis, we feel that it is at least possible to briefly reflect on each of these points in light of our broader discussion of detention and to try and illuminate a path toward a realistic detention framework for OAGs.

The first question to be resolved is whether detention by OAGs should be status-based or threat-based. If status-based detention were even conceivable in a NIAC, the analogy with the Third Geneva Convention regarding the obligation to release detainees without delay at the end of active hostilities poses a conceptual challenge: in principle, a NIAC lasts until the cumulated criteria of intensity and organization are no longer being met.[175] In practice—to avoid an on/off approach—many IHL experts tend to consider that the NIAC lasts until the armed group is either disbanded or defeated or until a "peaceful settlement is achieved." As the existence of an OAG is by definition linked to the existence of an armed conflict, allowing OAGs to detain fighters until the end of active hostilities could imply allowing them to detain for as long as they exist. The fact that some NIACs turn into Forever Wars also speaks against introducing status-based detention for OAGs for the same reasons that States should not resort to it.

Second, as regards threat-based detention, it comes across as a far more appropriate solution to detention by OAGs. Thus, OAGs would be allowed to detain individuals only for as long as they have reasonable grounds to consider them a security threat. The necessity of detention should be reviewed by a body that is as far as possible analogous to State bodies. As the very existence of an OAG violates domestic law in most national jurisdictions, States typically consider any detention they engage in as being unlawful as well. However, an adequate threat-based

---

173. *Id.* The "home governments" in question are those of European countries such as Belgium, Britain, France, and Germany, but also those belonging to the "Muslim world," such as Egypt, Tunisia, and Yemen.

174. *Id.*

175. See on this question JULIA GRIGNON, L'APPLICABILITÉ TEMPORELLE DU DROIT INTERNATIONAL HUMANITAIRE (2014); Milanović, *supra* note 103, at 163–88; Rogier Bartels, *Temporal Scope of Application of IHL: When Do Non-International Armed Conflicts End? Part 1*, OPINIO JURIS (Feb. 18, 2014), http://opiniojuris.org/2014/02/18/guest-post-bartels-temporal-scope-application-ihl-non-international-armed-conflicts-end-part-1/.

framework could allow for OAG internment to be seen as acceptable under the IHL of NIACs and non-arbitrary under IHRL, as argued by Clapham.[176]

Third, from a human rights perspective, security detention is an extreme measure that can only be justified in circumstances where less intrusive means to achieve the same result are not available.[177] This means that internment is only permissible if detention based on other grounds, particularly for reasons of criminal prosecution and punishment, is not possible. Applying the same standards to OAGs is a complex matter, as it raises the question of the validity and mere practical possibility of OAG trials and criminal sanctions.[178] It is currently unclear whether OAG trials and sanctions could even in principle conform to the requirements of the right to a fair trial or the principle of legality and whether the outcome of a trial, even if regarded as fair, should be subjected to the principle of *ne bis in idem*.[179] Some better-organized armed groups with control over territory do hold criminal trials—for example, in Syria or Sudan.[180] The trials and sanctions could be based on the legislation currently in force in the State in question (some armed groups use existing State infrastructure, which often includes local courts, in territories they control) or "legislation" passed by the OAG or international law (with regard to international crimes). In our view, applying the principle of necessity to OAG internment also requires OAGs to subject detention to the same requirements, with a few caveats: (a) it has to be taken into account, before resorting to security detention, whether an armed group is capable of conducting a criminal trial and meting out sanctions in a way analogous to States—if so, this should be *required* of the group before it is allowed to intern individuals; (b) OAGs entertaining good relations with one or more States may also consider transferring their detainees to those States for criminal punishment (assuming that the transfer would not endanger the individual and the State accepts to receive them, this may be a preferable to option (a)); if neither of these possibilities is available, then (c) the OAG could resort to threat-based detention.

Fourth, a specificity of counterterrorism is that there may be an obligation to detain suspected terrorists for the purposes of criminal punishment (we discuss this

---

176. Clapham, *supra* note 170, at 15–16.

177. *See, e.g.*, General Comment No. 35, *supra* note 151, ¶ 15: "Such detention would normally amount to arbitrary detention as other effective measures addressing the threat, including the criminal justice system, would be available."

178. *See* Ezequiel Heffes, *Administration of Justice by Armed Groups: Some Legal and Practical Concerns*, Humanitarian Law & Policy (Nov. 22, 2018), https://blogs.icrc.org/law-and-pol icy/2018/11/22/administration-of-justice-armed-groups-some-legal-practical-concerns/.

179. See Jan Willms, *Justice Through Armed Groups' Governance—An Oxymoron?* 13ff. (SFB-Governance Working Paper Series, No. 40, 2012).

180. Heffes, *supra* note 178. In relation to Syria, see also U.N. Human Rights Council, *Report of the Independent International Commission of Inquiry on the Syrian Arab Republic* ¶¶ 67–68, U.N. Doc. A/HRC/37/72 (Feb. 1, 2018), https://www.securitycouncilreport.org/atf/cf/%7B6 5BFCF9B-6D27-4E9C-8CD3-CF6E4FF96FF9%7D/a_hrc_37_72.pdf.

matter in Part IV). The counterterrorism regime currently in force is contained in sectoral treaties and in a number of Security Council resolutions. The latter are formally binding on all U.N. members, but we see no reason why non-State actors should not be held to the same requirements where possible.[181] Accordingly, OAGs may even be required to act in accordance with options (a) and (b) in the paragraph above to the extent that this is feasible under the prevailing circumstances. The fact that some States have expressed fears that Kurdish forces in Syria might release ISIS detainees lends credibility to this approach.

Fifth, the possibility for States—particularly foreign States—to take over detainees from OAGs in some situations also raises complex matters under domestic law, human rights law, humanitarian law, and the U.N. Charter itself (regarding noninterference in the domestic affairs of the territorial State). Excluding the last of these from our analysis, we must ask whether States are obliged to take over custody of such individuals if presented with the opportunity (whether for the purposes of these individuals' repatriation, to effect their release, or for further criminal punishment). If they are in a position to receive suspected terrorists, it is reasonable to assume that States are bound by counterterrorism law to ensure their prosecution and punishment or to further extradite them (we discuss this in the following part). It is more difficult to posit the existence of such an obligation in the context of the release and repatriation of detainees who are not, or are no longer, suspected of terrorism. Some States, such as France, have refused to accept the repatriation from Kurdish forces of their own nationals having fought for ISIS.[182] Such an obligation would have to be sought in IHRL or domestic legislation. Although this matter deserves more extensive research and reflection, it seems to us that such an obligation may exist under the right to enter one's own country[183] and, insofar as an obligation to repatriate may be read into NIAC law by analogy to IAC law, the obligation to ensure respect for the Geneva Conventions under their Common Article 1.[184]

---

181. On the question of whether NSAs are bound by U.N. Security Council resolutions, see further Kristen Boon, *The UN Security Council and Non-State Actors*, 113 PROCEEDINGS OF THE ASIL ANNUAL MEETING 209 (2019).

182. *See, e.g.*, Catherine Gouëset, *Daech: quel sort pour les djihadistes français détenus en Irak et en Syrie?*, L'Express, Nov. 11, 2017. For an overview of the positions of different European countries to this matter, see RIGHTS & SECURITY INTERNATIONAL, *supra* note 3.

183. As provided for in, for example, International Covenant on Civil and Political Rights, *supra* note 148, art. 12(4): "No one shall be arbitrarily deprived of the right to enter his own country."

184. There is ongoing debate concerning the applicability of Common Article 1 to NIACs: see, in particular, the discussion of this matter in Carlo Focarelli, *Common Article 1 of the 1949 Geneva Conventions: A Soap Bubble?*, 21 EUROPEAN JOURNAL OF INTERNATIONAL LAW 125, 159–60 (2010); Michael N. Schmitt & Sean Watts, *Common Article 1 and the Duty to "Ensure Respect,"* 96 INTERNATIONAL LAW STUDIES 674, 700–02 (2020). The authors of both articles conclude that NIACs are excluded from this provision. For opposing views, see Laurence Boisson de Chazournes & Luigi Condorelli, *Common Article 1 of the Geneva Conventions Revisited: Protecting Collective Interests*, 82 INTERNATIONAL REVIEW OF THE RED CROSS 67, 68ff.

Sixth, once detainees are to be released (having served a prison sentence and/or no longer being considered a security threat), then we must consider the question of their transfer and possibly repatriation. As discussed earlier, it makes sense to consider these matters even outside the context of an IAC: contemporary NIACs often involve "foreign fighters," and often their family members, who are not nationals of the State in which they are fighting and where they could be detained. In our view, foreign detainees should be repatriated upon release, provided that their own State accepts to take them back. The State is obliged to receive its own nationals, but if it nevertheless refuses, this is not something that the detaining OAG could change. If the detainees are local or if they are foreign detainees whose repatriation is impossible, the OAG should relocate them to their place of habitual residence or, if this is not possible, provide alternative accommodation. This would again flow from an analogy with the law of IACs.[185] In all cases where transfer and relocation happen, international standards must be respected. This includes notably the human rights principle of *non-refoulement* and standards of humane transfer that may be established by analogy with relevant provisions of the Third Geneva Convention.[186]

The OAG's obligations in this regard should be framed realistically. What is "feasible" would depend on many factors, such as whether the group exercises territorial control, including over the points of relocation; its relations with the territorial State and third States for the purposes of transfer and repatriation; its ability to provide alternative accommodation if repatriation/relocation upon release is impossible; and so on. At least better-organized groups exercising territorial control and maintaining relations with certain States—such as the Kurdish forces in Northern Syria or various armed groups in Colombia—should be able to implement them in full.

Sassòli has famously proposed that what obligations are incumbent on an OAG should be determined according to a "sliding scale": the more an OAG is capable of implementing standards by analogy with a State, the stricter the requirements by which it should be held bound.[187] This theory is pragmatic and convenient, although it admittedly leaves wide room for interpretation as to what would be an OAG's obligations in a specific case. That being said, it also provides a useful yardstick for determining obligations related to release and repatriation. Naturally,

---

(2000); Oona A. Hathaway, Emily Chertoff, Lara Domínguez, Zachary Manfredi & Peter Tzeng, *Ensuring Responsibility: Common Article 1 and State Responsibility for Non-State Actors*, 95 TEXAS LAW REVIEW 539 (2017). In our view, there is no convincing reason why the obligation to ensure respect should not extend to Common Article 3 a provision of the Geneva Conventions.

185. *See* Third Geneva Convention, *supra* note 8, art. 118; Fourth Geneva Convention, *supra* note 9, arts. 132, 133.

186. *See* Third Geneva Convention, *supra* note 8, arts. 12, 46–48.

187. Marco Sassòli, *Introducing a Sliding-Scale of Obligations to Address the Fundamental Inequality Between Armed Groups and States?*, 93 INTERNATIONAL REVIEW OF THE RED CROSS 426 (2011).

certain standards apply regardless of the group's capacity to implement them, notably in relation to humane treatment, detention conditions, and the existence of minimal procedural safeguards in relation to detention (that is, a review by an independent and impartial body).

IV. THE IMPACT OF COUNTERTERRORISM LEGISLATION ON CONFLICT-RELATED DETENTION

In addition to IHL and IHRL, a third element to be considered in relation to the armed-conflict-related detention of suspected terrorists is the international counterterrorism regulatory apparatus. The various acts perpetrated by groups and individuals labeled as terrorists are criminalized under international law. Therefore, authorities will be legally obliged to investigate and prosecute their suspected perpetrators. There may thus be an indirect obligation to detain terrorist suspects (in either a criminal justice or a security context). It remains to be seen how such an obligation interacts with IHL and IHRL provisions on the deprivation of liberty.

International law primarily deals with international terrorism as a criminal phenomenon traversing State borders; purely domestic matters remain within the sovereign jurisdiction of territorial States and may still be criminalized under domestic law.[188] There is an increasing tendency to perceive all types of terrorism as an international problem, and not just one limited to individual States—especially where the underlying acts coincide with other international crimes such as war crimes, crimes against humanity, torture, and so on. International counterterrorism treaties[189] define around fifty offenses (such as terrorist bombing, the taking of hostages, and the financing of terrorism) that States are required to incorporate into domestic criminal legislation.[190] The treaties foresee universal jurisdiction in relation to these crimes, although this has commonly been interpreted as an incidence of the principle *aut dedere aut judicare* (the difference is namely that universal jurisdiction *allows* States to prosecute a crime happening outside of their borders and with no connection to their own nationals, whereas the latter principle *requires* them to do so or extradite the suspect(s) to another State willing to launch criminal proceedings).[191] This is an accurate understanding

---

188. ANTONIO CASSESE, INTERNATIONAL CRIMINAL LAW 128–30 (2003).

189. For a list, *see* Daniel O'Donnell, *International Treaties Against Terrorism and the Use of Terrorism During Armed Conflict and by Armed Forces*, 88 INTERNATIONAL REVIEW OF THE RED CROSS 853 (2006).

190. *Id.*, at 855ff.

191. *See* Declan Costello, *International Terrorism and the Development of the Principle* Aut Dedere Aut Judicare, 9 IRISH JURIST 209 (1974); Antonio Cassese, *Terrorism as an International Crime, in* ENFORCING INTERNATIONAL LAW NORMS AGAINST TERRORISM 213, 224–25 (Andrea Bianchi ed., 2004); M. CHERIF BASSIOUNI, INTERNATIONAL CRIMINAL LAW 695ff. (2008).

of the obligation to "adopt such measures as may be necessary" to criminalize and punish terrorist offenses as contained in some of the treaties. Although not all relevant treaties explicitly embody an obligation to prosecute or extradite (some, for example, do not mention extradition),[192] practice today supports the full application of *aut dedere aut judicare* to crimes defined by the international counterterrorism regulatory framework. Thus, the Security Council issued several resolutions condemning Libya for failing to extradite its nationals involved in the 1988 Lockerbie bombing.[193]

Apart from the convention regime, the U.N. counterterrorism regime is complemented by significant legislative work by the Security Council. Unlike the treaties, which are of a general scope, the Security Council resolutions primarily enumerate specific State obligations toward designated terrorist groups and their supporters, such as the Taliban, Al Qaeda, and ISIS. The measures imposed are also not solely of a criminal nature. Thus, the Security Council ordered an air and financial embargo of the Taliban in resolution 1267 (1999);[194] the freezing of assets of suspected terrorists in resolution 1373 (2001);[195] the prosecution and punishment of foreign terrorist fighters in resolution 2178 (2014);[196] and so on. A common thread in the Council's resolutions is to recall the obligation of all States to prosecute and punish terrorists in line with international law and to cooperate in this regard. Therefore, there is no doubt that the *aut dedere aut judicare* principle has been imported into the counterterrorism framework if it was not already universally present in treaty law.

It is possible to understand the obligation to prevent acts of terrorism in a very broad manner—for example, as entailing an obligation to detain suspected terrorists for security reasons.[197] This could open the door for States either to abuse the resolutions or to genuinely misinterpret them as requiring that individuals be detained even if they cannot be prosecuted for terrorist crimes in various modalities. In its submission to the European Court of Human Rights in the *Al-Jedda* case, the British government argued that it was under an obligation to detain individuals in Iraq in light of resolution 1546 (2004)[198] in order to safeguard

---

192. See Costello, *supra* note 191, at 210ff.

193. See ALEX CONTE, HUMAN RIGHTS IN THE PREVENTION AND PUNISHMENT OF TERRORISM 51 (2010).

194. S.C. Res. 1267, U.N. Doc. S/RES/1267 (Oct. 15, 1999).

195. S.C. Res. 1373, U.N. Doc. S/RES/1373 (Sept. 28, 2001).

196. S.C. Res. 2178, U.N. Doc. S/RES/2178 (Sept. 24, 2014).

197. We recall in this regard that States are also obliged by IHRL to protect the right to life of persons within their jurisdiction from risks posed by private individuals and non-State entities. *See* U.N. Human Rights Comm., *General Comment No. 36: Article 6 (Right to Life)*, ¶¶ 7, 21, U.N. Doc. CCPR/C/GC/36 (Oct. 30, 2018).

198. S.C. Res. 1546, U.N. Doc. S/RES/1546 (June 8, 2004).

the population under its occupation.[199] The Court easily rejected this argument, stating that it did not consider that:

> the language used in this Resolution indicates unambiguously that the Security Council intended to place member States within the Multinational Force under an obligation to use measures of indefinite internment without charge and without judicial guarantees, in breach of their undertakings under international human rights instruments . . . Internment is not explicitly referred to in the Resolution.[200]

As far as we are aware, none of the Security Council resolutions calls explicitly for internment. Rather, they seem to support the criminal justice avenue for suspected terrorists, as does resolution 1373 when it urges States to "[e]nsure that any person who participates in the financing, planning, preparation or perpetration of terrorist acts or in supporting terrorist acts is brought to justice."[201]

In our view, both the conventional and secondary "legislation" making up the U.N. counterterrorism framework require States to prevent and punish terrorism, but this may only create an obligation to detain insofar as detention is related to criminal punishment: there is certainly no obligation to intern. Internment *may* be a way in which a State meets its obligations under counterterrorism law, in line with its other obligations under international law, but it is not itself an obligation. This means that the lawfulness of internment must always be decided according to the rules of IHL and IHRL applicable to a specific case of deprivation of liberty, and that the existence of an obligation in a Security Council resolution, unless explicit, cannot be invoked to override the rules presently in force.

Lastly, a few remarks should be made on the return/release regime and the U.N. counterterrorism framework, as the latter requires that individuals listed as terrorists by the Security Council be subjected to a travel ban. This could create a tension between the rules on repatriation and counterterrorism legislation—for example, if the listed individual is a POW entitled to repatriation in line with the Third Geneva Convention. The first thing to bear in mind, should this occur, is to minimize the possibility of a conflict of norms: not even the Security Council resolutions are so inflexible as to prohibit *all* foreign travel.[202] For example, resolution 2161 (2014) requires States to:

---

199. Al-Jedda v. United Kingdom, App. No. 27021/08, ¶ 87 (2011) (ECtHR).

200. *Id.*, ¶ 105.

201. S.C. Res. 1373, ¶ 2(e), U.N. Doc. S/RES/1373 (Sept. 28, 2001).

202. This remark is illustrative of the approach of human rights bodies, such as the European Court of Human Rights, which have tended to avoid the question of the relationship between U.N. Security Council resolutions and IHRL treaties by interpreting the former "harmoniously" with the latter, thereby avoiding a conflict of norms. See the Court's reasoning in Nada

[p]revent the entry into or transit through their territories of [listed] individuals, provided that nothing in this paragraph shall oblige any State to deny entry or require the departure from its territories of its own nationals and this paragraph shall not apply where entry or transit is necessary for the fulfilment of a judicial process or the [Al-Qaida Sanctions] Committee determines on a case-by-case basis only that entry or transit is justified . . .[203]

A conflict of norms may still sometimes arise: let us imagine that the State of "repatriation" is the power to which the POW belongs (from an IHL perspective),[204] but not their State of nationality. One could certainly have recourse to Article 103 of the U.N. Charter to resolve the conflict or norms in favor of the Security Council resolution, but great care should be taken that the application of this mechanism may not always be appropriate.[205]

V. PRACTICAL RECOMMENDATIONS FOR CONFLICT-RELATED DETENTION OF TERRORISTS

A. General Remarks

The various approaches presented earlier demonstrate the tensions inherent in the creation of an adequate internment regime for "counterterrorist" NIAC situations. On the one hand, States are required to take all possible steps to protect their population from terrorism, which is a very real and grave threat in today's world. On the other hand, attempts at fighting terrorism must not compromise the very foundations of the rule of law and democratic society that terrorists are seeking to

---

v. Switzerland, App. No. 10593/08 (2012) (ECtHR), https://hudoc.echr.coe.int/fre#{%22itemid%22:[%22001-113118%22]}.

203. S.C. Res. 2161, ¶ 1(b), U.N. Doc. S/RES/2161 (June 17, 2014).

204. According to the ICRC's Commentary to Article 118 of the Third Geneva Convention, "The term 'repatriation' generally refers to the returning of individuals to their places of origin, nationality or residence. Where prisoners of war are concerned, account must be taken of the duty of allegiance which binds members of the armed forces to the Power on which they depend. Repatriation in this context therefore means handing prisoners of war over to this Power. In most instances, this will be the prisoners' State of nationality. However, in cases where individuals fought on behalf of, or otherwise belonged to, the military of a State other than their State of nationality, origin or residence, this is the Power on which they depend." 2020 GC III COMMENTARY, *supra* note 26, ¶ 4446, https://ihl-databases.icrc.org/applic/ihl/ihl.nsf/Comment.xsp?action=openDocument&documentId=2E2384E30078EF5DC125858500426E02. For the definition of a POW, see Third Geneva Convention, *supra* note 8, art. 4.

205. For example, a strict application of this principle could be problematic if it led to violations of the individual's rights or if the obligation to repatriate were understood as a peremptory norm of international law.

destroy. It is, therefore, very difficult to strike a balance between these two poles and find a middle ground that is both purposeful and compliant with the law.

To achieve this goal, it is, in our view, necessary to consider *all* the legal provisions that come into play in such situations. Under international law, these include IHL, IHRL, and counterterrorism legislation. If the conflict involving terrorists is an IAC (which will only exceptionally be the case), then there are very few problems in applying the explicit rules of the Third and Fourth Geneva Conventions, in addition to IHRL, to internment. But, as no equivalent rules exist in NIACs, any detention must largely be modeled after IHRL. This is not a moral supposition: it is simply taking heed of the applicable norms of positive law. In fact, attempts at extending IAC rules to NIAC situations are themselves *lex ferenda*, as treaty NIAC law does not foresee this possibility; there is very little evidence that the customary IHL of NIACs mirrors that of IACs on detention; and analogy itself is not a source of positive international law. To the contrary, the IHRL rules on deprivation of liberty, which continue to apply in situations of armed conflict, are without doubt positive law norms pertinent to internees and thus interact with those IHL norms whose existence can be demonstrated. We would like to make a few remarks in this regard.

First, in situations where IAC law and counterterrorism rules overlap, suspected terrorists will be entitled to protection under either the Third or Fourth Geneva Convention. In the former case, they may be detained until the end of active hostilities, as foreseen by Article 118 of the Third Geneva Convention. In the latter, they may be subjected to the internment regime for civilians based on a threat assessment. In both cases, the detaining power will be obliged to prosecute them if it has reason to believe that they have engaged in international crimes, specifically terrorism. If the suspect is a civilian, then the possibility of pressing criminal charges must figure in the analysis of the necessity of internment. Only if it is objectively not possible to start criminal proceedings without delay, but the individual concerned is genuinely believed to pose a real and imminent threat, may that individual be interned, which may not at any rate happen after the cessation of hostilities. In either case, both POWs and civilians must be released and returned/repatriated as soon as their continued detention is unjustifiable under IHL.

Second, in NIACs, the detention regime will be dictated by IHRL rules accommodating for the circumstances of the ongoing armed conflict. IHL is not a sufficient legal basis for internment and a State will need to enact domestic legislation to state with precision the grounds and procedure for detention. IHL may allow that the grounds of *military necessity* be imported into IHRL as a legitimate aim for a limitation of the right to liberty. Such detention will not in principle be arbitrary from an IHRL standpoint, although States parties to certain human rights treaties, such as the European Convention on Human Rights, must derogate to the right to liberty in order to allow for the expanded grounds for detention.[206] Internment will nevertheless be subjected to a necessity analysis and thus

---

206. So far, the European Court has not interpreted Article 5 of the ECHR in light of the IHL of NIACs as it did regarding IAC law in the *Hassan* case, so it is currently impossible to see if derogations in NIACs would be necessary.

always subsidiary to criminal prosecution, especially if the detainee is suspected of having committed international crimes. States are also required to consider the possibility of extending broad amnesties at the end of a NIAC insofar as the pardoned acts are not international offenses, including terrorism.

Third, the end of detention, whether for criminal or security reasons, is effectuated not merely through release but also through return and repatriation. We understand by "return" the released individual's transport to their former place of permanent or habitual residence, if possible; this may or may not be abroad, especially in a NIAC situation. The obligation to return home detainees in a NIAC may, according to the ICRC, be of a customary nature (its violation is certainly treated as an offense in the legislation of some countries).[207] If the detainee is a foreign national, then certainly they are also entitled, as a matter of IHRL, to leave the country and return to their own.[208] It is admittedly difficult to pinpoint the full extent of the return/repatriation obligation in positive law. States certainly cannot hinder such detainees arbitrarily, and in our view should also take reasonable steps to facilitate them—particularly if the individual has not been detained following a criminal conviction.

B. A Proposed Framework for NIACs Involving Groups Designated as Terrorist

Based on our analysis, we suggest the following framework for detention and internment of suspected terrorists in situations of NIAC. When a suspected terrorist falls within the power of a State, the following steps would ensure a detention regime that is compliant with international law.

1. The detaining authorities must first examine the possibility of pressing criminal charges against the individual as per their obligations under international counterterrorism legislation.[209] Whether or not charges will be filed is not a policy matter: it depends exclusively on the available evidence and the objective circumstances related to the ongoing armed conflict. If charges are filed, a judge must nevertheless review the lawfulness and necessity of remand detention as in ordinary criminal cases. The basis for pre- and (possibly) post-conviction detention will lie in a State's criminal legislation as implementing international law, or

---

207. 1 CUSTOMARY INTERNATIONAL HUMANITARIAN LAW, *supra* note 95, at 451ff.

208. See, on this topic, Rosalyn Higgins, *The Right in International Law of an Individual to Enter, Stay in and Leave a Country*, 49 INTERNATIONAL AFFAIRS 341 (1973); Elspeth Guild & Vladislava Stoyanova, *The Human Rights to Leave Any Country*, *in* EUROPEAN YEARBOOK ON HUMAN RIGHTS 373 (Wolfgang Benedek, Philip Czech, Lisa Heschl, Karin Lukas & Manfred Nowak eds., 2018).

209. As discussed in Part III.C of this chapter.

directly in international law, depending on the domestic legal system. The body ordering detention will then normally be a civilian or military prosecutor and further review will be administered by a civilian or military tribunal.[210]

2. If prosecution is temporarily impossible, then internment may be an exceptional and provisional alternative: the detainee might still be a "suspect" for criminal purposes even though, in the absence of a judicial decision, they may not yet be an "accused." In any event, the detainee's release from internment or transfer into criminal proceedings should be a matter of days and weeks, not months.[211] States should consider derogating from their IHRL treaty obligations to allow for such internment and should in any case enact domestic legislation authorizing the internment and spelling out the requisite grounds and the procedural and judicial safeguards.

3. With respect to detention for the purposes of a criminal trial, the detaining authorities should also take into consideration whether the individual is accused of a domestic law crime which has been subjected to an amnesty. If an amnesty has been given, the individual cannot be held in internment solely in relation to the act that has been excluded from criminal prosecution by means of an amnesty.[212] It must, however, be borne in mind that amnesty cannot be given for international crimes, such as acts of terrorism as defined in the international counterterrorism treaties. Furthermore, States cannot prosecute—and therefore also cannot consider as a threat to their security—actions which are specifically permitted under IHL, such as offering assistance to the wounded and sick or providing humanitarian aid.[213]

4. The body ordering or at least reviewing internment should be a court if the circumstances permit and the judicial system in the given region is functioning. Alternatively, internment may be ordered/reviewed by a body possessing competencies, composition, and characteristics analogous to a court performing habeas corpus review. It must provide sufficient guarantees of independence and impartiality and have the power to order immediate release if internment is not warranted. Its staff should primarily consist of legal experts.[214] In extreme circumstances, a purely administrative body may be sufficient, but it must be independent

---

210. As discussed in Part III.B.4, but also Part II.A.2 in relation to civilian internees in IACs.

211. As discussed generally in Parts III.B.2 and III.B.4.

212. As discussed in Part III.C.

213. As discussed in Part II.B.

214. As discussed in Parts II.A.2 and III.B.4.

from the authority requesting detention and, again, the State should have previously derogated from its IHRL obligations.[215]

5. The review must consider both (domestic) lawfulness and the necessity to intern: the onus to demonstrate the necessity of internment, in light of the momentary impossibility of opening criminal proceedings, will be on the authority requesting detention, and it will always be of a prospective, not punitive, nature (because of a well-founded threat of something that the detainee might do in the foreseeable future, not solely because of something they are believed to have done earlier). The review must also consider whether less extreme measures were considered (such as a restriction of freedom of movement or surveillance) and why they would be inadequate in a given case. It should also take into consideration the individual circumstances of the detainee (their health, age, gender, whether they are pregnant or the mother of a small child, and so on). The standard of proof required for internment should be comparable to the one required for initiating criminal proceedings or, if internment is done to collect further information and evidence, for initiating an investigation, and should become progressively higher at subsequent reviews.

6. The internees must be promptly informed of the reasons for their internment and must be given access to counsel and, if necessary, an interpreter. If this is impossible, they must be informed of their rights at least by the reviewing body itself. They must also be acquainted, as far as possible, with the evidence supporting internment, or at least its essence if withholding some elements may be exceptionally justified to safeguard the public order or the rights of others.[216] Although peacetime regularity of review may be impossible, biannual review will likely be inadequate unless such low periodicity is justifiable under the circumstances: there should typically be no more than several weeks between each review.[217] The initial review should be scheduled ex officio as soon as the individual has been deprived of their liberty and should not depend on their own initiative.

7. Internees should not be held in penitentiary facilities. If this is not possible, they should at least be kept separate from convicts.

8. Once release has been ordered and if the internee has not been transferred to the criminal justice system, the detaining authorities should facilitate their return home or their repatriation if they are not nationals or residents of the territory in which they were interned.[218]

---

215. As discussed in Parts III.B.4 and V.A.
216. As discussed in Part III.B.2.
217. As discussed in Parts III.B.1 and III.B.4.
218. As discussed in Parts II.A and III.A.

9. Release, repatriation, and transfer of internees must take place under humane conditions respecting their physical and mental well-being and in accordance with the principle of *non-refoulement*.[219]

In our view, a framework respecting the principles enumerated above would be fully compliant with international law but would also address the legitimate needs of States to prevent and punish the perpetrators of terrorist acts. This should, of course, primarily be done though the criminal justice avenue. Internment will be still possible, but only as a measure of last resort if the criminal route is temporarily unavailable.

VI. CONCLUSION

Internment is a powerful tool in the counterterrorism arsenal, but it must be used both sparingly and purposefully. It is not a means for keeping undesirable individuals locked away for good: this is an outdated and unjustifiable practice that is thoroughly at odds with positive international law.

In situations where IHL and counterterrorism legislation overlap, only a framework that takes both into account, in addition to the rules of IHRL, may be deemed compliant with international law. States are obliged to prosecute, not intern, suspected terrorists. Thus, even under the arduous conditions of counterterrorism, the traditional framework of IHL and IHRL needs to be respected. Except for the IAC rules on POWs, both legal branches require that internment be treated as a measure of last resort. There is no reason why this should be any different if the detainee is a suspected terrorist but criminal prosecution is not possible, as the present chapter has attempted to demonstrate.

A major aspect of any internment regime is, of course, the question of the release and repatriation of internees. This matter has, in our view, been neglected in doctrine. There are rules of IHL and IHRL that are relevant to this matter either directly or indirectly, and in our view, it is not difficult to demonstrate that States are at least obliged not to hinder return and/or repatriation, even in situations of NIAC. This obligation will not be deterred by the international counterterrorism framework unless the individual is standing trial for or convicted of terrorist acts, which neither IHL nor IHRL prevents.

---

219. As discussed in Parts II.A.1 and II.A.2.

PART THREE

History and Perspectives

13

The Lieber Code and Prisoners of War: A Legacy of Practical Humanitarianism

DAVID WALLACE AND SHANE REEVES* ■

I. INTRODUCTION

The 1860s marked a watershed decade in the formation and development of the law of armed conflict (LOAC). During this roughly ten-year time frame, the seeds of the modern LOAC were planted with the innovative and vital contributions of three documents—two treaties and one regulatory code for military forces. In August of 1864, representatives of sixteen States met in Geneva to negotiate and reach an international accord on protecting wounded and sick soldiers on the battlefield and all of those caring for them.[1] A mere two pages and ten articles in

---

*. The views expressed here are the authors' personal views and do not necessarily reflect those of the Department of Defense, the United States Army, the United States Military Academy, or any other department or agency of the United States government. The analysis presented here stems from their academic research of publicly available sources, not from protected operational information. Brigadier General (ret.) Wallace is a Professor Emeritus, United States Military Academy; and the Class of 1971 Distinguished Military Professor of Law & Leadership, United States Naval Academy. Brigadier General Shane Reeves is the 15th Dean of the Academic Board at the United States Military Academy.

1. GARY D. SOLIS, THE LAW OF ARMED CONFLICT: INTERNATIONAL HUMANITARIAN LAW IN WAR 53 (2d ed. 2016). Of the sixteen States present at the convention, only twelve initially signed it. *Id.* A representative of the United States participated in the convention but did not sign. *Id.* The United States finally ratified the First Geneva Convention in 1882. *Id.*

David Wallace and Shane Reeves, *The Lieber Code and Prisoners of War: A Legacy of Practical Humanitarianism* In: *Prisoners of War in Contemporary Conflict*. Edited by: Michael N. Schmitt and Christopher J. Koschnitzky, Oxford University Press.
© Oxford University Press 2023. DOI: 10.1093/oso/9780197663288.003.0013

length,[2] the First Geneva Convention reflected the vision of Henri Dunant, the Swiss businessman, author of *A Memory of Solferino*, and co-recipient of the first Nobel Peace Prize for his humanitarian efforts.[3]

The second foundational LOAC treaty of the decade was the 1868 St. Petersburg Declaration Renouncing the Use, in Time of War, of Explosive Projectiles Under 400 Grammes Weight. This accord marked the first multilateral agreement prohibiting the use of certain weapons in war.[4] More specifically, the Declaration was the first international agreement "in which the use of a weapon developed through advances in technology was banned on humanitarian grounds."[5] However, the lasting impact of the Declaration was not the specific ban itself but rather the statement of principle upon which it was based.[6]

---

2. *See generally* Convention for the Amelioration of the Condition of the Wounded in Armies in the Field, Aug. 22, 1864, 22 Stat. 940. The main purpose of the treaty is to provide relief to the wounded without any distinction as to nationality; neutrality (inviolability) of medical personnel and medical establishments and units; and the designation of the distinctive sign of the red cross on a white ground.

3. JOHN FABIAN WITT, LINCOLN'S CODE: THE LAWS OF WAR IN AMERICAN HISTORY 338–40 (2013). *See also 100th Anniversary of the Nobel Peace Prize Awarded to Henry Dunant*, INTERNATIONAL COMMITTEE OF THE RED CROSS (Apr. 1, 2005), https://www.icrc.org/en/doc/resources/documents/misc/57jrdg.htm. In 1859, Dunant witnessed the carnage and human suffering in the aftermath of a battle that took place between French, Sardinian, and Austrian troops. *Id.* More than forty thousand were left dead or dying after that battle and, together with local inhabitants of the area, Dunant attempted care for and alleviate the suffering of the wounded and injured soldiers. *Id.* When Dunant returned to Geneva, he wrote and published a short, but moving and vivid account of what he observed in the book *A Memory of Solferino*. *Id.* Based upon his personal experience, he made two main proposals in the book. First, he called for States to formulate some international principles, sanctioned by a convention inviolate in character, giving legal protection to the wounded and sick in the field. Second, he proposed the creation of national societies to provide help to the wounded and sick. *Id. See also* ROBERT KOLB & RICHARD HYDE, AN INTRODUCTION TO THE INTERNATIONAL LAW OF ARMED CONFLICT 38 (2010)(discussing the motivation behind Dunant's humanitarian efforts).

4. Declaration Renouncing the Use, in Time of War, of Explosive Projectiles Under 400 Grammes Weight, Nov. 29/Dec. 11, 1868, 138 Consol. T.S. 297, 18 MARTENS NOUVEAU RECUEIL (ser. 1) 474, http://www.icrc.org/applic/ihl/ihl.nsf/Article.xsp?action=openDocument&documentId=568842C2B90F4A29C12563CD0051547C. The Declaration renounced, in case of war among themselves, the employment by their military or naval troops of any projectile of a weight below 400 grammes, which is either explosive or charged with fulminating or inflammable substances.

5. SOLIS, *supra* note 1, at 54.

6. Christopher Greenwood, *Historical Development and Legal Basis*, *in* THE HANDBOOK OF INTERNATIONAL HUMANITARIAN LAW 23 (Dieter Fleck ed., 2d ed. 2009). The preamble to the 1868 St. Petersburg Declaration states, in part, as follows:

> That the only legitimate object which States should endeavor to accomplish during war is to weaken the military forces of the enemy. That for this purpose it is sufficient to disable the greatest possible number of men; That this object would be exceeded by the employment of arms which uselessly aggravate the sufferings of disabled men, or render their

Notwithstanding the significant and lasting contributions of the First Geneva Convention and the 1868 St. Petersburg Declaration to the early corpus of the LOAC, the so-called Lieber Code of 1863 did considerably more to enhance, shape, and define the future trajectory of the law. On April 24, 1863, U.S. President Abraham Lincoln issued "General Orders No. 100: Instructions for the Government of the Armies of the United States in the Field." This 157-article effort is often referred to as the "Lieber Code" after its principal drafter, Francis Lieber, a German American professor of law and political science at Columbia College in New York City.

The Lieber Code succinctly and comprehensively clarified and summarized the customary laws of war that provided Union officers an introductory education in a wide range of law of war topics.[7] The real genius of General Orders No. 100 "lay in the gathering—in one accessible document—of the gist of the writings of publicists and the customs of armed forces of the day: customs and usages of war that Lieber had not only studied, but experienced."[8] Or as stated by another commentator:

> No nation, kingdom or empire had ever before placed such strictures on its warriors; no previous government had ever bound itself formally in voluntary policy to practice humane treatment towards its enemies; and few documents in western history were to have such an impact on the modern law of land warfare as Francis Lieber's Code.[9]

---

death inevitable; That the employment of such arms would, therefore, be contrary to the laws of humanity;...

Id.

7. D.H. Dilbeck, *"The Genesis of This Little Tablet with My Name": Francis Lieber and the Wartime Origins of General Orders No. 100*, 5 JOURNAL OF THE CIVIL WAR ERA 231, 232 (2015). In a letter to Charles Sumner within a month of the issuances of the Lieber Code, Lieber expressed his contemporaneous thoughts as follows:

> The genesis of this little tablet with my name is this: When the war broke out, our government hesitated to exchange POWs fearing that it would amount to an acknowledgement of the rebels. I wrote an article in the Times, to show that this was not the case. At the same time, I concluded the lecture on the law of war in the law school. Then came the abuse of flags of truce, the arrogant pretensions of the enemy to lay down absurd rules of the law of war, and then the "guerrilla" business and confusion of ideas. Gen Halleck called upon me, after my correspondence with him, to write a pamphlet on guerrillas, which I did. The fearful abuse of paroling, becoming a premium on cowardice, went on. The Harpers Ferry affair happened. At last I wrote to Halleck that he ought to issue a Code on the Law of Nations so far as it relates to the armies in the field. I was approached, and here is the thing.

Id. See also Francis Lieber to Charles Sumner, May 19, 1863, box 43, Papers of Francis Lieber, Huntington Library, San Marino, California.

8. SOLIS, *supra* note 1, at 45.

9. RICHARD SHELLY HARTIGAN, LIEBER'S CODE AND THE LAW OF WAR 25 (1983).

At that time, the sources of information on the customs and usages of war were found only in scattered textbooks and treatises, few of them readily accessible.[10] For this reason, Lieber's ambitious attempt to comprehensively distill the positive law for those engaged in warfare stood apart from the First Geneva Convention and the Declaration of St. Petersburg, which were narrow in scope with decidedly humanitarian aims. Further, the Lieber Code's broad legal framework—which regulated the means and methods of warfare while providing protections for the victims of war— laid the foundation for the entirety of the modern LOAC.

Of particular contemporary relevance is how the Lieber Code addresses prisoners of war (POWs). Though some of the thirty-eight articles in the Code on POWs are undoubtedly anachronistic, the provisions on categorization and treatment continue to inform the LOAC. Understanding why, after over 150 years, this remains the case requires a summary, found in Part II, of Francis Lieber and the genesis of his code. This overview will illustrate why Lieber wrote the code as a practical humanitarian guide to warfare and will help contextualize Part III's detailed analysis of the POW provisions. Finally, Part IV will discuss the ongoing legacy of the Lieber Code with regard to the status and treatment of POWs and the contemporary understanding of the LOAC.

II. FRANCIS LIEBER AND THE LIEBER CODE

Francis Lieber was born in Berlin, Germany, in 1798.[11] At the age of seventeen, Lieber and his three brothers enlisted in the legendary Colberg Regiment of the Prussian Army. Lieber fought against Napoleon's forces and was severely wounded in the neck and chest at the Battle of Namur near Waterloo.[12] Miraculously, he survived his wounds[13] and, after a lengthy recovery, returned to Berlin.[14] Discharged from the Army, Lieber studied at several universities, eventually receiving a doctorate in mathematics from the University at

---

10. E. Root, *Francis Lieber*, AMERICAN JOURNAL OF INTERNATIONAL LAW 453, 453 (1913). Lieber's earliest and most important inspiration for writing the code came in May 1861, when Major General Benjamin F. Butler declared fugitive slaves at Fortress Monroe, Virginia, contraband of war. *Id.* Butler's proclamation created great controversy and confusion. According to Lieber, General George B. McClellan made things worse and added to the confusion created by Butler when he stated that the Union army would assist in putting down servile insurrection and then step back and fight the masters again. *Id.* Lieber believed that because there was such a lack of knowledge of the laws of war, he was inspired to write and speak on the subject. *Id. See also* Dilbeck, *supra* note 7, at 233.

11. WITT, *supra* note 3, at 173.

12. Richard Salomon, The Unsuspected Francis Lieber 5 (May 2018) (M.A. thesis, The Graduate Center, City University of New York).

13. WITT, *supra* note 3, at 174–75.

14. SOLIS, *supra* note 1, at 43.

Jena.[15] Lieber's deep attraction to war led him to join an international brigade of Danes, Poles, Frenchmen, Italians, and Germans to fight for Greek independence against the Turks. Disappointedly, bandits robbed Lieber's group, and it was unable to fight the Turkish military.[16] Returning to Prussia, Lieber was jailed for his political views, eventually leading him to flee to England and, in 1827, immigrate to the United States.[17]

In the United States, Lieber began to make his reputation as an academic and a prolific writer. Initially, he took a position as the first permanent director of a new gymnasium in Boston. He became friends with several prominent and influential Americans, including many who opposed slavery.[18] To monetize his intellectual background, Lieber edited the first edition of the thirteen-volume *Encyclopedia Americana* (1829–33).[19] Searching for greater financial security for his family, he became a history and political economics professor at South Carolina College in 1835.[20]

In 1856, Lieber resigned from South Carolina College and moved to New York City, where he was appointed a professor of history and political science at Columbia College.[21] In the fall of 1861, Lieber unveiled his thinking on the laws and customs of war, including the treatment of POWs, in lectures at Columbia College's new law school. These lectures were carried in the *New York Times* and reprinted in newspapers across the United States.[22] General Henry W. Halleck, appointed General-in-Chief of the Union forces in 1862, learned of Lieber's lectures and asked for copies.[23] Due to Halleck's interest in his work, Lieber suggested to Halleck that he be allowed to write a pamphlet for the Union officers on guerrilla or

---

15. *Id.*

16. Jordan J. Paust, *Dr. Francis Lieber and the Lieber Code*, 95 PROCEEDINGS OF THE ASIL ANNUAL MEETING 112, 112 (2001).

17. Salomon, *supra* note 12, at 6.

18. Paust, *supra* note 16, at 112.

19. WITT, *supra* note 3, at 176.

20. SOLIS, *supra* note 1, at 43. During his time on the faculty at South Carolina College, Lieber continued to thrive as a scholar. Of note, in 1853, he published the two-volume *On Civil Liberty and Self-Government*. This publication is still considered the first systemic work on political science to appear in the United States.

21. WITT, *supra* note 3, at 179–80. The Lieber family was also deeply divided by the Civil War. Lieber's oldest son, Oscar, enlisted in the Confederate Army while his sons Hamilton and Norman would join the Union forces. *Id.*

22. *Id.* at 181.

23. SOLIS, *supra* note 1, at 44. Halleck, an 1839 graduate of the United States Military Academy, was, by the 1850s, a successful lawyer, businessman, and author of scientific books and pamphlets. *See* Milton H. Shutes, *Henry Wager Halleck: Lincoln's Chief-of-Staff*, 16 CALIFORNIA HISTORICAL SOCIETY QUARTERLY 195, 199 (1937).

irregular fighters.[24] Halleck agreed, and Lieber wrote *Guerrilla Parties Considered with Reference to the Law and Usages of War*. This led Lieber to propose to Halleck that he be assigned to write a compilation of the customary rules of warfare.[25] The War Department agreed and appointed a board of senior officers to work with Lieber on the project.[26]

On April 24, 1863, the War Department issued General Orders No. 100. Thus, the date of issue was almost the halfway point in the Civil War.[27] From the War Department's perspective, the Lieber Code was a response to the massive expansion of the Army during the Civil War. The pre-Civil War Army had been a small but professional frontier force of approximately thirteen thousand soldiers and officers; during the War, it expanded to a million men led by thousands of inexperienced volunteer officers ignorant of the laws and customs of war.[28] The Lieber Code provided the needed guidance.

Divided into ten sections, the Lieber Code covered a dazzling array of topics. An essential aspect of the Code is that it is far more than just a statement of broad LOAC principles. It is a detailed, proscriptive regulatory code outlining permitted and prohibited conduct in wartime. For example, the exchange of prisoners, truce, and armistice are subject to detailed regulation in the code.[29] While many of the Lieber Code provisions are orthodox law as developed by the eighteenth century, much of the document also reflected Lieber's personal views of the LOAC. Of note, "[t]he treatment of prisoners . . . elaborately reproduced the most civilized terms with respect to captured enemy soldiers. The previous summer, Lieber had worried that his son Norman might have been captured in the Seven Days' Battle."[30] The Lieber Code was particularly remarkable because there was nothing else like it at the time. Commenting on writing the Code, Lieber stated, "I had no guide, no groundwork, no textbook. . . . No country . . . has anything of the kind."[31]

Arguably, the most important aspect of the Lieber Code is its conceptualization and articulation of the principle of military necessity. Some publicists maintain

---

24. SOLIS, *supra* note 1, at 44. *See also* Francis LIEBER, GUERRILLA PARTIES CONSIDERED WITH REFERENCE TO THE LAWS AND USAGES OF WAR: WRITTEN AT THE REQUEST OF MAJOR-GEN. HENRY W. HALLECK (1862).

25. SOLIS, *supra* note 1, at 44.

26. *Id.* The board was made up of Francis Lieber, LL.D., and four volunteer officers: Generals Hitchcock, Cadwalader, Hartsuff, and Martindale. *See also* Root, *supra* note 10, at 454 (discussing the drafting of the Lieber Code).

27. *See* Adam Roberts, *Foundational Myths in the Laws of War: The 1863 Lieber Code, and the 1864 Geneva Convention*, 20 MELBOURNE JOURNAL OF INTERNATIONAL LAW 158, 164 (2019).

28. Burrus M. Carnahan, *Lincoln, Lieber and the Laws of War: The Origins and Limits of the Principle of Military Necessity*, 92 AMERICAN JOURNAL OF INTERNATIONAL LAW 213, 214 (1998).

29. Greenwood, *supra* note 6, at 21.

30. WITT, *supra* note 3, at 231.

31. *Id.* at 232.

that Lieber's views on military necessity are his most significant theoretical contribution to the modern law of war.[32] Article 15 of the Code states as follows:

> Military necessity admits of all direct destruction of life or limb of armed enemies, and of other persons whose destruction is incidentally unavoidable in the armed contests of the war; it allows of the capturing of every armed enemy, and every enemy of importance to the hostile government, or of peculiar danger to the captor; it allows of all destruction of property, and obstruction of the ways and channels of traffic, travel, or communication, and of all withholding of sustenance or means of life from the enemy; of the appropriation of whatever an enemy's country affords necessary for the subsistence and safety of the army, and of such deception as does not involve the breaking of good faith either positively pledged, regarding agreements entered into during the war, or supposed by the modern law of war to exist. Men who take up arms against one another in public war do not cease on this account to be moral beings, responsible to one another and to God.

His views on military necessity, a concept far from settled in the early 1860s, animated the Code and distinguished Lieber's views on warfare and humanitarianism from others like Henri Dunant, who focused exclusively on protecting the victims of war and those who served them. Lieber's expansive view on military necessity is encapsulated in one sentence, namely that "[m]ilitary necessity, as understood by modern civilized nations, consists in the necessity of those measures which are indispensable for securing the ends of war, and which are lawful according to the modern law and usages of war."[33]

For Lieber, though, military necessity was not without limitation. He notes:

32. Carnahan, *supra* note 28, at 213.

33. U.S. Department of War, Instructions for the Government of Armies of the United States in the Field, General Orders No. 100, art. 14, Apr. 24, 1863 [hereinafter Lieber Code]. Lieber's use of the term "indispensable" in Article 14 can be traced to President Lincoln's response to an emancipation proclamation issued by Union Major General David Hunter. In May 1862, Hunter, commanding general in Union enclaves along the Carolina and Georgia coasts, issued a general order declaring all slaves held in Georgia, Florida, and South Carolina to be free. Lincoln himself would issue a preliminary emancipation proclamation, but in May, Lincoln was not ready to declare emancipation a war aim. Therefore, Lincoln declared Hunter's order void, noting that the government had not authorized any military commander to declare slaves free. Lincoln stated as follows:

> I further make known that whether it be competent for me, as Commander-in-Chief of the Army and Navy, to declare the Slaves of any state or states, free, and whether at any time, in any case, it shall have become a necessity *indispensable* to the maintenance of the government, to exercise such supposed power, are questions which, under my responsibility, I reserve to myself, and which I cannot feel justified in leaving to the decision of commanders in the field.

Carnahan, *supra* note 28, at 216 (emphasis added).

> Military necessity does not admit of cruelty—that is, the infliction of suffering for the sake of suffering or for revenge, nor of maiming or wounding except in fight, nor of torture to extort confessions. It does not admit of the use of poison in any way, nor of the wanton devastation of a district. It admits of deception, but disclaims acts of perfidy; and, in general, military necessity does not include any act of hostility which makes the return to peace unnecessarily difficult.[34]

Although it is widely acknowledged and accepted today that military necessity is a legal precondition for destructive acts during armed conflict, that was not the case in the first half of the nineteenth century. At that time, the law of war permitted the capture or destruction of any property belonging to persons owing allegiance to an enemy regardless of military needs.[35]

Inextricably linked to military necessity in warfare is the handling and treatment of POWs. In the U.S. Civil War, the number of POWs taken on both sides was enormous. When the War began, neither side was well-positioned to handle POWs. As such, the common practice was to exchange prisoners after the battle. Over time, a formal exchange system developed and was accepted by both sides. However, that exchange system eventually broke down over procedural disagreements and slavery-related issues.[36]

Throughout the conflict, approximately the same number of Union and Confederate forces were held as POWs: Union (211,400) and Confederacy (220,000). Of those, 30,218 Union soldiers died while in captivity compared to 26,436 Confederates.[37] Widespread abuse of prisoners occurred at a number of notorious POW camps, the best known of which was the Confederate camp at Andersonville, Georgia. Formally called Camp Sumter,[38] it is more widely known as Andersonville.

When Camp Sumter opened in February 1864, its stockade was designed to hold about six thousand Union prisoners.[39] As the prison population grew to

---

34. Lieber Code, *supra* note 33, art. 16.

35. Carnahan, *supra* note 28, at 217.

36. SOLIS, *supra* note 1, at 63.

37. ROBERT C. DOYLE, "PRISONERS OF POLITICS: A VERY UNCIVIL WAR." THE ENEMY IN OUR HANDS: AMERICA'S TREATMENT OF POWS FROM THE REVOLUTION TO THE WAR ON TERROR 90 (2010).

38. Roger L. Rosentreter, *Surviving That "Dismal Hole" in Georgia*, MICHIGAN HISTORY MAGAZINE, May–June 2009. Andersonville Prison appeared to be an ideal site, as it was in a pine-forested area and divided by a small stream and a railroad serviced the nearby Andersonville. *Id.* The Confederacy held many Union soldiers in prisons around Richmond, Virginia, and Camp Sumter was opened to relieve pressure on other prisons. *Id.* Conditions quickly deteriorated as more and more northern soldiers arrived. *Id.*

39. *Id.* Some sources claim that Andersonville had the capacity to hold up to a maximum of ten thousand prisoners.

more than forty-five thousand,[40] conditions quickly deteriorated. Hunger and sickness were rampant, with diarrhea, dysentery, scurvy, and pneumonia taking their toll.[41] The number of prisoners to die is unknown, but the number given at the Andersonville National Cemetery is 12,914. After the war, Captain Heinrich Hartman Wirz, the camp's commandant, was tried by a Union military commission for his conduct at the camp. Convicted, Wirtz was sentenced to death and hanged on gallows erected in front of the U.S. Capitol. He was the only Civil War soldier on either side to be convicted of war crimes.[42] The Union and Confederate war veterans also reported their maltreatment at other camps. Therefore, it is understandable that the treatment of POWs featured prominently in the Lieber Code, a reflection of Lieber's views on warfare and humanitarianism.

III. POWS AND THE LIEBER CODE

Francis Lieber previewed his view on the status and treatment of Confederate prisoners four months before the Civil War began. Lieber wrote an open letter in the *New York Times* about the nature and treatment of Confederate prisoners.[43] He stated, in part, as follows:

> So soon as it became evident that war would be waged between the United States and the insurgents of the South, men who have experience in war asked, "What can we and ought we to do with the prisoners we may make?" It is a question of peculiar difficulty in our present civil war.[44]

The status and treatment of Confederate prisoners was anything but a foregone conclusion. In his first inaugural address, President Lincoln took the position that secessionists were not enemies but criminals.[45] Specifically, Lincoln stated, "acts of violence within any State or States against the authority of the United States are insurrectionary or revolutionary."[46] Without expressing sympathy for those

---

40. *Id.*

41. *Id.*

42. SOLIS, *supra* note 1, at 62–68.

43. Francis Lieber, *The Disposal of Prisoners: Would the Exchange of Prisoners Amount to Partial Acknowledgment of the Insurgents as Belligerents, According to International Law?*, NEW YORK TIMES, Aug. 19, 1861 at 5, *cited in* Paul Finkelman, *Francis Lieber and the Law of War*, NEW YORK TIMES (Mar. 2, 2013), https://opinionator.blogs.nytimes.com/2013/03/02/francis-lieber-and-the-law-of-war/, *archived at* https://perma.cc/7JSC-W7DV.

44. *Id.*

45. WITT, *supra* note 3, at 142.

46. President Abraham Lincoln, First Inaugural Address (Mar. 4, 1861), *available at* https://avalon.law.yale.edu/19th_century/lincoln1.asp.

who rebelled against the United States, Lieber took the position that laws of war should be applied to prisoners not as a formal or diplomatic recognition of the Confederacy but as a recognition of reality.[47] That position ultimately prevailed.

Of the 157 articles in the Lieber Code, approximately one-quarter address POW issues. Section III, "Deserters—Prisoners of War—Hostages—Booty on the battle-field," focused on POWs. Four important themes permeate these articles that have been foundational to subsequent LOAC treaties regulating the status and treatment of POWs, including the Third Geneva Convention.[48]

The first theme involves defining POWs, categorizing them, and bounding their conduct. Lieber defined and categorized POWs as a predicate to other matters related to their captivity. In Article 49 of the Code, he defines and describes a POW as a

> public enemy armed or attached to the hostile army for active aid, who has fallen into the hands of the captor, either fighting or wounded, on the field or in the hospital, by individual surrender or by capitulation.
>
> All soldiers, of whatever species of arms; all men who belong to the rising en masse of the hostile country; all those who are attached to the army for its efficiency and promote directly the object of the war, except such as are hereinafter provided for; all disabled men or officers on the field or elsewhere, if captured; all enemies who have thrown away their arms and ask for quarter, are prisoners of war, and as such exposed to the inconveniences as well as entitled to the privileges of a prisoner of war.[49]

Beyond the provision, Lieber specified categories of individuals designated as POWs. His contribution to the development of the LOAC was particularly significant in this regard, as it was the first instrument to contain a clear articulation of which persons were entitled to protection as POWs and which were not.[50] Of note, Lieber provided that POW status should be recognized for citizens who accompany an army for whatever purpose, such as sutlers,[51] editors, or reporters of

---

47. Roberts, *supra* note 27, at 170.

48. *See generally* Convention (III) Relative to the Treatment of Prisoners of War, Aug. 12, 1949, 6 U.S.T. 3316, 75 U.N.T.S. 135 [hereinafter Third Geneva Convention]. The Third Geneva Convention is the most comprehensive international agreement for the protection of POWs in international law. It replaced the Convention Relative to the Treatment of Prisoners of War, July 27, 1929, 47 Stat. 2021, 118 L.N.T.S. 343 [hereinafter 1929 POW Convention].

49. Lieber Code, *supra* note 33, art. 49.

50. INTERNATIONAL COMMITTEE OF THE RED CROSS, COMMENTARY ON THE THIRD GENEVA CONVENTION: CONVENTION (III) RELATIVE TO THE TREATMENT OF PRISONERS OF WAR art. 4 (2020), https://ihl-databases.icrc.org/applic/ihl/ihl.nsf/Comment.xsp?action=openDocument&documentId=1796813618ABDA06C12585850057AB95#_Toc42431467 [hereinafter 2020 GC III Commentary].

51. *Id.* Sutlers are civilian merchants who sell provisions to the armed forces.

journals, or contractors.[52] Additionally, Lieber included members of a duly authorized *levée en masse* as entitled to POW status.[53]

A *levée en masse* describes a situation in which inhabitants of non-occupied territory spontaneously take up arms, without forming units, to resist invading forces. These persons were, according to Lieber, lawful combatants and POWs upon capture, provided they carried arms openly and respected the laws and customs of war.[54] As noted in the 2020 Commentary to the Third Geneva Convention, a *levée en masse* is a unique category under the LOAC.[55] It is the only group of persons recognized as having full autonomy from the State, and which did not require a command structure or have to display a fixed distinctive sign, that was granted POW status.[56] Lieber also expressly prohibited treating members of a *levée en masse* as brigands or bandits.[57] Finally, Lieber cautioned that if the territory on which an uprising occurs is already occupied, those participating would be violating the laws of war and are not entitled to their protections, as they did not qualify as members of a *levée en masse*.[58]

The second major theme involves the treatment of POWs. The Lieber Code provided that "[a POW] is subject to no punishment for being a public enemy, nor is any revenge wreaked upon him by the intentional infliction of any suffering, or disgrace, by cruel imprisonment, want of food, by mutilation, death, or

---

52. *Id. See also* Lieber Code, *supra* note 33, art. 50. A category of civilians accompanying the armed forces entitled to POW status has existed in each of the early codifications of humanitarian law.

53. Lieber Code, *supra* note 33, art. 51.

54. *Id.*

55. 2020 GC III Commentary, *supra* note 50, art. 4. The concept of a *levée en masse* may seem obsolete in an era where invading forces use advanced weaponry. However, the approach of an invading army still occasionally prompts civilians to take up arms out of a sense of patriotism or self-preservation. *See, e.g.*, Emily Crawford, *Tracing the Historical and Legal Development of the Levée en Masse in the Law of Armed Conflict*, 19 JOURNAL OF THE HISTORY OF INTERNATIONAL LAW 329, 353 (2017) (discussing the International Criminal Tribunal for the former Yugoslavia's examination of whether a *levée en masse* took place in the vicinity of Srebenica in 1992).

56. 2020 GC III Commentary, *supra* note 50, art. 4.

57. Lieber Code, *supra* note 33, art. 51. Lieber's cautionary reference to not treating members of a *levée en masse* should be put in the larger context of guerrilla warfare that was being prosecuted by elements in the Confederacy. Lieber addressed that form of warfare in his essay to General Halleck entitled "Guerrilla Parties Considered with Reference to the Laws and Usages of Warfare." In that essay, he states the following on brigands: "[t]he Brigand is, in military language, the soldier who detaches himself from his troop and commits robbery, naturally accompanied in many cases with murder and other crimes of violence. His punishment, inflicted even by his own authorities, is death." *See* Francis Lieber, *Guerrilla Parties Considered with Reference to the Laws and Usages of Warfare* 10 (1862).

58. Lieber Code, *supra* note 33, art. 51.

any other barbarity."[59] Addressing this issue of combatant immunity or privilege, Lieber noted,

> [s]o soon as a man is armed by a sovereign government and takes the soldier's oath of fidelity, he is a belligerent; his killing, wounding, or other warlike acts are not individual crimes or offenses. No belligerent has a right to declare that enemies of a certain class, color, or condition, when properly organized as soldiers, will not be treated by him as public enemies.[60]

Lieber recognized, however, that belligerents remain answerable for their pre-capture crimes.[61]

Given the underlying reason for the Civil War and Lieber's ardent antislavery views,[62] it is unsurprising that the Lieber Code included a provision related to race and the treatment of prisoners. Article 58 confirms that the law of nations knows of no distinction of color.[63] But, of course, Lieber was not writing the Code in a vacuum. The treatment of Black soldiers by Confederates was horrendous.

Some Confederate leaders simply summarily executed Black soldiers. In some cases, entire units of Black soldiers were murdered on the pretext that they were attempting to escape. Arguably, the most notorious racially motivated mass killing occurred in April 1864 at Fort Pillow, Tennessee. Major General Bedford Forrest's

---

59. *Id.*, art. 56. Lieber addressed the treatment of POWs with some granularity. For example, the Code mandates that POWs shall be treated with humanity and fed upon plain and wholesome food wherever practicable. *See id.*, art. 76. Additionally, POWs are subject to confinement or imprisonment on account of safety; however, they are not to be subjected to other international suffering or indignity. *See id.*, art. 75. Moreover, every captured wounded enemy shall be medically treated. *See id.*, art. 79. Money and other valuables on the person of POWs is private property and taking it is dishonorable and prohibited. *See id.*, art. 72. Finally, Lieber makes clear that violence shall not be permitted against POWs in order to extort the desired information or to punish them for having given false information. *See id.*, art. 80.

60. *Id.*, art. 57.

61. *Id.*, art. 59.

62. As noted by author Richard Salomon, it is impossible to reconcile the many provisions of the Lieber Code that radically favored the dignity and humanity of Black people with the fact that Lieber himself was a slaveholder for two decades. On the one hand, the Lieber Code contained provisions such as Article 57, which explicitly provided that the color of a soldier could not be used as a basis to disqualify him as a lawful combatant. Similarly, Article 58 authorized the death penalty for anyone who enslaved and sold Union POWs. On the other hand, during Lieber's tenure in South Carolina, he had slaves as domestic servants. *See* Salomon, *supra* note 12, at 39–43.

63. *Id.*, art. 58. According to Professor Witt, Lieber's "crisp" terms with respect to race provided Union officials with a script for the remainder of the war. *See* WITT, *supra* note 3, at 259–60 (noting, for example, that General Halleck committed the Union to offering protection to all persons duly).

cavalry force of 2,500 assaulted the Union garrison, which was guarded by approximately 600 soldiers, of whom 262 were Black. Most of the Black soldiers had recently been slaves; some were even known to members of Forrest's cavalry. When the Confederate force overran the garrison, they allowed the white Union soldiers to surrender while the Black soldiers were murdered.[64]

The Lieber Code's third major theme concerning the treatment of POWs dealt with reprisals. Arguably, belligerent reprisals have constituted the most important means of coercion available to States in the conduct of hostilities.[65] During the 1860s, they were considered a lawful method of enforcing the laws and customs of war, with both sides making frequent use of reprisals.[66] The Lieber Code even permitted retaliation against POWs, with Article 59 providing, "[a]ll POWs are liable to the infliction of retaliatory measures."[67]

Reprisals against POWs are one notable aspect of the Lieber Code that did not survive the test of time. The 1929 Geneva Convention Relative to the Treatment of Prisoners of War was the first treaty to prohibit reprisals against them,[68] followed by a similar provision in the 1949 Third Geneva Convention.[69] This contemporary prohibition is a pragmatic recognition that, despite Lieber's position to the contrary, reprisals against POWs are not necessarily effective in forcing a lawbreaking State to abide by the LOAC.[70] Reprisals have proven prone to abuse, sometimes claiming to be a justification for LOAC violations.[71] The Lieber Code's position on reprisals is clearly out of step with the modern LOAC.

---

64. WITT, *supra* note 3, at 256–57. Major General Nathan Bedford Forrest was a ruthless slave trader and the first grand wizard in the Ku Klux Klan. See DeNeen L. Brown, *The Civil War Massacre That Left Nearly 200 Black Soldiers "Murdered"*, WASHINGTON POST (Oct. 28, 2018), https://www.washingtonpost.com/history/2018/10/28/civil-war-massacre-that-left-nearly-black-soldiers-murdered/.

65. COMMENTARY ON THE ADDITIONAL PROTOCOLS OF 8 JUNE 1977 TO THE GENEVA CONVENTIONS OF 12 AUGUST 1949, ¶ 3428 (Yves Sandoz, Christophe Swinarski & Bruno Zimmermann eds., 1987).

66. Patryk I. Labuda, *The Lieber Code, Retaliation and the Origins of International Criminal Law*, *in* 3 HISTORICAL ORIGINS OF INTERNATIONAL CRIMINAL LAW 299, 304, 306 (Morten Bergsmo et al. eds., 2015).

67. Lieber Code, *supra* note 33, art. 59.

68. *See* 1929 POW Convention, *supra* note 48, art. 2 (stating "[p]risoners of war are in the power of the hostile Government, but not of the individuals or formation which captured them. They shall at all times be humanely treated and protected, particularly against acts of violence, from insults and from public curiosity. Measures of reprisal against them are forbidden.").

69. *See* Third Geneva Convention, *supra* note 48, art. 13.

70. *See* 2020 GC III Commentary, *supra* 50, art. 13 ¶ 1642.

71. *See* Stefan Oeter, *Methods and Means of Combat*, *in* THE HANDBOOK OF INTERNATIONAL HUMANITARIAN LAW 232 (Dieter Fleck ed., 2d ed. 2008).

The final POW theme in the Lieber Code concerned parole and prisoner exchanges. These provisions were of great import during the Civil War, with the Confederacy adopting a policy of paroling thousands of U.S. troops on the battlefield. For example, at the battles of Harpers Ferry and Richmond, Confederate officials paroled thirteen thousand Union soldiers in just one month.[72] According to the Lieber Code, the term "parole" designates a pledge of individual good faith and honor to do or not do certain acts.[73] A paroled POW was permitted to return to his home or to live in greater freedom in the captor's country, subject to the conditions of the parole.[74] Under the Lieber Code, the sanction for violating parole was death.[75]

From Lieber's perspective, the release of prisoners by exchange was the general rule, while releasing by parole was the exception.[76] By mid-1862, an agreement between the Union and the Confederacy provided for a system of prisoner exchanges. However, the following year the system began to break down.[77] Unsurprisingly, one underlying problem was that the Confederacy refused to regard Black soldiers and their white officers as eligible for exchange. Instead, Jefferson Davis and the Confederate Congress treated them as fugitive slaves, insurrectionists, and criminals.[78]

The Lieber Code's expansive treatment of POWs was a pragmatic response to the realities of the Civil War's battlefield conditions. However, as demonstrated by the four themes discussed above, Section III of the Code also captured Lieber's humanitarian aim to protect and respect prisoners during that brutal war. While

---

72. WITT, *supra* note 3, at 230–32. Lieber had specific concerns about mass paroles on the battlefield, as he believed that only the captured soldier's government could approve. *Id.* This clearly created a problem, as no soldier could trade away his country's interest by making private agreements. Articles 121 and 128 of the Code addressed these issues. *See* Lieber Code, *supra* note 33, arts. 121, 128.

73. Lieber Code, *supra* note 33, art. 120.

74. *Id.*, art. 122.

75. *Id.*, art. 124. Describing the pledge, Article 130 of the Code provides, in part, as follows:

> This pledge refers only to the active service in the field, against the paroling belligerent or his allies actively engaged in the same war. These cases of breaking the parole are patent acts, and can be visited with the punishment of death; but the pledge does not refer to internal service, such as recruiting or drilling the recruits, fortifying places not besieged, quelling civil commotions, fighting against belligerents unconnected with the paroling belligerents, or to civil or diplomatic service for which the paroled officer may be employed.

Id.

76. *Id.*, art. 123.

77. WITT, *supra* note 3, at 254.

78. *Id.*

portions of the Code are no longer relevant, the practical humanitarianism approach taken by Lieber toward POWs—and throughout the entirety of the document—laid the foundation for the modern LOAC. Accordingly, the legacy of the Lieber Code is extraordinary.

IV. THE LEGACY OF THE LIEBER CODE

By all accounts, the Lieber Code should have been a footnote in history, as it was written to regulate one side of a civil war and was enforceable only as a general order. Yet, the impact of this short text on the laws of war, written almost 160 years ago,[79] cannot be overstated. The Lieber Code became the basis for similar codes issued by Great Britain, France, Prussia, Spain, Russia, Serbia, Argentina, and the Netherlands.[80] It later directly inspired international agreements on the law of war, including the Third Geneva Convention.[81] In fact, much of the Lieber Code reflects customary international law on the contemporary battlefield.[82]

The Code has had such a profound legacy, in part, due to Francis Lieber's practical humanitarian approach to warfare. As someone who was severely wounded in combat and the father of sons fighting on both sides of the Civil War, Lieber understood war and soldiering. Although he wrote the Code as a practical legal document intended for regulating warfare, his connection to its savagery explains why the Code goes beyond simply reciting the current law and reflects the hope of a humanitarian.

This hope appears in his provisions regarding enemy prisoners. Taking enemy prisoners has been a common practice for centuries. Lieber's thirty-eight-article regulatory scheme for POWs is built around the fundamental obligation that captured public enemies are to be treated humanely. Many of its provisions are as relevant today as they were in 1863.

---

79. Gary D. Solis, *Introduction, in* GENEVA CONVENTIONS 9 (2010)(noting that the Lieber Code was written as a set of rules for the Union Army).

80. *Id.* In terms of the United States, the Lieber Code remained America's war-fighting directive until 1914, *id.,* and continues to greatly influence modern law of war manuals. *See, e.g.,* U.S. DEPARTMENT OF ARMY, FIELD MANUAL 6-27/U.S. MARINE CORPS 11-10C, THE COMMANDER'S HANDBOOK ON THE LAW OF LAND WARFARE, at 1–7 (defining military necessity and referencing the Lieber Code Articles 15 and 16 for historical reference).

81. *See* Erik Ringmar, *Francis Lieber, Terrorism, and the American Way of War,* 3 PERSPECTIVES ON TERRORISM 52, 52 (2009).

82. *See* GEOFFREY S. CORN, VICTOR HANSEN, RICHARD B. JACKSON, CHRIS JENKS, ERIC TALBOT JENSEN & JAMES A. SCHOETTLER, JR., THE LAW OF ARMED CONFLICT: AN OPERATIONAL APPROACH 39 (2012).

The "echo of Lieber is clear and distinct,"[83] not only in how POWs are treated in contemporary warfare but also in how hostilities are conducted more broadly.[84] Of course, some provisions of the Code did not survive the test of time. But, for those that did, commanders, legal advisers, policymakers, and scholars will continue to look to them as they shape the LOAC into the twenty-first century.

---

83. Hartigan, *supra* note 9, at 23.

84. Yoram Dinstein, The Conduct of Hostilities Under the Law of International Armed Conflict 1 (2004)noting:

> Some people, no doubt animated by the noblest humanitarian impulses, would like to see zero-casualty warfare. However, this is an impossible dream. War is not a chess game. Almost by definition, it entails human losses, suffering and pain. As long as it is waged, humanitarian considerations cannot be the sole legal arbiters of the conduct of hostilities.

Id.

14

The Role of Judge Advocates in Prisoner of War and Detention Operations in the U.S. Army: A Short History

FRED L. BORCH III*

I. INTRODUCTION

During the Revolution, American soldiers captured enemy fighters on the battlefield and detained them and other individuals while at war with Great Britain. In all subsequent armed conflicts, the U.S. Army has continued to detain persons in the course of its military operations, and judge advocates have played an

*. Fred L. Borch III is the Regimental Historian and Archivist for the U.S. Army Judge Advocate General's Corps and the Professor of Legal History and Leadership at The Judge Advocate General's Legal Center and School. He served as an active-duty Army judge advocate from 1980 to 2005, when he retired as a colonel. Fred Borch has an A.B. in history from Davidson College, a J.D. from the University of North Carolina at Chapel Hill, an LLM in international and comparative law from the University of Brussels, Belgium; an LLM in military law from The Judge Advocate General's School; an M.A. in national security studies from the Naval War College; an M.A. in U.S. history from the University of Virginia; and an M.A. in military history from Norwich University. From 2012 to 2013, he was a Fulbright Scholar to the Netherlands and a Visiting Professor at the University of Leiden's Center for Terrorism and Counterterrorism and a Visiting Researcher at the Netherlands Institute of Military History. He is the author of a variety of books and articles, including MILITARY TRIALS OF WAR CRIMINALS IN THE NETHERLANDS EAST INDIES 1946–1949 (2017).

Fred L. Borch III, *The Role of Judge Advocates in Prisoner of War and Detention Operations in the U.S. Army: A Short History* In: *Prisoners of War in Contemporary Conflict*. Edited by: Michael N. Schmitt and Christopher J. Koschnitzky, Oxford University Press. © Oxford University Press 2023. DOI: 10.1093/oso/9780197663288.003.0014

important role in determining the status and treatment of these prisoners of war and other detainees.[1]

This chapter first looks at the role played by judge advocates in the history of prisoner of war (POW) operations in the Army, starting with the Civil War and concluding with the armed conflict in Iraq. It looks at the evolution of POW status and treatment—and the role played by lawyers in the Army in that evolution—through the lens of the Lieber Code of 1863, The Hague Convention of 1907, the Geneva Conventions of 1929 and 1949, and Additional Protocol I. After discussing Army lawyers in POW operations during the Civil War, the Second World War, Vietnam, and Iraq, the chapter then explores the role played by judge advocates in detention operations. It focuses chiefly on the emergence of detainee operations in the last decade of the twentieth century and the early years of the twenty-first century, when U.S. involvement in international armed conflicts—and corresponding POW operations—diminished substantially and was replaced by Army operations in non-international armed conflicts. Since persons captured or detained in non-international operations could not be POWs as a matter of law, the Army had to create procedures governing the status and treatment of detainees. Starting with Army deployments to Somalia and Haiti, Army lawyers were heavily involved in the detainee operations that were part and parcel of these deployments. Additionally, as operational law as a legal discipline emerged as the raison d'être for the Army's Judge Advocate General's Corps, uniformed lawyers have become more and more central to detention operations in recent history.

II. PRISONER OF WAR OPERATIONS

A. Civil War through the Second World War

As the United States Supreme Court recognized in 2004, the detention of individuals who fight against the United States "for the duration of the particular conflict in which they are captured" is simply "fundamental and accepted as incident to war."[2] But while the Army did take combat captives during the Revolution, the War of 1812, and the Mexican–American War, there was no legal regime

---

1. Today, those persons detained by the Army fall into three legal categories: belligerents, retained personnel, and civilian internees. Retained personnel are dentists, surgeons and other physicians, and chaplains; as noncombatants, they are not prisoners of war (POWs) but they receive the same treatment as POWs. Convention (II) for the Amelioration of the Condition of the Wounded, Sick, and Shipwrecked Members of Armed Forces at Sea art. 28, Aug. 12, 1949, 6 U.S.T. 3217, 75 U.N.T.S. 85. Additionally, there are two subcategories of belligerent detainees: privileged—who are POWs—and unprivileged. Unprivileged detainees take a direct part in hostilities but have no POW status if captured; they are civilians who take up arms without any authorization under international law. GARY D. SOLIS, THE LAW OF ARMED CONFLICT 222–27 (2d ed. 2016).

2. Hamdi v. Rumsfeld, 542 U.S. 507 (2004).

(other than customary law) governing their treatment as prisoners until the Civil War, when President Abraham Lincoln's promulgation of General Orders No. 100 ushered in fundamental change.[3] Francis Lieber, the principal author of this General Orders, was not a judge advocate, but he was a lawyer and law professor. The Army's top officer, Major General Henry W. Halleck,[4] employed Lieber to perform an important legal assignment: write a legal treatise that would guide the actions and conduct of Union commanders and soldiers in the field. Lieber, who taught international, civil, and common law at Columbia University in New York City, was ideally suited to take on this project.[5]

The import of Lieber's regulations on the usages of war, titled *Instructions for the Government of Armies of the United States in the Field* and officially adopted as General Orders No. 100 on April 24, 1863, cannot be stressed too much. Soon known as the "Lieber Code," it was the first modern codification of the law of armed conflict issued to a national army for its guidance and compliance.[6]

The Code consisted of ten sections dealing with such subjects as military necessity, flags of truce, hostages—and POWs. Article 49 defined a POW as "a public enemy armed or attached to the hostile army ... who has fallen into the hands of the captor." Any person falling into this category was "entitled to the privileges of a POW," which Article 56 explained meant that a POW could not be punished "for being a public enemy." He also could not have "any revenge wreaked upon him by the intentional infliction of any suffering, or disgrace, by cruel imprisonment, want of food, by mutilation, death, or any other barbarity."[7]

The Lieber Code influenced the future development of POW operations. It remained at the foundation of U.S. Army doctrine on the treatment of combat captives in the late nineteenth century and was central to judge advocate Colonel William Winthrop's *Military Law and Precedents*. First published in 1886 with the

---

3. There does not appear to have been any judge advocate involvement in the capture or detention of POWs in these early conflicts. There were only a few uniformed lawyers in the Army and they were mostly involved with courts-martial. *See generally* THE JUDGE ADVOCATE GENERAL'S CORPS, THE ARMY LAWYER: A HISTORY OF THE JUDGE ADVOCATE GENERAL'S CORPS, 1775–1975 1–47 (1975) [hereinafter THE ARMY LAWYER].

4. President Lincoln appointed Henry Halleck (1815–1872) as General-in-Chief of the Army in 1862. A U.S. Military Academy graduate, Halleck served as a lieutenant in the Mexican-American War. He resigned his Regular commission in 1854, settled in California, and became a successful lawyer. Halleck had a special interest in the law of war, as evidenced by his 1861 treatise, *International Law: Or Rules Regulating the Intercourse of States in Peace and War*. This explains Halleck's interest in having Francis Lieber write what would be adopted by the Union Army as General Orders No. 100.

5. Born in 1800 in Berlin, Germany, Francis Lieber came to the United States in 1826. His son, Guido Norman Lieber, served as an Infantry officer during the Civil War and was the Army's Judge Advocate General from 1895 to 1901. THE ARMY LAWYER, *supra* note 3, at 84–86.

6. *Id.* at 62.

7. U.S. Department of War, Instructions for the Government of Armies of the United States in the Field, General Orders No. 100, arts. 49, 56, Apr. 24, 1863.

title *Military Law*, this book was the authoritative legal treatise in the Army of the era and it provided specific guidance on the status and treatment of POWs. Under the heading "Rights and Obligations of Warfare in General," Winthrop noted that "prisoners of war are to be treated humanely" and that it was unlawful to "commit violence" against prisoners or those who surrender "in good faith."[8] Later, when discussing the issue of POWs with more specificity, Winthrop explained that individuals entitled to POW status included more than enemy combatants. As he put it, all "civil persons engaged in military duty," such as clerks, telegraphists, teamsters, laborers, and messengers in the employment of an enemy armed force, were entitled to be "treated similarly." Finally, Winthrop insisted that the law did not permit the holding of POWs as some type of punishment. Rather, captivity was "merely temporary detention which is devoid of all penal character."[9]

The Lieber Code and Winthrop's writings on the subject of POWs had an influence beyond the U.S. Army. The Germans followed the Lieber Code in the Franco-Prussian War and Lieber's work "had a profound influence" on the men drafting The Hague Convention of 1899 and The Hague Regulations of 1907.[10] In this regard, Brigadier General George B. Davis, who had seen combat in the Civil War before graduating from the U.S. Military Academy, and who served as the Judge Advocate General from 1901 to 1911, was a delegate plenipotentiary to The Hague Conference of 1907. Like the first Hague Conference of 1899, the chief goal of the 1907 Conference was to negotiate international agreements that would codify customary rules and laws of warfare on land and sea. Davis, who was well known as a legal scholar from his *Elements of International Law*, a textbook used at West Point and other colleges, almost certainly was involved in discussions about the status and treatment of POWs in international armed conflicts.[11]

As a result of the work of Davis and other delegates, the Annex to 1907 Hague Convention IV, Regulations Respecting the Laws and Customs of War on Land, speaks directly to the status and treatment of POWs. Article 1 defines the status of POWs— that is, they are captured fighters who qualify as "belligerents."[12] Article 4 then sets out the treatment that must be afforded all POWs. They "must be humanely treated" and "their personal belongings . . . remain their property." Additionally, while POWs may be "interned in a town, fortress, camp or other

---

8. WILLIAM WINTHROP, MILITARY LAW AND PRECEDENTS 778 (2d ed. 1920).

9. *Id.*

10. THE ARMY LAWYER, *supra* note 3, at 62.

11. For more on George Davis, *see* Fred L. Borch, *From Frontier Cavalryman to the World Stage: The Career of Army Judge Advocate General George B. Davis*, ARMY HISTORY, Winter 2010, at 6–19.

12. Belligerents are "commanded by a person responsible for his subordinates," wear "a fixed distinctive emblem recognizable at a distance," "carry arms openly," and "conduct their operations in accordance with the laws and customs of war." Annex to Convention No. IV Respecting the Laws and Customs of War on Land, Oct. 18, 1907, 36 Stat. 2227, T.S. No. 539, *reprinted in* DOCUMENTS ON THE LAWS OF WAR 73 (Adam Roberts & Richard Guelff eds., 3d ed. 2000).

place," they "can not be confined except as an indispensable measure of safety."[13] Articles 6 through 20 detail with great specificity the type of labor that POWs may be required to perform (including how much they must be paid) and explain that POWs must receive the same food, lodging, and clothing "as troops of the Government who captured them."[14]

Seven years after the signing of Hague 1907, the Army's Judge Advocate General's Department, recognizing that soldiers needed written instructions on their responsibilities under international law, published the *Rules of Land Warfare—1914*. While this manual was helpful, and ensured that soldiers throughout the Army had some guidance on the treatment of POWs (it followed the Lieber Code and Hague requirements), the experience of the Allies in the First World War "highlighted the need to strengthen protections accorded POWs." This is because there were "gaps, deficiencies and imprecision in the 1907 Hague regulations regarding prisoners."[15]

As a result, delegates from forty-seven nations, meeting in Geneva in 1929 at a conference convened by the Swiss Federal Council, adopted the first convention for the protection of POWs. Then Lieutenant Colonel Allen Gullion, an Army lawyer who would later serve as The Judge Advocate General (TJAG) from 1937 to 1941, was the senior War Department representative at this conference. According to an Army press release, Gullion was "chiefly responsible for the creation of" the Geneva Prisoners of War Convention signed on July 27, 1929.[16]

Gullion's role in defining the status and treatment of POWs is important not only because of his work as a key author of the 1929 Geneva Prisoners of War Convention but also because, during the Second World War, it was then Major General Gullion who was primarily responsible for all POW operations in the U.S. Army. While Gullion's oversight of POW operations was in his capacity as the Army's Provost Marshal General, the position to which he was appointed shortly before he relinquished his duties as TJAG in 1941, Gullion had spent the majority of his career as an Army lawyer. Consequently, it is fair to claim that Second World War POW operations were very much the product of judge advocate participation.

---

13. *Id.* at 74.

14. *Id.* at 73.

15. SOLIS, *supra* note 1, at 84.

16. Press Release, War Department, Bureau of Public Relations, Press Branch, Maj. Gen. Allen W. Gullion Retires, (Jan. 1, 1945) at 1. Gullion's son, Allen Wyant Gullion, Jr., graduated from the U.S. Military Academy in 1943. Commissioned in the Air Corps, he was a pilot assigned to the 416th Bombardment Group when he was shot down and taken prisoner. After being released from captivity in 1945, he remained on active duty and served in a variety of Air Force assignments until retiring as a lieutenant colonel in 1966. He died in Cadiz, Spain, in 1985. *Allen W. Gullion, Jr., in* REGISTER OF GRADUATES AND FORMER CADETS OF THE UNITED STATES MILITARY ACADEMY 352 (1992).

Gullion created and implemented America's first POW program. When one considers that nearly four hundred thousand German POWs and another fifty thousand Italian POWs arrived in the United States between 1942 and 1945 from battlefields in North Africa, Sicily, and Italy, and that Gullion was responsible for overseeing their custody and care in more than five hundred prison camps throughout the United States, this remains both a unique and remarkable achievement.[17]

Gullion recognized that the 1929 Geneva Prisoners of War Convention set the legal parameters for POW operations but, as the Convention had never been tested in war, there were many unanticipated problems. POWs needed to be sheltered and so Gullion implemented a "massive $50 million construction program" to build more than 150 POW camps. The camps needed guards, but there was a shortage of personnel to perform this mission. There were never enough German- and Italian-speaking guards who could communicate with prisoners who did not speak English. Finally, there was always the fear of sabotage, especially from German POWs who remained true believers in the tenets of National Socialism.[18]

Gullion not only had to wrestle with these issues, but also had to decide how best to use POW labor to work in American agriculture. The many American farm workers who had enlisted and were overseas fighting had resulted in a critical shortage of labor. Ultimately, in compliance with the Geneva articles governing POW labor, more than 115,000 enemy prisoners, earning between 80 cents and $1.50 a day, labored in fields throughout the United States. In Texas, they gathered pecans. In Mississippi, they picked cotton. In Maine, they harvested potatoes. In Illinois, they cut asparagus.[19]

In the aftermath of the Second World War, with its horrific casualties among both POWs and civilians, four new Geneva Conventions emerged. Today, no serious scholar disputes that these 1949 Conventions are the cornerstone of the law of armed conflict and that they have greatly strengthened battlefield law.[20] The four 1949 Conventions exist to protect the victims of armed conflict—the sick and wounded, POWs, and civilians. Of the four, the Third Geneva Convention is devoted to POWs.[21]

---

17. ARNOLD KRAMMER, NAZI PRISONERS OF WAR IN AMERICA vii (1979).

18. *Id.* at 27–28.

19. *Id.* at 87–89.

20. SOLIS, *supra* note 1, at 88.

21. Convention (III) Relative to the Treatment of Prisoners of War, Aug. 12, 1949, 6 U.S.T. 3316, 75 U.N.T.S. 135 [hereinafter Third Geneva Convention].

B. Korea and Vietnam

When the Korean War began in 1950, the 1949 Geneva Conventions were not yet in force as a matter of international law. The United States and the other United Nations forces in Korea, however, conducted their POW operations as if the Conventions had been fully ratified. In this regard, since the war on the peninsula was an international armed conflict, all the detailed rules on the status and treatment of POWs enunciated in the 1949 Geneva Convention Relative to the Treatment of Prisoner of War were followed in POW operations involving Chinese and North Korean combat captives. The military police were in charge of day-to-day POW activities, as they had been during the Second World War, with judge advocates providing guidance and interpreting the Third Geneva Convention at the strategic level.

The Vietnam War presented new challenges for Army lawyers when it came to POW operations. This is because when Army judge advocate Colonel George S. Prugh arrived in Saigon around Thanksgiving 1964, he discovered that South Vietnam viewed the war as an insurgency—a non-international armed conflict to which the 1949 Prisoners of War Convention was inapplicable, except arguably for Common Article 3.

There are some twenty articles that are "common" to all four Conventions, and Common Article 3 alone governs the status of persons captured and detained in conflicts that are not between states. At the time the 1949 Conventions were signed, the delegates assumed that all significant armed conflict would continue to be state-on-state, and the requirements laid down in Common Article 3 reflect this assumption. Warfare after the Second World War, however, has been less and less international in character—as was the situation on the ground when Colonel Prugh arrived in Vietnam.

By the end of 1964, there were more than twenty-four thousand Americans in uniform in Vietnam.[22] Some of these men were participating in combat operations as advisers to South Vietnamese Army units, and a small number of these advisers were being captured by the enemy. What was happening to these Americans? Although some survived, Colonel Prugh learned that it was more likely for the Viet Cong to kill them rather than take them prisoner. One captured American advisor, for example, had been beheaded. Another had had his hands tied behind his back before being shot in the head.[23]

---

22. In 1964, U.S. military personnel in Vietnam were still very much in an advisory role. The build-up of American military strength did not begin until the spring of 1965 and, by 1969, there were more than five hundred thousand U.S. military personnel in Vietnam—a far cry from the twenty-four thousand Americans present in Colonel Prugh's era.

23. GEORGE S. PRUGH, LAW AT WAR: VIETNAM 1964–1973 63 (1975) (Vietnam Studies). *See also* FRED L. BORCH, JUDGE ADVOCATES IN VIETNAM: ARMY LAWYERS IN SOUTHEAST ASIA 1959–1975 19 (2003).

Having obtained permission from his boss, General William C. Westmoreland, to question soldiers departing Vietnam at the end of their advisory tours, Prugh learned that both sides—Viet Cong and South Vietnamese—often killed enemy wounded and those captured. The fratricidal nature of the war explained these killings, at least in part. Some guerrillas were executed by the South Vietnamese, however, because the latter viewed them as "Communist rebel combat captives" deserving summary treatment as illegitimate insurgents acting against a legitimate government. In short, the South Vietnamese government was refusing to treat Viet Cong captives as POWs. Rather, as POW status afforded by the Third Geneva Convention applied only to armed conflict between nation-states, and as the fighting in Vietnam was regarded by the South Vietnamese as a civil insurrection, leaders in Saigon insisted that the Convention was inapplicable and that captured enemy personnel were not entitled to POW status. Consequently, those Viet Cong who did survive capture in the field were not sent to POW camps. Instead, they were imprisoned "in provisional and national jails along with political prisoners and common criminals."[24] In sum, the government viewed the enemy as criminals and treated them accordingly. The Viet Cong, however, were usually even harsher in their treatment of captives, executing South Vietnamese soldiers falling into their hands as a matter of routine. Initially, captured U.S. advisers were spared, but when the government of South Vietnam publicly executed some enemy agents, the Viet Cong killed captured American advisers in retribution.[25]

Colonel Prugh and his legal staff realized that American advisers captured in South Vietnam and U.S. pilots shot down and taken prisoner in North Vietnam would not survive captivity unless these men received POW status. Believing that the Viet Cong and North Vietnamese might reciprocate with better treatment of U.S. captives if South Vietnam were to reverse its position on the status of Viet Cong prisoners, Prugh and his staff worked to convince Colonel Nguyen Monh Bich, the Army of South Vietnam's Director of Military Justice, that it was in South Vietnam's best interests to construct prison camps for enemy captives and to ensure their humane treatment during imprisonment.[26]

The more enemy POWs there were in custody, the more likely that an exchange of South Vietnamese and American POWs could be worked out. Additionally, a unilateral decision by the Saigon government to acknowledge the applicability of the Third Geneva Convention "would also ameliorate domestic and international criticism of the war."[27]

In December 1964, Colonels Prugh and Bich visited Vietnamese confinement facilities throughout South Vietnam. By American standards, conditions were

---

24. Jeffrey J. Clarke, Advice and Support: The Final Years, 1965–1973, U.S. Army in Vietnam 119 (1987).

25. Prugh, *supra* note 23, at 63.

26. Borch, *supra* note 23, at 19–20.

27. Clarke, *supra* note 24, at 120.

very poor—overcrowding, insufficient food, and a shortage of qualified security personnel prevailed. In Da Nang, for example, Prugh saw that one jail, built by the French to house 250 individuals, in fact had some 750 people incarcerated in it. Not only were far too many people locked up in the facility, but combat captives were mingled with prostitutes, thieves, and other criminals, along with juveniles, popularly known as "slicky boys" because of their streetwise ways.[28]

In the end, persuading the South Vietnamese to reverse course was agonizingly slow. Yet, by mid-1966, the South Vietnamese had set up facilities suitable for the confinement of POWs, and the number of such prisoners held by South Vietnam went from near zero to nearly thirty-six thousand by the end of 1971. Prugh and the judge advocates who followed him deserve much of the credit for reversing South Vietnam's "no POW" policy and the resulting better treatment for enemy POWs. Moreover, as more U.S. troops were surviving capture and the humane treatment afforded Viet Cong and North Vietnamese Army prisoners exerted constant pressure on the enemy to reciprocate, Prugh's initiative was of real benefit.

C. Persian Gulf War

Following the withdrawal of all U.S. personnel from Vietnam in 1973, there was no significant American POW operation until the Persian Gulf War. After Iraqi tanks rolled into Kuwait in August 1990, and the United States and its allies decided to oppose Iraqi aggression with an invasion, Army planners began thinking about how they would handle the large number of Iraqi POWs that were almost certain to be captured.

In the fall of 1990, General Norman Schwarzkopf concluded that U.S. Central Command (CENTCOM) did not have the in-country assets to care for POWs. Consequently, he decided that all enemy personnel captured by U.S. and Allied forces would be transferred to Saudi control. Although an agreement to this effect was not required by law, U.S. Army policy did call for one prior to the transfer of POWs.[29] As a result, a U.S. negotiating team, with Army Colonel Raymond P. Ruppert, the CENTCOM staff judge advocate as a member, met with the Saudi government to reach an agreement on the terms that would govern the transfer, custody, and administration of such prisoners.

Colonel Ruppert advised that the United States must retain the right to inspect any Saudi-run camps containing transferred POWs. This was because transferring Iraqis to Saudi custody did not relieve the United States of its responsibility under the law of armed conflict. Rather, the United States had a continuing obligation

---

28. PRUGH, *supra* note 23, at 63.

29. Joint Universal Lessons Learned System (JULLS) Long Report 62159-45948, July 2, 1991, subj: International Agreements for EPW [Enemy Prisoners of War] Transfer, Historians files, OTJAG.

to ensure that Saudi Arabia's treatment of enemy POWs complied with the Third Geneva Convention. After the United States and Saudi Arabia reached an understanding on POW transfer issues, Colonel Ruppert personally briefed the Saudi Red Crescent, the Saudi Foreign Office, and additional members of the Saudi military establishment on their obligations under the Geneva Conventions. Later, following Ruppert's counsel, American inspectors did visit Saudi-operated POW camps.[30]

Army judge advocates at CENTCOM also authored legal documents dealing with the transfer of POWs between the allied contingents. On January 31, 1991, for example, the CENTCOM Provost Marshal and his British counterpart at British Forces Middle East signed an agreement drafted by Army lawyers. Under the terms of this two-page protocol, "An Arrangement for the Transfer of Enemy Prisoners of War and Civilian Internees from the Custody of the British Forces to the Custody of the American Forces," the Americans agreed to accept all individuals captured or interned by the British, while the British agreed that the United States would later transfer these POWs to Saudi control.[31]

With POW policy formulated at CENTCOM—with robust help from uniformed lawyers—the detail of the processing and treatment of enemy soldiers captured by American, British, and French forces was left to subordinate units. Ultimately, after the start of ground combat in Operation Desert Storm, 22d Support Command had overall responsibility for processing POWs. Actual day-to-day operations fell to the 800th Military Police (Enemy Prisoners of War) Brigade, a major subordinate element of the Support Command. This unit, with over seven thousand soldiers, was a composite Army National Guard and Army Reserve unit from the northeastern United States specializing in POW operations.[32]

Initially, a judge advocate major and captain comprised the legal staff of the brigade, but as thousands and thousands of Iraqi POWs were taken into custody, three additional judge advocates were assigned to the 800th. Their mission was to handle legal issues surrounding the transfer of POWs from American to Saudi control. They also were to identify Iraqis alleged to have committed war crimes. Finally, Army lawyers were heavily involved in Article 5 hearings, which exist to determine POW status in accordance with the Geneva Conventions.[33] Under Army regulations, these tribunals require that a judge advocate be present to act

---

30. Interview, author with Colonel Raymond P. Ruppert, Dec. 2, 1996, Regimental Archives, TJAGLCS.

31. Protocol, CENTCOM and British Forces Middle East, Jan. 31, 1991, sub: An Arrangement for the Transfer of Enemy Prisoners of War and Civilian Internees from the Custody of the British Forces to the Custody of the American Forces, Regimental Archives, TJAGLCS.

32. THE WHIRLWIND WAR 162 (Frank N. Schubert & Theresa L. Kraus eds., 1995).

33. The title derives from Article 5 of the Third Geneva Convention, *supra* note 21. That article stipulates that a "competent tribunal" should resolve any doubts about the status of persons who "commit a belligerent act" and who have "fallen into the hands of the enemy."

as recorder and presenter of evidence on the issue of POW status. Ultimately, the United States conducted 1,196 Article 5 hearings in the Persian Gulf War.[34]

Many unusual questions surfaced at the 800th, all of which came to judge advocates for opinions. Could commanders accept offers from enemy POWs and civilian detainees to spy for U.S. forces? Could they be utilized in psychological operations? Could captured soldiers be used as gravediggers for enemy dead? After coordinating with other judge advocates in the theater, the 22d Support Command attorneys advised that Articles 49 and 52 of the Third Geneva Convention permitted prisoner labor as long as the work was not unhealthy, dangerous, or humiliating. Consequently, using enemy prisoner volunteers as intelligence collectors, translators, and interpreters was lawful, and such service also entitled them to compensation. Furthermore, the use of POWs for burial details also was permitted. The expeditious burial of enemy dead helped preserve a healthy environment, was not contrary to the Islamic faith, and ensured that the burial was in accordance with Islamic religious beliefs.[35]

From January 18, 1991, when the first Iraqi soldier was captured, to May 2, 1991, when the last prisoner in U.S. custody was transferred to Saudi Arabian control, the Army processed 69,822 Iraqi POWs. Relative to the length of the military operation, this was the most extensive U.S. POW operation since the Second World War.[36] During the entire period, judge advocates at the Support Command periodically traveled to the four POW camps being run by the Saudis, providing oversight and advice on an ad hoc basis. Their work "prevented the camps from turning into legal and public relations nightmares."[37] Later, when the U.S. custody of Iraqi captives ended, ICRC officials reported that the treatment of these POWs by the American forces had complied more fully with the Geneva Conventions than the treatment afforded by any nation in any previous conflict in history. Army lawyers deserved much of the credit, particularly since, in advising on the policies and procedures for handling POWs, judge advocates ensured that there was no adverse effect on the planning and execution of military operations.[38]

D. Iraq

The most recent POW operations involved the early months of Operation Iraqi Freedom, when U.S. forces invaded Iraq on March 20, 2003. The international

---

34. Solis, *supra* note 1, at 245.

35. United States Army Legal Services Agency, Desert Storm Assessment Team's Report to The Judge Advocate General of the Army 21 (Apr. 22, 1992).

36. U.S. Department of Defense, Conduct of the Persian Gulf War: Final Report to Congress app. O at 617 (Apr. 1992).

37. Interview, author with Colonel William Hagan, Jan. 23, 1997, Historian's files, TJAGLCS.

38. Final Report to Congress, *supra* note 36, app. O at 620.

nature of the conflict meant that the Geneva Conventions applied in their entirety—and that Iraqi soldiers captured in combat were POWs.

By the time American and coalition troops entered Baghdad in early April, some eighty thousand Iraqis had been taken prisoner. Many had put up little to no resistance on the battlefield, as American aircraft had "rained millions of surrender leaflets" on the Iraqis, "prompting many to surrender at the first sight of coalition troops."[39]

From the outset, complying with the Third Geneva Convention was problematic. During the Persian Gulf War in 1991, Saudi Arabia had agreed to accept all Iraqi POWs, which meant that the Army was responsible only for transferring these combat captives to Saudi camps. The Americans never had to concern themselves with the day-to-day operation of POW camps. In 2003, however, no other nation offered to accept Iraqi POWs, which meant that the United States was completely responsible for the safety, security, housing, and feeding of thousands and thousands of enemy captives.

Lacking a secure location outside of Iraq to which POWs might have been moved, the United States necessarily had to intern them in Iraq. But the rise of an insurgency meant that no location on Iraqi soil was safe—and safeguarding POWs from hostilities is a core requirement of the Third Geneva Convention.[40] Facing this quandary, American commanders made a practical, but ultimately wrong, decision to house Iraqi POWs in existing Iraqi prisons. This was how some Iraqi POWs came to be detained in Abu Ghraib, a large prison facility near Baghdad. As one historian notes, the decision to use the prison "indicated the improvised nature of POW operations [in Operation Iraqi Freedom] and a clear lack of understanding: that Abu Ghraib was a hated symbol of Saddam Hussein's regime." Iraqis knew that Abu Ghraib had held thousands of political prisoners "who were subjected to unspeakable tortures," and deciding to house Iraqi POWs in Abu Ghraib—and other Iraqi prisons—would turn out to be a grave error in judgment and a public relations disaster for the United States.[41]

By the fall of 2003, there were some eight thousand Iraqis in Abu Ghraib, six hundred of whom were POWs. This commingling of POWs with civilian detainees was a violation of the Third Geneva Convention, but the crisis in POW operations did not emerge until April 2004, when CBS News broadcast a number of photographs showing American soldiers abusing Iraqis in Abu Ghraib. The photographs, which had been taken by American soldiers tasked with guarding the POWs and detainees, showed naked prisoners chained together; simulated homosexual acts; and a hooded man, connected to electrical wires, standing on

---

39. PAUL J. SPRINGER, AMERICA'S CAPTIVES 197 (2010).

40. Article 20 states that "all suitable precautions" shall be taken to ensure the safety of POWs being evacuated from the battlefield. Third Geneva Convention, *supra* note 21.

41. SPRINGER, *supra* note 39, at 198.

a box with his arms outstretched. The resulting investigation confirmed that "a small group of morally corrupt soldiers and civilians" had abused the Iraqis.[42]

In the days that followed the revelations at Abu Ghraib, judge advocates became heavily involved in Iraqi POW operations. The 800th Military Police Brigade—as during the Persian Gulf War—had been responsible for ensuring that Iraqi POWs were being treated in accordance with the Third Geneva Convention. But soldiers in that unit had been using harsh interrogation techniques in the questioning of detainees at Abu Ghraib, as evidenced by the photographs broadcast on CBS News. Army Colonel Marc Warren, who was the Staff Judge Advocate for Coalition Forces in Iraq and had been serving on the Security Internee Review and Appeal Board since August 2003,[43] now worked to ensure that the abuse of POWs and civilian detainees at Abu Ghraib ceased. Army lawyers at III Corps also conducted a series of high-profile prosecutions against soldiers who had abused detainees. Those convicted included Staff Sergeant Ivan Frederick (eight years' imprisonment), Specialist Charles Graner (ten years' imprisonment), and Private First Class Lynndie England (three years' confinement).[44]

The lesson for Army lawyers after Abu Ghraib was clear: judge advocates must be more integrated into POW operations to ensure that captured privileged belligerents are treated in accordance with the Third Geneva Convention and Additional Protocol I, at least to the extent that the latter is binding as customary international law.[45]

---

42. SPRINGER, *supra* note 39, at 200.

43. This Board, established in August 2003, determined whether detainees should be released from custody, either because they were no longer a security threat or because they lacked intelligence value.

44. For more on the crimes committed at Abu Ghraib, *see* MICHAEL CLEMENS & CHRISTOPHER GRAVELINE, THE SECRETS OF ABU GHRAIB REVEALED (2010). For details on the judge advocates who served as prosecutors and defense counsel in the courts-martial, *see* Jennifer L. Crawford, *Abu Ghraib Trials, 15 Years Later*, 4 ARMY LAWYER 48 (2019).

45. Protocol Additional to the Geneva Conventions of 12 August 1949, and Relating to the Protection of Victims of International Armed Conflicts, June 8, 1977, 1125 U.N.T.S. 3. Additional Protocol I alters the traditional rules on POW status by diminishing the distinction between privileged and unprivileged belligerents. For example, the Geneva requirement that a lawful or privileged combatant wear "a fixed distinctive emblem recognizable at a distance" was changed in Additional Protocol I to require only that a combatant wear such an emblem while "engaged in an attack or in military operation preparatory to an attack." SOLIS, *supra* note 1, at 135. The United States has never ratified Additional Protocol I. Over time, however, much of Additional Protocol I has come to be understood as part of customary law, and consequently binding on the United States. But, even if one does not accept that the POW provisions of Additional I are now part of the customary law of armed conflict, since most of our allies have ratified Additional Protocol I, military operations conducted by the U.S. Army in concert with those allies necessarily require U.S. military personnel to comply with Additional Protocol I. SOLIS, *supra* note 1, at 148.

III. DETENTION OPERATIONS

By the last decade of the twentieth century, with the end of the Cold War, the collapse of the Soviet Union, and the American and allied victory in Iraq, it appeared that *international* armed conflicts were at an end. But war had not ceased. Non-international armed conflicts were ascendant, and the American Army now discovered that those individuals—combatants and noncombatants—whom it detained in military operations did not have the status of POWs who enjoyed the robust protections of the Geneva Conventions. On the contrary, it seemed that *only* Common Article 3, and Additional Protocol I for parties to that instrument, provided guidance for the treatment of detainees. Consequently, starting with Somalia and Haiti in the 1990s, and continuing with the wars in both Iraq and Afghanistan, the Army constructed new legal regimes governing the status and treatment of detainees. Judge advocates have been key participants in detainee operations for two reasons. First, the emergence of operational law in the 1980s meant that Army lawyers now deployed with commanders and used their legal talents to help commanders fulfill the mission—and successful detainee operations were critical to mission success. Second, since detainee operations involved the creation and implementation of a process, and as lawyers are well suited to create and implement any process, it made sense for judge advocates to be heavily involved in detainee operations.

A. Somalia and Haiti

Given that the Persian Gulf War was a Common Article 2 conflict, and that the status and treatment of enemy captives was spelled out in the Geneva Conventions, judge advocates who deployed to Somalia in Operation Restore Hope or Haiti in Operation Uphold Democracy (or both) and found themselves in a non-international armed conflict had very limited experience when it came to the status and treatment of non-POW captives and detainees. The 1949 Conventions were not of much use, as Common Article 3 speaks to the status and treatment of detainees only in general terms. While the Third Geneva Convention provides exhaustive rules for the status and treatment of POWs in international conflict, Common Article 3 states only that combat captives and other detainees shall "be treated humanely, without any adverse distinction founded on race, colour, religion or faith, sex, birth or wealth."[46]

In Somalia, judge advocates were part of the multinational coalition known as the Unified Task Force (UNITAF, or Task Force). It deployed to Somalia in December 1992 under the terms of United Nations Security Council Resolution 794. For the humanitarian mission in Somalia to succeed, there had to be some degree of law and order. Yet Somalia had no police and no prisons, much less

---

46. Common Article 3 to the Geneva Conventions of 1949.

a judicial system. This meant that UNITAF would have to create and operate a law enforcement infrastructure. Effective policing would require the detention of Somalis who had committed serious criminal offenses or who had attacked Task Force personnel and whose continued freedom likely would endanger Task Force personnel forces or innocent third parties. The result was that as soon as these uniformed lawyers arrived in Somalia, they featured prominently in the formulation of a detainee policy.

Judge advocates decided that the legal basis for UNITAF's law enforcement operations—and the authority to create a detainee policy—flowed form the general principles of international law and Security Council Resolution 794. The absence of a government in Somalia made the Task Force a de facto sovereign, and the inherent powers of a sovereign included the power to arrest and detain wrongdoers in order to protect the population. Additionally, Resolution 794 directed that UNITAF use "all necessary means" to ensure the passage of relief supplies. This logically implied the power to arrest and detain those interfering with or otherwise jeopardizing the delivery of humanitarian goods. Still another legal basis was the military commander's inherent authority to take those actions necessary to protect the personnel under his command and those civilians present in areas under his control.[47]

Using these legal bases, and recognizing that all detainee procedures must adhere to certain due process standards, judge advocates advised that Somalis who committed serious offenses, such as murder and rape, could be detained. Additionally, those who attacked Task Force personnel or who posed a future threat to troops or innocent Somali citizens also could be detained. In formulating rules for detainee treatment, judge advocates insisted that all detentions in excess of twenty-four hours would require a probable cause determination that would be reviewed and approved by UNITAF's Chief of Staff. Detainees were to be housed in a facility under the control of the Task Force's Support Command, and an Army judge advocate assigned to that command was to monitor activities at the detention center in order to ensure compliance with minimum humanitarian standards as enunciated in Common Article 3, particularly the provision of adequate food and medical care for all detainees.[48]

Additionally, when newly formed Somali law enforcement forces were ready to accept the transfer of detainees in the UNITAF facility, judge advocates were to inspect the Somali facilities to ensure that adequate food was available. These same lawyers also insisted that the Somalis adhere to minimum standards of humane treatment. Some of these judge advocates later accompanied representatives of the ICRC during their inspections of these Somali prisons.[49]

---

47. Frederic L. Borch, Judge Advocates in Combat: Army Lawyers in Military Operations from Vietnam to Haiti 217–18 (2001).

48. *Id.*

49. After Action Report, SJA 10th Mountain Division, n.d. [1993], sub: US Army Legal Operations, Operation Restore Hope, 5 December 1992–5 May 1993, at 26.

In September 1994, U.S. troops landed in Haiti without firing a shot and captured no POWs. But it was clear within a few days that certain Haitians posed a threat to the Americans, as well as to their fellow citizens. As a result, Army judge advocates assigned to Combined Task Forces 180 and 190 advised that U.N. Security Council Resolution 940, combined with the inherent authority of Lieutenant General Henry H. Shelton and Major General David C. Meade to protect their forces, constituted sufficient authority to detain Haitian troublemakers.[50] Additionally, they advised that as existing Haitian jails and prisons were neither humane nor reliable locations to house these detainees, the Americans could lawfully detain them in a U.S.-operated facility.

Some American officers proposed detaining Haitians in the brig aboard the aircraft carrier *USS America*. But, following the advice of judge advocates, this idea was rejected, as it would have tied the naval vessel to Haitian waters and would have used space required to confine sailors facing courts-martial. Additionally, this arrangement would make visits by representatives of the ICRC difficult. Finally, while detainees would not be considered POWs, and were not legally entitled to such status, a policy decision had already been made that U.S. forces would treat Haitian detainees as having a status "equivalent" to POWs. The fact that the Third Geneva Convention required internment "only in premises located on land" provided yet another reason to avoid using the *America*'s brig.[51]

Instead, the Americans made a decision to locate a detention facility at the Light Industrial Complex in Port-au-Prince. Operations at the so-called Joint Detention Facility began on September 30, 1994. A military police company commander was placed in charge of the facility and his unit provided the manpower necessary to run its daily operations. A small military intelligence cell operated in the facility as well, and its several interrogation teams gathered intelligence from the detainees.[52]

As Task Force 190 was responsible for the detention facility, its judge advocates assumed the lead in ensuring that humane treatment and due process were afforded to all detainees. These uniformed lawyers, aware of the lessons learned by 10th Mountain troops detaining Somalis during Restore Hope, designed a procedure for detaining Haitians. As a matter of policy, these military attorneys determined that detainees should be afforded the same treatment accorded detained persons under the Third Geneva Convention. Such treatment included decent clothing; an examination by a medical doctor and a dentist; and adequate food in the form of a meal, ready to eat like that consumed by U.S. military personnel. As a practical matter, these standards of treatment resulted in some problems; poor living conditions in Port-au-Prince meant that some Haitians preferred detention

---

50. Shelton, the XVIII Airborne Corps Commander, headed Combined Task Force 180; Meade, the 10th Mountain Division Commander, headed Combined Task Force 190. For more on the operational features of Operation Uphold Democracy, *see* BORCH, *supra* note 47, at 229–33.

51. *Id.* at 243.

52. *Id.*

to freedom, and a number of Haitians admitted that they committed minor criminal acts hoping to be caught and detained.[53]

A list containing the name of each detainee was maintained and updated daily. A judge advocate conferred with each detainee on the list and, while not acting as a defense counsel, provided the detainee with an opportunity to offer any reason why he should be released from the facility. This information was relayed to the Task Force Staff Judge Advocate. At the same time, a second Army lawyer, who acted as legal adviser to the facility, obtained information from law enforcement and intelligence personnel as to why a particular Haitian should be detained. Thus, for example, the judge advocate who had conferred with the detainee might argue for his immediate release. The judge advocate advising the facility—who represented the command—would present the views of the police and intelligence personnel concerning a particular Haitian and often argued that continued detention was necessary. After hearing from both attorneys, the Staff Judge Advocate would brief the Commanding General with a recommended course of action. The Commanding General would then determine who merited release and who should continue to be detained. Between forty and fifty individuals were in the detention facility and, while the Commanding General and Staff Judge Advocate made no written record of their discussions, the commanding general made daily decisions regarding detainees.[54]

The Joint Detention Facility in Haiti was an unqualified success. Its operation protected the force and, because detaining those who would harm their fellow Haitians also enhanced law and order generally, it also aided the return of a civilian government. Additionally, the procedural safeguards implemented by Army judge advocates stood in sharp contrast to Haiti's legacy of arbitrary and sometimes brutal detention. This demonstrated to the Haitian people that the law could be a source of some good, rather than a tool of oppression. The ICRC stated publicly that the Joint Detention Facility adhered to the highest standards of humane treatment. Later, when some members of the media joined relatives of detainees in criticizing detention facility operations, Red Cross personnel spoke out in the facility's defense.[55]

B. Afghanistan

Department of Defense Directive 2311.01 requires American military commanders to "comply with the law of war during all conflicts, *however characterized*" (emphasis added).[56] This Directive, however, did not mean that captured Taliban and

---

53. *Id.*

54. *Id.* at 244.

55. *Id.*

56. Department of Defense Directive 2311.01, DoD Law of War Program, Jul. 2, 2020. Directive 2311.01 updates DoD Directive 5500.77, the original Directive creating the Law of War Program in November 1974. The language in 2311.01 is essentially the same as in the original 5500.77.

al Qaeda fighters were POWs. On the contrary, the George Bush administration initially insisted that the Geneva Conventions were completely inapplicable to the armed conflict in Afghanistan.[57] After the Supreme Court's 2006 decision in *Hamdan v. Rumsfeld*, however, the U.S. government accepted that Common Article 3 applied to these belligerents and to the War on Terrorism being fought outside the United States. Consequently, those enemy fighters captured on the battlefield in Afghanistan had to be afforded humane treatment.[58]

Long before the ruling in *Hamdan*, however, the United States had transferred al Qaeda and Taliban fighters to Guantánamo Bay, Cuba, for long-term detention. Guantánamo had been chosen, in the words of Bush administration lawyer John Yoo, because it was the "legal equivalent of outer space."[59] The first detainees arrived in January 2002, after the U.S. military offered bounties of between $5,000 and $25,000 for the names of persons with ties to al Qaeda and the Taliban. Since the average income in Afghanistan at the time was less than $300 a year, this unbelievable incentive resulted in hundreds of men being detained, some of whom were shipped to Guantánamo Bay. Ultimately, there were 779 detainees from forty-eight countries in Guantánamo. The U.S. government's intent—at least initially—was to prosecute most of these detainees for war crimes at military commissions. Almost twenty years later, however, there has been only a handful of military commission prosecutions and much less has been accomplished than was envisaged.

The status of detainees held at Guantánamo continues to be controversial, and the involvement of Army lawyers such as Lieutenant Colonel Diane E. Beaver has done nothing to instill confidence in detention operations on the island. Beaver was the Staff Judge Advocate and the senior legal adviser to the Joint Task Force Commander at Guantánamo Bay. In October 2002, she authored a legal opinion in which she concluded that proposed coercive interrogation techniques for detainees did "not violate applicable federal law." Significantly, Beaver's opinion advised that it was lawful to use waterboarding ("use of wet towel and dripping water to induce the misperception of suffocation"), as well as "scenarios designed to convince the detainee that death or severely painful consequences are imminent for him and/or his family."[60]

Beaver's legally incorrect and morally wrong advice indicates that Army lawyers do sometimes commit grievous errors in providing legal advice. Today, the

---

57. The rationale was that Afghanistan was a "failed state" and the Taliban militia consequently were not governing a state. As for al Qaeda, it was a non-state actor, and international agreements generally do not apply to non-state actors. JILL LAPORE, THESE TRUTHS: A HISTORY OF THE UNITED STATES 746 (2018).

58. Hamdan v. Rumsfeld, 548 U.S.557 (2006); Geoffrey S. Corn, *Hamdan, Fundamental Fairness, and the Significance of Additional Protocol II*, ARMY LAWYER, Aug. 2006, 1, 2.

59. LAPORE, *supra* note 57, at 746.

60. Memorandum from Lieutenant Colonel Diane E. Beaver for Commander, Joint Task Force 170, Guantánamo Bay, Cuba, subj: Legal Review of Aggressive Interrogation Techniques (Oct. 11, 2002).

Detainee Treatment Act of 2005 precludes an opinion like Beaver's, since it sets clear guidance for judge advocates on the treatment of detainees: "[n]o individual in the custody or under the physical control of the United States Government, regardless of nationality or physical location, shall be subject to cruel, inhuman, or degrading treatment or punishment."[61]

While the treatment of detainees at Guantánamo was problematic, it was equally troublesome in the early days of Operation Enduring Freedom.[62] In 2002, an Afghan taxi driver named Dilawar being held by the Army at Bagram Airfield died after five days in custody. His death, which resulted from repeated blows to his legs by those personnel guarding him, was ruled a homicide. A documentary about the homicide of this detainee, *Taxi to the Dark Side*, won the 2007 Academy Award for Best Documentary.[63] While the military police had the primary mission of care and custody of detainees at Bagram, judge advocates participated in the investigation into the mistreatment of Dilawar and another detainee who had also died in custody. As a result of this investigation, and courts-martial that followed, the Army made important changes to detainee operations at Bagram.

By 2009, with substantial Army judge advocate involvement, the treatment of detainees in Afghanistan had improved significantly with the establishment of Detainee Review Boards with robust due process protections. These Boards, which include a legal adviser, hold a hearing with each detainee to determine if "the facts support the detention of each detainee as an unprivileged enemy belligerent, the level of threat the detainee represents, and the detainee's potential for rehabilitation and reconciliation."[64]

C. Iraq

Military operations in Iraq initially were governed by Common Article 2. Consequently, Iraqi armed forces personnel detained in fighting in the early days of Operation Iraqi Freedom were POWs. After the establishment of an independent and sovereign Iraqi government in June 2004, however, the newly formed Multi-National Force–Iraq began helping Iraq rebuild its judicial, correctional, and law enforcement system. Iraqis detained in the anti-government

---

61. Detainee Treatment Act of 2005, Pub. L. No. 109-148, § 1003(a), 119 Stat. 2680, 2739 (2005) (codified at 42 U.S.C. § 2000dd) (2006).

62. Operation Enduring Freedom was the official name given to the invasion of Afghanistan. It began on October 7, 2001, when airstrikes hit al Qaeda and Taliban targets. Enduring Freedom ended on December 28, 2014, and was followed by Operation Freedom's Sentinel.

63. TAXI TO THE DARK SIDE (Alex Gibney, Eva Orner & Susannah Shipman 2007).

64. Jeff A. Bovarnick, *Detainee Review Boards in Afghanistan: From Strategic Liability to Legitimacy*, ARMY LAWYER, June 2010, at 24.

insurgency were entitled to humane treatment under Common Article 3, as the insurgency constituted a non-international armed conflict.

After the debacle at Abu Ghraib, the Army wanted to transfer all its detention responsibilities to the Iraqis. This was difficult, however, because the Iraqi Ministry of Justice was still in its infancy and consequently neither willing nor able to take over detention operations. By the end of 2006, the Army held some thirteen thousand detainees in Iraq, including four thousand at Abu Ghraib and seven thousand at Camp Bucca.[65]

Ultimately, some of the detainees were identified as criminals and convicted in the Central Criminal Court of Iraq. Judge advocates expended "an enormous amount of time and resources" working with this tribunal to improve its procedures. A so-called Combined Review and Release Board, with a judge advocate legal adviser, also regularly reviewed detainee status.

IV. CONCLUSION

The history of POW and detention operations in the Army generally has been a story of hastily planned and quickly implemented processes and procedures. As one scholar notes, the Army has never "clearly established" POW policies before the capture of enemy troops.[66] Even today, it lacks clear guidance on who qualifies as a POW and who does not. But expecting the Army—or the Defense Department—to make POW and detainee operations a "top priority" is not going to happen, if only because the focus of the U.S. armed forces always is on winning the battle. What happens post-conflict will always be subordinate to victory.

Judge advocate participation in POW and detention operations shows that, with the exception of POW operations during the Second World War, the status and treatment of combat captives and detainees has been an ad hoc process. But this is to be expected, since the Army itself has given a lower priority to the POW and detainee operations.

Yet, these observations aside, judge advocate participation in POW operations in Army history deserves much praise. In regard to detention operations, however, judge advocates arguably have been less successful, with Somalia and Haiti being the exceptions. The future will no doubt bring new challenges for Army lawyers in the status and treatment of persons captured and detained in military operations.

---

65. Cheryl Benard et al., *Detainee Operations in Iraq*, in THE BATTLE BEHIND THE WIRE 49 (2011), *available at* https://www.jstor.org/stable/10.7249/mg934osd.13.

66. SPRINGER, *supra* note 39, at 305.

15

The Updated ICRC Commentary on the Third Geneva Convention

A New Tool to Protect Prisoners of War in the Twenty-First Century

JEMMA ARMAN, JEAN-MARIE HENCKAERTS, HELEEN HIEMSTRA, AND KVITOSLAVA KROTIUK* ∎

In 2011, the International Committee of the Red Cross (ICRC) embarked on an ambitious project to update the Commentaries on the Geneva Conventions of 1949 and their Additional Protocols of 1977.[1] The updated Commentaries seek

---

*. Jemma Arman is a regional legal adviser of the ICRC based in Nairobi; Jean-Marie Henckaerts is head of the Commentaries Update Unit of the Legal Division of the ICRC; Heleen Hiemstra is legal adviser in the Commentaries Update Unit; and Kvitoslava Krotiuk is an adviser in the Office of the President of the ICRC. Jemma Arman and Kvitoslava Krotiuk were legal advisers in the Commentaries Update Unit before their current assignments. This article summarizes some of the key findings of the updated Commentary on the Third Geneva Convention. The authors wish to acknowledge the input of many experts involved in the drafting and review of the Commentary, including their colleagues Bruno Demeyere, Yvette Issar, Eve La Haye, and Heike Niebergall-Lackner. The article was originally published in 102 INTERNATIONAL REVIEW OF THE RED CROSS 389 (2020) and is reprinted here with permission. It has been edited to fit the style of this publication, with some additional minor changes.

1. THE GENEVA CONVENTIONS OF 12 AUGUST 1949: COMMENTARY, vols. I–IV (Jean S. Pictet ed., 1952–1960). The ICRC wrote the original commentaries and is now updating them pursuant to its role as guardian and promoter of international humanitarian law. This role, in particular the ICRC's role "to work for the understanding and dissemination of knowledge of international humanitarian law applicable in armed conflicts and to prepare any development thereof," is recognized in the Statutes of the International Red Cross and Red Crescent Movement art. 5(2)(c) and (g), adopted by the 25th International Conference of the Red Cross at Geneva in 1986, amended in 1995 and 2006. On the ICRC's role in the interpretation of international

to reflect developments in how the law is applied and interpreted in practice, recognizing that over seventy years have passed since the Geneva Conventions were adopted. Previous milestones of this project include the completion of the updated Commentaries on the First and Second Geneva Conventions in 2016 and 2017 respectively.[2] In 2020, the project reached another major milestone with the completion of the updated Commentary on the Third Geneva Convention Relative to the Treatment of Prisoners of War (hereinafter "the Third Geneva Convention").[3]

The Third Geneva Convention protects members of the armed forces and other defined categories of persons who fall into the power of the enemy in times of international armed conflicts.[4] Prisoners of war are not to be punished for their mere participation in hostilities; their detention is not a punishment but an act to prevent their further participation in hostilities. This understanding underpins the whole of the Third Geneva Convention.[5]

The Third Geneva Convention sets out a number of fundamental protections that apply to all prisoners of war. These fundamental protections serve as a foundation for the more prescriptive articles, which provide that prisoners of war must at all times be treated humanely, with respect for their persons and their honor; and treated equally, without discrimination.[6] These principles in turn are supplemented by detailed provisions regulating the treatment of prisoners of war. These include provisions relating to the beginning of captivity, the provision of prisoners' basic needs, the transfer of prisoners, the use of prisoners' labor, the imposition of disciplinary or judicial proceedings, and the final release and repatriation of prisoners. The level of detail provided for the protection of prisoners of war at the time of drafting the Third Geneva Convention in 1949 was unprecedented, and it continues to provide comprehensive protection to prisoners of war.

humanitarian law, *see also* FRANÇOIS BUGNION, THE INTERNATIONAL COMMITTEE OF THE RED CROSS AND THE PROTECTION OF WAR VICTIMS 914 (2003).

2. For more details, *see* Bruno Demeyere et al., *The Updated ICRC Commentary on the Second Geneva Convention: Demystifying the Law of Armed Conflict at Sea*, 98 INTERNATIONAL REVIEW OF THE RED CROSS 401 (2016); and Lindsey Cameron et al., *The Updated Commentary on the First Geneva Convention—A New Tool for Generating Respect for International Humanitarian Law*, 97 INTERNATIONAL REVIEW OF THE RED CROSS 1209 (2015).

3. INTERNATIONAL COMMITTEE OF THE RED CROSS, COMMENTARY ON THE THIRD GENEVA CONVENTION: CONVENTION (III) RELATIVE TO THE TREATMENT OF PRISONERS OF WAR (2020), https://ihl-databases.icrc.org/applic/ihl/ihl.nsf/vwTreaties1949.xsp [hereinafter 2020 GC III COMMENTARY].

4. It should be noted that in non-international armed conflict, international humanitarian law foresees no entitlement to prisoner of war status as it exists for international armed conflict.

5. 2020 GC III COMMENTARY, *supra* note 3, Introduction, ¶ 20 and commentary on Article 21, ¶ 1932.

6. Convention (III) Relative to the Treatment of Prisoners of War arts. 13, 14, 16, Aug. 12, 1949, 6 U.S.T. 3316, 75 U.N.T.S. 135 [hereinafter Third Geneva Convention].

Updating the commentaries on each of the 143 articles of the Third Geneva Convention required consideration of a wide range of historical, legal, military, ethical, sociocultural, and technological issues. As with the updated Commentaries on the First and Second Geneva Conventions, the development of the updated Commentary on the Third Geneva Convention involved a collaborative effort, with input from ICRC and non-ICRC lawyers; specialists with subject-matter expertise, including military personnel; protection officers specializing in detention, academics, and others. In addition, the development of this Commentary has benefited from the fact that the ICRC has been able to draw on archival records of its work visiting prisoners of war over the last seventy years. This work has enabled it to witness measures taken to comply with the Third Geneva Convention, and also challenges in its implementation.

The Third Geneva Convention remains relevant today as there continue to be prisoners of war. Its rules have informed parallel provisions protecting civilian internees under the Fourth Geneva Convention. No article of the Third Geneva Convention was found to have fallen into desuetude, although it was sometimes more difficult to find recent practice in relation to certain topics, such as the financial resources of prisoners of war.[7]

The update of the Commentary on the Third Geneva Convention follows the same methodology as that applied for the updated Commentaries on the First and Second Geneva Conventions, based on the rules of treaty interpretation set out in the 1969 Vienna Convention on the Law of Treaties, and in particular Articles 31–33.[8] Pursuant to these rules, the contributors started from the ordinary meaning of the terms of the Third Geneva Convention in their context and in light of the object and purpose of the treaty. Although the updated Commentary has been drafted in English, the authors have consistently consulted and compared the English text of the Convention with the French text, which is equally authentic.[9] Close examination was also made of the preparatory work for each article of the Convention.

Where relevant, the updated Commentary also takes into account developments in other branches of international law, such as international criminal law and international human rights law. Other treaties are referred to on the understanding

---

7. In international armed conflicts since 1949, Article 61 on supplementary pay for prisoners of war does not appear to have been resorted to. On absence of practice and desuetude, *see also* 2020 GC III COMMENTARY, *supra* note 3, Introduction, sec. C.8.

8. Vienna Convention on the Law of Treaties, May 23, 1969, 1155 U.N.T.S. 331. Articles 31–33 are generally considered to reflect customary international law. *See, e.g.*, Kasikili/Sedudu Island (Botswana v. Namibia), Judgment, 1999 I.C.J. 1045, ¶¶ 18–20 (Dec. 13); Application of the Convention on the Prevention and Punishment of the Crime of Genocide (Bosn. & Herz. v. Serb. & Montenegro), Judgment, 2007 I.C.J. 43, ¶ 160 (Feb. 26); International Law Commission, *Report on the Work of its Seventieth Session*, U.N. Doc. A/73/10, chap. IV, conclusion 2.1 (2018), https://legal.un.org/ilc/reports/2018/english/a_73_10_advance.pdf.

9. Third Geneva Convention, *supra* note 6, art. 133; Vienna Convention on the Law of Treaties, *supra* note 8, art. 33.

that they apply only to States that have ratified or acceded to them, and only if the conditions relating to their geographic, temporal, and personal scope of application are fulfilled. Reference is made to international human rights law where relevant to interpret shared concepts (for example, cruel, inhuman, and degrading treatment) as well as to provide practitioners with further information about certain topics, and in certain circumstances where the Third Geneva Convention may be affected by international human rights obligations.[10] This does not mean that international human rights law and interpretations can be transposed mechanically to international humanitarian law provisions, and differences have also been pointed out where relevant.[11]

This chapter highlights key points of interest covered in the updated Commentary on the Third Geneva Convention. It is divided into three parts. Part I covers the fundamentals of the Third Geneva Convention: the historical background, the personal scope of application of the Third Geneva Convention, and the fundamental protections that apply to all prisoners of war. Part II provides a framework for understanding when certain obligations are triggered, which may be broadly grouped as the obligations of a Detaining Power prior to holding prisoners of war; obligations triggered by the taking of prisoners of war and during their captivity; and obligations at the end of a prisoner of war's captivity. Part III summarizes key substantive protections provided in the Third Geneva Convention, providing examples of the depth of detail in the Third Geneva Convention when it comes to the protection of prisoners of war. A brief conclusion is provided in Part IV.

I. THE FUNDAMENTALS OF THE THIRD GENEVA CONVENTION

A. Historical Background of the Third Geneva Convention

Customs and codes regulating the capture and detention of enemy soldiers have existed for thousands of years, drawing on a variety of cultural, religious, and ethical frameworks.[12] The development of an international treaty, however, began in earnest in the eighteenth and nineteenth centuries, at which time many States began to establish and consolidate professional armies, to enter bilateral

---

10. For example, a discussion on the application of Article 100 on the death penalty would not be complete without acknowledging the existence of international treaties by which many States have committed to abolish the death penalty. *See* 2020 GC III COMMENTARY, *supra* note 3, commentary on Article 100, ¶ 3979.

11. For an example in relation to the definition of torture, *see id.*, commentary on Article 3, sec. G.2 and commentary on Article 130, sec. D.2.a. For more information on the use of other relevant rules of international law, *see id.*, Introduction, sec. C.5.

12. *Id.*, Introduction, ¶ 4.

agreements regarding the conditions of warfare,[13] and to include protections for prisoners of war in their military manuals.[14]

In 1874 a conference of fifteen European States adopted a draft text submitted by the Russian government, now known as the Brussels Declaration, which included twelve articles on the protection of prisoners of war. The Brussels Declaration never became a binding treaty, but many of its definitions were adopted essentially without change at the 1899 Hague Peace Conference.[15] The Hague Regulations annexed to the Hague Conventions of 1899 was the first binding multilateral agreement dealing with prisoners of war.[16] Seventeen articles of the Regulations dealt with prisoners of war, addressing inter alia the obligation to treat prisoners humanely and without distinction, to feed and clothe prisoners at a standard at least on par with the soldiers of the Detaining Power, and to ensure speedy repatriation of prisoners upon the end of the conflict.[17]

The provisions in the Hague Regulations proved to be insufficiently detailed, and during World War I some belligerents signed temporary agreements to clarify disputed points.[18] Further, the changing character of warfare, technological developments, and the increased size of armies and wars led to significantly larger numbers of persons being taken captive during armed conflicts of this period, most notably in World War I.[19] On the basis of general principles developed by the Tenth International Conference of the Red Cross, the 1929 Convention Relative

---

13. For example, during the Napoleonic Wars, the United Kingdom and France entered into an agreement that allowed for a "protecting power" to visit prisoners and provide additional food. In 1896 Italy and Ethiopia entered into the Treaty of Addis Ababa, which included the requirement of release of all prisoners, as well as an obligation on the part of Ethiopia to allow a detachment of the Italian Red Cross to facilitate this process. 1 ALEXANDER GILLESPIE, A HISTORY OF THE LAWS OF WAR: THE CUSTOMS AND LAWS OF WAR WITH REGARDS TO COMBATANTS AND CAPTIVES 149, 164 (2011); JAMES MOLONY SPAIGHT, WAR RIGHTS ON LAND 37 (1911).

14. ALLAN ROSAS, THE LEGAL STATUS OF PRISONERS OF WAR: A STUDY IN INTERNATIONAL HUMANITARIAN LAW APPLICABLE IN ARMED CONFLICTS 69, 72–73 (1976, reprinted 2005). See, in particular, U.S. Department of War, Instructions for the Government of Armies of the United States in the Field, General Orders No. 100, Apr. 24, 1863 (Lieber Code).

15. Convention No. II with Respect to the Laws and Customs of War on Land, July 29, 1899, 32 Stat. 1803, T.S. No. 403, sec. II. Provisions dealing with prisoners of war can also be found in Institute of International Law, The Laws of War on Land arts. 21–22, 61–78 (1880) (Oxford Manual), reprinted in THE LAWS OF ARMED CONFLICTS 29 (Dietrich Schindler & Jiri Toman eds., 4th ed. 2004).

16. ROSAS, supra note 14, at 70.

17. 2020 GC III COMMENTARY, supra note 3, Introduction, ¶ 7.

18. See, e.g., Agreement between the British and Ottoman Governments respecting Prisoners of War and Civilians, Dec. 1917, H.M.S.O., 1918.

19. During World War I, for example, an unprecedented estimated seven to eight million soldiers were taken as prisoners of war. On treatment issues for prisoners of war in World War I, see GILLESPIE, supra note 13, at 166–172.

to the Treatment of Prisoners of War was adopted, considerably supplementing the Hague Regulations.[20] Its eighty substantive articles included provisions on the prohibition of measures of reprisal and collective penalties; the organization of labor of prisoners of war; the ability of prisoners to elect their representatives; the codification of judicial procedures and punitive measures; and the official recognition of the role of the ICRC, generally and in regard to the organization of a central information agency. Forty-seven States were party to the 1929 Convention at the outbreak of World War II.[21] While the protections conferred by the 1929 Convention had an important impact in several theaters of World War II, in others they did not, in part as they were interpreted to not be applicable. For example, a narrow interpretation of the definition of prisoner of war was used to deny prisoner of war status to soldiers of several countries who surrendered following the capitulation of their State.[22]

The negotiations for what would become the Third Geneva Convention were in turn heavily influenced by the experiences of World War II. As in World War I, quarter was regularly denied on a devastating scale.[23] Further, World War II witnessed the use of detention itself as a means to enable the killing of innumerable soldiers, including by summary execution, extreme acts of violence, ill-treatment, starvation, and malnutrition.[24] Prisoners were treated differently depending on their nationality and which State detained them and, at the end of the war, the repatriation of prisoners was significantly drawn out.[25]

In the immediate aftermath of World War II, several expert conferences were convened in Geneva, where preparatory material gathered by the ICRC and first drafts for the new conventions were discussed. The most important of these conferences were the Preliminary Conference of National Red Cross Societies in 1946 and the Conference of Government Experts in 1947. The drafts prepared by these conferences were presented to the 1948 International Conference of the Red

---

20. See BUGNION, supra note 1, at 121 for more details on the preparatory steps that led to the adoption of the 1929 Convention.

21. In addition, Japan declared that it was ready to apply the Convention during World War II "under conditions of reciprocity and *mutatis mutandis*." INTERNATIONAL COMMITTEE OF THE RED CROSS, REPORT OF THE INTERNATIONAL COMMITTEE OF THE RED CROSS ON ITS ACTIVITIES DURING THE SECOND WORLD WAR (SEPTEMBER 1, 1939–JUNE 30, 1947), vol. I, 229 (1948).

22. 2020 GC III COMMENTARY, *supra* note 3, commentary on Article 4, sec. D.1. *See also id.*, ¶ 1041 in relation to the denial of prisoner of war status to soldiers of governments or authorities not recognized by the Detaining Power.

23. *See, e.g.*, GILLESPIE, *supra* note 13, at 186.

24. *See, e.g.*, ROSAS, *supra* note 14, at 78; GILLESPIE, *supra* note 13, at 192–200; Sandra Krähenmann, *Protection of Prisoners in Armed Conflict, in* THE HANDBOOK OF INTERNATIONAL HUMANITARIAN LAW 362 (Dieter Fleck ed., 3rd ed. 2013).

25. For example, it is estimated that there were still 630,000 German prisoners of war in France in 1947: Krähenmann, *supra* note 24, at 363.

Cross in Stockholm, where further amendments were adopted. The Stockholm Drafts served as the basis for negotiation at the Diplomatic Conference which met in Geneva from April 21 to August 12, 1949. Fifty-nine States were officially represented by delegations with full powers to discuss the texts; four States sent observers.

In general terms, the Third Geneva Convention of 1949 is considerably more detailed than the 1929 Convention. It clarifies and expands the scope of persons to whom it applies; it provides clearer regulation to keep prisoners in good health; it elaborates on the guarantees they are due in cases of disciplinary or penal sanction; it provides stricter regulation on the use of prisoner of war labor; and it clarifies the obligation to repatriate prisoners at the end of active hostilities. The Third Geneva Convention also contains, like the other three conventions, a system for the suppression of breaches of the Convention, by defining the concept of "grave breaches" against prisoners of war, by creating obligations on States to pass legislation criminalizing grave breaches, and by obliging States to search for and to try or extradite those who are suspected of having committed such breaches. It provides for a greater role for relief societies and acknowledges the "special position" of the ICRC in this respect. Finally, the Third Geneva Convention allows for the ICRC to visit prisoners of war and forms the basis for its Central Tracing Agency.[26]

B. The Personal Scope of Application of the Third Geneva Convention

Article 4 is perhaps the best known and most debated provision of the Third Geneva Convention. This article defines prisoners of war and, accordingly, is central to understanding the personal scope of application of the Third Geneva Convention. It provides, in short, that a prisoner of war is a person belonging to one of six categories defined in Article 4A at the time that they "fall into the power of the enemy" in an international armed conflict.[27] Article 4A mirrors the list of protected persons in Articles 13 of the First and Second Geneva Conventions, which provide protection for wounded, sick, and shipwrecked military personnel. Wounded, sick, and shipwrecked persons covered by the First or Second Geneva Convention who fall into the power of the enemy are simultaneously protected by the First or Second and Third Geneva Conventions.[28]

---

26. The requirement that the ICRC be allowed to visit "all places where prisoners of war may be" is provided for in Third Geneva Convention, *supra* note 6, art. 126. The Central Tracing Agency operating under the responsibility of the ICRC is based on Article 123 of the Third Geneva Convention.

27. For a discussion on the expression "fallen into the power of the enemy," *see* 2020 GC III COMMENTARY, *supra* note 3, commentary on Article 5, ¶¶ 1100–01.

28. For details, *see* Convention (I) for the Amelioration of the Condition of the Wounded and Sick in the Armed Forces in the Field art. 14, Aug. 12, 1949, 6 U.S.T. 3114, 75 U.N.T.S. 31 and

1. Members of the Armed Forces

The first of the six categories is "members of the armed forces." Numerically, this is likely to be the most significant category. "Members of the armed forces" refers to all military personnel under a command responsible to a party to the conflict. The requirements for membership in the armed forces are not prescribed in international law, but rather are a matter of domestic regulation.[29] This first category also includes members of militia or volunteer corps forming part of the armed forces, that is to say, formally incorporated into the armed forces and under the responsible command of a party to the conflict.[30] It may also include paramilitary and armed law enforcement agencies that are formally incorporated into the armed forces through the national law of a State.[31] Members of the armed forces are required to distinguish themselves from the civilian population during military operations. Under customary international humanitarian law, failure to do so while engaged in an attack or in a military operation preparatory to an attack results in their forfeiting the right to prisoner of war status.[32] This provides an example of how the updated Commentary refers to customary international humanitarian law where it may be considered a "relevant [rule] of international law applicable in the relations between the parties."[33]

2. Members of Other Militias and Members of Other Volunteer Corps, Including Those of Organized Resistance Movements, Belonging to a Party to the Conflict and Fulfilling the Four Conditions

The second category of prisoners of war encompasses members of "other militias and members of other volunteer corps, including those of organized resistance movements, belonging to a Party to the conflict" and fulfilling four prescribed conditions. This category concerns groups that are not incorporated into the armed forces but otherwise "belong" to a party to the conflict.

A group belongs to a party to the conflict for the purpose of Article 4A(2) if the group fights on behalf of that party and that party accepts such fighting role. This

---

Convention (II) for the Amelioration of the Condition of the Wounded, Sick, and Shipwrecked Members of Armed Forces at Sea art. 16, Aug. 12, 1949, 6 U.S.T. 3217, 75 U.N.T.S. 85.

29. 2020 GC III Commentary, *supra* note 3, commentary on Article 4, ¶ 977.

30. *Id.*, ¶ 979.

31. *Id.*, ¶¶ 979–82.

32. 1 Customary International Humanitarian Law, Rule 106 (Jean-Marie Henckaerts & Louise Doswald-Beck eds., 2005) [hereinafter ICRC Customary IHL Study]. For further discussion on this point, *see* 2020 GC III Commentary, *supra* note 3, commentary on Article 4, ¶¶ 983–87.

33. Vienna Convention on the Law of Treaties, *supra* note 8, art. 31(3). *See also* 2020 GC III Commentary, *supra* note 3, Introduction, ¶¶ 92–95.

acceptance can be express, for example when a party gives a formal authorization to the group or acknowledges that the group fights on its behalf. It can also be implicit or tacit, for example, when a group fights alongside the State and claims to be fighting on its behalf and the State does not deny this relationship when given the opportunity. The acceptance of a "belonging to" relationship can also be demonstrated by the overall control that the party exercises over the group.[34]

For members of such militia or volunteer corps to be considered prisoners of war upon falling into the power of the enemy, the militia and volunteer corps must collectively fulfill four conditions, each of which serves a protective purpose: they must be commanded by a person responsible for their subordinates; they must have a fixed distinctive sign recognizable at a distance; they must carry arms openly; and they must conduct their operations in accordance with the laws and customs of war. A structured hierarchy can ensure internal discipline and that operations are planned, coordinated, and carried out in a way that is consistent with the laws and customs of war. Having a fixed distinctive sign and carrying arms openly facilitate distinguishing combatants from the civilian population. The condition that the militia or volunteer corps conduct operations in accordance with the laws and customs of war serves as an additional encouragement for the groups to comply with international humanitarian law, in order for their members to receive the protective prisoner of war status in the event they fall into the power of the enemy.

The Commentary also considers the question of whether these four conditions, which appear in Article 4A(2) but not in 4A(1), nevertheless also apply to 4A(1) forces.[35] In the ICRC's view, while the four conditions are obligations for regular armed forces, they are not *collective conditions* for prisoner of war status.[36] The four conditions reflect the usual practice of State armed forces. By definition, such forces are commanded by a person responsible for their subordinates.[37] Further, as mentioned above, members of the armed forces are under an obligation to distinguish themselves sufficiently from the civilian population and not to conceal their weapons during military operations. The ICRC's understanding is that a combatant loses eligibility for prisoner of war status if they fail to distinguish themselves. Such loss of eligibility, however, only applies on an individual basis and not to the group as a whole.[38] Compliance with the laws and customs of war is a standard requirement under the Geneva Conventions and general international law,[39] and Article 85 of the Third Geneva Convention makes it clear that

---

34. For a more in-depth discussion of the meaning of "belonging to" under Article 4A(2), *see* 2020 GC III COMMENTARY, *supra* note 3, commentary on Article 4, ¶¶ 1001–09.

35. *Id.*, ¶¶ 1028–39.

36. *Id.*, ¶ 1039.

37. *Id.*

38. *Id.*, ¶¶ 983 and 1039.

39. *Id.*, ¶ 1039.

prisoners of war keep their protected status if convicted for acts committed prior to capture.[40] If and when regular armed forces are perceived as not fulfilling these obligations, avenues other than a collective denial of prisoner of war status are available to States under international law to endeavor to induce compliance.[41] The ICRC recognizes, however, that there are diverging views as to whether the four conditions under Article 4A(2) are collective conditions for prisoner of war status for members of a State's regular armed forces.[42]

3. Members of Regular Armed Forces Who Profess Allegiance to a Government or Authority Not Recognized by the Detaining Power

The third category are members of regular armed forces who profess allegiance to a government or authority not recognized by the Detaining Power. Members of the regular armed forces of a party to an international armed conflict are included within the definition of prisoners of war under the first category described above. World War II saw, however, the denial of prisoner of war status to certain groups on the basis that the authorities or governments to which those armed forces pledged allegiance were not recognized by the enemy State.[43] To avoid a repetition of this abusive interpretation, the definition of prisoner of war in the Third Geneva Convention expressly includes all members of regular armed forces, irrespective of whether the enemy recognized the legitimacy of their government or authority.[44]

4. Persons Authorized to and in Fact Accompanying the Armed Forces without Being Members Thereof

The fourth and fifth categories of prisoners of war are the only two categories of persons entitled to prisoner of war status without equally being entitled to combatant status, immunity, or privileges. The fourth category pertains to persons authorized to and in fact accompanying the armed forces without being members thereof.[45] The inclusion of this category recognizes that the proximity of

---

40. *See also id.*, ¶ 1033.

41. *Id.*, ¶ 1039.

42. *Id.*, ¶ 1036.

43. For example, Germany denied prisoner of war status to French forces operating under the command of General de Gaulle and to Italian units in southern Italy following the signing of an armistice between the Allies and Italy in September 1943: 2 INTERNATIONAL COMMITTEE OF THE RED CROSS, COMMISSION OF GOVERNMENT EXPERTS FOR THE STUDY OF CONVENTIONS FOR THE PROTECTION OF WAR VICTIMS (GENEVA APRIL 14 TO 26, 1947): PRELIMINARY DOCUMENTS SUBMITTED BY THE ICRC 4 (1947).

44. *Id.*

45. For more information, *see* 2020 GC III COMMENTARY, *supra* note 3, commentary on Article 4, ¶¶ 1047–50.

such persons to the armed forces increases the risks of their being interned with combatants and makes explicit the protective framework that applies to them. It might include, for example, civilian contractors authorized to accompany the armed forces providing services such as laundry or transportation.[46] The authorization of a person to accompany the armed forces is evidenced by the provision of an identity card of a similar model to that in Annex IV.A of the Third Geneva Convention, as well as by co-location, shared logistical arrangements, contractual arrangements, and/or apparel.[47]

5. Members of the Crew of the Merchant Marine or Civil Aircraft of the Parties to the Conflict Who Do Not Benefit from Other More Favorable Treatment in International Law

The fifth category concerns members of the crew of the merchant marine or civil aircraft of the parties to the conflict who do not benefit from other more favorable treatment in international law. The inclusion of the crew of the merchant marine sought to remedy uncertainty as to their status and inconsistencies in the protection provided to such persons during World War II. Civilian members of aircraft crews were also included, recognizing the increasing role of aircraft in providing deliveries to combat areas.[48]

In relation to treatment, the Third Geneva Convention makes no distinction between prisoners of war who are combatants and those who are civilians. However, some provisions of the Third Geneva Convention presume the existence of membership in the armed forces and are silent as to their application in relation to the other categories of prisoners of war. For example, certain provisions in relation to the use of prisoner of war labor, such as the rate of payment, are framed around the rank of prisoners of war.[49] If a Detaining Power interns prisoners of war who are civilians, it must apply these provisions in good faith and in line with the rationale behind the provisions in question.[50]

6. LEVÉE EN MASSE

The sixth, and final, category of prisoners of war applies to participants in what is commonly referred to as a *levée en masse*. More precisely, this category comprises any inhabitants of a non-occupied territory, who on the approach of the enemy spontaneously take up arms to resist the invading forces, without having had time to form themselves into regular armed units, provided they carry arms openly and respect the laws and customs of war. This is the only category of prisoners of

---

46. For a more detailed discussion, *see id*. See also *id*., ¶ 1051 in relation to private military and security companies.

47. *Id*., ¶ 1050.

48. *Id*., ¶¶ 1052–60.

49. *See* Third Geneva Convention, *supra* note 6, art. 60.

50. 2020 GC III Commentary, *supra* note 3, commentary on Article 4, ¶ 1046.

war that is entirely autonomous from the State. The persons under this category do not "belong to" the State, nor do they require any level of organization, command structure, or fixed distinctive sign.[51]

The circumstances in which the conditions for a *levée en masse* apply are limited. First, it refers only to those that take up arms during an invasion period, where territory is not yet occupied, or in an area where the previous Occupying Power has lost control over the administration of the territory and is attempting to regain it. Second, the persons must have spontaneously taken up arms in response to the invading army. This category does not include persons or groups who organize or are organized in advance of the invasion. Finally, the persons who take up arms must carry arms openly and respect the laws and customs of war.

In addition to these six categories, Article 4 also sets out two categories of persons who are not prisoners of war per se but are to be treated as prisoners of war.[52]

The definition in Article 4 is supplemented in this respect by Additional Protocol I (and customary international humanitarian law), which exclude spies, saboteurs, and mercenaries from prisoner of war status.[53]

The drafters of the Third Geneva Convention gave considerable attention to defining which categories of persons qualify for prisoner of war status, and in many ways reduced uncertainties that existed within previous definitions under the Hague Regulations and 1929 Convention. Notwithstanding this, doubt as to the status of persons may still arise. An important innovation in the Third Geneva Convention was to provide a mechanism to address these situations. Article 5(2) of the Third Geneva Convention provides that in case of doubt regarding the status of persons who have committed belligerent acts and fall into the hands of the enemy, such persons enjoy the protection of the Convention until a determination of their status has been made by a competent tribunal. The term "competent tribunal" was employed to encompass review by a court or military tribunal and to prevent "arbitrary decisions [being made] by a local commander, who may be of a very low rank."[54] In practice, the status of individuals has been decided by civil courts, military tribunals or courts, and boards of inquiry.[55]

---

51. *Id.*, ¶ 1062.

52. Third Geneva Convention, *supra* note 6, art. 4B(1) and (2) and 2020 GC III COMMENTARY, *supra* note 3, commentary on Article 4, ¶¶ 1069–90.

53. For more information on the exclusion of "spies and saboteurs", *see* 2020 GC III COMMENTARY, *supra* note 3, commentary on Article 4, ¶¶ 988–91. For more information on the exclusion of "mercenaries," *see id.*, ¶ 998.

54. II-B FINAL RECORD OF THE DIPLOMATIC CONFERENCE OF GENEVA OF 1949, 270 (1949). *See also* H.W. William Caming, *Nuremberg Trials: Partisans, Hostages and Reprisals*, 4 JUDGE ADVOCATE JOURNAL 16, 19 (1950) in relation to the infamous Barbarossa Jurisdiction Order issued on May 13, 1941. This order directed that "partisan suspects" be brought before an officer who would determine whether they were to be shot. This was considered during the Nuremberg Trials as "patently criminal" as it "permitted the immediate killing of alleged partisans and 'partisan suspects' without investigation and at the discretion of a junior officer."

55. 2020 GC III COMMENTARY, *supra* note 3, commentary on Article 5, ¶ 1126.

A determination should be made within a reasonable time frame, in good faith, and on a case-by-case basis, as mentioned. The requirement of determinations to be made by a "competent tribunal" prevents arbitrary, "on the spot" decision-making. That noted, the particular procedural guarantees applicable to status determinations are not regulated by international humanitarian law but are a matter of domestic law.[56]

Doubt as to a person's status arises when it is not clear whether the person belongs to any of the categories discussed above. For example, it can arise in relation to persons who accompany the armed forces and have lost their identity cards, persons engaged in belligerent acts without wearing a uniform in zones of active hostilities, or persons suspected of being spies. It may also arise where a person or the Power on which they depend asserts prisoner of war status and this is not immediately accepted. Conversely, it may arise where a person asserts not to be a prisoner of war. The existence of a doubt that triggers a determination by a competent tribunal must not depend solely on the subjective belief of the Detaining Power; rather a Detaining Power must consider each situation in good faith, on a case-by-case basis, with a proper assessment of facts.[57]

Any person determined to be a prisoner of war will continue to enjoy the protections of the Third Geneva Convention. A person determined not to fall within the categories of Article 4 of the Third Geneva Convention will otherwise be a civilian and is protected by the Fourth Convention (including Articles 43 and 78) and/or Article 75 of Additional Protocol I, as applicable, and customary international humanitarian law.[58]

C. Fundamental Principles for the Protection of Prisoners of War

The Third Geneva Convention embodies a balance between the requirements of humanity and military necessity. Its overall object and purpose are to ensure that prisoners of war are humanely treated at all times, while allowing belligerents to intern captured enemy combatants to prevent them from returning to the battlefield.[59] The authorization to intern, contained in Article 21 of the Convention, gives expression to military necessity: interning prisoners of war for the duration of active hostilities aims to ensure that captured enemy personnel are not able to participate again in the hostilities, which would pose a military threat to the Detaining

---

56. *Id.*, ¶ 1127.

57. *Id.*, ¶¶ 1119–21.

58. *Id.*, ¶ 1115.

59. 2020 GC III COMMENTARY, *supra* note 3, Introduction, ¶ 89.

Power.[60]

Reflecting the requirements of humanity, the Third Geneva Convention provides a set of general protections for prisoners of war, setting standards below which the treatment afforded to and conditions enjoyed by prisoners of war must not fall. These overarching protections include the obligations of humane and equal treatment, the prohibition of adverse distinction, and respect for prisoners' persons and honor. The Convention deals with an extremely broad range of issues, and many articles in the Convention are more specific iterations of these obligations. The drafters did not intend, however, to set out detailed rules or codes for every single area covered. Instead, the Convention refers in certain articles, through the principle of assimilation, to rules and regulations that are applicable to the Detaining Power's own armed forces. In those cases, prisoners of war are to be treated in accordance with these rules and regulations, while the Convention's standards on humane treatment continue to apply and act as a minimum standard.

The requirement to treat prisoners of war humanely is stated in Article 13. It is complemented by the obligation to respect prisoners of war's persons and honor in Article 14, as well as the requirement to treat prisoners of war equally and the prohibition of discrimination in Article 16. These provisions provide for the minimum standard of treatment. They are interconnected and underpin all protections owed to prisoners of war.

The requirement to treat a prisoner of war humanely (or in the equally authentic French version, *avec humanité*) involves respect for the prisoner's inherent human dignity and inviolable quality as a human being.[61] Article 13 provides certain express articulations of what this means, including the prohibition of physical mutilation, medical or scientific experiments, acts of violence, intimidation, insults, and public curiosity. The protection against public curiosity is particularly relevant in the age of mass media and social media, given the ease in which images and comments can be spread around the world.[62]

This obligation clearly cannot be separated from the obligation to respect a prisoner's person and honor. Respect for the person of a prisoner of war relates not only to their physical integrity, prohibiting acts of violence and physical torture, but also to their moral integrity, namely the essential attributes that make up a person, including their religious, political, intellectual, and social convictions, gender, and sexual orientation.[63] Respect for the honor of a prisoner of war more

---

60. 2020 GC III COMMENTARY, *supra* note 3, commentary on Article 21, ¶ 1932. Further expressions of military necessity can be found in the rules that serve the maintenance of security, discipline, and good order in prisoner-of-war camps. *See, e.g.*, Third Geneva Convention, *supra* note 6, arts. 42 (use of weapons against prisoners of war), 76 (censorship and examination), 92 (unsuccessful escape) and 95 (disciplinary procedure), which specifically mentions "camp order and discipline."

61. 2020 GC III COMMENTARY, *supra* note 3, commentary on Article 13, ¶ 1570.

62. *Id.*, ¶ 1563.

63. *Id.*, commentary on Article 14, ¶ 1665.

specifically entails due respect for the sense of value that every person has of themselves.[64] The Third Geneva Convention expressly protects certain aspects of honor with regard to military structures, distinctions, and codes of honor, for example, in providing that badges of rank and decorations may not be taken away from prisoners of war and that prisoners of war may not be deprived of their rank.[65] How a prisoner of war's person and honor are to be respected depends on a wide range of factors, including their cultural, social, or religious background, gender, and age.[66]

This, in turn, relates to the protection provided in Article 16, which provides for the equality of treatment of prisoners of war and the prohibition of "adverse distinction based on race, nationality, religious belief or political opinions, or any other distinction founded on similar criteria."

Equal treatment does not necessarily require identical treatment. Prisoners of war in different situations and with different needs may need to be treated differently to achieve substantive equality of treatment.[67] Article 16 expressly lists health, age, and professional qualifications as potential grounds for "privileged treatment"; it also requires consideration of provisions relating to rank and sex in the Third Geneva Convention.[68] These considerations should not be taken as an exhaustive list upon which non-adverse distinction may be permitted, or is required.[69]

In relation to discrimination, the prohibition in Article 16 identifies a number of grounds on which adverse differentiated treatment is prohibited: race, nationality, religious belief, or political opinion, as well as "any other distinction founded on similar criteria." Additional Protocol I provides a longer list of prohibited grounds: "race, colour, sex, language, religion or belief, political or other opinion, national or social origin, wealth, birth or other status, or on any other similar criteria."[70] Adverse distinctions founded on other grounds, such as ethnicity, disability, level of education, or family connections of a prisoner of war, and as noted above, age or state of health, would equally be prohibited. Any list of prohibited criteria will necessarily be incomplete and should be interpreted in light of legal

---

64. *Id.*, ¶ 1658.

65. Third Geneva Convention, *supra* note 6, arts. 18(3), 44.

66. 2020 GC III COMMENTARY, *supra* note 3, commentary on Article 14, ¶ 1659.

67. *Id.*, commentary on Article 16, ¶ 1742.

68. In relation to different treatment in relation to sex, Third Geneva Convention, *supra* note 6, art. 14(2) provides that female prisoners of war are to be treated "with all the regard due to their sex" and, most importantly, that their treatment may in no case be inferior to that of male prisoners of war.

69. *See* 2020 GC III COMMENTARY, *supra* note 3, commentary on Article 16, ¶¶ 1743–44.

70. Protocol Additional to the Geneva Conventions of 12 August 1949, and relating to the Protection of Victims of International Armed Conflicts art. 75(1), 1125 UNTS 3, June 8, 1977 [hereinafter AP I]. *See also* ICRC CUSTOMARY IHL STUDY, *supra* note 32, Rule 88.

and social developments. The residual category of "any other distinction based on similar criteria" makes express provision for this.

It is in conjunction with the minimum standards and safeguards provided in the Convention that the principle of assimilation operates. It reflects an understanding that, with respect to certain issues, prisoners of war are to be treated in the same or a similar manner as members of the Detaining Power's own forces.[71] In this way, it complements the prohibition of adverse distinction as it ensures that all prisoners of war interned by a Detaining Power are subject to the same or similar conditions and standards, irrespective of their country of origin. This would not necessarily be the case if the Detaining Power treated prisoners of war from different countries according to the standards and conditions prevailing in each of the respective armed forces.

The principle of assimilation also facilitates the task of administering the internment of prisoners of war, since the Detaining Power has to apply to them some of the rules and standards that are already in force for its own troops. The Detaining Power is necessarily familiar with and has preexisting experience with implementing those rules and standards and thus can readily apply them to prisoners of war as well.

The principle of assimilation does not operate in a vacuum but in conjunction with the minimum standards and safeguards spelled out in the rest of the Convention, in particular those concerning the humane treatment of prisoners of war discussed above.[72] This is made explicit in several rules, including Article 82.[73] The approach to protecting prisoners of war by reference to the rules of both national and international law is also reflected in the provisions on penal and disciplinary sanctions (discussed below). Several of these provisions expressly make the principle of assimilation subject to compliance with minimum standards that must be applied to all prisoners of war, irrespective of the standards or conditions applicable to members of the armed forces of the Detaining Power. Accordingly, when the treatment afforded by a Detaining Power to its own armed forces falls

---

71. *See*, in particular, Third Geneva Convention, *supra* note 6, arts. 20 (conditions of evacuation), 25 (quarters), 46 (conditions for transfer), 82 (applicable legislation), 84 (courts), 87 (penalties), 88 (execution of penalties), 95 (confinement awaiting hearing), 102 (conditions for validity of sentence), 103 (confinement awaiting proceedings), 106 (the right to appeal), and 108 (the establishments and conditions for serving a sentence). The principle is also implicit in arts. 33 (rights and privileges of retained personnel), 52 (dangerous or humiliating labor), and 60 (advances of pay).

72. Third Geneva Convention, *supra* note 6, art. 13 and the provisions that give expression to the requirement of humane treatment in specific areas, such as quarters (art. 25), food (art. 26), clothing (art. 27), and hygiene (art. 29).

73. Third Geneva Convention, *supra* note 6, art. 82: "However, no proceedings or punishments contrary to the provisions of this Chapter shall be allowed." For further examples, *see* Third Geneva Convention arts. 25 (quarters), 46 (conditions of transfer), 50 (authorized work), 84 (courts), 87 (penalties), 95 (confinement awaiting hearing), 102 (conditions for validity of sentence), 103 (confinement awaiting trial), and 108 (execution of penalties).

short of the minimum standards set out in the Convention, the latter standards apply with respect to prisoners of war.

II. TIMING OF OBLIGATIONS

A. Planning and Preparation

Because of the wide range of issues dealt with in the Third Geneva Convention, proper planning and preparation, including making sure the domestic legal framework is up to date, are indispensable for its successful implementation.[74] An important part of this planning and preparation is the requirement for the Detaining Power to instruct the armed forces in their duties.[75] In this respect, Article 127(1) provides for the dissemination of the text of the Convention in time of peace and in time of armed conflict "so that the principles thereof may become known to all their armed forces and to the entire population," and Article 127(2) requires that authorities who assume responsibility for prisoners of war must possess the text of the Convention and be specially instructed in its provisions.

The implementation of some provisions of the Third Geneva Convention require action to be taken prior to the capture of prisoners. For example, the Convention requires that prisoners of war be interned on land, with every guarantee afforded for their hygiene and health, that they must not be held in penitentiaries except in particular cases where it is in the interests of the prisoners themselves,[76] and that they be quartered under conditions as favorable as those of the Detaining

---

74. This is consistent with the reference to provisions to be implemented in peacetime in Third Geneva Convention, *supra* note 6, art. 2(1).

75. This point was emphasized in the U.K. Baha Mousa Public Inquiry Report. Although the Inquiry concerned the treatment of Iraqi civilian internees by U.K. armed forces, it contained general conclusions and recommendations that are also relevant to prisoners of war. With regard to training, the Inquiry concluded that the general training the soldiers received in the law of armed conflict "lacked specific guidance on how to handle a prisoner; what the permitted treatment of a prisoner actually was in practical terms; and most importantly what type of treatment was expressly forbidden": 2 Sir William Gage, The Report of the Baha Mousa Inquiry ¶ 6.67 (2011), https://www.gov.uk/government/publications/the-baha-mousa-public-inquiry-report. In addition, the Inquiry identified deficiencies in specific teaching courses, including the training given to tactical questioners and interrogators. Accordingly, it made several recommendations, both general (Recommendations 47–58) and specific (Recommendations 59–73), on training soldiers in the handling of prisoners: *id.*, ¶¶ 6.66–73 and 6.339–49 and 3 Sir William Gage, The Report of the Baha Mousa Inquiry ¶¶ 1279–82 and 1282–86 (2011), https://www.gov.uk/government/publications/the-baha-mousa-public-inquiry-report. The Al Sweady Public Inquiry Report referred to several of these recommendations. *See* 2 Sir Thayne Forbes, The Report of the Al Sweady Inquiry ¶ 5.101 (Dec. 2014), https://www.gov.uk/government/publications/al-sweady-inquiry-report.

76. Third Geneva Convention, *supra* note 6, art. 22(1).

Power.[77] Providing accommodation that meets these standards requires infrastructure, equipment, logistics, trained staff, a budget, and operating procedures. This may be challenging for the Detaining Power once it is engaged in an international armed conflict. Successfully establishing humane, compliant internment of prisoners of war requires States to develop plans, even in peacetime, about how it would hold such potential prisoners, including for the types and location of internment facilities.

B. On Taking Prisoners of War Captive

Once a person in one of the categories of Article 4 falls into the power of the enemy, the Third Geneva Convention applies as a whole. The Third Geneva Convention does, however, take the different stages of captivity into consideration. It has, for example, a section dedicated to the beginning of captivity outlining the obligations of the Detaining Power immediately after prisoners fall into its power: Article 17 deals with the questioning of prisoners; Article 18 governs the property of prisoners; and Articles 19 and 20 concern the evacuation of prisoners from the combat zone. While these articles are most relevant soon after combatants fall into the power of the enemy and during the initial processing of prisoners, they continue to apply beyond the immediate time and location of the point of capture, including in some cases throughout captivity. For example, the prohibition of torture and coercion during questioning set out in Article 17 remains valid during the entire time of internment.[78]

The principle of humane treatment discussed above underpins these articles as they seek to ensure that, where prisoners are taken, they are brought to safety and are properly identified and processed. Often the first obligation for a Detaining Power is to evacuate the persons who have fallen into its power to an area that is far enough removed from the combat zone for the prisoners to be out of danger.[79] This evacuation must be carried out humanely and in conditions similar to those for the forces of the Detaining Power when they change positions.[80]

Depending on the circumstances, such as the distance and available means of transport, it may be that prisoners of war pass through transit camps during their evacuation. Such camps may be established temporarily and even close to the combat zone. Considering these ad hoc circumstances, it will usually be difficult for a Detaining Power to fulfill all the material conditions of the entire Convention. Accordingly, the stay in such camps must be as brief as possible.[81] These camps can

---

77. *Id.*, art. 25. This is discussed further below.

78. *See* 2020 GC III COMMENTARY, *supra* note 3, commentary on Article 17, ¶ 1822.

79. Third Geneva Convention, *supra* note 6, art. 19(1).

80. *Id.*, art. 20(1).

81. *Id.*, art. 20(3).

be distinguished from permanent transit camps. If a Detaining Power has such permanent establishments that it uses to screen and process prisoners, they must offer conditions similar to those of other prisoner of war camps, and prisoners in those camps must benefit from the same treatment as in other camps.[82]

After their evacuation and processing, prisoners of war typically arrive in a permanent prisoner of war camp. However, they do not always stay in one place nor under the responsibility of the same Power. During their captivity, they may be transferred to other camps and/or to other Powers. The Convention regulates both the physical transfer of prisoners of war to another location irrespective of whether they remain under the control of the same Power, as well as the transfer of prisoners of war from one Power to another.[83] For the transfer of a prisoner to another location, the Convention has a similar provision as for evacuation: the transfer must be effected in a humane manner and in conditions not less favorable than those under which the forces of the Detaining Power are transferred. It is slightly more stringent, however, than the provision on evacuation, as the conditions in the former case must only be "similar." This is understandable considering the more predictable nature of a transfer than of an evacuation from the battlefield.[84]

A prisoner may during captivity also be transferred to another Power, if that receiving Power is also a party to the Convention[85] and after the original Detaining Power can satisfy itself of the willingness and ability of the receiving Power to apply the Convention.[86] Because of the general understanding that only States can be High Contracting Parties to the Geneva Conventions, this means that prisoners of war may not be transferred to entities other than States—such as non-State armed groups and paramilitary and non-military organizations.[87]

An important obligation for the transferring Power is that if the receiving Power "fails to carry out the provisions of the Convention in any important respect," it must "take effective measures to correct the situation or shall request the return of the prisoners of war."[88] The Convention does not explain what "important respect" means. One benchmark for determining whether a breach is "important"

---

82. 2020 GC III COMMENTARY, *supra* note 3, commentary on Article 24, ¶¶ 2058, 2063–65.

83. Third Geneva Convention, *supra* note 6, arts. 12(2) and (3), 46–48.

84. Keiichiro Okimoto, *Evacuation and Transfer of Prisoners of War*, *in* THE 1949 GENEVA CONVENTIONS: A COMMENTARY 965 (Andrew Clapham, Paola Gaeta & Marco Sassòli eds., 2015), *cited in* 2020 GC III COMMENTARY, *supra* note 3, commentary on Article 46, n. 16.

85. This does not serve as a limitation today, as the Geneva Conventions are universally ratified.

86. Third Geneva Convention, *supra* note 6, art. 12(2). This includes neutral States. *See* 2020 GC III COMMENTARY, *supra* note 3, commentary on Article 12, sec. C.2.a.

87. *See*, however, 2020 GC III COMMENTARY, *supra* note 3, commentary on Article 12, ¶¶ 1530–32, for a discussion on transfers to non-State entities (including armed groups under the overall control of a State), international organizations, or international courts and tribunals.

88. Third Geneva Convention, *supra* note 6, art. 12(3).

is whether it violates the general obligation of humane treatment as articulated in Article 13. This covers, in any case, acts that qualify as grave breaches. Failure to provide for the basic needs of prisoners with respect to their quarters, food, water, and medical care in a way that would endanger the health of the prisoners or denying prisoners contact with the outside world, including visits from the ICRC, would also be covered. These examples are not exhaustive.[89]

There are different ways for a transferring Power to rectify such a failure to comply. As the Convention itself specifies, in some situations the transferring Power must request the return of the prisoners. Where the failure is due to inadequate material conditions of internment, such as lack of space, food, water, or medical care, measures to correct the situation may consist of direct assistance provided by the transferring Power, such as food, medical staff, and equipment. In situations where the failure is more systemic, for example when it relates to a denial of judicial guarantees or ill-treatment by camp staff, a request for the return of the prisoner may be the only adequate measure.[90]

C. On the End of Captivity

The Third Geneva Convention also regulates the end of captivity of prisoners of war. For most prisoners of war, captivity will cease at the end of active hostilities. Article 118 establishes a unilateral and non-reciprocal obligation on Detaining Powers to release and repatriate prisoners of war without delay after the cessation of active hostilities.[91] This obligation logically follows from the purpose of internment, which is to prevent further participation in hostilities.[92] Once hostilities between the two or more States have ended, there is no longer a need to keep prisoners of war interned.[93] Release and repatriation at the end of active hostilities marks the end of application of the Third Geneva Convention for these prisoners. Repatriation at the end of hostilities must take place "without delay." While this implies that repatriation does not have to be instantaneous, it must happen as soon as feasible considering the circumstances. It may depend, for example, on the number of persons to be repatriated, the security situation, the location of the camp(s) and available logistical means,

---

89. For a discussion and examples, *see* 2020 GC III Commentary, *supra* note 3, commentary on Article 12, sec. E.2.

90. For further discussion, *see id.*, sec. E.4.

91. Prisoners of war against whom criminal proceedings are pending or who are serving a criminal sentence may be kept back. See 2020 GC III Commentary, commentary on Article 119, sec. G.

92. *See id.*, commentary on Article 21, sec. C.1., in particular ¶ 1932.

93. *Id.*, commentary on Article 118, ¶ 4444.

and the ability of the State on which the prisoners depend to receive the prisoners.[94]

The Third Geneva Convention does not address the situation in which a prisoner of war does not want to be repatriated. As already recognized in the original ICRC Commentary, and reiterated in the updated Commentary, an exception to the obligation to repatriate prisoners of war may be made if, determined on an individual case-by-case-basis, there are "serious reasons for fearing that a prisoner of war who is himself opposed to being repatriated may, after his repatriation, be the subject of unjust measures affecting his life or liberty, especially on grounds of race, social class, religion or political views, and that consequently repatriation would be contrary to the general principles of international law for the protection of the human being."[95] An interpretation of Article 118 allowing for such an exception is in line with the principle of *non-refoulement* under international law, by which States cannot transfer persons within their control to another State if there is a real risk that they may face violations of certain fundamental rights.[96]

The updated commentary on Article 118 also discusses the obligation to release and repatriate in situations where a legal classification changes from an international to a non-international armed conflict, because of a change of circumstances on the ground. In such circumstances a party to the conflict is unlikely to be willing to release and repatriate any prisoners of war it holds. This is an example of a situation where the updated Commentary indicates divergent views and highlights issues not yet settled. There are two main approaches to this issue. Under the first approach, the obligation to release and repatriate prisoners of war is not triggered because the hostilities between the same actors have not ceased, even if the legal classification of the armed conflict has changed. Accordingly, the Third Geneva Convention remains the legal basis for the internment of prisoners of war and for their protection. Under the second approach, the hostilities related to the international armed conflict and the non-international armed conflict are considered to be distinct. Because the hostilities related to the international armed conflict have ceased, the obligation to release and repatriate prisoners of war is triggered on the basis of Article 118 of the Third Geneva Convention. In that case, the Convention no longer provides a legal basis for the internment of the prisoners, and if the

---

94. *Id.*, ¶ 4462.

95. 3 THE GENEVA CONVENTIONS OF 1949: COMMENTARY 547 (Jean S. Pictet ed., 1960) and 2020 GC III COMMENTARY, *supra* note 3, commentary on Article 118, ¶ 4469.

96. *See* Cordula Droege, *Transfers of Detainees: Legal Framework,* Non-Refoulement *and Contemporary Challenges*, 90 INTERNATIONAL REVIEW OF THE RED CROSS 671 (2008); Emmanuela-Chiara Gillard, *There's No Place Like Home: States' Obligations in Relation to Transfers of Persons*, 90 INTERNATIONAL REVIEW OF THE RED CROSS 704 (2008); Christopher Michaelsen, *The Renaissance of Non-Refoulement? The Othman (Abu Qatada) Decision of the European Court of Human Rights*, 61 INTERNATIONAL & COMPARATIVE LAW QUARTERLY 753 (July 2012). *See also* 2020 GC III COMMENTARY, *supra* note 3, commentary on Article 3, sec. G.7.

party believes it must continue to hold such persons for imperative reasons of security, another legal basis for their internment is required.[97]

In addition to the obligation to release and repatriate prisoners of war at the end of active hostilities, certain prisoners of war must be released and repatriated earlier than this. The Third Geneva Convention dedicates a number of articles to the repatriation of seriously wounded or sick prisoners of war during hostilities.[98] Again, this is a logical consequence of the purpose of internment. The assumption is that such prisoners of war are no longer able to participate in hostilities and therefore their continued internment would no longer be justified by military necessity.[99] A safeguard is built into the Convention though, as it includes an explicit prohibition of re-employing such repatriated prisoners on active military service, which is particularly important in modern warfare given the wider variety of assignments that might make the redeployment of seriously wounded or sick prisoners possible.[100]

Finally, the Third Geneva Convention also contains rules applicable to the Detaining Power when a prisoner dies during captivity. Needless to say, full compliance with the Third Geneva Convention may reduce the instances of fatalities, both through proper care of prisoners and also ensuring the repatriation of the seriously wounded and sick. In the event that a prisoner does pass away during internment, the Detaining Power retains certain obligations toward the deceased, which indirectly benefit their family. First, as an important means of accountability and to prevent people going missing, death certificates or certified lists must be prepared for any person who dies while a prisoner of war, recording the identity of the dead, the circumstances of death, and the burial site (or details of cremation, if applicable).[101] These must be forwarded to the national information bureau as rapidly as possible, which today generally means electronically.[102] At the same time, if not done previously, the will of the deceased should be transmitted to the Protecting Power, with a certified copy to the Central Tracing Agency.[103] These processes are not only important for the families' "closure" but may also have important legal implications.

Respecting the honor of a prisoner extends to the dead: Detaining Powers are required to ensure that prisoners of war who have died in captivity are honorably

---

97. For a detailed discussion, *see* 2020 GC III COMMENTARY, *supra* note 3, commentary on Article 118, ¶¶ 4459–60 and commentary on Article 5, sec. C.4.

98. Third Geneva Convention, *supra* note 6, art. 110.

99. 2020 GC III COMMENTARY, *supra* note 3, commentary on Article 109, ¶ 4245.

100. On the temporal scope of the obligation, *see id.*, commentary on Article 117, sec. C.3.

101. Details should be included as to why cremation was chosen (e.g., religious reasons, the wishes of the deceased), given the presumption in the Third Geneva Convention in favor of burial. *See id.*, commentary on Article 120, ¶ 4576.

102. *Id.*, ¶ 4563.

103. Third Geneva Convention, *supra* note 6, art. 120(1).

buried, if possible, according to the rites of their religion, and that their graves are respected, suitably maintained, and marked.[104] Additional Protocol I goes further, requiring parties to conclude agreements as soon as circumstances permit "to facilitate the return of the remains of the deceased and of personal effects to the home country."[105] The ICRC can and has acted as a neutral intermediary in the return of bodies to the families of the deceased.[106]

III. SUBSTANTIVE PROTECTIONS

As discussed above, in addition to setting out fundamental principles for the protection of prisoners of war, the Third Geneva Convention elucidates express protections on many facets of the life of a prisoner of war. The following discussion summarizes a number of these protections.

A. Internment in a Prisoner of War Camp

In the event that a prisoner of war is interned, they should not be held in penitentiaries unless it is in the best interests of the prisoner themselves.[107] Further, unless prisoners are subjected to penal or disciplinary sanctions, which are further discussed below, or when necessary to safeguard their health, prisoners of war may not be held in close confinement.[108]

While it is not an obligation for the Detaining Power, generally it will choose to intern prisoners of war, and the Convention provides detailed conditions for such internment. Below is a summary of some of the provisions governing interned prisoners of war.

B. Quarters

Article 25 provides that prisoners of war who are interned must be "quartered under conditions as favorable as those of the forces of the Detaining Power who are billeted in the same area." Again, this provision is underpinned not only by the fundamental protections described above (including respecting the person and

---

104. This includes the establishment of an official graves registration service: Third Geneva Convention, *supra* note 6, art. 120(6).

105. AP I, *supra* note 70, art. 34(2)(c). *See also* ICRC Customary IHL Study, *supra* note 32, Rule 114.

106. 2020 GC III Commentary, *supra* note 3, commentary on Article 120, ¶ 4598.

107. Third Geneva Convention, *supra* note 6, art. 22(1).

108. *Id.*, art. 21(1).

honor of the prisoner of war) but also by the consideration that holding prisoners of war is not intended to be punitive. Furthermore, allowance must be made for the customs and habits of prisoners of war, as well as ensuring that the accommodation is not "prejudicial to their health."[109]

While there can be wide disparities between the standards of quarters provided by the same Detaining Power to its own forces, quarters provided for prisoners of war must be at least of the standard genuinely used by the Detaining Power to accommodate a significant number of its own forces.[110] The quarters must also be protected from the vagaries of the weather and vermin and should be periodically visited by a doctor or other suitably qualified person to ensure that they are not prejudicial to the health of the prisoners.[111]

According to Article 25, women must be provided with dormitories separate from men, but it is not necessarily required that the quarters as a whole be separated.[112] In the event infants or very young children are present in prisoner of war camps (for instance, because they are born there), they must be accommodated with their parents.[113]

C. Food

Article 26 requires the Detaining Power to provide basic daily food rations that are "sufficient in quantity, quality and variety," as well as sufficient drinking water. Care must be taken of prisoners with health conditions by appropriately adapting food rations to their condition. Rations provided for older prisoners of war, pregnant or lactating prisoners, or any children present in prisoner of war camps have to be adapted to their needs.[114] Where prisoners of war carry out physical work, they will also need to be provided with additional rations to permit them to remain in good health.[115]

---

109. *Id.*, art. 25(1).

110. 2020 GC III COMMENTARY, *supra* note 3, commentary on Article 21, ¶ 2076.

111. *Id.*, commentary on Article 25, ¶¶ 2078–79.

112. In comparison, see Third Geneva Convention, *supra* note 6, art. 108(2), which requires women prisoners of war undergoing confinement to be held in separate quarters. See also AP I, *supra* note 70, art. 75(5) and ICRC CUSTOMARY IHL STUDY, *supra* note 32, Rule 119, which refer to separate quarters for women.

113. *See also* AP I, *supra* note 70, arts. 75(5) and 77(4); and 2020 GC III COMMENTARY, *supra* note 3, commentary on Article 25, ¶ 2104.

114. 2020 GC III COMMENTARY, *supra* note 3, commentary on Article 26, ¶ 2113.

115. Third Geneva Convention, *supra* note 6, art. 26(2) and 2020 GC III COMMENTARY, *supra* note 3, commentary on Article 26, ¶ 2126.

Article 26 further requires the Detaining Power to take into account the habitual diet of the prisoners.[116] One means to implement this provision is to involve them in the preparation of their own meals.[117]

The Convention requires that "[t]he use of tobacco shall be permitted." At the time the Third Geneva Convention was drafted, the hazards to health of tobacco use were not commonly known. Today, it would be appropriate and consistent with the requirement to provide for a healthy environment for internees for a Detaining Power to impose reasonable restrictions on tobacco use, such as measures to protect people against passive smoking and to prevent access of tobacco to minors.[118] This may also be required by other applicable rules of international law.[119]

Parties to an armed conflict are also required to provide canteens, where "foodstuffs, soap and tobacco and ordinary articles in daily use" are available for purchase.[120] However, in certain situations, for example, in conflicts of short duration or where prisoners of war are to be transferred to another camp or to another party to the conflict, it may be unnecessary or unreasonable to establish such a canteen.[121]

D. Clothing

Article 27 requires the Detaining Power to supply clothing, underwear, and footwear to prisoners of war. To ensure that the health of the captives is not affected, the Detaining Power must provide sufficient clothing adapted to the climate where the prisoners are interned, such as sweaters, hats, and gloves in cold climates.[122] Prisoners of war generally require at least two sets of clothing and sleepwear to enable a change when one set is being washed or repaired.[123]

---

116. *See, e.g.*, NATIONAL DEFENCE HEADQUARTERS (CANADA), B-GJ-005-110/FP-020, PRISONER OF WAR HANDLING: DETAINEES AND INTERROGATION & TACTICAL QUESTIONING IN INTERNATIONAL OPERATIONS, JOINT DOCTRINE MANUAL ¶ 3F-10 (2004): "Ration scales are to be tailored, as far as is possible, to the national dietary requirements of PW, bearing in mind that a diet which is totally suited to PW from one nation may be inadequate or unsuitable for those from a different nation. There may also be religious or ethnic dietary requirements for which, whenever possible, provision should be made." *See also* 2020 GC III COMMENTARY, *supra* note 3, commentary on Article 26, ¶ 2121.

117. Third Geneva Convention, *supra* note 6, art. 26(4).

118. 2020 GC III COMMENTARY, *supra* note 3, commentary on Article 26, ¶ 2131.

119. *See, e.g.*, WHO Framework Convention on Tobacco Control, May 21, 2003, 2302 U.N.T.S. 166.

120. Third Geneva Convention, *supra* note 6, art. 28.

121. 2020 GC III COMMENTARY, *supra* note 3, commentary on Article 28, ¶ 2164.

122. *Id.*, commentary on Article 27, ¶ 2149.

123. *Id.*, ¶ 2148.

The type of clothing provided must also be in line with the fundamental protections described above, and in particular the obligation to respect the person's honor. Clothing must be adapted, for example, to the prisoner's age, gender, and religious and cultural background.[124] Prisoners of war may not be compelled to wear the uniform of their enemies or other clothing that may negatively impact their sense of allegiance or honor.[125]

E. Medical Care and Sanitation

Every prisoner of war camp must have its own infirmary to tend to the healthcare needs of prisoners. Prisoners of war requiring medical attention are entitled to receive it at the cost of the Detaining Power.[126] Meeting the healthcare needs of prisoners may require, in some circumstances, transferring prisoners with health conditions that warrant specialized treatment to a military or civilian medical unit where such treatment can be given.[127] All medical care must comply with the applicable standards of medical ethics, which include the duty to provide medical care impartially/without adverse distinction. Such standards also address the principle of voluntary and informed consent.[128]

The Third Geneva Convention also refers to the use of isolation wards for "contagious or mental disease." Any decision to use isolation wards must be taken exclusively on the advice of a medical doctor or other appropriately qualified health professional and should only be for as long as necessary. The reference in Article 30 to isolating people with mental health conditions "if necessary" should be read in line with the other obligations of the Detaining Power, including the fundamental protections mentioned above.[129] Imposing isolation on prisoners of war with mental health conditions should be avoided as it may aggravate their condition, be inconsistent with the prohibition on adverse distinction, and may amount to torture or other ill-treatment as it can lead to psychotic symptoms and/or significant functional impairments, self-harm, or even suicide.[130]

In order to prevent illness, the Third Geneva Convention also provides an obligation on Detaining Powers to take all necessary sanitary measures to ensure the cleanliness and "healthfulness" of camps and to prevent the spread of infectious

---

124. *Id.*, ¶ 2151.

125. *Id.*

126. Third Geneva Convention, *supra* note 6, art. 15.

127. *Id.*, art. 30(2).

128. 2020 GC III COMMENTARY, *supra* note 3, commentary on Article 30, ¶¶ 2232 and 2245.

129. *Id.*, ¶ 2242.

130. *Id.*, ¶ 2243.

diseases.¹³¹ Upholding hygienic standards and reducing the risk of disease transmission within places of detention is of immediate practical value to the Detaining Power, as it reduces the risk of transmission to personnel of the Detaining Power, such as guards, as well as to the neighboring community.¹³²

F. Recreation and Religion

Maintaining the health of a prisoner of war and respect for their person requires attention not only to their physical but also their mental well-being. One of the ways that this is acknowledged and addressed in the Third Geneva Convention is through the requirement of allowing prisoners "complete latitude" to exercise their religious duties (or in the equally authentic French, *l'exercise de leur religion*), provided this complies with any disciplinary routine prescribed by the military authorities. The Third Geneva Convention also requires the Detaining Power to encourage "the practice of intellectual, educational, and recreational pursuits, sports and games amongst prisoners."¹³³

Allowing prisoners to practice their faith is an important way through which the Detaining Power can enable prisoners of war to process their current situation and the hardships that come with it.¹³⁴ It is also consistent both with the obligations to treat them humanely and to respect their persons and honor. Detaining Powers must take into account religious practices in many aspects of camp life, such as setting up the place of internment (e.g., providing facilities for washing), food preparation (consistent with religious precepts and taboos), and work schedules (e.g., allowing for prayer time).¹³⁵ Various armed forces employ cultural advisers to help them better understand the environment in which they operate.¹³⁶

In relation to recreational activities, Article 38 specifies that the individual preferences of each prisoner must be respected to ensure that the provision is not used as a pretext to oblige prisoners to take part in ideological or political propaganda under the guise of "recreation."¹³⁷ The Detaining Power must provide prisoners with adequate premises and the necessary equipment for this purpose, including sufficient open spaces for physical exercise.

---

131. Third Geneva Convention, *supra* note 6, art. 29(1).

132. 2020 GC III COMMENTARY, *supra* note 3, commentary on Article 29, ¶ 2185.

133. Third Geneva Convention, *supra* note 6, arts. 34 and 38.

134. 2020 GC III COMMENTARY, *supra* note 3, commentary on Article 34, ¶ 2359.

135. *Id.*, ¶ 2365.

136. *Id.*, ¶ 2366.

137. *See* Third Geneva Convention, *supra* note 6, art. 16. *See also* 2020 GC III COMMENTARY, *supra* note 3, commentary on Article 14, ¶ 1671.

Educational opportunities are particularly important for prisoners of war who are interned for long periods of time. In some international armed conflicts, the ICRC has been allowed to supply notebooks and writing materials, textbooks, and other books, subject to the Detaining Power's approval, as well as sporting equipment.[138]

G. Relations with the Exterior

Maintaining connection with the outside world is another vital means of maintaining morale for prisoners of war, as well as serving as a check on their treatment and preventing disappearances.

Article 70 provides that a prisoner of war's capture, sickness, hospitalization, and transfer be communicated at the earliest possible moment to the prisoner's family and also to the Central Prisoners of War Agency (now known as the Central Tracing Agency, which is operated by the ICRC). This is facilitated by enabling prisoners of war to write "capture cards," which are forwarded as rapidly as possible to the Central Tracing Agency and to the family of the prisoner of war.

For more substantive communications, Article 71 provides for the right of prisoners of war to send and receive letters and cards. The importance of being connected to families was well understood at the time of drafting the Third Geneva Convention. As expressed by the ICRC shortly after the adoption of the Geneva Conventions, "[e]ven the most favourable living conditions do not compensate, in the eyes of the prisoner, for absence of news or slowness in mail delivery."[139] In practice, where postal services are not functioning, the ICRC regularly facilitates correspondence through its "Red Cross messages" service, enabling families to connect and share content of a strictly private and familial nature.[140]

Article 71 also recognizes that in circumstances where prisoners of war have been without news for a long period of time, or who are unable to receive news from their next of kin or by the ordinary postal route, they "shall be permitted to send telegrams." Clearly this is a product of the time of drafting, but the purpose behind this provision should be respected with the use of more modern means of communication, such as email, telephone, or video calls.[141]

---

138. *See* 2020 GC III COMMENTARY, *supra* note 3, commentary on Article 34, ¶ 2377 and commentary on Article 38, ¶ 2461.

139. 2 ICRC, THE GENEVA CONVENTIONS OF AUGUST 12, 1949: ANALYSIS FOR THE USE OF NATIONAL RED CROSS SOCIETIES 27 (1950).

140. For more information, *see* 2020 GC III COMMENTARY, *supra* note 3, commentary on Article 71, ¶ 3215.

141. *Id.*, ¶ 3218.

Another additional protection provided for prisoners of war is that they may receive relief shipments. Detaining Powers cannot charge "import, customs or other dues" or "postal dues" on such shipments.[142]

H. The Use of Prisoners of War's Labor

The ability to use a prisoner of war's labor is of potential benefit to the Detaining Power. The framework provided for prisoner of war labor also supports the well-being of the prisoners, by maintaining them in a good state of physical and mental health. The absence of meaningful activity, coupled with isolation and uncertainty about the future, can lead to boredom and impact prisoners' mental and physical well-being.[143]

Prisoners of war may only be engaged in certain types of work and may not be engaged in work that is unhealthy or dangerous unless they volunteer. In addition, for permitted labor, certain health and safety measures are expressly prescribed, such as the requirement of suitable accommodation, food, clothing, and equipment for the tasks that the prisoners are employed in (which may not be inferior to the conditions enjoyed by nationals of the Detaining Power employed in similar work). In relation to the duration of labor, three essential safeguards are provided for: the duration of labor must not be excessive;[144] the maximum duration of work is fixed at the maximum allowed under the domestic legislation of the Detaining Power for civilians in the same work; and the time taken to travel to and from the place of work must be counted within the working hours. Detaining Powers must allow for a minimum of one hour's rest in the middle of the day, a day of rest per week, and a period of eight consecutive rest days every year.[145]

Article 62 provides that prisoners of war must be paid "a fair working rate of pay by the detaining authorities direct" that shall be fixed by the authorities "but shall at no time be less than one-fourth of one Swiss franc for a full working day."[146] Even factoring in the Swiss consumer price index, 0.25 Swiss francs in 1949 corresponded to just 1.25 Swiss francs in 2019.[147] In many contexts around the globe, this amount would not be considered a fair working rate, and accordingly the Detaining Power must consider in good faith an adequate increase.[148]

---

142. Third Geneva Convention, *supra* note 6, art. 74.

143. 2020 GC III COMMENTARY, *supra* note 3, commentary on Article 49, ¶ 2675.

144. *Id.*, commentary on Article 53, ¶ 2762.

145. Third Geneva Convention, *supra* note 6, art. 53.

146. 2020 GC III COMMENTARY, *supra* note 3, commentary on Article 62, ¶ 2952.

147. *See* Indice des prix à la consommation: La calculatrice du renchérissement, http://www.portal-stat.admin.ch/lik_rechner/f/lik_rechner.htm (last visited Oct. 15, 2021).

148. For further discussion on fixing a fair rate, *see* 2020 GC III COMMENTARY, *supra* note 3, commentary on Article 62, ¶¶ 2952–55.

I. Relations with the Detaining Authorities

The Third Geneva Convention contains three categories of provisions regarding the relationship between prisoners of war and the detaining authorities. These cover the circumstances where the prisoners have complaints about their conditions of captivity; the mechanism to facilitate communication between prisoners and the detaining authorities (namely, through prisoners' representatives); and the circumstances where the detaining authorities have complaints about the conduct of detainees (penal and disciplinary sanctions).

Prisoners of war have a right to "make known" their requests about the conditions of their captivity to the prison authorities, as well as to the prisoners' representative or even directly to the Protecting Powers. They cannot be punished for making these requests. In practice, complaints are often communicated to the ICRC through channels including confidential interviews with ICRC delegates pursuant to Article 126. The role of the ICRC in this regard is important given the absence of Protecting Powers in most international armed conflicts since 1949.[149]

Prisoners' representatives represent prisoners before military authorities, Protecting Powers, the ICRC, and any other organization that might assist them. They work for the well-being of prisoners of war and carry out a number of defined other duties in the Third Geneva Convention.[150] The Detaining Power must support prisoners' representatives in this role, by affording them "all material facilities,"[151] the ability to appoint advisers or assistants,[152] an exemption from work if it makes fulfilling their duties difficult,[153] and the freedom to move about the camp or visit other locations to fulfill their duties.[154]

In some circumstances, there may be cause for a Detaining Power to pursue disciplinary or judicial proceedings against a prisoner of war. Underlying the framework for disciplinary and judicial proceedings is the principle of assimilation, according to which prisoners of war are "subject to the laws, regulations and orders in force in relation to the armed forces of the Detaining Power."[155]

---

149. 2020 GC III COMMENTARY, *supra* note 3, commentary on Article 78, ¶ 3433. On the absence of Protecting Powers in general, *see also id.*, Introduction, ¶¶ 49–51.

150. *Id.*, commentary on Article 80, sec. D.

151. *Id.*, ¶ 3528.

152. *See id.*, ¶ 3525 in relation to the different usage of the terms "adviser" and "assistant."

153. Prisoners' representatives and their assistants/advisers are paid out of canteen funds, unless there are not such funds available, in which case they are paid by the detaining authorities; 2020 GC III COMMENTARY, *supra* note 3, commentary on Article 62, ¶ 2944.

154. Third Geneva Convention, *supra* note 6, art. 81(2).

155. *Id.*, art. 82(1). For a detailed discussion on the principle of assimilation in relation to disciplinary or judicial proceedings, *see* 2020 GC III COMMENTARY, *supra* note 3, commentary on Article 82, sec. C. For a wider discussion of the principle of assimilation in the Third Geneva Convention, *see id.*, Introduction, sec. A.3.c.

In deciding whether to proceed with disciplinary or judicial proceedings, Detaining Powers are required to apply "the greatest leniency," recognizing that prisoners owe no allegiance to the Detaining Power.[156] The only four types of disciplinary punishments allowed for are fines, discontinuance of privileges, fatigue duties, and confinement.[157] More arduous labor may not be imposed as a disciplinary punishment.[158]

If a prisoner of war is to face prosecution for an offense, they can only be tried in a court that offers the essential guarantees of independence and impartiality, and in particular the procedure of which affords the accused the necessary rights and means of defense.[159] While the principle of assimilation will ordinarily ensure the application of a robust framework for judicial guarantees and due process, the Third Geneva Convention expressly sets out a number of protections, including the prohibition against double jeopardy, the principle of legality (the prisoner may not be tried or sentenced for an act which was not prohibited by the law of the Detaining Power or by international law at the time the act was committed), and the right to present one's own defense with the assistance of a qualified advocate or counsel.[160] In the event that the standards provided for in the domestic law of the Detaining Power fall short of these minimum standards, the rules of the Convention prevail and prisoners of war must benefit from the protections it offers.

IV. CONCLUSION

The Third Geneva Convention provides a robust framework for the protection of prisoners of war, whereby prisoners of war must be treated humanely, their persons and honor are to be respected, they must be treated equally, and discrimination is prohibited.

The articulation of these principles within the Third Geneva Convention is detailed. Learning from the experiences of previous conflicts, and in particular World War II, the drafters recognized the essential application of the principles that are needed to ensure humane treatment and respect for prisoners' persons and honor. The drafters understood from experience what was essential to keep prisoners of war in good mental and physical health. They also understood the realities of providing for the care of the prisoners in the midst of active hostilities. The 143 articles provide a rich framework of realistic but essential protections

---

156. Third Geneva Convention, *supra* note 6, art. 83.

157. *Id.*, art. 89.

158. 2020 GC III COMMENTARY, *supra* note 3, commentary on Article 51, ¶¶ 2737–38

159. Third Geneva Convention, *supra* note 6, art. 84(2); *see also* art. 105.

160. *Id.*, arts. 86 and 99.

covering all aspects of a prisoner's capture until their final release and repatriation. Some articles refer to outdated technologies or understandings of science, but after many decades of visiting prisoners of war, the ICRC is firmly convinced that the provisions remain as relevant and important for prisoners of war today as they were when first drafted.

The updated Commentary on the Third Geneva Convention is the third of the series of updated Commentaries to be published by the ICRC. Research continues with respect to the protection of civilians in times of war (covered by the Fourth Geneva Convention), on which an updated commentary will be published in the coming years, as will updated commentaries on Additional Protocols I and II.

16

ICRC Perspectives on the Interpretation of the Third Geneva Convention More Than Seventy Years after Its Adoption

JEAN-MARIE HENCKAERTS, KUBO MAČÁK, MIKHAIL ORKIN, AND ELLEN POLICINSKI*

1. INTRODUCTION

The International Committee of the Red Cross (ICRC) is an impartial, neutral, and independent organization whose exclusively humanitarian mission is to protect the lives and dignity of victims of armed conflict and other situations of violence and to provide them with assistance. The ICRC also endeavors to prevent suffering by promoting and strengthening international humanitarian law (IHL).[1] Fulfilling this mission implies, inter alia, working for the faithful application of

---

*. Jean-Marie Henckaerts is head of the unit charged with updating the Commentaries on the 1949 Geneva Conventions and their 1977 Additional Protocols. Kubo Mačák, Mikhail Orkin, and Ellen Policinski are legal advisers within this unit. The authors wish to thank their colleagues Yvette Issar and Matt Pollard for their valuable comments and suggestions and Stella Nasirumbi and Serhat Öztürk for their research assistance. Parts of this chapter are based on Jean-Marie Henckaerts & Elvina Pothelet, *The Interpretation of IHL Treaties: Subsequent Practice and Other Salient Issues*, in LAW-MAKING AND LEGITIMACY IN INTERNATIONAL HUMANITARIAN LAW 150–69 (Heike Krieger ed., 2021) and have been used with the agreement of the authors. The opinions expressed in this chapter do not necessarily reflect those of the ICRC or its Legal Division but are based on the authors' experience updating the Commentaries.

1. International Committee of the Red Cross, Mission Statement, www.icrc.org/en/mandate-and-mission (last visited Oct. 19, 2021).

IHL and for its clarification, dissemination, and development.[2] To this end, the ICRC has been engaged for over 150 years in efforts to clarify, disseminate, and develop IHL.

In the context of its work to clarify and disseminate IHL, the ICRC published "commentaries" on the four Geneva Conventions in the 1950s.[3] Treaty commentaries are a specific type of legal scholarship.[4] They differ from other scholarly publications such as monographs or law review articles in that they aim to give detailed insights into the interpretation of a given treaty by the States Parties, rather than setting out an author's opinion on how the law applies (or should apply) in a given area. They are meant to be consulted in the same way as a dictionary or an encyclopedia, as a starting point for understanding how a treaty provision should be interpreted and applied.

The original Commentaries aimed to clarify the scope and content of the then newly adopted Conventions, in particular in the light of the preparatory work and previous experience in armed conflicts, especially during World War II. The so-called Pictet Commentaries (named after the ICRC lawyer, Jean Pictet, under whose general editorship the Commentaries were drafted) became, over time, a key reference for interpreting the Conventions, frequently cited by military lawyers, international and national courts, and scholars around the world.[5] However, the original Commentaries were drafted in the 1950s and do not reflect the developments in law and practice since then.

---

2. Statutes of the International Red Cross and Red Crescent Movement, art. 5(2)(c) and (g), adopted by the 25th International Conference of the Red Cross at Geneva in 1986, amended in 1995 and 2006.

3. *See* COMMENTARY ON THE GENEVA CONVENTIONS OF 12 AUGUST 1949, vols. I–IV (Jean S. Pictet ed., 1952–1960).

4. *See further* Christian Djeffal, *Commentaries on the Law of Treaties: A Review Essay Reflecting on the Genre of Commentaries*, 24 EUROPEAN JOURNAL OF INTERNATIONAL LAW 1223 (2013); Jean-Marie Henckaerts, *The Impact of Commentaries on Compliance with International Law*, *in* 115 PROCEEDINGS OF THE ASIL ANNUAL MEETING 55–58 (2021).

5. For references to the Pictet Commentaries by scholars and international courts, *see*, *e.g.*, Theodor Meron, *The West Bank and International Humanitarian Law on the Eve of the Fiftieth Anniversary of the Six-Day War: Notes and Comments*, 111 AMERICAN JOURNAL OF INTERNATIONAL LAW 357, 364 (2017); Fionnuala Ni Aolain, *Hamdan and Common Article 3: Did the Supreme Court Get It Right?*, 91 MINNESOTA LAW REVIEW 1523, 1529; Prosecutor v. Tadić, Case No. IT-94-1-A, Appeals Chamber Judgment, ¶ 93 (Int'l Crim. Trib. for the former Yugoslavia July 15, 1999). On the status of the Pictet Commentaries in general, *see*, *e.g.*, W. Hays Parks, *Pictet's Commentaries*, *in* STUDIES AND ESSAYS ON INTERNATIONAL HUMANITARIAN LAW AND RED CROSS PRINCIPLES IN HONOUR OF JEAN PICTET 495, 495–97 (Christophe Swinarski ed., 1984); and Julia Grignon, *Les Commentaires des Conventions de Genève rédigés sous la direction de Jean Pictet*, in HOMMAGE À JEAN PICTET PAR LE CONCOURS DE DROIT INTERNATIONAL HUMANITAIRE JEAN-PICTET 127–50 (Julia Grignon ed., 2016).

Against this background, in 2011 the ICRC embarked on a major project to update the Commentaries on the Geneva Conventions of 1949.[6] By updating them, the ICRC intends to provide current interpretations and guidance that take into account the issues and challenges encountered in armed conflicts in recent decades, as well as developments in technology and in international and national law.

The nature and status of the original and updated Commentaries are the same. They seek to provide a scholarly, and at the same time practical, contribution to clarifying the Conventions; they do not amount to an "authentic" interpretation because only the States party to an international treaty are qualified to give an authentic interpretation of that treaty.[7] Nonetheless, they are the "official" ICRC Commentaries on the Geneva Conventions as they present the ICRC's interpretation of the law while indicating main diverging views, as well as issues requiring further discussion and clarification.[8] As noted by ICRC President Peter Maurer in the forewords to the Commentaries, the ICRC will duly take the updated Commentaries into account in its daily work, while being aware that practice and interpretations may evolve still further.[9]

The updated Commentaries set out to honor and continue the legacy of the original Commentaries. To achieve their purpose, the updated Commentaries follow a methodology of interpretation based on the 1969 Vienna Convention on

---

6. The project also includes an update of the Commentaries on the Additional Protocols of 1977. See COMMENTARY ON THE ADDITIONAL PROTOCOLS OF 8 JUNE 1977 TO THE GENEVA CONVENTIONS OF 12 AUGUST 1949 (Yves Sandoz, Christophe Swinarski & Bruno Zimmermann eds., 1987) [hereinafter COMMENTARY ON THE 1977 ADDITIONAL PROTOCOLS]. The ICRC Commentary on the 2005 Additional Protocol III was published in 2007 and does not yet require updating. *See* Jean-François Quéguiner, *Commentary on the Protocol Additional to the Geneva Conventions of 12 August 1949, and Relating to the Adoption of an Additional Distinctive Emblem (Protocol III)*, 89 INTERNATIONAL REVIEW OF THE RED CROSS 175 (2007).

7. This was explicitly stated in the forewords to each of the original Commentaries, *supra* note 3. The notice was reformulated in the updated Commentaries but remains equally valid: *see* INTERNATIONAL COMMITTEE OF THE RED CROSS, COMMENTARY ON THE FIRST GENEVA CONVENTION: CONVENTION (I) FOR THE AMELIORATION OF THE CONDITION OF THE WOUNDED AND SICK IN THE ARMED FORCES IN THE FIELD, ¶¶ 1–99 (2016) [hereinafter 2016 GC I COMMENTARY] INTERNATIONAL COMMITTEE OF THE RED CROSS, COMMENTARY ON THE SECOND GENEVA CONVENTION: CONVENTION (II) FOR THE AMELIORATION OF THE CONDITION OF THE WOUNDED, SICK AND SHIPWRECKED MEMBERS OF ARMED FORCES AT SEA, ¶¶ 1–121 (2017) [hereinafter 2017 GC II COMMENTARY]; INTERNATIONAL COMMITTEE OF THE RED CROSS, COMMENTARY ON THE THIRD GENEVA CONVENTION: CONVENTION (III) RELATIVE TO THE TREATMENT OF PRISONERS OF WAR, ¶¶ 1–131 (2020) [hereinafter 2020 GC III COMMENTARY].

8. For examples of issues requiring further clarification, *see* ICRC, 2020 GC III COMMENTARY, *supra* note 7, commentary on art. 2, ¶ 289, commentary on art. 3, ¶ 497, and commentary on art. 42, ¶ 2554.

9. *See* 2020 GC III COMMENTARY, *supra* note 7, at xii. *See also* 2016 GC I COMMENTARY, *supra* note 7, at xii; and 2017 GC II COMMENTARY, *supra* note 7, at xii.

the Law of Treaties [hereinafter "Vienna Convention"], in-depth research, and a rigorous review process. The methodology is further addressed in Parts II–VII.

With regard to the review process, the updated Commentaries go several steps further than the original versions. First, the updated Commentaries were not drafted by ICRC lawyers alone but involved more than a dozen external contributors recognized for their expertise in IHL. For the Third Geneva Convention, the external contributors drafted more than a third of the commentaries (57 out of 143 articles). They also reviewed the drafts produced by ICRC lawyers as part of their role in the reading committee.[10] Additionally, a peer review group composed of some fifty experts from around the world, roughly half military and half academic, reviewed the drafts and gave critical and constructive feedback based on their regional and/or professional perspectives.[11] Experts from fields as diverse as health, telecommunications, and private international law were also consulted.[12] Finally, an editorial committee of renowned experts, comprising senior ICRC lawyers and external experts reflecting governmental, military, and academic backgrounds, discussed the peer reviewers' feedback and reviewed the final drafts.[13] The original Commentaries did not undergo such an extensive consultation with an unprecedented level of external involvement.

The process of treaty interpretation does not come to a halt when a commentary on a treaty is published. Indeed, legal interpretation in international law is a continuous, iterative, and pluralistic process that bestows particular weight on the legal views expressed by States.[14] Scholars have noted that State responses to IHL scholarship contribute to the "pluralistic process of formation and development" of IHL[15] and that they help "ensure that the law remains realistic and that the

---

10. For the composition of the reading committee, *see* 2020 GC III COMMENTARY, *supra* note 7, Acknowledgements, at xvi–xvii.

11. For the list of peer reviewers, *see id.*, at xvii–xxii.

12. *See id.*, at xxiv. This was relevant, for example, with respect to the WHO Framework Convention on Tobacco Control, May 21, 2003 2302 U.N.T.S. 166 (2020 GC III COMMENTARY, *supra* note 7, commentary on art. 26, ¶ 2131); International Telecommunications Union, *Final Acts of the World Conference on International Telecommunications* (2012), http://www.itu.int/en/wcit-12/Documents/final-acts-wcit-12.pdf (*see* 2020 GC III COMMENTARY, *supra* note 7, commentary on art. 74, sec. G.2); Hague Convention on the Conflicts of Laws Relating to the Form of Testamentary Dispositions, Oct. 5, 1961 (*see* 2020 GC III COMMENTARY, *supra* note 7, commentary on art. 120, ¶ 4543).

13. For the composition of the editorial committee, *see* 2020 GC III COMMENTARY, *supra* note 7, Acknowledgements, at xv.

14. *See generally* INTERPRETATION IN INTERNATIONAL LAW (Andrea Bianchi, Daniel Peat & Matthew Windsor eds., 2015).

15. Michael N. Schmitt & Sean Watts, *The Decline of International Humanitarian Law Opinio Juris and the Law of Cyber Warfare*, 50 TEXAS INTERNATIONAL LAW JOURNAL 189, 209 (2015).

law on the books is the same as that applied on the ground."¹⁶ We welcome such contributions and further engagement with practitioners as well as academics on the subject matter covered by the Commentaries.

This chapter aims to share the ICRC's experience and insights in applying the treaty interpretation methodology set out in the Vienna Convention to the interpretation of the Geneva Conventions.[17] It draws on the work accomplished in updating the first three Commentaries, focusing on the Third Geneva Convention. It explains how the rules for treaty interpretation have been applied in this process.

Part II provides an overview of the Vienna Convention's framework for treaty interpretation. Part III looks at the requirement that an interpretation be carried out in good faith. In Part IV, we take a closer look at the concepts of the "ordinary meaning of terms" and the "object and purpose" of a Convention. Part V examines the impact of subsequent developments in practice and law on the interpretation of the Geneva Conventions. Part VI surveys the supplementary means of interpretation set out in the Vienna Convention. Part VII focuses on the particular issues of treaties authenticated in two or more languages, as is the case for the Geneva Conventions. Finally, Part VIII examines how the Commentaries have drawn a distinction between the law as it stands today (*lex lata*) and the law as it should be (*de lege ferenda*). Part IX contains a short conclusion.

II. THE VIENNA CONVENTION INTERPRETIVE FRAMEWORK: A FULL-COURSE MENU

The rules governing treaty interpretation are codified in Articles 31–33 of the Vienna Convention and are accepted as reflecting customary international law.[18]

The Vienna Convention interpretive framework consists of a general rule expressed in Article 31 and a provision on supplementary means of interpretation in Article 32. It further includes a specific provision in Article 33 related to the interpretation of treaties authenticated in two or more languages, as is the case for the Geneva Conventions.

---

16. Sandesh Sivakumaran, *Making and Shaping the Law of Armed Conflict*, 71 CURRENT LEGAL PROBLEMS 119, 157 (2018).

17. Vienna Convention on the Law of Treaties, arts. 31–33, May 23, 1969, 1155 U.N.T.S. 331.

18. *See, e.g.*, Territorial Dispute (Libyan Arab Jamahiriya v. Chad), 1994, Judgment, I.C.J. 6, ¶ 21 (Feb. 3); Kasikili/Sedudu Island (Botswana v. Namibia), Judgment, 1999 I.C.J. 1045, ¶¶ 18–20 (Dec. 13); Application of the Convention on the Prevention and Punishment of the Crime of Genocide (Bosn. & Herz. v. Serb. & Montenegro), Judgment, 2007 I.C.J. 43, ¶ 160 (Feb. 26); Question of the Delimitation of the Continental Shelf between Nicaragua and Colombia beyond 200 Nautical Miles from the Nicaraguan Coast (Nicaragua v. Colombia), Judgment, 2016 I.C.J. 100, ¶ 33 (Mar. 17); International Law Commission, *Report on the Work of Its Seventieth Session*, U.N. Doc. A/73/10, chap. IV, conclusion 2.1, at 13 (2018) [hereinafter ILC, *Report on the Work of Its Seventieth Session*]; RICHARD K. GARDINER, TREATY INTERPRETATION 13–14 (2nd ed. 2015); ANTHONY AUST, MODERN TREATY LAW AND PRACTICE 207 (3rd ed. 2013).

Article 31 of the Vienna Convention provides that a treaty must be interpreted "in good faith in accordance with the ordinary meaning to be given to the terms of the treaty in their context and in the light of its object and purpose." This rule of interpretation has different elements, and the interpretation itself must combine all the elements.[19]

In other words, the Vienna Convention does not offer a choice of different—let alone conflicting—methods. Rather, it contains one general rule of interpretation in Article 31, complemented by the supplementary means of interpretation in Article 32 and by the rules of Article 33 applicable to treaties authenticated in multiple languages. Any interpretation has to fit the Vienna Convention framework and "tick all the boxes," that is to say, the interpreter has to go through all the courses on the Vienna Convention menu. It is not a "pick-and-choose" menu; it is a set menu of which no course may be skipped. It is also a coherent menu that combines different, not conflicting, elements that lead to the most informed interpretation because it objectively takes all relevant information into account. Interpreters have to be clear about *what* they are doing and *when* and make sure that they follow *all* of the steps required by the Vienna Convention. That is the approach we have taken in updating the Commentaries on the Geneva Conventions. All the elements in Articles 31–33 of the Vienna Convention have served as an interpretive compass throughout our work. The exact combination of elements and the emphasis on one or other element depend on the provision and issue at hand[20] but always need to be applied in good faith (see further Part III).

To illustrate this approach, consider the unsettled question of whether and how the transports used for the non-medical evacuation of prisoners of war may be marked to ensure the prisoners' safety. The interpretive approach used to clarify the relevant provisions reflects a careful application of the Vienna Convention methodology in its entirety and can be unpicked as follows. The starting point for the Commentary is the text of Article 20(2) of the Third Geneva Convention, which prescribes that the Detaining Power must take "all suitable precautions" to

---

19. *See* International Law Commission, *Documents of the Second Part of the Seventeenth Session and of the Eighteenth Session Including the Reports of the Commission to the General Assembly*, reprinted in [1966] 2 YEARBOOK OF THE INTERNATIONAL LAW COMMISSION 1966, U.N. Doc. A/CN.4/SER.A/1966/Add.1 [hereinafter ILC, *Documents of the Second Part of the Seventeenth Session and of the Eighteenth Session*]; ILC, *Report on the Work of Its Seventieth Session, supra* note 18, conclusion 2.5 (2018); GARDINER, *supra* note 18, at 31–32; AUST, *supra* note 18, at 205.

20. For a similar (although not identical) view, *see* ULF LINDERFALK, ON THE INTERPRETATION OF TREATIES: MODERN INTERNATIONAL LAW AS EXPRESSED IN THE 1969 VIENNA CONVENTION ON THE LAW OF TREATIES 3–6, 373–75 (2007): "[T]he regime laid down in Vienna Convention Articles 31–33 amounts to a system of rules, but the system would still have to be described as to some extent open-textured. The rules provide a framework for the interpretation process; but within this framework, the political judgment of each individual applier is still allowed to play a part (although, of course, not the leading part . . .)." (at 374). *See also* Ulf Linderfalk, *Is Treaty Interpretation an Art or a Science? International Law and Rational Decision Making*, 26 EUROPEAN JOURNAL OF INTERNATIONAL LAW 169 (2015).

ensure the safety of prisoners of war during evacuation.[21] The Commentary then situates this provision within its normative context, which provides some important limitations on the markings available for this purpose. This context includes, first, Articles 35 and 39 of the First Geneva Convention, according to which the distinctive emblem may be displayed on military medical "equipment"—a term that includes military medical transports—but not on non-medical equipment.[22] This means that the emblem may be displayed on transports used to evacuate wounded and sick prisoners from the combat zone but not on transports used for non-medical evacuations.[23] The context also includes Article 23(4) of the Third Geneva Convention, according to which "[o]nly prisoner of war camps" may be marked by the letters PW or PG, which therefore also precludes the use of these markings on non-medical transports for prisoners.[24] It is the teleological step of the analysis that reveals a pragmatic solution endorsed by the Commentary: "If it is considered that marking the transport *in some other manner* will reduce the likelihood of it being attacked and better ensure the safety of the prisoners, this may, and should, be done."[25] The Commentary thus identifies a practical solution that respects both the black letter of the Convention and its overall object and purpose.[26] This is in line with the framework of the Vienna Convention, which

---

21. 2020 GC III COMMENTARY, *supra* note 7, commentary on art. 20, ¶ 1901.

22. *See* 2016 GC I COMMENTARY, *supra* note 7, commentary on art. 35, ¶ 2403 and commentary on art. 39, ¶¶ 2576–77.

23. 2020 GC III COMMENTARY, *supra* note 7, commentary on art. 20, ¶ 1903, n. 36.

24. *Id.*, commentary on art. 20, ¶ 1903 and commentary on art. 23, ¶ 2056. A number of military manuals similarly emphasize that these letters must not be used for any other purpose than marking prisoner-of-war camps: *see, e.g.*, AUSTRALIAN DEFENCE HEADQUARTERS, ADDP 06.4, LAW OF ARMED CONFLICT ¶ 10.26 (2006); NORWEGIAN MINISTRY OF DEFENCE, MANUAL OF THE LAW OF ARMED CONFLICT ¶ 6.62 (2013); UNITED KINGDOM MINISTRY OF DEFENCE, THE MANUAL OF THE LAW OF ARMED CONFLICT ¶ 8.39 (2004); OFFICE OF THE GENERAL COUNSEL, U.S. DEPARTMENT OF DEFENSE, LAW OF WAR MANUAL § 5.24.3 (rev. ed., Dec. 2016); U.S. NAVY, U.S. MARINE CORPS & U.S. COAST GUARD, FM 6-27/MCTP 11-10C, THE COMMANDER'S HANDBOOK ON THE LAW OF LAND WARFARE § 2-166 (2019). The U.K. manual, however, also notes that prisoners' transports "should be marked with large letters 'PW' or 'PG' so that they are not unwittingly attacked"; UNITED KINGDOM MINISTRY OF DEFENCE, THE MANUAL OF THE LAW OF ARMED CONFLICT ¶ 8.35(c) (2004). Finally, the New Zealand manual opts for what could be described as a middle ground, when it notes that transports should be "marked 'PW' *or with another agreed emblem* so that they are not mistakenly attacked by the opposing force"; 4 NEW ZEALAND DEFENCE FORCE, DM 69, MANUAL OF ARMED FORCES LAW: LAW OF ARMED CONFLICT ¶ 12.7.3(F) (2nd ed., 2019) (emphasis added).

25. 2020 GC III COMMENTARY, *supra* note 7, commentary on art. 20, ¶ 1903 (emphasis added).

26. *See id.*, Introduction, ¶ 89, noting that "[t]he overall object and purpose of the Third Convention is to ensure that prisoners of war are humanely treated at all times, while allowing belligerents to intern captured enemy combatants to prevent them from returning to the battlefield." *See also infra*, Part IV, for a discussion on identifying the object and purpose of the Geneva Conventions.

reflects both the "literal" approach (where the ordinary meaning of the text is the main factor of interpretation) and the "teleological" approach (where the object and purpose of the treaty is the main factor) to ascertain the parties' intention accurately.[27]

III. GOOD FAITH

In its work to update the Commentaries, the ICRC was guided by the principle of good faith, as required by the Vienna Convention.[28] Appearing at the very beginning of Article 31,[29] good faith can be considered to be "at the centre of the application of the General Rule [in Article 31 of the Vienna Convention]"[30] and "prevails throughout the process of interpretation."[31] Good faith is said to have several distinct meanings in international law.[32] For the purposes of treaty interpretation, it has two main prongs. The first prong of the good faith in Article 31 can be expressed as a certain subjective quality, specifically that the interpreter undertakes their task "honestly, without fraud or intent to deceive,"[33] or in the *absence* of bad faith.

Second, the instruction in Article 31 that a treaty be interpreted "in good faith" relates not only to the subjective element of the interpreting entity but also more directly to the task of interpretation itself, more specifically to "*how* the task of interpretation is to be undertaken."[34] The second prong of good faith[35] under Article

---

27. ILC, *Documents of the Second Part of the Seventeenth Session and of the Eighteenth Session*, supra note 19, at 221, ¶ 12; GARDINER, supra note 18, at 8; MARK E. VILLIGER, COMMENTARY ON THE 1969 VIENNA CONVENTION ON THE LAW OF TREATIES 427–28 (2009).

28. On good faith in international law generally, *see further* ROBERT KOLB, GOOD FAITH IN INTERNATIONAL LAW (2017); and Ulf Linderfalk, *What Are the Functions of the General Principles? Good Faith and International Legal Pragmatics* 78 ZEITSCHRIFT FÜR AUSLÄNDISCHES ÖFFENTLICHES RECHT UND VÖLKERRECHT 1, 9 (2018).

29. For more discussion specifically on good faith in the interpretation of treaties, *see* VILLIGER, supra note 27, at 425–26; GARDINER, supra note 18, at 167–81; Jean-Marc Sorel & Valérie Boré Eveno, *Article 31 Convention of 1969*, in 1 THE VIENNA CONVENTIONS ON THE LAW OF TREATIES: A COMMENTARY 817–18 (Olivier Corten & Pierre Klein eds., 2011); ROBERT KOLB, GOOD FAITH IN INTERNATIONAL LAW 62–67 (2017).

30. VILLIGER, *supra* note 27, at 426.

31. *Id.*, at 426.

32. For a detailed account, *see* KOLB, *supra* note 29.

33. GARDINER, *supra* note 18, at 17. *See also* VILLIGER, *supra* note 27, at 425: "Good faith requires the parties to a treaty to act honestly, fairly and reasonably, and to refrain from taking unfair advantage."

34. GARDINER, *supra* note 18, at 171 (emphasis in original).

35. *Id.*: "Good faith, therefore, means more than simply *bona fides* in the sense of absence of *mala fides*. . . . It signifies an element of reasonableness qualifying the dogmatism that can result

31 then involves applying a set of other considerations, notably reasonableness,[36] the importance of balancing different treaty elements,[37] and the principle of effectiveness of the treaty.[38] These considerations are concerned with preserving the integrity of the drafters' intention, and we have consistently taken them into account in updating the Commentaries.

IV. THE ORDINARY MEANING OF THE TEXT IN THE LIGHT OF THE OBJECT AND PURPOSE OF THE TREATY

To determine their ordinary meaning, we must consider the terms of a treaty "in their context and in light of [the treaty's] object and purpose."[39] However, they are complementary elements forming one course of the full interpretive menu under the Vienna Convention. Indeed, it is impossible to define a treaty term in isolation. Rather, the broader context and the object and purpose of the treaty must be considered to give full meaning to the language used so that the drafters' intent is reflected in the interpretation of the terms.[40]

The "ordinary meaning of the terms" in the Geneva Conventions does not generally raise major issues since the language was intended to be easily understood both by military personnel and their commanders, as well as by civilians, who either have to apply them or who benefit from their protection. This is especially true of the Third Geneva Convention, which must be "posted in the prisoners' own language, at places where all may read them" in every prisoner of war camp.[41] Where necessary, the Commentary refers to authoritative, standard English and legal dictionaries.[42] The French version of the Geneva Conventions, which is

---

37. *Id.*, at 178–79.

38. *Id.*, at 179–81.

39. Vienna Convention on the Law of Treaties, *supra* note 17, art. 31(1).

40. *See supra* note 27.

41. Convention (III) Relative to the Treatment of Prisoners of War art. 41, Aug. 12, 1949, 6 U.S.T. 3316, 75 U.N.T.S. 135 [hereinafter Third Geneva Convention].

42. Such as the *Concise Oxford English Dictionary* or *Black's Law Dictionary*. For example, as the Conventions do not provide a specific definition of "violence" for the purposes of Article 13, which protects prisoners of war from "acts of violence" at all times, the Commentaries use the definition "behaviour involving physical force intended to hurt, damage, or kill." CONCISE OXFORD ENGLISH DICTIONARY 1614 (12th ed. 2011). *See also* BRYAN A. GARNER, BLACK'S LAW DICTIONARY 1881 (11th ed. 2019), *cited in* 2020 GC III COMMENTARY, *supra* note 7, commentary on art. 13, ¶ 1619. In another instance, "suitable" for the purposes of the Article 51 requirement

from purely verbal analysis. . . . [T]he term is also capable of a sufficiently broad meaning to include the principle of effective interpretation."

36. *Id.*, at 176–77.

equally authentic, has also consistently been consulted in line with Article 33 of the Vienna Convention (Part VII discusses this in more detail).[43]

The words "object"[44] and "purpose"[45] are strikingly similar in meaning, and the phrase "object and purpose" is used as a single term.[46] Thus, a treaty's object and purpose is said to refer to its "raison d'être,"[47] its "fundamental core,"[48] or "its essential content."[49]

The Vienna Convention does not expressly state how to identify the object and purpose of a given treaty. It is sometimes, but not always, found in the preamble.[50]

In any case, the preamble is a good source of information as part of the context of the treaty, and even where it does not expressly state the treaty's object and purpose, it can serve as a starting point, the object and purpose becoming clear in the

---

that prisoners of war be given "suitable working conditions" is defined as "fit and appropriate for the intended purpose." GARNER, *supra*, at 1735, *cited in* 2020 GC III COMMENTARY, *supra* note 7, commentary on art. 51, ¶ 2721.

43. *See* CONVENTION (I) FOR THE AMELIORATION OF THE CONDITION OF THE WOUNDED AND SICK IN THE ARMED FORCES IN THE FIELD art. 55, Aug. 12, 1949, 6 U.S.T. 3114, 75 U.N.T.S. 31 [hereinafter GC I] and ICRC, UPDATED COMMENTARY ON GENEVA CONVENTION I, *supra* note 7. For example, where the meaning of "fatigue" in Article 89(3) was potentially unclear, the Commentary uses the French text to determine that "fatigue duties . . . do not refer to duties intended to lead to a state of fatigue." *See* ICRC, UPDATED COMMENTARY ON GENEVA CONVENTION III, *supra* note 7, ¶ 3751.

44. Referring to the rights and obligations contained in the treaty. *See* PAUL REUTER, INTRODUCTION TO THE LAW OF TREATIES 186, ¶ 283 (2nd ed. 1995). *See also* Isabelle Buffard & Karl Zemanek, *"The Object and Purpose" of a Treaty: An Enigma?* 3 AUSTRIAN REVIEW OF INTERNATIONAL & EUROPEAN LAW 311, 331–32 (1998).

45. Referring to the aim to be achieved by the treaty's provisions. *See* Buffard & Zemanek, *supra* note 44, at 331–32.

46. VILLIGER, *supra* note 27, at 427, with further references; GARDINER, *supra* note 18, at 212–13 ("a composite item"); David S. Jonas & Thomas N. Saunders, *The Object and Purpose of a Treaty: Three Interpretive Methods*, 43 VANDERBILT JOURNAL OF TRANSNATIONAL LAW 565, 578 (2010) ("a unitary concept").

47. Reservations to the Convention on the Prevention and Punishment of the Crime of Genocide, Advisory Opinion, 1951 I.C.J. 15, ¶ 23 (May 28).

48. Alain Pellet, *Article 19. Formulation of Reservations*, *in* 1 THE VIENNA CONVENTIONS ON THE LAW OF TREATIES—A COMMENTARY 405, 450–51 (Olivier Corten & Pierre Klein eds., 2011).

49. Jonas & Saunders, *supra* note 46, at 576.

50. Case Concerning Rights of Nationals of the United States of America in Morocco (France v. United States of America), Judgment, 1952 I.C.J. 176, at 196 (Aug. 27). *See also* Sir Gerald Fitzmaurice, *The Law and Procedure of the International Court of Justice 1951-4: Treaty Interpretation and Other Treaty Points*, 33 BRITISH YEARBOOK OF INTERNATIONAL LAW 203, 228 (1957); IAN SINCLAIR, The Vienna Convention on the Law of Treaties 125–26 (2nd ed. 1984).

provisions of the treaty.⁵¹ However, Gardiner urges caution as "preambles are not always drafted with care and a preamble itself may need interpreting."⁵²

There was intense debate over the suggested preamble among the committees formed to discuss the draft Geneva Conventions. In particular, it was hard to reach agreement on the Holy See's proposal that "there should be some reference to the Deity in each Preamble"⁵³ or on the importance to be given to the prohibition and punishment of violations of the Geneva Conventions.⁵⁴ Ultimately, the drafters of the Third Geneva Convention chose not to include a substantive preamble.⁵⁵ This is not to say that there is no object and purpose to the Convention, as that would be a logical impossibility.

In fact, an interpreter must look at the whole of the treaty and especially the substantive provisions to identify the object and purpose of a treaty.⁵⁶ The text of the treaty itself, including the title, preamble (if any), headings, and substantive provisions, is the primary resource to determine its object and purpose.⁵⁷ The other elements of interpretation laid out in the Vienna Convention, including the preparatory work, can then be used to confirm that prima facie object and purpose.⁵⁸

On this basis, the Commentary on the Third Geneva Convention identifies the overall object and purpose of the Convention as being "to ensure that prisoners of war are humanely treated at all times, while allowing belligerents to intern captured enemy combatants to prevent them from returning to the battlefield."⁵⁹ All the rules of the Convention are geared toward this end, and several provisions provide more detail on how to put it into practice. These include the rules on prisoners' labor, financial resources, and relations with the exterior and with the authorities.⁶⁰ The object and purpose cannot have been simply to allow States to intern captured enemy combatants to prevent their return to the fight, as a treaty would not then have been necessary.⁶¹ The negotiation of the Third Geneva

---

51. *See* Oil Platforms (Islamic Republic of Iran v. United States of America), Judgment, 1996 I.C.J. 803, ¶¶ 27–28 (Dec. 1996).

52. GARDINER, *supra* note 18, at 217.

53. *See* II-A FINAL RECORD OF THE DIPLOMATIC CONFERENCE OF GENEVA OF 1949 112–14 (1949).

54. *Id.*, at 165.

55. 2020 GC III COMMENTARY, *supra* note 7, Preamble, ¶¶ 134–39.

56. VILLIGER, *supra* note 27, at 428, with further references; GARDINER, *supra* note 18, at 217–18.

57. GARDINER, *supra* note 18, at 197.

58. Buffard and Zemanek, *supra* note 44, at 333. VILLIGER, *supra* note 27, at 428.

59. 2020 GC III COMMENTARY, *supra* note 7, Introduction, ¶ 89.

60. *Id.*, ¶¶ 49–108.

61. Marco Sassòli, *Is the Time for Law of War Treaty Commentaries Over?*, ARTICLES OF WAR (Feb. 26, 2021) https://lieber.westpoint.edu/time-law-war-treaty-commentaries-over-2/.

Convention took place against the backdrop of the suffering of huge numbers of prisoners during World War I and II, something the drafters were intimately familiar with (as is evident from the drafting history). This, combined with the context of the Convention as a whole and the underlying imperative of the Geneva Conventions regime (and IHL more generally) on a balance between humanitarian considerations and military necessity, facilitates the process of identifying the object and purpose of the Third Geneva Convention. Further certainty may be reached by consulting the 1929 Geneva Convention Relative to the Treatment of Prisoners of War,[62] which the 1949 Convention replaced. The 1929 Convention did contain a substantive preamble. As the predecessor to the 1949 Convention, this preamble is informative:

> Recognizing that, in the extreme event of a war, it will be the duty of every Power, to mitigate as far as possible, the inevitable rigours thereof and to alleviate the condition of prisoners of war;
> Being desirous of developing the principles which have inspired the international conventions of The Hague, in particular the Convention concerning the Laws and Customs of War and the Regulations thereunto annexed,
> Have resolved to conclude a Convention for that purpose.[63]

Similar formulations are found in the preambles to IHL treaties that preceded, respectively, the First and Second Geneva Conventions.[64] This is also noted in the updated commentaries on the preambles to those Conventions.[65] However, those commentaries do not intend to formulate an alternative object and purpose for the relevant Conventions, as suggested elsewhere in this volume;[66] the controlling

---

62. Convention Relative to the Treatment of Prisoners of War, July 27, 1929, 47 Stat. 2021, 118 L.N.T.S. 343.

63. *Id.*, preamble (emphasis added).

64. Convention for the Amelioration of the Condition of the Wounded in Armies in the Field, Preamble, Aug. 22, 1864, 22 Stat. 940, 129 Consol. T.S. 361; Convention for the Amelioration of the Condition of the Wounded and Sick in Armies in the Field, Preamble, July 6, 1906, 35 Stat. 1885, 202 Consol. T.S. 144 ("Being equally animated by the desire to lessen, so far as lies in their power, the evils inseparable from war and desiring, for this purpose, to perfect and complete the provisions agreed to at Geneva on 22 August 1864, and 6 July 1906, for the amelioration of the condition of the wounded and sick in armies in the field."). *See also* Convention No. X for the Adaptation to Maritime Warfare of the Principles of the Geneva Convention, Preamble, Oct. 18, 1907, 36 Stat. 2371, T.S. No. 543 ("Animated alike by the desire to diminish, as far as depends on them, the inevitable evils of war; [a]nd wishing with this object to adapt to maritime warfare the principles of the Geneva Convention of 6 July 1906.").

65. *See* 2016 GC I COMMENTARY, Preamble, *supra* note 7, ¶ 112; ICRC, 2017 GC II COMMENTARY, *supra* note 7, Preamble, ¶ 134. For the Third Convention, *see* 2020 GC III COMMENTARY, *supra* note 7, Preamble, ¶ 144.

66. Michael W. Meier, *A Perspective on the Updated Third Geneva Convention Commentary from a United States Practitioner, infra*, ch. 17 in this volume, C17P42 ("In the 2020 GC III

formulation is found in the "object and purpose" section of the introduction to each updated Commentary.⁶⁷ In our view, there is no conflict between those two sets of passages in each of these Commentaries. The passage in the Commentaries on the preambles merely confirms that in adopting the treaties in question, States were motivated by an overarching desire to "lessen"/"diminish"/"mitigate" the evils of war.⁶⁸ This is fully in line with the more precise formulation, which is carefully adjusted to each Geneva Convention and which can be found in the introduction to each Commentary.⁶⁹

One example where the object and purpose of the treaty, in addition to State practice, informed the interpretation of the text is found in the section on the geographical scope of application of Article 3 common to the four 1949 Geneva Conventions [hereinafter "common Article 3"]. The section concludes that the object and purpose of the Conventions supports an interpretation according to which common Article 3 applies to armed conflicts that cross the borders of a State.⁷⁰

Another example where the object and purpose of a treaty has informed the literal interpretation of the text can be found in the commentary on Article 92 of the Third Geneva Convention where the notion of "recapture" is discussed.⁷¹ The interpretation of this notion is important to determine what sanctions a Detaining Power may impose for an attempted escape. The plain language of Article 92 seems not to extend to instances where an attempted escape fails before the prisoner can evade the Detaining Power's custody.⁷² However, as noted in the Commentary, such a strictly textual interpretation would mean that a prisoner who, for instance, was stopped by guards at the gate while trying to escape could be punished more severely than a prisoner who managed to leave the camp but was then recaptured. Such an interpretation would be unreasonable and "run counter to the spirit of the Convention."⁷³ Several other examples can be found throughout the

---

Commentary, the ICRC attempts to set forth the 'object and purpose' of the Third Convention not once, but twice.") and ("Later, in the preamble, the ICRC provides a second, and *different* 'object and purpose.'") (emphasis added).

67. *See* 2016 GC I COMMENTARY, *supra* note 7, Introduction, sec. C.4; 2017 GC II COMMENTARY, *supra* note 7, Introduction, sec. C.4; 2020 GC III COMMENTARY, *supra* note 7, Introduction, sec. C.4.

68. *Supra* note 65.

69. *Supra* note 67.

70. 2020 GC III Commentary, *supra* note 7, commentary on art. 3, ¶ 504.

71. 2020 GC III COMMENTARY, *supra* note 7, commentary on art. 92, ¶ 3819.

72. *See* Third Geneva Convention, *supra* note 41, art. 92(1): "A prisoner of war who *attempts to escape and is recaptured before having made good his escape* in the sense of Article 91 shall be liable only to a disciplinary punishment in respect of this act, even if it is a repeated offence." (emphasis added).

73. 2020 GC III COMMENTARY, *supra* note 7, commentary on art. 92, ¶ 3819.

Commentary.[74]

V. SUBSEQUENT DEVELOPMENTS

The interpretation of treaty terms may evolve over time. Accordingly, the Vienna Convention recognizes the need to take into account the passing of time through subsequent agreements, subsequent practice, and other relevant rules of international law (Article 31(3)).

On the one hand, "subsequent agreements" did not prove relevant for the updated Commentary on the Third Geneva Convention. The Additional Protocols do not as such constitute "subsequent agreements between the parties regarding the interpretation of the treaty or the application of its provisions."[75] They are separate treaties that have not been ratified by all parties to the Geneva Conventions, as Article 31(3)(a) of the Vienna Convention would require. However, this does not exclude that the provisions of the Additional Protocols—which complement the Geneva Conventions—may be taken into account in interpreting the Geneva Conventions under Article 32 of the Vienna Convention. In addition, those rules in the Protocols that reflect customary international law bind all States, regardless of whether or not they are party to the Protocols.[76] Because treaty and customary rules have equal status in international law, the later customary rule (reflected in the Protocols) takes precedence over incompatible treaty rules (laid down by the Conventions).[77]

---

74. *See, e.g., id.*, commentary on art. 12, ¶ 1532, commentary on art. 11, ¶ 1486, commentary on art. 41, ¶ 2508, commentary on art. 86, ¶ 3655, commentary on art. 129, ¶¶ 5134 and 5148, and commentary on art. 142, ¶ 5511.

75. Vienna Convention on the Law of Treaties, *supra* note 17, art. 31(3)(b).

76. This is sometimes criticized in the literature: *see, e.g.*, Iain Scobbie, *The Approach to Customary International Law in the Study*, *in* PERSPECTIVES ON THE ICRC STUDY ON CUSTOMARY INTERNATIONAL HUMANITARIAN LAW 34 (Elizabeth Wilmshurst & Susan Breau eds., 2007), who asks the following rhetorical question: "Can States be expected to accept as customary that which they have rejected as a conventional obligation?" However, it is submitted that the answer is, in some cases, affirmative. This is because States may have refused the entirety of the treaty in question for different reasons and accept a particular rule therein as customary without much difficulty. For specific examples, *see, e.g.*, the acceptance by the United States of Article 75 of Additional Protocol I as customary (most recently *in* OFFICE OF THE GENERAL COUNSEL, U.S. DEPARTMENT OF DEFENSE, LAW OF WAR MANUAL § 8.1.4.2 (rev. ed., Dec. 2016)) or Israel's acceptance of Article 70 of Additional Protocol I as customary (*see* HCJ 9132/07 *Jaber Al-Bassiouni Ahmed and Others v. Prime Minister and Minister of Defence*, Judgment, ¶ 15 (2008) (Isr.)).

77. *See, e.g.*, Michael Akehurst, *The Hierarchy of the Sources of International Law*, 47 BRITISH YEARBOOK OF INTERNATIONAL LAW 273, 275 (1975); MARK E. VILLIGER, CUSTOMARY INTERNATIONAL LAW AND TREATIES 58–59 (2nd ed., 1997); Rebecca Crootof, *Change Without Consent: How Customary International Law Modifies Treaties*, 41 YALE JOURNAL OF INTERNATIONAL LAW 237, 285 (2016).

To illustrate this mechanism, consider Article 70 of Additional Protocol I, which requires the free passage of a wide range of essential humanitarian supplies to all civilians.[78] The content of this provision reflects customary international law, as noted in Rules 55 and 56 of the ICRC's Customary IHL Study.[79] The rule is considerably broader than its corresponding provision in the Fourth Geneva Convention, Article 23, which lists a narrower set of items and beneficiaries.[80] Accordingly, to the extent that Article 23 of the Fourth Geneva Convention is incompatible with Article 70 of Additional Protocol I, the latter must prevail.[81] This approach was tacitly adopted by the Israeli Supreme Court sitting as the High Court of Justice in the 2008 *Al-Bassiouni* case, in which the court referred to the customary nature of Article 70 of Additional Protocol I to affirm the obligation of Israel—a non-party to the Protocol—"to allow the passage of essential humanitarian goods to the Gaza Strip."[82]

On the other hand, subsequent practice and other relevant rules of international law have been particularly important when interpreting the Third Geneva Convention.

A. Subsequent Practice in the Application of a Treaty

Subsequent practice by States in the application of a treaty is an important source of interpretation.[83] As Aust explains, "[h]owever precise a text appears to be, the way in which it is actually applied by the parties is usually a good indication of what they understand it to mean, provided the practice is consistent and is common to, or accepted, expressly or tacitly, by both or all parties."[84]

---

78. Protocol Additional to the Geneva Conventions of 12 August 1949, and Relating to the Protection of Victims of International Armed Conflicts (Protocol I), art. 70(1) and (2), June 8, 1977, 1125 U.N.T.S. 3.

79. 1 Customary International Humanitarian Law 194 and 200 (Jean-Marie Henckaerts & Louise Doswald-Beck eds., 2005) [hereinafter ICRC Customary IHL Study].

80. Commentary on the 1977 Additional Protocols, *supra* note 6, ¶¶ 2813–22.

81. Crootof, *supra* note 77, at 272–74.

82. HCJ 9132/07 *Jaber Al-Bassiouni Ahmed and Others v. Prime Minister and Minister of Defence*, Judgment, ¶ 15 (2008) (Isr.).

83. According to the ILC, '[s]ubsequent agreements and subsequent practice under article 31, paragraph 3 (*a*) and (*b*), being objective evidence of the understanding of the parties as to the meaning of the treaty, are authentic means of interpretation, in the application of the general rule of treaty interpretation reflected in article 31,' ILC, *Report on the Work of Its Seventieth Session*, *supra* note 18, conclusion 3.

84. Aust, *supra* note 18, at 215. Or in the words of Yasseen: "Appliquer le traité, cela suppose l'avoir compris, donc interprété. La pratique suivie dans l'application du traité a, par conséquent, pour fondement un certain sens accepté par ceux qui la suivent." ("Applying a treaty implies that it has been understood, and therefore that it has been interpreted. Practice in the application of the treaty is, therefore, based on a specific understanding accepted by the authors of the practice" (our translation)): Mustafa Kamil Yasseen, *L'interprétation des traités d'après la*

This has been particularly pertinent in the update of the original Commentaries, which were drafted in the light of the preparatory work and previous conflicts, most notably World War II. The update provides an opportunity to take into account the way the Geneva Conventions have been applied and interpreted by States in the seven decades since their adoption. This is a perspective the original Commentaries could not offer and is endorsed, indeed required, by the Vienna Convention.

The International Law Commission (ILC) defines subsequent practice as an authentic means of interpretation under Article 31(3)(b), as "consist[ing] of conduct in the application of a treaty, after its conclusion, which establishes the agreement of the parties regarding the interpretation of the treaty."[85]

The threshold for subsequent practice to qualify as an authentic means of interpretation under Article 31(3)(b) is high. The said practice must establish "the agreement of the parties." According to the ILC, this requires "a common understanding regarding the interpretation of a treaty which the parties are aware of and accept."[86] This is generally understood as implying the agreement of *all* parties to the treaty.[87] However, the agreement of all parties does not mean that there must be practice by all parties as, in some circumstances, silence can constitute acceptance of a subsequent practice.[88] For example, the fact that States generally did not object to the absence of the appointment of Protecting Powers in recent decades can be taken as tacit agreement of this practice. Hence, the ICRC concluded that the obligation expressed in Article 8/8/8/9 common to the four Geneva Conventions should today be interpreted as optional.[89]

---

convention de Vienne sur le droit des traités, 151 COLLECTED COURSES OF THE HAGUE ACADEMY OF INTERNATIONAL LAW 47 (1976).

85. ILC, *Report on the Work of Its Seventieth Session, supra* note 18, conclusion 4.2.

86. *Id.*, conclusion 10.1.

87. For an explanation why Article 31(3)(b) should be understood as such despite the absence of an explicit reference to the agreement of "all" parties, *see* ILC, *Report on the Work of Its Seventieth Session, supra* note 18, commentary on draft conclusion 10.2, ¶ 13. In doctrine, *see* GARDINER, *supra* note 18, at 266, 270; AUST, *supra* note 18, at 216; Gerhard Hafner, *Subsequent Agreements and Practice: Between Interpretation, Informal Modification, and Formal Amendment, in* TREATIES AND SUBSEQUENT PRACTICE 112–13 (Georg Nolte ed., 2013).

88. ILC, *Report on the Work of Its Seventieth Session, supra* note 18, conclusion 10.2: "The number of parties that must actively engage in subsequent practice in order to establish an agreement under article 31, paragraph 3 (*b*), may vary. *Silence on the part of one or more parties may constitute acceptance of the subsequent practice when the circumstances call for some reaction*" (emphasis added). *See also* GARDINER, *supra* note 18, at 270 ("[I]t is sufficient if there is practice of one or more parties and good evidence that the other parties have endorsed the practice.").

89. 2016 GC I COMMENTARY, *supra* note 7, commentary on art. 8, ¶¶ 1114–19; 2017 GC II COMMENTARY, *supra* note 7, commentary on art. 8, ¶¶ 1152–57; 2020 GC III COMMENTARY, *supra* note 7, commentary on art. 8, ¶¶ 1296–1302.

Nevertheless, subsequent practice as understood under Article 31(3)(b) is not easy to establish in relation to treaties that have been universally ratified, such as the Geneva Conventions (196 States Parties). Other subsequent practice—that is, that which does not, or not clearly, establish the agreement of the parties regarding the interpretation of a treaty—remains relevant, however, as a supplementary means of interpretation under Article 32 and did play a role in the updating of the Commentaries (for more details, Part VI, section A).

B. Other Relevant Rules of International Law

The principle enshrined in Article 31(3)(c) of the Vienna Convention aims to achieve coherence among different parts of international law.[90] This provision, by mandating that "any relevant rules of international law applicable in the relations between the parties" be taken into account, in effect envisages treaty interpretation against the background of the entire body of international law.[91] It has been cited in a number of decisions of international courts and tribunals.[92] It has also proved instrumental in interpreting the Geneva Conventions.

Importantly, the provision does not refer to the law as it stood at the moment the treaty was adopted but rather to the law as it stands at the moment of interpretation.[93] This is confirmed by the drafting history of the provision, during which the ILC deleted the words "in force at the time of its conclusion" from an earlier draft.[94] It is also the approach of the International Court of Justice, which held in the *Namibia* case that "an international instrument has to be interpreted and applied within the framework of the entire legal system prevailing *at the time of the interpretation*."[95] This approach is especially apposite when it comes to

---

90. For more on the meaning and history of this rule, *see* GARDINER, *supra* note 18, at 473–74.

91. VILLIGER, *supra* note 27, at 432.

92. *See, e.g.*, International Law Commission, *Fragmentation of International Law: Difficulties Arising from the Diversification and Expansion of International Law*, Report of the Study Group of the International Law Commission, sec. F.3 (¶¶ 433–60), with references, U.N. Doc A/CN.4/L.682 (Apr. 13, 2006); Ivo Tarik de Vries-Zou, *Divided But Harmonious? The Interpretations and Applications of Article 31(3)(C) of the Vienna Convention on the Law of Treaties*, 16 UTRECHT LAW REVIEW 86 (2020), with references. As a recent example, *see* Maritime Delimitation in the Indian Ocean (Somalia v. Kenya), 2017, Preliminary Objections, Judgment, 2017 I.C.J. ¶¶ 87–91 (Feb. 2).

93. KOLB, *supra* note 29, at 158; GARDINER, *supra* note 18, at 467–69; AUST, *supra* note 18, at 216; VILLIGER, *supra* note 27, at 433.

94. [1966] 2 YEARBOOK OF THE INTERNATIONAL LAW COMMISSION 222, ¶ 167.

95. Legal Consequences for States of the Continued Presence of South Africa in Namibia (South West Africa) notwithstanding Security Council Resolution 276 (1970), Advisory Opinion, 1971 I.C.J. 16, at 19, ¶ 53 (June 21) (emphasis added).

treaties regulating warfare, a matter subject to continuous operational and legal developments.[96] As Michael Meier notes in this volume, "an interpretation may require regard to not only international law in 1949 when the Geneva Conventions were adopted, but also may look to contemporary law of today."[97] In the framework of the interpretation of the Geneva Conventions, this contemporary law of today, or the "relevant rules of international law" in the parlance of the Vienna Convention, includes not only the Additional Protocols but also customary international humanitarian law and other bodies of law, such as the law of State responsibility, international criminal law, human rights law, and refugee law.[98] It may be instrumental at this point to look at some of these areas to illustrate how they have influenced the ICRC's interpretation of the Conventions.

To begin with, the law of State responsibility was far from being consolidated when the original Commentaries were being drafted. As late as the 1990s, a leading commentator noted that "[i]n the law of state responsibility one might be forgiven for thinking that there is almost nothing that is certain."[99] However, since then the articulation of the rules on State responsibility by the ILC in 2001[100] has brought a welcome degree of legal clarity that permeates all specific areas of international law, including IHL.[101]

In the context of the Geneva Conventions, the law of State responsibility helps clarify, for instance, the legal consequences of the material inability to fulfill certain positive obligations prescribed by the Conventions. These include the duty to

---

96. As Kolb puts it, "[The UN Charter and the European Convention on Human Rights] tend to be interpreted in the light of the law as it stands at the moment of interpretation. These treaties are intended to inform social life as it evolves. Their purpose could not be fulfilled if they were to be construed in an 'obsolete' surrounding. The same is true for IHL treaties and for a series of other subject matters." KOLB, *supra* note 29, at 158.

97. Meier, *supra* note 66, at 8, C17P38.

98. *See* 2020 GC III COMMENTARY, *supra* note 7, Introduction, ¶¶ 92–116. The drafting history of Article 31(3)(c) of the Vienna Convention confirms that the "relevant rules" are not restricted to customary rules but also include treaty rules. *See, e.g.*, GARDINER, *supra* note 18, at 301–02; VILLIGER, *supra* note 27, at 433.

99. ROSALYN HIGGINS, PROBLEMS AND PROCESS: INTERNATIONAL LAW AND HOW WE USE IT 146 (1995).

100. International Law Commission, *Report on the Work of Its Fifty-Third Session*, U.N. Doc. A/56/10, at 43 (2001), *reprinted in* [2001] 2 YEARBOOK OF THE INTERNATIONAL LAW COMMISSION 32, U.N. Doc. A/CN.4/SER.A/2001/Add.1 (Part 2).

101. Kubo Mačák, *Strengthening the Rule of Law in Time of War: An IHL Perspective on the Present and Future of the Articles on State Responsibility*, EJIL:TALK! (Aug. 6, 2021) https://www.ejiltalk.org/strengthening-the-rule-of-law-in-time-of-war-an-ihl-perspective-on-the-present-and-future-of-the-articles-on-state-responsibility/; Federica Paddeu and Christian Tams, *Dithering, Trickling Down, and Encoding: Concluding Thoughts on the "ILC Articles at 20" Symposium*, EJIL:TALK! (Aug. 9, 2021), https://www.ejiltalk.org/dithering-trickling-down-and-encoding-concluding-thoughts-on-the-ilc-articles-at-20-symposium/.

provide prisoners of war and civilian internees with sufficient daily food rations[102] or access to clean bathroom and laundry facilities.[103] When the conduct of the Detaining Power falls short of what is required of it by any of these primary obligations, it will have committed what the ILC characterizes as an internationally wrongful act of a continuing character.[104] This, in turn, triggers the responsible State's secondary obligations, including the obligation to cease its wrongful conduct[105] through any means available to it.[106]

In such situations, the first solution should, of course, be for the State concerned to reallocate resources without delay so as to meet its primary obligations. But if that cannot be done, the updated Commentary on the Third Geneva Convention highlights a range of alternative "appropriate measures" that the Detaining Power may take. These may be, for example, requesting or accepting assistance from other States; requesting or accepting assistance from an impartial humanitarian organization such as the ICRC; or transferring the prisoners to another Power.[107] If none of these measures are available and if there is no other option for the Detaining Power to cease the continuing breach of its primary obligations under the Convention, then, ultimately, it is obliged to release and repatriate the prisoners in question.[108] The interpretation of the relevant Geneva Convention provisions "within the wider context of international law"[109]—which includes the contemporary law of State responsibility—thus allows the updated Commentaries to propose a practical answer to a difficult legal question not directly addressed by the Conventions while respecting both their text and spirit.[110]

---

102. Third Geneva Convention, *supra* note 41, art. 26(1); Convention (IV) Relative to the Protection of Civilian Persons in Time of War art. 89(1), Aug. 12, 1949, 6 U.S.T. 3516, 75 U.N.T.S. 287 [hereinafter Fourth Geneva Convention].

103. Third Geneva Convention, *supra* note 41, art. 29(3); Fourth Geneva Convention, *supra* note 102, art. 85(3).

104. International Law Commission, Draft Articles on Responsibility of States for Internationally Wrongful Acts, with commentaries, *reprinted in* [2001] 2 YEARBOOK OF THE INTERNATIONAL LAW COMMISSION, Part Two, commentary on art. 14, ¶ 3.

105. *Id.*, commentary on art. 30(a).

106. Olivier Corten, *The Obligation of Cessation*, *in* THE LAW OF INTERNATIONAL RESPONSIBILITY 548 (James Crawford, Alain Pellet & Simon Olleson eds., 2010), noting that "[i]n law, a State must and can always put an end to a continuing breach."

107. 2020 GC III COMMENTARY, *supra* note 7, Introduction, ¶ 114.

108. For a specific application of this analysis to the relevant articles of the Third Convention, *see id.*, commentary on art. 9, ¶ 1357, commentary on art. 12, ¶ 1526, commentary on art. 15, ¶ 1721, commentary on art. 21, ¶ 1940, commentary on art. 26, ¶ 2119.

109. Meier, *supra* note 66, at 8, C17P38.

110. *See further* Kubo Mačák, *GCIII Commentary: If I Can't Feed You, Do I Have to Let You Go?*, HUMANITARIAN LAW & POLICY (Oct. 22, 2020), https://blogs.icrc.org/law-and-policy/2020/10/22/gciii-commentary-if-i-cant-feed-you/.

The other branches of international law mentioned earlier, that is, international criminal law, human rights law, and refugee law, were still in their infancy when the original Commentaries were being drafted but have developed significantly since. This new legal environment has inevitably resulted in evolutions in the way the law is interpreted and applied by States, and this is also reflected in the updated Commentaries.

For example, in 1952 the original Commentary on the First Geneva Convention recommended that common Article 3 "be applied as widely as possible."[111] This recommendation was based on the fact that there were, at the time, no other clearly defined bodies of international law protecting persons affected by situations of violence short of armed conflict. Since 1949, however, the protection provided by human rights law in such situations has considerably developed. The updated Commentaries reflect today's prevailing interpretation that IHL should apply only to the situations it was intended to regulate: armed conflicts, but not beyond.[112] This view is, furthermore, more faithful to the terms of the treaty itself.

An important caveat is that only other treaty rules "applicable in the relations between the parties" can inform the interpretation of a given treaty. When interpreting the Geneva Conventions, this has meant, for example, that reliance on the Additional Protocols has to be very carefully considered since they are not, contrary to the Conventions, universally ratified. Michael Meier notes in this volume that the Protocols "may have some usefulness but are not particularly relevant until all the parties of the 1949 Geneva Conventions are also parties to those agreements."[113] One important exception to this observation is that specific rules in other treaties can be referred to as a matter of general interpretation when they reflect customary international law.[114] Examples include the definition of who is "hors de combat" in Article 41 of Additional Protocol I or the definition of military objectives in Article 52(2) of the Protocol.[115] Other rules are referred to in the updated Commentaries on the understanding that they apply only to States that have ratified or acceded to the treaties in question, and this is expressly noted in

---

111. 1 COMMENTARY ON THE GENEVA CONVENTIONS OF 1949, *supra* note 3, at 50 (1952).

112. *See* ICRC, UPDATED COMMENTARY ON GENEVA CONVENTION III, *supra* note 7, commentary on art. 3, ¶ 390.

113. Meier, *supra* note 66, at 14, C17P58.

114. International Law Commission, *supra* note 92, ¶ 21, noting that "Article 31 (3) (c) also requires the interpreter to consider other treaty-based rules so as to arrive at a consistent meaning. Such other rules are of particular relevance . . . where the treaty rule has passed into or expresses customary international law."

115. On the customary status of these rules, *see* ICRC Customary IHL Study, *supra* note 79, Rules 41 and 8 respectively. For their specific application in the interpretation of the provisions of the Conventions, *see, e.g.*, 2020 GC III COMMENTARY, *supra* note 7, commentary on art. 3, ¶ 571 and commentary on art. 23, ¶ 2028. For examples related to Additional Protocol II, *see, e.g.*, 2020 GC III COMMENTARY, *supra* note 7, commentary on art. 3, ¶¶ 593, 720 and 797.

the introductions to the Commentaries.¹¹⁶ The Additional Protocols, for example, are only legally applicable to the States that have ratified them. However, since these number 174 for Additional Protocol I and 169 for Additional Protocol II, the Protocols are relevant for the vast majority of States party to the 1949 Geneva Conventions. The Commentaries might in many respects be incomplete and less useful for these States if they had ignored the Protocols or other relevant treaties.

VI. SUPPLEMENTARY MEANS OF INTERPRETATION

The general rule of interpretation in Article 31 of the Vienna Convention is complemented by the rule in Article 32 on supplementary means of interpretation, which include—but are not restricted to—the "preparatory work of the treaty and the circumstances of its conclusion."

A. The Importance of Supplementary Means

Although Article 32 suggests that supplementary means are optional—"recourse *may* be had" (emphasis added)—and thus of secondary importance, experience suggests otherwise.

According to the text of Article 32, supplementary means of interpretation may be used for two purposes: *confirming* the meaning of a term resulting from the application of Article 31 or *determining* the meaning, when the application of Article 31 "(a) leaves the meaning ambiguous or obscure; or (b) leads to a result which is manifestly absurd or unreasonable."¹¹⁷ Whether a given interpretation needs "confirmation" implies some discretion for the interpreter to decide whether to have recourse to supplementary means.¹¹⁸ In fact, the preparatory work (or *travaux préparatoires*) is used routinely by interpreters,¹¹⁹ and not only

---

116. *See, e.g.*, 2020 GC III Commentary, *supra* note 7, Introduction, ¶ 95.

117. For a view that Article 32 could also be used to "correct" the meaning of a treaty provision, *see* Stephen M. Schwebel, *May Preparatory Work Be Used to Correct Rather Than Confirm the "Clear" Meaning of a Treaty Provision?*, *in* Theory of International Law at the Threshold of the 21st Century 173–81 (Jerzy Makarczyk ed., 1996).

118. This was acknowledged by the principal architect of the Vienna rules, Sir Humphrey Waldock: "This formulation [the precursor to Article 32] seemed to the Commission about as near as it is possible to get to reconciling the principle of the primacy of the text . . . with frequent and quite normal recourse to *travaux préparatoires* without any too nice regard for the question whether the text itself is clear. Moreover, the rule . . . is inherently flexible, since the question whether the text can be said to be 'clear' is in some degree subjective." International Law Commission, *Sixth Report on the Law of Treaties*, *in* [1966] 2 Yearbook of the International Law Commission 99 [20], *cited in* Gardiner, *supra* note 18, at 347.

119. Aust insists that international tribunals, and the parties arguing before them, have for long had recourse to the preparatory work: Aust, *supra* note 18, at 217–18, citing Lockerbie (Libya

in cases where the general rule of interpretation yielded an unsatisfactory result. Most interpretations, including many commentaries on other treaties,[120] systematically examine the preparatory work and not just where the meaning is ambiguous or obscure or where interpretation under Article 31 leads to a result that is manifestly absurd or unreasonable.[121]

In addition, recourse to the preparatory work helps to understand "the terms of the treaty in their context", which is a requirement under the general rule (Article 31(1) and (2) of the Vienna Convention).

Article 32 is not limited to preparatory work and the circumstances of a treaty's conclusion. As explained below, it can also include subsequent practice that does not meet the requirements of Article 31(3)(b), as well as judicial decisions and the teachings of the most highly qualified publicists. We now turn to the question: Which supplementary means are most relevant for the interpretation of the Geneva Conventions?

B. Preparatory Work

Preparatory work should be understood broadly as including successive drafts of the treaty, conference records, and explanatory statements made in drafting committees.[122] During treaty negotiations, important discussions may also occur outside of any formally recorded arena. However, in the case of the Geneva Conventions and their Additional Protocols, a significant amount of documentation has been collected, ranging from drafts and reports preparatory to the 1949 and 1974–1977 Diplomatic Conferences to the stenographic notes (minutes) of the Conferences and their final/official records.[123] These documents have been helpful to the authors of the original and updated Commentaries in clarifying the meaning and context of certain provisions.

---

v. UK), Preliminary Objections, 1998 I.C.J. 9, ¶¶ 4.17–4.18; [1998] ILM 587; 117 ILR 1 and 664; LORD MCNAIR, THE LAW OF TREATIES 413, 422 (1961); and examples given in Martin Mennecke & Christian Tams, *The Right to Consular Assistance under International Law*, in [1999] 42 GERMAN YEARBOOK OF INTERNATIONAL LAW 192, 223–24. *See also* Martin Ris, *Treaty Interpretation and ICJ Recourse to Travaux Préparatoires: Towards a Proposed Amendment of Articles 31 and 32 of the Vienna Convention on the Law of Treaties*, 14 BOSTON COLLEGE INTERNATIONAL AND COMPARATIVE LAW REVIEW 111, 131 (1991).

120. For a representative list, *see* 2020 GC III COMMENTARY, *supra* note 7, Introduction, ¶ 119, n. 167.

121. 2016 GC I COMMENTARY, *supra* note 7, Introduction, ¶ 48.

122. For more on preparatory work as a supplementary means of interpretation, *see* AUST, *supra* note 18, at 218; GARDINER, *supra* note 18, at 349–56.

123. For a full list of (and access to) the documents constituting the preparatory work of the 1949 Geneva Conventions and their 1977 Additional Protocols, *see* International Committee of the Red Cross Library website, https://library.icrc.org/library/search/shortview?searchType=PredefinedSearch&name=1949 Geneva Conventions for the 1949 Geneva Conventions and

In addition, a comparison with the predecessor of the Third Geneva Convention, the 1929 Convention Relative to the Treatment of Prisoners of War, has been useful in understanding the origin of many provisions in the 1949 Convention. Indeed, the 1929 Convention was already a detailed code of protection for prisoners of war (97 articles), upon which the 1949 version builds (143 articles). Accordingly, a commentary on the 1929 Convention was also used as a reference to understand the meaning of the 1929 Convention and, thereby, the changes brought about by the 1949 Convention.[124]

C. Subsequent Practice in the Broad Sense

As stated above, State practice that does not fulfill the requirements of "subsequent practice" under Article 31—that is, practice for which it is not possible to identify the agreement of all parties—may be examined as a supplementary means of interpretation. This is recognized by the ILC,[125] which explains that "any practice in the application of the treaty that may provide indications as to how the treaty is to be interpreted may be a relevant supplementary means of interpretation under article 32" (this is what the ILC calls "subsequent practice in the broad sense").[126]

"Subsequent practice" is generally understood as being limited to the practice of the parties to the treaty (usually States, but depending on the treaty can also include international organizations).[127] The weight of such practice may depend on its clarity and specificity and whether and how it is repeated.[128] Thus, in the

---

https://library.icrc.org/library/search/shortview?searchType=PredefinedSearch&name=1977 Additional Protocols for the 1977 Additional Protocols (both last visited Dec. 1, 2021).

124. For the commentary on the 1929 Convention used, *see* GUSTAV RASMUSSEN, CODE DES PRISONNIERS DE GUERRE: COMMENTAIRE DE LA CONVENTION DU 27 JUILLET 1929 RELATIVE AU TRAITEMENT DES PRISONNIERS DE GUERRE (1931).

125. ILC, *Report on the Work of Its Seventieth Session, supra* note 18, conclusion 2.4: "Recourse may be had to other subsequent practice in the application of the treaty as a supplementary means of interpretation under article 32." For references to case law and doctrine supporting this, *see id.*, commentary on draft conclusion 2.4, ¶ 9, n. 36–37 and commentary on draft conclusion 4.3, ¶¶ 25–32. Practice not accompanied by an agreement of all parties is examined *in* International Law Commission, *Fourth Report on Subsequent Agreements and Subsequent Practice in Relation to the Interpretation of Treaties*, ¶¶ 107–09, U.N. Doc. A/CN.4/694 (2016) Sixty-eighth session (May 2–June 10 and July 4–Aug. 12, 2016).

126. ILC, *Report on the Work of Its Seventieth Session, supra* note 18 commentary on draft conclusion 4, ¶ 24.

127. *Id.*, conclusion 5 on attribution of subsequent practice: "1. Subsequent practice under articles 31 and 32 may consist of any conduct of a party in the application of a treaty, whether in the exercise of its executive, legislative, judicial or other functions; 2. Other conduct, including by non-State actors, does not constitute subsequent practice under articles 31 and 32. Such conduct may, however, be relevant when assessing the subsequent practice of parties to a treaty."

128. *Id.*, conclusion 9.

case of conflicting positions between various State organs or between different instances of a State's practice, that practice is considered internally inconsistent, and its weight may be diminished.

Physical acts relevant to the interpretation of IHL treaty rules include conduct on the battlefield; the use of weapons, means, and methods of warfare; the treatment of persons in the power of a party to the conflict; or the display of the emblem. Evidence of the implementation of the law during armed conflicts—official practice—can be found in documents such as domestic legislation, military manuals, instructions to armed and security forces, communiqués during armed conflicts, national case law, diplomatic protests, opinions of State military and civilian legal advisers, official State pronouncements on the drafts of subsequent IHL treaties, executive decisions and regulations, pleadings before international tribunals, and official statements made within international organizations and at international conferences.

In addition, in the context of the Third Geneva Convention, useful sources of publicly available State practice include UN reports, awards of the Eritrea-Ethiopia Claims Commission, and ICRC publications.[129] Additional practice can be gleaned from publications that report and comment on specific armed conflicts.[130]

The sources of subsequent practice mentioned above are available in the public domain, notably through the ICRC databases on customary international humanitarian law and national implementation.[131] The ICRC archives are also a valuable resource. The Commentaries draw on research in the archives while respecting their confidential nature. For the Third Geneva Convention, reports from ICRC visits to a prisoner-of-war camp relating to a range of international armed conflicts were analyzed.[132]

---

129. *See, e.g.*, U.N. Security Council, *Prisoners of War in Iran and Iraq: The Report of a Mission Dispatched by the Secretary-General*, UN Doc. S/16962 (Feb. 22, 1985); Prisoners of War, Eritrea's Claim, Partial Award, and Prisoners of War, Ethiopia's Claim, Partial Award (Eritrea-Ethiopia Claims Commission, 2004); International Committee of the Red Cross, *ICRC Activities in Favour of Prisoners of War during the Iraq-Iran War and the Gulf War* (Mar. 11, 2003); INTERNATIONAL COMMITTEE OF THE RED CROSS, ANNUAL REPORT 172 (2017) (*see, e.g.*, ICRC, UPDATED COMMENTARY ON GENEVA CONVENTION I, *supra* note 7, ¶ 3186, n. 27).

130. *See, e.g.*, THE GULF WAR 1990–91 IN INTERNATIONAL AND ENGLISH LAW (Peter Rowe ed., 1993); THE 1998–2000 WAR BETWEEN ERITREA AND ETHIOPIA (Andrea de Guttry, Harry H.G. Post & Gabriella Venturini eds., 2009). For practice related to several conflicts, *see* CATHERIN MAIA, ROBERT KOLB & DAMIEN SCALIA, LA PROTECTION DES PRISONNIERS DE GUERRE EN DROIT INTERNATIONAL HUMANITAIRE (*see, e.g.*, ¶ 1834, n. 55) (2015).

131. *See* International Committee of the Red Cross, IHL database search, https://ihl-databases.icrc.org/applic/ihl/ihl-search.nsf/home.xsp?lang=EN (last visited Oct. 8, 2021).

132. These conflicts include: the Six-Day War between Israel and Egypt, Syria, Jordan, and Iraq in June 1967 and the conflicts between Armenia and Azerbaijan (period covered: 1988–1994), Eritrea and Ethiopia (1998–2000), India and Pakistan (period covered: 1970–1971), Iran and Iraq (1980–1988), Russia and Georgia (2008), and the international armed conflict between the U.S.-led coalition and Iraq (2003–2004). Other conflicts in which the ICRC visited prisoners of

The examples gleaned from practice involve a variety of attitudes toward the Geneva Conventions. The ILC specifies that "an element of good faith is necessary in any 'subsequent practice in the application of the treaty.'"[133] In that sense, many references exemplify this approach and are given as instances of respect for the Convention.[134] Other references are cited as best practices, providing relevant guidance to other States.[135] In this way, the Commentaries constitute a repository of practice for States about how the Conventions have been implemented. These examples do not thereby become "binding" on all other States but provide relevant information that can assist practitioners in their work.

Conversely, a manifest misapplication of a treaty is not an "application of the treaty" in the sense of Articles 31 and 32.[136] Violations of the Conventions, therefore, do not count as practice informing their interpretation. For example, a situation in which prisoners were forced to run laps around a camp courtyard until exhaustion is a violation of Article 38 of the Third Geneva Convention, not a bona fide application.[137] Several other examples have been highlighted throughout the Commentary on the Third Geneva Convention.[138]

The ILC carefully nuances the value of subsequent practice not fulfilling the requirement of Article 31(3)(b): "In any case, the distinction between agreed subsequent practice under article 31, paragraph 3 (b), as an authentic means of interpretation, and other subsequent practice (in a broad sense) under article 32, implies that a greater interpretative value should be attributed to the former."[139]

The lower interpretive value of practice under Article 32 is *relative* to that of subsequent practice under Article 31(3)(b), assuming that the latter is available. Yet, as highlighted above, the agreement of third States vis-à-vis the practice of parties to an armed conflict cannot always be easily established, particularly for

---

war include, for example, the 1991 First Gulf War and the international armed conflict in the Democratic Republic of the Congo (1998–2002). *See also* 2020 GC III COMMENTARY, *supra* note 7, Introduction, ¶ 74.

133. ILC, *Report on the Work of Its Seventieth Session*, *supra* note 18, commentary on draft conclusion 4.2, ¶ 19.

134. *See, e.g.*, 2020 GC III COMMENTARY, *supra* note 7, commentary on art. 34 ¶ 2364 and commentary on art. 38, ¶¶ 2456, 2461, and 2463.

135. For such examples, *see id.* commentary on art. 34, ¶ 2365, n. 18 and accompanying text, and commentary on art. 38, ¶¶ 2464–66.

136. ILC, *Report on the Work of Its Seventieth Session*, *supra* note 18, commentary on draft conclusion 4.2, ¶ 19.

137. ICRC, UPDATED COMMENTARY ON GENEVA CONVENTION III, *supra* note 7, commentary on art. 38, ¶ 2473.

138. For examples, *see id.*, commentary on art. 13, ¶ 1582, n. 38, commentary on art. 20, ¶ 1896, commentary on art. 22, ¶¶ 1993 and 2006, n. 62, commentary on art. 29, ¶ 2125, commentary on art. 27, 2150, n. 10, and commentary on art. 29, ¶ 2194.

139. ILC, *Report on the Work of Its Seventieth Session*, *supra* note 18, commentary on draft conclusion 4.3, ¶ 33.

specific points of interpretation. Therefore, "subsequent practice in the broad sense" falling under Article 32 may be the only subsequent practice available. Its weight in confirming or determining the meaning of the Geneva Conventions should therefore not be underestimated.

When discussing subsequent practice (or any other element of interpretation), one should not lose sight of the fact that each element is only one aspect of the Vienna Convention framework for interpretation. All the other elements of that framework have to be taken into account. For example, the fact that prisoners of war may be allowed to communicate through modern means of communication is supported by some subsequent practice in the broad sense, but it is also in line with the purpose of the provisions related to family contact. In this context, the Commentary acknowledges that the words of the Convention are "updated" in light of modern technology: for example, the function of sending letters and cards, as well as telegrams, can now be accomplished through email, as recognized in some military manuals.[140]

D. Other Supplementary Elements

"[J]udicial decisions and the teachings of the most highly qualified publicists of the various nations" constitute "subsidiary means for the determination of rules of law."[141] As such, they may also constitute relevant supplementary elements for the interpretation of treaties. The consideration of these elements is exemplified in many other commentaries.[142]

The decisions of judicial and quasi-judicial bodies applying the Geneva Conventions constitute a relevant reference point when interpreting these treaties in general.[143] International criminal courts and tribunals, in particular, have conducted substantial interpretive work in relation to the Geneva Conventions, and their pronouncements have proven especially important in confirming or determining the meaning of specific terms in the Conventions. For example, the definitions of torture, cruel or degrading treatment, or hostage-taking under the Geneva Conventions are largely informed by those developed by such courts and

---

140. 2020 GC III COMMENTARY, *supra* note 7, Introduction, ¶ 40 and commentary on art. 71, ¶ 3186. For references to military manuals in this context, *see id.* ¶ 3186, n. 26.

141. Statute of the International Court of Justice, art. 38(1)(d), June 26, 1946, 33 U.N.T.S. 993.

142. For a representative list, *see* 2020 GC III COMMENTARY, *supra* note 7, Introduction, ¶ 119, n. 167.

143. International criminal tribunals have jurisdiction over war crimes, the primary rules of which are IHL rules. As to human rights law bodies, they may be called upon to interpret notions that are similar under human rights law and IHL (e.g., the prohibition of ill-treatment); or, when applying human rights law in times of armed conflict, they may interpret human rights law in the light of IHL rules or apply IHL rules directly.

tribunals.¹⁴⁴ National courts have also applied the Geneva Conventions on numerous occasions in the past seventy years, and their pronouncements have been looked at as a supplementary means of interpretation.¹⁴⁵ This does not mean that the interpretation by one State's courts automatically binds other States. Rather such decisions are looked at as relevant examples of how the provisions have been interpreted. Over time, such pronouncements can become accepted by other courts and tribunals and more widely in State practice and thus become a more widely accepted interpretation.

The teachings of the most highly qualified publicists of the various nations refer to scholarly publications, such as books, academic reports, and law review articles. Such publications have been recognized as supplementary means of interpretation¹⁴⁶ and are often used by courts and tribunals.¹⁴⁷ Scholarly publications are a relevant means of interpretation, notably when they themselves collect and interpret State practice. In addition to the examples mentioned above,¹⁴⁸ this is the case with the seminal work on prisoners of war by Howard Levie, which was inspired by the author's practical experience and is replete with examples drawn from such practice.¹⁴⁹ More recently, many authors have discussed in great detail the meaning of various aspects of the Geneva Conventions, for example, the geographical scope of application of common Article 3.¹⁵⁰ They often do so, not in a vacuum, but by reviewing State practice. Hence, the updated Commentaries review this literature, alongside all other elements of interpretation.

Legal publications on the Geneva Conventions have proliferated in recent decades. In the case of the ICRC's updated Commentaries, significant time and

---

144. For example, the updated Commentary on the First Convention largely refers to the ICTY case law for the definition of torture under common Article 3; *see* 2016 GC I COMMENTARY, *supra* note 7, commentary on art. 3, ¶¶ 626–45. Similarly, when defining "hostage taking," the ICRC's updated Commentary on the Third Convention refers to case law from the Special Court for Sierra Leone (Prosecutor v. Sesay, Case No. SCSL-04-15-A, Appeal Judgment, ¶ 598 (Oct. 26, 2009)); *see* 2020 GC III COMMENTARY, *supra* note 7, commentary on art. 3, ¶ 648.

145. More than 120 decisions of national courts have been referenced in the Updated Commentary on the Third Geneva Convention. For a complete listing, see 2020 GC III COMMENTARY, *supra* note 7, at 2119–36. For specific examples, *see, e.g., id.*, commentary on art. 34, ¶ 2381 and commentary on art. 130, ¶ 5249, n. 161 and ¶ 5285, n. 233.

146. GARDINER, *supra* note 18, at 401–04.

147. *See, e.g.*, Sandesh Sivakumaran, *The Influence of Teachings of Publicists on the Development of International Law*, 66 INTERNATIONAL AND COMPARATIVE LAW QUARTERLY 1, 26–29 (Jan. 2017).

148. *See* the publications mentioned *supra* note 130.

149. Howard S. Levie, *Prisoners of War in International Armed Conflict*, 59 INTERNATIONAL LAW STUDIES 315 (1978); *Documents on Prisoners of War*, 60 INTERNATIONAL LAW STUDIES (Howard S. Levie ed., 1979).

150. *See, e.g.*, 2020 GC III COMMENTARY, *supra* note 7, commentary on art. 3, ¶ 497 and references.

effort have been invested in collecting and analyzing relevant publications to reflect the diversity of legal writing.[151] Peer reviewers have proved very helpful in this process, signaling doctrine (and practice) from their regions and/or fields of expertise. This is important as the Statute of the International Court of Justice makes clear that the publications of the most highly qualified publicists of the "various nations" must be considered.[152] Doing so is a challenge in today's legal-academic landscape, and in the course of research for the updated Commentaries, particular effort has therefore been made to include publicists from various countries and backgrounds, as well as publications in different languages.

The legal writings of the ICRC itself and its legal advisers are part of the scholarly publications that may be relevant to the interpretation of treaties, particularly in areas where they review State practice, summarize (diverging) expert opinions, or reflect ICRC institutional positions.[153] It is logical for a commentary issued by the ICRC to refer to the organization's previous publications setting out interpretations on IHL. In this way, the updated Commentaries constitute a coherent repository of ICRC positions, combined with references to State practice, judicial decisions, and legal writings.

VII. TREATIES AUTHENTICATED IN TWO OR MORE LANGUAGES

Article 33(1) of the Vienna Convention provides that "[w]hen a treaty has been authenticated in two or more languages, the text is equally authoritative in each language, unless the treaty provides or the parties agree that, in case of divergence, a particular text shall prevail." This provision is relevant to the interpretation of the Geneva Conventions, the English and French versions of which are equally authentic.[154] Neither the Geneva Conventions nor the parties thereto indicate that one language version should prevail over another in the event of a divergence.[155] According to Article 33(1) of the Vienna Convention, both language versions of the text of the Conventions are therefore equally authoritative. Furthermore, pursuant to Article 33(3), the terms of the English and French versions of the Conventions are presumed to have the same meaning. Therefore, in updating the Commentaries, we have consistently consulted both language versions to ascertain the meaning of the

---

151. For example, on the discussion of the geographic scope of application of IHL in non-international armed conflict, *see* the discussion about practice combined with references to legal writings in 2020 GC III COMMENTARY, *supra* note 7, commentary on art. 3, sec. C.3.

152. Statute of the International Court of Justice, *supra* note 141, art. 38(1)(d).

153. On the role of the ICRC in this respect, *see also* ILC, *Report on the Work of Its Seventieth Session*, *supra* note 18, commentary on draft conclusion 5, ¶ 16.

154. Third Geneva Convention, *supra* note 41, art. 133.

155. For details, *see* 2020 GC III COMMENTARY, *supra* note 7, commentary on art. 133, sec. B.2.

text.¹⁵⁶ Where the French and the English versions of a provision have differed in meaning, we have followed the approach outlined in Article 33(4).¹⁵⁷ First, recourse is had to Articles 31 and 32. Where this does not resolve the difference, "the meaning which best reconciles the texts, having regard to the object and purpose of the treaty," has been adopted.¹⁵⁸

VIII. ON THE LAW AS IT IS AND THE LAW AS IT SHOULD BE

The purpose of the ICRC's updated Commentaries, like other commentaries, is to clarify the meaning of the Geneva Conventions so that they may be better understood and implemented. In this regard, the updated Commentaries have been criticized for clarifying ambiguities in the Conventions and for going further than the original Commentaries (and too far) in seeking clarity in their interpretation.¹⁵⁹

As noted above, the drafters of the Conventions aspired to produce texts that were clear and understandable to promote the use and implementation of the Conventions during armed conflict. It is true that the text of the Conventions is, at times, worded generally and that this, also at times, reflects the intention of the drafters. For example, Article 42 of the Fourth Geneva Convention allows for internment or placing in assigned residence if the security of the Detaining Power makes it absolutely necessary. The original Commentary explains that "[i]t did not seem possible to define the expression 'security of the state' in a more concrete fashion" and that "[i]t is thus left very largely to Governments to decide the measure of activity prejudicial to the internal or external security of the State which justifies internment or assigned residence."¹⁶⁰ It is possible to contrast the interpretation of the original Commentary in relation to the phrase "security of the state" with that in relation to "measures of control and security" as it appears in Article 27(4) of the Fourth Geneva Convention. While the original

---

156. *See* First Geneva Convention, *supra* note 43, art. 55 and 2016 GC I COMMENTARY, *supra* note 7, commentary on art. 55. For example, where the meaning of "fatigue" in Article 89(3) was potentially unclear, the Commentary uses the French text to determine that "fatigue duties... do not refer to duties intended to lead to a state of fatigue." *Id.*, commentary on art. 89, ¶ 3751.

157. *See, e.g.*, 2020 GC III COMMENTARY, *supra* note 7, commentary on art. 3, n. 277, commentary on art. 13, ¶ 1573, commentary on art. 32, ¶ 2306, commentary on art. 56, ¶ 2806, commentary on art. 83, ¶ 3593, commentary on art. 106, ¶¶ 4147, 4154 and 4156, and commentary on art. 129, ¶ 5161.

158. *See id.*

159. Sean Watts, *Interpretation in the Updated GC III Commentary*, ARTICLES OF WAR (Dec 15, 2020) https://lieber.westpoint.edu/interpretation-updated-gciii-commentary/.

160. COMMENTARY ON THE GENEVA CONVENTIONS 12 AUGUST 1949, vol. 4, *supra* note 3, at 257 (1958).

Commentary acknowledges that the phrase "measures of control and security" is purposefully general, it does consider further what sorts of measures this phrase refers to.[161] In so doing, it provides a series of examples of security measures that were common practice at the time, with a view to further clarifying which measures were intended. Indeed, from an interpretive perspective, such clarification of ambiguity is often an essential facet of interpretation. Ambiguity poses a potential problem to the interpretation and implementation of treaties. Recourse to supplementary means of interpretation pursuant to Article 32 of the Vienna Convention expressly aims to solve this problem, permitting recourse to such means when interpretation according to Article 31 "leaves the meaning ambiguous or obscure." It is to be expected that the updated Commentaries would go further than the original Commentaries in clarifying the Conventions. The very nature of treaty-making, as well as the passing of time, requires that treaty provisions be explained and clarified through treaty interpretation. This need has only increased since the publication of the original Commentaries more than sixty years ago.

Moreover, State practice and jurisprudence have contributed to further clarifying the meaning of the Conventions' provisions. It must be recalled that the primary addressees of the Commentaries are those who are seeking to apply the Conventions in practice. It is hoped that these practitioners will gain a clearer and more rounded understanding of the Conventions from a review of the various sources presented in the Commentaries using the Vienna Convention framework as the organizing method.

To return to the example of "measures of control and security" in Article 27(4) of the Fourth Convention: based on the Vienna Convention methodology, an updated commentary on this provision requires revisiting the interpretation that appears in the original Commentary to take stock of subsequent developments in law and practice, including security measures that did not exist when the Convention or the original Commentary was drafted. Thus, the general formulation ("measures of control and security") used by the drafters of the Convention has to be read in light of subsequent developments and may not be read as being limited to those measures that were available at the time of drafting.

It has also been suggested that the updated Commentaries present lex ferenda ('the law as it should be') as lex lata ('the law as it is')[162] and in so doing depart from the appropriate role to be played by law of war commentaries as produced by non-State actors.[163] In fact, the Commentaries aim to explain and clarify the meaning of existing treaty provisions. However, although the distinction between

---

161. COMMENTARY ON THE GENEVA CONVENTIONS OF 12 AUGUST 1949, vol. 4, *supra* note 3, at 207 (1958).

162. *See* Michael M. Meier, *The Updated GCIII Commentary: A Flawed Methodology?*, ARTICLES OF WAR (Feb. 3, 2021).

163. *See* Eric Jensen & Carolyn Sharp, *Non-State Commentaries: Law-Making or Law-Suggesting?*, ARTICLES OF WAR (Apr. 8, 2021) https://lieber.westpoint.edu/non-state-commentaries-law-making-law-suggesting/ (last visited Nov. 30, 2021).

lawmaking and treaty interpretation is clear in principle, the line may at times appear blurred in practice. For example, interpretation may involve identifying a rule in a text that does not explicitly state it. For example, the updated commentary on common Article 3 includes a section on sexual violence, although the article does not specifically mention this type of violence. However, in so doing the commentary does not create new law. Rather, it reflects the developments in law and practice, as well as contemporary recognition of factual contexts that were obscured, whether through discriminatory attitudes, exclusionary processes, or simple ignorance, at the time the Conventions were concluded. For example, sexual violence is now universally recognized as conduct that constitutes "violence to life and person, in particular murder of all kinds, mutilation, cruel treatment and torture" or "outrages upon personal dignity, in particular humiliating and degrading treatment," acts explicitly prohibited by common Article 3. In particular, although common Article 3 does not mention rape, international and national case law has nonetheless recognized rape as an act of torture.[164] It would not be realistic or desirable for treaty provisions to mention all foreseeable types of prohibited or required conduct. Thus, the Commentary clarifies and illustrates which specific conduct may fall under the broad categories of conduct identified in the treaty on the basis of the Vienna Convention methodology for treaty interpretation.

While in its conclusions on subsequent agreements and subsequent practice the ILC highlights that treaty interpretation cannot amount to the modification of a treaty (which requires a formal process regulated by distinct rules of the Vienna Convention),[165] in practice interpretation following the Vienna Convention rules may still lead in rare cases to a result approaching modification. For example, Article 8/8/8/9 common to the four Geneva Conventions provides that the Conventions "shall be applied with the co-operation and under the scrutiny of the Protecting Powers" (emphasis added). However, the practice of States Parties since 1949 has led the ICRC to conclude that States came to a change

---

164. *See* Prosecutor v. Delalić et al., Case No. IT-96-21-T, Judgment, ¶¶ 495–497 (Int'l Crim. Trib. for the former Yugoslavia Nov. 16, 1998); Prosecutor v. Kunarac, Case Nos. IT-96-23 & IT-96-23/1-A, Judgment, ¶ 151 (Int'l Crim. Trib. for the former Yugoslavia June 12, 2002); Prosecutor v. Akayesu, Case No. ICTR-96-4-T, Judgment, ¶ 682 (Sept. 2, 1998); Aydin v. Turkey, 57/1996/676/866 (ECtHR), ¶¶ 82–86 (1997); T.A. v. Sweden, Decisions, UN Committee against Torture ¶¶ 2.4 and 7.3 (2005); Case 10.970 (Peru), Inter-Amer. Comm'n on H.R., Report No 5/96, at 185 (1996). *See also* Pieter Hendrik Kooijmans (Special Rapporteur on Torture and Other Cruel, Inhuman or Degrading Treatment or Punishment), *Report*, ¶ 119, UN Doc. E/CN.4/1986/15 (Feb. 19, 1986). *See further* ICRC, 2016 GC I COMMENTARY, *supra* note 7, commentary on art. 3, ¶ 637.

165. *See* ILC, *Report on the Work of Its Seventieth Session*, *supra* note 18, conclusion 7(3): "It is presumed that the parties to a treaty, by an agreement or a practice in the application of the treaty, intend to interpret the treaty, not to amend or to modify it. The possibility of amending or modifying a treaty by subsequent practice of the parties has not been generally recognized. The present draft conclusion is without prejudice to the rules on the amendment or modification of treaties under the Vienna Convention on the Law of Treaties and under customary international law."

of understanding of this provision, now viewing the appointment of Protecting Powers as optional rather than mandatory.[166] Similarly, Article 38(2) of the First Convention provides that the only States able to use the red crescent emblem or the red lion and sun emblem were those already doing so at the time the 1949 Geneva Conventions were adopted. But the fact that a number of States chose to use one of these two emblems upon or subsequent to their adherence to the Convention, without formal objection by other parties to the Convention, has led the ICRC to "conclude that a practice or custom at variance with the rule set out in Article 38 has thus been allowed to take root."[167]

Relatedly, care has been taken in the wording of the updated Commentaries to distinguish between binding obligations and recommendations as they arise in interpretation related to the Conventions. Accordingly, the Commentaries reserve the word "must" for obligations that the ICRC considers mandatory under the law. By contrast, words such as "may" or "should" are reserved for recommendations and best practices, thereby recognizing that they are not legally required. Thus, the ICRC has been very mindful of its choice of wording in the Commentaries, with a view to expressly distinguishing between binding obligations and recommendations in its interpretation of the Conventions.

IX. CONCLUSION

Interpretation is an essential part of the application of any treaty.[168] IHL treaties, including the Geneva Conventions, are no exception. In a context where the adoption in the near future of new treaties supplementing the Geneva Conventions does not seem to be a realistic prospect, the interpretation of the existing Conventions and Additional Protocols will remain crucial. At the same time, it is important to ensure that the Conventions and Protocols continue to be interpreted and applied in a manner that is consistent with their wording and with their object and purpose.

---

166. "Over the decades since 1949, however, States have come to a different understanding of this provision. . . . [T]he appointment of Protecting Powers since 1949 has been the exception rather than the rule in international armed conflicts. Absent any protest, therefore, it would seem that the failure to appoint a Protecting Power is not, at least in the eyes of most States, seen as a violation of their treaty obligations. At the same time, there is no indication that the High Contracting Parties consider that Article 8 has fallen into desuetude." ICRC, 2016 GC I COMMENTARY, *supra* note 7, commentary on art. 8, ¶ 1045. For another example, *see* ILC, *Report on the Work of Its Seventieth Session*, *supra* note 18, at 54, ¶ 12 (with regard to the obligation to display the distinctive emblem in Article 12 of Additional Protocol II).

167. 2016 GC I COMMENTARY, *supra* note 7, commentary on art. 38, ¶ 2548.

168. For the reasons why we need treaty interpretation, *see* Panos Merkouris, *Introduction: Interpretation Is a Science, Is an Art, Is a Science*, in TREATY INTERPRETATION AND THE VIENNA CONVENTION ON THE LAW OF TREATIES: 30 YEARS ON 1, 5–7 (Malgosia Fitzmaurice, Olufemi A. Elias & Panos Merkouris eds., 2010).

A challenge linked to relatively older treaties such as the Geneva Conventions is that certain aspects of their language may not be adapted to today's societal, technological, and operational realities. While in such cases the purpose behind the rules often remains valid and relevant, there is a need to refresh the understanding of the treaty text to take account of current law and practice. The Vienna Convention allows for, indeed mandates, such an updated reading. Part of this interpretive work necessarily involves clarifying ambiguity where such ambiguity stands as an obstacle to interpretation and application. In this endeavor, commentaries cannot make new law, only clarify existing law.

The Vienna Convention offers a coherent legal framework for the interpretation of treaties, including IHL treaties. More than seventy years after the adoption of the Geneva Conventions and sixty years since the initial Commentaries were published, the updated Commentaries rely on developments in law and subsequent practice as important sources of interpretation. However, identifying subsequent practice meeting the requirements of Article 31(3)(b) of the Vienna Convention is challenging, especially in relation to universally ratified treaties such as the Geneva Conventions. Through the ILC's work, recourse to subsequent practice under the supplementary rule of interpretation in the sense of Article 32 of the Vienna Convention has been clarified and is now understood to apply broadly.

Using the methodology set out in the Vienna Convention, the ICRC has undertaken a once-in-a-generation study to update its Commentaries on the Geneva Conventions in light of developments in law and practice since their adoption. The result of this study to date confirms that the Geneva Conventions are living instruments that continue to play an essential role in preventing and alleviating the suffering caused by contemporary armed conflicts.

17

A Perspective on the Updated Third Geneva Convention Commentary from a United States Practitioner

MICHAEL W. MEIER*

In June of 2020, the International Committee of the Red Cross (ICRC) launched its updated Commentary on the Third Geneva Convention: Convention (III) Relative to the Treatment of Prisoners of War (2020 GC III Commentary).[1] It follows the release of the ICRC's 2016 Commentary on the First Geneva Convention: Convention (I) for the Amelioration of the Condition of the Wounded and Sick in the Armed Forces in the Field (2016 GC I Commentary)[2] and the 2017 Commentary on the Second Geneva Convention: Convention (II) for the Amelioration of the Condition of the Wounded, Sick and Shipwrecked

---

*. Michael W. Meier is the Special Assistant to the Judge Advocate General for Law of War Matters with the Department of the Army. The views expressed in this chapter are those of the author in his personal capacity and should not be understood as representing those of the Department of the Army or any other United States government entity.

1. INTERNATIONAL COMMITTEE OF THE RED CROSS, COMMENTARY ON THE THIRD GENEVA CONVENTION: CONVENTION (III) RELATIVE TO THE TREATMENT OF PRISONERS OF WAR (2020), https://ihl-databases.icrc.org/applic/ihl/ihl.nsf/Treaty.xsp?action=openDocument&documentId=77CB9983BE01D004C12563CD002D6B3E [hereinafter 2020 GC III COMMENTARY].

2. INTERNATIONAL COMMITTEE OF THE RED CROSS, COMMENTARY ON THE FIRST GENEVA CONVENTION: CONVENTION (I) FOR THE AMELIORATION OF THE CONDITION OF THE WOUNDED AND SICK IN THE ARMED FORCES IN THE FIELD (2016), https://ihl-databases.icrc.org/applic/ihl/ihl.nsf/Treaty.xsp?documentId=4825657B0C7E6BF0C12563CD002D6B0B&action=openDocument [hereinafter 2016 GC I COMMENTARY].

Members of Armed Forces at Sea (2017 GC II Commentary).³ According to the ICRC, the updated 2020 GC III Commentary aims to provide an understanding of the law as it is interpreted today so it can be applied effectively in current and future armed conflicts.⁴ It analyzes how the experiences gained over the past seventy years have "generated a detailed understanding of how they operate in armed conflicts all over the world and in contexts very different from those that led to their adoption."⁵ The ICRC readily acknowledges that this updated 2020 GC III Commentary is very different from the Commentary to Geneva Convention III Relative to the Treatment of Prisoners of War under the general editorship of Jean Pictet (Pictet Commentary),⁶ as "the new Commentaries go far beyond their first editions from the 1950s, which were largely based on the preparatory work for the Conventions and on the experience of the Second World War."⁷ The ICRC Commentaries project, led by Jean-Marie Henckaerts, has put tremendous work into this multi-year project and it is an impressive undertaking. The 2020 GC III Commentary is the largest effort to date at two thousand pages.⁸

A commentary can be an excellent resource for practitioners as it is often the first resource one would consult for treaty interpretation. Commentaries can provide a way to help discern State practice and review academic writings on a particular topic, and they are an invaluable bedrock tool for academic analysis and products.⁹ A noted academic, Sean Watts, has called the 2020 GC III Commentary a "remarkable feat of scholarship worthy of academic attention."¹⁰ However, he also cautioned that it is a "fraught source for the military, diplomatic,

---

3. INTERNATIONAL COMMITTEE OF THE RED CROSS, COMMENTARY ON THE SECOND GENEVA CONVENTION: CONVENTION (II) FOR THE AMELIORATION OF THE CONDITION OF THE WOUNDED, SICK AND SHIPWRECKED MEMBERS OF ARMED FORCES AT SEA (2017), https://ihl-databases.icrc.org/applic/ihl/ihl.nsf/Treaty.xsp?documentId=2F5AA9B07AB61934C12563CD002D6B25&action=openDocument [hereinafter 2017 GC II COMMENTARY].

4. *Updated Commentary Brings Fresh Insights on Continued Relevance of Geneva Conventions for Treatment of Prisoners of War*, INTERNATIONAL COMMITTEE OF THE RED CROSS (July 10, 2020), https://www.icrc.org/en/document/updated-commentary-third-geneva-convention.

5. *Id.*

6. COMMENTARY TO GENEVA CONVENTION III RELATIVE TO THE TREATMENT OF PRISONERS OF WAR (Jean Pictet ed., 1960) [hereinafter 1960 GC III COMMENTARY].

7. *Updated Commentary*, *supra* note 4. Pictet's commentary on the First Geneva Convention was published in 1952. His commentaries on the Second and Third Geneva Conventions followed in 1960.

8. Sean Watts, *Interpretation in the Updated GCIII Commentary*, ARTICLES OF WAR (Dec. 15, 2020), https://lieber.westpoint.edu/interpretation-updated-gciii-commentary/.

9. INTERCROSS: THE ICRC IN THE US & CANADA—THE PODCAST, *Episode #108 Updated Commentary on the Third Geneva Convention: The Treatment of Prisoners of War* (Sept. 8, 2020), https://intercrossblog.icrc.org/intercross-icrc-podcast-episodes/episode-108-geneva-conventions-commentaries-3#sthash.5csaxZTa.dpbs=.

10. Watts, *supra* note 8.

and judicial practitioners" who have to interpret and implement the Third Geneva Convention on behalf of a State Party.[11]

As I am a United States Army practitioner in this area, this chapter will look at the 2020 GC III Commentary from the United States' perspective on treaty interpretation. However, it is not intended as an official response of the United States to the 2020 GC III Commentary. It simply reflects my personal views of how the United States should respond to this ICRC effort. It is my hope that the United States, as well as other States Parties to the Third Geneva Convention, will provide a formal response to the 2020 GC III Commentary. A formal U.S. response would provide much needed clarity with respect to both State practice and interpretation of the Third Geneva Convention.[12]

The chapter examines several aspects of the 2020 GC III Commentary. Part I addresses the "authoritative" status of the Commentary. Part II raises particular concerns regarding the ICRC's methodology in preparing it. Part III compares the ICRC interpretation of various articles of the Third Geneva Convention with how the United States has interpreted those articles in practice. This will be done by reviewing the Department of Defense (DoD) Law of War Manual[13] and other official documents and writings by senior U.S. officials. Finally, Part IV considers the implications of the 2020 GC III Commentary for U.S. military and government personnel who must interpret the Third Geneva Convention.

I. THE "AUTHORITATIVE" STATUS OF THE ICRC COMMENTARY

As a practitioner, I keep numerous commentaries in arm's reach, such as the Tallinn Manual 2.0 on Cyber Operations,[14] the ICRC Customary International Humanitarian Law study,[15] and the Manual of the Law of Armed Conflict by the United Kingdom Ministry of Defence.[16] The most prominent and in easiest reach is the Pictet Commentary. This four-volume set is highlighted, has tabs and notes, and is torn in places from heavy use over the years. Although commentaries are

---

11. *Id.*

12. Convention (III) Relative to the Treatment of Prisoners of War, Aug. 12, 1949, 6 U.S.T. 3316, 75 U.N.T.S. 135 [hereinafter Third Geneva Convention].

13. OFFICE OF THE GENERAL COUNSEL, U.S. DEPARTMENT OF DEFENSE, LAW OF WAR MANUAL (rev. ed., Dec. 2016) [hereinafter DoD LAW OF WAR MANUAL].

14. TALLINN MANUAL 2.0 ON THE INTERNATIONAL LAW APPLICABLE TO CYBER WARFARE (Michael N. Schmitt ed., 2017).

15. CUSTOMARY INTERNATIONAL HUMANITARIAN LAW (Jean-Marie Henckaerts & Louise Doswald-Beck eds., 2005).

16. UNITED KINGDOM MINISTRY OF DEFENCE, THE MANUAL OF THE LAW OF ARMED CONFLICT (2004).

extremely useful to a U.S. military or government practitioner, it is important also to understand a commentary's limitations. The most important limitation is that a commentary is not an official part of the corresponding treaty. One commentator noted that "law of war commentaries, and international law commentaries more generally . . . play a pivotal role in formulating key questions and providing thoughtful, informed opinions on those questions."[17]

The role of government practitioners is to provide accurate legal advice to policy makers. Lieutenant General Charles N. Pede, the 40th Judge Advocate General of the United States Army, says it is the role of Judge Advocates to make clear what the law is to commanders. However, he also cautions that "the sheer volume and density of writing and publishing and commentary on the law of armed conflict presents the very real danger that people will no longer be able to tell the difference between what the law is, and what someone wants the law to be."[18] Accordingly, a practitioner must be able to distinguish what the law is from someone's unofficial view of the law.

The 1960 Pictet Commentary made this distinction clear. Its foreword plainly set out the views of its authors regarding the status of their work:

> Although published by the International Committee, the Commentary is the personal work of its authors. The Committee, moreover, whenever called upon for an opinion on a provision of an international Convention, always takes care to emphasize that only the participant States are qualified, through consultation between themselves, to give an official and, as it were, authentic interpretation of an intergovernmental treaty.[19]

Unfortunately, similar language was not carried forward by the authors of the updated Commentaries. In the introductions to the 2016 GC I Commentary and the 2017 GC II Commentary, the ICRC described its previously published commentaries to the 1949 Geneva Conventions and their 1977 Additional Protocols as "authoritative."[20] The 2020 GC III Commentary contains a revised and much longer introduction section than those two previous editions. Importantly,

---

17. Eric Jensen & Carolyn Sharp, *Non-State Commentaries: Law Making or Law Suggesting?*, ARTICLES OF WAR (Apr. 8, 2021), https://lieber.westpoint.edu/non-state-commentaries-law-making-law-suggesting/.

18. Charlie Dunlap, *LTG Pede on the "COIN/CT Hangover"; ROE, War Sustaining Targets, and Much More!*, LAWFIRE (Mar. 7, 2020), https://sites.duke.edu/lawfire/2020/03/07/ltg-pede-on-the-coin-ct-hangover-roe-war-sustaining-targets-and-much-more/.

19. 1960 GC III COMMENTARY, *supra* note 6, at 1.

20. 2016 GC I COMMENTARY, *supra* note 2, ¶ 3 ("Over the years, these six ICRC Commentaries have come to be recognized as well-respected and authoritative interpretations of the Conventions and their 1977 Additional Protocols, essential for the understanding and application of the law."); 2017 GC II COMMENTARY, *supra* note 3, ¶ 3.

the ICRC no longer refers to the previously published commentaries as "authoritative," but instead reflects:

> The ICRC mandated the writing of the original Commentaries pursuant to its role as guardian and promoter of humanitarian law. The same is true for the current updated edition. This role is recognized in the Statutes of the International Red Cross and Red Crescent Movement, in particular the ICRC's role "to work for the understanding and dissemination of knowledge of international humanitarian law applicable in armed conflicts and to prepare any development thereof."[21]

The ICRC argues that what sets its commentaries apart from other academic commentaries is that "the contributors were able to draw on research in the ICRC archives, while respecting their confidential nature, to assess the application and interpretation of the Conventions and Protocols since their adoption." And the unique role the ICRC plays as "guardian and promoter of humanitarian law" requires it to interpret humanitarian law treaties, which is at the heart of its daily work.[22]

It is well accepted that States' views remain dispositive with respect to interpretations of treaties to which they are a party.[23] As the United States has said:

> It is a fundamental and long-standing principle of customary international law that treaties are authoritatively interpreted by the Parties themselves through mutual agreement, either directly through the ordinary channels of international relations or indirectly as the result of recourse to good offices, mediation, or conciliation.[24]

The former General Counsel to the DoD, Paul C. Ney, Jr., in a 2019 speech at the Israeli Defense Forces Conference, noted that "international law is law made by States and for States. Other actors, such as nongovernmental organizations (NGOs) and academics, can play an important role, but States have the primary responsibility for developing and implementing international law."[25] Within the

---

21. 2020 GC III COMMENTARY, *supra* note 1, ¶ 71.

22. *Id.*, ¶¶ 71, 73.

23. Jensen & Sharp, *supra* note 17.

24. Observations of the United States of America on the Human Rights Committee's General Comment 33: The Obligations of States Parties under the Optional Protocol to the International Covenant on Civil and Political Rights, Dec. 22, 2008, https://2009-2017.state.gov/documents/organization/138852.pdf.

25. Quinta Jurecic, *Defense Department General Counsel Remarks at IDF Conference*, LAWFARE (May 28, 2019), https://www.lawfareblog.com/defense-department-general-counsel-remarks-idf-conference.

DoD, that "authoritative statement on the law of war" is set out in the DoD Law of War Manual.[26]

Although the ICRC attempts to distinguish itself from "academic" commentaries because of its extensive experience in interpreting the Conventions, its commentaries still do not rise to the level of an authoritative interpretation of the 1949 Geneva Conventions. Both the Pictet Commentary and the 2020 GC III Commentary reflect the important role the ICRC played during the negotiations and subsequent implementation of the Conventions, but it is not a High Contracting Party to them.

Accordingly, it is important for the ICRC to clarify that the 2020 GC III Commentary reflects its views regarding State practice, but that it is not an authoritative source of interpretation. It should also acknowledge that States' views still remain dispositive on the content of the law of armed conflict (LOAC). Thus, instead of viewing its interpretation of the 2020 GC III Commentary as "authoritative" or suggesting that its role as "the guardian" of IHL gives it special status with respect to interpretation, the ICRC should include a statement similar to the Pictet Commentary that the views expressed are its alone. The organization should recognize that the 2020 GC III Commentary is a way to influence State views and encourage the evolution of the law.[27] Such a clarification would better align how practitioners should use the 2020 III GC Commentary with the ICRC's proper recognition of the Commentary's persuasive authority.

II. THE METHODOLOGY OF TREATY INTERPRETATION BY THE ICRC

In addition to the concern noted above regarding the ICRC's assertion of the 2020 GC III Commentary's "authoritative" status, there are concerns with the methodology used in preparing it. The ICRC departed from the established principles of treaty interpretation in its flawed application of the 1969 Vienna Convention on the Law of Treaties (Vienna Convention).[28] This part addresses three ways where the ICRC methodology used in the 2020 GC III Commentary departs from established principles. They include (1) substituting its own interpretation of the "object and purpose" of the Third Geneva Convention when the original drafters specifically declined to provide one; (2) affording too much weight to statements and writings of the ICRC, academics, and NGOs, while giving insufficient weight to the text itself and State practice in applying the Convention; and (3) reliance on subsequent treaties to which certain States are not a party.

---

26. *See* U.S. Department of Defense, DoD Directive 2311.01, DoD Law of War Program, ¶ 3.1.b. (July 2, 2020).

27. Jensen & Sharp, *supra* note 17.

28. Vienna Convention on the Law of Treaties, May 23, 1969, 1155 U.N.T.S. 331 [hereinafter Vienna Convention].

The ICRC states that "[t]he updated Commentary applies the methodology for treaty interpretation as set out in the 1969 Vienna Convention on the Law of Treaties, in particular Articles 31–33."[29] In drafting the 2020 GC III Commentary, the ICRC acknowledged that the Third Geneva Convention needed to be interpreted in accordance with Article 31(1) of the Vienna Convention "in *good faith* in accordance with the *ordinary meaning* to be given to the terms of the treaty in their *context* and in light of its *object and purpose*" (emphasis added).[30] In Article 31(2), the context to be considered for treaty interpretation comprises not only the text of the treaty, but also its preamble and annexes.[31] Additionally, the 2020 GC III Commentary, pursuant to Article 31(3), would consider any subsequent agreement between the parties regarding the interpretation of the treaty or the application of its provisions; any subsequent practice in the application of the treaty that establishes the agreement of the parties regarding its interpretation; and any relevant rules of international law applicable in the relations between the parties.[32] The ICRC specifically mentions international criminal law, international human rights law, the Additional Protocols, customary international law, and the law of State responsibility as "relevant rules" it considered.[33] The question then is what does this really mean and did the ICRC, in compiling the 2020 GC III Commentary, properly apply these accepted precepts of treaty interpretation?

A. The Vienna Convention on the Law of Treaties

The Vienna Convention provides the general rules for treaty interpretation in Articles 31 and 32, which have been recognized as customary international law by the United States.[34]

Article 31 states:

1. A treaty shall be interpreted in good faith in accordance with the ordinary meaning to be given to the terms of the treaty in their context and in light of its object and purpose.[35]

---

29. 2020 GC III COMMENTARY, *supra* note 1, ¶ 75.

30. *Id.*, ¶ 77.

31. *Id.*, ¶ 83.

32. *Id.*, ¶ 92.

33. *Id.*, ¶ 94.

34. *See* William P. Rogers, Letter of Submittal, Oct. 18, 1971, in *Message of the President of the United States Transmitting the Vienna Convention on the Law of Treaties Signed for the United States on April 24, 1970,* 92 Congress, Executive L, p. 1 (1971) ("Although not yet in force, the Convention is already generally recognized as the authoritative guide to current treaty law and practice.").

35. Vienna Convention, *supra* note 28, art. 31(1).

2. The context for the purpose of the interpretation of a treaty shall comprise, in addition to the text, including its preamble and annexes:
   (a) any agreement relating to the treaty which was made between all the parties in connexion with the conclusion of the treaty;
   (b) any instrument which was made by one or more parties in connexion with the conclusion of the treaty and accepted by the other parties as an instrument related to the treaty.[36]
3. There shall be taken into account, together with the context:
   (a) any subsequent agreement between the parties regarding the interpretation of the treaty or the application of its provisions;
   (b) any subsequent practice in the application of the treaty which establishes the agreement of the parties regarding its interpretation;
   (c) any relevant rules of international law applicable in the relations between the parties.[37]
4. A special meaning shall be given to a term if it is established that the parties so intended.[38]

Article 32 provides:

Recourse may be had to supplementary means of interpretation, including the preparatory work of the treaty and the circumstances of its conclusion, in order to confirm the meaning resulting from the application of Article 31, or to determine the meaning when the interpretation according to Article 31:

(a) leaves the meaning ambiguous or obscure; or
(b) leads to a result which is manifestly absurd or unreasonable.[39]

Article 31 is entitled the "general rule" of interpretation. The singular noun emphasizes that this article contains only one rule, albeit with three main elements: the text, its context, and the object and purpose of the treaty. Although it may appear to create a hierarchy of interpretation, Article 31's three paragraphs represent a logical progression in the way one should interpret a treaty. Accordingly, one would first look at the text of the treaty, followed by context, and then look to other matters, in particular subsequent material, in order to determine the intention of the parties.[40]

Anthony Aust makes clear that interpreting a treaty in good faith, the first principle of Article 31(1), follows the principle of *pacta sunt sevanda* set forth in Article 26, which states that "[e]very treaty in force is binding upon the parties

---

36. *Id.*, art. 31(2).

37. *Id.*, art. 31(3)

38. *Id.*, art. 31(4).

39. *Id.*, art. 32.

40. Anthony Aust, Modern Treaty Law and Practice 208 (3d ed. 2013).

and must be performed in good faith."⁴¹ Mark Villiger argues that good faith "raises at the outset the presumption that the treaty terms were intended to mean something rather than nothing."⁴² Accordingly, parties to the treaty must act in an honest, fair, and reasonable manner and refrain taking unfair advantage. Further, Villiger concludes good faith requires that even when the treaty terms seem clear, the words cannot be interpreted so literally that it would lead to an absurd result. The parties must look to the context and seek another interpretation.⁴³ Giving a term its ordinary meaning is the most likely reflection of the intention of the treaty parties, absent evidence to the contrary.

Article 31(2) deals with context and is a key component for treaty interpretation. The ICRC correctly notes that in addition to the text of the treaty, consideration must be given to the preamble and any annexes to the treaty.⁴⁴ It also includes consideration of any agreement between all the parties in connection with the conclusion of the treaty or of an instrument by one or more of the parties in connection with its conclusion.

Finally, Article 31(3) provides that, together with the context, there shall be taken into account any subsequent agreement between the parties regarding interpretation of the treaty or application of its provisions. This provision talks about an "agreement," so there is no requirement that the subsequent agreement itself be a treaty. However, it must be an agreement "between the parties."⁴⁵

The most important aspect of paragraph (3) for treaty interpretation is consideration of subsequent practice by the parties. As Aust notes, "however precise a text appears to be, the way in which it is actually applied by the parties is usually a good indication of what they understand it to mean, provided the practice is consistent and common to, or accepted, expressly or tacitly, by both or all the parties."⁴⁶ The rule also provides that other relevant rules of international law applicable in the relations between the parties be considered. Therefore, a treaty must be interpreted within the wider context of international law. This means that an interpretation not only may require regard to international law in 1949 when the Geneva Conventions were adopted, but also may look to contemporary law of today.

Article 32 of the Vienna Convention addresses supplementary means of interpretation, such as a *travaux préparatoires*,⁴⁷ which are not included in the

41. *Id.*

42. Mark E. Villiger, Commentary on the 1969 Vienna Convention on the Law of Treaties 425–26 (2009).

43. *Id.*

44. 2020 GC III Commentary, *supra* note 1, ¶¶ 83–85.

45. Vienna Convention, *supra* note 28, art. 31(3).

46. Aust, *supra* note 40, at 215.

47. *Id.* at 218 (a *travaux préparatoires* is "generally understood to include written materials, such as successive drafts of the treaty, conference records, explanatory statements by an expert

consideration of Article 31, which is limited to the primary means of interpreting a treaty. Article 32 sets forth circumstances where it is necessary to consider supplementary elements to confirm the meaning of a treaty provision based on application of Article 31.[48] The second part of Article 32 also provides for a review of supplementary elements as a means of interpretation when the primary source leaves the meaning "ambiguous or obscure" or leads to a "manifestly absurd or unreasonable" result. Here, unlike the first part of Article 32, the analysis is not to "confirm" the meaning but rather to determine the meaning.[49]

B. Concerns with ICRC Interpretation of Vienna Convention to the Third Geneva Convention

1. OBJECT AND PURPOSE

The phrase "object and purpose" is frequently used with respect to treaties. However, efforts to effectively define it have left authors admitting "regret" that it remains an "enigma."[50] This is unfortunate, since Article 31, the general rule of treaty interpretation, requires that the object and purpose serve as one of the three sources that practitioners use to determine the meaning of a treaty.

However, Article 31 provides the necessary framework for interpreting the Vienna Convention itself. To determine the "object and purpose," Article 31 requires that one look to the ordinary meaning of the words. One author has noted that the word "object" is defined as "the purpose, aim, or goal of a specific action or effort." The word "purpose" is defined as "the object toward which one strives for or for which something exists." The term "object and purpose" therefore refers to "the goals that the drafters of the treaty hope to achieve."[51] Looking to context does not provide much help as there are no supplemental agreements to the Vienna Convention that define "object and purpose," nor is subsequent State practice helpful.[52] Finally, "object and purpose" reflects a "holistic mode of interpretation that accounts for more than the goals of the specific treaty provisions and encompasses the normative logic" when the entirety of the treaty's provisions are considered.[53] Therefore, "object and purpose" can be described as the "treaty's

---

49. *Id.* at 218.

50. Isabelle Buffard & Karl Zemanek, *The Object and Purpose of a Treaty: An Enigma?*, 3 AUSTRIAN REVIEW OF INTERNATIONAL AND EUROPEAN LAW 311, 343 (1998).

51. David S. Jones & Thomas N. Sanders, *The Object and Purpose of a Treaty: Three Interpretive Methods*, 43 VANDERBILT JOURNAL OF TRANSNATIONAL LAW 565, 578 (2010).

52. *Id.* at 579.

53. *Id.*

---

consultant at a codification conference, uncontested interpretative statements by the chairman of a drafting committee").

48. *Id.* at 217.

goals and the character of the means employed to achieve them."[54] As one of the fundamental principles of treaty interpretation is to discern the intention of the parties, it is unfortunate that the ICRC failed to do so with respect to the "object and purpose" of the Third Geneva Convention.

In the 2020 GC III Commentary, the ICRC attempts to set forth the "object and purpose" of the Third Geneva Convention not once, but twice. First, the introduction section defines the term "object and purpose" as follows:

> Strictly speaking the object of a treaty may be said to refer to the rights and obligations stipulated by the treaty, while the purpose refers to the aim which is to be achieved by the treaty provisions. However, the phrase "object and purpose" is used as "a combined whole." Thus, a treaty's object and purpose is said to refer to its "raison d'être," its "fundamental core" or "its essential content."[55]

The ICRC then describes the "object and purpose" of the Third Geneva Convention: "The overall object and purpose of the Third Convention is to ensure that prisoners of war are humanely treated at all times, while allowing belligerents to intern captured enemy combatants to prevent them from returning to the battlefield."[56] Later, in the preamble, the ICRC provides a second, and different, "object and purpose":

> The preamble provides no further reasons for the adoption of the Third Convention, rendering it of limited use in determining the Convention's object and purpose. One may, however, deduce its object and purpose by considering the preamble to the 1929 Convention. Thus, the object and purpose of the 1949 Convention would also be "to mitigate as far as possible, the inevitable rigours [of a war] and to alleviate the condition of prisoners of war."[57]

It is certainly correct that a treaty will often use the preamble to set out its "object and purpose." The Pictet Commentary notes that the preamble to the Third Geneva Convention (as well as all of the other three 1949 Conventions) was extremely brief and provided only limited guidance.[58] The Pictet Commentary explained that this is because "it is not always a matter of indifference whether a treaty does or does not open with a statement of motives and a [sic] exact definition of its object."[59] Some delegations, along with the ICRC, pushed for an

---

54. *Id.* at 580.

55. 2020 GC III COMMENTARY, *supra* note 1, ¶ 87.

56. *Id.*, ¶ 89.

57. *Id.*, ¶ 144.

58. 1960 GC III COMMENTARY, *supra* note 6, at 12.

59. *Id.* at 14.

expansive preamble while others disagreed. In the end, the delegations concluded that it was better not to have a preamble without consensus and the question of inserting a preamble was put to the vote and rejected by a large majority.[60]

The 2020 GC III Commentary provides a very perfunctory overview of the historical background that leaves out much of the rich discussion in the Pictet Commentary regarding the intentions of the negotiating States. Despite acknowledging that the preamble to the Third Geneva Convention is of limited use in determining the "object and purpose," the ICRC asserted, "one may, however, deduce its object and purpose by considering the preamble to the 1929 Convention,"[61] which ignores the intention of the drafters. Further, that preamble provides an "object and purpose" that is different from the introduction.

The concern is not with the formulation of the "object and purpose" crafted by the ICRC, but rather with the methodology used and the lack of discussion regarding the disagreement among the parties in 1949. The updated Commentary's failure to address the fact that States intentionally did not include a preamble specifically setting forth the "object and purpose" disregards the parties' intent. Instead, the ICRC substitutes its own conclusion and interpretation in their place.

2. STATE PRACTICE

In the 2020 GC III Commentary, the ICRC correctly describes the appropriate approach to assessing State practice. However, as with its 2005 Customary International Humanitarian Law study,[62] the ICRC fails to rigorously apply that approach. In November 2006, then DoD General Counsel, William J. Haynes II, and then Department of State Legal Adviser, John B. Bellinger III, penned a joint letter setting forth the official U.S. government response to the study.[63] Two of the methodological flaws noted by the United States are repeated with the 2020 Commentary: (1) undue weight is given to NGOs and the ICRC itself, as distinct from relying on actual practice by States parties; and (2) undue emphasis is placed on written materials, such as military manuals or other guidelines by States, in contrast to actual operational practice.[64]

---

60. *Id.* at 16.

61. 2020 GC III COMMENTARY, *supra* note 1, ¶ 144.

62. *See* CUSTOMARY INTERNATIONAL HUMANITARIAN LAW, *supra* note 15.

63. John B. Bellinger III & William J. Haynes II, *A US Government Response to the International Committee of the Red Cross Study Customary International Law*, 89 INTERNATIONAL REVIEW OF THE RED CROSS 443 (June 2007), *available at* https://international-review.icrc.org/sites/default/files/irrc_866_11.pdf.

64. *Id.* at 444–46. In the U.S. response to the Customary International Law Study, there are five concerns regarding the methodology:

- First, for many rules proffered as rising to the level of customary international law, the State practice cited is insufficiently dense to meet the "extensive and virtually uniform" standard generally required to demonstrate the existence of a customary rule.

(a) Reliance on Academic Writings and Writings by the ICRC Versus State Practice

Article 31(3) of the Vienna Convention provides that any interpretation should consider subsequent practice by the parties. As noted above, even when the text of a treaty appears precise, how that text is applied by the States parties is a strong indication of what they understand it to mean.[65] State practice can help clarify how terms should be understood, even if not defined in the treaty, as well as resolve textual uncertainties. A State Party's interpretation should be given appropriate weight, for it negotiated and concluded the treaty and is primarily responsible to implement it.

The 2020 GC III Commentary, like the 2005 Customary International Humanitarian Law study, does not afford the requisite weight to the subsequent practice of the States parties. Instead of looking to the practice of States in construing and applying the Third Geneva Convention, the 2020 GC III Commentary appears to place undue weight on the ICRC's interpretations and academic writings. For example, a review of the 2020 GC III Commentary with respect to Common Article 1 finds only three footnotes that directly reference State practice (by Norway and the United States).[66] However, there are over twenty footnotes referencing decisions by the International Court of Justice, seven

- Second, the United States is troubled by the type of practice on which the Study has, in too many places, relied. The initial U.S. review of the State practice volumes suggests that the Study places too much emphasis on written materials, such as military manuals and other guidelines published by States, as opposed to actual operational practice by States during armed conflict. Although manuals may provide important indications of State behavior and *opinio juris*, they cannot be a replacement for a meaningful assessment of operational State practice in connection with actual military operations. The United States also is troubled by the extent to which the Study relies on nonbinding resolutions of the General Assembly, given that States may lend their support to a particular resolution, or determine not to break consensus in regard to such a resolution, for reasons having nothing to do with a belief that the propositions in it reflect customary international law.
- Third, the Study gives undue weight to statements by non-governmental organizations and the ICRC itself, when those statements do not reflect whether a particular rule constitutes customary international law accepted by States.
- Fourth, although the Study acknowledges in principle the significance of negative practice, especially among those States that remain non-parties to relevant treaties, that practice is in important instances given inadequate weight.
- Finally, the Study often fails to pay due regard to the practice of specially affected States. A distinct but related point is that the Study tends to regard as equivalent the practice of States that have relatively little history of participation in armed conflict and the practice of States that have had a greater extent and depth of experience or that have otherwise had significant opportunities to develop a carefully considered military doctrine. The latter category of States, however, has typically contributed a significantly greater quantity and quality of practice.

Id. at 444–46.

65. *See* AUST, *supra* note 40, at 215.
66. *See* 2020 GC III COMMENTARY, *supra* note 1, Article 1 nn.50, 67, 93.

citations to the ICRC Customary International Humanitarian Law study, more than a dozen to academic writings, and over ten to other ICRC documents.[67]

Scholarly articles can be useful to the extent they help identify relevant State practice, but the views of those authors or the ICRC do not outweigh State practice. Additionally, the ICRC's work in developing the commentaries does not constitute evidence of subsequent agreement or State practice, which is most relevant for the interpretation of the Third Geneva Convention.

The 2020 GC III Commentary does provide examples of State practice and citations to various military manuals of States.[68] However, those citations are outnumbered by academic and ICRC writings. It appears that the ICRC has given more weight to the latter than the former. These scholarly articles, which include articles written by State practitioners, can be a useful way to determine a particular State's interpretation or practice, but care must be taken. Many articles, even when written by a military or government practitioner, are intended to advocate a certain view of the law or argue for a change in it. They are often written in the personal capacity of the author and generally come with a disclaimer. Accordingly, these articles do not necessarily reflect the official view of the practitioner's government.

(b) Other Military Manuals

The 2020 GC III Commentary also includes many references to military manuals and handbooks. Although these sources may be preferable to the reliance on academic writings or the ICRC's own publications, care must be taken as certain military manuals and regulations are not necessarily an accurate reflection of a State's view of its legal obligations under a particular treaty. Military manuals and handbooks are not created equal.

For the U.S. Department of Defense, the DoD Law of War Manual is the authoritative statement on the law of war.[69] In a positive note, the 2020 GC III Commentary cites the DoD Law of War Manual 128 times. However, there are instances where the 2020 GC III Commentary cites out-of-date U.S. publications, such as the 2017 Operational Law Handbook[70] or the 1956 Army Field Manual

---

67. *Id.* at Article 1 nn.1, 3, 5, 10, 12, 14–16, 22, 25, 28–30, 34–35, 50–51, 66, 71–73, 75–77, 80, 83–84, 87–94, 96, 99, 105–09, 112–14, 122–25, 130–42, 151, 153.

68. *See* 2020 GC III COMMENTARY, *supra* note 1, Article 3 nn.309–17, which provide references to military manuals from States such as Australia, Canada, Chad, Denmark, Djibouti, Nepal, Sri Lanka, Turkey, the United Kingdom, and the United States.

69. DOD LAW OF WAR MANUAL, *supra* note 13.

70. *See* INTERNATIONAL AND OPERATIONAL LAW DEPARTMENT, THE JUDGE ADVOCATE GENERAL'S LEGAL CENTER & SCHOOL, U.S. ARMY, OPERATIONAL LAW HANDBOOK (2020). The 2020 Operational Law Handbook is the current version.

27-10, The Law of Land Warfare.[71] In August 2019, the Army Field Manual was superseded by the Army and Marine Corps publication The Commander's Handbook on the Law of Land Warfare.[72] That publication provides guidance to soldiers and marines on the doctrine and practice related to customary international law and treaty law applicable to the conduct of land warfare. However, it clearly notes that it "summarizes the law and practice under LOAC" and provides "general and sometimes more narrow guidelines than may be allowed for a matter of law."[73] Similarly, the Operational Law Handbook includes a statement that "[t]he Handbook is NOT an official representation of U.S. policy regarding the binding application of various sources of law, and should not be used as such."[74]

One commentator found it "astonishing[]" that such manuals should not be used in the 2020 GC III Commentary because they reflect policy versus the law, given the difficulty getting States to make their positions known.[75] The author recognizes that it can be difficult to ascertain State practice even under the best of circumstances. However, military manuals and handbooks that are often used to provide guidance to forces may present, for operational and policy reasons, a more restrictive view than a particular treaty or rule under the law of war may allow. The fact that it can be difficult to sift through all these publications to ascertain State practice does not give the ICRC license to mischaracterize a State's legal interpretation of a treaty.

3. Reliance on Subsequent Treaties

Third, the ICRC references subsequent treaties—such as the 1977 Additional Protocols, human rights treaties, customary international law, and the law of State responsibility—as evidence of other relevant rules of international law. The updated 2020 GC III Commentary specifically cites the Rome Statute of the International Criminal Court,[76] the Convention Against Torture,[77] the International Covenant on Civil and Political Rights,[78] and the European Convention on Human Rights.[79] When trying to determine if the Additional Protocols or other specified treaties

---

71. This publication was replaced by DEPARTMENT OF THE ARMY AND UNITED STATES MARINE CORPS, FM 6-27/MCTP 11-10C, THE COMMANDER'S HANDBOOK ON THE LAW OF LAND WARFARE (Aug. 2019).

72. Id.

73. Id. at vii.

74. OPERATIONAL LAW HANDBOOK, supra note 70, Preface.

75. Marco Sassòli, Is the Time for Law of War Treaty Commentaries Over?, ARTICLES OF WAR (Feb. 26, 2021), https://lieber.westpoint.edu/time-law-war-treaty-commentaries-over-2/.

76. Rome Statute of the International Criminal Court, July 17, 1998, 2187 U.N.T.S. 90.

77. Convention Against Torture and Other Cruel, Inhuman or Degrading Treatment or Punishment, Dec. 10, 1984, 1465 U.N.T.S. 85.

78. International Covenant on Civil and Political Rights, Dec. 19, 1966, 999 U.N.T.S. 171.

79. Convention for the Protection of Human Rights and Fundamental Freedoms, Nov. 4, 1950, 213 U.N.T.S. 222.

constitute "relevant rules of international law applicable in the relations between the parties," they can be interpreted within the wider context of international law. But that process has limitations.

The 2006 International Law Commission report[80] offers some guidance. Article 31(3)(c) allows an interpreter to consider other treaties to help determine a consistent meaning of a term or provision. The report notes that these other rules are of "particular relevance where parties to the treaty under interpretation are also parties to the other treaty, where the treaty rule reflects customary international law, or where it provides evidence of the common understanding of the parties as to the object and purpose of the treaty or as to the meaning of a particular term."[81] Therefore, while the Additional Protocols and other treaties cited by the ICRC may have some usefulness, they are not directly relevant for interpretation purposes until all the parties to the 1949 Geneva Conventions are also parties to those agreements.

III. COMMENTS ON SELECT ARTICLES OF THE 2020 GC III COMMENTARY

This part will look at select articles of the Third Geneva Convention and the 2020 GC III Commentary to illustrate how the methodological concerns about the 2020 GC III Commentary are inconsistent with U.S. interpretation and its State's practice.

A. Common Article 1 — Respect for the Convention

No provision has drawn as much attention since publication of the 2016 GC I Commentary as Common Article 1.[82] Common Article 1 to the 1949 Geneva Conventions states that "[t]he High Contracting Parties undertake to respect and to ensure respect for the present Convention in all circumstances."[83] The 2020

---

80. International Law Commission, Report on the Works of its Fifty-eighth Session (2006), General Assembly, Official Record, Sixty-First Session, Supplement No. 10, U.N. Doc. A/61/10.

81. *Id.* at 41-15, ¶ 21.

82. Michael N. Schmitt & Sean Watts, *Common Article 1 and the Duty to "Ensure Respect,"* 96 INTERNATIONAL LAW STUDIES 674 (2020); Marten Zwanenburg, *The "External Element" of the Obligation to Ensure Respect for the Geneva Conventions: A Matter of Treaty Interpretation*, 97 INTERNATIONAL LAW STUDIES 621 (2021).

83. Convention (I) for the Amelioration of the Condition of the Wounded and Sick in the Armed Forces in the Field art. 1, Aug. 12, 1949, 6 U.S.T. 3114, 75 U.N.T.S. 31 [hereinafter First Geneva Convention]; Convention (II) for the Amelioration of the Condition of the Wounded, Sick, and Shipwrecked Members of Armed Forces at Sea art. 1, Aug. 12, 1949, 6 U.S.T. 3217, 75 U.N.T.S. 85 [hereinafter Second Geneva Convention]; Third Geneva Convention, *supra* note 12; Convention (IV) Relative to the Protection of Civilian Persons in Time of War art. 1, Aug. 12, 1949, 6 U.S.T. 3516, 75 U.N.T.S. 287 [hereinafter Fourth Geneva Convention].

GC III Commentary, in discussing the obligation to ensure respect by others, provides:

> The obligation to ensure respect also has an external dimension related to ensuring respect for the Conventions by others that are Party to a conflict. Accordingly, States, whether neutral, allied or enemy, must do everything reasonably in their power to ensure respect for the Conventions by others that are Party to a conflict.[84]

The 1949 Geneva Conventions added the obligation to ensure respect to the text of the corresponding provision of the 1929 Geneva Convention relative to the Treatment of Prisoners of War.[85] Common Article 1 originated from an ICRC draft submitted in May 1948 at the International Conference of the Red Cross and Red Crescent, as well as the draft provisions discussed at the diplomatic conference for the 1949 Conventions. Common Article 1 was adopted after minor changes and little discussion.[86]

The 2016 GC I and 2017 GC II Commentaries took a categorical approach to the assertion that Common Article 1 includes an external obligation.[87] However, the 2020 GC III Commentary has modified its stance and concedes that "[t]here is disagreement as to the legal nature of the positive component of the duty to ensure respect by others because the content of the obligation is not clearly defined and its concretization to a large extent left to the High Contracting Parties."[88] The United States has clearly rejected the expansive external obligation asserted by the ICRC as inconsistent with both its own interpretation of Common Article 1 and that of the drafters and the Pictet Commentary.

Turning first to the U.S. view of Common Article 1, then U.S. State Department Legal Adviser, Brian Egan, spoke directly to the issue at the April 2016 meeting of the American Society of International Law:

> Some have argued that the obligation in Common Article 1 of the Geneva Conventions to "ensure respect" for the Conventions legally requires us to undertake such steps and more vis-à-vis not only our partners, but all States and non-State actors engaged in armed conflict. Although we do not share

---

84. 2020 GC III COMMENTARY, *supra* note 1, ¶ 186.

85. Convention Relative to the Treatment of Prisoners of War, July 27, 1929, 47 Stat. 2021, 118 L.N.T.S. 343.

86. Zwanenburg, *supra* note 82, at 625.

87. 2016 GC I COMMENTARY, *supra* note 2, ¶ 153 ("The obligation to ensure respect also has an external dimension related to ensuring respect for the Conventions by others that are Party to a conflict. Accordingly, States, whether neutral, allied or enemy, must do everything reasonably in their power to ensure respect for the Conventions by others that are Party to a conflict."); 2017 GC II COMMENTARY, *supra* note 3, ¶ 175.

88. 2020 GC III COMMENTARY, *supra* note 1, ¶ 202.

this expansive interpretation of Common Article 1, as a matter of policy, we always seek to promote adherence to the law of armed conflict generally and encourage other States to do the same. As a matter of international law, we would look to the law of State responsibility and our partners' compliance with the law of armed conflict in assessing the lawfulness of our assistance to, and joint operations with, those military partners.[89]

Similarly, then General Counsel to the DoD, Paul C. Nye Jr., addressing the Israeli Defense Forces 3rd International Conference on the LOAC in 2019, stated:

> The ICRC has argued that Common Article 1 of the 1949 Geneva Conventions reflects a customary obligation for a State to take measures to implement other parties' obligations under international humanitarian law.
>
> The United States has been very clear that, although we always seek to promote compliance with the law of war by others as a matter of policy, we do not agree with this legal interpretation.[90]

This U.S. position has not changed since the drafting of the 1949 Geneva Conventions. As noted in the 2020 GC III Commentary, "statements made by delegates of Norway and the United States during the Diplomatic Conference leading to the adoption of the Conventions indicate that they understood the phrase 'to ensure respect' essentially as an undertaking by States to ensure respect for the Conventions by their populations as a whole."[91]

In addition to the ICRC view being inconsistent with the U.S. interpretation, it also appears to be contrary to the 1960 Pictet Commentary. Addressing the "ensure respect" provision, the 1960 Commentary provided:

> The Contracting Parties do not undertake merely to respect the Convention, but also to "ensure respect" for it. It is self-evident that it would not be enough for a Government to give orders or directions and leave the military authorities to arrange as they pleased for their detailed execution. It is for the Government to supervise the execution of the orders it gives. Furthermore, if it is to fulfil the solemn undertaking it has given, the Government must of necessity prepare in advance, that is to say in peace-time, the legal, material or other means of ensuring the faithful enforcement of the Convention when the occasion arises.[92]

---

89. Brian Egan, Legal Adviser, U.S. Department of State, Keynote Address at the American Society for International Law: International Law, Legal Diplomacy, and the Counter-ISIL Campaign (Apr. 1, 2016), https://www.justsecurity.org/wp-content/uploads/2016/04/Egan-ASIL-speech.pdf; https://www.asil.org/resources/audio/2016-annual-meeting (audio).

90. Jurecic, *supra* note 25.

91. 2020 GC III COMMENTARY, *supra* note 1, ¶ 188.

92. 1960 GC III COMMENTARY, *supra* note 6, at 18.

The Pictet Commentary suggests that the drafters understood "ensure respect" to be an internal duty of parties to an armed conflict to train and properly supervise individuals under their control to ensure compliance with the Conventions.[93] There does not seem to be any disagreement that this was the intention of the States when the Conventions were adopted in 1949.[94] The 2020 GC III Commentary does not provide any reference to State views that are contrary to that of the United States and Norway.[95]

The Pictet Commentary further supports the proposition that the authors of the Commentary did not view "ensure respect" as an external binding obligation for those States that were not party to the conflict, as it uses suggestive rather than mandatory terms. For example, it provides, "in the event of a Power failing to fulfil its obligations, each of the other Contracting Parties (neutral, allied or enemy) *should endeavour* to bring it back to an attitude of respect for the Convention" (emphasis added).[96] The Pictet Commentary clarifies that Common Article 1 cannot be read to suggest a legal obligation by States that are not party to an armed conflict. As noted by Brian Egan, even though it is not a legal obligation, the United States will seek to promote compliance with the LOAC and would "encourage" all other States to do the same.[97]

B. Common Article 2—Application of the Convention

Common Article 2(1) of the 1949 Geneva Conventions states that the Conventions will apply to "all cases of . . . armed conflict which may arise between two or more of the High Contracting Parties, even if the state of war is not recognized by one of them."[98] An international armed conflict (IAC) will exist when one State resorts to armed force against another State regardless of the scope, intensity, or duration of the violence, even if one of the parties to the conflict denies the existence of a state of war.[99] The 2020 GC III Commentary concludes that armed conflicts for purposes of Common Article 2(1) are "limited to armed conflicts [that involve] opposing States"[100] and that "statehood remains the baseline against which the existence of an armed conflict under Article 2(1) will be

---

93. Schmitt & Watts, *supra* note 82, at 683.

94. *Id.*

95. 2020 GC III Commentary, *supra* note 1, ¶ 188.

96. 1960 GC III Commentary, *supra* note 6, at 18; Schmitt & Watts, *supra* note 82, at 684.

97. Egan, *supra* note 89.

98. First Geneva Convention, *supra* note 83; Second Geneva Convention, *supra* note 83; Third Geneva Convention, *supra* note 12; Fourth Geneva Convention, *supra* note 83.

99. 1960 GC III Commentary, *supra* note 6, at 23.

100. 2020 GC III Commentary, *supra* note 1, ¶ 253.

measured."[101] Accordingly, the 2020 GC III Commentary concludes that IACs are those between opposing States, which is generally accepted.

The ICRC then takes an expansive view of what may constitute an IAC by stating that a nonconsensual military operation by one State in the territory of another State against non-State armed groups, even where no force is directed against the armed forces or government of the State, will trigger Common Article 2.[102] As explained further below, this is not the interpretation of the United States or consistent with its practice.

The 2020 GC III Commentary acknowledges that "contemporary armed conflicts show that increasingly States carry out military operations in the territory of another State."[103] In certain instances, the "use of armed force in the territory of another State . . . would . . . not necessarily be classified as an international armed conflict" where a State would consent to the use force on its territory.[104] According to the 2020 GC III Commentary, "the presence or absence of consent is essential for delineating the applicable legal framework between the two States."[105] In an instance where "the third State's intervention [is] carried out without the consent of the territorial State, it would amount to an international armed conflict between the intervening State and the territorial State."[106] The Commentary explains its rationale as follows:

> Some consider that in situations in which a State attacks exclusively members of a non-State armed group or its property on the territory of another State, no parallel international armed conflict arises between the territorial State and the State fighting the armed group. While that view is consequential in some respects, it is useful to recall that the population and public property of the territorial State may also be present in areas where the armed group is present and some group members may also be residents or citizens of the territorial State, such that attacks against the armed group will concomitantly affect the local population and the State's infrastructure. For these reasons and others, it better corresponds to the factual reality to conclude that an international armed conflict arises between the territorial State and

---

101. *Id.*, ¶ 254.

102. *Id.*, ¶ 293 ("The presence or absence of consent is essential for delineating the applicable legal framework between the two States as it affects the determination of the international or non-international character of the armed conflict involving those States. Should the third State's intervention be carried out without the consent of the territorial State, it would amount to an international armed conflict between the intervening State and the territorial State.").

103. 2020 GC III COMMENTARY, *supra* note 1, ¶ 290.

104. *Id.*, ¶ 292.

105. *Id.*, ¶ 293.

106. *Id.*

the intervening State when force is used on the former's territory without its consent.¹⁰⁷

In December 2016, the United States released the Report on the Legal and Policy Frameworks Guiding the United States Use of Military Force and Related National Security Operations.¹⁰⁸ The report details both the international and domestic legal authority for the United States engaging in armed conflict in various locations, such as Syria, where the United States has been conducting military operations against ISIS¹⁰⁹ in the collective self-defense of Iraq and other States since 2014.¹¹⁰ In doing so, it has engaged in a systematic campaign of airstrikes against ISIS and provided U.S. military equipment, ammunition, and other assistance to indigenous ground forces conducting operations against the group in Syria. The United States also deployed special operations forces to Syria to help coordinate U.S. operations with some of these indigenous ground forces.¹¹¹

When operations in Syria against ISIS began, the United States submitted a letter to the UN Security Council consistent with Article 51 of the UN Charter, explaining the international legal basis for its use of force.¹¹² As the letter explained, the government of Iraq has asked the United States to lead international efforts to strike ISIS strongholds in Syria in order to end the continuing armed attacks on Iraq, to protect Iraqi citizens, and ultimately to enable Iraqi forces to regain control of Iraqi borders. The United States noted that ISIS was also a threat to other U.S. partners in the region and to the United States itself. Finally, the letter explained that Syria is unable or unwilling to confront effectively the threat that ISIS posed, and the Syrian government had shown that it could not or would not confront ISIS effectively.¹¹³

The report also set forth the U.S. view on the applicable legal regime for Syria and the other locations across the globe where it was engaged in hostilities. It states:

---

107. *Id.*, ¶ 295.

108. THE WHITE HOUSE, REPORT ON THE LEGAL AND POLICY FRAMEWORKS GUIDING THE UNITED STATES' USE OF MILITARY FORCE AND RELATED NATIONAL SECURITY OPERATIONS(Dec. 2016), https://obamawhitehouse.archives.gov/sites/whitehouse.gov/files/documents/Legal_Policy_Report.pdf [hereinafter 2016 LEGAL AND POLICY FRAMEWORKS REPORT].

109. ISIS stands for the Islamic State of Iraq and Syria.

110. 2016 LEGAL AND POLICY FRAMEWORKS REPORT, *supra* note 108, at 10.

111. *Id.* at 16.

112. United Nations Security Council, Letter Dated 23 September 2014 from the Permanent Representative of the United States of America to the United Nations Addressed to the Secretary-General, S/2014/695 (Sept. 23, 2014), http://www.securitycouncilreport.org/atf/cf/%7B65BFCF9B-6D27-4E9C-8CD3-CF6E4FF96FF9%7D/s_2014_695.pdf.

113. 2016 LEGAL AND POLICY FRAMEWORKS REPORT, *supra* note 108, at 10.

Because the United States is currently engaged in hostilities against only non-State actors, the applicable international legal regime governing these U.S. military operations is the law of armed conflict covering non-international armed conflicts, including Common Article 3 of the 1949 Geneva Conventions and other treaty and customary international law rules governing the conduct of hostilities in non-international armed conflicts.[114]

As part of Operation Inherent Resolve, a coalition of States participated in the strikes in Syria. They included Australia, Bahrain, Canada, Denmark, France, Jordan, the Netherlands, Saudi Arabia, Turkey, the United Arab Emirates, and the United Kingdom.[115] Iran and the Russian Federation have also been involved in Syria.[116] Commentators have concluded that the hostilities are primarily non-IACs, as most States have avoided State-on-State hostilities.[117]

C. Article 4—Prisoners of War

The 2020 GC III Commentary addresses the status of nationals of a State who are captured while fighting for the opposing side. It notes that there are divergent State interpretations, including in domestic case law and doctrine.[118] One view is that any person who falls into one of the categories enumerated in Article 4(A) is in the power of the enemy regardless of nationality. Under this view, a national or dual national of the detaining power would be entitled to the full protections under the Third Geneva Convention, including belligerent immunity for lawful acts of war.[119] The opposing view is that the term "enemy" excludes a national of the detaining power because they are considered "traitorous subjects." They would not be entitled to the privileges and immunities of members of the armed

---

114. *Id.* at 19.

115. *See Operation Inherent Resolve: Targeted Operations against ISIS Terrorists*, DEPARTMENT OF DEFENSE, https://web.archive.org/web/20170331011424/http://www.defense.gov/News/Special-Reports/0814_Inherent-Resolve.

116. David Wallace, Amy McCarthy & Shane R. Reeves, *Trying to Make Sense of the Senseless: Classifying the Syrian War Under the Law of Armed Conflict*, 25 MICHIGAN STATE INTERNATIONAL LAW REVIEW 556, 591 (2017). *See* Terry D. Gill, *Classifying the Conflict in Syria*, 92 INTERNATIONAL LAW STUDIES 353, 375 (2016) ("This author takes the position that this . . . conflict is also non-international, notwithstanding the lack of consent by the Syrian government. Coalition actions are directed almost exclusively against ISIS, which is in firm control of a significant portion of Syrian territory, population and infrastructure, rather than Syrian government-held territory, population or infrastructure.").

117. Wallace, McCarthy & Reeves, *supra* note 116, at 593. (The authors also conclude that the United States and Syria are engaged in an IAC based on the U.S. strikes in 2017.)

118. 2020 GC III COMMENTARY, *supra* note 1, ¶ 964.

119. *Id.*, ¶ 965.

forces and may be treated as criminals and prosecuted for their acts.[120] Although acknowledging the diversity of practice and views, the ICRC "considers that nationality should not be a factor in the determination of prisoner-of-war status."[121]

The DoD Law of War Manual takes the opposite interpretation and has determined that "certain categories of persons are not entitled to POW status." They include "persons who are nationals of the Detaining Power or its co-belligerents, such as a defector who subsequently is captured by the force from which he or she defected."[122] Its rationale is that the privileges international law affords combatants generally do not apply between a national and his or her State of nationality. The Third Geneva Convention provisions assume that POWs are not nationals of the detaining power. The DoD Law of War Manual also provides that:

> although, as a matter of international law, nationals may not assert the privileges of combatant status against their own State, they may be subject to the liabilities of combatant status in relation to their own State under that State's domestic law. For example, under U.S. law, U.S. nationals who join enemy forces have been subject to the liabilities of combatant status, such as potentially being made the object of attack or detained.[123]

Finally, it is important to note that the 2020 GC III Commentary not only fails to interpret properly the DoD Law of War Manual, but misinterprets the two domestic law cases it cites in support of the position that a national of the detaining power is entitled to POW status.[124] Although a national of the United States is "not entitled to POW status," the DoD Law of War Manual does provides that the "policy of the United States has been to afford detainees certain POW protections even when they may not apply as a matter of law."[125] Additionally, the 2020 GC III Commentary mischaracterizes Ex parte *Quirin*[126] and *In re Territo*,[127] for neither case held that U.S nationals were entitled to POW status. Ex parte *Quirin* held

---

120. *Id.*, ¶ 966.

121. *Id.*, ¶ 970.

122. DoD Law of War Manual, *supra* note 13, § 9.3.2.1.

123. *Id.*, § 4.4.4.2. (citing Ex parte *Quirin*, 317 U.S. 1, 37 (1942) ("Citizenship in the United States of an enemy belligerent does not relieve him from the consequences of a belligerency which is unlawful because in violation of the law of war."); *In re Territo*, 156 F.2d 142, 145 (9th Cir. 1946) (rejecting the argument of petitioner, an Italian army draftee, that he could not be subject to the liabilities of combatant status and detained because he was a U.S. citizen).

124. *See* 2020 GC III Commentary, *supra* note 1, Article 4 n.45, https://ihl-databases.icrc.org/applic/ihl/ihl.nsf/Comment.xsp?action=openDocument&documentId=1796813618ABDA06C12585850057AB95.

125. DoD Law of War Manual, *supra* note 13, § 9.3.1.

126. Ex parte *Quirin*, 317 U.S. 1, 30 (1942).

127. *In re Territo*, 156 F.2d 142 (9th Cir. 1946).

that the United States could prosecute certain persons, including a U.S. citizen, for espionage and sabotage by military commission.[128] The U.S. citizen was not determined to be a POW, which would have precluded prosecution because he would have combatant immunity. Similarly, *In re Territo* rejected an argument by the petitioner, who was born in the United States but lived the majority of his life in Italy and was captured while serving in the Italian army, that he could not be detained because he was a U.S. citizen.[129] The issue was not whether the petitioner could assert the privileges of POW status against the United States; rather, the petitioner was arguing that he could not be held as a POW because he was a U.S. citizen. As the DoD Law of War Manual explains in the extract above, "U.S. nationals who join enemy forces have been subject to the liabilities of combatant status, such as potentially being made the object of attack or detained."[130]

D. Article 12 — Responsibility for the Treatment of Prisoners

Article 12 of the Third Geneva Convention deals with who is responsible for the treatment of prisoners. In one of its clearer statements, Article 12 provides that POWs "may only be transferred by the Detaining Power to a Power which is a party to the Convention and after the Detaining Power has satisfied itself of the willingness and ability of such transferee Power to apply the Convention."[131]

Therefore, it was astonishing to read in the 2020 GC III Commentary that POWs may be transferred from one High Contracting Party to a non-State armed group under the "overall control"[132] of another High Contracting Party to the Convention.[133] This is problematic for three reasons: (1) it is inconsistent with the

---

128. Ex parte *Quirin*, 317 U.S. at 30.

129. *In re Territo*, 156 F.2d at 144.

130. DoD Law of War Manual, *supra* note 13, § 4.4.4.2.

131. Third Geneva Convention, *supra* note 12, art. 12.

132. Prosecutor v. Tadić, Case No. IT-94-1-A, Appeals Chamber Judgment (Int'l Crim. Trib. for the former Yugoslavia). The Tadić case set out the "overall control" test as follows: "[The State] *has a role in organising, coordinating or planning the military actions* of the military group, in addition to financing, training and equipping or providing operational support to that group. . . . [The standard required for] *overall control* [goes] beyond the mere financing and equipping of such forces and involving also participation in the planning and supervision of military operations." ¶¶ 137, 145.

133. 2020 GC III Commentary, *supra* note 1, ¶ 1530 ("Because of the general understanding that only States can be High Contracting Parties to the Geneva Conventions, the first requirement implies that prisoners of war may not be transferred to entities other than States—such as non-State armed groups and paramilitary and non-military organizations. A 'transfer' of prisoners to such an entity that is under the overall control of the Detaining Power would not qualify as a transfer under Article 12(2) because the prisoner would remain under the responsibility of the Detaining Power. On the other hand, a transfer to such an entity that is under

plain reading of Article 12; (2) it is hard to see how the low bar of "overall control" will provide the necessary guarantees that the non-State armed group will properly apply the Convention; and (3) it is inconsistent with other provisions of the Third Geneva Convention.

The language of Article 12 makes it clear that POWs must be transferred to a "Power which is a Party to the Convention," which means a State party. The Commentary to Article 12 reinforces this position: "Prisoners of war may be transferred only to a Power that is a Party to the Convention. This condition is absolute and is designed to ensure that prisoners of war are not deprived of the protection of the Convention by the mere fact of a transfer, no matter its purpose."[134] The rationale seems obvious; the drafters determined that only States parties to the Third Geneva Convention could be entrusted with the lives and welfare of POWs. This is likely due to the interests States have in ensuring that prisoners under their charge are properly cared for so their own forces can expect to receive similar treatment. Further, a review of the 2020 GC III Commentary does not provide any State practice to support the ICRC's position that POWs may be transferred to a non-State group under the "overall control" of another High Contracting Party. In fact, the ICRC points to no academic or ICRC writings supporting its novel reading of Article 12.

Second, there is little in the "overall control" standard that supports the requirement of willingness and ability to apply the Convention set forth in the text of Article 12. The overall control standard requires a lower degree of oversight and does not require involvement by a State in specific decisions or courses of action by a non-State group. It is satisfied simply by evidence of support and capacity to influence. This is hardly a sufficient guarantee of proper treatment on the part of the non-State group under the Third Geneva Convention.

Finally, this interpretation appears to conflict with other articles in the Third Geneva Convention. For example, Article 39 requires that "[e]very prisoner of war camp shall be put under the immediate authority of a responsible commissioned officer belonging to the regular armed forces of the Detaining Power."[135] Non-State armed groups are not part of the regular armed forces of the detaining power and therefore cannot be placed in command of POW camps.

The ICRC interpretation that POWs may be transferred from one High Contracting Party to a non-State group under the "overall control" of another High Contracting Party also conflicts with the State practice, and guidance, of the United States. The DoD Law of War Manual correctly notes that the Third Geneva Convention specifies numerous rules applicable to the transfer of prisoners of

---

135. Third Geneva Convention, *supra* note 12, art. 39.

the overall control of another High Contracting Party would qualify as a transfer under Article 12(2), as it would constitute a transfer to that High Contracting Party.").

134. *Id.*, ¶ 1527.

war from a detaining power to another detaining power.[136] The Manual makes clear that:

> POWs may only be transferred by the Detaining Power to a Power that is a Party to the [Third Geneva Convention] and after the Detaining Power has satisfied itself of the willingness and ability of such receiving Power to apply the [Third Geneva Convention]. U.S. policy may prescribe additional requirements.
>
> To ensure accountability, a POW should not be transferred before his or her formal processing and submission of all required information to the National POW Information Bureau.[137]

There appears to be no support under U.S. treaty interpretation or State practice for the ICRC's interpretation of Article 12.

E. Article 17 — Questioning of Prisoners

The final rule to be discussed is Article 17 on questioning prisoners. The 2020 GC III Commentary states: "Conversely, if during questioning prisoners claim a rank superior to their actual status and the Detaining Power subsequently finds out this was not the case, they may be deprived *throughout their captivity* not only of the privileges which until then had been accorded them, but also of all the privileges to which their actual rank would have entitled them."[138] Although the Pictet Commentary makes the same point almost verbatim, this is nevertheless a surprising conclusion.[139] The interpretation, which seems to be punitive, runs counter to the principles espoused throughout the Geneva Conventions. It also raises the question of whether the United States (or any State Party) has ever done this to a prisoner or incorporated it into training or doctrine.

Unfortunately, the 2020 GC III Commentary is of no help, for the footnote to paragraph 1806 merely references the Pictet Commentary without further explanation or reference to State practice or military legal doctrine. Therefore, the next step is asking whether the United States has incorporated this provision into its training and doctrine.

The DoD Law of War Manual sets forth the accountability information that POWs are bound to provide upon questioning:

---

136. DoD Law of War Manual, *supra* note 13, § 9.30.

137. *Id.*, § 9.30.1.

138. 2020 GC III Commentary, *supra* note 1, ¶ 1806.

139. 1960 GC III Commentary, *supra* note 6, at 161.

Every POW, when questioned on the subject, is bound to give only his or her surname, first names and rank, date of birth, and army, regimental, personal or serial number, or, failing this, equivalent information. If POWs willfully infringe this rule, they may render themselves liable to a restriction of the privileges accorded to their rank or status. However, POWs who refuse to provide this information may not be coerced or exposed to any other unpleasant or disadvantageous treatment of any kind for failing to respond.[140]

This lacks the assertion in the 2020 GC III Commentary as to the deprivation of privileges related to claims of rank. A review of the panoply of detention and interrogation publications for the DoD—such as the DoD Law of War Program;[141] the DoD Detainee Program;[142] DoD Intelligence Interrogations, Detainee Debriefings, and Tactical Questioning;[143] Detainee Operations;[144] Program for Detainee Operations;[145] and Enemy Prisoners of War, Retained Personnel, Civilian Internees and Other Detainees[146]—failed to find a single reference on this topic. Accordingly, it appears that the United States has not incorporated the ICRC's interpretation of Article 17 into its training or doctrine. In my view, the failure to do so more closely hues to the plain language of Article 17.

IV. IMPLICATIONS FOR PRACTITIONERS

For the past two decades, the United States and its allies have been engaged in counterinsurgency and counterterrorism operations in Afghanistan, Iraq, Syria, and elsewhere. The United States Army identified seventeen warfighting capability gaps that have emerged as a result of these operations. Lieutenant General Pede has detailed what he refers to as an "eighteenth gap"—legal maneuver space.[147]

---

140. DoD LAW OF WAR MANUAL, *supra* note 13, § 9.8.4.

141. U.S. Department of Defense, DoD Directive 2311.01, DoD Law of War Program (July 2, 2020).

142. U.S. Department of Defense, DoD Directive 2310.01E, DoD Detainee Program (Aug. 19, 2014, incorporating change 2, effective Sept. 18, 2020).

143. U.S. Department of Defense, DoD Directive 3115.09, DoD Intelligence Interrogations, Detainee Debriefings, and Tactical Questioning (Oct. 11, 2012, incorporating change 3, effective Oct. 29, 2020).

144. Joint Chiefs of Staff, Joint Publication 3-63, *Detainee Operations* (Nov. 13, 2014).

145. Chairman, Joint Chiefs of Staff, Instruction 3290.01D, *Program for Detainee Operations* (June 1, 2012, incorporating Change 1, Feb. 17, 2015).

146. Army Regulation 190-8 on Enemy Prisoners, Retained Personnel, Civilian Internees and Other Detainees, Oct. 1, 1997.

147. Charles N. Pede & Pete Hayden, *The Eighteenth Gap—Preserving the Commander's Legal Maneuver Space on "Battlefield Next,"* MILITARY REVIEW (Mar.–Apr. 2021), https://www.arm

He describes it as a lack of understanding the difference between the LOAC as codified in treaty or reflective of customary international law and more restrictive policy overlays that result from the counterinsurgency/counterterrorism fight.[148]

There is an internal and external aspect to this gap. The external component is the gap between the actual content of the law adopted and interpreted by States and the aspirational evolution of the law advocated by academics; nongovernmental organizations; and, of course, the ICRC, through publications such as the 2020 GC III Commentary.[149] The internal component is where commanders and legal advisers conflate law and policy. To counter the internal component, commanders and their legal advisers must ensure that both know where the gap lies between the two.[150]

A. *Lex Ferenda Versus Lex Lata*

There are many instances in the 2020 GC III Commentary where statements of *lex ferenda* (law as it should be) are presented as *lex lata* (law as it is). The most prominent example is the 2020 GC III Commentary to Common Article 1, which was discussed above.[151] However, this is not the only instance where the 2020 GC III Commentary takes an expansive view. The ICRC's conclusion that military operations conducted on the territory of a State without its consent constitutes an IAC is contrary to both the U.S. interpretation and that of other States Parties. It would have been helpful, and would have afforded the 2020 GC III Commentary greater credibility, had the ICRC been clear when statements reflected *lex ferenda*, instead of making declarative statements disguised as *lex lata*.

When reviewing the 2020 GC III Commentary, military practitioners must ensure that they understand the law as set forth in the 1949 Geneva Conventions, to which the United States is party. Thus, it is critical that the 2020 GC III Commentary be cross-referenced to the DoD Law of War Manual and other U.S. government documents. Understanding that certain aspects of the 2020 GC III Commentary do not reflect the law as interpreted by the United States will ensure that U.S. legal advisers can explain what is legally required to decision makers.

---

149. *Id.* at 7–8.

150. *Id.* at 9.

151. 2020 GC III COMMENTARY, *supra* note 1, ¶¶ 152–54.

yupress.army.mil/Journals/Military-Review/English-Edition-Archives/March-April-2021/Pede-The-18th-Gap/.

148. *Id.* at 7.

B. Law versus Policy

Military practitioners understand that, in contrast to the LOAC, policies are often implemented through rules of engagement, DoD directives, regulations, and certain military manuals and handbooks.[152] Over the past twenty years, these policies have helped minimize civilian casualties and damage to civilian objects. For instance, for policy reasons and employing advanced technologies, operators sometimes were able to wait hours or days before engaging a target. Humanitarian actors and scholars who advocate for new policy and legal constraints are well aware of such technological advances and the surgical strikes they sometimes enable.[153]

Yet, policies and constraints implemented for the counterinsurgency/counterterrorism fight may not be appropriate for a large-scale combat operation of the future. Therefore, practitioners must remain "vigilant, to identify and highlight misstatements of the law, to clarify the distinctions between LOAC and more restrictive policies,"[154] and to ensure that decision makers have the tools necessary to make decisions based on the law.

V. CONCLUSION

It is critical that those who are practitioners get the law right; but it is equally essential for the ICRC to get the 2020 GC III Commentary right. There are many aspects of the Commentary that are useful to military or government practitioners. It is, however, a resource that must be used in conjunction with the Pictet Commentary when trying to properly interpret the 1949 Conventions. Even then, there are areas of concern where both the ICRC's methodology in crafting the 2020 GC III Commentary and its expansive interpretations of the Convention's provisions have fallen short.

---

152. Pede & Hayden, *supra* note 147, at 10.

153. *Id.* at 12.

154. Pede & Hayden, *supra* note 147, at 12.

INDEX

For the benefit of digital users, indexed terms that span two pages (e.g., 52–53) may, on occasion, appear on only one of those pages.

Abu Ghraib prison in Iraq, 334–35, 342
act of hostility, 137, 138–40, 314
active hostilities, cessation of, 36–37, 258–60, 283–85
Afghan Transitional Authority, 268
Afghanistan
  Al Qaeda members captured in, 268
  Bagram detention facility, 288–89
  counterterrorism operations in, 434–35
  detention of terrorists, 268–70
  judge advocates in U.S. Army, 339–41
  transition from an IAC to NIAC, 28–29, 33, 39–44, 51–52, 255
  US and Coalition Special Forces in, 77n.118, 249–50
Al Qaeda, 77n.118, 267–70, 280, 284, 296
Al-Warafi v. Obama, 280
Alexander II, Tsar of Russia, 103
Altmark incident (1940), 146
American Civil War
  judge advocates in U.S. Army, 324–28
  Lieber, Francis and, 312
  military assimilation and, 188, 189–90
  parole of POWs in, 239–40, 241, 242
American Revolutionary War, 186–87, 324–25
Amnesty International, 39n.45
armed conflict. *See also* international humanitarian law (IHL) of international armed conflict (IAC);
  law of armed conflict (LOAC); non-international armed conflicts (NIACs)
  international armed conflict, 3–4, 31–44, 271–79
  levée en masse in, 106–16
Article 5 tribunals, 11
artificial intelligence (AI), 99
astronauts and personnel, 152–54
atrocity crimes, 176, 289
Aust, Anthony, 415–16
Australian Defence Force, 227
Australian Japanese POW breakout, 211–12, 227–28
aut dedere aut judicare, 295–96
authority of detaining power, 19–21, 28
Authorization for Use of Military Force (AUMF), 280–81
autonomous warfare, 99–101

Bagram detention facility, 288–89
Basardh v. Obama, 282
battlefield suffering, 190–91
Beaver, Diane E., 340–41
belligerent occupation incident, 162–63
Bellinger, John B., III, 419
Black soldiers, 318–19
Boer War, 239–40
Bosnian Muslim resistance fighters, 105
Bothe, Michael, 56, 75
Bradley-Goldsmith theory, 283–84

British Military Court at Hamburg (1949), 62
Brown, Gary, 239
Brussels Declaration (1874), 61, 83, 87, 103–5, 189–90, 191–92
Bush, George W., 268–69

camouflage, legitimacy of, 77–78
Carron, Djemila, 7–8
carry arms openly requirement, 114–15
Carthaginians, 236–37
Central Criminal Court of Iraq, 342
Central Prisoners of War Agency, 370
cessation of hostilities, 36–37, 258–60, 283–85
chivalry, 237
Christian POWs, 237
civilian, defined, 165
civilian internees, 48n.69, 143, 256, 262–68, 324n.1, 345, 359n.75, 392–93
civilians/non-military personnel as POWs
    accompanying armed forces, 83–85, 90–94
    cyber operations and, 90, 91–92, 94
    function approach to, 93–94
    geographic proximity and function, 86–90, 93–94
    identification cards, 87–88
    introduction to, 81–83
    summary of, 95
clothing rations, 367–68
Clover, Joshua, 249–50
Colberg Regiment, Prussian Army, 310–11
Cold War, 336
combat drones, 97–98
combatant immunity, 167, 178–79
command requirement for POW status, 113–14
commander of POW camp, 10–11
The Commander's Handbook on the Law of Land Warfare (2019), 53
Commentary to the Third Geneva Convention. *See* International Committee of the Red Cross (ICRC) Commentary to the Third Geneva Convention
common access card (CAC), 88

Confederate POWs, 314–15
Conference of Government Experts (1947), 348–49
Continental Congress, 186–87
controlling State
    armed groups linked to, 5, 16–19, 21–24, 25
    IAC IHL proxy and, 3–4, 8
    POWs and, 9–15
Convention for the Protection of Human Rights and Fundamental Freedoms. *See* European Convention on Human Rights
Convention of Copenhagen (1917), 192–93
counterterrorism, 253–54, 259, 268–71, 288–90, 295–98
criminal sanction alternatives, 264–65
criminal trials, 11–12, 257n.23, 261–62, 292, 301
Customary International Humanitarian Law study (ICRC), 71, 219, 220, 419, 420–21
customary international law
    distinction from the civilian population, 56–57
    fluid conflicts and, 27–28
    fundamental guarantees provisions, 172–73
    Lieber Code, impact on, 321
    members of the armed forces, 350
    military assimilation, 183–84
    other militias and members of other volunteer corps, 350–52
    POWs captured out of uniform, 53, 56
cyber operations
    civilians/non-military personnel as POWs, 90, 91–92
    combat drones, 97–98
    hackers in cyber resistance movements, 108, 115–16
levée en masse, 99–101, 106–16

Davis, George B., 326
deprivation of rank, 176–77
Detainee Review Boards, 341
Detainee Treatment Act (2005), 340–41
detention for ransom, 185–86

Index

detention of terrorist suspects
  active hostilities, cessation of, 283–85
  civilian internees, 262–68
  conflict transformation, 271–77
  counterterrorism and, 253–54, 259, 268–71, 288–90, 295–98
  doctrinal solutions, 288–90
  general remarks on, 298–300
  IHRL-based approaches, 285–87
  introduction to, 253–55
  NIAC gap in doctrine, 280–87
  in NIACs, 290–95, 298–303
  NIACs *vs.* IACs, 31–44, 271–79
  practical recommendations for, 298–303
  release and repatriation in IACs, 255–77
  release and repatriation in Third and Fourth Geneva Conventions, 256–68
  status-based detention, 280–82
  summary of, 303
  threat-based detention, 282–83
Dinstein, Yoram, 56, 66, 75
Diplomatic Conference (1949), 202–3
direct participation in hostilities, 121
distinction from the civilian population, 55–58
Dix-Hill Cartel, 239
domestic criminal law, 121
Dunant, Henri, 307–8, 313

Egan, Brian, 424–25
electronic monitoring systems, 251
Elements of International Law (Davis), 326–27
end of active hostilities, 36–37, 283–85
enemy flag, 122
enemy merchant vessels, 121–25
England, Lynndie, 335
Eritrea, 260–61
Eritrea-Ethiopia Claims Commission, 398
escape/attempted escape of POWs
  breaches of discipline, 232–33
  from camps, 233
  extreme measures, 228–29
  in the field, 233
  Japanese POW breakout, 211–12, 227–28

  law enforcement paradigm, 213–14, 230–32
  preparations to escape, 222–27
  prevention of, 182n.6, 217–29
Ethiopia's release of POWs, 260–61
European Convention on Human Rights (ECHR), 172–73, 278–79, 422–23
European Court of Human Rights (ECtHR), 263–64, 278–79

fair trial rights, 169
fallen into the power of the enemy, 42–43
final, meaning of, 38–41
First World War. *See* World War I
fluid conflicts
  cessation of active hostilities, 36–37
  fallen into the power of the enemy, 42–43
  final, meaning of, 38–41
  introduction to, 27–30
  most protected status, 46–49
  nature of, 44–49
  NIACs *vs.* IACs, 31–46
  POW release and repatriation, 34–36
  status determinations, 30–44
  summary of, 49–50
food rations, 366–67
force majeure, 14
Forrest, Bedford, 318–19
Fourth Geneva Convention. *See* Geneva Convention (IV) Relative to the Protection of Civilian Persons in Time of War,
franc-tireurs, 103, 105–6, 138–39
Franco-Prussian War, 103, 190, 326
Frederick, Ivan, 335
French National Convention, 102
fundamental guarantees
  provisions, 169–75

Geneva Convention (II) on Wounded, Sick and Shipwrecked of Armed Forces at Sea, 120, 146–47
Geneva Convention (III) Relative to the Treatment of Prisoners of War
  Article 1, respect for the convention, 423–26
  Article 2, application of the convention, 426–29

Geneva Convention (III) Relative to the Treatment of Prisoners of War (*cont.*)
  Article 4, prisoners of war, 429–31
  Article 5, on tribunals, 11
  Article 12, treatment of POWs, 431–33
  Article 17, questioning of POWs, 433–34
  commander of POW camp, 10–11
  criminal trials, 11–12
  detention, release and repatriation of POWs, 23–24, 256–62
  detention, release and repatriation of terrorist suspects, 256–71
  detention conditions in outer space, 150–51
  exceptions for nationals of detaining power, 19–21
  fundamental guarantees provisions, 169–75
  humanity principle in protection of POWs, 165–69
  IAC IHL and, 3–9
  internment law in outer space, 146–48
  military assimilation under, 196–203
  neutral merchant vessels, 132–39
  NIACs *vs.* IACs, 31–44, 271–79
  other rules, 13–15
  overall control standard, 431–33
  POW status, 9–10, 15–22, 106n.45
  summary of, 24–25
  treatment of POWs, 10–15, 142n.4
  treatment of proxy-armed group members, 15–22
Geneva Convention (III) Additional Protocol I, Relative to the Protection of Victims of International Armed Conflicts, 15–16, 57, 60, 64
  development of, 388–95
  distinction requirement for uniforms, 79
  fundamental guarantees provisions, 169–75
  IAC *vs.* NIAC, 271–72
  incompleteness of, 394–95
  military assimilation under, 203–4
  protection of POWs under IHL, 161
  regular armed forces failure to wear uniforms, 72–73
Geneva Convention (III) Additional Protocol II, Relative to the Protection of Victims of Non-International Armed Conflicts, 169–75
  detention, release and repatriation of terrorist suspects, 277–79, 286–87, 290–95
  incompleteness of, 394–95
  travaux préparatoires on, 289–90
Geneva Convention (IV) Relative to the Protection of Civilian Persons in Time of War, 37, 90–91, 271–77, 282–83, 388–95
German Prize Ordinance (1939), 133–34, 136
German unlawful submarine warfare, 138–39
Graner, Charles, 335
Guantánamo Bay detention center, 250–51, 253–54, 268–69, 280–81, 339–41
guerilla warfare, 111–12n.67
Guerrilla Parties Considered with Reference to the Law and Usages of War (Lieber), 311–12
Guillory, Michael, 86–87
Gullion, Allen, 327–28

habeas corpus, 257, 263–64, 280, 282, 286–87, 301–2
habitable space objects, 143–49
habitation requirement, 108–9
hackers in cyber resistance movements, 108, 115–16
Hague Convention II Regulations concerning the Laws and Customs of War on Land (1899)
  civilians accompanying armed forces, 83–84
  expanding ammunition, 220–22
  historical background, 347
  irregular groups in armed forces, 54
  Lieber Code and, 326–27
  military assimilation and, 190–95, 198–99
  modeled after Third Geneva Convention, 61, 66
  parole of POWs under, 243–44
Hague Convention IV Regulations concerning the Laws and Customs of War on Land (1907)

Index

Article 21 of, 245–47
civilians accompanying armed forces, 83–84
irregular groups in armed forces, 54
judge advocates and, 324
levée en masse, 105
Lieber Code and, 326–27
military assimilation and, 190–95, 198–99
modeled after Third Geneva Convention, 61, 62, 64
parole of POWs under, 243–44, 245–46
unlawful perfidy, 60
Hague Convention XI Relative to Certain Restrictions with Regard to the Exercise of the Right of Capture in Naval War (1907), 133–34, 137
Hague Peace Conference (1899), 104–5, 190–91, 347
Haiti, 336–39
Hall, William, 101–2, 105–6
Halleck, Henry W., 311–12, 324–25
Hamdan v. Rumsfeld, 339–40
Hamdi case, 280–81
Handbook on the Law of Land Warfare, 58
Hardy, B.G., 212
Haynes, William J., II, 419
hereditary nobility of knighthood, 237
honor and duty for parolees, 239
hors de combat, 56, 161, 163–64, 170, 217, 256–62
Human Rights Committee, 285–86
human rights law. *See also* international humanitarian law
  Article 3 and, 172–73, 286
  Article 42 and, 227–28
  criminal offences and, 265
  developments of, 345–46
  First Geneva Convention, 394
  indefinite detention, 249–50
  international criminal tribunals, 400n.143, 414
  international human rights law, 255–56
  military assimilation and, 206–9
  POW status and, 160n.4
  suspected terrorists and, 286–87, 293
  use of force in, 230
  Vienna Convention and, 391–92

humane treatment of POWs
  Common Article 3, 170–71, 173–74
  in detention, 150, 294–95
  NIAC detention regime, 277–78, 279
  perceived affiliation with the enemy, 163–64, 169
  in prison camps, 330, 331, 337, 338–40, 341–42
  protection regime for, 13, 160, 161–62, 169
  protections beyond humanity principle, 175–80
  proxy-armed groups, 14–15
  in Third Geneva Convention, 165–75, 356, 358–59, 360, 361–62, 373–74
  voluntary policy toward, 309
humanitarianism, 162–63, 313, 314–15, 320–21

identification card for civilians, 87–88
In re Territo, 430–31
indigenous attire, 77n.118
injury payments and compensation, 200
Institute of International Law, 189–90
Instructions for the Government of Armies of the United States in the Field (Lieber). *See* Lieber Code
international armed conflict (IAC), 3–4, 31–44, 271–79. *See also* international humanitarian law (IHL) of international armed conflict (IAC); outer space IAC POW regime
international banking system, 13–14
International Committee of the Red Cross (ICRC)
  access to the POWs, 13
  Central Tracing Agency, 22
  civilian uprising possibility, 117
  civilians/non-military personnel as POWs, 86
  Customary International Humanitarian Law study, 219, 220, 410–11
  detention, release and repatriation of POWs, 258, 260, 263–64, 278, 300
  evacuation matters, 202–3
  internment in outer space, 144–45, 146–48
  introduction to, 5

International Committee of the Red Cross (ICRC) (*cont.*)
  military assimilation under, 196, 205–6
  neutral merchant vessels, 132
  ongoing internment in space, 144–45
  overall control test, 7
  parole of POWs, 249, 251
  penal and disciplinary matters, 201
  status of detainees, 39–41
  treatment of Iraqi POWs, 333
  use of weapons against POWs, 214, 216
International Committee of the Red Cross (ICRC) Commentary to the Third Geneva Convention 28, 53, 63, 71–72, 76. *See* ICRC interpretation of Third Geneva Convention; Pictet Commentary
  authoritative status of, 410–13
  on captive POWs, 360–62
  civilians/non-military personnel as POWs, 82n.7
  clothing rations, 367–68
  on ending POW captivity, 362–65
  escape/attempted escape of POWs, 222–28
  food rations, 366–67
  fundamental protections, 355–59
  fundamentals of, 346–59
  historical background, 346–49
  implications for practitioners, 434–36
  internment camps, 365
  internment quarters, 365–66
  introduction to, 343–46, 408–10
  law *vs.* policy, 436
  levée en masse, 353–55
  lex ferenda (law as it should be), 435
  lex lata (law as it is), 435
  medical care and sanitation, 368–69
  members of the armed forces, 350
  members of the armed forces pledging allegiance to unrecognized authority, 352
  members of the crew of the merchant marine or civil aircraft, 353
  methodology of, 413–23
  personal scope of application, 349–55
  persons authorized to and in fact accompanying the armed forces without being members thereof, 352–53
  Pictet Commentary, 66–67, 68–69, 411, 426
  planning and preparation, 359–60
  recreation and religion, 369–70
  relations with detaining authorities, 372–73
  relations with exterior, 370–71
  select articles of, 423–34
  substantive protections, 365–73
  summary of, 373–74, 436
  timing of obligations, 359–65
  updating of, 375–79
  use of POW labor, 371
International Committee of the Red Cross (ICRC) interpretation of Third Geneva Convention
  concerns over Vienna Convention interpretation, 414–23
  good faith and, 382–83
  introduction to, 375–79
  measures of control and security, 403–4
  military manuals and, 421–22
  object and purpose of, 417–19
  ordinary meaning, 383–88
  purpose of, 403–6
  relevant rules of international law, 391–95
  reliance on subsequent treaties, 422–23
  reliance on writings, 420–21
  State practice, 419–21
  subsequent developments, 388–95
  subsequent practice, 389–91, 397–400
  supplementary means of, 395–402
  travaux préparatoires of, 395–97, 416–17
  treaty authentication in two or more languages, 402–3
  Vienna Convention on the Law of Treaties, 60–61, 69, 377–78, 379–82, 385, 391, 406–7, 414–23
International Committee of the Red Cross (ICRC) interpretation of Vienna Convention on the Law of Treaties
  concerns with ICRC interpretation, 414–23
  military manuals and, 421–22
  object and purpose of, 417–19

Index

reliance on subsequent treaties, 422–23
reliance on writings, 420–21
State practice, 419–21
International Conference of the Red Cross in Stockholm (1948), 348–49
International Court of Justice (ICJ), 5, 7, 56–57, 391–92, 420–21
International Covenant on Civil and Political Rights (ICCPR), 172–73, 285–86, 422–23
International Criminal Court (ICC), 5, 167–68
International Criminal Tribunal for the former Yugoslavia (ICTY)
  criminalization of violations of POW rules, 167–68
  IAC vs. NIAC, 273–74, 275–76
  introduction to, 3–4, 5
  levée en masse, 105
  overall control test, 6–7
international human rights law (IHRL), 255–56
international humanitarian law (IHL). *See also* protection of POWs under IHL
  detention of terrorist suspects, 285–87, 298–303
  ICRC and, 375–79
  parole of POWs under, 241–47
  regular armed forces failure to wear uniforms, 51–55
  weapons use against POWs in, 218–22
international humanitarian law (IHL) in international armed conflict (IAC)
  adapting to non-State armed groups, 14
  belligerent occupation incident, 162–63
  cessation of active hostilities, 36–37
  controlling State and, 16–19
  counterterrorism and, 268–71
  detention, release and repatriation of terrorist suspects, 3–277
  difficulties in applying, 8–9
  exceptions for nationals of detaining power, 19–21
  fluid conflicts and, 27–49
  internment regime, 264–65
  introduction to, 3–4
  non-international armed conflict and, 31–41
  non-State armed groups and, 28–29
  POW release and repatriation, 23–24, 34–36
  POW status, 9–10
  POW treatment, 10–15
  proxy warfare and, 3–9
  summary of, 24–25
International Law Commission (ILC), 390, 392–93, 423
international refugee law, 261–62
International Review of the Red Cross, 55–56
internationalization of armed conflict, 271–72, 275
internment camps, 365
internment law in outer space, 143–49
internment quarters, 365–66
intransgressible principle of distinction, 69–70
Ipsen, Kurt, 55–56
Iran-Iraq War, 260
Iraq
  hostilities in, 66
  judge advocates in U.S. Army, 341–42
  Multi-National Force, 341–42
  as NIAC, 33
  Operation Iraqi Freedom, 333–35
  POWs from, 331–35
  transition from an IAC to NIAC, 51–52
Islamic State (ISIS), 290–91, 296, 428
Israeli Defense Forces Conference (2019), 412–13
Israeli Military Court, 74

Japan, 195
Japanese POW breakout, 211–12, 227–28
Joint Detention Facility in Haiti, 338–39
Jones, R., 212
Judge Advocate General (TJAG), 327
judge advocates in U.S. Army
  Afghanistan, 339–41
  American Civil War, 324–28
  detention operations, 336–42
  Haiti, 336–39
  introduction to, 323–24
  Iraq, 341–42
  Korean War, 329–31
  Operation Iraqi Freedom, 333–35
  Persian Gulf War, 331–33

judge advocates in U.S. Army (*cont.*)
    POW operations, 324–35
    Somalia, 336–39
    summary of, 342
    Vietnam War, 329–31
    World War I, 324–28
    World War II, 324–28
jus ad bellum, 181n.1
jus in bello, 56, 181–82nn.1–2

knighthood, 237
Korean War, 329–31

law enforcement paradigm, 213–14, 230–32
law of armed conflict (LOAC)
    application of, 28–29, 33
    civilians/non-military personnel as POWs, 83, 84, 86–87, 91
    development of, 307–9, 310
    fundamental tenet of, 45
    levée en masse under, 98–99, 107, 112
    Lieber Code and, 312, 316–17
    States' views on, 413
The Law of Land Warfare (1956), 53, 59
Law of War Manual (DoD) (2015), 53, 58–59, 60, 64, 67–68, 76, 421–22
    distinction requirement, 77–79
    expanding ammunition, 221
    military practitioners, 435
    prisoner-of-war status, 430–31
    questioning of POWs, 433–34
lawofwar rules, 109–10
lawful military objectives, 126–30
levée en masse
    autonomous warfare and cyber operations, 99–101
    carry arms openly requirement, 114–15
    in category of prisoners of war, 353–55
    command requirement for POW status, 113–14
    cyber operations, 99–101, 106–16
    defined, 101–2, 107
    in future armed conflict, 106–16
    habitation requirement, 108–9
    history and overview, 101–6
    introduction to, 97–99
    Lieber, Francis and, 316–17
    spontaneity requirement, 109–12

    status of regular forces, 63
    summary of, 117
lex ferenda (law as it should be), 141–42, 435
lex lata (law as it is), 435
lex specialis (law governing a specific subject matter), 286
Lieber, Francis, 309–15, 324–25
Lieber Code (1863)
    introduction to, 307–10
    judge advocates and, 324, 325–26
    legacy of, 321–22
    levée en masse, 102–3, 104
    Lieber, Francis and, 309–15
    military assimilation under, 188–90
    military necessity and, 312–14, 325
    non-military personnel on battlefield, 81, 83
    parole of POWs under, 241–43, 246n.84
    POWs and, 315–21
    in Third Geneva Convention, 64
Lincoln, Abraham, 324–25
London Declaration (1909), 121n.11, 123–25, 126, 130–31
London Submarine Protocol (1936), 126–27
Lorimer, James, 190

Manstein, Erich von, 62
Manual of Armed Forces Law (New Zealand Defense Force), 219–20
maritime neutrality. *See* neutral merchant vessels
Massoud, Ahmad Shah, 77n.118
Meade, David C., 338
measures of control and security, 403–4
medical care and sanitation, 368–69
members of the armed forces, 350
members of the armed forces pledging allegiance to unrecognized authority, 352
members of the crew of the merchant marine or civil aircraft, 353
A Memory of Solferino (Dunant), 307–8
Mexican-American War, 238–39, 324–25
Middle Ages, 237
military assimilation in POW regulation
    current and future doctrine, 203–9

Index 445

early instruments and custom, 185–90
early twentieth century codification, 190–95
of food and clothing, 198–99
Geneva Convention (III) and, 196–203
in historical practice, 185–95
introduction to, 181–84
of labor and pay, 199–201
miscellaneous protections, 202–3
penal and disciplinary matters, 201–2
of quarters, 197–98
summary of, 209–10
Military Law and Precedents (Winthrop), 325–26
military necessity, 207–8, 286, 299–300, 312–14, 325, 355–56, 364, 386
military operations
civilians/non-military personnel as POWs, 84
distinction requirement for uniforms, 71–72, 72n.94, 78, 79–80
nonconsensual military operations, 427
militias, 67–70, 350–52
minimum standards of humane treatment, 337
Mohamed Ali case, 74–75
most protected status, 30, 45, 46–49, 50
Multi-National Force, Iraq, 341–42
multilateral agreements on hostility regulations, 190

Namibia case, 391–92
Napoleonic Wars, 238–39
National-Socialist Party, 38
nationality exception, 19–21
nationals of detaining power, 19–21
naval intelligence, 126–27
Naval Warfare Information Publication (NWIP) 10-2, 133–34
neutral merchant vessels
acquisition of enemy character, 124–25
attack or capture of, 126–31
criminal liability of personnel, 138–39
enemy flag and, 122
enemy merchant vessels *vs.*, 121–25
German Prize Ordinance, 133–34, 136
Hague Convention (XI), 133–34, 137
introduction to, 119–21

as lawful military objectives, 126–30
legal status of masters and crews, 132–39
London Declaration, 121n.11, 123–25, 126, 130–31
neutral flag and, 122–24
Oxford Manual, 126–27, 135–36
personnel captured as prize, 133–35
preliminary conclusions, 125
same treatment as enemy merchant vessels, 127–29
San Remo Manual, 129–30, 131, 135, 137
summary of, 139–40
U.S. Naval Manual, 127–29
New Zealand Defense Force (NZDF), 219–20, 248
Ney, Paul C., Jr., 412–13
Nguyen Monh Bich, 330–31
non bis in idem, 174–75
non-international armed conflicts (NIACs). *See also* Additional Protocol II, Relative to the Protection of Victims of Non-International Armed Conflicts
belligerent occupation incident, 162–63
detention of terrorist suspects in, 290–95, 298–303
gap in doctrine, 280–87
IACs *vs.*, 31–44, 271–79
IHL rules of, 4
release and repatriation of detainees, 277–95
sovereign party affiliation, 165
non-mission-essential personnel, 89
non-occupied territories, 105, 110
non-refoulement principle, 261–62, 294, 303, 363
non-standard uniform, 78
non-State armed groups, 28–29
nonconsensual military operations, 427
nongovernmental organizations (NGOs), 412–13
nuclear weapons, 91
nullum crimen sine lege, 20, 47–49
Nuremberg Tribunal, 126–27
Nye, Paul C., Jr., 425

OAG detention regime, 290–95
occupational injuries, 200
Office of Legal Counsel, 71
Operation Desert Storm, 332
Operation Enduring Freedom, 341
Operation Inherent Resolve, 429
Operation Iraqi Freedom, 333–35
Operation Overlord, World War II, 108
Operation Restore Hope, 336
Operation Uphold Democracy, 336
operationalizing the law, 232–33
other militias and members of other volunteer corps, 350–52
outer space POW regime
   detention conditions, 150–52
   habitable space objects, 143–49
   internment law, 143–50
   internment on moon/celestial bodies, 149
   introduction to, 141–43
   military astronauts and personnel, 152–54
   ongoing internment, 144–48
   Outer Space Treaty, 141–42nn.2–3, 149
   Rescue Agreement, 153–56
   summary of, 156
   transport of POWs, 148–49
Outer Space Treaty, 141–42nn.2–3, 149
overall control standard, 431–33
Oxford Manual (1913), 126–27, 135–36, 191–92, 214

pacta sunt sevanda, 415–16
Pakistani-Indian conflict, 260
Parks, Hays, 55–56, 63–64, 65
parole of POWs
   historical background, 236–40
   in international law, 241–47
   introduction to, 235–36
   summary of, 251–52
   in twenty-first century, 247–51
Partch, Karl, 56, 75
Peace of Westphalia, 238–39
Pede, Charles N., 411, 434–35
penal repression regime protections, 175
perfidious acts, 60
Persian Gulf War, 331–33

personal status categories, 162–65
persons authorized to and in fact accompanying the armed forces without being members thereof, 352–53
Pfanner, Toni, 55–56, 62–63, 64–65
Pictet, Jean, 199
Pictet Commentary, 66–67, 68–69, 411, 426
Preliminary Conference of National Red Cross Societies (1946), 348–49
principle of legality, 12
Privy Council, 74–75
Project of an International Declaration concerning the Laws and Customs of War (1874), 242
protected civilians, 20
protection of POWs under IHL
   beyond humanity principle, 175–80
   fundamental guarantees provisions, 169–75
   humanity principle in, 165–69
   introduction to, 159–62
   penal repression regime protections, 175
   personal status categories, 162–65
proxy-armed groups, 3–4, 14–22
proxy warfare and Third Geneva Convention
   IAC IHL and, 3–9
   introduction to, 3–4
   Tadić theory, 3–9
Prugh, George S., 329–31

ransoming prisoners, 238
recreation and religion, 369–70
regular armed forces failure to wear uniforms
   distinction from the civilian population, 55–58
   distinction requirement, 77–79
   individual *vs.* collective application, 75–76
   introduction to, 51–55
   militia groups, 67–70
   spies and saboteurs, 58–59
   State's armed forces and, 60–79
   summary of, 80
   unlawful perfidy acts, 60

Index

Regulus, Marcus Atilius, 236–37
Reid v. Covert, 88
relations with exterior, 370–71
release of POWs, 23–24, 34–36
repatriation of POWs, 23–24, 34–36, 200, 238–39
Republika Srpska in Bosnia, 28
Rescue Agreement (1967), 153–56
resistance fighters, 108–9
respect for the convention (Article 1), 423–26
revolutionary mobilization of *levée en masse*, 111–12
riot control agents, 219–20
Rogers, A.P.V, 64
Rome Statute of the International Criminal Court, 422–23
Rousseau, Jean-Jacques, 238
Rules of Land Warfare-1914 manual, 327
Ruppert, Raymond P., 331–32
Russian forces in Ukraine, 51–55
Russo-Japanese War (1904), 240
Russo-Turkish War, 190

same treatment as enemy merchant vessels, 127–29
San Remo Manual (1994), 129–30, 131, 135, 137
Sassòli, Marco, 75
Saudi Arabia, 334
Schwarzkopf, Norman, 331
Sea Mob project, 99–100
Second Italian War of Independence, 190
Second World War. *See* World War II
self-defense law, 227
self-evident *(selbstverständlich)* obligation, 55–56
Serdar Mohammed case, 278–79
Shelton, Henry H., 338
Slavin, Nikolai, 61–62
Sofaer, Abraham, 73–74
Solf, Waldemar, 56, 75
Somalia, 336–39
sovereign party affiliation, 165
Soviet Union, 195
specialized military courts, 187–88

spies and saboteurs, 58–59
spoils of war, 236–37
spontaneity requirement, 109–12
St. Petersburg Declaration Renouncing the Use, in Time of War, of Explosive Projectiles Under 400 Grammes Weight (1868), 308–9
status-based detention, 280–82
STM *Kargu-2* system, 99–100
subsequent practice, 389–91, 397–400
Swarka case, 74
Swiss Federal Council, 327
Swiss francs as payment, 183

Tadić case
  controversies surrounding, 5–6
  definition of protected civilians, 20
  IAC *vs.* NIAC, 271–72, 275–76
  overall control test, 6–8
  proxy-armed groups and, 12, 15–16
  proxy warfare and, 3–9
Taliban, 268–70, 274
Taxi to the Dark Side (documentary), 341
temporary detention of POWs, 145
temporary protection, 46
terrorist suspects. *See* detention of terrorist suspects
Third Geneva Convention. *See* Geneva Convention (III) Relative to the Treatment of Prisoners of War.
Third Lateran Council, 237
threat-based detention, 282–83
threat-based determination, 256
tobacco use, 367
Tracked Hybrid Modular Infantry System (THeMIS), 99–100
transition from an IAC to, 28–29, 33, 39–44, 51–52, 255
travaux préparatoires, 11, 13, 289–90, 395–97, 416–17
treaty authentication in two or more languages, 402–3
Treaty of Amity (1785), 187
troops at base camps, 194

U.K. *Law of Armed Conflict Manual*, 72–73, 79

Ukraine, Russian forces in, 51–55
ultima ratio, 265
U.N. Convention Against Torture and Other Cruel, Inhuman or Degrading Treatment or Punishment, 422–23
U.N. Security Council, 268, 296–98, 336–38, 428
U.N. Working Group on Arbitrary Detention, 263–64
Unified Task Force (UNITAF), 336–37
Union POWs, 314–15
United States Army General Orders. *See* Lieber Code
United States v. Buck (1988), 74
universal jurisdiction over perpetrators, 167–68
unlawful perfidy acts, 60
unlawful submarine warfare by Germany, 138–39
unlawful weapons, 218–22
unlawfulness of force majeure, 14
unrestricted release of POWs, 236
U.S. Army. *See* judge advocates in U.S. Army
U.S. Central Command (CENTCOM), 331–32
U.S. Department of Defense. *See also Law of War Manual*
   command requirement for POW status, 113
   detention conditions in outer space, 150
   ongoing internment in space, 144
   proximate civilians, 88–89
U.S. Department of Justice Office of Legal Counsel, 70
U.S. Manuals (1997, 2007, 2107), 134
U.S. National Security Agency, 91–92
U.S. Naval Manual (1955), 127–29
U.S. Supreme Court, 231, 324–25
use of weapons against POWs. *See* weapons use against POWs in Article 42
USS *America*, 338

Vienna Convention on the Law of Treaties, 60–61, 69, 377–78, 379–82, 385, 391, 406–7. *See also* International Committee of the Red Cross (ICRC) interpretation of Vienna Convention on the Law of Treaties
Vietnam War, 329–31
Villiger, Mark, 415–16
volunteer corps, 350–52

war crimes, 11–12, 60, 62, 175, 178–79, 256n.15, 257–58, 270–71, 295–96, 314–15, 332–33, 340, 400n.143
War of 1812, 238–39, 324–25
War on Terror, 257–58
Warren, Marc, 335
Washington, George, 186–87
waterboarding, 340
Watts, Sean, 409–10
weapons use against POWs in Article 42
   deconstruction of, 217–29
   discipline, 232–33
   escape/attempted escape of POWs, 222–28
   expanding ammunition, 220–22
   extreme measures, 228–29
   general principles, 218
   in IHL, 218–22
   introduction to, 213–14
   Japanese prisoner of war breakout, 211–12
   law and pragmatism, 214–17
   law enforcement paradigm, 213–14, 230–32
   operationalizing the law, 232–33
   riot control agents, 219–20
   specifically unlawful weapons, 218–22
Westmoreland, William C., 330
Whitley v. Albers, 231
Winthrop, William, 325–26
World War I, 187, 192–94, 240, 324–28, 347–48
World War II
   Hague Regulations and, 347–48
   judge advocates in U.S. Army, 324–28
   Operation Overlord, 108
   parole of POWs, 240
   ratification of 1929 Geneva Convention, 195
   repatriation of internees, 266
   Third Geneva Convention and, 348–49